© Copyright 2000
J.P. van der Walt & Son (Pty) Ltd
380 Bosman Street, Pretoria
Set in 11 on 12.5pt Palatino
Reproduction and jacket design by Mandi Printers CC, Murrayfield, Pretoria
Printed by ABC Press (Pty) Ltd, 21 Kinghall Ave, Epping, Cape Town

First impression: 2000

ISBN 0 7993 2632 1

All rights reserved. No part of this publication may be reproduced or stored in a retrieval system, or transmitted in any form by any means mechanical or electronic; by photocopying, recording or otherwise, without the prior written permission of the publisher.

Cover: Lord Methuen rallying his broken forces at Tweebosch. Artwork by Peet Venter based on a drawing by C.M. Sheldon.

THE ANGLO-BOER WAR
A CHRONOLOGY

Pieter G. Cloete

J.P. van der Walt
Pretoria

SOUTHERN AFRICA - 1899

PORTUGUESE EAST AFRICA

RHODESIA

GERMAN SOUTH-WEST AFRICA

BECHUANALAND (BRITISH PROTECTORATE)

BRITISH BECHUANALAND (1885)

SOUTH AFRICAN REPUBLIC
Z.R.

SWAZILAND Z.A.R. PROTECTORATE

ZULULAND (1887)

NATAL (1843)

ORANGE FREE STATE

BASUTOLAND (1868)

GRIQUALAND WEST (1879)

EAST GRIQUALAND (1879)

PONDOLAND (1894)

TRANSKEI (1866-1886)

CAPE COLONY

INDIAN OCEAN

ATLANTIC OCEAN

Places:
Tuli, Pietersburg, Warmbaths, Dwarsdrift, Lydenburg, Middelburg, Nelspruit, Komati Poort, LOURENCO MARQUES, Barberton, Standerton, PRETORIA, JOHANNESBURG, Rustenburg, Lichtenburg, Potchefstroom, Klerksdorp, MAFEKING, Vryburg, Kuruman, Volksrust, Newcastle, LADYSMITH, Colenso, Estcourt, DURBAN, Pietermaritzburg, Heilbron, Lindley, Bethlehem, Harrismith, Kroonstad, Senekal, Winburg, Ladybrand, Brandfort, Thaba Nchu, BLOEMFONTEIN, Boshof, Wepener, Dewetsdorp, Rouxville, Bothaville, Belmont, Norval's Pont, De Aar, Colesberg, Naauwpoort, Stormberg, Dordrecht, Queenstown, Molteno, Graaff Reinet, Cradock, Port Alfred, PORT ELIZABETH, EAST LONDON, GRIQUALAND WEST KIMBERLEY, Prieska, Upington, Calvinia, Beaufort West, Mossel Bay, Stellenbosch, CAPE TOWN, Okiep, St Helena Bay, Lambert's Bay, Port Nolloth

Legend:
BRITISH TERRITORIES
( ) Date of British Annexation

N

500
400
300
200
100
0
Kilometres

CONTENTS

AUTHOR'S NOTE		6
FOREWORD	Professor Albert Grundlingh	7
PREFACE		8

CRISIS	to OCTOBER 1899	9
OPENING BLOWS	OCTOBER to DECEMBER 1899	38
HAMMER BLOWS	JANUARY to MARCH 1900	79
MARCHES AND RETREATS	APRIL to JUNE 1900	129
CHANGES	JULY to DECEMBER 1900	167
GUERRILLA	JANUARY to JUNE 1901	214
ATTRITION	JULY to DECEMBER 1901	251
THE BITTER END	JANUARY to JUNE 1902	292
AND THEN . . .		336

MAPS AND DIAGRAMS

SOUTHERN AFRICA 1899	5
COMPOSITION OF A TYPICAL BRITISH INFANTRY DIVISION	33
THE BATTLE OF MAGERSFONTEIN — 11 December 1899	68
THE BATTLE OF COLENSO — 15 December 1899	71
THE BATTLE OF SPIOENKOP — 24 January 1900	88
FIELD-MARSHAL LORD ROBERTS' CAMPAIGN	188
THE BATLLE OF NOOITGEDACHT — 13 December 1900	206
THE BLOCKHOUSE SYSTEM	246
GENERAL SMUTS' RAID INTO THE CAPE COLONY	278
LORD KITCHENER'S 'NEW MODEL' DRIVES	299
THE BATTLE OF YSTERSPRUIT — 25 February 1902	305
THE BATTLE OF TWEEBOSCH/DE KLIPDRIFT — 7 March 1902	310
THE BATTLE OF BOSCHBULT — 31 March 1902	315
THE BATTLE OF ROODEWAL — 11 April 1902	320

ADDENDA

ANGLO-BOER WAR RIFLES — A COMPARISON	339
ANGLO-BOER WAR ARTILLERY	340
A RECKONING — THE BALANCE SHEET	341
A RECKONING — THE BUTCHER'S BILL	342
THE CONCENTRATION CAMPS — THE INNOCENTS	343
THE CONCENTRATION CAMPS — JUNE 1901 TO MAY 1902	344

BIBLIOGRAPHY	345
INDEX	348

AUTHOR'S NOTE

CONTENTS:

This is a chronology. It does not presume to be complete or to uncover astounding new facts or perspectives on the war. It attempts to give a concise, day by day and blow by blow account of the eleven months preceding the Republican ultimatum and the 963 days from the start of hostilities to the final peace treaty.

The work covers:

The origins of the conflict, the peace attempts and the ultimatum.

The first Republican offensive, the famous sieges and the first British counter-offensive resulting in 'Black Week'.

The second British offensive under Lord Roberts, the lifting of the sieges and the occupation of the Republican capitals.

The apparent British victory and their attempts to mop up pockets of resistance.

The Republican revival, the start of unconventional warfare and the first British countermeasures.

The British 'scorched earth' and 'clearing the country' policies resulting in the blockhouse lines and the concentration camps.

The second Republican invasion of British territories and the guerrilla phase.

The 'Bitter End' and the peace negotiations.

Expanded entries on the key battles are accompanied by distinct maps and interesting facts and statistics are included as addenda.

FORMAT:

The book relates the political and military events of the Anglo-Boer War in a strict chronological order with daily diary type entries.

The daily entries are grouped under regional, campaign and other headings, enabling the reader to follow specific events, campaigns and other aspects of the war.

Where possible, direct quotations from speeches, letters, telegrams, etc., have been used to keep the events 'live' as seen through the eyes of the participants.

'Trivia' entries record other events during the period to give a wider historical perspective to the war, putting it in a world-wide setting.

FOREWORD

In a society characterised by continuous strife, the Anglo-Boer War at the turn of the century represents a period of particularly sustained violence. A devastating war, fought mainly by white protagonists, ravaged South Africa and especially the Transvaal and Orange Free State for nearly three years. The British scorched earth policy during the latter part of the conflict reduced the country almost to a wasteland. With the possible exception of the wholesale destruction during the Mfecane in the twenties and thirties of the 19th century, the Anglo-Boer War was the closest that South Africa came to total war and its effects.

At the same time, the war presented a watershed in British imperialism and was an early indication, though not necessarily recognised at the time, that overlordship in Africa would be increasingly challenged in the 20th century.

Not surprisingly, the war spawned a vast literature dealing with a variety of dimensions of the conflict. This book, however, is unique in that it is the first comprehensive attempt in the 100 years since the outbreak of the war, to provide a full chronological exposition of hostilities and related matters. It is carefully researched and provides a wealth of easily accessible detail to the specialist as well as the general reader.

Professor Albert Grundlingh
Department of History
University of South Africa
Pretoria

PREFACE

History consists, for the greater part, of the miseries brought upon the world by pride, ambition, avarice, revenge, lust, sedition, hypocrisy, ungoverned zeal, and all the train of disorderly appetites... These vices are the causes of those storms. Religion, morals, laws, prerogatives, privileges, liberties, rights of men, are the pretexts. *The pretexts are always found in some specious appearance of a real good.*

— E Burke, *Reflections on the Revolution in France.*

War must be mankind's most senseless pursuit — yet the history of war never ceases to fascinate.

Soon after the start of the Anglo-Boer War in October 1899, a British parliamentarian remarked: *"If the Rand had been a potato field, there would have been no war."* But the Rand was no potato field — it was the richest goldfield the world had ever seen and it was not part of the greatest empire the world had ever seen. So there was a war. A small war — a very interesting war.

A war with all the elements that makes wars interesting: David versus Goliath, amateurs versus professionals, heroes and villains, gallantry and cowardice, brilliant victories and ignominious defeats. The war involved interesting people: Cecil John Rhodes, Mahatma Ghandi, Winston Churchill, Arthur Conan Doyle, Rudyard Kipling, Edgar Wallace, Emily Hobhouse and the brothers of famous people, Von Zeppelin, Van Gogh and Mondrian. It brought innovations: aerial observation, armoured vehicles, wireless telegraphy, moving pictures, trench warfare, guerrilla warfare, concentration camps and 'Total War' — war against civilians and the land itself. It gave new words to the English language: Uitlander, pom-pom, drift, kopje, kraal, trek, blockhouse, mafficking; and to Afrikaans: 'dum-dum', 'Kakie', 'joiner', 'hendsopper'... and 'bittereinder'.

For a brief moment, South Africa was at the centre of world attention. Men came here from all over the British Empire, from America, from Europe and Asia — even an Algerian Arab. The new profession of war correspondent sent their stirring accounts to the corners of the world and the war was discussed, praised, condemned, analysed and then, like all unhappy interludes, forgotten... almost.

The Anglo-Boer War is sometimes referred to as 'the last of the gentlemen's wars', but this label is only found in British works. Strangely, it is also a British custom to name their wars after their opponents.

It is also called the 'Second War of Independence' or the 'Second Liberation War', but neither side gained their independence and nobody was liberated.

THE ANGLO-BOER WAR — A CHRONOLOGY (1899-1902)

CRISIS

'That war is an evil is something that we all know, and it would be pointless to go on cataloguing all the disadvantages involved in it. No one is forced into war by ignorance, nor, if he thinks he will gain from it, is he kept out of it by fear. The fact is that one side thinks that the profits to be won outweigh the risks to be incurred, and the other side is ready to face danger rather than accept an immediate loss.'

— Thucydides (c 471BC)

1898	SPRING	NOVEMBER
Day -343 Wed **1898-11-02**	Cape Town	Sir Alfred Milner, the British High Commissioner in South Africa and Governor of the Cape Colony, embarks at Cape Town for a 'holiday' in Britain. He tells GV Fiddes, the Imperial Secretary in Cape Town, that he intends to interview *all the leading politicians and pressmen... and to stamp on rose-coloured illusions about S. Africa.*[1]
Day -323 Tue **1898-11-22**	United Kingdom	Sir Alfred Milner meets Colonial Secretary Joseph Chamberlain at the Colonial Office in London, and puts the case for *working up to a crisis* in South Africa.[2] Subsequently, he holds interviews with the editors of all the major newspapers and prominent politicians and he is reported to be happy with the results.[3]

GOLD MINING IN SOUTH AFRICA

Alluvial gold was discovered in the eastern Transvaal during the 1870s, but the biggest strike was made when the Australian, George Harrison, discovered signs of a reef in an outcrop on the farm Langlaagte on the Witwatersrand. In 1886, when the first gold-fields on the Rand were declared a 'public digging', the Transvaal produced only 0,16% of the world's gold. In 1889 the ZAR was the largest single source of supply of the metal, accounting for no less than 27,55% of the world's output.

In 1899, the gold output of the ZAR gold-fields was as follows:

Witwatersrand	4 008 325,85 oz
Lydenburg	94 664,90 oz
De Kaap	65 546,30 oz
Klerksdorp	25 774,85 oz
Other districts	1 645,95 oz
TOTAL	4 195 960,85 oz About 130 metric tonnes.

In less than 15 years Johannesburg grew from a mining camp to the biggest city in South Africa, its population swelled by men from all over the world, seeking their fortune in the new El Dorado. The mining industry was dominated by powerful men and money houses intent on gleaning maximum profits from the ever-deepening mines. The back-breaking and dangerous labour was provided by a black population from all over the subcontinent that soon numbered almost 100 000 men.[4]

1899	SUMMER	DECEMBER
Day -314 Thu **1898-12-01**	South Africa	The number of British Imperial troops garrisoned in South Africa was as follows: Cape Colony 3 785 ; Natal 4 671; Total: 8 456 men with 24 artillery pieces.[5]
Day -305 Sat **1898-12-10**	*Trivia*	*The signing of the Treaty of Paris formally ends the Spanish-American War. Spain turns Puerto Rico, Guam and the Philippines over to the United States and relinquishes control over Cuba.*
Day -299 Fri **1898-12-16**	United Kingdom	Sir Alfred Milner has a long meeting with the Johannesburg millionaire Julius Wernher, who is looking for an editor for his newspaper, the Johannesburg *Star.*[6]
	Trivia	*The Day of the Covenant or the Day of the Vow. The 50th anniversary of the Voortrekkers' (Boer pioneers) victory against the Zulus in the Battle of Blood River in Natal.*

Day -297 Sun 1898-12-18	ZAR	**THE EDGAR INCIDENT** An Uitlander called Foster, relieving himself against a wall, swears at a small dog. Tom Jackson Edgar, a powerfully built Johannesburg Uitlander, on his way home from a bar, assumes that Foster is swearing at him and knocks him down with a single blow. Foster's wife and neighbours call for help and four ZAR policemen promptly arrive, chasing Edgar, who flees home. A ZAR policeman, Constable Bart Jones, forces an entrance and the suspect, wielding an iron-shod stick, charges at him. Jones is forced to shoot and Edgar is killed. The assault victim Foster subsequently dies of his injuries.[7]
Day -296 Mon 1898-12-19	ZAR	Constable Jones is arrested on a charge of murder. The charge is later changed to manslaughter and he is released on bail. *The Star*, a Johannesburg newspaper with an imperial bias, starts their own investigation and launches an 'Edgar Relief Fund' with the support of the SA League.[8]
Day -295 Tue 1898-12-20	ZAR Black involvement	The ZAR police launch a raid on Coloured inhabitants in Johannesburg as part of a 'cleanup' campaign in terms of the pass laws. Several 'Cape Coloureds', as well as a few from St. Helena who, as British subjects, are not subject to the law, are jailed. In a clear miscarriage of justice, the accused are later fined and the South African League, a pro-imperialist pressure group, decides to champion their cause.[9] Field-cornet Lombaard, the officer in command of the raids, is suspended but later reinstated.[10]
Day -294 Wed 1898-12-21	United Kingdom	The British War Office instructs Lieutenant-General Sir William Butler, Commander of Her Majesty's Forces in South Africa, to consider a scheme of defence for the Cape Colony and Natal in the event of a sudden outbreak of hostilities.[11]
Day -291 Sat 1898-12-24	ZAR	**THE FIRST PETITION** A crowd of almost 5 000 gathers at the British Vice-Consul's office and prepares a petition to the Queen beseeching her to secure "*a full and impartial trial*" against Constable Jones and to protect their lives and liberties urging the taking of "*such steps as may be necessary*".[12] Mr Emrys Evans, the Vice-Consul, refuses to accept the petition purporting to represent the views of 5 000 but signed by only 40.[13] Police arrest some of the leaders on a technical charge relating to illegal public meetings and they are later released on bail set at five times that of Constable Jones.
Day -290 Sun 1898-12-25		CHRISTMAS
Day -286 Thu 1898-12-29	ZAR	Third anniversary of the start of the ill-fated Jameson Raid (29-12-1895).
	THE JAMESON RAID 1895 Arch-capitalist and imperialist Cecil John Rhodes, Prime Minister of the Cape Colony, determined to fulfil his 'mission' to paint the map of Africa red, saw the Witwatersrand gold-fields as the ultimate glittering prize. Reports of his failing health spurred him on and he decided to use the Uitlanders to bring down the government of the Republic. To carry out his plans, Rhodes, with the knowledge and approval of the British Prime Minister, Lord Rosebery, the Minister for Colonies, Joseph Chamberlain, and the High Commissioner in South Africa, Sir Hercules Robinson, started organizing an uprising in Johannesburg. Weapons were smuggled to the Rand and a secret base camp was established at Pitsane in Bechuanaland. Here a military force, made up of 500 British South African policemen under Dr LS Jameson and Colonel Frank Rhodes (CJR's brother), was waiting for the signal to cross the border to 'rescue' the Uitlanders. At the last moment, the Uitlander conspirators flinched. Dissension in their ranks, serious developments on the Stock Exchange and a lack of any enthusiasm for such an orchestrated uprising compelled them to send urgent messages to Jameson and Rhodes cancelling, or at least postponing, the operation. Jameson, engrossed in his role as the conquering hero, disregarded all messages to wait, and on the evening of 29 December 1895, he crossed the border on his way to Johannesburg. His men neglected to cut all the telegraph wires and by the following morning, the Transvaal government was fully informed of the situation. The western commandos under General PA Cronje were called up and the invaders were shadowed all the way to the Witwatersrand. On 2 January 1896, at Doornkop, near Roodepoort, Jameson was confronted and forced to surrender. At the same time the Republican authorities swooped on the plotters in Johannesburg and arrested 64 members of the Reform Committee.	

		Chamberlain and Robinson immediately repudiated Jameson's raid, and by denying their knowledge or support of the scheme, turned him into a freebooter. President Kruger magnanimously (or shrewdly) handed Jameson and his officers over to the British government for punishment. Jameson was sentenced to 15 months imprisonment. He was released after a few months on grounds of ill-health. Rhodes, who was forced to resign as Prime Minister of the Cape Colony, gave evidence to the British Parliamentary Committee of Inquiry into the Raid. Rosebery, Chamberlain and Robinson's complicity was not revealed. The British opposition referred to the inquiry as the 'lying-in-state' or the 'committee of no enquiry'. The 64 arrested members of the Reform Committee were tried for high treason by Judge Rheinhold Gregarowski of the Orange Free State and the leaders, Lionel Phillips, J Hays Hammond, Frank Rhodes and George Farrar, pleaded guilty and were sentenced to death. President Kruger commuted the sentence to a fine of £25 000 each. The fines were paid by Cecil Rhodes. Other conspirators were sentenced to terms of imprisonment, fines of up to £2 000 and banned from participating in political activities. Two (Woolls-Sampson and 'Karri' Davies) refused to pay — but were released in honour of Queen Victoria's Diamond Jubilee. The gulf between Boer and Briton widened and Afrikaners throughout South Africa were drawn together by the emergence of a new nationalism spawned by the unmasking of a common adversary.[14]
Day -285 Fri **1898-12-30**	United Kingdom	Mr J Chamberlain remarks: *"The Edgar affair may be very important & may give us the right of remonstrance & action — outside the Convention — which we have not hitherto had."*[15]
1899	SUMMER	**JANUARY**
Day -283 Sun **1899-01-01**		NEW YEAR'S DAY
Day -270 Sat **1899-01-14**	ZAR	A protest meeting, this time held with all the appropriate official approvals in the Amphitheatre near Johannesburg, is interrupted by a road repair gang working in the vicinity, incensed by what they perceive to be a traitorous gathering. ZAR policemen present do nothing either to stop the interruption or to protect the speakers and are carried around shoulder-high by the intruders.[16]
Day -268 Mon **1899-01-16**	United Kingdom	In a note to the ZAR government, Colonial Secretary J Chamberlain demands the suspension of the Dynamite Concession which he deems to be a breach of the 1884 London Convention.[17]
		THE SUZERAINTY ISSUE Dr Peter Warwick explains this issue as follows: The Republican victory at Majuba in February 1881 led to the signing of the Pretoria Convention in August 1881 which granted the Transvaal *"complete self-government, subject to the suzerainty of Her Majesty Queen Victoria"*. Suzerainty was a word without precise meaning. Lord Kimberley, Gladstone's Colonial Secretary, explained that the word had been used as *"a convenient mode of expressing generally that certain stipulations existed in the Convention which limited the sovereignty of the Transvaal State"*. The most important stipulations gave Britain control of the Transvaal's external relations and a right of veto over legislation affecting the Republic's black population. The Pretoria Convention was replaced in 1884 by the London Convention, which did not mention suzerainty, restored to the Transvaal the name of the South African Republic, removed the British right of veto over 'native' legislation, and contained only one specific prohibition, namely, that *"The South African Republic will conclude no treaty or engagement with any State or nation other than the Orange Free State, nor with any native tribe to the eastward or westward of the Republic, until the same has been approved by Her Majesty the Queen"*. During the 1890s (after the discovery of gold) the imperial government maintained that British suzerainty still existed since it had not been expressly withdrawn by the later agreement (this was a somewhat tenuous argument to say the least, for Lord Derby, the then Colonial Secretary, had himself crossed out the entire preamble of the 1881 document when the London Convention was being prepared). Conversely, the government of the South African Republic insisted that it retained full control over its internal affairs and that British claims to suzerainty were spurious.[18]

Day -267 Tue **1899-01-17**	United Kingdom	Sir Alfred Milner interviews William F Moneypenny in connection with the editorship of the Johannesburg *Star*. He later urges Wernher and Beit to appoint him.[19]
Day -266 Wed **1899-01-18**	Cape Town	Lieutenant-General Sir William Butler, Acting High Commissioner in Milner's absence, defends Vice-Consul Evans' refusal to accept the petition, calling the Edgar-incident *"a drunken brawl"*.[20] It is also his opinion that the subsequent agitation, and indeed, *"All political questions in South Africa and nearly all information being sent from Cape Town to England, are now worked by... a colossal syndicate for the spread of systematic misrepresentation...* "controlled by a *"small and noisy group... who have got all the telegraphic and most of the press power in their hands"*.[21]
Day -265 Thu **1899-01-19**	United Kingdom	Sir Henry Cambell-Bannerman succeeds Sir William V Harcourt as leader of the Liberals in the House of Commons.
Day -264 Fri **1899-01-20**	*Trivia*	*Commandant-General Petrus (Piet) J Joubert's 68th birthday.*
1899	SUMMER	**FEBRUARY**
Day -249 Sat **1899-02-04**	*Trivia*	*Filipinos demand their independence from the United States of America.*
Day -239 Tue **1899-02-14**	ZAR	The Chamber of Mines offers the ZAR government a loan of £600 000 if the dynamite concession is cancelled. This offer leads to 'confidential' meetings between the Government and the major mining houses which are later to be known as the 'Great Deal'.[22]
	Cape Town	Sir Alfred Milner arrives back in Cape Town after his holiday in Britain.[23]
Day -228 Sat **1899-02-25**	ZAR	Constable Bart Jones is acquitted on the charge of culpable homicide by a jury. Judge Antonie Kock, the presiding judge, publicly announces his satisfaction with the verdict.[24] The public prosecutor FRM Cleaver comments, *"We have not heard the last of this. The Judge has knocked a big nail into our coffin today."*[25]
Day -227 Sun **1899-02-26**	ZAR	Mr WF Moneypenny arrives in Johannesburg to take up his position as the editor of Wernher and Beit's newspaper, *The Star*.[26]
1899	AUTUMN	**MARCH**
Day -222 Fri **1899-03-03**	ZAR	Mr Percy Fitzpatrick communicates details of the 'Great Deal' to the British Agent in Pretoria. According to him, the ZAR government offers *"to make peace with the whole Uitlander population"* if the financial houses would (i) support the government in the Asiatic Immigration Question, (ii) disown the South African League, (iii) cease press agitation in the Republic and in Europe. In return, the ZAR government would (i) settle the Dynamite and other mining questions, (ii) appoint a European financier and auditor, (iii) refrain from imposing new taxation without approval, and (iv) grant burgher rights after five years from the passing of the Act.[27]
Day -217 Wed **1899-03-08**	Cape Colony	Milner, reviewing the ZAR's policy on 'The Asiatic Question', writes, *"As I understand they are willing to allow Asiatics, who are already established in the country, to remain undisturbed, provided the Govt. can obtain a right which it does not now possess, of restricting their immigration in the future. With that principle in general I agree."*[28]
Day -208 Fri **1899-03-17**	ZAR	At a public meeting at Heidelberg, President Stephanus Johannes Paulus Kruger announces his intention to submit revisions to the Franchise Act to the Volksraad.[29]

		THE FRANCHISE ISSUE Act No 1 of 1876 was the first Transvaal law to determine the prerequisites for voting rights in that state. A distinction was drawn between men born in the country, who automatically obtained the right to vote at the age of 21, and persons born elsewhere. New arrivals qualified to vote if they owned fixed property or resided in the country for one year or longer. They were also expected to abide by the laws, prove good conduct and to swear an oath of allegiance to the people, the government and independence of the country. This allowed new citizens older than 21 years to vote for the Volksraad. After the Transvaal War of Independence, this act was replaced by Act No 7 of 1887. The oath of allegiance was modified and the residential qualification was extended to five years before the newcomer could apply for naturalisation. Persons who were exempted from military service through treaties, for example, British subjects who were not prepared to waive their citizenship, were not allowed to take the oath of allegiance. The influx of foreigners occasioned by the discovery of gold in 1886, caused the Republican government, concerned about the possibility of being swamped by foreigners with foreign loyalties, to amend their laws again. Firstly, Act No 4 of 1890 established a Second Volksraad (House of Assembly) with limited legislative powers in the fields of mining, road construction, copyright, certain commercial affairs, etc., all subject to ratification by the First Volksraad — clearly an attempt to appease the new citizens. This was followed by a new Franchise Law, Act No 5 of 1890. New immigrants could now apply for naturalisation after two years, thereby earning the right to participate in elections for the Second Volksraad. Only after a further 10 years could they, if they owned fixed property and were members of a Protestant church, qualify to vote for the First Volksraad. Very few Uitlanders, however, were at all interested in citizenship or the franchise and very few English surnames are evident among the 6 900 naturalised aliens. In July 1894, Lionel Phillips, Chairman of the Chamber of Mines, declared, *"As to the franchise. I do not think many people care a fig about it."*[30]
Day -205 Mon **1899-03-20**	United Kingdom	Mr Chamberlain defends the Government's policy of non-intervention in the ZAR on the grounds that intervention has never been sought by British subjects there.[31]
Day -204 Tue **1899-03-21**	ZAR	After secret discussions with the SA League and Moneypenny, Sir W Conyngham Greene cables the final timetable to be followed with the new Uitlander petition to Milner. Greene is to accept the petition on Friday, in time for it to reach Milner on Monday. Moneypenny tips off the London *Times* that an important message for Monday's issue is to follow.[32]
	Trivia	*An Anglo-French convention on the hinterland of Tripoli ends the Fashoda crisis, but Italy protests at the large concessions made to France in the Sahara.*
Day -201 Fri **1899-03-24**	ZAR Queen Victoria *(War Museum of the Boer Republics)*	**THE MARCH PETITION** A petition to the Queen, initiated by Percy Fitzpatrick (who is still barred from participating in political activities because of his involvement in the Jameson Raid) and the South African League, signed by 21 684 British subjects (the validity of some signatures is later to be questioned) is handed to the British Agent, Sir W Conyngham Greene.[33] It sets out *"in sober language the grievances of a community who"* feels that it *"formed the majority of the country's population and paid five-sixth of its taxes yet are denied any voice in this government".*[34] The petitioners conclude by beseeching *"Your Most Gracious Majesty to extend Your Majesty's protection to Your Most Gracious Majesty's loyal subjects resident in this State, and to cause an inquiry to be made into grievances and complaints enumerated and set forth in this humble petition, and to direct Your Majesty's Government to take measures which will secure the speedy reform of the abuses complained of, and to obtain substantial guarantees from the Government of this State for recognition of their rights as British subjects".*[35] Strangely, in asking the Queen to help them to get the franchise, *"they are asking her to divest themselves of allegiance to her".*[36]

Day -197 Tue 1899-03-28	ZAR	The Rand mining houses submit their reply to the ZAR government's confidential negotiations about concessions and reforms relating to the mining industry known as the 'Great Deal'.[37]
	Cape Colony	The Uitlander petition, personally taken to Cape Town by Fitzpatrick, is sent to London via Milner's office.[38] Milner adds a note, *"I hope they have taken great care to ensure the genuineness of the signatures."* In his covering letter he points out that there may be duplicate signatures, some of women, a large number of marks made by coloured people, but that, *"at a rough guess... at least three-fourths... were those of men of pure European Race".*[39]
1899	AUTUMN	**APRIL**
Day -193 Sat 1899-04-01	ZAR	At a public meeting at Rustenburg, President Kruger reaffirms his intention to revise the Franchise Act and to make certain concessions to the mining industry. [40]
Day -189 Wed 1899-04-05	Cape Colony *Sir Alfred Milner* *(War Museum of the Boer Republics)*	Milner writes to William Palmer, Lord Selborne, Under Secretary of State for the Colonies: *"... I don't want to give you the impression that I want to rush you. And I am painfully conscious that what is to us all here an all-overshadowing nightmare... is to people at home a matter of faint interest exciting only a very small degree of public attention. It is odd that it should be so, seeing the enormous material value of the thing involved, as well as the plainness of the moral issues... Will you not publish a Blue Book and see that Edgar shootings and Jones trials, amphitheatre meetings, Lombaard incidents, etc., etc., etc., get rubbed into the public mind. I wish to goodness some of my vitriol could get in too. P.S.— Don't be afraid of publishing anything lest it should annoy the Transvaal and Africanders. They are already furious with you. But, on the other hand, if we never mean ... to do anything, it is useless to call general attention to our impotence by barking. Of course, I always assume that the time will and must come. Otherwise life would be unbearable."*[41]
Day -188 Thu 1899-04-06	ZAR *State Secretary FW Reitz* *(War Museum of the Boer Republics)*	State Secretary FW Reitz complains that the confidentiality of the talks with the mining houses have been violated. As no official sanction has been obtained for the negotiations, he is forced to state that he, the Foreign Secretary and the State Attorney have acted *"on their own initative".*[42] Mr Fiddes reports to Milner, *"Eckstein* (a Rand Uitlander-Capitalist) *said twice, when I saw him yesterday, with great emphasis, I want a* peaceful *solution. (Fitzpatrick) is what I may call the political member of our firm; and I have told him to hold back. ...I don't want the franchise; wouldn't take it at any price. I represent millions of capital, and I can't forget my fiduciary position."*[43]
Day -182 Wed 1899-04-12	ZAR	The 22nd anniversary of the first annexation of the Transvaal. On this date in 1877, Sir Theophilus Shepstone, furthering British plans for a federation in South Africa, raised the Union Jack in Pretoria, annexing the Transvaal against the wishes of the majority of its citizens. Desperate efforts were made to win the support of the Republicans and to create the right climate for a federation. Shepstone saw British control of all Black territories in South Africa and the destruction of Zulu power as a prerequisite. His interference in Zulu tribal affairs led to the Anglo-Zulu War of 1879, the ignominious British defeat at Isandlwana, the heroic defence at Rorke's Drift and the massacre at the royal capital of Ulundi.[44]
	THE FIRST ANGLO-BOER WAR or TRANSVAAL WAR OF INDEPENDENCE 1880-1881 After months of failed negotiations, petitions and counterpetitions, deputations to London and protest meetings for the reinstatement of the independence of the Transvaal, the war finally broke out. On 16 December 1880, the first shots were fired at Potchefstroom and the *Vierkleur* (the Transvaal flag) was raised at Heidelberg. The British garrisons at Pretoria and Potchefstroom	

		were besieged and an infantry column was defeated at Bronkhorstspruit. The British invasion under Sir George Pommeroy Colley was stopped at Laing's Nek and Schuinshoogte on the Natal border. Colley's occupation of a hill dominating the Boer positions resulted on 27 February 1881 in the humiliating British defeat at Majuba during which 285 soldiers were killed or wounded for the loss of two burghers killed and four wounded. Sir Evelyn Wood arranged a truce and the provisional peace terms were ratified by the Pretoria Convention on 3 August 1881. The Transvaal, under the leadership of the triumvirate comprising SJP Kruger, MW Pretorius and PJ Joubert, regained its independence, subject to certain conditions. The Transvaal accepted British 'suzerainty', a British resident to oversee Black affairs, British control over the eastern border districts (Swaziland) and British approval of foreign affairs. The British had suffered a major military and political defeat.[45]
Day -177 Mon **1899-04-17**	ZAR	Mr Fiddes reports to Milner on a dinner-meeting with Uitlander leaders, *"I put the question: 'As regards Indians and Cape Boys. I know you don't love them much, and I know that there is something to be said on your side which I am sure HMG would take into account if properly approached. But the (Transvaal) don't approach us properly. I may tell you in strict confidence (I always like to tell people open secrets in strict confidence) that at the moment this question might assume a serious shape. Now if HMG made up their minds that it was necessary to take a firm stand on it, would Johannesburg be likely to take up a hostile or embarrassing attitude on it?'"* Fiddes' dinner companions 'chorused', *"Certainly not. Any stick is good enough to beat Kruger with, and though we don't love the Indian, we wouldn't say a word, and we would use our influence for all it's worth, to prevent others from saying a word against you."*[46]
Day -174 Thu **1899-04-20**	OFS	In a letter to President Kruger, the President of the Republic of the Orange Free State, President Marthinus Theunis Steyn, expresses his support for the proposed revision of the ZAR Franchise Act and concessions to the mining industry. He also confirms that the Reciprocal Recognition of Citizenship Agreement between the two republics will be accepted by the Orange Free State. (The discrepancy in qualifications for citizenship between the republics is an obstacle and it is unlikely that the above agreement can be workable without fundamental changes to the ZAR Franchise Act.)[47]
Day -171 Sun **1899-04-23**	United Kingdom	Colonial Secretary Mr. J Chamberlain requests reports from the High Commissioner which can be used to influence British public opinion.
Day -170 Mon **1899-04-24**	United Kingdom	Mr Chamberlain is of the opinion *"that the British public is... more likely to be stirred by concrete cases of oppression than by the general injustice of non-representation of the Uitlanders in the Legislature".*[48]
Day -169 Tue **1899-04-25**	ZAR	Danie Theron, a Krugersdorp attorney, is found guilty and fined £20 for assaulting Mr WF Moneypenny, the editor of *The Star*. Moneypenny, now in the country for less than two months, has written a derogatory editorial against the *"ignorant Dutch"*. Theron pleads extreme provocation and his fine is quickly paid by supporters in the courtroom.[49]
Day -164 Sun **1899-04-30**	ZAR	Despairing about the possibilities of successful negotiations, JC Smuts writes to WJ Leyds, *"England would still find a cause for hostilities in other points of dispute."*[50]
1899	AUTUMN	**MAY**
Day -159 Fri **1899-05-05**	Cape Colony	**THE 'HELOTS' TELEGRAM** High Commissioner Sir Alfred Milner sends his famous 'helots' telegram (*one of the most masterly State documents ever penned*) to Mr Joseph Chamberlain:

		"It seems a paradox but it is true that the only effective way of protecting our subjects is, to help them to cease to be our subjects... It is idle to talk of peace and unity... The case for intervention is overwhelming... The spectacle of thousands of British subjects kept permanently in the position of helots, constantly chafing under undoubted grievances and calling vainly to Her Majesty for redress, does steadily undermine the influence and reputation of Great Britain and the respect for the British Government within its own dominions."[51]
Day -158 Sat **1899-05-06**	Cape Colony	Mr William P Schreiner, Prime Minister of the Cape Colony, in a letter to President Steyn, informs him that the dispute between the British government and the ZAR is viewed in a very serious light in Britain. It would be in the interest of the subcontinent if Steyn could be instrumental in facilitating a meeting between Kruger and Milner to discuss the situation.[52] Mr Schreiner, a German-born English-speaking politician, elected with the support of Cape Afrikaners, is in a very difficult position. His cabinet is equally divided between supporters and bitter enemies of Rhodes and the imperial cause. His sister, Olive Schreiner, is vehemently anti-imperialist, or rather anti-Rhodes, while his wife, Fanny, is ex-President FW Reitz's sister.[53]
Day -156 Mon **1899-05-08**	United Kingdom	Mr Chamberlain, referring to Milner's 'helots' telegram, writes, *"This is tremendously stiff, and if it is published it will make either an ultimatum or Sir A Milner's recall necessary..."*[54]
	Cape Colony	Dr TNG te Water, the Cape Foreign Minister, urges President Steyn to act on Schreiner's suggestion with the utmost urgency. Steyn responds immediately, expressing his concern that the proposed meeting can create a platform where either of the parties can confront the other with demands of such an unacceptable nature that an unreconcilable breakdown is forged and blamed on the meeting. He immediately sends a telegram to Kruger to assess his feeling about such a meeting.[55]
Day -155 Tue **1899-05-09**	ZAR	President Kruger informs President Steyn that if the proposed meeting is acceptable to the High Commissioner, he would be pleased to attend.[56]
	Cape Colony	Sir A Milner receives a cypher cable from Chamberlain confirming that the Cabinet has decided to intervene — peacefully at present— on the side of the Uitlanders. This decision of a government to enter the struggle of its subjects to gain full citizenship of another country is unprecedented in world history.[57]
	ZAR	A counterpetition started by labour leaders on the Witwatersrand, states that, although there may be a need for reform, there are *"no grievances... which could justify any extreme measures on the part of Her Majesty's Government"*.[8]
Day-154 Wed **1899-05-10**	Cape Colony	Schreiner informs President Steyn that Milner accepts the desirability of a meeting with President Kruger, but asks for a postponement while he considers the relationships on which such a meeting should be based.[59]
	United Kingdom	Chamberlain instructs Milner to demand a settlement of the franchise question from Kruger that will be acceptable to the British government and which can be offered to the Uitlanders, whose treatment he considers to be in violation of the London Convention, as a *"reasonable concession to their just demands"*.[60]
Day -149 Mon **1899-05-15**	Cape Colony	Cape Afrikanerbond leader Jan Hendrik ('Onze Jan') Hofmeyr, informs the ZAR State Attorney, 27-year-old Jan Christiaan Smuts, that a large-scale armed insurrection in support of their cause by Cape Afrikaners, is unlikely.[61]
Day-148 Tue **1899-05-16**	OFS	President Steyn formally invites President Kruger and British High Commissioner Milner to a conference to promote good relations on issues of common interest in South Africa, to be held on 30 May in Bloemfontein.[62]

	ZAR	One of several counterpetitions (this one with 13 943 signatures) refers to the March petition as being by *"capitalists and not the public"*. The republican government has no major faults, but even if it has, they can be rectified without the intervention of foreign powers or *"the advice of capitalists"*. The signatures on counterpetitions received by the ZAR government eventually total about 23 500.[6]
Day-147 Wed **1899-05-17**	ZAR	President Kruger accepts Steyn's conference invitation. He is willing to discuss any proposals conducive to better relations between Britain and the South African Republic, *"provided that the independence of this Republic is not impugned"*.[64] He will be accompanied by SW Burger, ADW Wolmarans and State Attorney JC Smuts.[65]
	Cape Colony	Milner writes to Lord Selborne, the Colonial Under-Secretary: *"The conference really is a good stroke of business on part of the enemy, as it holds up dispatch and spoils, or at least delays, a great stroke on our part."* He is afraid of a *"plausible offer of reform"* which may be difficult to reject and postpone the *"day of reckoning"*.[66] *"Now I don't want war, but I admit I begin to think it may be the only way out ... No use saying now what I shall try to get out of old Kruger... But, as at present advised, I think I ought to be very stiff about Uitlander grievances and put my demands on this subject high and get him to break off, if he does break off, on these, rather than on any one of the 101 other differences, which, though they may afford better technical casus belli, do not really mean so much or excite so much interest... If I fail, it will be your turn... The Boers and their sympathizers have never been in such a funk for many years — never since Warren's expedition.* *"Therefore my advice to you is, if I fail with Kruger, to assume at once the diplomatic offensive and to back it with a strong show of material force... My view is (1) that absolute downright determination plus a large temporary increase of force will ensure a climb down. It is 20 to 1. And (2) that, if it didn't and there was a fight, it would be better now than 5 or 10 years hence... Bold words these, you will say. But remember I myself am risking a lot — indeed everything..."*[67]
Day -146 Thu **1899-05-18**	Cape Colony	High Commissioner Sir A Milner accepts President Steyn's invitation but objects to Steyn being a party to the conference. Cape Prime Minister Schreiner also *"does not see his way clear"* to attend. Milner requests that the date of the conference be changed to 31 May. [68]
	International	The World Conference opens at The Hague, in the Netherlands. At this first Peace Conference, 26 nations meet at Tsar Nicholas II's suggestion, to extend the Geneva Convention to naval warfare, to ban the use of explosive bullets and to authorise the establishment of a permanent Court of Arbitration to settle disputes.
Day -140 Wed **1899-05-24**	Cape Colony	Sir A Milner again writes a *"very secret letter"* to Lord Selborne: *"... if the conference fails... The exact amount of extra force required is for the military experts. ... with 30 000 additional troops we should have a means of pressure which would be irresistible ... My view has been and still is... that if we are perfectly determined we shall win without a fight or with a mere apology for one."*[69]
	Trivia	*Queen Victoria's 80th birthday.*
Day -139 Thu **1899-05-25**	ZAR	President Kruger accepts that President Steyn will not be a party to the conference, but insists that he acts as chairman.[70]
	Natal Colony	Sir A Milner assures the Natal Ministry that the colony will, if necessary, be defended by *"the whole force of the Empire"*. [71]
Day -133 Wed **1899-05-31**	OFS	**THE BLOEMFONTEIN CONFERENCE** Without *"apportioning blame"* for the *"deplorable situation"* in which both countries find themselves, it is Milner's opinion that the ZAR's policy towards the Uitlanders is the

		main problem, which, if removed, will lead to the solution of all other outstanding questions. He assures Kruger that Britain has no designs on the independence of the Republic.[72] President Kruger points out that the political demands of the Uitlanders conflict with the national rights of the ZAR.
1899	WINTER	**JUNE**
Day -132 Thu **1899-06-01**	OFS	**THE BLOEMFONTEIN CONFERENCE** On Milner's reference to the *"unjustified"* arming of the ZAR, Kruger counters that the traitorous behaviour of the Uitlanders and the eagerness of foreign powers to assist in plots against his government, as evidenced by the Jameson Raid, have precipitated rearming.[73] Milner returns to the franchise issue and asks for voting rights after five years with a retrospective clause. Kruger cannot comply as this would be *"suicide for the Volk"*.
	South Africa	The number of imperial British troops garrisoned in South Africa have increased by about 20% since December and are now as follows: Cape Colony 4 462; Natal 5 827; Total: 10 289 men with 24 artillery pieces.[74]
	ZAR	At about the same time the ZAR's permanent uniformed forces consist of the following: 575 men and a reserve of 158 in the Staatsartillerie including the Field Telegraph Service, Medical Department and the Music Corps; 1 545 policemen including detectives and foot police.[75]
Day -131 Fri **1899-06-02**	OFS	**THE BLOEMFONTEIN CONFERENCE** President Kruger surprises all with a fully detailed draft Reform Bill offering franchise after seven years. In return he wants compensation for the Jameson Raid, control over Swaziland and arbitration on the rival interpretations of the London Convention of 1884.[76] Milner is not interested in conditional reforms and wants to see arbitration as a separate issue. Milner raises the possibility of self-government (home rule) for the Rand knowing that it will be unacceptable to both parties. (Chamberlain's split with his own party stems from his opposition to home rule for Ireland.) Milner writes in his diary, *"Things have become critical now. Butler or I will have to go."*
Day -130 Sat **1899-06-03**	OFS	**THE BLOEMFONTEIN CONFERENCE** Sir A Milner submits a long list of objections to President Kruger's Reform Bill, although he admits in private that it is a *"great advance"*. The conference adjourns and Milner cables London, expressing his view that the conference will fail.[77] Chamberlain is concerned about public opinion if termination of the negotiations by Britain is seen as intolerance. Talking informally at a reception, President Steyn encourages Sir A Milner to also consider other issues like the Dynamite question where concessions are possible. Milner refuses, saying, "What is the Dynamite question after all? It is the franchise that must do it."[78]
	Trivia	*The French Court of Review (cour de cessation) annuls Alfred Dreyfus' first trial and orders a retrial.* *Johann Strauss dies at the age of 74.*
Day -129 Sun **1899-06-04**	OFS	**THE BLOEMFONTEIN CONFERENCE** The Dean of the Bloemfontein Anglican cathedral delivers a sermon with the theme *"Blessed are the Peacemakers"*.[79]

Day -128 Mon 1899-06-05	OFS	**THE BLOEMFONTEIN CONFERENCE** Sir A Milner decides to break off negotiations unless President Kruger gives in. Chamberlain's cable from London counselling restraint and advising against this, arrives too late and Milner closes the conference, saying, *"This Conference is absolutely at an end and there is no obligation on either side arising out of it."*[80] President Paul Kruger's final comment is, *"It is our country you want!"*[81]
Day -127 Tue 1899-06-06	OFS	The OFS Volksraad adopts a motion supporting President Kruger's franchise proposals as an *"extremely fair concession"* and supporting the reference of future disputes to arbitration for continuous peace and co-operation in South Africa.[82]
Day -125 Thu 1899-06-08	United Kingdom	Mr Chamberlain announces in the House of Commons that *"a new situation"* has arisen in South Africa.[83] Lord Selborne wires Milner, *"The crisis has come and we are not going to fail you. Thank God we have you as our High Commissioner."*[84] Lord Garnet Wolseley, the Commander-in-Chief of the British Army, initiates secret preparations for the mobilisation of *"a force consisting of an Army Corps, a battalion of mounted infantry and four battalions to guard communications"* (about 50 000 men).[85]
Day -124 Fri 1899-06-09	ZAR	The ZAR government accepts a motion condoning the President's actions in Bloemfontein. The motion regrets the fact that the High Commissioner could not favourably consider the President's *"extremely fair"* franchise proposals and supports the arbitration proposals. It further requests the President to submit his reform bill for consideration by the Raad.[86]
Day -123 Sat 1899-06-10	ZAR	A mass meeting of about 5 000 Uitlanders is held at the Wanderers sports field in Johannesburg. Amid vehement anti-Boer rhetoric, it is decided to establish an Uitlander Council and to confirm Milner's proposal at Bloemfontein as their minimum demands.[87]
	United Kingdom	Mr Chamberlain instructs the High Commissioner to present to the South African Republic a claim for £4 000 compensation on behalf of Edgar's widow.[88]
Day -122 Sun 1899-06-11	OFS	President Steyn offers to travel to Cape Town, if it can further the peace effort. Schreiner, in an interview with Milner, states that Kruger's proposals are fair and enforceable, although it could be improved on in certain details. Milner disagrees on what could be termed 'main issues' and 'details' and suggests that Schreiner submit his suggestions to Kruger.[89]
Day -119 Wed 1899-06-14	United Kingdom	Delayed until after the conclusion of the Bloemfontein Conference to achieve maximum impact on public opinion, Milner's 'helots' dispatch is finally published by way of a Blue Book.[90] Milner complains to Chamberlain about Major-General Sir William Butler, Officer Commanding Her Majesty's Forces in South Africa, and his *"policy of obstructive pacifism"*.[91]
Day -118 Thu 1899-06-15	ZAR	Commandant-General Petrus (Piet) Joubert addresses a long letter to Queen Victoria: *"An Earnest Representation and Historical Reminder to Her Majesty... in view of the Prevailing Crisis."*[92] In what Michael Davitt describes as *"one of the most eloquently pathetic letters ever written,"* Joubert describes the history of the 'Boer race' and British imperialism

		since 1806, the Voortrekkers, the First Boer War, Jameson's Raid, the greed of the Capitalists and the circumstances leading up to the present crisis.
		"Will Your Majesty permit a small weak State to be oppressed and overthrown by the world-renowned power and might of Great Britain simply owing to the misrepresentations of the people I have already mentioned? Such is the inquiry of him who considers it an honour and a privilege to extol Your Majesty, the Queen of Great Britain and Ireland and Empress of India... He will never believe that Your Majesty will suffer the sacred rights of a weak, peace loving people to be violated in your name, and South Africa to be cast into grief and mourning. Such is the wish and prayer of Your Majesty's most humble petitioner —P.J. JOUBERT." He also sends copies to the Kaiser and the Czar.
	OFS	President Steyn sends Abraham Fischer, a member of the OFS Executive Council, to Cape Town to consult with the High Commissioner and the Cape Government.[93]
	Cape Colony	Mr Schreiner submits the Cape Ministry's proposals, finalised in conjunction with Fischer, to Milner stressing that in their opinion, the situation is not serious enough to warrant interference in the internal affairs of the ZAR
Day -116 Sat **1899-06-15**	Cape Colony	In a letter to Milner Major-General Sir William Butler discounts any evidence that the Republic may attack and instead points to British preparedness and provocation. *"I find in the balance of things no reason to suppose that the Dutch could be desirous of a war with us. Can they think the same about us?"* Milner forwards this letter to Chamberlain, who is displeased: *"Milner is really rather trying. Think of our difficulties and how they would be enhanced by recalling Butler at this juncture... I shall do my best for Milner, and for the policy which is mine as well as his... but he is overstrained. I wish he would remember the advice to the lady whose clothes caught fire, to keep as cool as possible."*[94]
Day -111 Thu **1899-06-22**	OFS *Abraham Fischer* *(War Museum of the Boer Republics)*	After reporting to President Steyn, Abraham Fischer departs for Pretoria to inform President Kruger of the results of his meetings with the High Commissioner and the Cape government.[95] President Steyn requests Dr Te Water, the Cape Foreign Minister, to confirm or deny the rumour that 40 000 British troops have been sent to South Africa.[96]
	Cape Colony	Dr Te Water is convinced that no troops will be sent to South Africa without consultation with the Cape Prime Minister.[97] Major-General Sir William Butler, ordered to report on the purchasing of South African horses and mules and asked for his observations, uses the opportunity to give his opinion: *"I believe war between the white races... would be the greatest calamity that ever occurred in South Africa."*[98]
Day -108 Sun **1899-06-25**	United Kingdom	Lord Selborne, Colonial Under-Secretary, writes to Milner: *"The publication of the Blue Book produced a great effect but not so great an effect as we had hoped. The idea of war with the S.A. Republic is very distasteful to most people. Consequently the Cabinet have undoubtedly had to modify the pace that they contemplated moving at immediately after the Bloemfontein Conference. There is no idea of receding from the intervention which was commenced by your action at Bloemfontein and our reply to the petition, but we simply cannot force the pace. We have between us moved public opinion, almost universally, forward to the position of accepting the eventual responsibility of seeing a remedy applied, and this is a great step forward; but we have not convinced them yet either that you cannot believe a word Kruger says, or that he has never yielded and never will yield till he feels the muzzle of the pistol on his forehead, or that the surest way to avoid war is to prepare openly for war."*[99]

1899	WINTER	JULY
Day-102 Sat **1899-07-01**	United Kingdom	Cecil John Rhodes leaves Britain to return to South Africa.
Day-100 Mon **1899-07-03**	OFS	In Bloemfontein, President Steyn tells Jan H Hofmeyr, the Afrikanerbond leader and Cape politician, that further pressure on the ZAR government will fail. It is now time for the Cape government to state clearly that it does not want a war in South Africa and will not allow Britain to conduct a war on Cape soil. Hofmeyer fears that the Schreiner ministry will be dismissed and that Rhodes and Sprigg, who are not well-disposed to the Republics, will gain power with predictable results. Steyn expects this to happen in any case, but that Milner will not then be bold enough to pursue his aims without the support of the Cape Afrikaners.[100]
Day -95 Sat **1899-07-08**	Cape Colony	In an article in the *South African News*, Mr. Schreiner summarises the pressure that has been brought to bear by his government on the ZAR, and stresses, *"We are at liberty to say that the Government regards these* (Kruger's) *proposals as adequate, satisfactory and as such should secure a peaceful settlement."*[101]
Day -94 Sun **1899-07-09**	*Trivia*	*Britain purchases the possessions of the Niger Company.*
Day -93 Mon **1899-07-10**	International	Queensland offers military aid to Great Britain.[102]
Day -91 Wed **1899-07-12**	International	Lord Brassey of Victoria offers volunteers for service in South Africa.[103]
Day -86 Mon **1899-07-17**	ZAR	Sir A Milner to Chamberlain: *" 'Raad' has been in session all day and report is current that Franchise Bill is once more to be altered... if this scheme... approach our demands, say 7 years retrospective and 5 new seats, it will be difficult to reject it...* *"Franchise will thus be a fiasco while we shall have got no further about anything else. We could not accept that position without suffering diplomatic defeat at any rate in the eyes of our supporters in South Africa. I suggest that we should at once and before new measure is presented to us as a fait accompli, inform South African Republic that after all that has passed no franchise measure will be accepted as satisfactory unless its provisions are agreed upon between the two Governments...* *"It makes all the difference... to our position in South Africa whether measure is shaped and secured by Her Majesty's Government or whether it is arranged independently... by the South African Republic Government...* *"To assert our power and retain confidence of loyalists are after all two main objects to view."*[104]
	International	An offer of 300 men of the Malay States Guides arrives but the High Commissioner intimates that they cannot be spared.[105]
Day -85 Tue **1899-07-18**	ZAR	The Aliens Act (Franchise Law), Act No 3 of 1899, is passed by the ZAR Volksraad, refusing Milner's suggestion that the Act must first be submitted to the British Government.[106] This Act allows naturalization of aliens after five years with limited voting rights and full franchise after a further two years. The Act incorporates all the amendments as suggested by Fischer after his consultations in Cape Town:[107] 1. Full voting rights after seven years. 2. Immediate, full voting rights to everybody who has resided in the country for nine years or more.

		3. Full voting rights after five years to persons who have been in the country for two years.
		4. Full voting rights for the sons of aliens born in the country on achieving his majority.
		5. Four additional seats for the mining districts.
	United Kingdom	Joseph Chamberlain telegraphs Milner, *"I congratulate you on great victory. No one would dream of fighting over two years in qualification period."*[108] The political correspondent of *The London Times* reports that *"The crisis must be regarded as at an end"*.[109]
	International	Three hundred Hausas from Lagos volunteer their services.[110]
	Trivia	*Scientist RW Bunsen dies at the age of 88.*
Day -83 Thu **1899-07-20**	Cape Colony	Almost in a panic, Milner replies, *"Telegraphic summary of inspired article Times intimating that HM Government was satisfied with amended Franchise Law has created consternation among British party here."*[111]
Day -82 Fri **1899-07-21**	International	New South Wales offers 1 860 officers, noncommissioned officers and men for service in South Africa.[112]
Day -81 Sat **1899-07-22**	ZAR	As instructed by Chamberlain, Milner transmits the following to Conyngham Greene in Johannesburg: *"Please give the following advice to our friends: British Government could not afford to admit largeness of advance made by President without alienating public opinion in England. This does not mean that they are going to climb down. No need for discouragement but moderation of tone desirable. There is danger of Uitlander adopting a too uncompromising attitude and being thought to be for 'War at any price'."*[113] Colonel RSS Baden-Powell, a Special Service officer sent by the Colonial Office, lands at Cape Town with instructions to secretly raise two infantry regiments, to organise the defence of the Rhodesian and Bechuanaland frontiers and to keep the enemy occupied and away from the main British forces.[114]
Day -77 Wed **1899-07-26**	ZAR	The Aliens Act (Franchise Law), Act No 3 of 1899, is promulgated.[115]
	Cape Colony	Trying to maintain the pressure, Milner informs Chamberlain: *"Opinion growing that Government S.A.R. and its sympathisers are still bluffing and will yield further if pressure kept up."*[116]
Day -76 Thu **1899-07-27**	Cape Colony	In a diplomatic note to the ZAR Milner states that the new Aliens Act includes unacceptable regulations. He proposes that it must be subjected to a Joint Inquiry consisting of delegates from both governments whose recommendations will be submitted to both governments. Furthermore, at a future conference, this issue and the question of arbitration can be discussed, with the proviso that an arbitration court includes no 'international' elements and that the preamble to the Pretoria Convention of 1881 will not be subject to arbitration.[117]
Day -74 Sat **1899-07-29**	**THE INTERNATIONAL CONVENTION WITH RESPECT TO LAWS AND CUSTOMS OF WAR BY LAND** is signed at The Hague.[118] The approved clauses include the following: Article 23. It is prohibited to make improper use of a flag of truce, the national flag, or military insignia and the enemy's uniform, as well as the distinctive badges of the Geneva Convention.	

> Article 42. Military rule by an occupying force can only be exercised once the area is *materially* under the control of the invading force.
>
> Article 44. Any compulsion of the population of occupied territory to take part in military operations against their own country is prohibited.
>
> Article 45. The civilian population cannot be forced to swear allegiance to an occupying force. The dignity, family rights, lives of persons, private property, religious rights and customs of the occupied people must be respected and the confiscation of property is prohibited.
>
> Article 50. Collective punishment resulting from the actions of individuals is prohibited.
>
> Article 52. Requisition of goods and services of the civilian population is prohibited.[119]

1899-08-00	WINTER	**AUGUST**
Day -71 Tue **1899-08-01**	United Kingdom	The Colonial Secretary, Mr J Chamberlain, demands that the new ZAR Franchise Act must be submitted to a Joint Inquiry.[120]
Day -68 Fri **1899-08-04**	Europe	Dr Willem Johannes Leyds, the ZAR's Special Diplomatic Representative in Europe, warns his government not to expect any assistance from the major European powers.[121]
Day -60 Sat **1899-08-12**	ZAR *State Attorney JC Smuts* *(War Museum of the Boer Republics)*	During negotiations with State Attorney JC Smuts, Sir W Conyngham Greene, the British Agent in Johannesburg, expresses the opinion that full compliance with the franchise proposals as put forward by Milner at the Bloemfontein Conference, will no longer satisfy the British government. Smuts offers a simplified Franchise Draft Bill, allowing full voting rights after five years with a retrospective clause and increased representation for the mining districts on the Witwatersrand. *"In putting forward the above proposals, the Government of the Z.A.R. will assume that HM Government will agree that their present intervention shall not form a precedent, etc. Further that HM Government will not further insist on the assertion of Suzerainty, the controversy on this subject being tacitly allowed to drop. Lastly, arbitration, from which foreign element is excluded, to be conceded as soon as franchise scheme has become law."*[122]
Day -58 Mon **1899-08-14**	ZAR	The memorandum of the negotiations between JC Smuts and Sir W Conyngham Greene is wired to London.[123]
Day -57 Tue **1899-08-15**	Cape Colony	On the strength of Milner's repeated complaints about him (especially a telegram to Chamberlain stating, *"I am sorry to say that in my opinion the strength of the General's political opinion impairs his efficiency, whatever his military capacity."*) Sir William Butler is finally recalled. He is succeeded by Lieutenant-General Sir FWEF Forestier-Walker.[124]
Day -56 Wed **1899-08-16**	United Kingdom	Chamberlain instructs Milner to request official proposals from the ZAR government.[125]
	Cape Colony	Milner writes to Chamberlain: *"The last movement of the S.A.R. shows... their absolute determination not to admit our claim to have a voice in their affairs as the Paramount Power in South Africa... They will collapse if we don't weaken, or rather if we go on steadily turning the screw."*[126] Milner predicts that *"a successful blow dealt against that force* (the combined republican forces) *would be followed by a general debacle"*.[127]

	United Kingdom	The ZAR government receives the assurance that their proposals will not be taken as a rejection of the joint inquiry proposal and that the proposals will be considered on merit.[128]

Day -53 Sat **1899-08-19**	ZAR	**THE ZAR PROPOSALS**
		The ZAR formally submits the proposals worked out between State Attorney Smuts and British Agent Sir W Conyngham Greene.
		The proposals include the following:
		1. Franchise with a five year residency provision as demanded by Milner at Bloemfontein.
		2. Eight additional representatives for the mining districts (making it 10 out of 36).[129]
		3. Franchise to include the right to elect the State President and Commandant-General.
		4. The ZAR government will accept friendly advice from HMG on the issue of franchise legislation.
		5. The ZAR accepts:
		  (a) that Her Majesty's Government will agree that the present intervention will not constitute a precedent, and will not interfere in the internal affairs of the Republic,
		  (b) that Her Majesty's Government will not insist on the assertion of suzerainty, and will allow this dispute to lapse,
		  (c) that arbitration, without foreign elements (the Orange Free State excepted) be assented to for the settlement of future disputes.
		6. On Her Majesty's Government's acceptance of these proposals, the ZAR Volksraad will dissolve and go to the voters to finalise the proposed act within weeks.
		7. In the interim, discussion on the Arbitration Court can proceed and be provisionally agreed on to bring the present situation of tension to a speedy conclusion. [130]

	United Kingdom	In a telegram to Milner, Chamberlain describes the proposals as *"... an immense concession and even a considerable advance on your Bloemfontein proposals"*.[131]
Day -51 Mon **1899-08-21**	ZAR	The ZAR government stresses that its five-year franchise proposal will be subject to the stated conditions. Franchise and representation for the Uitlanders are made *"expressly conditional"* upon preliminary assurances from the Queen's Government on three points: *(a) In future not to interfere in internal affairs of the South African Republic.* *(b) Not to insist further on its assertion of existence of suzerainty.* *(c) To agree to arbitration."*[132]
Day -49 Wed **1899-08-23**	Cape Colony	Sir A Milner, urging the despatch of an expeditionary force, writes to Chamberlain: *"The problem here is, to my mind, now a purely military one. We have got the S.A.R. to go as they will go without not merely the threat but the actual application of force. I do not say war, for there is always a probability that with an Army actually on their borders they will submit to anything and everything including disarmament. But to a mere display of force at a distance they will pay no further heed."*[133]
Day -45 Sun **1899-08-27**	International	An 'abnormally large' crowd turns up at what may be the first pro-Boer rally, in Foster Place, Dublin. They chant *"Long live the Boers"* and speakers call on Irishmen in South Africa to take up arms in defence of their adopted country. [134]
Day -44 Mon **1899-08-28**	United Kingdom	Mr Joseph Chamberlain announces that the British government is willing to accept the five-year franchise proposal, but that most of the conditions either are unacceptable or have to be negotiated.[135] He also refers to 'other differences' which have to be settled concurrently. What these differences are, are not stated.[136]

Day -41 Thu **1899-08-31**	Cape Colony	Sir Alfred Milner, keeping the aggressive spirit alive, cables Chamberlain: *"British South Africa is prepared for extreme measures, and is ready to suffer much in order to see British authority conclusively vindicated. What is dreaded is prolongation of negotiations ending in indecisive results. I have serious fear that, if matters drag, there will be strong reaction of feeling against policy of HM's Govt."*[137]
	Trivia	*Princess Wilhelmina's 19th birthday.*[138]
1899-09-00	SPRING	**SEPTEMBER**
Day -40 Fri **1899-09-01**		*Lieutenant-General Paul Sanford, third Baron Methuen of Corsham, known as Lord Methuen, celebrates his 54th birthday.*
Day -39 Sat **1899-09-02** *Colonial Secretary J Chamberlain* *(War Museum of the Boer Republics)*	United Kingdom	Colonial Secretary J Chamberlain to Sir A Milner: *"I am really astonished at the progress we have made... Three months ago we could not go to war on this issue — now, although with a large majority against us — we shall be sufficiently supported. But please bear all this in mind if we move more slowly than you think wise."*[139] He also submits a list of demands for Milner's comment. These include the following: *"1. Explicit recognition of Suzerainty.* *2. Foreign affairs to be conducted through H.M. Government.* *3. Acceptance of Judicial Committee of Privy Council, with Transvaal judge added, to deal with all future questions of interpretation.* *4. Franchise, etc., as in the Cape Colony.* *5. Municipal rights for gold mining districts.* *6. All legislation since 1884 restricting rights and privileges of Uitlanders to be repealed.* *7. Disarmament.* *8. Indemnity for expenses incurred since refusal of franchise proposals.* *9. Federation of South African Colonies and States.* (Including the Orange Free State) *I give these as a list of possible demands, but whether it would be a good policy to put all of them forward before the war may well be a question..."*
Day -38 Sun **1899-09-03**	International	Princess Wilhelmina of the Netherlands writes to her aunt, Queen Victoria: *"I venture to hope that this circumstance will explain and excuse in your eyes, dear Aunt, my addressing you in this matter, by appealing to your well-known feeling of humanity and magnanimity, and entreating you to use your powerful influence to prevent this war, that would, I know, fill your heart with sorrow, because it will bring mourning and misery into many families on both sides by the inevitable bloodshed and destruction of property. God grant that your wisdom, experience and greatness of mind may find the way to avert this impending calamity!"* Queen Victoria, maybe not quite understanding that an acceptable franchise and citizenship settlement would make the Uitlanders foreign subjects, or maybe already anticipating the addition of a new colony to her Empire, answers: *"I sympathise most deeply with your expressions of the horrors of war, than which no one can feel more strongly than I do; and earnestly hope that it may be averted. But I cannot abandon my own subjects who have appealed to me for protection. If President Kruger is reasonable, there will be no war, but the issue is in his hands..."*[140]
Day -37 Mon **1899-09-04**	Cape Colony	Sir A Milner, responding to Chamberlain's cable, suggests the following demands: *"We must ask repeal of franchise laws since 1881, when independence was granted. Personally I should prefer to ask directly what we really want:* *1. Absolute equality of political status for all resident whites.* *2. Recognition of British paramountcy, affording not only control of foreign relations but ultimate right of interference even in internal affairs, where welfare of all SA is affected.* *3. Abandonment of policy of militarism including (a) dismantling of forts at Johannesburg and Pretoria and promise not to erect any; (b) no permanent military force except two field batteries. Number of men and guns not to be increased without consent of HM Government."*

	ZAR	*"... I am averse to claiming expenses in ultimatum, though if we are compelled to bring our Army Corps to enforce it, I think we might then claim something... I entirely agree that ultimatum should be accompanied by despatch of troops — not necessarily main body of expeditionary force, but number required to secure position in Colony... and make Natal impregnable with Laing's Nek occupied. I assume that these troops could come promptly and that their despatch and preliminary arrangements for sending a large force from England would not have to await summoning of Parliament."*[141] State Attorney JC Smuts drafts a war plan in which he envisages *"a long and exhausting struggle"*. It is essential that the Republicans get the upper hand early by taking the offensive and advance deep into the Cape Colony and Natal before the arrival of British reinforcements. If successful, the Republicans can expect *"many thousands of Afrikaners from the Cape Colony would flock to join the republican armies"* and soon an Afrikaner republic may be established in South Africa *"stretching from Table Bay to the Zambesi"*.[142]
Day -35 Wed **1899-09-06**	*Trivia*	*The 19-year-old Princess Wilhelmina is crowned as Queen of the Netherlands.* *Vice-president Schalk W Burger's 47th birthday.*
Day -34 Thu **1899-09-07**	ZAR	President Paul Kruger tells the Volksraad in Pretoria, *"They have asked for my trousers, and I have given them; then for my coat, I have given that also; now they want my life, and that I cannot give."*[143]
Day -32 Sat **1899-09-09**	*Trivia*	*At Alfred Dreyfus's retrial at Rennes a court martial finds him guilty 'with extenuating circumstances'.*
Day -28 Wed **1899-09-13**	Cape Colony	Lieutenant-Colonel RG Kekewich arrives in Kimberley to assess the military situation and to advise the new General Officer Commanding British Troops in South Africa, Lieutenant-General FWEF Forestier-Walker, on the steps to be taken regarding the defence of the town, in the event of war.[144]
Day -25 Sat **1899-09-16**	Cape Colony	Sir A Milner to Mr J Chamberlain: *"I hope orders will quietly be given to all troopships to come at the greatest possible speed."*[145]
	United Kingdom	General Sir George Stuart White VC, newly appointed General Officer Commanding British Troops in Natal, accompanied by Colonels Hamilton and Rawlinson, sail for South Africa on board the *Tantallon Castle*.[146]
Day -23 Mon **1899-09-18**	International	The first British Army contingent from India embarks at Bombay for South Africa.
Day -22 Tue **1899-09-19**	*Trivia*	*Alfred Dreyfus is pardoned by presidential decree, which with premier Waldeck-Rousseau's intervention in the Le Creosot strike, helps to heal divisions in France.*
Day -20 Thu **1899-09-21**	OFS	An extraordinary session of the OFS Volksraad is opened by President Steyn in Bloemfontein. He gives a complete summary of the recent developments

		and its implications for the Orange Free State. Because every concession on the part of the ZAR is greeted with further demands and increased military preparations, he cannot see his way clear to advise the ZAR government to accept the proposed joint inquiry unconditionally. President Steyn, however, is still convinced *"that nothing has yet happened that justifies military action. A war over the points of contention, which can be solved by negotiation or arbitration, would not only be an insult to Christianity and civilisation, but would be a crime against humanity"*.[147]
	International	Hong Kong offers military assistance to Great Britain.[148]
Day -19 Fri **1899-09-22**	United Kingdom	Mr J Chamberlain terminates the negotiations with the ZAR and states that the British government will *"formulate their own proposals for a final settlement... They will communicate to you the result of their deliberations in a later despatch"*.[149] **THE BRITISH ULTIMATUM** Mr Chamberlain submits his *"first incomplete draft"* of what he calls *"proposals for a final settlement"* to the British Cabinet. Wits refer to the document as Chamberlain's *"Penultimatum"*.[150] The conditions include the following: 1. All legislation adopted since 1881 deemed to be prejudicial to Uitlanders must be repealed, full rights must be granted after residence of one year, proportional representation and the official status of English must be guaranteed. 2. Full municipal rights must be granted to mining districts. 3. An impartial judiciary must be guaranteed. 4. All 'religious disabilities' must be removed. 5. The ZAR must agree to arbitration without any international elements. 6. British paramountcy and most-favoured-nation status must be recognized, not only in commercial affairs but in all issues relating to British interests and British subjects, whether white or coloured. 7. Agreements between the ZAR and Portugal must be terminated and an agreement must be arrived at for the reduction of the excessive armaments of the ZAR.[151] *"If these conditions are agreed to, H.M.G. will still be prepared to give a complete guarantee against any attack upon the independence of the S.A.R., either from within any part of the British Dominions or from the territory of a foreign state."* As these conditions will amount to the ZAR becoming nothing more than a British Protectorate — which will not be acceptable — it amounts to an ultimatum. It is decided that, with the approval of the Cabinet and after submission to the Queen, it will be sent at the end of October. In a 'secret and personal' cable Mr Chamberlain informs Milner: *"Cabinet unanimous and resolves to see matter through. All preparations for expeditionary force will be proceeded with as quickly as possible but without public announcement at present. Our proposals for settlement will be agreed on by Cabinet next week and if forwarded by mail will allow four weeks' interval for reinforcements which are now underway to arrive."*[152]
	OFS	Responding to a formal diplomatic question, President Steyn informs the British High Commissioner that the OFS Executive Council is unanimous in its intention to honour its obligations under the 1897 Defence Agreement with the ZAR. President Steyn again offers to act as mediator in the dispute with the ZAR.[153]
	ZAR	State Attorney JC Smuts submits his extensive secret memorandum on the proposed conduct of a war with Britain to the ZAR government. In this document he outlines how the Republic must exploit its initial numerical superiority through fast, decisive offensive action.

		His recommendations also include a special war tax to be levied on the gold mining company to finance the Republican war effort.[154] The ZAR takes over control of the railway lines and workshops of the Nederlandsche Zuid-Afrikaansche Spoorweg-Maatschappij or NZASM-railway company.[155]
Day -16 Mon **1899-09-25**	United Kingdom	Mr J Chamberlain informs the ZAR government, in an official dispatch via Milner's office: *"Her Majesty's Government is now compelled to consider the situation afresh and to formulate her own proposals for a final settlement... She will communicate to you the result of the deliberations in a later despatch. Communicate as above to Govt. S.A.R."*[156]
	Natal	Major-General Sir William Penn Symonds, commander of the British garrison at Ladysmith, in an operation that seems provocative, takes a brigade of just more than 4 000 men with 18 field-guns to Dundee, 120 kilometres closer to the ZAR border, to protect the coal mines and to reassure loyalists in the vicinity.[157]
Day -15 Tue **1899-09-26**	United Kingdom	In a bellicose speech in Birmingham, Chamberlain says: *"We have tried waiting, patience, and trusting to promises which were never kept. We can wait no more. It is our duty, not only to the Uitlander, but to the English throughout South Africa, to the native races, and to our own prestige in that part of the world, and to the world at large, to insist that the Transvaal falls into line with the other states in South Africa, and no longer menaces the peace and prosperity of the world."*[158]
	Cape Colony	Milner sends Chamberlain a secret telegram: *"Everything points to likelihood that the Boers will anticipate ultimatum by some action or declaration. British Agent wires that Executive have to-day been considering proposal to take offensive on Natal border at once. Even if this is not done, I feel sure that some step will be taken. This being so, consideration of ultimatum becomes unnecessary... We shall have our work cut out for us to hold on for three weeks pending arrival of troops now on water and even after that."*[159]
	ZAR	The ZAR government formally requests military assistance from the Orange Free State in accordance with the 1897 Political and Defence Agreement.[160]
Day -14 Wed **1899-09-27**	OFS	In Bloemfontein, a draft proposal prepared by a select commission in deliberation with the Executive Council, is submitted to the OFS Volksraad. It insists that all avenues must be explored to maintain the peace of the two republics without violating their honour and independence. Furthermore, the ZAR is requested to continue to pursue a peaceful solution, failing which, the Orange Free State will honour its obligations in accordance with its Political and Defence Agreement with the ZAR The proposal is carried unanimously.[161] **THE ZAR CALL-UP** The South African Republican Burgher Force is called up. The number of burghers liable for active service (i.e. between 16 and 60 years old) totals 32 353, but the initial call-up is limited to men between 18 and 35 years of age. Members of the Volksraad, only sons of widows, key government officials, ministers, church officials and even members of church committees can apply for exemption of military service. This means that the initial call-up involves between 56% and 65% of the eligible burghers — about 18 100 to 21 000 men.[162] The Burgher Force is organised in regions and all officers are elected by their men. There are 21 District Commandants plus a Special Commandant for Johannesburg. The bigger districts are subdivided in wards, commanded by 80 Field-cornets with 57 Assistant Field-cornets for the bigger wards. The Commandant-General, the supreme

| | | commander, is also elected by the voters and earns £2 500 per year, while all other Burgher Force officers are unpaid. The Commandant-General is assisted by six Generals and 10 Combat-Generals as 'Higher Officers'.[163] |
| | | The ZAR Staatsartillerie (State Artillery) possesses four 155mm Creusot fortress guns ('Long Toms'), 52 modern field-guns, 25 pom-poms and 14 obsolete artillery pieces with 34 machine guns.[164] |

THE ZAR COMMANDOS[165]

District	Ward	Burghers 18-34 years	Commandant	Volunteers	Men
Bethal	2 wards	448	Grobler (HS)		
Bloemhof	3 wards	553	De Beer (Tollie)	**Colonials**	
Carolina	3 wards	274	Joubert (D)	Cape Colony	1 704
Ermelo	3 wards	499	Grobler (JNH)	Natal	43
Heidelberg	4 wards	915	Weilbach (JD)	Griqualand	22
Krugersdorp	3 wards	320	Kemp (JCG)	Bechuanaland	271
Lichtenburg	3 wards	580	Celliers (JG)	Western border	319
					2 359
Lydenburg	3 wards	551	Burger (SW)		
Marico	4 wards	670	Snyman (JP)		
Middelburg	5 wards	1 126	Fourie		
Piet Retief	2 wards	212		**Foreigners**	
Potchefstroom	6 wards	1 878	Cronje (APJ)	Russia & Germany	311
Pretoria	6 wards	2 320	Erasmus (D)	Holland	17
Rustenburg	4 wards	1 368	Steenkamp (PS)	France	75
Standerton	3 wards	646	Alberts (JJ)	Italy	8
Swaziland	1 ward	181	Opperman	America	40
Utrecht	3 wards	317		Scandinavia	249
Vryheid	4 wards	481		Others	249
Wakkerstoom	3 wards	584	Alberts (JJ)		735
Waterberg	3 wards	455	Grobler (?)	**Total**	3 093
Wolmaransstad	2 wards	447	Du Toit (SB)		
Zoutpansberg	4 wards	676	Snyman (H)		
Goldfields	2 wards	515	Viljoen (B)		
Total		16 016		**Grand Total**	19 109

Day -13 Thu 1899-09-28	ZAR	A joint secret meeting of ZAR First and Second Volksrade debates the issuing of the ultimatum.
		President Kruger, infuriated by opposition from those who support continued negotiations and who are against offensive operations, charges JH (Koos) de la Rey with cowardice. De la Rey retorts, *"I shall do my duty as the Raad decides, and you, you will see me in the field fighting for our independence long after you and your party who make war with your mouths have fled the country."*[166]
		The motion to issue the ultimatum is eventually carried by fifty votes to seven. Amongst those casting dissenting votes are Commandant-General Piet Joubert and Generals Koos de la Rey, Lucas Meyer and Louis Botha.[167]
Day -12 Fri 1899-09-29	United Kingdom	The last meeting of the British Cabinet approves Chamberlain's draft ultimatum and it is decided to summon Parliament for 17 October.[168]
	Cape Colony	Milner sends a secret telegram to Chamberlain: *"I am sending you another telegram on proposed ultimatum, in case you still desire to send despatch on Saturday. But personally I am still of opinion not to hurry in sending ultimatum, as events of next few days may supply us with a better one than anybody can compose..."*[169]

Day -11 Sat **1899-09-30**	ZAR	The ZAR government asks for the 'final' British proposals which Chamberlain, in his despatch of 22 September, has stated will be communicated in a later despatch.[170] The major mines on the Reef cease operations including the Simmer & Jack, the Wolhuter, the Geldenhuys Deep and the Henry Nourse.[171]
	Trivia	*Field Marshal Frederick Sleigh Lord Roberts' 67th birthday.*
1899	SPRING	**OCTOBER**
Day -10 Sun **1899-10-01**	South Africa	The number of imperial British troops in South Africa have increased by 115% since June and 260% since December and is now as follows, with further reinforcements already at sea: Cape Colony 7 400; Natal 14 704; Total: 22 104 men with 60 artillery pieces. Additionally, the Cape Colony has permanent uniformed military and police forces consisting of about 900 Cape Mounted Rifles (about 400 in the eastern districts) and about 800 Cape Police (226 in the Kimberley district, 103 in Mafeking and the rest stationed throughout the colony).[172] In Natal, the local forces consist of 1 919 Natal Volunteers, about 300 Natal Mounted Police and the newly formed Imperial Light Horse, a unit recruited by Wools-Sampson amongst Uitlanders from the ZAR, is about 500 strong.[173]
	International	In Dublin, over 20 000 people flock to Beresford Place to protest *"the attack of England upon the libertios of the Transvaal"*. [174]
Day -9 Mon **1899-10-02**	United Kingdom	In a reply to the ZAR government's inquiry, Chamberlain states that it will be some time before the British *"final proposals will be ready"*.[175]
	OFS	**THE OFS CALL-UP** Orange Free State burghers are called up. The total number of burghers liable for active service (i.e. between 18 and 60 years old) totals 22 314. About the same percentage as for the ZAR is included in the initial call-up, this means between 12 500 and 14 500 men.[176] In the Orange Free State, the President acts as Commander-in-Chief, assisted by a Chief Commandant who is paid £1 per day. The country is divided into 19 districts commanded by 19 District Commandants and 14 of the bigger districts are subdivided into wards commanded by 42 Ward Field-cornets and Assistant Field-cornets. There are also 18 Town Field-cornets for the main towns in every district. All these officers are elected by their men and are unpaid. The same rules for exemption from military service as in the ZAR apply and persons unable to report for duty are allowed to send substitutes.[177] The Free State Artillery possesses only 24 serviceable and two obsolete artillery pieces with three machine guns.[178]
	Trivia	*President Marthinus Theunis Steyn's 42nd birthday.*

		THE OFS COMMANDOS			
		District	**Ward**	**Burghers** 18-34 years	**Commandant**
		Bloemfontein	3 wards	1 253	Du Plooy
		Winburg	3 wards	1 616	Vilonel
		Kroonstad	1 ward	2 068	Nel (C)
		Ladybrand	2 wards	749	Crowther (R)
		Ficksburg	1 ward	235	De Villiers (IJ)
		Bethlehem	1 ward	1 142	Prinsloo(M)
		Fauresmith	1 ward	988	Visser (PJ)
		Harrismith	1 ward	751	De Villiers (CJ)
		Heilbron	1 ward	1 857	Steenekamp (L)
		Vrede	1 ward	1 038	Botha (H)
		Boshof	1 ward	780	Badenhorst (CCJ)
		Rouxville	1 ward	528	Olivier (JH)
		Thaba Nchu		98	
		Hoopstad	1 ward	494	
		Smithfield	1 ward	299	Swanepoel (J)
		Bethulie	1 ward	337	Du Plooy (FJ)
		Wepener	1 ward	253	Roux (JP)
		Philippolis	1 ward	209	Hertzog (JAM)
		Jacobsdal	1 ward	139	Pretorius (HPJ)
		Total		14 834	

Day -8 Tue **1899-10-03**	ZAR	The Ferreira and the Robinson Deep mines decide to close down.[180]
	Cape Colony	General Sir George White arrives in Cape Town.
	United Kingdom	The War Office informs the (white) colonies that they can contribute some volunteers, but *"in view of the numbers already available, infantry is most, cavalry least serviceable"*.[181]
	Basutholand Black involvement	The British Resident Commissioner in Basutoland, Sir Godfrey Lagden, tells Basuto chiefs at a 'pitso' (meeting) in Maseru that the coming conflict would be *"a white man's war"*.
Day -7 Wed **1899-10-04**	ZAR	Mr JS Marwick, a representative of the Natal Native Affairs Department, leaves Johannesburg with six Republican policemen, escorting more than 7 000 Black mine workers on their way home to Natal and Zululand. In an epic journey, necessitated by the unavailability and expense of berths on trains, the people walk about 56 kilometres a day. The policemen travel ahead to warn inhabitants of their approach and, except for a few cases of theft and drunkenness ascribed to a number of released criminals in the group, the march proceeds peacefully without any widespread looting.[182]
Day -6 Thu **1899-10-05**	ZAR	The Mining Commissioner lists 66 major mines that have closed and only 17 applications to continue operations have been received. Business in Johannesburg is virtually at a standstill and there are serious concerns about the thousands of Black mine workers who have lost their jobs and whose contracts have expired.[183]
	OFS	President Steyn sends the following dispatch to Milner:

	United Kingdom	*"I consider it would not be practical to induce the Government of the ZAR to make or entertain (further) proposals or suggestions unless not only the troops menacing their State are withdrawn further from their borders, that an assurance be given by HM Government that all further despatch and increase of troops will at once and during the negotiations be stopped, and that those now on the water should either not be landed or, at least, should remain as far removed as can be from the scene of possible hostilities... If so, I would be prepared to take steps at once to try and obtain any needful assurance to safe-guard against any act of invasion or hostility any portion of HM colonies or territories, pending the negotiations."*[184] Chamberlain writes to Milner: *"To me, it seems incredible that the Boers should be able to make a successful offensive attack on any British force whether at Mafeking or in Natal.* *"What I fear is some suggestion of compromise from them which will be totally inadequate to provide a permanent settlement... Matters have come to such a pitch that unless there is a complete surrender on the part of the Boers either as a result of agreement or of war, we shall never again be able to put forward any demands for redress of any grievances however great. The people of England will not provide an armament of fifty or sixty thousand men at the expense of five or six million every time the Boers pass a bill that we do not like or extract money from the Uitlanders. Even outrages on British subjects, unless very serious, will not be redressed at such a cost. I suppose that you will have your reinforcements in a course of about a fortnight. I doubt under existing circumstances whether the Boers will really take the offensive... Of course, if they do, they will materially lessen the political difficulties as I do not suppose Harcourt or Morley (anti-war politicians) would expect us to go on negotiating after an actual invasion of our territories. Every provision for the Army Corps is now going on as rapidly as possible."*[185]
	International	Western Australia offers military assistance.[186]
	Trivia	*Ex-Orange Free State President (now ZAR State Secretary) Francis William Reitz's 56th birthday.*
Day -4 Sat **1899-10-07**	United Kingdom	**THE BRITISH MOBILISATION** The British Army is ordered to mobilise. The Cabinet, realising at the end of September that Lord Wolseley's repeated requests for an order to mobilise an army corps must be granted, postpones the issuing of such a mobilisation order until October.[187] The first army corps to be mobilised for service in South Africa consists of a cavalry division, three infantry divisions and corps troops with a total strength of 47 551 officers and men with 122 guns. The force includes eleven field hospitals, a railway company, a pontoon troop and two balloon sections. General Sir Redvers Buller VC, Adjutant-General at the War Office, previously commander at Aldershot, a 60-year-old soldier with extensive African experience, is selected as Commander-in-Chief South Africa.[188] The total number of permanent force (standing army) troops available to Britain worldwide are 1 053 865 officers and men. The regular army consists of 229 806 men, a regular army reserve of 87 937, with additional forces such as the militia, the yeomanry and the Honourable Artillery Company, constituting the home army, totalling 656 865 officers, noncommissioned officers and men. Additionally, Britain can rely on enormous numbers of volunteers from Britain itself and all its colonies, covering a sixth of the globe's surface area.[189]
	Natal Colony	Lieutenant-General Sir George White disembarks from the *SS Scott* in Durban harbour.[190]
	Trivia	*CR de Wet's 45th birthday.*

COMPOSITION OF A TYPICAL BRITISH INFANTRY DIVISION
November 1899

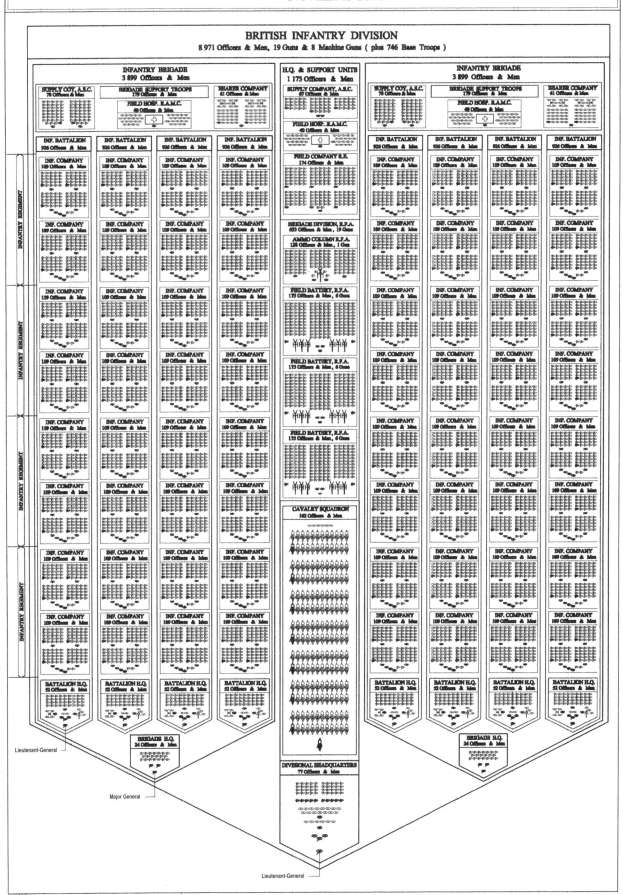

| Day -2 Mon 1899-10-09 | Pretoria | **THE ULTIMATUM**
At 17:00 State Secretary Francis William Reitz hands the ZAR ultimatum to the British Agent, Sir William Conyngham Greene.
"Her Majesty's unlawful intervention in the internal affairs of this Republic, in conflict with the London Convention of 1884, by the extraordinary strengthening of her troops in the neighbourhood of the borders of this Republic, has caused an intolerable condition of things to arise, to which this Government feels itself obliged, in the interest not only of this Republic, but also of all South Africa, to make an end as soon as possible; and this Government feels itself called upon and obliged to press earnestly, and with emphasis, for an immediate termination of this state of things, and to request Her Majesty's Government to give assurances upon the following four demands:
First — That all points of mutual difference must be regulated by friendly recourse to arbitration or by whatever amicable way may be agreed upon by this Government and Her Majesty's Government.
Second — That all troops on the borders of this Republic shall be instantly withdrawn.
Third — That all reinforcement of troops which have arrived in South Africa since June 1, 1899, shall be removed from South Africa within a reasonable time, to be agreed upon with this Government, and with the mutual assurance and guarantee on the part of this Government that no attack upon or hostilities against any portion of the possessions of the British Government shall be made by this Republic during the further negotiations, within a period of time to be subsequently agreed upon between the Governments; and this Government will, on compliance therewith, be prepared to withdraw the armed burghers of this Republic from the borders.
Fourth — That Her Majesty's troops which are now on the high seas shall not be landed in any part of South Africa.
This Government presses for an immediate and affirmative answer to these four questions, and earnestly requests Her Majesty's Government to return an answer before or on Wednesday October 11, 1899, not later than five o'clock p.m.
It desires, further, to add in the unexpected event of an answer not satisfactory being received by it within the interval, it will, with great regret, be compelled to regard the action of Her Majesty's Government as a formal declaration of war, and will not hold itself responsible for the consequences thereof, and that, in the event of any further movements of troops occurring within the above-mentioned time in a nearer direction to our borders, this Government will be compelled to regard that also as a formal declaration of war."[191]

REACTIONS
Mr J Chamberlain (delighted), *"They have done it!"*
Lord Lansdowne, Secretary of War (writing to Chamberlain), *"Accept my felicitations, I don't think Kruger could have played our cards better than he has... My soldiers are in ecstasies."*
Lord Salisbury, "(The ZAR ultimatum) *liberated us from the necessity of explaining to the people of England why we are at war."*[192]
The Telegraph, "Of course there can be only one answer to this grotesque challenge... Mr Kruger has asked for war, and war he must have."[193]
Moberly Bell of *The Times*, *"The ultimatum was excellent in every way. An official document is seldom both eminently amusing and useful but this was both."*[194]
President Steyn, *"I believe that nothing happens without the will of the Almighty and that He, who helped our forefathers in such a marvellous way, will take pity on us. In any case, His will be done."*[195]
President Kruger, quoting Psalm 108:7, *"God hath spoken in His Holiness; I will rejoice."*[196] |

	Swaziland Black involvement	In a letter to King Bhunu of Swaziland, Commandant-General Piet Joubert grants the king full powers, thus virtually independence, for the duration of the expected conflict. Swaziland has been a dependancy of the ZAR with British approval, since 1894.[197]
	International	Tasmania offers a military unit for service in South Africa.[198]
	Natal front	General Sir George White proceeds to Ladysmith, where he takes overall command of the British forces in Natal.
	Northern front	Colonel HCO Plumer arrives at Tuli, Rhodesia, with 500 men, all locally recruited, including 100 British South African Policemen with a 12,5-pounder field gun, two muzzle-loading guns and a machine gun.[199]
	Western front	Cecil John Rhodes and friends, including his secretary, Philip Jourdan, and Dr Thomas Smartt, son of a Cape Cabinet Minister, arrive in Kimberley.[200]
	Trivia	*On the next day, the ultimatum expires and the Anglo-Boer War, the Second Boer War, the Boer War, the Great Boer War, Kruger's War, Milner's War, Chamberlain's War, the Gold War or the South African War starts.* *If all wars, campaigns and punitive expeditions are considered, this is the 226th of 230 such conflicts involving the British Army during Queen Victoria's 64 year reign. There was indeed no single year of her reign that passed without Britain being involved in military conflict.[201]* *State President SJ Paul Kruger's 74th birthday.*
Day -1 Tue **1899-10-10**	Natal	The remarkable mine workers' march arrives in Newcastle where some embark on trains for their homes while others move off to Zululand on foot.[202]
	United Kingdom ZAR	**THE ULTIMATUM EXPIRES AT 17:00** The reply of the British government is delivered to the ZAR government, *"... Her Majesty's Government have received with great regret the peremptory demands of the Government of the South African Republic... and I am to inform you in reply that the conditions demanded... are such as Her Majesty's Government deem it impossible to discuss."[203]*

NOTES: CRISIS

1. PORTER, AN, The Origins of the South African War, p 180
2. PAKENHAM, T, The Boer War, p 30
3. STRYDOM, CJS, Kaapland en die Tweede Vryheidsoorlog, p 42
4. WARWICK, P, The South African War: The Anglo-Boer War, 1899-1902, p 19.
5. *Ibid*, p 58
6. PORTER, *op cit*, p 181
7. STRYDOM, CJS, *op cit*, p 52
8. *Ibid*, p 52
9. PAKENHAM, T, *op cit*, p 50.
10. HEADLAM, C, The Milner Papers, vol 1, p 306
11. *Ibid*, vol 1, p 302
12. CAMMACK, D, The Rand at War 1899-1902, p 28
13. *Ibid*, p 28
14. MULLER, CFJ, 500 Years — A History..., pp 291-292, 323; SAUNDERS, C, Illustrated History of S.A., pp 235-237; PRESTON, A, Pictorial History of South Africa, pp 88-91
15. PORTER, *op cit*, p 184
16. PAKENHAM, T, *op cit*, p 52
17. BREYTENBACH, JH, Die Geskiedenis van die Tweede Vryheidsoorlog in Suid-Afrika 1899-1902, vol 1, p 17
18. WARWICK, P, The South African War — The Anglo-Boer War, p 13
19. PORTER, *op cit*, p 181
20. *Ibid*, p 181.
21. BARBARY, J, The Boer War, p 49
22. HEADLAM, *op cit*, vol 1, p 319
23. AMERY, LCMS (ed), The Times History of the War in South Africa 1899-1902, vol 1, p 244
24. HOLT, Edgar, The Boer War, p 67
25. CAMMACK, D, *op cit*, p 21
26. PORTER, *op cit*, p 190
27. HEADLAM, *op cit*, vol 1, p 321
28. *Ibid*, vol 1, p 313
29. VAN SCHOOR, MCE (ed). 'n Bittereinder aan die Woord, Marthinus Theunis Steyn, p 92.
30. PLOEGER, Dr J, Die Lotgevalle van die Burgerlike Bevolking gedurende die Anglo-Boereoorlog, 1899-1902, pp 2:7-2:22
31. HEADLAM, *op cit*, vol 1, p 399
32. PORTER, *op cit*, p 191
33. PLOEGER, *op cit*, p 1:12
34. FARWELL, B, The Great Boer War, p 30
35. HEADLAM, *op cit*, vol 1, p 340; McCORD, JJ, South African Struggle, p 256
36. KRUGER, R, Good-bye Dolly Gray, p 45
37. PORTER, *op cit*, p 193
38. PAKENHAM, T, *op cit*, p 50
39. HEADLAM, *op cit*, vol 1, pp 340-341
40. VAN SCHOOR, *op cit*, p 92
41. CALDWELL, TC, The Anglo-Boer War — Why was it fought? Who was responsible?, p 97
42. HEADLAM, *op cit*, vol 1, p 331
43. HEADLAM, *op cit*, vol 1, p 347
44. MULLER, *op cit*, p 310;   SAUNDERS, *op cit*, pp 182-189
45. SAUNDERS, *op cit*, p 88; PRESTON, A, Pictorial History..., pp 79-80
46. CAMMACK, D, *op cit*, p 20
47. *Ibid*, p 92
48. PORTER, *op cit*, p 188
49. BREYTENBACH, JH, Kommandant Danie Theron, p 65
50. HANCOCK, WK., Selections from the Smuts Papers 1, p 228
51. FARWELL, *op cit*, p 33
52. VAN SCHOOR, *op cit*, p 93
53. CAMMACK, *op cit*, p 31
54. LE MAY, GHL, British Supremacy in South Africa ..., p 23
55. VAN SCHOOR, *op cit*, p 94
56. *Ibid*, p 95
57. PAKENHAM, *op cit*, p 60
58. CAMMACK, *op cit*, p 31
59. VAN SCHOOR, *op cit*, p 99
60. BREYTENBACH, *op cit*, vol I, p 118
61. PLOEGER, *op cit*, p 1:12.
62. VAN SCHOOR, *op cit*, p 103
63. CAMMACK, D, *op cit*, p 31
64. HEADLAM, *op cit*, vol 1, p 31
65. VAN SCHOOR, *op cit*, p 374
66. HEADLAM, *op cit*, vol I, p 103
67. GRONUM, MA, Die Ontplooiing van die Engelse Oorlog, 1899-1900, (3) p 16
68. VAN SCHOOR, *op cit*, pp 104 & 108
69. GRONUM, *op cit*, (3) p 17
70. VAN SCHOOR, *op cit*, p 113
71. AMERY, *op cit*, vol (ii), p 103
72. PAKENHAM, *op cit*, p 66
73. *Ibid*, p 66
74. STRYDOM, *op cit*, p 58
75. BREYTENBACH, *op cit*, vol (i), pp 52-60
76. PAKENHAM, *op cit*, p 67
77. *Ibid*, p 67
78. VAN SCHOOR, *op cit*, p 117
79. PAKENHAM, *op cit*, p 68
80. *Ibid*, p 68
81. GRONUM, *op cit*, (3) p 19
82. VAN SCHOOR, *op cit*, p 120
83. HEADLAM, *op cit*, vol 1, p 430.
84. GRONUM, MA, Die Engelse Oorlog. 1899-1902, (2) p 4
85. GRONUM, *op cit*, (3) p 19
86. VAN SCHOOR, *op cit*, p 123
87. FERREIRA, ... SPE Trichard, p 112
88. HEADLAM, *op cit*, vol 1, p 314
89. VAN SCHOOR, *op cit*, p 123; STRYDOM, *op cit*, p 46
90. HEADLAM, *op cit*, vol 1, p 445
91. FARWELL, B, *op cit*, p 37
92. MEINTJES, J, The Commandant-General, p 162
93. VAN SCHOOR, *op cit*, p 132
94. LE MAY, *op cit*, p 22
95. VAN SCHOOR, *op cit*, p 134
96. *Ibid*, p 135
97. *Ibid*, p 136
98. FARWELL, *op cit*, p 137
99. HEADLAM, *op cit*, vol 1, p 445

100. VAN SCHOOR, op cit, p 145
101. STRYDOM, CJS, op cit, p 48
102. CRESWICKE, L, South Africa and the Transvaal War. vol III, p 137
103. *Ibid*, vol III, p 137
104. McCORD, JJ, South African Struggle, p 261
105. CRESWICKE, *op cit*, vol III, p 137
106. PLOEGER, *op cit*, p 3:12
107. ANDRIESEN, WJ, Gedenkboek van die Oorlog in Zuid-Afrika, p 73
108. HEADLAM, *op cit*, vol 1, p 468
109. STRYDOM, CJS, *op cit*, p 49
110. CRESWICKE, *op cit*, vol III, p 137
111. HEADLAM, *op cit*, vol 1, p 468
112. CRESWICKE, *op cit*, vol III, p 137
113. HEADLAM, *op cit*, vol 1, p 469
114. MIDGLEY, JF, Petticoat in Mafeking, p 2
115. PLOEGER, *op cit*, p 2:17
116. HEADLAM, *op cit*, vol 1, p 471
117. BREYTENBACH, *op cit*, vol I, p 122
118. PLOEGER, *op cit*, p 13:4
119. PRETORIUS, F, Kommandolewe tydens die Anglo-Boereoorlog, p 97
120. McCORD, *op cit*, p 226
121. PLOEGER, *op cit*, p 3:13
122. HEADLAM, *op cit*, vol 1, p 488
123. BREYTENBACH, JH, Gedenkalbum van die Tweede Vryheidsoorlog, p 55
124. FARWELL, *op cit*, p 37; AMERY, *op cit*, (ii)p 120
125. BREYTENBACH, Gedenkalbum, *op cit*, p 55
126. HEADLAM, *op cit*, vol 1, p 516
127. GRONUM, *op cit*, (3) p 25
128. BREYTENBACH, Gedenkalbum, *op cit*, p 55
129. ANDRIESEN, *op cit*, p 74
130. *Ibid*, p 74
131. GRONUM, *op cit*, (3) p 20
132. CALDWELL, *op cit*, p 91
133. HEADLAM, *op cit*, vol 1, p 518
134. McCRACKEN, DP, The Irish Pro-Boers, p 46
135. BREYTENBACH, Gedenkalbum, *op cit*, p 55
136. McCORD, *op cit*, p 265
137. GRONUM, *op cit*, (3) p 20
138. OBERHOLSTER, AC (red), Dagboek van H.C. Bredell 1900-1904, p 97
139. GRONUM, *op cit*, p 20
140. KEMP, JGC, Vir Vryheid en Reg, pp 342-343
141. GRONUM, *op cit*, (3) pp 21-22
142. HANCOCK, *op cit*, vol 1, pp 322-329
143. GRIFFITH, K, Thank God We Kept The Flag Flying, p xvii
144. PEDDLE, Col. DE, Long Cecil, the story of the Gun made during the Siege of Kimberley, 15 October 1899 to 15 February 1900, p 1
145. McCORD, *op cit*, p 269
146. GRIFFITH, *op cit*, p 14
147. VAN SCHOOR, *op cit*, p 155
148. CRESWICKE, *op cit*, vol III, p 137
149. McCORD, *op cit*, p 266
150. BREYTENBACH, *op cit*, vol I, p 26
151. *Ibid*, vol I, p 26
152. GRONUM, *op cit*, (3) p 23
153. PLOEGER, *op cit*, p 1:18

154. KRUGER, DW, Die Krugermiljoene, p16
155. VAN SCHOOR, MCE (Red), Christiaan De Wet-Annale Nommer 7, p 17
156. GRONUM, *op cit*, (3) p 23
157. PAKENHAM, *op cit*, p 98
158. FARWELL, B, *op cit*, p 35
159. HEADLAM, *op cit*, vol 1, p 545
160. PLOEGER, *op cit*, p 1:18
161. VAN SCHOOR, *op cit*, p 163
162. BREYTENBACH, *op cit*, vol I, p 36
163. BREYTENBACH, *op cit*, vol I, pp 33-35
164. BREYTENBACH, *op cit*, vol I, pp 85-89
165. SLOCUM & REICHMAN, Boer War Operations..., pp 101-104
166. FARWELL, *op cit*, p 47
167. PAKENHAM, *op cit* p 192
168. KEMP, *op cit*, p 158
169. HEADLAM, *op cit*, vol 1, p 552
170. McCORD, *op cit*, p 270
171. CAMMACK, D, *op cit*, p 48
172. STRYDOM, *op cit*, p 58
173. BREYTENBACH, *op cit*, vol I, p 201
174. McCRACKEN, *op cit*, p 46
175. McCORD, *op cit*, p 270
176. BREYTENBACH, *op cit*, vol I, p 36
177. *Ibid*, vol I, pp 34-35
178. *Ibid*, vol I, p 89
179. SLOCUM, *op cit*, pp 101-104
180-. CAMMACK, *op cit*, p 48
181. FARWELL, *op cit*, p 40
182. CAMMACK, D, *op cit*, pp 51-52
183. *Ibid*, pp 48-49
184. DAVITT, M, The Boer Fight for Freedom, p 51
185. GRONUM, *op cit*, (3) p 25; HEADLAM, *op cit*, vol 1, p 554
186. CRESWICKE, *op cit*, (III) p 137
187. HOLT, *op cit*, p 84
188. AMERY, *op cit*, vol II, p 113
189. BREYTENBACH, *op cit*, vol I, p 153
190. GRIFFITH, *op cit*, p 17
191. DAVITT, *op cit*, p 55; COULTER, J & COOPER, JA (ed), Queen Victoria, p 571
192. PORTER, *op cit*, p 257
193. PAKENHAM, *op cit*, p 109
194. *Ibid*, p 109
195. FARWELL, *op cit*, p 47
196. HOLT, *op cit*, p 74
197. WARWICK, *op cit*, p 41
198. CRESWICKE, *op cit*, vol III, p 137
199. BREYTENBACH, *op cit*, vol I, p 419
200. FARWELL, *op cit*, p 419
201. WESSELS, A, Die Anglo-Boereoorlog 1899-1902. 'n Oorsig van die militêre verloop van die stryd, p 1
202. CAMMACK, *op cit*, p 52
203. DAVITT, *op cit*, p 55

OPENING BLOWS — 11 OCTOBER-DECEMBER 1899

War is the unfolding of miscalculations. — Barbara Tuchman.

1899	SPRING	
Day 1 Wed **1899-10-11** *Pres. SJP Kruger* *(War Museum of the Boer Republics)*	International	President Kruger sends a telegram to the New York newspaper, *The World*: *"Through* The World *I thank the people of the United States most sincerely for their sympathy. Last Monday the Republic gave Great Britain forty-eight hours' notice within which to give the Republic an assurance that the present dispute would be settled by arbitration or other peaceful means, and that the troops would be removed from the borders. This expired at five today. The British Agent has been recalled. War is certain. The Republics are determined, if they must belong to Great Britain, that a price will have to be paid which will stagger humanity. They have, however, full faith. The sun of liberty will arise in South Africa as it arose in North America."*[1]
	Pretoria	The British Agent in Johannesburg, Sir William Conyngham Greene, requests his passport and leaves Pretoria.
Pres. MT Steyn *(War Museum of the Boer Republics)*	OFS	In Bloemfontein, President Steyn issues a proclamation to the burghers of the Orange Free State, He says, '... *the Sister Republic is about to be attacked by an unscrupulous enemy, who has long looked for a pretext to annihilate the Africanders.*'[2] He emphasizes the many ties between the people of the two republics, as well as the formal treaty solemnly declared in the presence of the Almighty, that compel them to resist a powerful enemy owing to the injustice done to their kith and kin. He believes that no reliance can be placed on the solemn promises and obligations of Great Britain when the Administration at the helm is prepared to tread treaties underfoot. *"The original Conventions have been twisted and turned by Great Britain into a means of exercising tyranny against the Transvaal, which has not returned the injustice done to it in the past. No gratitude has been shown for the indulgence which was granted to British subjects, who, according to law, had forfeited their lives and property. Compliance with the British demands would be equivalent to the loss of our independence, which has been gained by our blood and tears. For many years British troops have been concentrating on the borders of the Transvaal in order to compel it by terrorism to comply with British claims. The crafty plans of those with whom love of gold is the motive are now being realised. While acknowledging the honour of thousands of Englishmen, who abhor deeds of robbery and violence, the Orange Free State execrates the wrongful deeds of a British statesman... Burghers of the Free State, stand up as one man against the oppressor and violator of right."*
	Cape Colony	Mr WP Schreiner, the Cape Prime Minister, seeks assurances that the Orange Free State will not violate that colony's territory. President Steyn expresses his willingness to comply, provided the colony remains neutral and is not used to transport Her Majesty's troops or as a springboard for military operations against the republics.[3] Sir A Milner informs Chamberlain: *"It is fearfully hampering to have to act with present Ministers, and involves certain grave risks. On the other hand risk of dismissing them at this juncture is greater. It would certainly lead to sporadic risings in the Colony, which, especially while our garrison is so weak, we must, as long as possible, avoid."*[4]
	Natal front	A council of war at Commandant-General Piet J Joubert's laager at Sandspruit discusses whether or not to cross into Natal. A motion by State Artillery Colonel SPE Trichard, proposing to proceed but that private property must be respected and that any fighting must be against British soldiers only, is accepted.[5]
	Trivia	*General JH (Koos) de la Rey's 51st birthday.*

DISPOSITION OF FORCES

REPUBLICAN FORCES:[6]
Commandant-General PJ Joubert.

Natal front:	Approx. 17 500 men	
Comdt.-Gen. PJ Joubert & Chief Comdt. M Prinsloo		
Western ZAR front:	Approx. 6 000 men	
General PA Cronje		
Western OFS front:	Approx. 4 800 men	
Chief Comdt. CJ Wessels & Gen. JJP Prinsloo		
Northern front:	Approx. 1 700 men	
General FA Grobler		
Southern (central) front:	Approx. 2 500 men	
Chief. Comdt. JH Olivier & Gen. ER Grobler		
Eastern ZAR & Zwaziland:	Approx. 1 500 -2 000	
General SW Burger		
Basutoland border:	Approx. 1 000 men	
TOTALS	35 000 - 35 500	

BRITISH FORCES:[7]
Lieutenant-General Sir FWEF Forestier-Walker

15 811	(including 2 781 locals)	Natal
	Lt.-Gen. Sir GS White & Maj. Gen. Sir WP Symonds	
1 016	(including 300 Town Guard)	Mafeking
	Lt.-Colonel RSS Baden-Powell	
4 129	(including local units)	Kimberley
	Lt.-Colonel RG Kekewich	
500	(all local units including BSAP)	Rhodesia
	Lt.-Colonel HCO Plumer	
3 150 - 3 450	Orange River, De Aar & Noupoort	
	Lt.-Colonels Money, Barton & Gough	
24 606 - 24906		

The Republican forces are also accompanied by between 7 000 and 9 000 black and coloured 'agterryers' – literally 'after-riders' – serving mostly voluntarily as orderlies, cooks and general assistants. They are not issued with firearms and they are used in a strictly noncombatant role.[8]

Day 2 Thu 1899-10-12	Natal front	**START OF THE FIRST REPUBLICAN OFFENSIVE** Commandant-General Piet J Joubert sends advance parties under General JHM Kock into Natal through Botha's Pass.[9]
	Western front 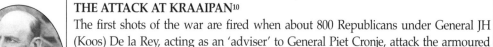 *Gen. JH de la Rey (National Cultural History Museum)*	Republican forces under General Piet A Cronje cross the western ZAR border. **THE ATTACK AT KRAAIPAN**[10] The first shots of the war are fired when about 800 Republicans under General JH (Koos) De la Rey, acting as an 'adviser' to General Piet Cronje, attack the armoured train *Mosquito* at Kraaipan, about 50 kilometres south of Mafeking. The locomotive tender derails where the burghers have broken up the track, the boiler is quickly damaged by accurate artillery fire and the track behind the train is also broken up. The train is subjected to accurate rifle fire and Lieutenant Nesbit and thirty-four soldiers including nine wounded surrender the next morning, while the Republicans report no casualties. De la Rey reports finding Mark IV (dumdum) ammunition on the train.
	Cape Colony	Mr Schreiner, speaking in the Cape House of Assembly, says, *"... it is the general duty of Her Majesty's Ministers in this colony... to save our country as much as possible from being involved in the vortex of war into which it is now apparently a certainty that South Africa has been drawn."*[11]
Day 3 Fri 1899-10-13	Natal front	ZAR forces enter Natal through Laing's Nek and via Volksrust and pass through the deserted Charlestown.[12]
	Western front	A locomotive pushes two railway trucks loaded with 22 tonnes of dynamite out of Mafeking, uncouples and steams back; the intention being that the dynamite is to be exploded as soon as curious burghers inspect the cargo. The Republicans, however, opens fire and a huge explosion destroys the railway line to the north more effectively than they could have done and no injuries are reported.[13]

	United Kingdom	A British commission is dispatched to Argentina to buy horses. This is the first of many such commissions to buy horses, mules and donkeys in South Africa (the largest single supplier), Canada, the USA, Austria-Hungary, Italy, Spain, Australasia, Cyprus and elsewhere.
		(Before the end of the war 669 575 horses, mules and donkeys would be in British service, of which 400 346 would be 'expended' during the war. In Port Elizabeth, a memorial is later dedicated to the memory of the horses that died in the Anglo-Boer War. The inscription reads, *"The greatness of a nation consists not so much in the number of its people or the extent of its territory as in the extent and justice of its compassion."*)
British soldier on horseback *(War Museum of the Boer Republics)*		The supply of horses from South America is significant because with the fodder arrives khaki-bush *(Alternanthera achyrantha)* and blackjacks — weeds that are still the enemy of the boer in South Africa a century later.[14]
	International	Offers of troops from South Australia and Canada are *"gratefully accepted"*.[15]
Day 4 Sat **1899-10-14**	Western front	**THE SIEGE OF MAFEKING BEGINS** Mafeking ('Place of stones'), situated on the main railway line to the north, is strategically important to the British because of the supplies stockpiled here and because it is seen as a symbol of British rule by the black tribes in the region. This small town with about 1 700 white and about 7 500 black and coloured inhabitants, is defended by 1 016 men, mostly locally recruited (including a 300-strong Town Guard) under Colonel RSS Baden-Powell. Among the besieged are Lord Edward Cecil, son of the British Prime Minister and husband of Lady Violet (who is to marry Milner after being prematurely widowed), Major Hamilton Goold-Hamilton, the Resident Commissioner of Bechuanaland, Captain Gordon Wilson, husband of Lady Sarah Spencer Churchill, and several other famous people.[16] A scouting party under Lord Charles Cavendish-Bentinck, clashes with Republicans north of Mafeking and he scampers back with a few men to fetch reinforcements. He orders an armoured train to steam out as far as the track is intact. Colonel Baden-Powell, now painfully aware that armoured trains are not as invincible as previously believed, realises that the train may be captured and orders Captain C Fitzclarence and 70 men to its assistance. This party is lured away from the railway line and is almost cut off before further reinforcements rush to cover their retirement. The British lose two killed and sixteen wounded, while the Republicans suffer five wounded.[17]
	Victoria Cross	Captain C Fitzclarence, Royal Fusileers, commanding partly trained, untried men of the Protectorate Regiment, earns a recommendation for the Victoria Cross for assisting in the relief of the hard-pressed train. Riverton, north of Kimberley, is occupied by Republican forces.[18]
	Natal front	Commandant-General PJ Joubert occupies Charlestown and General DJE Erasmus enters Natal via Engelbrechtsdrift. Louis Botha, an ordinary burgher, takes 14 men of Lucas Meyer's commando across the Buffels River and captures five members of the Natal Mounted Police.[19] Part of the Johannesburg commando and local inhabitants loot abandoned property in Charlestown.[20]
	OFS	As the Prime Minister of the self-governing Cape Colony cannot give any assurance of that colony's neutrality in HM Government's actions against the Republics, President Steyn issues a proclamation authorising his officers to cross the border in defence of the Republic and its independence. Strict orders are given to ensure the correct conduct of the Republican forces, the protection of lives, private property, the procurement of provisions, etc.[21] A Free State force crosses the western border and splits up, moving to Spytfontein and Modder River Station.[22]

	United Kingdom	General Sir Redvers Buller embarks at Southampton. On board the *Dunnottar Castle*, his fellow-passengers include Winston Churchill and a party of cinematographers led by WK Dickson with a 'biograph'.
	International	In accordance with the secret Second Treaty of Windsor, Portugal undertakes to prevent the passage of munitions from Delagoa Bay to the ZAR Unrest breaks out in Dublin, soldiers are jostled and police arrest several people for shouting pro-Boer slogans.[23]
Day 5 Sun **1899-10-15**	Western front	**Mafeking siege:** General PA Cronje and Koos De la Rey, his 'military advisor', disagree seriously about the conduct of the siege of Mafeking.[24]
	Black involvement	Before retiring from Taung, a small unit of about 75 Cape Police with a machine gun urges the local blacks to remain peaceful. The magistrate takes the eldest son of Chief Molala with him to Kimberley to ensure black loyalty to Britain.[25] Republican forces occupy Lobatsi (Bechuanaland) and Taung. A small patrol sent from Kimberley to assist the police at Riverton runs into a Free State commando and is captured.
	Western front	At Vryburg Police Commissioner Scott who has been tasked with local defence by Kekewich during September, is in command of 120 Cape Policemen. He reluctantly agrees at a meeting of 'leading citizens,' that it will not be wise to defend the town. The police leave town and the 'Vryburg Volunteers', a local unit raised by Scott, decides to disband. Scott feels deeply humiliated and commits suicide.[26] South of Kimberley, Free Staters fire on an armoured train and its escort. Nobody is hurt and the train returns to Kimberley.[27] **THE SIEGE OF KIMBERLEY BEGINS**[28] Kimberley, the second largest city in the Cape Colony, is of particular strategic and symbolic importance to the British. World-famous because of the richest diamond mines in the world, Kimberley is linked by rail to all the Cape harbours and the Great Northern Line. Called *"a seething mass of opulent iniquity"* by John X Merriman, Kimberley has a saloon for every sixteen inhabitants, women and children included. It is also viewed as 'Rhodes' city' and the mining magnate and former Prime Minister of the Cape Colony, reputed to be one of the richest men in the world, refuses to leave 'his' town. This added responsibility complicates the task of Lieutenant-Colonel RG Kekewich, the garrison commander, while making the town a very desirable prize for the Republicans.[29] At the start of the siege the population of Kimberley comprises 13 000 whites, 7 000 coloureds and Asians, and about 30 000 blacks. Refugees from elsewhere swell the total to about 55 000. Kekewich has at his disposal 4 219 men with 14 field-guns and 11 machine guns. Some of the machine guns, a number of rifles and a huge supply of ammunition have originally been acquired by the De Beers Company to be made available to the Jameson raiders.[30]
	Cape Colony	Compelled by their circumstances as a colony of the British Empire and to avoid a constitutional crisis, the Cape government is forced to take certain actions in support of the British war effort. Martial law is proclaimed in the northern Cape Colony and certain proclamations are countersigned by the Prime Minister. The Republican proclamations are declared null and void, the inhabitants are warned against committing high treason and are promised compensation for losses due to enemy action.[31]
	International	Walls, lampposts and billboards throughout Dublin are covered with large green posters proclaiming, *"Enlisting in the English Army is Treason to Ireland"* and *"Remember ninety-eight. Remember the Penal Laws. Remember the Famine."*[32]

Day 6 Mon **1899-10-16**	Natal front	Seriously delayed by wet, misty weather and slippery roads, Commandant-General Joubert reaches Newcastle and issues strict orders against looting.[33]
	Cape Colony	Local forces of the Cape Colony are called out. These forces include the town volunteers from the bigger cities and towns and shooting associations in the black districts. They total about 5 000 men and are initially only tasked to defend their own districts.[34]
	Western front Black involvement	**Mafeking siege:** General PA Cronje shells Mafeking and demands the surrender of the town. Only one casualty results from about 300 shells. After the bombardment, Silas Molemo, a spokesman for the Barolong tribe, visits the resident magistrate, Mr Bell, and informs him: *"Never mind this, we will stick with you and see it through."*[35] A 270-man strong local force, commanded by Police Inspector Snow, abandons Fourteen Streams and falls back to Kimberley.[36]
Day 7 Tue **1899-10-17**	ZAR	A proclamation prepared by Commandant-General PJ Joubert at Newcastle is published in an extraordinary Government Gazette in Pretoria. In language that almost seems out of place under the circumstances, Joubert says that although the war is forced upon the Republic by malicious capitalists and war-hungry British ministers, it will be conducted in a civilized manner. He urges the nation to act with the utmost discretion and to treat everybody in their persons and property with respect. [37]
	Natal front	Free State forces under Chief Commandant Marthinus Prinsloo and General CJ de Villiers, enter Natal through the Van Reenen's, De Beer's, Tintwa and Oliviershoek passes.[38] The main ZAR force under General DJE Erasmus and Lieutenant-Colonel SPE Trichard advances via Dannhauser Station towards Dundee. [39]
	Western front	**Mafeking siege:** Republicans take the Mafeking waterworks and the town has to rely on boreholes and wells from now on. Republicans under Field-cornet Bosman occupy Fourteen Streams and Warrenton.[40] The bridges over the Vaal and Modder Rivers are damaged by Republican forces. A skirmish occurs at Spytfontein near Kimberley.[41]
	United Kingdom	The British Parliament opens for the session during which the British ultimatum was to have been sent.
Day 8 Wed **1899-10-18**	OFS Black involvement	In a proclamation sent to Basutoland, President Steyn explains the defensive presence of commandos on the Basutoland border and stresses that the OFS is at peace with the Basuto and has no quarrel with them.[42]
	Natal Front	Free State forces under Commandant CJ de Villiers and Acting Field-cornet CR de Wet clash with Natal Carbineers at Bester's Station and force about 600 Colonial volunteers to fall back on Ladysmith.[43]
	United Kingdom	Mr Balfour announces that the militia and the militia reserves are to be called out.
	ZAR civilian life	The ZAR government institutes price control on basic consumer products.
Day 9 Thu **1899-10-19**	Natal front	Republican forces consisting of the Johannesburg commando and the German and Dutch Volunteers under General JHM Kock, occupy Elandslaagte and capture a supply train. The ZAR forces do not establish contact with the Free Staters as ordered by the Commandant-General.[44] General Penn-Symonds at Dundee, convinced that the Republicans will not be audacious enough to attack a British brigade, consisting of 5 028 men with 1 904 horses and 18 guns, is not worried by the occupation of Elandslaagte.[45] General Lucas Meyer enters Natal from the east via Doringberg and Landmansdrift.

	Western front	General Cronje appoints Koos de la Rey as Combat General and permits him to leave for Kimberley. Belmont Station is taken by about 300 burghers under Commandant Van der Merwe.[46]
	ZAR civilian life	Since October, 130 991 foreign subjects, including 53 000 whites, have voluntarily left the Rand, and have been transported by rail to the ZAR borders.[47]
Day 10 Fri **1899-10-20**	Natal front	**THE BATTLE OF TALANA**[48] In spite of the report of a night patrol running into Meyer's men, General Penn-Symonds' Dundee force takes no special defensive precautions. At about 05:50, in the clearing mist, General Lucas Meyer with 1 500 men and three guns emplaced on Talana Hill, Smith's Nek and Lennox Hill, open fire on the surprised camp. Recovering quickly, two batteries (12 guns) return fire. Penn-Symonds deploys three infantry battalions for a frontal assault on Talana Hill and orders his cavalry to prepare to cut off the enemy's retreat. The superior artillery fire-power forces Meyer to withdraw his guns. The infantry charge starts at 07:15 and increasing rifle fire pins them down in a clump of trees at a stone wall. Penn-Symonds pushes his artillery forward to close the range. Although the increased shelling forces some burghers to retreat, the assault is stalled. Ignoring all warnings, Penn-Symonds arrives at the stone wall, recklessly climbs it and is severely wounded in the stomach. The burghers, wary of threats to their line of retreat, notice the cavalry actions behind their right flank and stream down the rear slope in increasing numbers. This enables the infantry to renew their push to the crest where they arrive only to be subjected to own shelling. Meyer exploits this fiasco to withdraw and the British clear the hills in pouring rain at about 13:30. General DJE 'Marula' Erasmus on Impati Hill and Commandants Trichard and Grobler to the west of the town inexplicably remain inactive and do not attempt an attack on the vulnerable British camp. The British cavalry, keen to capture some horses, is hard pressed by the retreating burghers. They are forced to abandon a maxim and have to split up into two groups. Major Knox's unit reaches camp, but Lieutenant-Colonel Moller is cut off, runs into Captain Danie Theron's scouts and some of the Transvaal Irish Brigade, who surround them and force them to surrender. General White calls it *"hardly a satisfactory victory"* as the British lose 51 killed, 203 wounded and 246 captured. The Republicans suffer about 150 casualties including about 44 killed, about 90 wounded and a few missing. Lieutenant-General JDP French arrives in Ladysmith to take over command of White's cavalry.[49] Commandant Adolph Schiel of the German Volunteer Corps warns General Kock not to force an engagement with the enemy, but to cover the supply lines and to seek contact with the Free Staters as instructed by Joubert. Kock exclaims that he is there to fight the English and not to guard mountains. With 'luxuries' from the hotel and the supply train, Kock's men hold a 'smoking concert' with some of the prisoners joining in. *"God save Queen and the Volkslied (are) sung with vigourous impartiality."*[50]
	Western front	**Mafeking siege:** General PA Cronje notifies Colonel Baden-Powell of his intention to shell Mafeking within 48 hours and adds, *"You have to see that noncombatants leave Mafeking before the expiration of that time. If you do not comply with this I will not be answerable for the results."*[51]
	Northern front Black involvement	General FA Grobler writes a letter to Chief Khama stating that if Khama and his people refrained from assisting the British morally and physically, they would be left in peace. Khama informs him *"that I am a son of the white Queen (Victoria) and that I do as they instruct me. If I find you in my country I shall help the English to drive you out"*.[52]
	International	The first Australian contingent sails for South Africa.

Gen. Lucas Meyer (War Museum of the Boer Republics)

Gen. Penn-Symonds (War Museum of the Boer Republics)

Day 11 Sat **1899-10-21**	Western front	General De la Rey, with a commando of 1 200 men and three guns, occupies Vryburg, the administrative capital of the Bechuanaland Protectorate.[53] **Mafeking Siege:** Baden-Powell's famous laconic telegram from Mafeking: *"All well. Four hours' bombardment. One dog killed."*[54]
	Natal front	Major-General JH Yule, now in command at Dundee, moves part of his camp but discovers to his horror that at a distance of more than 7 000 metres, he is still not out of range of Trichardt's guns on Impati Hill.[55]
	 *Gen. JHM Kock* (War Museum of the Boer Republics)  *Col. Ian Hamilton* (War Museum of the Boer Republics)  *Commandant Adolf Schiel* (War Museum of the Boer Republics) **Victoria Cross**	**THE BATTLE OF ELANDSLAAGTE** As the morning mist lifts, General French's 750 men and six seven-pounder guns open fire on the activities around the Elandslaagte station buildings. The burghers, still unloading the train, local Indians in search of loot, British POWs and a Republican ambulance scatter in all directions. Falling back to his prepared positions overlooking the railway, General Kock orders his two field-guns to open fire. The excellently served Republican field-guns quickly damage two of their outranged British counterparts. French retires at 08:30, after rescuing a few POWs, thus gaining excellent information about the enemy's strengths and dispositions. The smug General JHM Kock, commanding about 1 000 men including the Johannesburg commando, about 140 of Commandant Adolf Schiel's German Corps and about 70 Hollander volunteers, is convinced that he has driven off the British. French retires to Modderspruit where reinforcements under Colonel Ian Hamilton are detrained out of sight of the Republican positions. The Republicans, now relaxed, are surprised when they are fired on by some detached mounted units. They quickly recover and deploy along a horseshoe-shaped ridge straddling the railway line. At about 15:00 they are opposed by a British force of 1 630 infantrymen with three machine guns, 1 314 mounted troops with three machine guns and 552 gunners with 18 field-guns. After an inspiring speech by Hamilton, the attack starts as a frontal attack by the British infantry and a flank attack along the ridge by mounted units. Both are supported by artillery with cavalry held in readiness to cut off the enemy's retreat. The Republican field-guns harass the cavalry moving towards the station, until the infantry crests the first ridge at about 15:30 and comes into view of their main position. As they descend into the depression between the ridges of the horseshoe, the Republicans shell them as well as they can, but cause very few casualties among the extended troops. At about 16:00 the British artillery opens up and silences their opposition before commencing the 'softening-up' of the main position. As the range closes, accurate Mauser fire takes its toll and the British guns have to engage this threat, allowing the Republican guns to come briefly into action again. The only reinforcements available to Kock, are Schiel's unit, who has earlier been sent to counter the cavalry. Schiel crosses the railway and tries to fall back to the main position. He is closely pursued and has to turn and fight, suffering heavy casualties. Schiel and those with him are almost all killed or wounded and the survivors fall into British hands. At 16:30 a fierce thunderstorm breaks, allowing the British infantry and the Imperial Light Horse, now unmounted, to approach the ridge as the burghers' fire weakens in the downpour. Several times the British attack falters when the light improves and the burghers counterattack in small groups. Captains R Johnstone and CH Mullins, of the Imperial Light Horse, save the flank attack by repeatedly rallying their men, thus earning recommendations for the Victoria Cross. Finally Republican resolve gives way and several groups retire down the back slopes. General Kock personally leads about 50 men in a fierce counter-attack as white handkerchiefs start to appear. He falls, seriously wounded in three places. Captain MFM Meiklejohn and Sergeant-Major W Robertson, both Gordon Highlanders, are instrumental in repulsing the final counterattacks and both are later to receive the Victoria

44

		Cross. The survivors of the Republican gun crews calmly await capture among the dead and wounded as the final position is overrun. The retreat down the back slope becomes a rout and the final bloody chapter of the battle begins. At about 18:30 the cavalry, hidden behind a coalmine dump in the right rear of the Republican position, comes into action against the fleeing burghers. Spearing and slashing they tear through the straggling mob. They wheel about and repeat the process again and again, mercilessly ignoring the burghers' attempts to surrender. The British victory costs them 52 killed and 213 wounded. The Republicans suffer heavy casualties, losing 38 killed, 113 wounded falling into British hands (of whom eight later die of their wounds) and 189, including four blacks, are captured. Besides four members of the Kock family, the casualties include H Coster (ex-State Attorney), BGV de Witt Hamer (Pretoria Town Clerk), Count H von Zeppelin, brother of the airship pioneer, and Commandant A Schiel (captured).[56] WF Mondriaan, brother of the Dutch graphic painter Piet Mondriaan, is wounded in the lung.[57]
Day 12 Sun **1899-10-22**	Natal front	Major-General Yule, his position at Dundee untenable, decides to retire to Ladysmith. He sneaks away at night leaving behind his wounded, including the fatally wounded General Penn-Symonds as well as stores, sufficient for almost a month, in the deserted camp.[58] General Penn-Symonds is promoted to the substantial rank of Major-General.[59]
Day 13 Mon **1899-10-23**	Natal front	Dundee is occupied by Republican forces. Incidents of looting are widespread and Major Donegan, commanding the abandoned British hospital, sentences one Indian medical orderly to death (later to be commuted) and three others to be publicly flogged for looting.[60] General Penn-Symonds dies at Dundee. Free Staters under Acting Field-cornet Christiaan R de Wet damage the railway about 20 kilometres north of Ladysmith, and Commandant JC de Villiers occupies positions at Rietfontein, on the Dundee railway line.[61]
	OFS	President MT Steyn visits Republican forces around Kimberley, returning to Bloemfontein on 27.[62]
	Western front	**Mafeking siege:** One of the ZAR 155 mm Creusot 'Long Tom' guns arrives at Mafeking. It is initially called 'Stemreg' (Franchise) but is later known as 'Ou Grietjie' or 'Old Creaky'.
	Northern front	Since the start of hostilities, the officers of the northern commandos, incited by Acting General HCJ van Rensburg, cannot believe that their commander, General FA Grobler, has been ordered to cross the border and to break up the railway line up to Bulawayo. They demand written confirmation from Commandant-General Piet Joubert and insist on artillery reinforcement. Field-cornet Briel crosses the Limpopo near Rhodes Drift and in a skirmish six British soldiers are killed while two burghers are wounded.[63]
	Natal Colony	Martial law is proclaimed throughout Natal and Zululand.[64] The Durban branch of the Transvaal National Bank is seized.
	United Kingdom	British Parlementarian Mr Duckworth remarks, *"If the Rand had been a potato field, there would have been no war."*[65]
	Trivia	*Unidentified Flying Objects are sighted at Vryheid, Paulpietersburg and Amsterdam in the southeastern ZAR.*

Day 14 Tue **1899-10-24**	Western front	**Kimberley siege:** A 600-strong commando attacks a British patrol under Major H Scott Turner as they escort an armoured train towards Dronfield, north of Kimberley. The British patrol is almost cut off but manages to extricate themselves. The attackers lose two men killed and seven wounded while the British lose three killed and 21 wounded.[66]
	Natal front	Due to the poor condition of his horses, General Lucas Meyer fails to make contact with Yule's force.[67] **THE BATTLE OF RIETFONTEIN** General Sir G White, attempting to cover Yule's retreat from Dundee via the Helpmekaar road, moves out with a force of 4 000 infantry, 1 100 mounted troops and 18 field-guns. In what is to be mostly an artillery action, he engages about 1,000 Free Staters, now under the command of General AP Cronje, deployed on two hills commanding the approach to Ladysmith. The shelling is mostly ineffectual against the widely dispersed burghers who open fierce small-arms fire on the British. White's force disengages at about 14:00 and falls back to Ladysmith having suffered 12 killed, 103 wounded and two missing. The Free Staters lose nine killed and 21 wounded. The Free Staters complain about the abuse of the white flag by the British and reports finding dumdum bullets on the battlefield.
	Gen. Sir G White (War Museum of the Boer Republics)	
	Black involvement	John Tengo Jabavu, editor of *Imvo Zabantsundu* (Black Opinion) and future ANC-founder member, writes: *"The British Government has succumbed to an irresponsible war party in Britain and South Africa. Meaningful negotiations could have taken place if only the government in London had not been persuaded that a military solution was the only alternative to a complete surrender of the ZAR government of its internal autonomy."*[68]
	Trivia	*UFOs, described as balloons with powerful searchlights, are sighted at Irene, Nylstroom, Biesiesvlei and Middelburg.[69]*
Day 15 Wed **1899-10-25**	Western front	**Mafeking siege:** The Republicans, supported by shelling, attack Mafeking from all sides. The assault is repulsed; the burghers are unable to approach closer than 1 370m to the British lines. Three burghers and two British soldiers are wounded.[70]
	Natal front	Commandant-General PJ Joubert sends a telegram of sympathy to Lady Penn-Symonds.
	United Kingdom	Mr Michael Davitt, Irish MP, rejects the Supplementary Army Estimates Bill in the House of Commons. He objects to Ireland having to contribute to a war she opposes. He will not *"purchase liberty for Ireland at the base price of voting against liberty in South Africa"*. He announces his retirement from the House in protest against British policy towards the Boers.[71]
Day 16 Thu **1899-10-26**	Western front Black involvement	General De la Rey arrives at Taung and transfers local civil authority to Chief Molala.[72]
	Natal front	The ZAR and Free State forces eventually join hands near Ladysmith. After their march of 65 kilometres, General Yule and his ragged column stagger into Ladysmith.[73]
	Northern front	Colonel Plumer, encouraged by the irresolution of his enemy, reoccupies Rhodes Drift after a skirmish in which four burghers are killed and one wounded at the loss of four own casualties. Field-cornets Briel and Alberts move their laagers back to the ZAR side of the river.[74]
	Cape Colony	Milner writes: *"... at whatever cost the armed oligarchy dominating all this subcontinent must be put an end to, if it is to be a place for civilized people to thrive in."*[75]

Day 17 Fri 1899-10-27	Western front	**Kimberley siege:** The Kimberley garrison engages Republican forces at Macfarlane's Siding.
	Victoria Cross	**Mafeking siege:** Captain C Fitzclarence and part of the Protectorate Regiment launch a night-time bayonet attack on a trench near the racecourse within 2 000 yards of Mafeking. This loathed type of assault first panics the defenders but then unleashes a furious fusillade on the British and the attack is repulsed.[76] Surprisingly the Boers lose only one man killed, while the British lose six killed, nine wounded and two taken prisoner. Among the wounded is Captain C Fitzclarence, Royal Fusilleers, who earns his second Victoria Cross recommendation for leading the night attack on enemy trenches.[77]
	Natal front	General John PD French leads a reconnaissance force consisting of a brigade of cavalry out of Ladysmith. He moves five battalions of infantry and four artillery batteries to a position east of town where they await further orders. Probing in all directions, he tries to determine the strengths and dispositions of the Republican forces around Ladysmith.[78]
Day 18 Sat 1899-10-28	Natal front	Ladysmith is surrounded on three sides by a Republican force of about 7 500 men with 16 field-guns and three pom-poms. General Sir GS White's Ladysmith garrison comprises about 14 500 men with more than 50 field-guns.[79]
	Cape Colony	The famous big-game hunter and pro-Boer FC Selous predicts that, if the war continues, *"we shall have entered upon a course which, though it may give us the gold-fields of the Transvaal for the present and the immediate future, will infallibly lose us the whole of South Africa as a British possession within the lifetime of many men who are now living"*.[80]
	Trivia	*UFO sightings are reported from Roodepoort, Springs, Rustenburg, Volksrust, Lydenburg and various other telegraph stations.*[81]
Day 19 Mon 1899-10-29	Western front	**Kimberley siege:** General De la Rey arrives at Kimberley.[82]
	Natal front	Emboldened by the apparent British victories at Dundee and Elandslaagte, General Sir G White is confident of achieving a decisive victory. He plans a complicated full-scale, three-pronged excursion out of Ladysmith with undefined objectives. After using his observation balloon to confirm the information gained by French the day before, White issues his orders: (1) Colonel GG Grimwood, with a strengthened brigade, is to seize Long Hill, about 6,5 kilometres northeast of town before joining up with Hamilton's brigade and attacking Pepworth Hill. (2) French's cavalry brigade is to occupy Lombard's Kop, about 7km east of Ladysmith from where he is to cover Grimwood's right flank. As the attack on Pepworth develops, French is to charge north and cut off the anticipated northward retreat of the enemy. (3) Lieutenant-Colonel FRC Carleton with 1 180 men and six mountain guns was to form the left flank and by occupying Nicholson's Nek, about 8 kilometres to the north, to threaten the enemy laagers. At about 17:00, one of the ZAR State Artillery's Creusot 'Long Tom' 155mm heavy guns arrives. It is immediately dragged up Pepworth Hill, where an emplacement has been prepared for it. [83]
	Natal Colony	Sir A Milner informs Sir Walter Hely-Hutchinson, the Governor of Natal, that *HMS Terrible* and *Magicienne* will reinforce *HMS Tartar* and *Powerful* in the endeavour to hold the port of Durban.[84]

Day 20 Mon **1899-10-30**	Natal front *Lt.-Col. SPE Trichard* (National Cultural History Museum) *Gen. Louis Botha* (National Cultural History Museum) **Victoria Cross**	**THE BATTLE OF MODDER SPRUIT AND NICHOLSON'S NEK** Lieutenant-Colonel Carleton with the longest distance to cover, leaves first and moves north along the Bell Spruit. He realizes that his progress is too slow and, to avoid being caught in the open at dawn, decides to occupy the closer Tchrengula or Cayinguba Hill. As his force climbs the hill, mules carrying the mountain guns and his heliograph stampede, charge through the infantry units and disappear in the darkness. Carleton reaches the summit and prepares defensive positions. At dawn, Lieutenant-Colonel SPE Trichardt of the ZAR Staatsartillerie on Pepworth Hill notices French's cavalry and immediately opens fire, preventing them from reaching their assigned positions. Grimwood in the centre, unaware that Long Hill is unoccupied, opens fire on the summit where he expects enemy artillery positions. He also comes under fire from his left, across the Modder Spruit where French is supposed to cover his flank. Grimwood postpones his assault on Long Hill, pivots slightly and extends his front towards Lombard's Kop to the east to protect his flank. The Long Tom also comes into action against Grimwood's artillery but later changes aim and starts shelling the station, where a train has just arrived, and the northern part of the town, causing great consternation. Grimwood, with his artillery outclassed by the few guns on Pepworth, is forced to extend his front increasingly eastwards where Louis Botha uses the burghers' excellent mobility to cross the Modderspruit and maintain pressure on the flank. At about 10:00 Hamilton, rather than waiting for Grimwood to support him in his planned frontal assault on Pepworth, moves east in support of the seriously engaged Grimwood and French. French is now also desperately fighting to prevent Grimwood's isolation by burghers pushing forward and moving towards his original objective, Lombard's Kop.[85] All efforts to contact Carleton's force fail and a patrol sent out to investigate, comes under severe fire and is forced to retire. 2nd Lieutenant J Norwood, 5th Dragoon Guards, turns around and gallops about 300 metres under fierce fire to rescue a fallen comrade, earning a Victoria Cross. When Knox, responsible for guarding the north and north-west of town, confirms earlier Imperial Light Horse reports of enemy movements in that sector, General White becomes concerned that the town is under threat from that quarter. At about 11:30, General White orders, *"Retire as opportunity offers"* and all units start falling back to Ladysmith. The retreat starts orderly but the infantry, seeing the cavalry rushing back, panics and the officers are hard pressed to maintain discipline. The Republican artillery now concentrates on their counterparts and soon damages four field-guns as they are falling back in stages over open ground. Displaying remarkable bravery, the British gunners retrieve all their field-guns, including the damaged ones. At about noon the Republican gunners on Pepworth Hill are surprised when they suddenly come under fire from two 4,7 inch (120mm) and three 12-pounder naval guns which have arrived on the morning train and are immediately pushed into action by their *HMS Powerful* naval crew under Captain Lambton. Transferring their attention to this direction, the Republican artillery soon damages two of the naval guns. With the British streaming back to town, Commandant-General Joubert is urged to order a pursuit, but he refuses, reputedly saying, *"When God holds out a finger, don't take the whole hand."* Earlier, on Tchrengula, Carleton discovers that the positions he has chosen in the dark are vulnerable to attacks from the north. Commandant LP Steenekamp and Field-cornet CR de Wet, investigating the noises made by the entrenching soldiers, immediately appreciate the situation and attack via Nicholson's Nek. In almost a re-enactment of Majuba, the burghers approach in small groups darting from rock to rock, while the British are unable to cover the 'dead ground' below the crest. The British soldiers, trained to fire in volleys, wait for their officers to give firing directions, while the burghers' independent fire keeps them down in their poorly sited positions. For sev-

	Western front	eral hours this part of the battle continues in the blazing sun. Casualties mount and ammunition and water start to give out. When Carleton and his men become aware of the army's retreat to Ladysmith, they realise their hopeless situation. At about 13:15, white flags start to appear and Carleton is forced to order 'cease fire' and surrender. On what is later described as '**Mournful Monday**', the British lose 106 killed, 374 wounded and 1 284 captured. The Republicans suffer 16 killed and 75 wounded.[86]
	Western front	**Mafeking siege:** An attack against a British fort led by the Scandinavian Volunteers advances to within 275 metres of the objective before it is repulsed. The British suffer eight casualties, while one burgher is killed and four are wounded. [87]
	International	The first Canadian contingent under the command of Lieutenant-Colonel Otter embarks at Quebec after a stirring speech by the Premier Sir Wilfred Laurier.
Day 21 Tue **1899-10-31**	Natal front	General Kock dies at Ladysmith of wounds received at Elandslaagte. CR de Wet is appointed as Acting Commandant of the Heilbron commando.[88]
	Western front	**Mafeking siege:** Preceded by severe shelling, using most of their guns, the Republicans launch an attack on a British fort at Kanon Kopje, southwest of Mafeking. The position is gallantly defended by 50 men of the BSA Police under Colonel Walford and the attack is repulsed, the British losing eight killed and three wounded. General PA Cronje's force suffers five wounded, including his own son, Piet, who is fatally wounded.[89]
	Northern front	Commandant SP Grobler arrives with a field-gun at Acting General van Rensburg's laager near Rhodes Drift, to be followed by two additional guns under Captain Sarel Eloff two days later.[90]
	Cape Colony	The new Commander-in-Chief of Her Majesty's troops in South Africa, Lieutenant-General Sir Redvers Buller, disembarks from the *Dunotter Castle* in Cape Town. Apart from the British troops already in South Africa and the locally recruited units, he has a full army corps at his disposal, consisting of a cavalry division, three infantry divisions and the usual support troops — a force of 46 665 men with 114 guns and 47 machine guns.[91]
1899	SPRING	**NOVEMBER 1899**
Day 22 Wed **1899-11-01**	Central front	Free Staters seize the Norval's Pont bridge, the Bethulie bridges and the Colesberg road bridge and invade the Cape Colony.[92]
	Western front	**Mafeking siege:** At Mafeking, Mr EG Perslow, war correspondent of the *Daily Chronicle*, is murdered by Lieutenant Murchison.
	Civilian life	The first edition of the *Mafeking Mail Special Siege Slip*, edited by GN Whales, appears and is to be issued daily, *"shells permitting"*. The remarkable 27-year-old Sol T Plaatje, fluent in eight languages and a future ANC founder member, assists as part-time typist and interpreter.[93]
	United Kingdom Civilian life	The South African Conciliation Committee is formed with Leonard Courtney as president and Emily Hobhouse as honorary secretary of its women's branch.[94]
Day 23 Thu **1899-11-02**	Central front	Acting General Van Rensburg, emboldened by the newly arrived artillery, finally crosses the river with his entire force and attacks two sections of Colonel Plumer's force. In both attacks the British are overpowered and resistance ceases as soon as the Republican guns find their range. Very few prisoners are taken, however, because the British disperse in the dense bush, in one case abusing the white flag to get away. The

		Republicans lose two killed and four slightly wounded, while the British lose ten captured including three wounded. Colonel Plumer retires to Tuli, leaving behind 70 horses, 100 mules, 18 oxen and several loaded supply wagons and an ambulance. Van Rensburg refuses to pursue the fleeing soldiers.[95]
	Natal front	Telegraph lines are cut and railway lines south of Ladysmith are broken up, but a planned attack on the town has to be cancelled, when the Free State burghers fail to arrive at the appointed position. The town is shelled without results.[96] **THE SIEGE OF LADYSMITH BEGINS** At the sack of Badajoz, Harry Smith, a Rifle Brigade officer, rescued a beautiful, young Spanish woman from his own troops, and subsequently married her. The town of Ladysmith is named after her. Ladysmith is the most important garrison town in the north of Britain's *"most loyal colony"* in South Africa. Huge quantities of supplies have been transported and stockpiled here during the previous months. British prestige in the face of the Natal loyalists and the Zulus are clearly linked to the defence of the town. To the Republicans, Natal will always be their 'Promised Land' for which they have fought the Zulus with God's help, only to be robbed of it by the British. The presence of Dr LS Jameson in town adds an additional incentive for them to capture the town and inflict a humiliating defeat on Britain in the full view of the entire world. Generals French and Hamilton leave on the last train out of Ladysmith.[97]
	Western front	**Mafeking siege:** General Snyman, besieging Mafeking, telegraphs his president in Pretoria: *"... the Mr CH Perrin sent here by the Government charged with the production of incendiary shells, filled an empty shell with sand and placed therein a note addressed to Baden-Powell asking for whiskey, whereupon he received his bottle of liquor this morning together with a letter. Thus I place not the slightest confidence in the man. What must I do? I had him court-martialled. He said he meant no harm."*[98] **Kimberley siege:** Republicans capture all the horses and mules of the Kimberley municipality's sanitary service. Until the De Beers Company manages to make alternative draught animals available, inhabitants are forced to dispose of their own nightsoil. Home-owners have to empty the pails on their own property, creating a health hazard.[99]
	ZAR	General JHM Kock, whose body has been returned by the British, is buried in Pretoria. As the dies for the coinage of the ZAR, produced by the Kaisermint, have been intercepted by British warships, the Director of the ZAR mint, Mr J Perrin, is forced to use the 1898 dies for new pounds to be struck. He modifies the dies and at 10:30, a coin with a single (oversized) '9' in place of '1899', is struck. It is the first coin to be struck during the war and he presents it to the State Secretary, Mr FW Reitz. The government decides to present it with dignified pomp and ceremony to the United States Consul-General Mr CE Marcum, for the sole purpose of ratifying the ZAR and the fact that it is producing coinage despite the war. [This totally unique coin has been part of King Farouk of Egypt's collection and is today in the possession of an anonymous collector. Due to its rarity the '1899 Kruger Single 9' is presently (1998) valued at R7 000 000, but is expected to command a price of over R100 000 000 if sold — one of the most valuable coins in the world.][100]
	International	Canada offers a second contingent. In Britain orders are issued for the mobilisation of the militia.[101] Dr Leyds receives a telegram of encouragement signed by about 4 000 Germans.

Day 24 Fri **1899-11-03**	Natal front	**Ladysmith siege:** A strong mounted force under Major-General JF Brocklehurst attacks the OFS commandos outside Ladysmith but is repulsed with five killed, 28 wounded and one missing. Lieutenant AE Brabant, son of Major-General Sir EY Brabant, is fatally wounded.[102] Commandant-General Joubert grants requests by the Town Council and the chief medical officer to establish a hospital and camp for civilians outside town. Joubert allows an armistice for the establishment of the so-called Intombi-camp and grants permission to allow a single train per day to steam from Ladysmith to the camp and back, under a flag of truce.[103] British troops evacuate Colenso on the Tugela, south of Ladysmith.
	Western front	**Kimberley siege:** Kimberley is completely surrounded. At this stage, about 7,000 Republicans, consisting of 4 800 Free Staters and 2 193 Transvalers, are concentrated around the town.[104]
	Northern front	A false alarm causes Acting General Van Rensburg to fall back across the Limpopo with his entire force, abandoning his guns until a few volunteers retrieve them.[105]
	Central front	British troops evacuate Burgersdorp and Stormberg and fall back to Queenstown. British troops evacuate Noupoort.
	Cape Colony	Martial law is proclaimed in the De Aar district.
Day 25 Sat **1899-11-04**	Western front	**Kimberley siege:** Chief Commandant CJ Wessels sends an ultimatum to Kekewich demanding the surrender of Kimberley and, in a humane gesture, offering to allow all women and children to leave the city, thus sparing them the privations and dangers of any future military action.[106] **Mafeking siege:** Outside Mafeking, in a demonstration authorised by General PA Cronje, a certain Mr Gumbold sets off an explosion using a mystery compound that is *"far stronger than dynamite"*.[107]
	Northern front	Acting General Van Rensburg realises his mistake and recrosses the Limpopo.
	Central front	Free State commandos invade the Cape Colony near Norval's Pont.[108]
	Cape Colony	**BULLER SPLITS THE ARMY CORPS** General Buller abandons his original operational plan of a direct assault along the central railway line through the Free State and decides to divide his forces.[109]
	International	In *Harper's Weekly*, American Finney Peter Dunne's fictional bar room philosopher, Mr Dooley, says, *"If I was Kruger, there'd've been no war. I'd give them the votes... But... I'd do the countin."*[110]
Day 26 Sun **1899-11-05**	Natal	**Ladysmith siege:** Commander Egerton of *HMS Powerful* dies of injuries received during a 'Long Tom' bombardment of Ladysmith.[111]
Day 27 Mon **1899-11-06**	Cape Colony	Chief Commandant JH Olivier, in command of the southern Free State forces on the central front, and member of the OFS Volksraad, holds discussions with the mayor of Aliwal North on the bridge spanning the Orange River at the town.[112]
	Western front	**Kimberley siege:** Kimberley is shelled for the first time.[113]
	Natal front	**Ladysmith siege:** Another Creusot 'Long Tom' arrives at Ladysmith and is positioned on Bulwana Hill.[114] A Free State commando under Commandant De Villiers enters the deserted Colenso where they are later joined by a ZAR commando.[115]

Day 28 Tue 1899-11-07	Western front	**Mafeking siege:** Major Godley and part of the Protectorate Regiment with two 7-pounders make a night attack on a laager west of Mafeking. The burghers are completely surprised by the unexpected bombardment but as the light improves, the attack is repulsed. Three burghers and six attackers, including Major Godley, are wounded.[116]
	Black involvement	**Kimberley siege:** From his conning tower Colonel Kekewich sees a *"living mass"* of men approaching from the north-east and his artillery opens up at almost point-blank range until they realise that the men are 3 000 unarmed black mine-workers released by De Beers from the compounds, without informing the military.[117]
	Natal front	**Ladysmith siege:** A planned attack on Ladysmith is cancelled without informing burghers south of town, who attack and are repulsed without loss.[118]
Day 29 Wed 1899-11-08	Western front Civilian life	**Kimberley siege:** After consultation with Rhodes, Kekewich releases a shortened version of Wessels' ultimatum for publication in the *Diamond Fields Advertiser*, in which Wessels' offer to civilians to leave Kimberley is revised, giving the impression that it is extended to Afrikaner families only. Only one family accepts the offer. All the remaining civilians are to suffer the hardships that could have been avoided by accepting the humane and generous offer.[119]
	Black involvement	**Mafeking siege:** President Steyn takes General Snyman to task for a cattle raid against Chief Montshiwa in which 203 head of cattle and 1 570 sheep and goats have been taken. In the President's view it is not advisable to alienate the blacks for the sake of a small herd of livestock. [120]
Day 30 Thu 1899-11-09	Natal front	**Ladysmith siege:** The planned Republican attack on Ladysmith eventually takes place. Preceded by a bombardment using all their guns, several commandos attack Platrand (Wagon Hill). Fierce rifle fire pins them down on the slopes and the attack loses momentum. At about 11:30 the burghers return to their camps having lost three killed and six wounded and inflicting British losses amounting to four killed and 27 wounded.[121]
	Cape Colony	Lord Methuen arrives in Cape Town aboard the *Moor*.[122]
	United Kingdom	**BRITAIN'S WAR AIMS** Lord Salisbury, speaking at the Lord Mayor of London's banquet, states that Britain's sole interest in the Witwatersrand mines is that they should be worked under good government: *"But that is the limit of our interest. We seek no gold-fields. We seek no territory. What we desire is equal rights for men of all races, and security of our fellow subjects and for the Empire."*[123]
	Trivia	*58th birthday of HM Albert Edward, Prince of Wales.*
Day 31 Fri 1899-11-10	Natal front	At a combined council of war near Ladysmith, the Free State officers express their reservations about the proposed combined Republican expedition into southern Natal, and the planned operation has to be scaled down to no more than a raid.[124]
	Western front	Two squadrons of Colonel Gough's 19th Lancers, a company and a half of Northumberland Fusiliers and North Lancashires, and a battery of field artillery undertake a reconnaissance operation in force north of the Orange River and run into Commandant van der Merwe's commando. The British are badly mauled in the first skirmish on this front. The Northumberlands lose all their officers almost as soon as firing starts, losing two killed and four wounded while no casualties are reported on the Republican side. This skirmish leads to the abandoning of all unnecessarily distinctive marks of rank, including the infantry officer's useless sword.[125]

Day 32 Sat **1899-11-11**	Western front	Republican forces occupy Barkley West **THE SIEGE OF KURUMAN** Commandant JH Visser with 200 men attacks Kuruman, British Bechuanaland, and demands the town's surrender. The defenders are only 35 members of the Cape Police, 33 local volunteers and a few armed blacks, but they stubbornly refuse to submit and the attack degenerates into a siege.[126]
	Natal front	Captain Percy Scott of *HMS Terrible* is appointed as commandant of the forces defending Durban.
	United Kingdom	Britain calls out a fifth division to be commanded by Lieutenant-Colonel Sir Charles Warren.
Day 33 Sun **1899-11-12**	Western front	Lieutenant-General Paul Sanford Lord Methuen assumes command at Orange River Station. His force, tasked with the relief of Kimberley and the protection of communication lines to Cape Town, now consists of the following:[127] **Artillery:** A strong detachment Royal Horse Artillery and a brigade division Royal Field Artillery with 1 086 men with 30 guns. **Infantry:** Three brigades and four regiments consisting of 12 013 men with 12 machine guns under Major-Generals HE Colvile and AG Wauchope. **Cavalry:** A regiment with 573 men and a machine gun. **Engineers and support troops:** 460 men and two field hospitals. **Total:** 14 841 men with 30 guns and 13 machine guns.
	Northern front	General FA Grobler arrives at Rhodes Drift with the 300-strong advance group of reinforcements and takes over command from Van Rensburg.[128]
Day 34 Mon **1899-11-13**	Natal front	A combined Republican force, commanded by the 69-year-old Commandant-General Joubert, consisting of 1 600 Transvalers and 500 Free Staters with only two guns, arrive at Colenso to start their planned invasion of southern Natal.[129]
	Western front	Republican forces occupy Douglas.
	Central front *Chief Comdt. JH Olivier* *(National Cultural History Museum)*	Chief Commandant JH Olivier, fearing that the Aliwal North bridge may be mined, sends a messenger into town to fetch the local magistrate, Mr Hugo, who is forced to stand in the middle of the bridge with his assistant and the chief constable as the commando files past. The Free State flag is hoisted in Aliwal North, immediately renamed *"Oliviersfontein"*.[130] As instructed by President Steyn, an occupation proclamation is read out and local supporters of the Republican cause are 'commandeered' to join up in an effort to protect them against future treason charges. On his own initiative, Olivier uses a fair amount of intimidation to swell his ranks.
	Black involvement	John Tengo Jabavu writes in *Imvo Zabantsundu* (Black Opinion) that the war is *"the very quintessence of unfairness"*.
Day 35 Tue **1899-11-14**	Natal front	A very nervous Colonel Long, acting commanding officer at Estcourt, packs up his tents and loads his guns into railway trucks, in preparation for a hasty retreat.[131]
	Central front	A combined Republican force numbering about 700 under Chief Commandant ER Grobler (OFS) and General HJ Schoeman (ZAR) enters Colesberg unopposed and they are enthusiastically welcomed by the local Afrikaners.[132] At Lady Grey some Free Staters and local supporters arrive and affix a copy of

		President Steyn's annexation proclamation to the Post Office notice board. Their leader demands the office keys from Mrs Sarah Glueck, the local postmaster. She not only refuses to oblige but also removes the Free State proclamation and pins up a reminder to all Cape Colonists that they are subjects of the Crown. She even underlines certain passages of the notice and writes *RULE BRITANNIA* in large letters on top.[133]
	Western front	**Mafeking siege:** A census conducted by Colonel Baden-Powell puts the population of Mafeking at 1 074 white men, 229 white women, 405 white children and 7 500 blacks *"all told"*.[134]
Day 36 Wed **1899-11-15**	Central front	Republican forces under Commandant FJ du Plooy enter Burgersdorp.[135]
	Natal front	**THE ARMOURED TRAIN INCIDENT NEAR FRERE** An armoured train steaming out of Estcourt is ambushed and partly wrecked by burghers with an excellently handled mountain gun, between Frere and Chieveley. In the ensuing fight four British soldiers are killed, 34 are wounded and 69 taken prisoner. Winston Churchill, the extremely well-paid war correspondent of *The Morning Post*, actively takes part in the action, assisting in the removal of wreckage from the track, allowing the locomotive and part of the train carrying the wounded to escape to Estcourt. Churchill, although claiming non-combatant status, is also captured and treated as a prisoner of war.[136] After this action, the Republican expedition to southern Natal splits into two groups. Moving in an eastward arc around Estcourt is a 600-man group commanded by Commandant David Joubert, a nephew of the Commandant-General, while the right hook is formed by the remainder, commanded by General Louis Botha.[137]
	Cape Colony	Martial law is extended to the central and northern districts of Cape Colony.
Day 37 Thu **1899-11-16**	Western front	**Kimberley siege:** An attack on a post manned by 30 Bloemfontein burghers outside Kimberley is repulsed after Major Albrecht reinforces them with 100 men and a single gun. After a skirmish lasting almost two hours, the attackers retreat with 11 casualties.[138] General JH de la Rey leaves Kimberley with about 1 500 reinforcements and heads south for Belmont. [139]
	Central front	Lieutenant-General Sir WF Gatacre lands at East London and takes over command of the eastern sector of the central front, responsible for the protection of the Eastern Cape Province and preparations for the British assault on the Republics in accordance with the original campaign plan. His force consists of the following:[140] **Artillery**: One brigade division of Royal Field Artillery with 678 men and 18 field-guns. **Infantry and mounted infantry:** Three infantry battalions and a half-battalion mounted infantry consisting of 3 246 men with three or four machine guns. **Engineers and support troops:** 303 men and a field hospital. **Total**: 4 227 men with 18 field-guns and about four machine guns.
	Cape Colony	Martial law is proclaimed in the Hay district.
	Natal front	A telegram from Commandant Viljoen, commanding the Johannesburg commando at Ladysmith, to Field-cornet De Vries, Fordsburg:

		"About twenty persons have arrived here from your ward. Some of them sick or disabled, others crippled, blind or cockeyed. The majority possess medical certificates which have been ignored either by you or the Acting Commandant. What the hell do you think I have here, a hospital, a reformatory or a war on my hands? These sick and disabled must suffer the greatest discomfort and privation amongst us, since not only are they quite unserviceable but they also need nursing and accommodation without which they must surely perish. Among others who arrived here with chronic and grave diseases are J Elliot who is blind, G van der Walt who has a large rupture and JF van der Merwe with a gastric ulcer, whereas G Roestof throws an epileptic fit every day. In addition there are many more. Why do you not commandeer plump, over-nourished persons like the officials, as well as Charlie du Plessis of Vrededorp? As for that big fat braggart G Bezuidenhout, I cannot leave him there, he must come and defend his country. Besides, you have enough scouts in skirts to help you. And if Field-Cornet Lombaard will not come himself, why does he not send his clerk Pienaar and such-like types? Give Field-Cornet Lombaard a copy of this."[141] Major-General HJT Hildyard arrives with reinforcements and assumes command at Estcourt.
Day 38 Fri 1899-11-17	Western front	**Kimberley siege:** Commandant Lubbe is involved in a skirmish near Alexanderfontein, outside Kimberley, during which three burghers are wounded.[142] Republican forces occupy Griekwastad.
	Natal front	**Ladysmith siege:** A soccer game between the Gordon Highlanders and the Imperial Light Horse is interrupted when a shell drops on the field. No one is hurt, but the Gordons 'sneak' a goal under cover of the dust and smoke. The ILH object but the Scots are *"immovably stubborn"*, and finally a message is sent to the Football Association in England, inquiring as to whether such a contingency is covered by the rules of the game.[143]
	Cape Colony	Republican forces under Commandant David Joubert occupy Weenen. Mr Schreiner protests to President Steyn, expressing his *"surprise and regret"* at the invasion and at the purported proclamations and annexation of Cape territory. *"The people of this Colony have not deserved such treatment. Some may thereby be misled into conduct for which they may in future suffer very heavily, and the consequences of such wrong action will be justly laid to Your Honour's charge, if it be not put a stop to without delay wherever it has taken place."*[144]
Day 39 Sat 1899-11-18	Central front	Chief Commandant Olivier occupies Jamestown with a Republican force numbering about 150 men.
	Northern front	The ZAR government orders the irresolute Grobler to send 600 burghers for service elsewhere and to return across the river and assume a purely defensive role.[145] The first edition of a siege newspaper, *The Ladysmith Bombshell,* appears.
	Western front *Gen. JP (Kootjie) Snyman (National Cultural History Museum)*	General PA Cronje departs for Kimberley, leaving General Kootjie Snyman in command of the besieging forces at Mafeking. Cronje and his force move to Klerksdorp, then by train via Johannesburg and Bloemfontein to Edenburg, and from there on horseback to the Kimberley front.[146] **Kimberley siege:** With most of their senior officers elsewhere, the ZAR forces west and south-west of Kimberley, repulse a strong force of 1 820 men under Lieutenant-Colonel Chamier. The British lose 24 killed and 32 wounded.[147] Major-General AG (Andy) Wauchope reoccupies Noupoort. This important railway town has been completely unprotected since 3 November, but Schoeman's inactivity in Colesberg enables the British to regain it, thus securing the supply lines to two fronts.[148]

Day 40 Sun **1899-11-19**	Central front	Republican supporters try to occupy Lady Grey. They demand the office keys from the formidable postmaster, Mrs Sarah Glueck. She refuses and instead reads aloud a telegram from the Cape Prime Minister, reminding all British subjects of their duty.[149]
	Western front	**Kuruman siege:** The siege of Kuruman is temporarily lifted as Commandant Visser is ordered to Vryburg.
	International	Kaizer Wilhelm II and Von Bülow arrives for a six-day visit to Britain to discuss the possibility of an Anglo-German alliance.
Day 41 Mon **1899-11-20**	Central front	Recently escaped from Ladysmith, Lieutenant-General JDP French, now tasked to protect the central Cape Colony and to prepare for the future assault on the Republics, arrives at Noupoort. His force consist of the following:[150] **Artillery:** Two batteries Royal Horse Artillery and one battery Royal Field Artillery consisting of 722 men with 18 field-guns. **Cavalry :** Five cavalry regiments and two companies mounted infantry consisting of 3 220 men with five machine guns. **Infantry and engineers:** 1 006 men with a single machine gun. **Total :** 4 948 men with 18 guns and six machine guns.
	Black involvement	At Lady Grey Mrs Glueck's defiant conduct is to no avail as the local magistrate hands over the keys to all public offices, and the Free State flag is hoisted. The *Daily Mail* later presents Mrs Glueck, who earns £120 per annum, with a cheque for £100 in appreciation of her pluck. She declines to use the gift for her own purposes.[151] Olivier sends a telegram to Major Hook, commanding officer of the Herschel Native Police — a force consisting of 70 Cape policemen, 30 white volunteers and 400 blacks. He offers to respect the neutrality of the Herschel territory on condition that Hook undertakes to maintain law and order in that district. [152] Republican forces occupy Venterstad.
	United Kingdom	The Kaizer arrives for a state visit to England, apparently proving Germany's neutrality. Lady Salisbury, wife of the British Prime Minister, dies.[153]
	Trivia	*Chief of OFS Artillery Major FWR Albrecht's 51st birthday.*
Day 42 Tue **1899-11-21**	Western front Lt.-Gen. Lord Methuen (War Museum of the Boer Republics)	**START OF THE FIRST BRITISH OFFENSIVE** Lieutenant-General Lord Methuen commences his advance on Kimberley. His column, almost five kilometres long, crosses the Orange River bridge and camps on the north bank. Methuen predicts, *"I shall breakfast in Kimberley on Monday."* The area of operations in front of him is British territory, presently occupied by the invaders. After the discovery of diamonds in this region, the Orange and Vaal Rivers, which formed the accepted borders, were suddenly regarded as too vague by the British government. They also felt a keen responsibility to some of their forgotten subjects, the Griquas, a people of mixed descent, who had been left to their own devices, mostly survival farming with a bit of cattle rustling and river pirating, for decades. Characteristically, the British champion the cause of the underdog. They declare a dispute, a Briton is appointed as arbitrator and a new colony is created with an eastern border formed by straight lines that form awkward angles and offsets to include several tribal graves and, of course, most of the diamond bearing formations. A token settlement amount is paid to the Orange Free State and Griqualand West is later integrated into the Cape Colony.
	Natal front	Republican forces under Commandant David Joubert occupy Willow Grange Station.

Day 43 Wed **1899-11-22**	Cape Colony	Since 17 November more than 22 000 troops have arrived in Cape Town. General Buller leaves Cape Town, travelling by train via Stormberg to East London, where he embarks for Durban.[154]
	Cape Colony	Lord Methuen is reinforced at Witputs by the 1st Coldstream Guards and two companies of Royal Munster Fusiliers. Republicans fire at his sappers who attempt to improve their water supply. Using long-range rifle fire, they also prevent him from making any detailed reconnaissance.[155]
	Natal front	Republican forces approaching from Willow Grange shell Mooi River. Bad weather limits visibility and only a few shells are fired.[156] **THE BATTLE OF WILLOW GRANGE** After alternately occupying and abandoning Willow Grange Station during the previous weeks, Major-General HJT Hildyard, commanding officer at Estcourt, indecisive and confused by conflicting reports and uncertain of the enemy's intentions, decides to take Brynbella Hill, overlooking the station with a force of about 5,200 men with 14 field-guns. He orders a force under Colonel FW Kitchener to occupy Beacon Hill from where he plans to make a night attack on Brynbella, supported by one of his naval guns. It is a very hot day and the unacclimatized troops are exhausted and thirsty before reaching the foot of Beacon Hill. A heavy thunderstorm first alleviate their plight, but it changes into a hailstorm that leaves them battered and bruised. The Republicans also notice their struggle in dragging the naval gun up the steep slope, and opens fire with their Creusot field-gun. The British persevere and are soon able to position their naval gun on the summit and return fire until the renewed thunderstorm and darkness suspend the action. After dark, a tremendous thunderstorm engulfs the landscape. Two British soldiers and two burghers are knocked unconscious by lightning and a burgher and six horses are killed on Brynbella.[157]
Day 44 Thu **1899-11-23**	Natal front	**THE BATTLE OF WILLOW GRANGE** Slipping and sliding, the British proceed with their night march despite the appalling conditions. After a short rest on the slope, they charge the summit at about 03:00. The small Free State picket abandons their position, blankets and a few ponies to avoid the loathed bayonets and flee down the back slope, leaving the summit in the hands of the jubilant British. At dawn, part of the Krugersdorp commando and General Louis Botha open fire on the summit. They are soon joined by the expedition's two field-guns and a pom-pom. As the light improves, Republican rifle fire increases and Kitchener's position on the summit become steadily worse. At about 09:00 he realises that he will have to retreat to avoid being cut off and surrounded. The retreating British troops are raked by Republican shellfire. Only when their own artillery return fire, can they fall back to Beacon Hill and from there to Estcourt, where they arrive at about 11:00. The British lose 11 killed (including Percy Fitzpatrick's brother, George), 67 wounded and eight captured. The Republicans lose two killed and two wounded.[158]
	Western front	**THE BATTLE OF BELMONT** The heights dominating Belmont Station to the east, are occupied by 2 950 Free State burghers under General J Prinsloo with two Krupp guns and a pom-pom. Lord Methuen, bivouacking at Thomas' farm, has 7 700 infantry with ten machine guns; 1 000 cavalry; 950 artillerists with 16 field-guns and 800 support troops — a total of about 10 500 men. The attack he has decided on is a classic night march followed by a dawn assault, supported by artillery, with flanking movements by his cavalry. After gaining their first objective, the force is to pivot slightly and take the higher feature from the south-east, with the cavalry ready to cut off the enemy's retreat. The night march starts late and is immediately delayed as they cut the fences along

		the rail lines. The troops are deployed five to six metres apart and it is soon clear that the distances have been underestimated. As dawn approaches, the Scots Guards are only about a metre apart and still more than 200 metres from their objective. At that moment the burghers open fire. The Grenadier Guards are in a worse position as they are 400 metres from their target and they are also subjected to fire from their flank. At the same time, the 9th Brigade crosses the railway line. The Scots and the Grenadiers charge, with their bands playing, determined to take Gun Hill at bayonet point. They are winded when they reach the top, only to see the Free Staters falling back to positions on Table Mountain. They are also exposed to their own artillery bombardment as the gunners fire with the sun in their eyes.
		The battle now deteriorates into a frontal assault on the Free Staters' main positions along the crest of Table Mountain and from there on the ridge called Mont Blanc, as Methuen commits more and more of his reserves. The Coldstream Guards abandon their planned assault and charge Razor Back Hill, the origin of the fire directed at them. The burghers keep up their fire all along the ridges until the attackers reach the dead ground at the foot of their positions. They then start retiring northwards, leaving small groups to cover their retreat. When the British clear the enemy positions, the Free Staters streaming northwards over the plain are already out of range.
		The British cavalry, assigned with the task of cutting off the retreat, are harassed by small mounted patrols and fail to make contact with the fleeing burghers. At 07:30 the battle is over. The cheering British troops are in possession of the battlefield and at 10:00 they return to their camp at Thomas's Farm. The burghers retreat unmolested, ready to fight another day.
		The British lose 54 killed and 243 wounded, while the Free Staters suffer 15 killed, 30 wounded and 36 taken prisoner. The British also destroy 64 wagons captured on the battlefield. Lord Methuen praises his soldiers, saying, *"With troops like you, no General can fear for the result of his plans."*[159]
		At about 13:00 some 365 marines of the Naval Brigade from *HMS Powerful, HMS Doris* and *HMS Monarch* arrive at Belmont. About 16 km north of Belmont, at Graspan, General De la Rey arrives with about 700 men and two field-guns.[160]
	Central front	A local rebel commando takes control of Barkly East in anticipation of the arrival of Olivier's Free State commando.[161]
Day 45 Fri **1899-11-24**	Western front	Lord Methuen undertakes a reconnaissance operation from Belmont, along the railway line, and estimates the enemy stationed around Graspan and Enslin at about 500. He moves his force to Swinkpan, leaving the Scots Guards and two companies of the Munster Fusiliers to guard Belmont. At Graspan, General De la Rey, now in command, is joined by about 1 300 Free Staters under General J Prinsloo.[162]
	Natal front	The 68-year-old Commandant-General Joubert is thrown by his horse near Beacon Hill. He suffers internal injuries of which he is never to recover fully.
Day 46 Sat **1899-11-25**	Western front Black involvement	**THE ATROCITY AT DERDEPOORT** Crossing the border the previous night and sent ahead by Colonel Holdworth, who fears that the enemy *"will hear the troops' boots"*, three Kgatla-Tswana regiments armed by the British, attack a burgher laager at Derdepoort, east of Gaberones. Holdsworth gives what he calls *"Maxim covering fire"* at extreme range and retreats early, leaving the tribesmen to their own devices. Twenty burghers, including a local member of the Volksraad and two women, are killed and 17 women and children are kidnapped and taken to Mochudi, for the loss of 14 Tswana killed and 16 wounded. A German trader, Engers, is also murdered, presumably to silence him. Commandant Kirsten later reports that the Tswana *"shot infinitely better than the British"*.[163]

| | Natal front | Commandant-General Joubert, disheartened by his injuries, advises President Kruger that it is now time to try and make peace with the enemy. President Kruger immediately rejects the notion.
A council of war meeting near Willow Grange is also influenced by Joubert's injuries and decides to return to the Tugela. According to Commandant Ben Viljoen the thunderstorm on 22 was also crucial to this decision. " *two Boers had been struck by lightning, which, according to his (Joubert's) doctrine, was an infallible sign from the Almighty that the commandos were to proceed no further.*"[164]
General Buller arrives at Durban and immediately moves to Pietermaritzburg to take over command of the right front (Natal) from Lieutenant-General Sir CF Clery. In doing this, he becomes fully involved on this front and seriously jeopardises his role as Commander-in-Chief.
In Natal, he now has (apart from White's force besieged at Ladysmith and several local units at several locations) the following forces at his disposal:[165]
Artillery: Two brigade divisions Royal Field Artillery consisting of 1 356 men with 30 field-guns under Colonel HV Hunt.
Infantry: Four brigades consisting of 16 497 men with 18 machine guns under Major-Generals HJT Hildyard, NG Lyttelton, A FitzRoy Hart and G Barton.
Cavalry: Two regiments consisting of 1 172 men with two machine guns.
Engineers and support troops : 725 men with five field hospitals.
Total: 21 587 men with 30 field-guns and 20 machine guns. |
| | Western front | **BATTLE OF ENSLIN OR GRASPAN**
General De la Rey positions his 700 Transvalers and their two field-guns on koppies west of the railway line and the rest of the available Free Staters as follows: on the koppies immediately to the east of the railway line he places 250 of Jordaan's Winburg commando, with a Krupp gun under the command of Major Albrecht. Next to them 500 men of the Bloemfontein commando under General Prinsloo take up position and on the easternmost koppies, fronting both to the south and the east, a mixed group of about 300 Free Staters, with two pom-poms, move in under Commandant Lubbe.
Lord Methuen, commanding a total of about 10 000 men, including about 7 700 infantry, 900 cavalry troops and 950 artillerists with 16 field-guns, believes that he is facing about 500 demoralised burghers. He plans to bombard the enemy's position, outflank him with cavalry and mounted infantry and capture the entire force.
His infantry leaves camp in the dark and the Belmont detachment is called in to act as a rearguard. An armoured train transports the naval guns to within 5 000 metres of the koppies. At 06:00, two batteries (12 guns) come into action astride the railway line and they are soon joined by the naval guns. This draws a spirited reply from five Republican field-guns and accurate rifle fire.
Methuen quickly realises that his plans are based on faulty information and, rather than retreating, he decides to change his line of attack to the eastern koppie, defended by Lubbe's men. He moves his infantry diagonally across the enemy's front to a new starting line almost 3 000 metres to the east. After a concentrated bombardment lasting two hours, the infantry assault proceeds in the face of increasingly accurate rifle and pom-pom fire. After reaching the dead ground at the base of the koppie, they scale the slope with the Naval Brigade in the lead. At 09:30 the crest is taken in a bayonet charge under cover of artillery fire. As Lubbe's men retire, the entire position becomes untenable and soon all the burghers, including De la Rey's men on the other side of the railway line, withdraw. Methuen's cavalry again fails to hamper the retreat. Actually, a group of the British cavalry is almost captured by a small party of burghers and they have to fight their way out. The disappointed Methuen replaces Colonel Gough, his cavalry commander.
The Republicans lose 19 killed in action, 40 wounded and 43 captured. The British casualties include 17 killed and 143 wounded. The Naval Brigade suffers especially high casualties, most of them during the early part of the assault.[166] |

Maj. Richard Albrecht
(National Cultural History Museum)

	Western front	**Kimberley siege:** The Kimberley garrison attempts a sortie, led by Major Henry Scott Turner, against the besieging forces's nine-pounders at Carter's Ridge (Lazaretskop). Although they fail to capture the guns, they inflict 28 casualties and take 32 prisoners at a cost to themselves of seven killed and 25 wounded.[167] At a council of war at Jacobsdal General De la Rey encourages and motivates the discouraged burghers. He explains his plans for the defence of the Modder River. The last two battles have shown that koppies are not good defensive positions because they offer the enemy an excellent artillery target and the rock-strewn crests amplify the effect of shell-bursts and shrapnel. Attackers can approach the foot of the koppie with light casualties, regroup and take a breather on the dead ground at the foot, before rushing up the slopes for a bayonet charge during which the defenders have to show themselves to fire down over the crest. It has also been clear that plunging fire from the hilltop is not as dangerous as rifle fire across the open veld.[168]
Day 47 Sun 1899-11-26	Western front *Gen. JH de la Rey* *(War Museum of the Boer Republics)*	Generals De la Rey and Prinsloo gather their men at the confluence of the Riet and the Modder Rivers near the damaged railway bridge, and start preparing positions under De la Rey's supervision. He extends his line on both sides of the railway lines, stretching from the loop in the Riet River, about 3 kilometres east of the bridge, to beyond the little village of Rosmead (now Ritchie) about 3 kilometres west of the bridge. Contrary to conventional tactics, he does not use the river as an obstacle in front of his defenders, but he places them on the enemy's side, south of the river. Here, they dig a series of short, detached six-man trenches in the soft banks. They camouflage the parapets and cut down some vegetation where necessary, to clear their arcs of fire. Whitewashed stones are scattered in the veld to give exact ranges to gunners and riflemen. On the north bank he orders some bombproof shelters to be dug for the horses, but here he on purpose makes no attempt at concealment. He also orders some sniper posts to be prepared in the tall trees on the north or right bank.[169]
	Natal front	General SW Burger sends 100 men with a field-gun and a howitzer to Colenso.[170]
	Central front	General Gatacre moves from Queenstown to Putter's Kraal. Republican forces occupy Stormberg Junction.
Day 48 Mon 1899-11-27	Western front *Gen. PA Cronjé* *(National History Museum)*	General Piet Cronje arrives at Modder River from Edenburg Station with two Krupp guns, three pom-poms and about 1 200 men and assumes command. He, however, decides not to interfere with De la Rey's plans. The Republican force now totals between 2 100 and 2 200 men with six or seven field-guns, three or four pom-poms and two machine guns. Lord Methuen, commanding about 10 000 men, including about 7 700 infantry, 900 cavalry troops and 950 artillerists with 16 field-guns, continues his march to about 10 kilometres south of Modder River Station. His first plan is to feint against Modder River, march against the Republican base at Jacobsdal. From here, he plans to sweep north and attempt to take Spytfontein, where he expects the main enemy position to be, in the flank. Incorrect maps and some cursory scouting convince him to change his plans and to force a crossing of the river along the railway line.[171]
	Black involvement	The women and children kidnapped by the Bakgatla-Tswana at Derdepoort, arrive at Mochudi, after having been forced to walk the distance of about 37 kilometres.[172]
	Natal front	**Ladysmith siege:** The *Ladysmith Lyre* appears for the first time. Written by the joint efforts of journalists in beleaguered Ladysmith, headed by GW Steevens, this newssheet, *"full of the latest shaves, the Jargon of the day, helped to raise a laugh and stimulate conversation; the want of news, combined with the anxiety for it, particularly during the 118-day investment, being the workings of fertile imaginations!"*[173] **THE END OF THE FIRST REPUBLICAN OFFENSIVE** Republican forces complete their sortie into the Natal midlands and retire to Chieveley and Colenso.

Day 49 Tue 1899-11-28	Cape Colony	Sir Alfred Milner writes in a 'very confidential' report to Percy Fitzpatrick, *"One thing is quite evident. The* ultimate *end is a self-governing white Community, supported by* well-treated *and* justly governed *black labour from Cape Town to Zambezi. There must be one flag, the Union Jack, but under it equality of races and languages. Given* equality *all round, English must prevail...There must be an interval, to allow the British population... to return and increase, and the mess to be cleared up, before we can apply the principle of self-government..."* On the war, he says, *"I pray for a decisive result. A patch up would be awful. But a decisive result means a tremendous and sustained effort on the part of the British people."*[174]
	Western front	**THE BATTLE OF MODDER RIVER OR TWEERIVIERE** At 04:30 Lord Methuen starts his march, deciding to let his troops take breakfast once they reach the river. At about 05:30 his cavalry draws fire from the river on his east flank, where Cronje brings a field-gun and a pom-pom into action to discourage a crossing at Bosman's Drift. The British, however, are not aware of the existence of the drift and they assume the fire is from enemy forces defending Jacobsdal. The infantry advance on a front of about five kilometres wide, with Pole-Carew's 9th Brigade on the west and Colvile's Guards Brigade to the east of the railway line. At about 08:00, they are about 1 300 metres from the river and, convinced that the enemy is not around, Methuen selects a suitable building to use as his new headquarters on the other side of the river. Suddenly, using smokeless ammunition, the Republicans open fire from their invisible positions. At this long range they cause few casualties, but the fusillade immediately pins down the British, and all attempts to dash forward fail. Amid the low scrub and anthills the three Guards regiments are safe enough while laying down, but any movement or attempt to return fire, draws remarkably accurate rifle and pom-pom fire. Colvile commits his rearmost battalions eastwards to test the Republican left flank but they run into the loop of the river not shown on their maps. They cannot find a crossing and extend their line along the river, fronting east. They are now under fire from the north and east and soon after about 09:00 Methuen's eastern flank is immobilised for the remainder of the battle. His left flank, consisting of Pole-Carew's 9th Brigade, pushed left by the veering Guards, find themselves further to the west than originally planned. They are also pinned down and at about noon Methuen's force is laying prone from about one and a half kilometre west of the railway line all the way to the river in the east. The British artillery has been in action since the shooting started, and although vastly superior guns, they are today facing a very mobile and elusive opponent. The Free State artillery commander, Major Albrecht, takes on the British might with his four Krupp guns by constantly changing position, something he has been unable to do in the hilltop positions they occupied in the previous battles. The 16 British field-guns including their four naval 12-pounders, can only shoot at what they can see, and soon the poplar trees suffer and most of the buildings are riddled with shrapnel. On the western flank Pole-Carew decides that a farmhouse on the south bank near the village may be the key to the Republican positions in this sector. His efforts are unsuccessful until he discovers a donga leading down to the river which enables him to advance some troops to within striking distance of the farmhouse and Republican positions on the south bank. Lord Methuen arrives at about 11:00 and approves his plans and he promises artillery cover and whatever reinforcements he can divert. The 18th Battery, Royal Field Artillery, is moved across the railway line and subjects the Free Staters responsible for the western flank and the defence of Rosmead to a tremendous barrage. The Free Staters are 'rattled'. They fear being isolated and give way, allowing a mixed British force to cross the river at a weir and take the village. By 14:00 the Republican right flank apparently collapses and a complete British victory seems likely. At the same time General De la Rey is struck in the shoulder by a shell fragment, but he continues to rally some men to counter the expected attack from Rosmead towards their centre. Methuen has difficulty in rounding up reinforcements. All over the battlefield his troops have been pinned down since 08:00. The temperature soars

Gen. Pole-Carew
(War Museum of the Boer Republics)

		to 43 degrees Centigrade, and the troops are subjected to constant sniping and are tormented by the vicious ants that attack them when their anthills are hit. Sunburn, thirst and fatigue make most incapable of answering his call. Methuen does manage to shift the weight of the shelling to the western flank to such an extent that Albrecht almost loses his field-guns. Eventually Pole-Carew starts his attack with a scratch force of about 500 men but they run into a fierce counterattack and a bombardment from Albrecht's field-guns, made worse by misdirected own shelling. At this crucial time Methuen is wounded and it takes a while before Colvile realises that he is in command. He spreads the shelling back to sweep the entire enemy position which, although it prevents De la Rey from shifting his forces to the threatened western flank, also reduces the softening up in front of Pole-Carew. He decides to call off his new attack, starts consolidating his position in Rosmead village and wait for dark. After dark the burghers start abandoning their positions with General Cronje's blessing. De la Rey's objections lead to a shouting match with Cronje while De la Rey's seriously wounded son is lying at the roadside. The Republicans lose at least 16 killed, 66 wounded and 13 captured. Their wounded includes General Koos de la Rey and his 19-year-old son Adriaan (Adaan), who is fatally wounded. De la Rey has to transport his son personally to the hospital at Jacobsdal, where he dies in his father's arms the next day. The British lose 71 killed in action and 389 wounded, including Lord Methuen, and 18 missing.[175]
	Western front	**Kimberley siege:** The Kimberley garrison launches a second attack on Carter's Ridge (Lazaretskop) to support Methuen's march. The attack fails miserably, with Major Scott-Turner and 23 others killed in action and 32 wounded.[176]
	Natal front	The Colenso railway bridge is blown up by railway experts and engineers of the ZASM (South African Railway Company).[177]
Day 50 Wed **1899-11-29** *A Boer ambulance* *(War Museum of the Boer Republics)*	Western front	After firing a few shells on Modder River Station without any reaction, the British are astounded to find that the Republicans have abandoned all their positions during the night. In his telegram to the War Office, Lord Methuen calls it *"one of the hardest and most trying fights in the annals of the British Army"*. Captain March Phillips says, *"... we had... suffered another crushing victory."*[178] A council of war chaired by General PA Cronje decides, in General De la Rey's absence, to occupy the heights at Scholtznek and Spytfontein.[179] Republican ambulance personnel consisting of seven doctors, a pharmacist and 28 medical orderlies and stretcher-bearers under Drs AEW Ramsbottom of the Free State and GA Mangold of the ZAR with their ambulances, vehicles and equipment are captured by British forces while attending the wounded after the battle. Despite their protestations and in clear violation of the Geneva Convention, to which the OFS is a signatory, they are treated as prisoners, ordered to leave their patients and sent under close armed guard by train to Cape Town.[180]
	International	The first Canadian contingent arrives in Cape Town.
Day 51 Thu **1899-11-30**	Western front	Returning from Jacobsdal where he has buried his son and has had his shoulder wound treated, De la Rey finds the council of war's decisions unacceptable and he decides to seek President Steyn's support by telegram.[181] The women and children kidnapped after the Derdepoort massacre are returned to Republican lines on board an armoured train under a white flag.[182]
	Natal front	With Commandant-General Joubert incapacitated and General SW Burger assuming command of the besiegers around Ladysmith, General Louis Botha takes command of the Republican forces on the Tugela. His force increases to about 3 000 with five field-guns near Colenso, with about 2 000 Free Staters guarding the upper Tugela.[183]

	Cape Colony	Sir A Milner writes to Selborne: *"It is evident that either we must absolutely smash them politically, or our own expulsion from this part of the Continent, even if not immediately effected, can only be a matter of time."*[184]
	United Kingdom	A Sixth division to be commanded by Major-General T Kelly-Kenny is announced for service in South Africa. Joseph Chamberlain's hostile speech at Leicester ends the rapprochement with Germany.
	Trivia	*Oscar Wilde dies in Paris.*
1899	SUMMER	**DECEMBER 1899**
Day 52 Fri **1899-12-01**	Natal front	Commandant-General PJ Joubert is taken to the Volksrust hospital to receive treatment for his injuries.[185]
	Northern front	Colonel HCO Plumer undertakes a reconnaissance mission into the northern ZAR.
	Cape Colony	The Canadian and Australian contingents leave Cape Town for the front.
Day 53 Sat **1899-12-02**	Central front	Republican forces under Commandant Olivier occupy Dordrecht and Rhodes. At Dordrecht the combined Republican flag, known as the Vyfkleur (five colour) is hoisted for the first time. This flag consists of the ZAR flag with a vertical orange stripe.[186]
	Northern front	A BSAP officer arranges with Republican forces near Crocodile Pools for the return of 17 women and children who have been kidnapped by Kgatla tribesmen after the Derdepoort incident on 25 November.[187]
	ZAR	The ZAR government informs its special representative in Europe, Dr JW Leyds, that agents Philips and Rooth have been sent to Europe to buy 30 additional artillery pieces and ammunition. (Although the Government makes a substantial payment to Schneider et Cie, Creusot, the orders are never to be carried out.)[188]
	Cape Colony	The Red Cross personnel captured after the battle of Twee Riviere, leave Cape Town by train on their way back to the front. Since their capture they have been threatened, mistreated, transported in cattle trucks to De Aar, where they spent the night in a filthy jail. On the voyage to Cape Town, their guards were ordered, *"You kick them if they move, and shoot them when they come to the door."* In Cape Town they were taken to the military hospital where after signing affidavits, they were at last recognised as Red Cross personnel. The military authorities admit that a *"huge blunder"* has been made.[189]
Day 54 Sun **1899-12-03**	Western front *Pres. MT Steyn* (*War Museum of the Boer Republics*)	On arrival at Spytfontein, President Steyn immediately grasps De la Rey's tactical plan and actively supports him. De la Rey's ideas centres on (i) the most effective use of dismounted burghers who have been regarded as useless in traditional Boer tactics, (ii) methods to avoid premature retirements and (iii) the optimal utilisation of the Mauser's range and flat trajectory. Furthermore, he is convinced that surprise can be achieved by deviating from the well-known Boer tactic of occupying higher ground, koppies and ridges.[190] The captured Red Cross personnel are blindfolded, led through the British positions on the Modder River, from where they must negotiate the no-man's land, on foot. Their ambulance vehicles have been captured and kept by the British. After their harrowing experiences in British hands, they eventually arrive back at the Republican headquarters, near Jacobsdal.[191]
	Cape Colony	The transport ship *Ismore* is wrecked without loss of life about 280 kilometres north of Cape Town. All the troops on board land safely.[192] (Remarkably, this is to be the only ship wrecked during the entire war. In total 1 027 ships are to be engaged to transport 386 081 troops, 352 864 horses and, excluding the soldiers' equipment, about 1 374 million tons of supplies.)[193]
	Trivia	*WF Gatacre's 56th birthday.*

Day 55 Mon 1899-12-04	Western front	At a council of war, with President Steyn's support, the previous plans are eventually revised and De la Rey's proposals are accepted. The Republican forces start preparing the new positions at Magersfontein under General De la Rey's supervision. Their line stretches for almost 14 kilometres diagonally across the route to Kimberley from Langeberg Farm, across the railway to Moss Drift on the Modder River. The main position is trenches about 1 000 metres in length on the plain about two to three hundred metres in front of the foot of Magersfontein Hill. To the east of this position is a gap, and from there to the river burghers position themselves behind stone ramparts or in shallow trenches, along a bushy ridge running in the direction of the river. At the same time dummy positions and sangars (stone breastworks) are prepared on the slopes and crest of the Magersfontein hills.[194]
Day 56 Tue 1899-12-05	Natal front	General Sir Redvers Buller arrives at Frere.
	Western front	**Kuruman siege:** Commandant Visser returns with 500 men and resumes the siege of Kuruman, with the defenders still refusing to surrender.
	Trivia	*Walt Disney is born in Chicago, Ill., USA.*
Day 57 Wed 1899-12-06	Western front	Lord Methuen has recovered sufficiently from his wounds to reassume command of his force from Major-General Colvile.[195]
	Natal front	General Buller's engineers replace the damaged bridge across the Bloukrans River, north of Frere, with a temporary structure.[196] General Botha sends 400 men of the Boksburg commando to occupy Hlangwane Hill on the other side of the Tugela, which he recognises to be the key to his Colenso positions.[197]
Day 58 Thu 1899-12-07	Natal front	**THE SORTIE AGAINST GUN HILL** **Ladysmith siege:** A British force of about 650 consisting mostly of Colonials under Major-General Sir A Hunter sneaks out of Ladysmith wearing soft shoes to avoid noise. While most of the troops act as screens protecting their flanks, the main party of about 100 Imperial Light Horse and 100 Natal volunteers surprises and chases off the sleeping Republican pickets and artillerists on Gun Hill. They explode gun cotton stuffed into the 'Long Tom' and a howitzer. They also remove and carry off the gun's breach blocks as well as a Maxim gun. The British return to Ladysmith with the loss of three killed and 21 wounded. The Republicans lose one killed and one wounded while four officers are suspended pending an investigation (which never happens).[198]
	Western front	**THE ATTACK ON ENSLIN** General JJP Prinsloo with a commando of 1 000 burghers and two guns move around Lord Methuen's right flank and attack about 200 British troops guarding Enslin Station in an effort to destroy Methuen's supply lines. Prinsloo's attack is half-hearted and the British detachment stubbornly resists until reinforcements arrive and force Prinsloo to withdraw. He suffers six wounded while the British lose 11 wounded and they repair the damaged railway line within a few hours. Prinsloo's ineffective and overly cautious actions cause President Steyn to replace him as Chief Commandant with General Ignatius S Ferreira.[199] General De la Rey, satisfied that preparations of the Magersfontein positions are proceeding satisfactory, leaves for the laager at Riverton to have his wound attended to.[200] **Mafeking siege:** Lady Sarah Wilson (nee Churchill, daughter of the Duke of Marlborough) is permitted to enter Mafeking in exchange for the release of a certain Viljoen who has been imprisoned for horse theft since before the start of hostilities.[201]

	Central front	General French occupies Arundel, northern Cape. In a skirmish at Halseton two burghers are wounded.[202] Chief Commandant HJ Olivier takes over command at Stormberg Junction. He is faced with a dispute with Commandant Du Plooy about control over the Krupp gun and a planned attack on Molteno has to be postponed.[203]
Day 59 Fri **1899-12-08**	Western front	Lieutenant-General Lord Methuen is reinforced by the Highland Brigade under Major-General AG Wauchope, the 12th Lancers and two batteries artillery, a quick-firing 4,7inch (120mm) naval gun and several officers and men of the Medical Corps and the Service Corps, totalling about 5 000 troops with 11 field-guns. This brings his total force to 14 964 men with 33 field-guns and 16 machine guns. Facing him, in their half-completed positions strung out along about 14 kilometres, are about 8 200 burghers of whom about 6 000 are 'battle-ready', with five Krupp guns and five pom-poms.[204]
	Cape Colony Black involvement United Kingdom	Sir Henry Elliot, Chief Magistrate of the Eastern Province, raises a unit of 2 500 Mfengu and Thembu tribesmen at Engcobo in the Border area. The 67-year-old Field Marshal Lord Roberts offers his services in a confidential letter to Lansdowne. *"I am much concerned to hear the very gloomy view which Sir Redvers Buller takes of the situation in South Africa... From the day he landed in Cape Town he seemed to take a pessimistic view of our position, and when a Commander allows himself to entertain evil forebodings, the effect is inevitably felt throughout the Army. I feel the greatest possible hesitation and dislike to expressing my opinion thus plainly, and nothing but the gravity of the situation and the strongest sense of duty would induce me to do so, or to offer — as I now do — to place my services at the disposal of the Government... If it is decided to accept the offer of my services, I shall hope, with God's help to be able to end the war in a satisfactory manner..."*[205]
Day 60 Sat **1899-12-09**	Natal front	At Frere, General Sir Redvers Buller has the following forces at his disposal: **Artillery:** Two brigade divisions Royal Field Artillery and a naval unit consisting of 1 441 men with 30 field-guns under Colonel HV Hunt as well as 14 naval 12-pounders and two 120mm naval guns. **Infantry:** Four brigades consisting of 15 888 men with 18 machine guns under Major-Generals HJT Hildyard, NG Lyttelton, A FitzRoy Hart and G Barton. **Cavalry:** A brigade consisting of 2 687 men with two machine guns under Col. Earl of Dundonald. **Engineers and support troops:** 1 160 men with five field hospitals. **Total:** 21 176 men with 46 field-guns and 20 machine guns.[206] The commando sent by Botha to occupy Hlangwane, on the opposite bank of the Tugela, attempts to use political influence to reverse his orders. Their spokesman in Pretoria, General Lucas Meyer, accuses General Botha of placing them in an untenable and dangerous position.[207] **Ladysmith siege:** Lack of vigilance by the besiegers allows the Ladysmith garrison to undertake another sortie. This time one of the spans of the railway bridge between Glencoe and Waschbank is slightly damaged.[208]
	OFS	Christiaan R de Wet is appointed Combat General by President MT Steyn.
	Western front	On Lord Methuen's orders the 4,7inch (120mm) naval gun, known as 'Joe Chamberlain', shells the Magersfontein hills and the unmanned Scholtznek.[209]

| Day 61 Sun 1899-12-10 | Central front **Black Week** | **BATTLE OF STORMBERG**

General Gatacre decides to attack Stormberg Junction, about 15 kilometres northwest of Molteno, to regain control of the most important railway junction in the region. He intends to hold it in preparation for the main invasion of the Republics on Buller's return from Natal, as originally planned.

Using trains to concentrate the forces at his disposal at Molteno, Gatacre undertakes a night march with about 2 700 men with 12 field-guns and four machine guns in the direction of Stormberg Junction. Despite the fact that some of his troops have spent more than three hours in open train trucks under the South African summer sun no postponement is contemplated and an Irish regiment is ordered to march the entire distance with fixed bayonets.

Gatacre's guides either lose their way, misunderstand the desired destination or underestimate the distance and lead the British force into the surprised Republicans under Chief Commandant JH Olivier with about 1 700 men and two field-guns stationed on Kissieberg. The Republican picket is just preparing breakfast when the British march into view, and immediately raises the alarm. They fire as fast as possible and Gatacre is completely disorientated and a very confused fight that *"can hardly be called a battle,"* follows. British troops immediately charge up the steep slopes but are halted at the foot of an unscalable cliff. The British artillery, blinded by the rising sun, fires on their own troops. Some of the exhausted troops fall asleep as soon as they find cover. Elsewhere, a local farmer shoots British soldiers slaughtering his sheep.

Within an hour and fifteen minutes, General Gatacre decides to call off his attack and withdraw his demoralised troops to Molteno. Alerted by the firing, Republican burghers under FJ du Plooy, stationed some way to the west, arrive and the disordered British troops are subjected to a murderous crossfire. Some of the artillery horses stampede and more and more Republican reinforcements arrive, adding to the utter confusion. The British withdraw (some say flee) in disorder.

British casualties amount to only 25 killed and 102 wounded and missing. Then Gatacre, to his horror, discovers that he has left 672 of his troops behind against the slopes of Kissieberg where they are rounded up and taken prisoner. Three or four field-guns are left on the battlefield. Republican casualties amount to five killed and 16 wounded.

The defeat at Stormberg is the first of the three serious British setbacks known as **Black Week.**[210] |
|---|---|---|
| | Western front | At Magersfontein, at about 15:00, in a move impossible to hide from the enemy scouts, or maybe deliberately planned to be an intimidating show of force, Lord Methuen moves the bulk of his force to a rendezvous behind a small rise on the plain which he calls Headquarter Hill.

Burghers, using Martini-Henry rifles with black powder ammunition and firing from the dummy positions on the hill, prevent British scouts from approaching closer and convince them that the hills form the main enemy position.

Using 28 guns including the 4,7inch naval gun nicknamed 'Joe Chamberlain' the British unleash a heavy bombardment on Magersfontein Hill. The bombardment starts at 16:30 and lasts more than two hours. It is described as the heaviest artillery bombardment since Sebastopol. Lord Methuen, who does not use his observation balloon to observe the fall of shot or the enemy positions, is convinced that nothing can live through such an inferno. Actually, the Republican casualties amount to three wounded. The ill-considered shelling gives the burghers ample warning of the impending attack and fills them with confidence in the protection offered by their trenches.[211]

Mafeking siege: A British outpost or fort is attacked, taken and destroyed by a small party of burghers.[212] |
| | Natal front | **THE SORTIE AGAINST SURPRISE HILL**

Ladysmith siege: Lieutenant-Colonel CTE Metcalfe with a force of 12 officers and 488 |

		men, leaves Ladysmith at midnight and scales Vaalkop, later to be known as Surprise Hill. When challenged by the pickets, they charge and chase off the sleepy Republican gunners. Lieutenant Digby-Jones immediately prepares the explosive charges. A fuse fails and the delay gives the Republicans time to recover and when the massive double explosion signals the destruction of a 120mm howitzer and some ammunition, they counterattack and threaten to cut off the British line of retreat. The attackers are especially hard pressed by a small group of Pretorians, and have to fight their way out. The British lose 20 killed, 38 wounded and six captured. The Republicans suffer two killed in action, two fatally wounded, five wounded and three gunners missing.[213]
	United Kingdom	Lord Salisbury, after reading Lord Roberts' offer, is of the opinion that Roberts is too old for the task. He points out that Buller has, as yet, not made any mistakes. Salisbury is indeed expecting a brilliant success from Buller on the Tugela within the next few days. He promises, however, to keep Roberts' offer in mind.[214]
Day 62 Mon 1899-12-11	Western front **Black Week**  *Black Watch on parade* (War Museum of the Boer Republics) **Victoria Cross**	**THE BATTLE OF MAGERSFONTEIN** At 00:30 General Wauchope's redoubtable Highlanders, guided by Major Benson, march from Headquarter Hill in 'massed quarter columns' which means that almost 3 400 men formed a rectangle about 38m x 155m. Despite a heavy downpour, lightning and difficult terrain, the troops arrive about 45 minutes late, at 03:30, remarkably close to the planned starting position for the assault on the hill. Benson suggests that extended formation be ordered, but Wauchope, still worried that his force may become disarranged, decides to carry on a bit further. They encounter a thorn thicket that can only be negotiated in twos and threes and the order to deploy is finally given at about 04:00 with the day rapidly dawning. Suddenly, from invisible positions less than 400 metres away, a fierce, continuous fusillade is poured into their ranks. In the half light before dawn, the initial salvoes are high, but the continuous hail of bullets, coming not from the hill crest where the enemy is expected but from somewhere on the plain, causes havoc and heavy losses especially to the Black Watch. During the first 15 minutes, General Andrew Wauchope, his adjutant, Lieutenant Arthur G Wauchope, and two battalion commanders are killed and the rear battalion commander is wounded. Without clear orders, the fleeing front troops add to the utter confusion that spreads panic to the rear, where some are still in the vulnerable massed formation. On the right a mixed group actually finds the gap in the Republican defence and starts to climb the hill only to be shot back by a small group of burghers led by Cronje. They also come under own fire from the British artillery which comes into action at this moment. Part of this group is forced to surrender while the others stream down the hill towards their comrades. Pandemonium is only prevented by a piper playing *"The Campbells are coming"*. Some brave officers try to force the invisible trenches by frontal assault, but fail with heavy casualties. On the Republican side, Field-cornet J Flygare's Scandinavian Corps, who has pushed forward to close the gap east of the main trench, is overwhelmed and wiped out in the Highlanders' efforts to outflank the trenches. At sunrise, the bulk of the Highland Brigade, without clear orders and with its regiments in complete disarray and mixed up, is pinned down in front of the trenches. Only the Horse Artillery's action from an exposed position prevents their annihilation. Methuen orders the Guards Brigade to cover the Highlanders' right flank and the battle develops southwards all along the ridge where the Republicans occupy hastily prepared positions. When the British observation balloon is eventually launched at about 06:00, the assault has stalled completely. At about 07:00 Methuen orders an advance by his reserve, the Gordon Highlanders, over open ground in an attempt to prod the prone troops into launching a new assault, but the tired, demoralised troops are not up to it.[215] Both stretcher-bearer Corporal JDF Shaul of the Highland Light Infantry and Lieutenant Dr HEM Douglas, Royal Army Medical Corps, bravely attend to the wounded under fire without regard for their own safety, performing heroic deeds for which they are to receive the Victoria Cross.

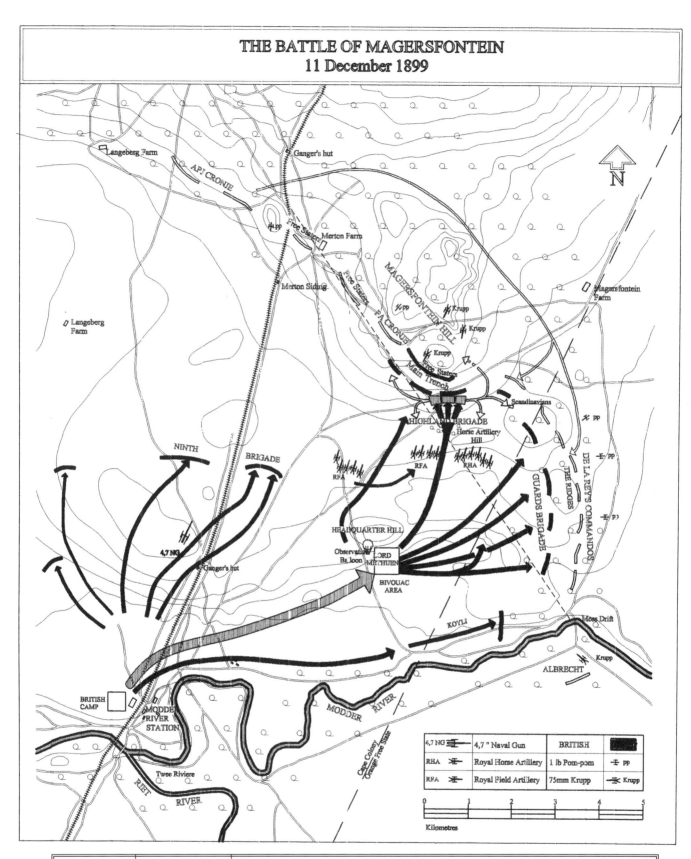

At Moss Drift, on the Republicans' extreme left, the Free State Artillery stops the 9th Lancers and the KOY Light Infantry. On the British left, Pole-Carew's half-hearted diversionary demonstration along the railway is so transparent that Cronje can transfer a large force to reinforce the ridge to such an extent that an attack on the Highlanders' flank develops at about 14:00. To counter this menace, part of the Highlanders is ordered to fall back in order to pivot towards the threat.

	Victoria Cross	The backward movement is contagious and becomes a general scramble to the rear and the water carts. Now, for the first time, the Republican field-guns open up and inflict serious casualties. The retreat becomes a rout. Captain EBB Towse of the Gordon Highlanders earns the Victoria Cross for carrying his mortally wounded commanding officer, Colonel Downman, to an aid post. By 16:00 only the dead and wounded are left in front of the trenches and the rest are streaming across the plain. The Republicans, subjected to constant shelling and thirst, are also at the limit of their endurance and incapable of following up their victory. At about 18:00 burghers, exhausted and tormented by the cries of the wounded, leave their trenches and tell those British soldiers who can, to leave their weapons and retire. They also assist the British doctors and share their water with the wounded.[216]
	Cape Colony	Sir A Milner to a friend, *"The state of the Colony is awful. It simply reeks of treason."*[217]
	United Kingdom	Lord Lorning writes to Lady Edward Cecil: *"This war is the biggest thing since the Mutiny. It is great in itself; it is great in its incidents; it is great in its issues."*[218]
	International	In a speech in the Reichstag in Berlin, Von Bülow rejects British advances for an Anglo-German Alliance.
Day 63 Tue **1899-12-12**	Western front **Black Week**	**THE BATTLE OF MAGERSFONTEIN** Lord Methuen's hope that the Republicans will again abandon their positions in a repeat of Twee Riviere is dashed when a patrol of Scots Guards daring too close is chased off. Probing actions in all sectors confirm the burghers' presence in strength. At about 08:00 a Republican orderly approaches the lines of the Scots Guards under a flag of truce offering to allow the British ambulances to remove the dead and the wounded. The offer is immediately accepted and a cease-fire is called. As the burghers leave their trenches to render assistance, the crew of the naval gun, unaware of the local armistice, opens fire. The Republican field-guns immediately retaliate against the Horse Artillery. With extreme discipline they hold their fire while the misunderstanding is cleared up. At about midday the appearance of an armoured train triggers a new artillery duel, but the shelling stops at about 14:00 and the British retire to their camp at Modder River. On the previous day the Republicans have lost 71 killed, including Field-cornet J Flygare and 42 Scandinavians, and 184 wounded. The British suffer at least 288 killed, 700 wounded and 100 missing, while many hundreds more, especially the kilted Scots, are rendered medical casualties through exposure and serious sunburn.[219]
	Natal front **Black Week**	General Buller writes to Lord Lansdowne, the Secretary of State for War: *"After a careful reconnaissance by telescope, I came to the conclusion that a direct assault upon the enemy's position at Colenso and the north of it would be too costly. The approach to the drift this side, is dead flat without any cover, and the enemy have a very strong position which they have systematically fortified just on the other side of the drift."* He also heliographs to the besieged White: *"I have definitely decided to advance by Potgieter's Drift. Expect to start on 12th December and take five days."*[220]
	ZAR	Abandoning two comrades with whom he planned an escape, Winston Churchill climbs over the yard wall of the State Model School in Pretoria where he has been imprisoned with British officers and walks to the Eastern line where he jumps a train.[221]
Day 64 Wed **1899-12-13**	Natal front **Black Week**	General Buller signals to White: *"Have been forced to change my plans; am coming through via Colenso and Onderbroek Spruit."*[222] He explains in a signal to the War Office: (The original plan) *"involved the complete abandonment of my communications, and, in the event of success, the risk that I might share the fate of Sir George White and be cut off from Natal. I had considered that with the enemy dispirited*

69

		by the failure of their plans in the west, the risk was justifiable, but I cannot think I ought now to take such a risk. From my point of view, it will be better to lose Ladysmith altogether than to throw open Natal to the enemy." General Buller, using his heavy calibre naval guns, orders a bombardment across the Tugela. The Republicans on Hlangwane Hill abandon their positions and retire across the river. General Botha immediately informs President Kruger and beseeches him to motivate the wavering burghers.[223]
	Western front	**Mafeking siege:** A grandchild and namesake of President Paul Kruger is killed in action near Mafeking.[224]
	Central front	Republican forces attack Arundel Siding, near Colesberg.
	Cape Colony	Sir Charles Warren and part of the Fifth Division arrive in Cape Town. Lord Wolesley has given General Warren a 'dormant commission' to replace Buller, should the latter be incapacitated.[225]
	United Kingdom	A seventh division under Major-General C Tucker is to be mobilized at Aldershot.
Day 65 Thu **1899-12-14**  *Gen. Christiaan Botha* (National Cultural History Museum)	Natal front **Black week**	At a council of war near Colenso, General Louis Botha reads the telegrams he has received from President Kruger, complete with appropriate Bible texts. After a long discussion, Botha convinces them of the importance of Hlangwane Hill. They decide to draw lots and the choice falls on Commandant Rooi (Red) Joshua Joubert of the Wakkerstroom commando. He declares: *"The choice of the lot is the choice of God! I go."* He and his men immediately swim the flooded river to occupy the key position. His 800 men, without field-guns or machine guns, constitute Botha's eastern flank. In the centre, from Fort Wylie to the mined, but still intact, road bridge, Botha places the commandos of Krugersdorp and Vryheid with a few ZAR Policemen, supported by a Krupp gun, a howitzer and a pom-pom. On the western flank, the Swaziland commando under his brother, General Christiaan Botha, Soutpansberg and Ermelo dig in, covered by two Creusot guns on Rooikop. They prepare short, deep, discontinuous trenches along the north bank and dummy positions against the slopes of the heights above Colenso. Using their own labourers, as well as locally commandeered blacks, they dig up or hide the drifts. For the first time in Boer military history, Botha employs the strange concept of a reserve —- that is, a force, not in the firing line, that can be employed by the commander where it may be needed as the battle develops. His entire force, including reserves, consists of less than 3 000 men with four field-guns and a pom-pom, covering a front extending about 13 kilometres. From Shooter's Hill, the British naval guns shell the heights on the north bank from about 08:30 to sunset, with a three-hour break at lunch time. They elicit no reaction and the gunners begin to suspect that the enemy has left. On the Republican side, the burghers gain confidence in their shelters and lose their fear of shelling. They are also forewarned of Buller's planned attack. Buller's orders to his officers are vague and ambiguous, especially concerning the enemy dispositions, the topography, ranges and landmarks as well as the objectives of the operation. He plans a three-pronged attack with close artillery support by Colonel Long's batteries. In the centre General Hildyard is ordered to cross the Tugela at the *"iron bridge"*. On his left General Hart must cross at the *"bridle drift"* and link up with Hildyard on the north bank. On the right, Lord Dundonald is *"to move in the direction of Hlangwane"*, while Generals Lyttleton and Barton will form a reserve.[226]
	Black involvement	King Bunu of Swaziland dies at Bremersdorp. In the following weeks a council of chiefs appoints Queen Regent Labotsebeni to rule on behalf of his young son Sobhusa II. Sobhusa is destined to become one of the longest-reigning monarchs in the world.[227]

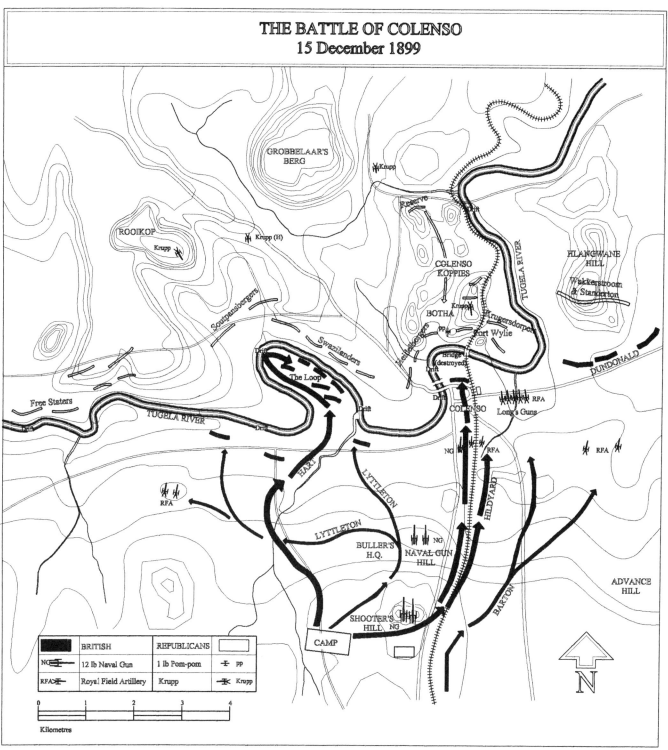

| Day 66 Fri
1899-12-15 | Natal front
Black Week | **THE BATTLE OF COLENSO**
Buller's heavy naval guns are in position on Naval Gun Hill and open up at 05:20. In the centre, Hildyard and Barton are late and the field artillery, following Colonel CJ Long's unconventional ideas on the deployment of guns, find themselves in front of the infantry they are supposed to support. They rush ahead, overshoot their appointed position and they eventually unlimber, align their guns parade ground fashion and come into action well within rifle range of the enemy. About 600 to 700 metres from the river the gunners soon suffer heavy casualties and within 15 minutes Long is also wounded. At about 07:00, the gun crews retire with their wounded to the shelter of a donga, where they await more ammunition, leaving their 12 field-guns standing in full view of the burghers. |

		General Buller is alarmed when the guns fall silent and he orders Hildyard to support the gun position. Hildyard, whose troops are arranged in battle formation for their assault towards the bridge, obliges, thus abandoning the main attack.

On the western flank General AF Hart marches his Irish Brigade in massed quarter columns in daylight towards the enemy. His native guide disappears and, searching for the ford where he is supposed to cross the river, he enters a loop of the Tugela not shown on his map. The burghers cannot resist such a target and ignoring Botha's explicit orders, they open fire. Despite the intensive crossfire, Hart manages to extend his troops somewhat and they take cover. A few of his men actually cross the fast flowing river, but by 07:00 the Irish Brigade is completely pinned down in the loop.

Lord Dundonald's attack against Hlangwane is proceeding slowly but he soon encounters Commandant Rooi Joshua Joubert's determined marksmen. Dundonald requests Barton to send troops west of the hill to threaten the defender's line of retreat, hoping that this move may dislodge them. Barton refuses to co-operate without explicit orders from Buller. At about 09:00 the entire battlefield is more or less static. With less than half of his force committed, Buller, upset by Hart's failure, is totally distraught when two officers, sent to expedite the artillery ammunition supplies, report that the guns have been knocked out. He decides to investigate personally and moves to the naval gun position. A shell bursts almost on top of him, killing his doctor and bruising his ribs. He shows a brave front but he is badly shaken, suffering from what would later be termed 'shell shock'. When he observes the apparently abandoned guns, he decides to call off the attack.

He halts the nine ammunition wagons going forward to resupply the guns. Hildyard's men, who have been well dispersed and steadily moving through the village towards the bridge, are ordered to abandon their attack and to cover the field-guns. Buller refuses to consider Hildyard's proposal to remain in the safety of the village until dark, and then to retrieve the guns. He is adamant that the attack must be terminated immediately. It is not yet 10:00.

Now the British Army's unshakeable dictum of never abandoning field-guns, is to exact a terrible toll. Buller asks for volunteers to fetch Long's guns and two teams of brave men are quickly made up. Captain HN Schofield and Lord Roberts' only son, the Hon Lieutenant FHS Roberts, are in the first group rushing across the open veld towards the field-guns. They succeed in hooking up two of the guns and gallop back. Roberts is struck early in the dash and wounded twice more as he lies in the open. He is dragged to shelter by Captain WN Congreve and Major W Babtie. The next attempt to save the guns under Captain HL Reed fails with 13 out of the 22 horses and seven out of 13 men shot down. Further attempts are called off.

Victoria Cross — Captain WN Congreve, 2nd Rifle Brigade, Captain HL Reed, Royal Field Artillery, Captain HN Schofield, Royal Field Artillery, The Hon Lieutenant FHS Roberts, the King's Royal Rifle Corps, Corporal GE Nurse, Royal Field Artillery, and Private G Ravenhill, Royal Scots Fusilliers, all earn the Victoria Cross for the attempts to rescue Long's guns. Major W Babtie, Royal Army Medical Corps, earns the VC for attending to the wounded artillerymen sheltering in the donga. He also assists Captain Congreve to bring in the wounded Lieutenant Roberts under heavy fire.[228]

Buller's final orders of the day are to recall Lord Dundonald's force from Hlangwane. At 11:00, all the British soldiers are on their way back to camp. The naval guns maintain a long-range barrage on the bridge until they are also limbered up and hauled away at 14:30. The burghers cross the river in small groups and capture the artillerymen in the donga behind the guns. At 17:00 they hook up the 10 guns and nine ammunition wagons and drag them across the bridge in full view of the retreating British army.

The German Staff historian declares: *"The general and not his gallant force was defeated."* The British lose 143 killed in action, 756 wounded and 240 missing. The Republicans capture 38 men and of course, 10 serviceable guns. Their own losses include seven killed in action, 30 wounded and one drowned.[229]

		Besides the eight Victoria Crosses awarded at Colenso, 18 noncommissioned officers and drivers are to receive the Distinguished Conduct Medal. General Louis Botha's report to the ZAR government in Pretoria starts: *"Today, the Lord of our forefathers has given us a brilliant victory."* He urges the government to declare a day of thanksgiving.[230]
Day 67 Sat **1899-12-16**	Natal front **Black Week**	On Buller's request, General Botha grants a 24-hour armistice to allow the British to remove their dead and wounded.[231] General Buller sends two unfortunate heliograph messages to the besieged White: *"I tried Colenso yesterday but failed; the enemy is too strong for my force, except with siege operations, and this will take one full month to prepare. Can you last so long? If not, how many days can you give me in which to take up defensive positions? After which I suggest you firing away as much ammunition as you can and making the best terms you can..."*[232] And later: *"Also add to end of message: Whatever happens, recollect to burn your cipher, and decipher and code books, and any deciphered messages."*[233] **Ladysmith siege:** Two British artillerymen are killed on the main street of Ladysmith by Republican shelling. General Buller requests 8 000 irregular mounted infantry and orders the construction of a railway from Modder River to Jacobsdal.
	Western front	**Kuruman siege:** Commandant Visser makes a determined attack on the 'forts' around Kuruman, but although they take one fort, the defenders fall back and further attacks fail.
	United Kingdom	The Lord Mayor of London's offer to raise a corps of City Imperial Volunteers is accepted.
	International	The offer of a second Canadian contingent is accepted.
	Trivia	*Dingaan's Day (Day of the Covenant).* *A total eclipse of the moon is observed in Natal.* *Noel Coward is born.*
Day 68 Sun **1899-12-17**	ZAR **Black Week**	The ZAR government declares this Sunday as a day of thanksgiving and it is observed throughout the Republics and by their forces in the field.[234] Dr Arthur Conan Doyle is to write: *"The week extending from 10th December to 17th December, 1899, was the blackest one during our generation, and the most disastrous for British arms during the century."*[235]
	United Kingdom	Lord Frederick Roberts is offered the overall command of the British forces in South Africa and receives the bitter news of his son's death on the same day.[236] At Windsor Castle, Queen Victoria, on receiving the news of Buller's reverse: *"There is no depression in this house. We are not interested in the possibilities of defeat. They do not exist"*[237] The War Office orders the remaining portion of the Army 'A' Reserves be called up and large reinforcements be sent to South Africa without delay. Offers of second contingents by the Colonies are accepted.[238]
Day 69 Mon **1899-12-18**	Natal front	**Ladysmith siege:** The British report some troopers of the Natal Carbineers, two sentries on Caesar's Camp and 'a few' blacks, employed as trench diggers, killed by Republican shelling.[239]
	United Kingdom	**LORD ROBERTS TAKES OVER** Field Marshal Lord Roberts of Kandahar is appointed Commander-in-Chief in South Africa with Major-General Lord Kitchener of Khartoum as his Chief of Staff. This is Lord Roberts' second appointment to the position of Commander in South Africa. In 1881, he had been appointed to succeed Sir George Colley after the Battle of Majuba,

		but 24 hours after his arrival in Cape Town, he was ordered to return home when the peace treaty was signed.[240] Kitchener immediately leaves Khartoum for Gibraltar. The British Government announces the raising of a mounted infantry unit, to be called the Imperial Yeomanry, and allows twelve battalions of militia to volunteer for service abroad.
	ZAR	A special law, authorized by a Volksraad decision (Art 1416 of 28 September), introduces a special war tax on the gold mines, based on State Attorney JC Smuts' prewar recommendations.[241]
	Cape Colony	The 20-year-old CK de Meillon escapes from the prison ship *Penelope* in Simon's Bay. He is eventually to rejoin General Chris Botha's commando.[242]
Day 70 Tue **1899-12-19**	ZAR	The escapee Winston Churchill crosses the Mozambique border, hiding in a train carrying wool to Lourenço Marques.[243]
	International	Further Australian contingents are offered.
Day 71 Wed **1899-12-20**	Natal front	**Ladysmith siege:** The tower of the Ladysmith Town Hall is damaged by a shell from the Long Tom on Bulwana. No one is injured.[244]
	United Kingdom	The formation of the City of London Imperial Volunteers, a 1 400-strong unit commanded by Colonel the Earl of Albemarle, is announced by Mr AJ Newton, the Lord Mayor.[245]
	International	A second New Zealand contingent is offered.
Day 72 Thu **1899-12-21**	Natal front	**Ladysmith siege:** General White's headquarters in Poort Road are damaged by a shell, forcing him to move to the house of the Christopher family on Convent Hill.[246]
	Western front	Lancers dynamite a private dwelling belonging to a certain Van Niekerk near Jacobsdal and burn down another in the same vicinity.[247]
	Cape Colony	Sir Charles Warren, Royal Engineers, an expert on the Northern Cape, founder/planner of Mafeking, solver of border disputes in the area and having the town Warrenton named after him, leaves Cape Town for Natal.
	ZAR	The Special War Tax on Gold Mines Act is promulgated. This act levies a 30% tax on gross gold production on mines kept in production by the owners, 50% where the Government has taken over production and 30% based on the previous three months' gold production of mines where the owners have suspended production.[248] News of this step is severely criticized in Europe and is blamed for undermining the ZAR cause in France and Germany. The government, however, is never really to be in a position to enforce this act and its effect on the state coffers is negligible.
Day 73 Fri **1899-12-22**	ZAR	A 'wanted poster', originally handwritten in Dutch, appears in Pretoria, £ 25 *(Twenty-five Pounds stg) REWARD is offered by the Sub-Commission of the fifth division, on behalf of the Special Constable Of the said division, to anyone who brings the escaped prisoner of war* C H U R C H I L L, *dead or alive to this office.* *For the Sub-Commission of the fifth division, (Signed) Lodk. De Haas. Sec.*[249]
	Natal front	**Ladysmith siege:** A shell explodes in the camp of the Gloucesters, killing five men.[250]

Day 74 Sat **1899-12-23**	Bechuanaland Black involvement	In reprisal for the Derdepoort massacre a 500-strong commando led by Du Plessis, Louw and Swarts, cross into Bechuanaland and attacks the Bakgatla-Tswana settlements armed by the British. The villages of Sikwane, Malolwane and Mmathubudukwane are laid waste. The raiders lose three men while 150 tribesmen are killed.[251]
	Natal	Winston Churchill arrives in Durban from Lourenço Marques aboard the *Induna*.[252]
	United Kingdom	Lord Roberts departs on board the *Dunnottar Castle*, the same ship that brought Buller to South Africa. He is joined by Lord Kitchener at Gibraltar. A member of his staff, N Chamberlain, no relation of the Colonial Secretary, is credited with having 'invented' the game of snooker.
Day 75 Sun **1899-12-24**	Western front	**Kuruman siege:** While all the other officers are holding a council of war near Kuruman, Field-cornet Wessels, responsible for the southern sector of the siege, grants an informal armistice to the defenders. The British leave their fort and mix freely with the Free State burghers, even swimming together in the river. Visser is furious, especially when he finds out that the armistice is misused to transport supplies to some of the forts. He immediately cancels the agreement and opens fire.[253]
	Central front	A part of Colonel Dalgety's force under Captain De Montmorency attacks Dordrecht.
	United Kingdom	The enlistment of the Imperial Yeomanry is confirmed.
	Trivia	*The Netherlands adopts the principle of proportional representation.*
Day 76 Mon **1899-12-25**	Western front	CHRISTMAS — the first Christmas of the war. **Kimberley siege:** At a Christmas party George Labram, an American mechanical engineer, incidentally trapped in Kimberley, suggests the possibility of manufacturing a field-gun to CJ Rhodes who immediately supports the idea and gives the go-ahead. Work starts the next day.[254]
	Natal front	**Ladysmith siege:** The Republicans fire shells, inscribed *"With the compliments of the Season,"* and filled with Christmas puddings, into the town. [255]
Day 77 Tue **1899-12-26**	Western front	BOXING DAY **Mafeking siege:** Black Boxing Day. An unsuccessful attack is made by Colonel Baden-Powell on Game Tree Fort (Platboomfort), 2,5 to 3 kilometres north of Mafeking. The British casualties include 25 killed, 23 wounded and three taken prisoner, while the Republicans lose two killed and seven wounded.[256]
	Victoria Cross	Three soldiers are nominated for the Victoria Cross: Captain C Fitzclarence, Royal Fusiliers, this time wounded in both legs, earns his third recommendation for the Victoria Cross. Sergeant HR Martineau, Protectorate Regiment, loses an arm while saving a wounded corporal very close to the enemy position. Trooper HE Ramsden of the Protectorate Regiment saves his wounded brother and carries him for about 600 yards under heavy fire.[257]
Day 78 Wed **1899-12-27**	Western front	Commandant Lubbe reports that an enemy patrol has destroyed five farms in the Jacobsdal district.[258]
	Natal front	**Ladysmith siege:** The shelling commences after the unofficial Christmas ceasefire and several officers of the Devons are killed at breakfast. [259]
	Central front	Republican forces evacuate Rensburg Siding.
	Northern front	Colonel Plumer leaves Tuli on the Bechuanaland/Rhodesia border.

Day 79 Thu **1899-12-28**	Central front	Dordrecht is occupied by Colonel Dalgety's force,[260] while the burghers fall back to a strong position in Labuschagne's Nek, where they await reinforcements.
	International	Lord Kitchener joins Lord Roberts on board of the *Dunottar Castle* at Gibraltar.[261]
Day 80 Fri **1899-12-29**	Western front	Republican forces invade the Upington district of the northern Cape Colony.
	International	The German mail steamer *Bundesrath* is seized in international waters near Delagoa Bay by *HMS Magicienne*.[262]
Day 81 Sat **1899-12-30**	Central front	General French occupies Rensburg Siding. At Labuschagne's Nek, near Dordrecht, some 500 Republicans, including 200 Cape rebels with a single field-gun, attack a mixed British patrol of about 500, commanded by Captain De Montmorency and Colonel Dalgety with four field-guns. Some 40 Cape volunteers are cut off from the main force and trapped in a donga, but they resist furiously and cannot be dislodged by the Republicans.[263]
Day 82 Sun **1899-12-31**	Central front	A rescue force from Dordrecht under Captain Goldworthy with four field-guns silences the Republican field-gun and extricates Montmorency's group, who flees, hotly pursued by the burghers, through the town of Dordrecht to Indwe and Sterkstroom.[264] The British suffer 90 killed and wounded, nine captured, 40 horses killed and some arms and ammunition fall into enemy hands. The burghers lose three killed and 16 wounded.[265]
	Northern front	Colonel Plumer reaches Palapye, Bechuanaland.

NOTES:

OPENING BLOWS (11 OCT - DEC 1899)

1. CRESWELL, *op cit*, vol 11, p 3
2. *Ibit*, Vol II, pp 4, 5
3. VAN SCHOOR, 'n Bittereinder aan die Woord..., p 170
4. HEADLAM, *op cit*, vol II, p 18
5. FERREIRA, OJO, ... SPE Trichard, p 118
6. BREYTENBACH, *op cit*, vol I, pp 153, 419, 386, 201, 148
7. BREYTENBACH, *op cit*, vol II, p 360
8. PRETORIUS, F, Kommandolewe tydens die Anglo-Boereoorlog, p 317
9. BREYTENBACH, *op cit*, vol 1, p 180
10. *Ibid*, vol 1, p 387
11. LE MAY, *op cit*, p 41
12. BREYTENBACH, *op cit*, vol 1, p 180
13. *Ibid*, vol 1, p 391
14. AMERY, *op cit*, vol VI, pp 418-419
15. CRESWELL, *op cit*, vol III, p 137
16. MIDGLEY, *op cit*, p 148
17. SMIT, AP & MARE, Die Beleg van Mafeking..., p 51
18. GRONUM, MA, Die Engelse Oorlog, p 334
19. BREYTENBACH, *op cit*, vol 1, p 181
20. SCHOLTZ, L, Beroemde Suid-Afrikaanse Krygsmanne, p 76
21. VAN SCHOOR, Bittereinder..., *op cit*, p 171
22. BREYTENBACH, *op cit*, vol 1, p 396
23. McCRACKEN, DP, The Irish Pro-Boers, p 50
24. SCHOLTZ, I, Beroemde Suid-Afrikaanse Krygsmanne, p 118
25. STRYDOM, CJS, Kaapland en die Tweede Vryheidsoorlog, p 62
26. BREYTENBACH, *op cit*, vol 1, p 394
27. *Ibid*, vol 1, p 397
28. FARWELL, B, The Great Boer War, p 196
29. AMERY, *op cit*, vol VI, p 543
30. BREYTENBACH, *op cit*, vol 1, p 361
31. STRYDOM, CJS, Kaapland en die Tweede Vryheidsoorlog, p 60
32. McCRACKEN, DP, The Irish Pro-Boers, p 50
33. BREYTENBACH, *op cit*, vol 1, p 183
34. STRYDOM, CJS, Kaapland en die Tweede Vryheidsoorlog, p 59
35. MIDGLEY, *op cit*, p 32
36. VAN RENSBURG, T, Oorlogsjoernaal van SJ Burger, p 34
37. MEINTJES, Anglo-Boer War..., p 33
38. BREYTENBACH, *op cit*, Vol 1, p 197
39. FERREIRA, OJO, ... SPE Trichard, p 119
40. BREYTENBACH, *op cit*, vol 1, p 393
41. MIDGLEY, *op cit*, p 19
42. WARWICK, P, Black People and the South African War, p 62
43. BREYTENBACH, *op cit*, vol 1, p 196
44. *Ibid*, vol 1, p 197
45. *Ibid*, vol 1, p 214
46. SCHOLTZ, I, *op cit*, p 118
47. PLOEGER, *op cit*, p 192
48. BREYTENBACH, *op cit*, vol 1, pp 214-236
49. *Ibid*, vol 1, p 199
50. KRUGER, R, Good-Bye Dolly Gray, p 81
51. COMAROFF, JL, The Boer War Diary of Sol. T Plaatje, p 142
52. WULFSON, L, Rustenburg at War, p 53

53. BREYTENBACH, *op cit*, vol 1, p 395
54. MIDGLEY, *op cit*, p 32
55. GRONUM, MA, Die Engelse Oorlog, p 346
56. BREYTENBACH, *op cit*, vol 1, pp 237-263; VAN SCHOOR, Bittereinder..., *op cit*, pp 117-119.
57. FERREIRA, OJO, Krijgsgevangenschap van LC Ruijsenaars, p 141
58. GRONUM, *op cit*, p 346
59. CRESWELL, *op cit*, vol II, p viii
60. PAKENHAM, T, The Boer War, p 147
61. GRONUM, *op cit*, p 353
62. MIDGLEY, *op cit*, p 34
63. BREYTENBACH, *op cit*, vol 1, pp 420-421
64. DE SOUZA, CW, No Charge for Delivery, p 160
65. WARWICK, P, The South African War, p 242
66. BREYTENBACH, *op cit*, vol 1, p 287
67. *Ibid*, vol I, p 212 & pp 293-298
68. WARWICK, P, Black People and the South African War, p 112
69. DE SOUZA, CW, No Charge for Delivery, p 161
70. BREYTENBACH, *op cit*, vol 1, p 281
71. McCRACKEN, DP, The Irish Pro-Boers, p 99
72. BREYTENBACH, *op cit*, vol 1, p 401
73. BELFIELD, E, The Boer War, p 19
74. BREYTENBACH, *op cit*, vol 1, p 422
75. KEMP, JCG, Die Pad van die Veroweraar, p 9
76. SMIT, AP & MARE, Die Beleg van Mafeking..., p 85
77. CRESWELL, *op cit*, vol VI, p 193
78. BREYTENBACH, *op cit*, vol 1, p 503
79. WESSELS, A, Die Anglo-Boereoorlog. 'n Oorsig..., p 11
80. WARWICK, P, The South African War, p 256
81. DE SOUZA, CW, No Charge for Delivery, pp 160-161
82. BREYTENBACH, *op cit*, vol I, p 314
83. BELFIELD, E, The Boer War, pp 19-20; BREYTENBACH, *op cit*, vol 1, pp 308-313
84. HEADLAM, *op cit*, vol II p 5
85. BREYTENBACH, *op cit*, vol 1, pp 303-338
86. FERREIRA, OJO, ... SPE Trichard, p 125
87. CRESWELL, *op cit*, vol III, p 142
88. BREYTENBACH, *op cit*, vol VI, p 13
89. MIDGLEY, *op cit*, p 41; SMIT, AP & MARE, *op cit*, p 94
90. BREYTENBACH, *op cit*, vol 1, p 423
91. BREYTENACH, *op cit*, vol II, p 1
92. BREYTENBACH, *op cit*, vol 1, p 441
93. COMAROFF, JL, *op cit*, pp 6 & 144
94. VAN REENEN, R, Emily Hobhouse, Boer War Letters, p 4
95. BREYTENBACH, *op cit*, vol 1, pp 423-425
96. *Ibid*, vol 1, p 351
97. TODD, P, Private Tucker's Boer War Dairy, p 88
98. DE SOUZA, CW, No Charge for Delivery, p 72
99. BREYTENBACH, *op cit*, vol II, p 412
100. THE COIN REPORT vol 1, no 5, Issue 5, 1998
101. FERREIRA, OJO, ... SPE Trichard, p 122
102. BREYTENBACH, *op cit*, vol 1, pp 353-355
103. *Ibid*, vol 1, p 356
104. *Ibid*, vol 1, pp 371-372
105. *Ibid*, vol 1, p 425
106. BREYTENBACH, *op cit*, vol II, pp 372-374
107. DE SOUZA, CW, No Charge for Delivery, p 34
108. BREYTENBACH, *op cit*, vol 1, p 427
109. BREYTENBACH, *op cit*, vol II, pp 6-14
110. WARWICK, P, The South African War, p 317

111. DOONER, MG, The 'Last Post', p107
112. MEINTJES, J, Stormberg..., p27
113. PAKENHAM, T, The Boer War, p 184
114. BREYTENBACH, *op cit*, vol 1, p 357
115. *Ibid*, vol 1, p 366
116. MIDGLEY, *op cit*, p 46
117. PAKENHAM, T, The Boer War, p 185
118. BREYTENBACH, *op cit*, vol II, pp 357-358
119. *Ibid*, vol II, pp 372-374
120. BREYTENBACH, *op cit*, vol VI, p 28
121. BREYTENACH, *op cit*, vol 1, pp 360-361
122. PAKENHAM, T, The Boer War, p 177
123. LE MAY, *op cit*, p 30
124. BREYTENBACH, *op cit*, vol 1, p 362
125. AMERY, *op cit*, vol II, p 95
126. WESSELS, A, Die Anglo-Boereoorlog. 'n Oorsig..., p 10
127. BREYTENBACH, *op cit*, vol II, pp 10-11
128. BREYTENBACH, *op cit*, vol 1, p 427
129. *Ibid*, vol 1, p 367
130. MEINTJES, J, Stormberg..., p 28
131. PAKENHAM, T, The Boer War, p 173
132. BREYTENBACH, *op cit*, vol 1, p 444
133. 'SETEMPE, March/April 1998, Article by D Olmesdahl, p 25.
134. PAKENHAM, T, The Boer War, p 406
135. MEINTJES, J, Stormberg..., p 47
136. WESSELS, A, Die Anglo-Boereoorlog. 'n Oorsig..., p 12
137. BREYTENBACH, *op cit*, vol 1, p 372
138. BREYTENBACH, *op cit*, vol II, pp 378-379
139. *Ibid*, vol II, p 18
140. *Ibid*, *op cit*, vol II, pp 12-13
141. DE SOUZA, CW, *op cit*, p 184
142. BREYTENBACH, *op cit*, vol II, pp 378-379
143. GRIFFITH, K, Thank God We Kept the Flag Flying, p 112
144. LE MAY, *op cit*, p 41
145. BREYTENBACH, *op cit*, vol 1, p 435
146. COMAROFF, JL, The Boer War Diary of Sol T Plaatje, p 146
147. BREYTENBACH, *op cit*, vol II, pp 382-389
148. *Ibid*, vol II, pp 194-195
149. 'SETEMPE', March/April 1998, Article by D Olmesdahl, p 25
150. BREYTENBACH, *op cit*, vol II, pp 13-14
151. 'SETEMPE', March/April 1998, Article by D Olmesdahl, p 25
152. OOSTHUIZEN, AV, Rebelle van die Stormberge, p 62
153. KRUGER, R, Good-Bye Dolly Gray, p 106
154. CRESWELL, *op cit*, vol II, p viii
155. DUXBURY, Die Slag van Magersfontein, p 22
156. BREYTENBACH, *op cit*, vol 1, pp 375-376
157. *Ibid*, vol 1, pp 375-376
158. *Ibid*, vol 1, pp 376-382
159. BREYTENBACH, *op cit*, vol 1, pp 23-34; PEMBERTON, *op cit*, pp 47-54
160. DUXBURY, Die Slag van..., pp 2-1&2
161. OOSTHUIZEN, AV, Rebelle van die Stormberge, p 66
162. DUXBURY, Die Slag van..., pp 2-1&2
163. WARWICK, P, Black People and the South African War, pp 40-41
164. BELFIELD, E, The Boer War, p 47
165. BREYTENBACH, *op cit*, vol II, pp 7-10
166. *Ibid*, vol II, pp 34-56; PEMBERTON, WB, *op cit*, pp 56-57
167. PAKENHAM, T, The Boer War, p 187
168. DUXBURY, Die Slag van..., pp 3-5
169. *Ibid*, p 3-1; PEMBERTON, WB, *op cit*, pp 60-61
170. BREYTENBACH, *op cit*, vol II, p 237

171. DUXBURY, Die Slag van..., p 3-1; PEMBERTON, *op cit*, pp 60-62

172. WULFSON, L, Rustenburg at War, p 59

173. PAMPHLET issued by the War Museum, Bloemfontein

174. HEADLAM, *op cit*, vol II, p 36

175. BREYTENBACH, *op cit*, vol II, p 238

176. PAKENHAM, T, The Boer War, p 187

177. BREYTENBACH, *op cit*, vol II, p 239

178. *Ibid*, vol II, pp 85-87

179. *Ibid*, vol II, p 96

180. *Ibid*, vol II, pp 85-86

181. *Ibid*, vol II, p 96

182. WULFSON, L, Rustenburg at War, p 60

183. BREYTENBACH, *op cit*, vol II, pp 238-240

184. KEMP, JCG, Die Pad van die Veroweraar, p 16

185. FERREIRA, OJO, ... SPE Trichard, p 128

186. OOSTHUIZEN, AV, Rebelle van die Stormberge, p 72

187. DE SOUZA, CW, *op cit*, p 29

188. KRUGER, DW, Die Krugermiljoene, p 51

189. CONRADIE, FW, Met Cronje op die Wesfront, pp 47-48

190. BREYTENBACH, *op cit*, vol II, pp 96-99

191. CONRADIE, FW, Met Cronje op die Wesfront, pp 47-48

192. CRESWELL, *op cit*, vol II, p viii

193. BELFIELD, E, The Boer War, p 167

194. BREYTENBACH, *op cit*, vol II, pp 96-99

195. *Ibid*, vol II, p 112

196. *Ibid*, vol II, p 233

197. *Ibid*, vol II, p 245

198. *Ibid*, vol II, pp 437-443

199. *Ibid*, vol II, pp 109-112

200. *Ibid*, vol II, p 121

201. SMIT, AP & MARE, Die Beleg van Mafeking..., p 134

202. WESSELS, A, War Diary of Herbert Gwynne Howell, p 22

203. OOSTHUIZEN, AV, Rebelle van die Stormberge, p 73

204. BREYTENBACH, *op cit*, vol II, p 113

205. *Ibid*, vol II, pp 341-342

206. *Ibid*, vol II, pp 231-232

207. *Ibid*, vol II, p 246

208. *Ibid*, vol II, pp 443-444

209. *Ibid*, vol II, p120

210. WESSELS, A, The War Diary of Herbert Gwynne Howell, p 24
     BREYTENBACH, *op cit*, vol 1, pp 196-225
     MEINTJES, J, Stormberg..., pp 84-89

211. PEMBERTON, *op cit*, p 86

212. BREYTENBACH, *op cit*, vol V, p 26

213. BREYTENBACH, *op cit*, vol II, pp 443-449

214. BREYTENBACH, *op cit*, vol 1, p 342

215. BREYTENBACH, *op cit*, vol II, pp 135-166

216. CRESWELL, *op cit*, vol VI, pp 192-192

217. HEADLAM, *op cit*, vol II, p 23

218. FARWELL, *op cit*, p ix

219. BREYTENBACH, *op cit*, vol II, pp 166-170

220. CHISHOLM, R, Ladysmith, pp 135-136

221. WOODS, F, Young Winston's Wars, pp 181-183

222. CHISHOLM, R, Ladysmith, p 136

223. BREYTENBACH, *op cit*, vol 1, p 247

224. SMIT, AP & MARE, Die Beleg van Mafeking..., p 151

225. BELFIELD, E, The Boer War, p 69

226. BREYTENBACH, *op cit*, vol 1, pp 249-250; PEMBERTON, *op cit*, pp 128-130

227. DE SOUZA, CW, *op cit*, p 172

228. BREYTENBACH, *op cit*, vol 1, pp 263-332; PEMBERTON, *op cit*, pp 130-151

229. CRESWELL, *op cit*, vol VI, pp 191-192

230. BREYTENBACH, *op cit*, vol 1, p 484

231. AMERY, *op cit*, vol II, p 456

232. CHISHOLM, R, Ladysmith, p 149

233. *Ibid*, p 162

234. PRETORIUS, F, Kommandolewe tydens die Anglo-Boereoorlog, p 189

235. GARDNER, B, The Lion's Cage, p 140

236. TODD, P, Private Tucker's Boer War Diary, p 33

237. CRESWELL, *op cit*, vol II, p viii; CHISHOLM, R, Ladysmith, p 154

238. CRESWELL, *op cit*, vol VII, p 201

239. CHISHOLM, R, Ladysmith, p 162

240. PAMPHLET issued by the War Museum, Bloemfontein

241. KRUGER, DW, Die Krugermiljoene, p 20

242. FERREIRA, OJO, Krijgsgevangenschap van LC Ruijsenaars, p 83

243. BARBARY, J, The Boer War, p 74

244. GRIFFITH, K, Thank God We kept the Flag Flying, p 165

245. CRESWELL, *op cit*, vol II, p viii

246. CHISHOLM, R, Ladysmith, p 162

247. PLOEGER, *op cit*, pp 27:2-3

248. KRUGER, DW, Die Krugermiljoene, p 20

249. MEINTJES, Anglo-Boer War..., p 49

250. CHISHOLM, R, Ladysmith, p 162

251. WARWICK, P, Black People and the South African War, p 42

252. WOODS, F, Young Winston's Wars, p 190

253. BREYTENBACH, *op cit*, vol I, p 407

254. PEDDLE, Col DE, Long Cecil, The Story of the Gun..., p 4

255. CHISHOLM, R, Ladysmith, p 165

256. SMIT, AP & MARE, Die Beleg van Mafeking..., p 173

257. CRESWELL, *op cit*, vol VI, p 192

258. PLOEGER, *op cit*, p 27:3

259. CHISHOLM, R, Ladysmith, p 165

260. WESSELS, A, The Boer War Diary of Herbert Gwynne Howell, p 26

261. GARDNER, B, The Lion's Cage, p 146

262. CRESWELL, *op cit*, vol VI, p 192

263. BREYTENBACH, *op cit*, vol IV, p 3

264. *Ibid*, vol IV, p 3

265. OOSTHUIZEN, AV, Rebelle van die Stormberge, p 81

JANUARY - MARCH 1900

HAMMER BLOWS

1900	SUMMER	JANUARY
Day 83 Mon **1900-01-01**	Western front Black involvement	NEW YEAR'S DAY **Kuruman siege:** Commandant JH Visser's besiegers shell Kuruman for the first time with the recently arrived seven-pounder (3kg) muzzle loading gun. The gunner is pathetic and he moves the gun from position to position and it takes 80 shells before the wall of a fort is hit and ten further shots before it collapses. The gallant British garrison at Kuruman surrenders after a 'siege' lasting 50 days. Captains Bates and Dennison, ten other officers and 120 Cape Policemen, including 70 black members, are taken prisoner. During the siege, the British has lost three men killed, while only one burgher has been slightly wounded.[1]
	Black involvement	**Mafeking siege:** Colonel Baden-Powell, suspecting that large stores of grain are hidden away in the black 'stat', refuses rations to all blacks *"to see if there is any real want"*.[2] Colonel Pilcher, with a mixed force consisting of Australians, Canadians and Brittons, capture a rebel laager at Sunnyside, 48 kilometres north of Belmont, taking 40 prisoners.
	Central front	General French attacks Republican forces at Colesberg, attempting to work around their right flank and threatening both their rear and their line of retreat to the Colesberg bridge. Simultaneous attacks on Jasfontein and Skietberg are launched to keep Schoeman's forces occupied and to divert their attention from the flanking move. The attack fails and the British lose one officer killed and 21 wounded with one officer missing compared to nine Republicans wounded. The Republicans, however, do not follow up their success.[3]
	United Kingdom	Enrolment of the first draft of the City Imperial Volunteers starts.[4]
	Trivia	*The day is almost universally wrongly celebrated as the first day of the 20th century.* *British protectorates are set up and Frederick Lugard becomes High Commissioner in Nigeria.*
Day 84 Tue **1900-01-02**	Western front	Colonel Pilcher occupies Douglas, northern Cape, and sends loyal inhabitants under an escort to Belmont Station.[5]
	Central front	French again attacks the Colesberg position, keeping the defenders pinned down with shelling and rifle fire while an 800-strong column cuts the telegraph line to the Colesberg road bridge. French also succeeds in pushing his positions and outposts closer to Colesberg. The brakes of a supply train at Rensburg Siding fail and the train runs downhill towards Plewmans near Colesberg where burghers spend a lot of time and effort attempting to capture supplies under fire. British artillery succeeds in setting the train on fire.[6]
Day 85 Wed **1900-01-03**	Western front	Colonel Pilcher evacuates Douglas for 'military reasons'.[7]
	Natal front	**Ladysmith siege:** A combined Republican council of war attended by 43 officers, chaired by Commandant-General Joubert and Chief Commandant Prinsloo, decides to take offensive action against Ladysmith. They decide on a combined attack on Platrand, a key position south of town, with simultaneous diversionary actions all along the perimeter.[8]
	Central front	Chief Commandant Olivier leads a patrol consisting of about 1 000 burghers with

	International	two field-guns from Stormberg via Molteno and runs into an armoured train sent by Gatacre from Sterkstroom. Republican artillery drives off the train and the burghers take up a position near Syfergat. A long-distance fight with the train ensues with no casualties on either side.[9] Republicans under General Olivier retake Dordrecht. John Redmond proclaims that, in view of the war in South Africa, there is no telling what advantages may not arise for Ireland if she pressed vigorously for her various demands. He adds, *"Here is the opportunity for which generations of Irishmen have longed..."*[10]
Day 86 Thu **1900-01-04**	Central front	General Piet de Wet launches a counterattack against French's troops threatening Colesberg. A group of his men surrounds a British detachment but due to a lack of support by General Schoeman and effective counter-measures by French, a group of burghers is cut off and forced to surrender after fighting a rearguard action. De Wet loses five killed, ten wounded and 21 captured while French lose seven killed and 15 wounded.[11]
	International	The German mail steamer, *General*, en route to Lourenço Marques with cargo suspected to be bound for the ZAR, is intercepted and impounded in international waters by the Royal Navy.[12]
Day 87 Fri **1900-01-05**	Central front **Victoria Cross**	While personally reconnoitring positions west of Colesberg in preparation for an attack on Graskop, General French and his bodyguard are fiercely attacked by a group of Johannesburg Police, who assumes their intention is the capture of supply wagons. French loses three seriously wounded and five taken prisoner. Lieutenant Sir JP Milbanke, French's ADC, 10th Hussars, is recommended for the Victoria Cross.[13]
	Natal front	**Ladysmith siege:** The planned Republican attack on Platrand is scheduled for Saturday, 6 January. They earmark 450 ZAR burghers and 400 Free Staters for the assault, while General Botha is to send 300 burghers from his Colenso line to serve as a mobile reserve. For the first time more than 20 Republican field-guns, including two 'Long Toms' and six pom-poms, will be available to support the attack. The final arrangements for the attack are concluded with prayer meetings. By coincidence, General Sir George White orders two additional guns, including a heavy naval gun, to be emplaced on Wagon Hill, the western crest of the Platrand position. This increases the normal garrison of Wagon Hill and Caesar's Camp, as the British call the position, to about 1 000 men with eight field-guns and the naval gun on the back slope. More important, the activities of the sappers preparing the gun emplacements raise the alertness all along the sector.[14]
	Trivia	*John Redmond, Irish Nationalist leader, calls for an uprising in Ireland.*
Day 88 Sat **1900-01-06**	Natal front	**THE BATTLE OF PLATRAND OR WAGON HILL** At about 01:00 the Harrismith commando, led by Combat General JC de Villiers, a Majuba veteran, starts climbing Platrand, aiming for the saddle between Wagon Hill and Wagon Point. In the centre the Transvaal commandos prepare to scale the southern slopes of Caesar's Camp and Commandants Hattingh and Spruyt's men, the eastern shoulder. Lieutenant RJT Digby Jones, 33 Royal Engineers and a working party of Gordon Highlanders and Manchesters are preparing the heavy timber gun platform for the naval gun which is being brought up by its crew. The wide awake pickets hear the approaching burghers and at 02:30 their challenge rings out, followed by the first fusillade into the darkness. De Villiers' men hesitate, and then rush upwards to reach the edge of the summit, where they tenaciously gain a foothold and pour fire in the direction of the defenders. Colonel Ian Hamilton rushes from his post on the eastern

		edge of Caesar's Camp just before about 50 burghers reach the crest at his back. He immediately calls for reinforcements from White as the burghers force the Manchesters along the summit. The British sangars and forts, positioned on the back edge of the summit, are a surprise to the attackers and as visibility improves, the weight of fire and the first shrapnel shells force them to return to the edge of the plateau.
		The Republican field-guns on Bulwana, reputedly ordered into action by Mrs Hendrina Joubert, *"the real Commandant-General"*, soon take on the British artillery behind Platrand and relieve the pressure on the Transvalers clinging to the eastern edge of Caesar's Camp. The central burgher attack does not become a serious threat, as some of the burghers elect not to join their comrades, others remain in the safety of the dead ground at the foot of Platrand, while some retreat and are happy to keep up *"a long-range fire more dangerous to their own men on the heights than the British"*.
		Elsewhere on the siege perimeter only the diversionary attack on Observation Hill north of town amounts to anything but White soon realises that Platrand is the main objective and he sends more and more reinforcements there. Colonel WH Dick-Cunnyngham VC, of the Gordons, is killed by a stray bullet almost three kilometres from the firing line, Lieutenant-Colonel Edwards of the ILH, Lord Ava and Major Karri Davis are wounded. As the morning proceeds the defenders push more and more men onto the summit, but they are unable to dislodge the burghers. On the other side, although the burghers are maintaining themselves and repulse the one counter-attack after the other, they cannot hope to gain the upper hand without being reinforced from below. Just after noon, both De Villiers and Ian Hamilton realise that Wagon Point on the western extreme is the key to victory. De Villiers sends Field-cornets Japie de Villiers and De Jager down the hill to collect as many burghers as possible to execute a left hook and assault Wagon Point from the west. The battle reaches a climax as parties from both sides charge at the half-completed gun emplacement. Hamilton reaches it first and a shoot-out ensues: De Villiers, De Jager, Miller-Wallnut, Digby-Jones and Trooper Albrecht all fall within the emplacement, the last two earning posthumous VC's.
	Victoria Cross	At 16:00, just as White was ordering the last reinforcements he could spare, Colonel Park's Devons, to cross the open ground on the rear slope of Platrand, a terrific thunderstorm breaks. On the summit, both sides fear an attack from out of the storm and both sides fire as hard as they can. Panic spreads and both sides falter. The soldiers run but they are rallied and ordered back. At 17:00 the Devons start their bayonet charge. They fall in droves as the burghers recklessly stand up to empty their magazines into them. They charge on, a subaltern winning the VC for continuing in spite of six wounds. The burghers fire up to the last possible moment before falling back to a new position. The firing continues until darkness allows the Republicans to melt away, General De Villiers being the last to leave.
		During this 'soldiers' battle' the losses are heavy: the British lose 148 killed in action, 26 fatally wounded and 275 wounded. The Republicans lose 56 killed in action, six fatally wounded and 110 wounded.[15]
	Victoria Cross	Five Victoria Crosses are awarded to the following: Privates R Scott and J Pitts, both of the Manchester Regiment, at Caesar's Camp, Lieutenant RJT Digby-Jones of the Royal Engineers, Trooper H Albrecht of the Imperial Light Horse and Lieutenant JEI Masterson of the Devonshire Regiment at Wagon Hill.[16]
		Under perilous conditions Rev JD Kestell, Republican Field Chaplain, attends to the wounded on both sides. *"A grievously wounded British sergeant said to him: 'You are preaching a good service to-day.'"* These words are engraved on the battlefield monument.[17]
	Central front	**ACTION AT GRASKOP** Trying to force the Republicans to abandon Colesberg, General French attempts outflanking their positions by sending 305 men of the Suffolk Regiment under Lieutenant-Colonel Watson to occupy Graskop (Grassy Hill). After a night march the

	International	troops scale the hill but clash unexpectedly with 100 men of the Heidelberg Commando. The Suffolks flee in disarray and those left behind surrender at sunrise, losing 37 killed, 52 wounded and 99 taken prisoner including 29 of the wounded.[18] The German post steamer *Herzog* en route to Lourenço Marques, with cargo bound for the ZAR, is intercepted in international waters by *HMS Thetis* of the Royal Navy.[19]
Day 89 Sun **1900-01-07**	Central front *Trivia*	A patrol of Cape Mounted Rifles is surprised by a party of Cape rebels between Dordrecht and Bird's River and they suffer two killed and six are captured.[20] *Sir Redvers H Buller's 61st birthday.*
Day 90 Mon **1900-01-08**	Western front Central front	**Kimberley siege:** Horse meat becomes part of the regular diet in Kimberley. [21] Ignatius S Ferreira is elected as Chief Commandant of the Free State forces on the Western front. [22] General JH de la Rey arrives at Colesberg to take over command from General Schoeman, who is tactfully recalled to take an administrative position in Bloemfontein.[23]
Day 91 Tue **1900-01-09**	Natal	The German steamer *Herzog* is released after being intercepted in international water north of Lourenço Marques by *HMS Thetis* and escorted to Durban.[24] The British government is later obliged to pay £18 500 in compensation to the German owners.[25] Australian and Canadian troops launch a raid into Orange Free State territory near Jacobsdal.[26]
Day 92 Wed **1900-01-10**	Cape Colony Natal front Western front Black Involvement	**THE ARRIVAL OF LORD ROBERTS** Field Marshall Lord Roberts and Major-General Lord Kitchener arrive in Cape Town, taking command of an army larger than the entire white population of the ZAR. **BULLER'S SECOND ATTEMPT** Leaving a strong garrison behind at Chievely and Frere, General Buller moves towards the upper Tugela to Springfield. His force, consisting of 24 356 troops with 58 field-guns, 21 machine guns, 350 convoy wagons and seven steam tractors, stretches 27 kilometres and moves at less than 2 kilometres per hour. When night falls, the tail end of this mighty force is still within sight of Frere.[27] Lord Dundonald, commanding the mounted troops, scouts ahead. He meets no opposition, leaves about 400 men at Springfield, and occupies Mount Alice, a koppie commanding Potgieter's Drift on the Tugela. The Republicans stationed on the upper Tugela are commanded by General AP Cronje (OFS) who has less than 1 500 burghers at his disposal. In the evening General Botha dispatches 500 men, all that he feels he can remove from his Colenso position, to reinforce him. [28] **Mafeking siege:** Wessel Montshiwa, a Barolong chief, advises his people not to assist the British. According to Hamilton: *"... he told them in his amiable fashion that the English wished to make slaves of them, and that they would not be paid for any services they rendered; nor would they, added he, taking advantage of an unfortunate turn in the situation, be given any food, but left to starve when the critical moment came."*[29]
Day 93 Thu **1900-01-11**	Natal front	Lord Dundonald seizes Potgieter's Drift. In spite of heavy long-range rifle fire, his men also succeed in capturing the ferry boat on the opposite bank.[30] **Ladysmith siege:** Archibald James Leofric Temple Blackwood, Earl of Alva, dies of wounds sustained during the Battle of Platrand or Wagon Hill on 6 January.[31]

	Central front	In a remarkable feat Major Butcher succeeds in dragging a 15-pounder Armstrong gun to the top of the 250 metres high Coleskop, which dominates the town and environs.[32]
	United Kingdom	DA Smith, now Lord Strathcona, Canadian High Commissioner in London, offers to raise a Canadian regiment of 500 mounted men.
Day 94 Fri **1900-01-12**	Central front	The British shell Colesberg town from Coleskop, and although results are limited, the Republicans are unnerved and forced to retire out of range.[33]
Day 95 Sat **1900-01-13**	Natal front	**Ladysmith siege:** Chief Commandant M Prinsloo relays a plan to flood Ladysmith, devised by a Free Stater named Krause, to President Steyn. The plan, based on Ladysmith's location on the banks of the Klip River, calls for a wall between nine and 14 metres high to be built across the narrows south-west of Bulwana.[34] There are 2 150 men in Intombi Camp Hospital at Ladysmith.[35]
	ZAR	A Belgian-German volunteer ambulance arrives in Pretoria.
Day 96 Sun **1900-01-14**	Natal front	General Buller starts the bombardment of Republican positions on the upper Tugela. The Republicans now have to defend a line from Hlangwane in the east to heights west of Trichardt's Drift, a distance of more than 80 kilometres.[36]
	Northern front	Colonel HCO Plumer occupies Gaberones, Bechuanaland.
	Trivia	*The first performance of Puccinni's opera* Tosca *in Rome.*
Day 97 Mon **1900-01-15**	Natal front	**Ladysmith siege:** The *Daily Mail* correspondent and editor of the *Ladysmith Lyre*, George Steevens, dies of enteric fever.[37] The British report a skirmish at Rensburg Siding. Martial law is extended to Philipstown and Hopetown.
Day 98 Tue **1900-01-16**	Natal front	As part of an elaborate feint, almost 8 000 men with 1 600 horses and 22 field-guns move towards Potgieter's and Meul Drifts. They throw a pontoon across the river and move two full battalions complete with artillery support across, without opposition. This effort is devised to allow Sir Charles Warren to move to Trichardt's Drift with 15 382 men, about 5 000 horses and 36 guns. They reach the river after midnight.[38] **Ladysmith siege:** President Steyn gives his blessing to the dam building project and requests General M Prinsloo to co-ordinate the effort with Commandant-General Joubert as the officer in overall command of this front.[39] There are more than 2 400 men in the hospital at Ladysmith.[40]
	Trivia	*ISM Hamilton's 47th birthday.*
Day 99 Wed **1900-01-17**	Natal front	Commandant-General Joubert appoints General Botha as commander on the upper Tugela. He succeeds in sending more burghers to this sector, and there are now between 4 000 and 5 000 men with seven guns under General AP Cronje and Commandant Ben Viljoen.[41] Sir Charles Warren, an ex-Royal Engineer, becomes absorbed in the river crossing operation and orders the building of a pontoon bridge, complete with an approach road down to the water's edge, while his force looks on. Late in the afternoon, the first units cross, move beyond the opposite bank and camp for the night. Lord Dundonald crosses the river with his Mounted Brigade consisting of 2 270 men with two machine guns, at a deep ford about 2 kilometres away.[42]
	Cape Colony	Sir A Milner to Chamberlain: *"The only thing I ever really fear is a 'wobble' in British opinion."*[43]
	Trivia	*ZAR independence day (Sand River Convention 1852).* *D Lloyd George's 37th birthday.*

Day 100 Thu **1900-01-18**	Natal front	**THE ACTION AT ACTON HOMES** Sir Charles Warren continues to supervise the crossing of his force at Trichardt's Drift. Lord Dundonald, with vague orders to scout ahead, moves around Tabanyama and finds the road from Acton Homes to Ladysmith open. He is spotted by Opperman and Mentz, who immediately send 300 burghers to investigate. Dundonald ambushes them and inflicts about 50 casualties. He requests reinforcements but Warren immediately recalls part of his force to protect his oxen. Warren deliberately delays the crossing of Dundonald's baggage and says: *"If I let them go, Lord Dundonald will try to go on to Ladysmith."* Instead of reinforcing Dundonald's bold advance, Warren recalls him and ungraciously tells him that the role of the cavalry is to protect the baggage and not to *"indulge in semi-independent antics"*. Warren also rejects the possibility of advancing via Acton Homes and decides on the Fairview-Rosalie route. As this road is dominated by Tabanyama and Spioenkop, it is necessary to clear the heights [44] **Ladysmith siege:** A Diamant, an engineer, and PJ Malan, Chief of the ZAR Roads Department, with land surveyors and other experts inspect the proposed site of the dam wall in the Klip River. They immediately issue requests for sandbags and the recruiting of about 400 black labourers.[45]
	Western front Black Involvement	**Mafeking siege:** Two black cattle-herds are captured and summarily executed at Mafeking by burghers, in accordance with a council of war decision on cattle-rustlers. President Kruger immediately repudiates this decision and orders this practice to cease forthwith.[46]
	United Kingdom	The Eighth Division is to mobilize at Aldershot under the command of Lieutenant-General Sir HML Rundle.
Day 101 Fri **1900-01-19**	Natal front	Sir Charles Warren completes his crossing at Trichardt's Drift. All the British forces on the other side of the Tugela start a bombardment and long-range rifle fire to probe the heights commanding the river. The observation balloon is also launched, but the Republicans refuse to exchange shots. They prefer to wait for the expected assault and extend their right flank further westwards to prevent it being turned.[47]
	Western front	**Kimberley siege:** 'Long Cecil,' the 4 inch (104mm) field-gun, designed by American George Labram and manufactured in the De Beers workshop in Kimberley, is test fired. Rhodes gives the honour of the first shot to Mrs Pickering, wife of the Secretary of the De Beers Company.[48]
	Black Involvement	**Mafeking siege:** General JP Snyman sends a starving group of black women, who have been encouraged to attempt a breakout, back under a white flag. Colonel Baden-Powell objects, stating that it is against the customs of civilized warfare *"to receive anyone into a besieged town. The Colonel commanding therefore formally declines to receive this party and should they advance further, the white flag as above stated, being invalid, hostilities will be recommenced."*[49] General JP Snyman informs the ZAR government that he has armed about 180 of Makgobi Motsewakhumo's Barolong tribesmen to avoid a repeat of the Derdepoort attack by the Kgatla tribesmen (25 November 1899).[50]
	Trivia	*JJ Cheere Emmet's 33rd birthday (General L Botha's brother-in-law).*
Day 102 Sat **1900-01-20**	Natal front	**THE BATTLE OF TABANYAMA** General Sir CF Clery, commanding two infantry brigades, six field artillery batteries (36 guns) and three cavalry squadrons, leaves camp at 03:00 and assaults Three Trees Hill. After a fierce bombardment, the troops take the hill and an adjoining height at 06:00, only to discover that it has been undefended. They prepare positions across the slope of the hill and start dragging their guns to the summit. Between 07:00 and 08:00

		four batteries open fire against the crest of Tabanyama. Convinced of the demoralising effect of a sustained barrage, the gunners, soon joined by two more batteries, continue firing for four hours. They are, however, not clear about Republican dispositions and concentrate on the crest visible from their vantage point. The burghers hold their fire and retire to their main trench positioned along the rear edge of the summit. At 10:30 Clery advances his infantry, about 5 500 men, expecting to clear the summit of disheartened stragglers.
		The burghers patiently wait until the British are within range before opening a furious and accurate small-arms fire from the higher rear crest. The soldiers are caught on the open glacis, take cover where they can and the attack is stalled. The Republican field-guns, pom-poms and machine guns open up and Clery orders retirement. An attempted flank attack fails to find the enemy flank and the attackers end up in front of the Republican position and are seriously cut up. A group of Indian stretcher bearers, among whom is Mohandas Ghandi, a young Durban attorney, recklessly becomes intermingled with fighting troops and six of them are killed and 12 wounded in the cross-fire and shelling. The soldiers fall back to Bastion and Three Trees Hill and the battle becomes a desultory artillery duel until nightfall.
		The burghers lose five killed in action, 42 wounded of whom two die later of their wounds. About 30 British troops are killed in action and 280 are wounded.[51]
		At Potgieter's Drift Lyttleton again demonstrates against the Republican positions on the Brakfontein Heights. He loses three killed, 13 wounded and one man missing without inflicting any Republican casualties. He pulls back and contents himself with shelling the ridges.[52]
	International	The Second New Zealand contingent sails for South Africa.
	Trivia	*Commandant-General PJ Joubert's 69th birthday.* *John Ruskin, writer and critic, dies.*
Day 103 Sun **1900-01-21**	Natal front	**THE BATTLE OF TABANYAMA** Buller insists that Warren must follow his proposed tactical plan of launching a series of successive rolling attacks to the left, until the Republican western flank is turned. Warren orders Hart and Kitchener to attack and at 04:00 they move north from Bastion Hill. Kitchener is to make a wide flanking move, while Hart's men pin the enemy down in their trenches. After a fire fight lasting five hours, the order to charge is given at 10:30, but no sooner do the troops come to their feet or they are met by murderous and accurate Mauser fire. Despite their bravest efforts they can make no headway and suffer serious losses. The attack is called off after half an hour. From about noon a static fire fight develops: the British, using all their guns and the burghers intermittently harassing them with their deadly little pom-pom shells, constantly changing position. The British suffer about 24 killed, 223 wounded and four missing in action, while the Republicans lose four killed and 20 wounded[53]
	Western front	**Kimberley siege:** 'Long Cecil' is officially handed over to the Diamond Fields Artillery.[54]
Day 104 Mon **1900-01-22**	Natal front	**THE BATTLE OF TABANYAMA** Reluctant to retire, Warren spends the day considering alternative methods to clear the heights, but he does not make any serious attempts other than continuing the artillery barrage. His 36 field-guns are supplemented by four howitzers which high trajectory is more effective against the Republican trenches. General Botha's efforts to counter the first signs of faltering morale are immeasurably boosted by the unexpected appearance of President MT Steyn on the battlefield. The burghers are re-motivated, they return to their positions and maintain a lively fusillade on the enemy. The British lose one killed and 36 wounded, while one soldier is missing in action.

		Frustration and clashing personalities, compounded by the threat of Warren's 'dormant commission', create tension between the senior British officers. Warren is in a quandary: he has lost enthusiasm for the left flank advance as 'suggested' by Buller and cannot bring himself to consider the wide manoeuvre via Acton Homes that Dundonald exposed four days ago. Buller again 'suggests' that the Republicans may be concentrating for a counter-attack. He bluntly tells Warren to stop wasting time on demoralizing schemes: he must attack or pull back across the Tugela. Warren points out that the Fairview-Rosalie route is not feasible without taking the height dominating it on the east: Spioenkop. Almost flippantly, Buller replies, *"Of course you must take it."*[55] Warren immediately declares his readiness to finalize preparations for an attempt the same night, with himself leading. Buller decides that the newly arrived Major-General J Talbot Coke will command the assault. Coke accepts but requests a 24-hour delay to reconnoitre the mountain.[56]
	Western front	The siege of Mafeking enters its hundredth day.
Day 105 Tue **1900-01-23**	Natal front	**BATTLE OF SPIOENKOP** Talbot Coke's old leg injury makes him incapable of leading the assault on Spioenkop, and it is decided that Major-General ERP Woodgate will take over. At 19:30, 1 700 men assemble below Three Trees Hill. Lieutenant-Colonel TMG Thorneycroft's Mounted Infantry (on foot) lead the march, followed by the Lancashire Fusiliers and the Royal Lancasters. The night march is well executed and firm discipline is maintained. They climb the southern spur and arrive below the summit, where they fix bayonets. A small burgher picket of less than 200 men stationed on the summit shout out a challenge, and the British charge. In confused shooting, about ten soldiers are wounded and three burghers killed and the rest chased off the summit. The British give three cheers and start preparing a defensive position on the summit. Their entrenching tools are inefficient and no sandbags have been brought to the top. The darkness and a mountain mist make it impossible to do a detailed appreciation of the topography of the hill. The burghers scramble down the mountain and raise the alarm. General Botha, with his headquarters at Rosalie farms, immediately realises the danger to his Tugela line, and start to rally all the burghers he can find in the dark.[57]
	Western front	The siege of Kimberley enters its hundredth day. 'Long Cecil' fires its first rounds at the besiegers around Kimberley, outranging the Republican field-guns by several hundred metres. General Cronje immediately requests one of the big Creusot fortress guns from Pretoria.[58]
	Trivia	*Lieutenant-Colonel SPE Trichard's 53rd birthday.*
Day 106 Wed **1900-01-24** *Comdt. HF Prinsloo (National Cultural History Museum)*	Natal front	**BATTLE OF SPIOENKOP** The summit plateau of Spioenkop is about 16 hectares in extent. The main British trench is about 300 metres in length and resembles a boomerang running east-west with a slight salient to the north. The troops can only dig about 500 millimetres deep before striking solid rock and they have to incorporate the excavated soil, clods of earth and rocks to form a parapet. At about 08:00, when the morning mist suddenly lifts, Woodgate and Thorneycroft are shocked to discover that their main position is about a hundred metres from the edge of the plateau, and this is the distance they can cover with rifle fire. This means that the enemy can approach unseen and under cover to 45 to 180 metres from the British trench. Woodgate immediately sends his sappers to prepare trenches at the crest, but their equipment is not suitable for the rocky terrain, they run into a burgher counterattack and they have to fall back. The first Republican thrust is spearheaded by 84 men of Commandant Hendrik Prinsloo's Carolina commando who gain the north-eastern ridge. Prinsloo returns to Botha's laager and gives a situation report. They plan the positioning of their artillery

and direct the shelling onto the summit. From Tabanyama, where a Free State Krupp and pom-pom are stationed, to Twin Peaks near Brakfontein, the Republican artillery is positioned in an arc encompassing almost 120 degrees. Field-guns from Acton Homes and elsewhere are dragged closer and open up within easy range of their target, but invisible to and out of range of the British guns. The Republicans, for once, enjoy local superiority in artillery.

Botha rallies burghers from all along their line, musters them under cover and sends them up the back slopes of Spioenkop and adjoining features, from where they sweep the badly positioned British main trench. Prinsloo rejoins his men, accompanied by Commandant 'Rooi' Daniel Opperman's Pretoria commando. The burghers threaten the edge and keep the trench under fire.

Comdt. 'Rooi' Daniël Opperman
(National Cultural History Museum)

The British artillery is ineffective, except the naval guns' bombardment of Conical Hill, which has to be abandoned. North of Potgieter's Drift Lyttleton's gunners have shelled Spioenkop since daybreak, but at about 08:00 Warren orders him to stop for fear of shelling their own men. The heliograph on the summit is knocked out by shell fire, and at his headquarters at Three Trees Hill, Warren's information about conditions on the summit becomes increasingly hazy, despite efforts to use semaphore flags. The burghers' sustained fire increases in ferocity and more and more reinforcements are climbing the back slope, especially towards Aloe Knoll from where they enfilade the British trench at a range of less than 300 metres. (Fire from this position is deadly accurate and afterwards 70 of the men killed in the trench have been found with wounds on the right-hand side of their heads.)

At about 09:00, while observing this threat, General Woodgate is fatally wounded by shrapnel. A message to Warren from Crofton, the second ranking officer on the hill, reporting Woodgate's wound and requesting further reinforcements, is condensed by a signaller to, *"Reinforce at once or all is lost. General dead."* Warren is confused, because he receives this message soon after Woodgate's previous message (written at about 07:00) which states, *"We have entrenched a position, and are, I hope, secure."* He orders Coke to the summit with two battalions and the Imperial Light Infantry and concludes his orders with, *"You must hold on to the last. No surrender."*

Inexplicably, Warren does not consider attacks by either his left flank under Clery on Tabanyama, or his right flank under Lyttleton north of Potgieter's Drift and the attack on Spioenkop becomes an isolated battle rather than a combined offensive. While the troops on the summit are being decimated, more than 10 000 troops are idle all day, facing forces depleted as Botha transfers all available burghers to Spioenkop. Lyttleton actually offers his services and Warren vaguely asks him to do what he can. Receiving a cry for help from the summit, Lyttleton immediately orders some troops across a small ford and up the southern slope of Spioenkop and in the direction of Aloe Knoll and Twin Peaks. He also orders all his guns to shell the eastern slopes of Spioenkop and Aloe Knoll, only to receive the message from Warren, *"We occupy the whole summit and I fear you are shelling us seriously; cannot you turn your guns on the enemy's guns."*

Now Buller, who has been observing the battle like an umpire from his headquarters at Spearmans, interferes by 'suggesting', *"Unless you put some really good hard fighting man in command on the top you will lose the hill. I suggest Thorneycroft."* Warren awards Thorneycroft the local rank of Brigadier-General and confusion reigns among the officers on the summit as Thorneycroft and both Crofton and Coke assume to be in command. In the heat of battle it is impossible to clear up.

The British situation becomes critical as burghers approach the front crest in strength, expertly exploiting every bit of cover and closely supported by their artillery. As the entire summit is exposed to Republican rifle, pom-pom and shell fire, it is impossible to reinforce the summit edge. Thorneycroft personally leads a bayonet charge, but fails. At about noon all the troops are either in the main trench on the back crest or below the summit on the southern slope. In the main trench the soldiers use the bodies of their comrades to hide behind and water becomes critical. The close range car-

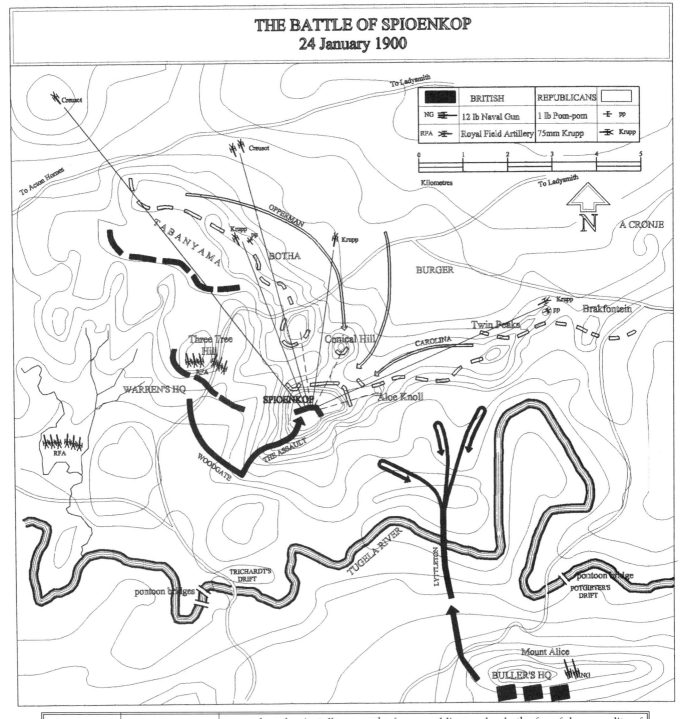

nage also takes its toll among the farmer-soldiers and only the forceful personality of Opperman encourages them to persist and to press closer. At about 13:00, a few Lancaster Fusiliers on the British right waves their handkerchiefs in surrender. Thorneycroft charges forward with a handful of his men, shouting at Opperman, *"I'm commander here; take your men back to hell, sir; there's no surrender!"*[59]

At 15:00 the arrival of Coke's reinforcements below the southern crest pushes more men into the congested killing field, but does not improve the position on the summit. There are soon 2 000 on the summit, where there is barely cover for 1 000. From below the rear crest, without a full assessment of the situation, he sends a message back to Warren, reading, *"We appear to be holding our own at present."*

In fact, all their efforts to push the burghers from the north and north-east crest fail. The withering rifle fire from Aloe Knoll stops any advance on the eastern summit and at about 16:00 the battle is static, with the British taking severe punishment and accurate Republican shells landing on their congested positions at a rate of seven to ten

*Gen. Schalk Burger* (National Cultural History Museum)		shells per minute, interspersed with almost continuous strings of pom-pom shells. On the extreme right, the Republican position on Twin Peaks is lightly held as most of the burgers have left to join the attack on Spioenkop. Lyttleton's attack is very successful and troops under Major Bewicke-Copley force the Republicans to retreat and remove their two field-guns. Politician/General Schalk Burger and Free State General AP Cronje are desperate for reinforcements, when Buller and Warren come to their aid. *"Snatching defeat from the jaws of victory"*, they mistake the fleeing burghers for their own troops and order the guns to stop their bombardment and, to his disgust, Bewicke-Copley's force is recalled. As the afternoon drags on, the British try the one bayonet charge after the other, only to be repulsed repeatedly, unable to dislodge the desperate burghers. As darkness falls, the limit of human endurance is reached — on both sides. At 18:00, Coke signals Warren, *"The situation is extremely critical... Please give orders and should you wish me to withdraw, cover retirement..."* Thorneycroft also reports, *"... if casualties go on at the present rate I shall barely hold out the night... The situation is critical."* Warren's reaction to this is to order Coke, limping with a leg injury, to report to him at Three Trees Hill. At about 19:30 Thorneycroft summons his senior officers to discuss the situation. He decides, *"Better six battalions safely off the hill than a mop up in the morning,"* and at 20:15, he gives the order to withdraw.[60] On the Republican side the burghers are also at their limit and start to drift down the mountain looking for food and water. Schalk Burger's commando strikes camp and moves off to Ladysmith. Even the brave men from Carolina and Pretoria saddle up and prepare to go home, convinced that the hill and thus the line on the upper Tugela is lost. Botha rides up and down the line beseeching his men not to desert.[61]
	Western front	**Kimberley siege:** Kimberley is subjected to a heavy bombardment that lasts, virtually without a break, for forty-eight hours. General Liebenberg leaves General PA Cronje's Magersfontein position with 130 men, two field-guns and a machine gun to occupy Prieska and to recruit rebels. [62]
Day 107 Thu **1900-01-25** *Field-cornet (later Gen.) JCG Kemp* (War Museum of the Boer Republics)	Natal front	**BATTLE OF SPIOENKOP** Before dawn Field-cornet JCG Kemp and a few burghers carefully scout the summit of Spioenkop, and to their surprise find only the wounded, the dead and seven hopelessly lost soldiers, whom they immediately capture. Waving their rifles and hats, they draw the attention of the men waiting at the foot. The jubilant burghers immediately rush up the slope to take possession of the hill, claiming one of the biggest victories of the war.[63] The casualties are high. Concentrated on what is to be called 'the acre of massacre', the carnage and the suffering of the wounded are overwhelming. The British lose about 225 killed, 122 missing, presumed dead, 550 wounded and 178 taken prisoner, a total of at least 1 075. The Republicans lose 58 killed and 140 wounded. The Carolina commando as a unit suffers one of the highest casualty rates of the war, suffering 55 killed and wounded out of the 85 men that participated, and 'Rooi' Daniel Opperman's Pretorians lose 16 killed and 20 wounded. All efforts by senior officers to convince Buller to reoccupy Spioenkop fail. Despite all their pleas he bluntly says, *"No! I have got the key to the position. We are going back."*[64] General Buller immediately orders the withdrawal of his forces across the Tugela, earning him the title of the *"Tugela ferryman"*.
Day 108 Fri **1900-01-26**	Western front	**Kimberley siege:** The military authorities in Kimberley start purchasing horses and mules for slaughtering purposes to supplement the diet of the besieged.[65]
	Central front	Major-General Brabant arrives in Queenstown to take command of the Colonial Division. General Kelly-Kenny, commanding the Sixth Division, occupies Teebus Station between Stormberg and Middelburg.[66]

89

Day 109 Sat **1900-01-27**	Natal front	Sir Redvers Buller completes the withdrawal of his forces across the Tugela and camps on Hattingh's Farm between Potgieter's and Trichardt's Drifts.[67]
	Cape Colony	Colonel Alderson reoccupies Prieska.
	Trivia	*Kaizer William II's 41th birthday.*
Day 110 Sun **1900-01-28**	Natal front	General Louis Botha departs from Modderspruit Station for a well-earned furlough with his family in Pretoria. He leaves General Schalk Burger in command on the upper Tugela.[68]
	Cape Colony	General French, recalled from the central front, arrives in Cape Town to confer with Lord Roberts.
Day 111 Mon **1900-01-29**	Western front	**Kimberley siege:** Colonel Kekewich has a serious meeting with the leading merchants in Kimberley. He meets a measure of resentment about rationing and he reports to Lord Roberts, *"Trust you will realise... not further possible to reduce rations."*[69]
Day 112 Tue **1900-01-30**	OFS	The Creusot 'Long Tom' 155mm fortress gun, damaged during the successful British raid on Gun Hill outside Ladysmith, arrives at Brandfort Station. After the December incident, this gun has been taken to Johannesburg where it has been repaired in the railway workshops under the supervision of the French engineer, Leon. Besides the manufacture of a breech-block, the repairs have entailed the cutting off of a section of the muzzle — earning the gun the obvious nickname 'the Jew'. Maybe slightly wary of the modifications, Commandant-General Joubert permits it to be sent to Cronje who has been wailing for a bigger gun since the first appearance of 'Long Cecil'.[70]
	Natal front	Addressing his burghers, Commandant-General Joubert says: *"Let the enemy rob and loot, as do barbarians, but refrain you from soiling your hands. It cannot carry God's approval, and He may withdraw His protecting hand from us. Struggle as Christians..."*[71]
	United Kingdom	The British Houses of Parliament assemble. The Opposition tables a motion of no confidence attacking the Government for *"the want of knowledge, foresight and judgement displayed by Her Majesty's Ministers".*[72]
	Trivia	*OFS independence day (Bloemfontein Convention 1854).*
Day 113 Wed **1900-01-31**	Natal front	On receiving the news of Buller's reverse, morale in Ladysmith reaches a low with a record 2 094 soldiers in hospital.[73]
	Western front	'The Jew', harnessed to double spans of oxen, leaves Brandfort for Kanfersdam, near Kimberley. At drifts up to 64 oxen have to be inspanned to move the heavy gun to its new destination.[74]
		After advocating his plan to destroy railway lines and communications behind enemy lines since soon after the Battle of Magersfontein, Republican Scout Koos Jooste finally obtains permission to proceed. During the previous six weeks he has been lobbying support from various people and travels from Magersfontein to Pretoria, Bloemfontein, Colesberg and back, only to find that Cronje has decided to send Liebenberg and that the objective has changed to a recruiting drive in the northern Cape.[75]
	United Kingdom	Future Labour MP Keir Hardie says: *"You cannot build up an Empire of free peoples by force."*[76]
	Trivia	*BD Bouwer's 25th birthday.*

1900	SUMMER	FEBRUARY
Day 114 Thu 1900-02-01	Cape Colony	The City of London Imperial Volunteers land in Cape Town.[77]
Day 115 Fri 1900-02-02	Natal front	General Schalk Burger is too sick to mount a horse and remains in his laager, unable to inspect his extended positions along the river.[78]
	International	Theodore Roosevelt writes to his sister: *"The trouble with the war is not that both sides are wrong, but that from their different standpoints both sides are right."*[79]
Day 116 Sat 1900-02-03	OFS	A joint dispatch addressed to Lord Roberts from Presidents Kruger and Steyn at Bloemfontein states, *"We learn from many sides that the British troops, contrary to the recognised usages of war, have been guilty of destruction by burning and blowing up with dynamite farmhouses and devastating farms and goods therein, whereby unprotected women and children have often been deprived of food and shelter. This happens not only in places where barbarians are encouraged by British officers, but even in Cape Colony and in this State where white brigands come out from the theatre of war with the evident intention of carrying on a general devastation without any reason recognised by the custom of war and without furthering the operations. We wish earnestly to protest against such practices."*[80]
	Natal front	**Ladysmith siege:** Without discussing it with either Prinsloo or Diamant, Commandant-General Piet Joubert places Roads Inspector PJ Malan in command of the dam-building project. [81]
	Western front	Scout Koos Jooste, Andries de Wet and their black grooms leave Magersfontein camp, trying to catch up with General Liebenberg's expedition to the northern Cape Colony. [82] General Hector MacDonald and the Highland Brigade leave Modder River for Koedoesberg Drift in a diversionary action and to isolate Liebenberg's force. The small picket of 15 burghers quickly retires at the approach of MacDonald's Highland Brigade, accompanied by two squadrons of lancers, a field battery and a company of Engineers.[83]
	Trivia	*Lord RATG Cecil Salisbury's 70th birthday.*
Day 117 Sun 1900-02-04	Natal front	General Tobias Smuts is convinced that the next British assault will be in the Kranskloof–Vaalkrantz sector, but he is unable to obtain reinforcements from either General Schalk Burger or General Lucas Meyer. [84] In desperation Presidents Steyn and Kruger propose the appointment of Free State Chief Commandant M Prinsloo as commander on the Tugela in Botha's absence. General Louis Botha leaves Pretoria on board a special train to reassume command and stop the feuding amongst the Republican generals. [85]

BULLER'S THIRD ATTEMPT

Buller's force consists of the following:

Headquarters staff : 266 men with 123 horses.

Naval brigade : 213 men with six horses and ten naval guns.

Artillery : Two brigade divisions of 1 879 men with 1 535 horses and 56 field-guns.

Infantry : Five brigades of 18 143 men with 908 horses and 16 machine guns.

Mounted troops : Two brigades of 2 753 men with 2 798 horses, six guns and three machine guns.

Engineers and support troops :

1 350 men with 1 148 horses.

Total : 24 220 men, 6 518 horses, 72 field-guns and 19 machine guns.

Gen. Tobias Smuts
(National Cultural History Museum)

		The Republican forces facing Buller consist of about 3 600 men spread over about 30 kilometres with ten field-guns and three pom-poms.[86]
	Western front	General CR de Wet, newly appointed commander of the Free State forces on the Western front, immediately sends Acting Commandant Du Plooy with 100 men to investigate MacDonald's movements. General Piet Cronje is convinced that the British are trying to draw his attention west, weaken his force, and then force his Magersfontein position. He orders De Wet to secure his right flank and dispel MacDonald's force, but cannot spare him more than 300 men. On arrival, Du Plooy notices lancers on Koedoesberg and prepares to attack them the following day.[87]
	United Kingdom	Mr J Chamberlain speaks in the House of Commons. He defends the Government's policies (*"we have been too anxious for peace"*), frankly admitting that mistakes have been made in practice. He promises that these will be rectified, pointing out that the combined effort of the Empire is *"advancing... to the realization of that great federation of our race which will inevitably make for peace and liberty and justice"*. The Queen sends him a personal note of congratulations on his fine speech. [88]
Day 118 Mon **1900-02-05**	Natal front	General Louis Botha meets one of his grooms, Yoni or Mpepa, at Elandslaagte and proceeds to Ben Viljoen's laager north of Meul Drift, in the Vaalkrantz sector. [89] **THE BATTLE OF VAALKRANTZ** Sir Redvers Buller's huge force comes into motion at 06:00, starting a diversionary action in the direction of Potgieter's Drift. Seven artillery batteries (42 guns) are unlimbered and drawn up in an almost straight line facing the Rooikoppies on the northern bank of the river. At about 07:00 a single shot from the 4,7 inch naval gun on Mount Alice signals the start of a terrible bombardment of the Free Staters on the Brakfontein Heights. Predictably, the Free Staters do not return fire, but they are pinned down in their trenches and do not notice as Buller repositions some batteries to cover the building of three pontoon bridges. The 11th Brigade who have crossed near Potgieter's Drift demonstrates northwards against the Brakfontein Heights until the Republican Krupps and a pom-pom come into action. At this, the troops take cover, their first purpose having been achieved. The British artillery systematically redeploy eastwards and they shift their aim to Vaalkrantz. At noon the third pontoon bridge downstream of Meul Drift, to the east of Vaalkrantz, is completed and the main force under Lyttleton moves there, while the bombardment of the heights intensifies. The diversionary force also withdraws eastwards, crosses to the right bank over the middle pontoon bridge and fans out against the Vaalkrantz Heights. Another diversionary demonstration in the direction of Colenso is so transparent that it does not prevent General Meyer from transferring burghers to General Tobias Smuts' sector. Vaalkrantz is occupied by only about 95 burghers, including Viljoen's Johannesburgers, who have to prove their worth after being accused of prematurely retiring at Elandslaagte. They valiantly hold out, maintaining a severe small arms and pom-pom fire on the sappers building the pontoon bridge and repulsing several attacks, despite the shelling from 72 British field-guns. Only at 14:00, after a bombardment lasting more than five hours, does Lyttleton's division succeed in breaking out over the river bank and they reach the dead ground at the foot of the hill after a series of short rushes. Supported by two of Hildyard's battalions, Lyttleton's troops rush up the slope and Viljoen, who is almost killed by a shell bursting almost on top of him, orders a retirement to Groenkop in their rear. Just after 16:00, cheering British appears on the crest of Vaalkrantz, capturing a small rearguard of five burghers and several armed blacks whom they immediately deal with — *"To these no quarter was given."* Subjected to accurate long-range rifle fire, however, the British are unable to exploit their victory and must seek cover behind the south-western ridges, where they prepare to spend the night. The night attack expected by the Commandant-General does not materialise, and he is able to reinforce Smuts and Viljoen with almost 1 000 men and to bring a Long Tom on Doringkop to bear on the British on Vaalkrantz. [90]

Gen.Ben Viljoen
(National Cultural History Museum)

		Ladysmith siege: The dam-building project is seriously jeopardised by a 'power struggle' between Prinsloo, Diamant and Malan. They argue and haggle about the overall command on the site, the responsibility for materials, the wages of the black workers, etc. After both Presidents have been involved, Prinsloo insists on written orders and Diamant leaves in protest. [91]
	Western front	**THE ACTION AT KOEDOESBERG** At dawn Du Plooy immediately attacks the lancers MacDonald has posted on Koedoesberg and succeeds in chasing them off the summit. MacDonald reinforces them with sappers and Du Plooy soon is in a life-and-death struggle against superior forces. General De Wet immediately comes to Du Plooy's aid on Koedoesberg. Leaving their horses at the foot, they split in three sections and climb the hill from three sides. The battle becomes static at the stone wall the sappers have built across the summit and both sides hold out until dark. In complete silence General De Wet evacuates his burghers after dark [92] Lord Roberts answers repeated complaints about his conduct of the war: *"The most stringent instructions have been issued to the British troops to respect private property, as far as it is compatible with the conduct of military operations. All wanton destruction or injury to peaceful inhabitants is contrary to British practice and tradition, and will if necessary be rigorously repressed by me."* He also objects to instances where loyal British subjects have been expelled from areas under Republican control for refusing to obey commandeering orders. He says, *"It is barbarous to attempt to force men to take sides against their own Sovereign and country by threats of spoilation and expulsion."* [93]
	United Kingdom	In the House of Commons, David Lloyd George states that the real blunder has not been made by the government, the War Office or the generals, but by Chamberlain alone for starting the war: A war entirely for the benefit of the Rand mine-owners who will be taxed less by a British government and thus be enabled to exploit labour more cheaply. *"It is simply — £. s. d."* The vote of no confidence is defeated by 352 to 139 votes. [94]
Day 119 Tue **1900-02-06**	Natal front	**THE BATTLE OF VAALKRANTZ** At daybreak the British are unpleasantly surprised when the Republican artillery, positioned in an arc around Vaalkrantz, open up on their half-completed entrenchments on the southern part of the hill. The forward troops as well as the reserves are severely shelled, and all efforts to silence the nine enemy field-guns and pom-poms, soon joined by Long Tom, fail. General Louis Botha, arriving back after his visit to Pretoria, quickly assesses the situation and, realising that Vaalkrantz is the centre of Buller's offensive, gathers burghers from all over the Tugela line and plans to recapture the British positions. Botha's countermeasures and the sustained Republican shelling and long-range rifle fire completely stop all forward movement by the British. At about 15:00 a group of burghers approach the British position under cover of smoke from a veld fire, started by the shelling. When they suddenly open fire, the Durham Light Infantry abandons its part of the hill and flee. Only the timely charge by the King's Royal Rifles forces the outnumbered burghers to retire and prevents the loss of a key position. Reporting to Lord Roberts, Buller vacillates, *"This operation will cost from 2 000 to 3 000 men, and I am hopeful but not confident of success. Do you think the chance of relieving Ladysmith worth the risk, and how would such a loss affect your plans?"* Roberts replies: *"Ladysmith must be relieved even at the loss you expect... Let troops know that in their hands is the honour of the Empire, and that of their success I have no possible doubt."* With the initiative lost and his troops subjected to continuous demoralizing shelling, however, Buller can only spend the rest of the day improving their positions

Field-Marshal Lord Roberts
(War Museum of the Boer Republics)

	Western front	on the slopes of Vaalkrantz. [95] **The Kimberley siege:** The Creusot 'Long Tom' known as 'the Jew,' arrives at Kimberley and work on its gun emplacement starts immediately. [96] At Koedoesberg De Wet again attacks the British position at the stone wall — this time with his burghers very widely dispersed and moving from rock to rock, exploiting every available cover. They come within 350 metres of the enemy, but De Wet realises that his men will not be able to execute a successful charge, and the battle again reaches a stalemate that lasts until dark. Just before dusk Commandant Andries Cronje arrives with a Krupp gun commanded by Major Albrecht of the Free State artillery. [97]
	Central front	Major-General RAP Clements takes over French's command in the Colesberg sector.
	Cape Colony	Field-Marshal Lord Roberts and Lord Kitchener leave Cape Town in secret for Modder River. A heavily guarded special train with their staff is sent ahead as a decoy, while they board the scheduled night mail train. [98]
Day 120 Wed **1900-02-07**	Natal front	**THE BATTLE OF VAALKRANTZ** The position on the north bank is virtually unchanged. Despite expending almost 10 000 shells the previous day, Buller is despondent when the Republican field-guns open with renewed vigour. All predictions by his officers foresee heavy casualties if the assault is resumed. Unknown to him, the Republicans are wavering under the demoralising effect of the heavy British bombardment and some officers urge the Commandant-General to start the preparation of positions to fall back on. Buller's resolve, however, cracks first and after a meeting at 16:00, he decides to withdraw. The order to evacuate is given at about 19:00 and at midnight the pontoon bridges are removed and there are no British troops left on the opposite bank of the Tugela. [99] Since crossing the river on 5 February, Buller has lost 25 killed, 344 wounded and five missing. The Republicans suffer a total of 38 killed, 45 wounded and four missing. The Johannesburg commando bears the brunt, suffering 30 killed, 23 wounded (including Commandant BJ Viljoen, who is concussed) and four missing. [100]
	Western front	**The Kimberley siege:** 'The Jew' shells Kimberley for the first time and serious damage is reported. The modifications have not seriously affected the gun's performance and 'Long Cecil' is again outranged. [101] **THE ACTION AT KOEDOESBERG** While De Wet occupies the defenders' attention, Major Albrecht completes the emplacement of his gun without being seen. He opens up at about 10:00, and with his third shot, he knocks a breach in the stone wall and torments the British with shrapnel fire. MacDonald's gunners engage Albrecht's lone field-gun with two, and later four, Armstrong guns, but are unable to silence him — in fact, they are forced to withdraw behind the mountain. On the summit De Wet, enjoying the lull in the shelling, seriously threatens the British position, forcing MacDonald to send more and more reinforcements up the hill. Even with about 2 000 troops engaged, the British are hard pressed and MacDonald requests help from Lord Methuen, who immediately dispatches Major-General Babington with an entire mounted brigade with two artillery batteries. De Wet spots their approach and acts fast. A small group of burghers open a furious fusillade on the leading cavalry. Reluctant to chance a night battle with De Wet's men, the British delay their plan to surround the burghers on the hill until the next day. [102]
	Gen. CR de Wet *(War Museum of the Boer Republics)*	
	Trivia	*Sir C Warren's 60th birthday.*

Day 121 Thu **1900-02-08**	Natal front	The Republicans reoccupy Vaalkrantz, but do not attempt to harass the retreating British force.
	Western front	Field-Marshal Lord Roberts reaches Modder River Station. **THE ACTION AT KOEDOESPOORT** Babington completes the envelopment of the hill, only to find that the burghers have abandoned their positions during the night. The Republicans, now reinforced to almost 1 000 men with two Krupps, have taken position on low ridges to the north, forcing a checkmate situation. During the previous few days the British have lost six killed and 47 wounded, while De Wet has suffered three killed and 14 wounded. Lord Roberts recalls MacDonald and Babington to Modder River in preparation for his planned offensive, but General Cronje is convinced that he has won a great victory.[103]
	Black involvement	**Kimberley siege:** Colonel Kekewich reports a 'serious situation' in Kimberley. **Mafeking siege:** Colonel Baden-Powell prohibits the sale of rations to blacks not needed for military duties. This happens after most of the trenches and fortifications around Mafeking have been completed.[104]
Day 122 Fri **1900-02-09**	Western front	**Kimberley siege:** Colonel Kekewich bans a public meeting planned by Cecil Rhodes to protest the delays and perceived inactivity of forces supposed to be relieving Kimberley. As most of the inhabitants are De Beers employees and almost half are Afrikaners, Kekewich judges Rhodes' meeting as dangerous. Informed of the ban, Rhodes is furious: *"Before Kimberley surrenders I will take good care that the English people shall know what I think about this!"*[105] George Labram, designer of 'Long Cecil', is killed in his room at the Grand Hotel in Kimberley, by the last round of the day fired by 'the Jew'.[106]
	Trivia	*General RAP Clements' 45th birthday.* *Dr LS Jameson's 47th birthday.* *Dwight Davis launches the Davis Tennis Cup Competition.*
Day 123 Sat **1900-02-10**	Natal front	The siege of Ladysmith enters its hundredth day and the first hundred cavalry horses are selected for slaughter. [107] A branch railway line to transport materials to the dam site on the Klip River is completed.[108] General Buller and his main army retreat to Chieveley.
	Western front	**Kimberley siege:** To the disgust of the people of Kimberley, 'the Jew' opens fire during Labram's funeral. It is, however, unlikely that this is on purpose. [109] An editorial in *The Diamond Fields Advertiser*, owned by Rhodes, titled *"Why Kimberley cannot wait"*, thunders, *"How utterly the public and military authorities have failed to grasp the claim which Kimberley, by the heroic exertions of its citizens, has established on the British Empire... We have stood a siege that is rapidly approaching the duration of the siege of Paris... Is it unreasonable, when our women and children are being slaughtered, and our buildings fired, to expect something better than that a large British army should remain inactive in the presence of eight or ten thousand peasants?"* When Kekewich attempts to arrest the editor, he discovers that Rhodes has hidden him in one of the mines. Rhodes also insists that a petition drafted at an illegal meeting attended by twelve of the leading citizens, be transmitted to Roberts. Kekewich offers to transmit a precis and Rhodes explodes, *"I know what damned rot your signallers are wasting their time in signalling. You low, damned, mean cur, Kekewich, you deny me at your peril!"* He storms out and promptly reads the top-secret cable, announcing the imminent start of Roberts' march, aloud to passers-by from the steps of the Kimberley Club.[110]

Day 124 Sun **1900-02-11**	Western front	**Kimberley siege:** Panic grips Kimberley and there is a frantic effort to complete the building of new bomb-proof shelters before 'Long Tom' (and the numerous new Republican guns falsely rumoured to be arriving) opens up on Monday. Mr Rhodes, without bothering to inform Kekewich, adds to the panic by offering De Beers' facilities and recommending that women and children be lowered down the mines for complete shelter.[111] At the same time he starts preparations for a victory banquet.

START OF THE SECOND BRITISH OFFENSIVE
LORD ROBERTS' GREAT FLANK MARCH BEGINS
The British force, concentrated at Modder River and Graspan, consists of the following:

Commander-in-Chief	:	Field Marshall Lord Roberts VC, KP.
Chief of Staff	:	Major-General Lord Kitchener.
Mounted troops	:	One combined division, commanded by Lieutenant-General French, consisting of — Three cavalry brigades, commanded by Porter, Broadwood and Gordon; and One division mounted infantry, commanded by Hutton.
Totalling	13 294 men with 42 field-guns and about 28 machine guns.	
Infantry	:	Four infantry divisions, as follows:
	:	1st Division, commanded by Lieutenant-General Lord Methuen, consisting of — Two infantry brigades, commanded by Pole-Carew and Douglas.
	:	6th Division, commanded by Lieutenant-General Kelly-Kenny, consisting of — Two infantry brigades, commanded by Knox and Stephenson.
	:	7th Division, commanded by Lieutenant-General Tucker, consisting of — Two infantry brigades, commanded by Chermside and Wavell.
	:	9th Division, commanded by Lieutenant-General Colvile, consisting of — Two infantry brigades, commanded by MacDonald and Smith-Dorrien.
Totalling	27 820 men with 66 field-guns and 33 machine guns.	

Headquarters staff, engineers, divisional staff, medical staff and miscellaneous support troops

Totalling	4 452 men with two field-guns.	
Convoy columns	:	1 134 mule wagons with about 11 000 mules.
	:	600 ox-wagons with about 9 600 oxen, handled by 4 020 convoy drivers.

A **grand total** of 49 586 men with 110 field-guns, about 61 machine guns, about 16 000 horses, about 1 735 vehicles and about 12 000 other draught animals.[112]

Early in the morning the enormous force comes into motion from Methuen's camp at Modder River and from Graspan. They head back to Enslin, cross the Free State border and head for their first resting place at the water-rich Ramdam Farm.[113]

Day 125 Mon **1900-02-12**	Natal front	**Ladysmith siege:** Inspector of Works Malan, in charge of the dam-building project, realises that the dam wall has to have a length of 40 metres long at the bottom and 100 to 140 metres on top and that 160 000 sandbags would be needed and not 30 000 as he originally calculated.[114] Lord Dundonald's cavalry attack Hussar Hill, about six kilometres south of Hlangwane on the south bank of the Tugela, with 700 men, the Welsh Fusiliers, supported by a field battery artillery and some machine guns. The 50 odd

		burghers on the hill retire after a token resistance and the British take the position, only to abandon it at about 13:00. During their retirement, burghers on adjoining features open fierce long-range rifle fire and the British are forced to bring their artillery into action. The burghers lose one killed and five wounded, while the British lose 12 wounded.[115]
	Western front	A party of 150 Fauresmith burghers under Commandant Jacobs, gallantly defend their position at Wolwekraal, west of Orange River Station, against a part of Roberts' overwhelming force and retire without loss after administering 40 casualties to Hannay's mounted infantry.[116] The march itself takes its toll and 21 British soldiers die of sunstroke. General French orders a demonstration against Waterval's Drift and occupies De Kiel's Drift on the Riet River and the heights on both banks.[117] The Austrian Foreign Volunteer, Count Sternberg, after a personal reconnaissance on Cronje's left flank, informs him of French's crossing of the Riet River and advises him to occupy the Modder River crossings as soon as possible. Cronje is convinced that is only a diversionary action, and that Roberts will attempt a frontal attack on his Magersfontein position. He refuses to believe that the cavalry can be a serious threat or that it is the vanguard of a huge force. He orders General CR de Wet with 450 men and two field-guns to prevent the enemy from crossing the Riet River.[118] **Kimberley siege:** Captain Leon, the French engineer who has accompanied the repaired 'Long Tom' to Kimberley, is wounded. The bullet lodges in his brain.[119]
	Central front	**THE ASSAULT ON KEEROMSKOP** While Commandant Van Dam with about 100 men, including a group of ZAR Police, leads an assault against the Worcester Regiment dug in on Keeromskop, two flanking groups of 100 and 75 men are sent to cut off the British retreat. Accurate shelling forces the Worcesters to abandon their positions. A spirited counter-attack is repulsed and they have to withdraw. British casualties amount to 37 killed, 81 wounded and 19 captured. The Republicans captures a machine gun, but lose eight killed and 19 wounded.[120]
	Northern front	Colonel Plumer makes an unsuccessful attack near Crocodile Pools, south of Gaberones.
Day 126 Tue **1900-02-13**	Black involvement	General Buller reports that, contrary to prisoners' statements that blacks are only used as 'after-riders', several officers have seen blacks firing on British troops.[121] General French's mounted troops start from De Kiel's Drift, moving forward on an eight-kilometre-wide front and closely followed by the Horse Artillery's 42 field-guns.[122] General De Wet is misled by the sheer size of Roberts' force. He mistakes a flanking movement by a mounted brigade at Watervalsdrift as the main assault and moves eastwards with 450 men to defend Koffiefontein, which he presumes to be the objective. He occupies positions at Wintershoek and is reinforced by about 750 men.[123] General French occupies Klip Drift on the Modder River. Showing remarkable military insight, President Kruger telegraphs Cronje from Pretoria, warning him not to cling to his Magersfontein position and to beware of British flanking movements.[124] Dr Dunlop of the Warrenton Hospital operates on the French engineer Leon and remarkably the patient makes a full recovery, also regaining sight in his left eye.[125]
	Central front	Republicans capture the abandoned British camp at Slingersfontein left intact as a ruse to allow the retreating troops a head start. About 70 tents and other supplies, including rifles and ammunition, are taken.[126]

		General Clements, his forces seriously weakened as units are diverted as part of Lord Roberts' build-up on the Modder River, abandons Colesberg and retires to Arundel Siding.[127]
Day 127 Wed **1900-02-14**	Western front	Reports reaching General Cronje at Magersfontein, warns that 4 000 to 5 000 British troops have entered the Orange Free State. Actually, the invasion force totals between 40 000 and 50 000.[128] **Kimberley siege:** Receiving information from black scouts that the Free Staters have left Alexanderfontein, Major Fraser with about 100 men of the Beaconfield Town Guard occupies their abandoned positions. Efforts by Generals Du Toit and Kolbe to dislodge him fail as reinforcements arrive.[129]
	Natal front	General Buller starts his fourth attempt to relieve Ladysmith. The first objective is Hussar Hill, abandoned by Dundonald two days ago. The attacking force consists of Warren's division on the left, Lyttelton's division on the right with Lord Dundonald's cavalry in the lead. The burghers' three field-guns are soon silenced and at 08:30 Dundonald takes the hill, virtually without opposition. Leaving the 5th Division to occupy the hill and a line to the west, the mounted troops move east along the Bloukrans River, with Lyttelton's 2nd Division following — extending the line towards Moord Drift. [130]
	Central front	Two companies of the Wiltshire Regiment are cut off during Clements' retreat to Arundel. After a brisk skirmish they surrender, losing 13 killed and 138 captured, including 45 wounded, against two Republicans killed and four wounded. [131]
Day 128 Thu **1900-02-15**	Western front	**GENERAL FRENCH'S BREAKTHROUGH** North of Klip Drift, at Roodekalkfontein, about 800 burghers with two field-guns sent by Cronje to stop General French's cavalry, are in an excellent position on heights overlooking his route. The 9th Lancers run into a fierce crossfire and French orders five of his seven batteries to unlimber and come into action — 18 field-guns on his left flank concentrating on Albrecht's pair and the rest against the burghers' on the heights. Although Albrecht's shells account for 24 casualties and about 36 artillery horses, the British might is overwhelming and the burghers resolve starts to waver. French, rather than clearing the opposition, orders a charge. In one of history's last great cavalry charges, the dust stirred up by the thundering hooves of 6 000 horses blinds the defenders who flee in terror. The breakthrough costs the British only about 40 casualties, while about 35 burghers, are killed while trying to surrender to the charging cavalry — a fatal attempt. [132] **KIMBERLEY IS RELIEVED** After 123 days the siege is finally lifted as 'the Jew' fires its last shell at about noon and advance parties of French's force enter the town at about 16:00. Despite the numerous attacks and sorties and the 5 800 shells fired at the town, Kimberley has suffered only 134 casualties among the armed defenders and 21 civilian casualties. However, some 1 500 people, mostly Coloureds and blacks, have died of famine and disease and the infant mortality rate during the four months of the siege has risen to 67,1% among whites and 91,2 % among Coloureds and blacks.[133] The efforts to liberate Kimberley cost the British at least 2 237 men of the relieving force.[134] Kekewich's efforts to capture the 'Long Tom' fails. On entering Kimberley, General French is directed to Rhodes at the Sanatorium Hotel where Colonel Kekewich, eventually finds him. Rhodes tries to retain centre stage by shouting at Kekewich, *"You shan't see French; this is my house, get out of it!"* [135]

		Lord Roberts' supply column cannot keep up with the infantry and is ordered to stay at Waterval Drift, near Bloubank, and to follow the main force as soon as the oxen have recovered sufficiently. General Kelly-Kenny details about 500 troops to escort the convoy which stretches more than 10 to 12 kilometres. As soon as the main force is out of sight, General De Wet attacks. His long-range shelling and rifle fire causes the draught animals to stampede and the escort commander realises that there is now no way of preventing the wagons from falling into enemy hands. He retreats, abandoning the convoy. De Wet takes 180 loaded wagons, about 2 800 oxen, a few horses and an enormous supply of food, as well as 58 prisoners. The loss of four days' precious rations and almost a third of all the oxen brought together for the advance, can jeopardize a massive operation in an inhospitable country, but Roberts is unfazed.[136] After a skirmish south of Jacobsdal, Major-General AG Wavell, commanding the 15th brigade of the Seventh Division, enters the first Free State town to fall into British hands. [137] General Cronje moves his encampment to Bossiespan, about six kilometres upstream from his eastern emplacements at Brown's Drift.[138] That evening a council of war decides not to take the safer route northwards and around Kimberley on the west, but rather to move eastwards, along the right bank of the Modder River. Cronje plans to place his force between Roberts and Bloemfontein, which he now believes to be the British objective.[139]
	Natal front	At dawn Sir Redvers Buller's artillery, comprising 72 field-guns stationed on Gun Hill, next to the railway line, and the newly occupied Hussar Hill, open up. They keep up a sustained, slow, day-long barrage on Green Hill, Monte Cristo, Cingolo, Hlangwane and suspected enemy positions in between.[140]
	Cape Colony	In Cape Town, news of the relief of Kimberley is celebrated by the proclamation of a holiday.
Day 129 Fri **1900-02-16**	Western front	At last General Cronje evacuates his Magersfontein positions, leaving behind about 78 wagons, his field hospital and a few pitched tents. He decides against leaving the women and children visiting their relatives in the laager, to the mercy of the enemy. Some depart along the safer northern route, but about 62, including Mrs Cronje, remain with his force.[141] Despite bright moonlight, his eight-kilometre-long train comprising 400 ox-wagons and other vehicles pass unseen within a few kilometres of General Kelly-Kenny's 6th Division.[142] At daybreak, when the British artillery opens fire on Bossiespan, a Red Cross official approaches with the news that they are shelling the undefended hospital. The British set off in pursuit and at about 08:00, they engage Cronje's rearguard with three guns near Klip Drift. A running battle develops and Kitchener desperately needs to delay Cronje so that he can concentrate his widely dispersed forces. Colonel Hannay's Mounted Infantry run into fierce rifle fire from the determined rearguard at Roodekalkfontein. They execute a right hook attempting a flank attack, but Cronje swiftly brings a single gun and a pom-pom into action and he traps the Mounted Infantry between the high banks of the river. Caught in a kilometre section of the river, several horses are hit, several drown and Hannay has to fall back to regroup. The British have to continue their pursuit using their exhausted foot soldiers to sweep the burghers off their hill positions from Drieputs to Roodekalkfontein. They succeed, only to be stopped and thrown back by an unexpected counter-attack and spirited shelling. The tired British fall back to better positions where they dig in. Cronje does not cross the

		river at Klipkraal Drift and waits for darkness. The day's action costs the British 11 killed, 105 wounded and seven prisoners of war.[143] After a brief rest, Cronje resumes his march eastwards along the north bank, shedding some wagons and animals that cannot keep pace.[144]
		Lord Roberts realises that Cronje is outstripping his pursuers. At about 20:00 General French in Kimberley receives orders to attempt to cut him off.
		North of Kimberley Republican forces fight rearguard actions at Dronfield and Macfarlane against French's cavalry and some of Kekewich's defenders. The Republicans get clear away northwards with all their field-guns, including the 'Long Tom', on which Rhodes and the directors of De Beers have placed a reward of £1 000. The exhausted cavalry suffers 28 casualties and loses at least 68 horses.[145]
	Natal front	Major-General Lyttleton's eastward movement to Moordkraal forces the defenders under General Lucas Meyer to occupy Cingolo Hill.[146] The British bombardment resumes and continues for the entire day. A single shell scores a direct hit on a burgher trench, killing seven burghers and wounding seven more. Notably, Cingolo is not shelled and a probing demonstration is made to within two kilometres of its foot. [147]
	Cape Colony	In the north-western Cape Colony, rebels enthusiastically join General Liebenberg's force, swelling their ranks to more than 400. He sends Commandant Steenkamp and 75 men to accept the surrender of Prieska.[148]
Day 130 Sat **1900-02-17**	Western front	Just after midnight, General Cronje reaches Perdeberg's Drift, where he calls a halt. At about the same time French's dash to cut off the Republican retreat starts and Colonel Broadwood, with a mounted force of 1 557 men and 12 field-guns, move from Alexanderfontein, south of Kimberley.
		After a rest of four hours, some 200 Republican ox-wagons ford the river and make for Bloemfontein with a small mounted escort. Cronje scouts ahead, but he feels that he is too close to his pursuers to attempt crossing the river with the rest of his exhausted draught animals. He decides to move to Wolwekraal, where they arrive and unharnesses at about 08:00. His escape seems to be proceeding successfully and he plans to take up position at Koedoesrand where he can cover his crossing at Koedoes Drift. He has however, completely lost touch with his detached forces under Chief Commandant IS Ferreira to his north and De Wet's force near Pramberg to the south. Actually, these officers have not even been informed that Cronje has left Magersfontein — both are only to learn of his plight during the day.[149] Ferreira, trying to link up with Cronje, almost runs into French's cavalry and retires northwards. Cronje expecting no threat from the north, only has a few signallers in that direction, and at about 10:15 they are surprised and captured by French's scouts. French immediately grasps Cronje's vulnerable positions and moves his artillery into position. At the same time Hannay's pursuing Mounted Infantry make contact with Cronje's rearguard under Commandant Froneman. General Cronje sends reinforcements to his rear and orders his convoy to inspan and to cross the river at Vandisie Drift. His men, while rounding up the oxen, notice French's cavalry and Commandant Tollie de Beer is sent to occupy Koedoesrand, the heights commanding the whole position.
		Just after 11:00, as the leading wagons approach the ford, French's gunners open up with 12 guns and the shells falling around them start a panic among the drivers. Albrecht's artillery quickly return fire and Froneman also sends snipers to a position from where they can harass the gunners, while De Beer, who has gained Koedoesrand also brings his pom-pom into action against the cavalry. French's tired troops are seriously threatened as the afternoon wears on, but huge clouds

		of dust herald the approach of the infantry. As the sun sets, Cronje reassesses his position. During the last two days he has lost only eight killed and 12 wounded, but he has lost most of his draught animals. Despite the pleas of his officers, he flatly refuses to abandon his wagons, his wounded or the women and children, and orders the digging of trenches on the river bank. [150] On arrival at his office, Colonel Kekewich is surprised to find that he has been replaced as Garrison Commander of Kimberley by Colonel Porter, CO of the 1st Cavalry Brigade.[151]
	OFS	**LORD ROBERTS' FIRST PROCLAMATION** Lord Roberts issues his first proclamation to the citizens of the Orange Free State. He asserts that, had the Orange Free State remained neutral, the British government would have respected its independence. He accuses the OFS government of unnecessary aggression by invading the British Colonies and, as the British government wishes to preserve the *"inhabitants from the evils brought upon them by the wrongful actions of their Government"*, he warns all burghers *"to desist from any further hostility* and promises that all who do so *"and who are found staying in their homes and quietly pursuing their ordinary occupations, will not be made to suffer in their persons or property on account of their having taken up arms in obedience to the order of their Government"*.[152]
	Central front	Republican forces, consisting of mostly Cape rebels under Commandant Schoeman, launch simultaneous attacks against several British positions; the main attack is directed against Colonel Dalgety's camp at Bird's River Siding. The British are reinforced from Sterkstroom and later number more than 1 600. The burghers lose one killed and eight wounded against seven British killed and eight wounded.[153] The Colonial Division under Major-General Brabant occupies Dordrecht.
	Natal front	**THE TUGELA BATTLES: CINGOLO** Although the heavy two-day bombardment causes very few casualties, the Republican morale is severely tested. The arrival of General Louis Botha from the upper Tugela bolsters their resolve, but the reinforcements expected from that sector are late. At dawn the bombardment is resumed, now reinforced by naval guns positioned on Hussar Hill. Major-General Lyttleton's Division advances eastwards, forming a five-kilometre wide front. The 200 defenders on Cingolo are unnerved and any possibility of surprise is lost when they nervously open fire. Dundonald's cavalry is alerted and, although reinforced, the Republican position becomes untenable and they have to retreat. Lord Dundonald, supported by both Norcott and Hildyard's brigades, seizes the hill in the early afternoon, losing only four killed and 32 wounded against one burgher killed and eight wounded.[154]
	Cape Colony	Commandant BJ Schutte, marching south from Prieska with a small force comprising mostly Griqualand rebels, takes the post office at Omdraaivlei ('Turnaround Moor'), about 70 kilometres south-east of Prieska and 100 kilometres north-west of the important railway town of De Aar. The name of the place is prophetic because it indicates the deepest penetration into enemy territory during the first Republican invasion.[155]
	International	The third New Zealand contingent sails for South Africa.
Day 131 Sun **1900-02-18**	Western front	**THE BATTLE OF PAARDEBERG (DAY 1)** Lord Roberts is indisposed and remains in Jacobsdal, transferring command to Major-General Lord Kitchener, to the displeasure of Lieutenant-General Kelly-Kenny, the ranking general. Rather than completing the encirclement of the laager and preparing to shell Cronje into submission, Kitchener decides to attack at once. He does not consult with the Divisional Commanders, who all

Maj. Gen. Lord Kitchener
(War Museum of the Boer Republics)

outrank him, and his orders seem to be unco-ordinated and confused and to lack the enthusiastic support of the senior officers.

At 03:00 he orders Lieutenant-Colonel Hannay, whose troops have been considered to be too untrained to accompany French on his dash to Kimberley, but are now the only mounted troops at Kitchener's disposal, to thrust upstream along the river in preparation of an attack from the east. Hannay is to be supported by Stephenson's 18th Brigade consisting of the Welsh and Essex battalions. En route to capture a drift east of the laager from where he plans to launch his attack, Hannay wisely detaches about 400 men of Kitchener's Horse to occupy heights directly south of the laager called Oskoppies, later known as Kitchener's Koppie. At sunrise the British guns come into action and the bombardment sets fire to some of Cronje's wagons. A fierce rifle fire from invisible positions in the direction of the laager soon shows several British units that they have approached too close. At 07:00 the main frontal attack by Kenny-Kelly's 6th Division starts, supported by 38 field-guns. From the laager, Major Albrecht's five guns cannot prevent the British artillery from moving closer and taking positions on a small rise, called Signal Hill, south-west of the laager. The infantry, Knox's 13th Brigade (four regiments) and the Yorkshires attack, deployed in three lines following each other with about 300-metre intervals with the Highland Brigade on their left in a long single line. At 500 to 800 metres from the riverbank, intense Mauser fire stalls the attack and they cannot even approach close enough to threaten Cronje's excellent defences — a series of concealed trenches dug in the soft soil of the river bank. Some of the Highlanders succeed in crossing the river, only to be pinned down in front of a wide donga, which has been integrated as part of the defences.

At about 08:00, Kitchener also orders Colvile's 9th Division to cross the river at Paardeberg Drift and to attack the laager from the west. The crossing is delayed by the fast flowing river, and the assault along the north bank starts at about 10:15, only to run into the same accurate fire from the wide donga. They succeed in taking the unoccupied Gun Hill and immediately emplace two batteries in an excellent position to enfilade the donga and almost overlooking the laager. Lack of co-ordination between the various attacks, however, prevents exploitation of this advantage, and checkmate situations develop on both the southern and western sectors. Lord Kitchener rides all over the battlefield and issues instructions to junior officers, to the irritation of divisional and brigade commanders.

Hannay and Stephenson's mounted force is distracted by the presence of Tollie de Beer's men on Koedoesrand and they also become aware of part of General Ferreira's commando that has crossed Koedoes Drift to the south and was taking cover on the Bankkoppies, south-east of the laager. The burghers make out a very small force, but the gunners of the 81st battery are surprised when Commandant Steyn's two field-guns open fire from an unexpected quarter. The British have to swing their guns round to counter this threat and Kitchener orders Hannay and Stephenson to continue their planned eastern attack, expecting French to deal with burghers outside the trap. Hannay, who has crossed at Vanderberg Drift, runs into fierce fire and the foot soldiers accompanying him have to form a front towards the east, facing the burghers at his rear. Stephenson's attack also withers against the accurate long-range rifle fire from Cronje's burghers in the dongas and gullies. The Essex and Welsh regiments are forced to seek cover on the south bank and are increasingly subjected to crossfire as Steyn and Ferreira's force increases. [156]

Victoria Cross

Lieutenant FN Parsons, 44th Essex Regiment, earns a recommendation for the Victoria Cross as he tends to a wounded private lying in an exposed position, under heavy fire. Parsons twice crawls to the river to fetch water for the wounded man and eventually carries him to safety. [157]

HANNAY: A SOLDIER'S PROTEST

At about 13:30, after being in action for more than eight hours, Lieutenant-Colonel OC Hannay, commanding the Mounted Infantry on the north bank, informs Kitchener that his men, with little rest after twenty-four hours of continuous marching without food, are utterly exhausted and that any further advance is out of the question.

Kitchener, frustrated by the stubborn resistance and so desperate that *"no consideration of flesh and blood would deter him"* replies, *"The time has now come for a final effort... the laager must be rushed at all costs. Try and carry Stephenson with you, but if they cannot go, the MI should do it. Gallop up and fire into the laager."* Hannay, who receives this order at 15:00, realises that *"these were the words of a madman blinded by bloodlust"*. He is unwilling to sacrifice his men by passing on this suicidal but clear and direct order and *"resolves upon a soldier's protest"*. He sends his staff away on various pretexts and personally complies with his orders. A small group of his men follows him, but Hannay, far outstripping them, charges the laager at full tilt. The defenders hesitate, baffled at the mad charge of a lone and defenceless horseman but then open fire. Hannay falls, riddled with bullets, almost within their lines. (His lone grave is preserved where he fell.)[158]

Victoria Cross

Kitchener's 'final effort' order exacts a heavy toll from the attackers — a Welsh and Essex bayonet charge fails to come within effective range of the defenders and several brave charges on all sides are repulsed by the determined defenders. During a charge across more than 700 yards completely devoid of cover, the gallant conduct of Sergeant A Atkinson, 1st Battalion, the Yorkshire Regiment, is rewarded with a Victoria Cross. General De Wet has been moving from Pramberg towards Paardeberg ever since the previous day, on receiving Lubbe's reports of Cronje's situation. He is joined by General Philip Botha and drawn by the noise of battle they approach from the south- and climb the Oskoppies. About 60 members of Kitchener's Horse are captured and the rest are forced to flee down the northern slope. De Wet's arrival and forceful actions bring a new element to the battle: his field-guns rake the British artillery south-west of the laager, encouraging Albrecht's guns, silent since early morning, to join in from inside the laager. Several units of Knox's Brigade have to turn around and face De Wet. One charge after the other is launched and repulsed.

At about 17:00, the vanguard of the Third Cavalry Brigade, arriving from Kimberley, engages De Beer to the east of Koedoesrand. Threatened with encirclement, De Beer is forced to retreat to the south bank, across Koedoes Drift and to take up position on Steyn's right. This brigade's 12 field-guns increase the number of British guns to 50.

As daylight fails the fighting dies down, but no side can claim victory after the day's hard fighting.

Kitchener's resolute tactics and Cronje's determined defence cause the war's highest British casualties for a single day. They lose 303 killed (including Lieutenant-Colonels Hannay and Aldworth), 906 wounded (including Major-Generals Knox and Hector MacDonald and Lieutenant-Colonel Banfield) and 61 men taken prisoner — a total of 1 270 men including 85 officers.

The Republican casualties are remarkably light, namely 50 killed and wounded in Cronje's laager, and six killed and 14 wounded among De Wet, Ferreira and Steyn's commandos.[159]

Gen. De Wet
(War Museum of the Boer Republics)

The utter exhaustion of Cronje's defenders, the depth of Vandisie Drift, the limited number of horses and their condition make any attempt of escape during the night impossible.

Natal front

THE TUGELA BATTLES: MONTE CRISTO

Buller moves his artillery closer and he places field-guns on the slope of Cingolo. An infantry attack follows a fierce bombardment and the burghers again reveal their positions by opening fire prematurely. Major-General Lyttelton is able to concentrate vastly superior forces and to gain a foothold on Monte Cristo after a halfhearted defence. Hildyard's troops move along the western ridge, supported by Dundonald's

		mounted men on the eastern flank, pushing the burgers steadily northwards. When Republican guns on Green Hill suddenly shell the main attack on Monte Cristo, Lyttleton orders Norcott and Barton to neutralise this threat. They are soon able to take the small Green Hill as the defenders fall back to avoid being cut off. The burgher retreat is infectious and an anxious situation develops as fleeing burghers from all sections congregate on the riverbank, too demoralised to hold their positions. A burgher laager falls into British hands and artillery sweeps all the Republican positions on the right bank. Even a 'Long Tom' firing from the Colenso Heights is ineffective and is soon silenced. Caution, however, prevents Buller from exploiting the situation and chasing them across the river.[160]
	Northern front Black involvement	A burgher convoy is attacked by 1 500 Bagatla tribesmen near Derdepoort, killing two of the ten burghers escorting it.[161] One of the burghers killed, is the rescourceful Marthinus Ras, the blacksmith who designed and built a cannon which was used at the siege of Rustenburg during the First Boer War.[162]
Day 132 Mon **1900-02-19**	Western front	**THE BATTLE OF PAARDEBERG (DAY 2)** At daybreak, the British are delighted to see that Cronje has contracted his defensive perimeter during the night and now only occupies about 3 kilometres of the river. Kitchener is keen to resume his assault on the laager, but the senior officers demur vigorously, upset by the previous day's carnage, and they appeal to Roberts for a decision.[163] Lord Roberts, upset by the reports reaching him, leaves Jacobsdal at 04:00 and reaches Paardeberg at about 10:00. He is appalled by the casualties and decides to consolidate his encirclement of the laager and to bombard Cronje into submission. General Cronje requests a twenty-four-hour armistice to tend to his wounded and bury his dead. Lord Roberts declines and demands unconditional surrender. Cronje answers, "*Since you are so unmerciful as not to accord the time asked for, nothing remains for me to do; you do as you wish.*" This is translated as "*nothing remains for me but to do as you wish*", and mistaken for an offer to surrender. Cronje's second message clears up any possible misunderstanding: "*During my lifetime I will never surrender. If you wish to bombard, fire away. Dixi.*"[164] The bombardment is resumed and intensified as 24 field-guns and three naval guns are emplaced on Gun Hill, within easy range of the target, to augment the 18 other guns and four naval guns south of the river and French's horse artillery to the north. The Gloucesters, who have kept up a long-range rifle duel with De Wet's men on Kitchener's Koppie, attempt an attack, supported by 37 field-guns, in the late afternoon. Their force gain a foothold but is insufficient to make headway against the burghers who have been reinforced by small parties arriving throughout the day. General De Wet urges Cronje to attempt a breakout with his best men during the night. The Republicans suffer a severe loss when Chief Commandant IS Ferreira is accidentally shot by a sleeping picket while he is inspecting his sentries. General De Wet takes over command of all Free Staters on the western front.[165]
	Natal front	**THE TUGELA BATTLES: HLANGWANE** Rather than pushing resolutely ahead, General Buller decides to mop up all resistance on the right bank. He concentrates all his forces on the defenders south of the river and delays his assault on Hlangwane Hill until Monte Cristo is completely cleared. His artillery pounds Hlangwane and fights a long-range duel with a few Republican guns on the opposite bank before he orders Warren's 5th Division to attack. At about 11:00 Hlangwane, the key to the Tugela positions that blocked Buller since December, was finally in British hands. A near-general panic grips the defenders, forces the Republicans to abandon all their positions and they flee across the river. Clearing his side of the river costs Buller 25 killed, 276 wounded and four missing, while 15 burghers are killed and 71 wounded.[166]
	Central front	At Dordrecht, General WF Gatacre dislodges Commandant Schoeman, forces him to retire to Labuschagne's Nek and the British reoccupy the town.[167]

Chief Comdt. IS Ferreira
(National Cultural History Museum)

| Day 133 Tue 1900-02-20 | Natal front | **THE BATTLE OF PAARDEBERG (DAY 3)**

Expecting Republican attacks on his forces or his lines of communications from outside the siege lines, and still smarting from the supplies lost when De Wet captured his supply convoy at Waterval, Lord Roberts cannot fire full out and only keeps up a limited bombardment of the laager.[168] All of Major Albrecht's five guns except his pom-pom are knocked out or without ammunition.[169]

The Gloucesters have entrenched themselves overnight and keep up a long-range fire fight with De Wet's men all day long. General De Wet has succeeded in dragging a Krupp gun to the top of Kitchener's Kopje during the night, and he opens fire to the surprise of the troops in his front. Commandants CC Froneman, JF Potgieter and JG v B Greyling exploit the British confusion to gallop out of the laager and break out with 64 burghers to join De Wet.[170]

Major-General Chermside's attempt to relieve Brigadier-General Stephenson's tired troops north of Vanderberg Drift, costs him 38 casualties and seven supply wagons.[171] |
|---|---|---|
| 
Comdt. JG van B Greyling
(National Cultural History Museum) | | |
| | Central front | De la Rey attacks Clements at Rietfontein near Arundel but fails to push him back, because Schoeman and Grobler's burghers fail to co-operate. Chief Commandant Piet de Wet is also ordered west to assist Cronje (without De la Rey's knowledge). De la Rey is forced to abandon his attempt to threaten Lord Roberts' supply lines near Noupoort. The Republican withdrawal from Colesberg begins.[172] |
| | Natal front | **THE TUGELA BATTLES**

Rather than vigorously exploiting his success and the panic, Buller, inexplicably, expects a Republican counterattack. He prepares defensive positions and decides to occupy the undefended Colenso, thus allowing the Republicans to regroup to some extent. During the afternoon, Major-General Hart's Irish Brigade occupies the town of Colenso. A small patrol of Thorneycroft's Mounted Infantry crosses the Tugela and finds the trenches which caused their defeat on 15 December deserted. Buller sends for the Royal Engineer pontoon section waiting at Chieveley.

During the period since 14 February, the British have lost 25 men killed, 276 wounded and four missing — a total of only 305 men. During the same period the Republican losses are calculated to be 17 killed and 78 wounded, indicating the halfhearted nature of their defence.[173] |
| | ZAR | President Paul Kruger urges his burghers, *"Stand fast in faith to fight, and you shall be convinced that the Lord shall arise and scatter his enemies. Our faith is now at its utmost test."* [174] |
| Day 134 Wed 1900-02-21 | Western front | **THE BATTLE OF PAARDEBERG, (DAY 4)**
Lord Roberts sends a message to Cronje: *"I have learned only today that there are women and children in your laager... I shall be happy to give them a safe-conduct through our lines to any place they may wish to go. I must express... my regret that during the recent actions they have been exposed to our fire, owing to the fact that we were ignorant of their presence with your forces. I have also heard that there is a lack of doctors and medicines, and if you are in need of them I shall have great pleasure in sending you either or both."*

Cronje replies: *"Safe-conduct declined; accept offer of doctors and medicines, but stipulate that once doctors have entered this laager, they will not be allowed to leave until such time as I shift it."*

Lord Roberts answers: *"... Seeing the conditions you attach thereto... I can not spare my medical officers for such an indefinite period, I am reluctantly compelled to withdraw my offer."*[175]

During the negotiations regarding the provision of medical assistance, the British offi- |
| 
Lord Roberts
(War Museum of the Boer Republics) | | |

cers who approach the Republican positions under the flag of truce, distribute copies of Roberts' proclamation offering lenient terms to surrendering burghers, thereby seriously undermining morale in the laager. [176]

At Kitchener's Koppie and other heights at Osfontein and Stinkfontein, the British abandon their gains of the previous night.[177] About three kilometres east of Kitchener's Hill, General French's mounted force prevents about 200 newly arrived burghers under General APJ Cronje from joining De Wet.[178]

The British intensify their bombardment of De Wet's positions and both French and Broadwood's cavalry execute wide flanking movements that threaten the burghers' line of defeat. Distracted by these manoeuvres, the burghers turn to face south-eastwards, allowing General Chermside's 14th Brigade to charge their hill positions from the north. When some of his burghers flee, De Wet has to abandon Kitchener's Koppie and make a fast retreat to avoid encirclement. He is forced to fight a running battle that lasts almost the entire day covers more than 15 kilometres and ends near Poplar Grove.[179]

Lord Kitchener is sent to Noupoort to 'expedite railway and bridge repairs'.

Natal front

Gen. Louis Botha
(National Cultural History Museum)

THE TUGELA BATTLES

General Buller signals the besieged White: *"... I think there is only a rearguard in front of me... I hope to be with you tomorrow night."*[180] His delay enables Botha to regroup his burghers and to prepare some kind of defensive line on the left bank of the river. Botha has again gathered more than 3 000 burghers with five field-guns and a pom-pom. He orders the occupation of the heights overlooking Colenso and the railway line, from the slopes of Rooikop, west of Colenso, to Pieter's Hill and Aasvoëlkrans in the north-east — a line nearly 16 kilometres in length.

The British start a severe bombardment on all the features dominating the river that lasts the entire morning. Although the shelling causes few casualties, it enables the Royal Engineers to construct a pontoon bridge over the river west of Hlangwane. At 14:00, on Warren's orders, part of Major-General Coke's 10th Brigade — six companies of the Somerset Light Infantry — crosses the river and spreads out, heading north-west in the direction of Grobbelaarskloof. The Republican field-guns open up, but at the extreme range, cause few casualties. Botha's riflemen allow the troops to approach to within 500 metres before pouring lead into their ranks, not only from their front, but also from Horseshoe Hill in their flank. They are pinned down and Coke pushes four companies of the Dorset Regiment against the hills on the Somersets' right. At 16:00 the Dorsets are also pinned down and even a furious artillery barrage does not shift the burghers. The troops are ordered to hold out until they can fall back under the cover of darkness.

They retire to consolidate their occupation of Fort Wylie and fortify positions on the Colenso Koppies. Their assault against the Republican 'rearguard' costs them 111 casualties while Botha loses a single burgher killed and seven slightly wounded.[181]

Botha is elated by his success, the burgher morale soars and several groups return to the firing line.[182]

Ladysmith siege: The British artillery on Wagon Hill shells the dam-building project and although the Long Tom on Bulwana soon silences or distracts the British guns, the project is seriously delayed and Malan requests more protection.[183]

Day 135 Thu 1900-02-22	Western front	**THE BATTLE OF PAARDEBERG (DAY 5)** General Cronje responds again to Lord Roberts' communication: *"On second thought, I beg to make the following suggestion: That you supply me with full hospital equipment, medicines and doctors, to whom free access will be given, and I am willing that the hospital should be erected 1 000 yards west of my laager."* Lord Roberts answers: *"I regret I have not sufficient hospital accommodations for our own men, and if my first offer can not be accepted none other can be made."*[184] Roberts does not offer to allow the Republican ambulance in occupied Jacobsdal to move closer to Paardeberg.[185]

106

		At 17:30, the British observation balloon is launched and an observer makes sketches of Cronje's positions.[186] British units from Kimberley occupy Barkly West.
	Natal front	**THE TUGELA BATTLES: WYNNE'S HILL** General Buller reopens his artillery barrage at dawn and Warren is ordered to clear the 'snipers' from Horseshoe Hill by taking the next feature in the chain of hills. Major-General Wynne's 11th Brigade is tasked to attack Hedge (later Wynne's) Hill. Troops pour across the pontoon bridge and attempt to advance along the railway line. At sunrise there are 40 battalions with 40 field-guns and supplies crowded into the narrow, low-lying space beyond the pontoon bridge. At 14:00, Wynne starts his march from the Colenso heights with Lyttleton's Division following at a great distance. The burghers fall back under the concentrated fire of four battalions, but, as usual, their stronger positions are behind the crest. When the troops crest the further hill, known as Wynne's East or Green Hill, they meet a staggering fire. It soon becomes clear that the flank protection is not sufficient. The adjoining hill, Wynne's West, will also have to be secured. The King's Own Lancasters, the King's Royal Rifles and the East Surreys capture the crests of both of Wynne's Hills, but realise that these positions are commanded by the still higher ground of Terrace or Hart's (Inniskilling) Hill. After being reinforced by the Royal Welsh Fusiliers and other regiments they consolidate and form the left flank. Further advance along the railway line is attempted but soon stops as it comes into view of Hart's Hill. The Republican guns — presumed to have been silenced or dislodged — open up on the concentrated British near the railway line. As the light fails, Wynne's troops along the crests have to be further reinforced to maintain their foothold for the night. Throughout the night the burghers push closer to the British positions and afford them no rest. [187] The British suffer 22 killed and 93 wounded.[188]
	Central front	General Clements is extensively reinforced and now commands about 6 500 troops with 28 field-guns and four machine guns against De la Rey's continually weakening forces.[189]
	Western front	**Mafeking siege:** General Snyman leaves his Mafeking positions with 300 burghers and some artillery to engage Plumer who is reported to be at Kanya.[190]
	International	The third telegraphic route linking South Africa to Europe via Cape Town, St Helena, and Ascencion Island comes into operation. The other routes are (1) via Durban, Delagoa Bay, Zanzibar, Aden, the Red Sea, and the Mediterranean to Gibraltar, and (2) Cape Town, Mossamedes, Luanda, St Vincent and Madeira to Lissabon.
	Trivia	*RSS Baden-Powell's 43rd birthday. Although he has already, during the first week of the siege, formed local boys into what is to become known as the 'Boy Scouts', this famous world-wide youth organisation is to celebrate this day as its founding date. The movement's motto, 'Be Prepared', is also linked to 'B-P's' initials.*
Day 136 Fri **1900-02-23**	Western front	**THE BATTLE OF PAARDEBERG (DAY 6)** The bombardment of General Cronje's laager continues. General De Wet, reinforced by burghers under General APJ Cronje and Commandants Theunissen and Vilonel, attempts to retake Kitchener's Koppie. Despite initial successes and determined attacks by General Philip Botha, the British have reinforced De Wet's old positions to such an extend that the Republican attack is repulsed. Commandant Theunissen and 87 men of his Winburg commando are captured through the reckless action of his men who fail to co-ordinate their attack with General Philip Botha's attempt.[191] Overcast conditions make co-ordination with Cronje impossible and De Wet's attack fails. During the afternoon it starts to rain and conditions in the laager are initially improved as the carcasses of dead animals are washed away. Later, the mud and water in the trenches add to the burghers' misery and discomfort.[192]
	Natal front	**THE TUGELA BATTLES: HART'S HILL** A group of burghers who has sneaked closer during the night, charges the tormented Royal Rifles and East Surreys on Wynne's Hill and the troops turn and run.

	Victoria Cross	Colonel Harris and a company of East Surreys launch a counter-attack with bayonets and are cut down, with Harris wounded in several places. Several other units are caught up in the panic and flee down the slope. Fatigue and a dwindling ammunition supply prevent the burghers from exploiting their success, enabling the British to stem the tide and push more reinforcements into the firing line.[193] Private AE Curtis, 2nd Battalion, the East Surrey Regiment, earns a Victoria Cross for rescuing Colonel Harris, who is brought down a perfectly open space under close fire of an enemy breastwork near Onderbroekspruit.[194] Using more than 70 field-guns, the British subject Wynne's, Terrace (Hart's or Inniskilling) and Railway Hills to a tremendous barrage. Surprisingly, Republican guns answer with such accurate counter-fire that the British have to concentrate on silencing them before continuing the softening up of the hills.[195] Major-General Hart's (Fifth) Irish Brigade (Dublins, Inniskillings and Connaughts) attempts to advance along the railway but is stopped by fierce resistance from Hart's Hill. They move into the cover offered by the river bank but their progress is slowed by the mud and stopped when they come to the flooded and impassable Langverwacht Spruit. They are forced to cross open ground and to cross the pom-pom bridge where they suffer heavily. Although it is already almost 17:00, Hart realises the urgency of taking up defensible positions and decides to storm Hart's (Inniskilling) Hill. The troops make a determined effort, but they again suffer the consequences of insufficient scouting. Again the troops capture a false crest commanded by Republican positions on higher ground. Two attempts to rush these positions are repulsed with heavy losses and, as night falls, the tired troops cannot do anything but hang on to their precarious position on the crest with their wounded abandoned in no man's land.[196] The British lose 59 killed, 238 wounded and 16 missing — a total of 313 men. [197]
	Central front	After reoccupying Molteno, General Gatacre, with a force of 4 000 troops, eight field-guns and supported by an armoured train, carries out a probing action in the direction of Stormberg Junction. On his own farm, Schoemanskop, rebel Commandant Danie Schoeman with 800 men and three guns repulse a British attack, greatly assisted by a violent hailstorm. A counter-attack in his flank forces Gatacre to retire before dark with casualties of 88 killed, wounded or missing against three killed and seven wounded. In a skirmish on the same front, the very popular Captain the Hon Raymond Harvey Lodge Joseph de Montmorency VC, leader of Montmorency's Scouts, and six of his men are killed in action.[198] A British attack near Arundel pushes the burghers back to Kuilfontein [199]
Day 137 Sat **1900-02-24**	Natal front	**THE TUGELA BATTLES** At dawn, the precarious position of the troops on the southern slope of Hart's Hill is obvious, and small groups of burghers are able to edge around their flank and suddenly open a fierce enfilading fire from their rear quarter. Their other flank is also threatened when they draw fire from a position that should have been secured by the Imperial Light Infantry. The British artillery tries to support their comrades, but their shells are badly directed and land amongst them. This is the last straw and they run, leaving their dead (including Colonel Sitwell) and wounded.
	Victoria Cross	Lieutenant ET Inkson, Royal Army Medical Corps (Royal Inniskilling Fusiliers), wins a Victoria Cross recommendation when he carries a wounded lieutenant for three or four hundred metres under heavy fire.[200] Major-General Hart's efforts to push back the burghers threatening his flanks are stopped by determined and accurate rifle fire. When the burghers open up with three or four well-placed field-guns that have just arrived from the upper Tugela, the forward movement of Buller's week-old offensive is stopped dead. The Republicans, not feeling strong enough for offensive action, do not follow up their success and miss an

		excellent opportunity to throw them back across the river. For the rest of the day the battle is static with the burghers undoubtedly holding the upper hand.[201] The British lose 115 killed, 682 wounded and 58 captured unhurt — a total of 855.[202]
		Ladysmith siege: Despite the increased shelling directed at it, the work on the Klip River dam project has been speeded up and more black workers are employed. Lack of rain in the catchment area, however, limits the inflow into the dam. The water level rises at a disappointingly slow rate and the project is abandoned as all efforts are directed against Buller's advance.[203]
	Western front	**THE BATTLE OF PAARDEBERG (DAY 7)** The rain continues and the rising river has a demoralising effect as the burghers see their chances of crossing the swollen river and escaping grow slimmer. The clouds again prevent any heliographic contact between Cronje and De Wet's force at Poplar Grove.[204] When it clears, the British observation balloon discovers four ammunition carts in the riverbed, which are soon destroyed by the 4,7inch naval guns. [205]
	Central front	General Clements, now reinforced further, starts offensive operations. He attacks Generals Schoeman and Grobler but is repulsed. Nineteen Lancers, nine of them wounded, fall into Republican hands while two burghers are killed and 14 wounded.[206]
	Victoria Cross	Sergeant W Firth, 1st Battalion, The Duke of Wellington's West Riding Regiment, Plewman's Farm, Arundel near Colesburg.
Day 137 Sun **1900-02-25**	ZAR	Anxious about the fate of General Cronje and his men, the ZAR government declares this Sunday a day of prayer and in Pretoria an all-night vigil is held in several churches.[207]
	Western front	**THE BATTLE OF PAARDEBERG (DAY 8)** Captain Danie Theron bravely crosses the British lines and enters Cronje's laager in an effort to co-ordinate a breakout. Captain Theron crawls for long distances and even talks to guards before swimming across the river. Although Cronje is willing to consider such an attempt, he is committed to submit the plan to a council of war. [208] Attempts to build a bridge across the flooded Modder River using chains and parts of the destroyed wagons, are abandoned when the British turn their guns on them.[209] The British trenches, mostly dug at night, reach closer and closer to the Republican lines. [210] Answering an inquiry from Roberts, Cronje confirms that he has 12 unhurt and four wounded British prisoners, as well as four own wounded. Lord Roberts offers, *"... if you will send our wounded out of your laager and four of your own wounded, the latter shall be sent to Jacobsdal to the German Red Cross Hospital and released as soon as cured."*[211]
		Mafeking siege: General Snyman discovers that Colonel Plumer has retreated to Crocodile Pools and he returns to Mafeking.[212] Outside the town, the peace of the Sabbath is broken when a slanging match erupts between the opponents. *"Cape Boys in advanced trenches, and Boers, engaged in an argument as to their respective mothers and other female relatives' merits and demerits."*[213]
	Central front	General De la Rey starts transferring forces to the western front by rail via Bloemfontein in an effort to assist Cronje at Paardeberg. De la Rey hands over command to General Lemmer and Republican forces start falling back on the Orange River.[214]
	Natal front	**TUGELA BATTLES: THE ARMISTICE** During the night, Buller realises, to his horror, that some of his wounded are still abandoned in no man's land. On Wynne's Hill they have been lying for three nights and two days without food or water; on Hart's Hill for two nights and a day. Bargaining on the burgher's aversion to fighting on a Sunday, Buller requests an armistice in

Danie Theron

		the *"interests of humanity"*. Botha immediately agrees and at about 11:00, *"the white flags* (rise) *shakily above both lines of trenches, and an eerie day of fraternization* (begins)".[215] The British casualties for the previous two days total 1 158 men while the burghers have lost 22 killed and 80 wounded during the same period. [216] Then ... *"with unbounded relief* (Botha sees) *that Buller* (is) *using the armistice to withdraw his force back across the river. If the British* (are) *once again pulling out he* (will) *have time to rest his men... and inject fresh resolution into the defence."*[217] However, General Buller is abusing the cease-fire, granted in the *"interests of humanity"*, to improve his tactical position. He extricates his troops who are crowded into the narrow strip of land on the left bank, dominated by Republican positions and unable to concentrate sufficiently to launch a decisive move against any of the hills above them. At 10:00 all the British guns have been withdrawn across the pontoon bridge on their way to emplacements from where they dominate the entire Republican line.[218]
Day 139 Mon **1900-02-26**	Western front	**BATTLE OF PAARDEBERG (DAY 9)** Four 150mm howitzers arrive. The laager is subjected to the heaviest bombardment to date, when all the British artillery pieces, now about 100 in total, keep up a continuous barrage. All supplies dwindle and almost all foodstuffs are contaminated by lyddite.[219] Captain Theron sneaks out of the laager and reports back to General De Wet. Cronje's council of war rejects De Wet's plan because most of the horses and draught animals have been killed and they are unwilling to abandon the laager.[220] The presence of about 62 women and children,[221] as well as the wounded in the laager, also influences the decision. Certain officers threaten to remain in their trenches and to surrender if Cronje gives the order to attempt a break-out. General Cronje pleads with his officers to hold out until the 28th to avoid the humiliation of surrendering on Majuba Day.[222] On General De Wet's request, President MT Steyn, A Fischer and ADW Wolmarans arrive at Poplar Grove to personally address the burghers in an attempt to stop the negative spirit amongst them.[223] Before nightfall, about 800 of De Wet's men move out from Poplar Grove in the direction of Paardeberg. They form two parallel lines about two and a half kilometre apart, straddling the route along which Cronje is expected to fight his way out, should he accept De Wet's plan as taken to him by Captain Theron.[224] They wait in vain.
	Natal front	**THE TUGELA BATTLES** In the morning 76 British field-guns are in position on the high ground on the right bank and a slow bombardment is opened, determining the ranges of the Republican positions. Units from Frere, Chievely and all over the front are concentrated, ready for offensive action on Majuba Day. After dark the Engineers demolish the pontoon bridge and transport it northwards.[225] Major John MacBride and 50 members of the Irish Volunteers arrive to reinforce the Ermelo commando at Pieter's Hill.[226]
	Central front	General FA Grobler abandons his positions and falls back to Colesberg [227]
	International	Lumsden's Horse sails from India.
Day 140 Tue **1900-02-27**	Western front	**THE BATTLE OF PAARDEBERG (DAY 10)** At 01:45, on the western side of the laager, about 450 Canadians move forward in a compact formation to dig in as far forward as they can. At about 03:00 they come under terrific fire, but the burghers' aim is too high and the Canadians go down and dig in. They reinforce and extend their trenches with sandbags and wait. At dawn, the British guns open fire and it is soon clear to Cronje and his men that the new Canadian trench and troop movements on the south bank have made some of their

Gen. PA Cronje
(War Museum of the Boer Republics)

Natal front

key positions untenable. As white handkerchiefs begin to flutter above some of his trenches, Cronje who has been determined to hold out until the next day, has no option other than to inform Lord Roberts that he is prepared to surrender.

GENERAL PA CRONJE SURRENDERS ON MAJUBA DAY

On receipt of Cronje's message, Lord Roberts sends an officer to escort General Cronje to the British Headquarters. When the bedraggled Cronje arrives on a grey, bony horse, Roberts greets him, saying, *"I am glad to see you. You have made a gallant defence, sir."*

Cronje surrenders with 3 919 men, including 24 ZAR officers and 2 568 men, 22 OFS officers and 1 305 men — almost 10% of the total Republican fighting strength. Since 15 February Cronje's force has lost 87 killed in action and 162 wounded.[228]

The British casualties for the ten-day battle since 18 February total 239 killed, 1 095 wounded, 67 missing in action, presumably killed, and one taken prisoner: a total of 1 402.

President Steyn travels all along the Republican positions outside the British cordon, personally talking to burghers and addressing them with inspiring speeches in the spirit of Majuba Day. Efforts to achieve heliographic communications with Cronje's laager, however, ominously fail.[229]

Mafeking siege: A 5,5-inch smooth-bore howitzer is made under the direction of Major Panzera.[230] The gun is to be called 'the Wolf' after a nickname given to Baden-Powell by Fingo tribesmen in Mafeking. Baden-Powell presumes this nickname to mean 'the wolf that never sleeps', but as there are no wolves in South Africa, it is more likely that it refers to a hyena — a much more unflattering epithet.

THE TUGELA BATTLES: THE BATTLE OF PIETER'S HILL

At dawn the Engineers start the construction of a pontoon bridge below the falls, north of Hlangwane, under the cover of the high river banks. A severe bombardment keeps the burghers' heads down while British preparations are finalized. For the first time during his campaign, General Buller has extensive knowledge of his enemy's positions — gained during the armistice — and, for the first time, he plans to commit his entire force. At 10:00, the bridge, almost 100 metres in length, is completed and Barton's brigade hears the news of Cronje's surrender as they start crossing. They march along the riverbed and inexplicably, they draw no fire until about noon, when they are fully extended and ready to start their assault on Pieter's Hill. They climb the hill, pushing the burghers back from one stone parapet to the next until they come under crossfire from Railway Hill.

At 14:00 Lyttleton's troops, forming the left wing of the operation and supported by the naval guns, open a heavy fusillade on the burghers on Wynne's Hill, Horseshoe Hill and positions further westwards, preventing reinforcements from there reaching Railway or Pieter's Hills. The artillery barrage from 91 guns of all calibers is so effective that the defenders do not notice when, at 14:00, Colonel Walter Kitchener, Lord Kitchener's brother, starts his assault on Railway Hill in extended order. At 14:45, Norcott's Brigade is also deployed along the railway and the British attacking force is fully extended and they open fire against the occupied heights. At 14:50, lack of ammunition forces one of the Republican guns to stop firing. At 16:00, Kitchener renews his attack against Railway Hill. Despite the overwhelming covering fire from 22 machine guns used in unison from the slopes of Hlangwane, accurate burgher fire slows his assault to a crawl. He pushes the last of his reserves into the firing line and requests Norcott's column to relieve pressure on his flank by attacking Hart's (or Terrace) Hill. Norcott immediately orders the East Surreys and the Scottish Rifles to assist by storming up the slope. Almost simultaneously Kitchener's West Yorkshires, moving along the cover of a gulley, reach the eastern crest of the hill, from where they can enfilade the defenders, making their position untenable. After a furious bayonet charge and hand-to-hand fighting with the last brave defenders, the cheering British

	Victoria Cross	finally take both Terrace (or Hart's) and Railway Hill. Captain C Mansel-Jones, the West Yorkshire Regiment, earns his recommendation for the Victoria Cross on Terrace Hill, when, in spite of a serious wound, he inspires his men to take the ridge. [231] The burghers on Wynne's and Horseshoe Hills are able to cover their retreating men from Railway Hill until they reach Langverwacht Spruit, where they turn and repulse their pursuers. This spirited burgher rearguard action and the failing light convince Buller to stop Dundonald's cavalry from crossing the pontoon bridge in pursuit of the retreating enemy. At 20:00 the battle dies down with the British in firm control of the heights and the road to Ladysmith is finally open as the burghers stream northwards. The British success is expensive. Buller loses at least 87 killed, 427 wounded and nine missing in action, while the Republicans lose 34 killed and fatally wounded. They succeed in recovering 115 of their wounded, while 83 — including several wounded — fall into British hands.[232] Among the Republican casualties is a mortally wounded 19-year-old girl in the same trench as her husband, who has been killed only moments previously.[233]
	Central front	Near Colesberg, General Grobler's rearguard is attacked at Vaalkop and General Clements reoccupies Rensburg Siding.[234]
	Trivia	*The British Labour Party is founded.* *JNH Grobler's 36th birthday (Commandant of Ermelo commando)*
Day 141 Wed **1900-02-28**	Natal front	The Republican demoralisation is complete. *"... the plain was covered with a multitude of men, wagons and guns ploughing across the sodden veld in the greatest disorder... it seemed as if the bulk of the transport would have to be abandoned, for the mounted men pressed steadily on without concerning themselves with the convoys. Had the British fired a single gun at this surging mob everything on wheels would have fallen into their hands."*[235] All efforts by Botha and Commandant-General Joubert to stem the tide of retreating burghers fails. 'Colonel' John YF Blake's Irish-American volunteers manage to save one of the Republican 'Long Toms' by hitching oxen to the gun and crawling past Ladysmith, almost within earshot of the British outposts.[236] **LADYSMITH IS RELIEVED** After a siege of 118 days, 'Long Tom' fires his final shot at 10:00 and the Republican forces abandon their positions. At about 16:00, Major Gough of the 17th Lancers enters Ladysmith.[237] The gallant garrison has suffered 244 killed, 61 fatally wounded, 636 wounded, 14 missing and captured, while 541 men have died of disease. General Sir George White VC: *"Thank God we have kept the flag flying."*[238] President Kruger, despite his age and a painful eye infection, leaves Pretoria by train for the Natal Front in an attempt to stem the tide of fleeing burghers streaming homewards.[239]
Col. John YF Blake *(War Museum of the Boer Republics)*	Central front	After repulsing a few British attacks, the Republican forces move their supply wagons to Colesberg Bridge and evacuate Colesberg, allowing General Clements to occupy the town unopposed.[240] Republican forces retire across the Orange River.
	Western front	During the past 13 days since 15 February, Lord Roberts' force has lost 1 474 horses.[241]
	Cape Colony	General PJ Liebenberg arrives at Swemkuil with about 400 men, half of whom are Griqualand rebels. The total Republican force in the north-western Cape Colony— mostly recruited locally — now stands at 750 men with a Krupp and a pom-pom.[242]
	International	The Russian foreign minister, Count Muraviev, suggests that France and Germany put joint pressure on Britain to end the war in South Africa.

	Trivia	*In the Gregorian calender, a century year is not a leap year unless the date is divisible by 400. Thus, 1900 is not a leap year.*
1900	AUTUMN	**MARCH**
Day 142 Thu **1900-03-01**	Natal front	President Kruger, joined by the ailing Commandant-General Joubert, addresses thousands of burghers in a stirring speech at Glencoe.[243] The Republican rearguard falling back on Modderspruit Station consists of only 150 men under Generals Louis Botha and Lucas Meyer.[244] General Sir Redvers Buller receives the following telegram: *"To: Sir Redvers Buller, 1st March, 1900* *Sincerest congratulations.* *Edward Albert."*[245] At Ladysmith, General White sends a small mounted force to harass the fleeing burghers, but their horses are not up to it, they fail to make contact and Buller orders them to return.[246]
Pres. SJP Kruger (National Cultural History Museum)	Western front	**Mafeking siege:** A burgher writes: *"Things must be getting pretty hard in Mafeking for every day numbers of quite emaciated Black women and children try to come out, but as always are turned back. Often they refuse to go until fired upon repeatedly. It is a most miserable affair, but orders are strict. Some of the Burghers flatly refuse to have a hand in it."*[247]
	Mafeking	Field-Marshal Lord Roberts arrives in Kimberley.
Day 143 Fri **1900-03-02**	Central front	The British report that the railway has been repaired up to Colesburg.[248] General HJ Olivier evacuates his Stormberg positions.[249]
	OFS	A council of war at Poplar Grove gives Danie Theron permission to form a Scout Corps consisting of about 100 men to be known by the initials 'TVK'.[250]
	ZAR	On his return in Pretoria, President Kruger receives a telegram from Commandant-General Joubert, reporting that the morale amongst the burgers has again deteriorated and is at a new low. Joubert suggests forming a defensive line north of the Biggarsberg, but that it is now the time to negotiate peace terms, while Republican forces are still on British soil. Although Kruger seriously admonishes Joubert, he starts arrangements to confer with President Steyn in Bloemfontein.[251]
	International	A formal Russian proposal by the Tsar to the Kaiser, states: *"In the opinion of the Imperial Cabinet and in view of the latest events and the successes of the English armies, it appears that the moment had arrived for the Continental states, particularly those interested in African affairs, to endeavour to prevent the serious consequences, which might be the result of the complete annihilation of the South African republics."*[252]
	Trivia	*London's Daily Mail, carrying news of the British successes, achieves a circulation of 1 000 000 for the first time.*
Day 144 Sat **1900-03-03**	Natal front	General Sir Redvers Buller finally enters Ladysmith.[253] Commandant-General Joubert delivers a stirring speech on the station platform at Glencoe Station, urging the retreating burghers to persist.[254]
	Western front	Colonel J Adye leaves De Aar for Britstown and General Settle marches from Orange River Station, both ordered to clear the Northern Cape of Republican and rebel commandos.[255]
		Mafeking siege: The howitzer 'Wolf', made in Mafeking, 'passes its trials' and is put into service.[256]

	Central front	Major General Brabant attacks the rebel forces holding Labuschagne's Nek outside Dordrecht. He launches two flank attacks, and the right attack, commanded by Major Maxwell, succeeds in capturing the key position of Bakenkop.[257] Retiring Republican forces dynamite the Norval's Pont railway bridge.[258] General Clements advances from Colesberg. A 200-strong British unit, supported by artillery, dislodges a Republican picket at the undamaged road bridge north of Colesberg but fails to establish an effective bridgehead.[259]
	International	Germany rejects the Russian proposal to put pressure on Britain to end the war.
Day 145 Sun **1900-03-04**	Central front	Labuschagne's Nek, outside Dordrecht, defended by about 400 Cape rebels under Commandant M de Wet, is captured after the main assault by about 1 200 men of the Colonial Division under General Brabant dislodges the defenders. A rebel attempt to retake Bakenkop fails after Maxwell has succeeded in dragging two field-guns to the summit during the previous night. The British lose 14 killed and 28 wounded against Republican losses of eight killed, 17 wounded as well as a few taken prisoner.[260]
	Cape Colony	General PJ Liebenberg reaches Omdraaivlei with 200 men and two field-guns and takes command of the men occupying the place.[261]
Day 146 Mon **1900-03-05**	Natal front	At Glencoe, a Republican council of war decides to establish a new line of defence along the Biggarsberg. [262]
	Central front	The British occupation of Labuschagne's Nek is completed when Barkly East rebels are forced to abandon Pappasnek.[263] General Gatacre occupies Stormberg Junction which has been evacuated by the Republicans.
	Cape Colony	Martial law is extended to Prieska, Britstown, Kenhart and Barkly East.
	OFS	President Kruger receives an enthusiastic reception on arrival at the Bloemfontein Station. After discussing the situation at the various fronts and reviewing Commandant-General Joubert's telegram, they decide, despite President Steyn's reluctance, to formulate a telegram to Lord Salisbury.[264] **THE REPUBLICAN PEACE OVERTURES** *"The blood and tears of thousands who have suffered in this war and the prospect of moral and material ruin that threaten South Africa, compels the belligerents to reflect, in the presence of ... God, why they are fighting and whether these reasons can justify the suffering and destruction."* The Republics reiterate that their war aims are limited to the defence and protection of their indisputable independence as sovereign international states. The undermining of Britain's role and British interests in the region are not contemplated, nor her elimination as a Colonial Power. The acquisition of her Colonies as part of an independent South Africa is not considered either. *"If their indisputable independence as sovereign international states can be recognised and respected and an assurance is obtained that those British subjects that supported the Republican cause will not be made to suffer in their persons or property, then and only then, do the Republics desire to make an end to the evil that now reigns. If, however, Great Britain is resolved on the destruction of the Republics, she must accept that, in spite of her superior power, she will be resolutely resisted, with the help of God that kindled the undying fire of patriotism."* It is also explained that reconciliation proposals could not have been considered while the Republican forces held the military advantage but now, with the capture of one of their armies, a more equitable situation makes it possible to consider negotiations. This communication is not sent via the military or the Colonial Secretary, but is sent directly to the British Prime Minister, the Marquis of Salisbury. Copies of this telegram are also sent to France, Russia, Germany and the United States.[265]

Day 147 Tue 1900-03-06	Western front	Chief Commandant De Wet now has about 5 000 burghers and seven field-guns at his disposal at Poplar Grove (or Modderrivierspoort) and he prepares to bar the British advance towards Bloemfontein. His positions stretch over 35 kilometres from Kanonfontein, about 20 kilometres north of the river, in an arc towards Tafelberg, west of the ford and then southwards to Sewekoppies.[266] President Paul Kruger visits the Republican forces near Poplar Grove and attempts to inspire the demoralised burghers. [267]
	Central front	General LAS Lemmer completes the withdrawal of his forces to the northern bank of the Orange River at the Colesberg road bridge. The railway bridge is charged with explosives by a railway engineer. [268]
	Cape Colony	**THE FIGHT AT HOUWATER** Colonel J Adye's column, marching to recapture Prieska with a force of between 500 and 700 men with six field-guns, attacks a rebel force at Houwater, the farm of the Cape politician, Dr Smartt. The Republicans under General Liebenberg are not ready and they have to drag their artillery for about 7 kilometres over completely open ground to take position on some ridges. A small commando, made up mostly of rebels under the 24-year-old Chaim David Judelewitz, an Uitlander,[269] and Field-cornet Van der Westhuizen, inspired by the artillerists' charge, launches a vigourous flank attack and Adye retreats. A running battle follows but the British succeed in falling back all the way to Britstown. According to official casualty figures they suffer three killed, 14 wounded and seven captured, while the Republicans lose two killed and three wounded.[270] Carnarvon is occupied by Colonel Parsons.
	ZAR	State Secretary FW Reitz informs the ZAR delegate in The Hague that it is the firm intention of his government to destroy the mines and mining machinery in Johannesburg, should the Republican situation become hopeless. It later becomes clear that Reitz does not have much support for this and that even President Kruger is against the destruction of the mines.[271]
	Northern front	Colonel Plumer's force arrives at Lobatsi, between Crocodile Pools and Mafeking.
	Trivia	*Gotlieb Daimler, the German designer and manufacturer of motor cars, dies.*
Day 148 Wed 1900-03-07	OFS	**THE BATTLE OF POPLAR GROVE OR MODDERRIVIERSPOORT** General French, ordered to execute a wide flanking movement to the south to cut off the enemy's line of retreat, starts later than intended and at dawn his cavalry is not at the burghers' rear. The burghers, with the encirclement of Cronje in mind, are in no mood to be outflanked and quickly change their front to the south. French is surprised when he runs into their extended positions and he is stopped at about 08:00 and urges Kelly-Kenny's 6th Division to use their naval guns and to clear the Sewekoppies.[272] At Poplar Grove, De Wet has to bundle President Kruger into a Cape cart and sends him away. On his return he finds that burghers are deserting their positions in small groups and his defence deteriorates into no more than a rearguard action.[273] North of the river, Colvile's 9th Division is delayed by a single Krupp gun on Loog Hill. It is only when Smith-Dorrien's Shropshires and Canadians start to envelop the hill that they flee eastwards, abandoning their gun. At about noon, the flanking movements by British cavalry on both sides of the river, force De Wet to abandon his positions. After covering actions at Slachtkraal and Boschkop, the Republicans retire towards Abrahamskraal, untroubled by the exhausted British mounted forces.[274] The British lose eight killed and 49 wounded while Chief Commandant De Wet loses at least one killed and one wounded.[275]

	Central front	The Colesberg road bridge is blown up by General Lemmer's retreating burghers.[276] General Gatacre occupies Burgersdorp and General EY Brabant's vanguard enters Jamestown.
	Northern front	Colonel Plumer captures a Republican laager near Gopani, Bechuanaland.
Day 149 Thu **1900-03-08**	OFS	General JH de la Rey, with less than 1 000 men from the Colesberg front, joins De Wet near Abrahamskraal. Despite an order to shoot deserters (which the responsible police officer cannot obey), these men and other reinforcements, cannot stem the tide. On President Steyn's request, De Wet departs for Bloemfontein, where he and Judge Hertzog plans the defence of the city. With the help of black labourers several rifle pits, short trenches and gun positions are prepared. General De la Rey takes over at Abrahamskraal, where he now commands only about 3 000 men — almost 2 000 less than at Poplar Grove.[277]
	Central front	General Clements occupies Norval's Pont. Major-General EY Brabant occupies Jamestown, abandoned by the Republicans on 6 March.
Day 150 Fri **1900-03-09**	OFS	De la Rey's defensive lines extend from the heights north of the Modder River at Oertel's Drift, southwards over Abrahamskraal, Helderfontein to Driefontein, where he takes guard, and from there to a position south of Bosrand. His 12 field-guns and pom-poms are distributed over the entire front measuring more than 30 kilometres.[278] A cavalry reconnaissance mission by French's men convinces him that the Transvaalers and Free Staters have split up and that the road to Bloemfontein is open.[279]
	Cape Colony	An attempt to escape from the Simon's Bay prisoner of war camp is thwarted when an almost completed escape tunnel is discovered.[280]
Day 151 Sat **1900-03-10**	OFS	**THE BATTLE OF ABRAHAMSKRAAL AND DRIEFONTEIN** At dawn, French's advance parties come under fire from Abrahamskraal and he, predictably, immediately orders his Cavalry Brigade south to occupy the Driefontein Koppies which he presumes to be the Republican flank. Driefontein, however, is occupied and is soon strengthened as De la Rey transfers a small group here, in anticipation of French's move. The flanking move by French and Kelly-Kenny's 6th Division thus becomes a frontal attack against a small but determined group of burghers and Rand policemen. Repeated charges, supported by artillery, fail to dislodge De la Rey. The furious rifle fire forces the British to fall back, even temporarily abandoning some of their guns. Another flank attack is launched and again De la Rey is able to pre-empt their move, preventing the cavalry threatening their line of retreat. Although Weilbach's Heidelbergers retire prematurely, the Republicans hold on until sunset, when De la Rey orders them to fall back to Bloemfontein. Although their resistance is more determined than at Poplar Grove, the vast British superiority forces them to retire eastwards, with at least 30 killed, 47 wounded and 20 captured. British losses amount to at least 60 killed and 361 wounded. After the battle both sides accuse the other of abusing the white flag and of using explosive bullets.[281] General Tucker enters Petrusburg with a part of his 7th Division.[282] A deputation of prominent citizens beseeches President Steyn not to defend Bloemfontein.[283] Commandant-General Joubert grants Colonel Count Georges de Villebois-Mareuil the rank of Combat General and requests him to reorganise the Foreign Volunteers.[284]
	Central front	A Republican party attacks the small British party stationed at the road bridge, north of Colesberg and they complete its destruction.[285]

116

Day 152 Sun **1900-03-11**	OFS	Despite the exhausted condition of their horses, French's cavalry push on and reach the railway line at Ferreira Siding, south of Bloemfontein.[286] The demoralised burghers take positions to the east and west of Bloemfontein.
	Central front	President Steyn formally issues instructions to recall his commandos from the Cape Province.[287] Forces under Gatacre capture the Bethulie road bridge in the face of heavy shelling and they succeed in removing dynamite charges before the bridge can be destroyed.[288] Major General Sir EY Brabant occupies Aliwal North and enters the Free State. Major Henderson and 150 of Montmorency's Scouts gallop through the main street and make for the Orange River bridge. Although holes have been drilled in the bridge piers, they are not yet charged with dynamite and the bridge falls into British hands undamaged after a brisk engagement involving artillery on both sides. The British lose five killed, 17 wounded and four captured while the burghers suffer five wounded.[289]
	Western front	**Mafeking siege:** A burgher writes, *"During the last few days... a large number of Black women have come out of Mafeking. As the order has at last been given prohibiting the Burghers to shoot at them, as all threats are of no avail to drive them back. The result is that they come through, and they are then sent on to different places in the Transvaal. I am very glad that we have got at least so far as to permit them to come out. It is really a pitiful sight to see all these poor starved wretches, and more especially the little children, who are nothing but walking skeletons. Some are so weak that they are unable to bring the food to their mouths."*[290]
Day 153 Mon **1900-03-12**	OFS	At a council of war outside Bloemfontein, Chief Commandant De Wet emotionally calls on the burghers to defend Bloemfontein to the last man. General De la Rey brings a touch of calm and sanity by pointing out that they are defending their freedom and independence and, while willing to sacrifice himself and his men for those ideals, he is not prepared to order the destruction of the Republican force for the possession of Bloemfontein or any other town or city. He moves off to take his position on the western approach to the city. The morale amongst the burghers deteriorates further and large-scale desertions take place. It is soon clear that a determined, long lasting defence is unlikely and supplies are sent north and eastwards. General French sends a proclamation to Bloemfontein, promising the peaceful inhabitants that they will be protected and remain unmolested. They are ordered to refrain from any offensive actions or resistance as this will be severely dealt with — leading to bloodshed *"which the Field-Marshal would regret"*.[291] President Steyn and the OFS government leave Bloemfontein for Kroonstad, now officially declared the new capital.[292] Lord Methuen occupies Boshof without firing a shot and installs a small garrison.
	United Kingdom	Lord Salisbury transmits the British government's reply in a long letter in which he reminds the Presidents that Republican forces started hostilities by invading Her Majesty's colonies. *"... the British Empire has been compelled to confront an invasion which has entailed a costly war, and the loss of thousands of precious lives. This great calamity has been the penalty which Great Britain has suffered for having in recent years acquiesced in the existence of the two republics."* Salisbury tells the Presidents in no uncertain terms that, *"Her Majesty's Government can only answer Your Honours' telegram that they are not prepared to assent to the independence either of the South African Republic or of the Orange Free State."*[293]
Day 154 Tue **1900-03-13**	OFS	When key positions south of town are abandoned, the defence is abandoned and the burghers retire north and eastwards. A group of leading citizens, including the mayor, Dr BO Kellner, Mr JG Brebner, Dr Wolffe Ehrlich, Mr J Fraser and magistrate Papenfus, ride out to greet the British

Maj. Gen. Sir EY Brabant
(National Cultural History Museum)

	Victoria Cross	**LORD ROBERTS ENTERS BLOEMFONTEIN** The British enter at about noon. At the station and railway yard, 25 locomotives, 20 passenger coaches and 124 goods wagons are captured through the treacherous collaboration of English-speaking railway officials.[295] The force marching into Bloemfontein with Lord Roberts includes 33 954 officers and men, 11 540 horses, 113 field-guns and 39 machine guns.[296] Unknown to the Republicans, the troops have an average of 34 cartridges and a single 'Army biscuit' each, with their supply columns still kilometres away.[297] Lord Roberts billets himself in Steyn's Presidency and appoints Major-General GT Pretyman as military governor of Bloemfontein.[298] A party of engineers, escorted by cavalry, sent to destroy the railway line north of Bloemfontein, is almost cut off and they have to charge though Republican lines. Sergeant HW Englehart, 10th Hussars, earns a Victoria Cross for turning back under fire to rescue a wounded sapper.[299]
	OFS	In a bold move, Chief Commandant De Wet, sensing that there will be a lull in activities while Roberts' forces rest, regroup and refit in Bloemfontein, and sensitive to the general demoralisation and fatigue, sends all the Free State burghers home on leave. All burghers are ordered to report back at the Sand River railway bridge on 25 March.[300] When seriously reprimanded by Commandant-General Joubert, De Wet answers: *"You cannot catch a hare with unwilling dogs."*
	Cape Colony	Republican forces under Generals FA Grobler and Lemmer, retreating from the Colesberg front, arrive at Springfontein.[301] Johanna Charlotte Walton becomes a loyalist civilian heroine when she refuses to hand the keys of the post office of the Karoo town, Van Wyksvlei, south-west of Prieska, to a group of 20 Cape rebels. She places herself in front of the door and taunts, *"Shoot, coward, and kill me!"* She is forcibly removed, the rebels break down the door and remove the telegraph equipment. The British magazine *Punch* later publishes a very jingoistic poem singing her praises.[302]
	International	A Republican delegation consisting of A Fischer, ADW Wolmarans and CH Wessels with JM De Bruin as secretary, embarks at Lourenço Marques for Europe, seeking international intervention or aid.
	Trivia	*HCO Plumer's 43rd birthday.*
Day 155 Wed **1900-03-14**	Northern front	Colonel HCO Plumer again retires to Crocodile Pools, south of Gaberones.
	Trivia	*USA goes on Gold Standard. The Currency Act declares paper and other money redeemable in gold.*
Day 156 Thu **1900-03-15**	Central front	General Clements crosses the Orange River at Norval's Pont and Gatacre crosses at Bethulie, and they enter the Orange Free State.
	OFS	Lord Roberts issues his second proclamation (Proclamation III) to Republican burghers. *"All burghers who have not taken a prominent part in the policy which has led to the war between HM and the OFS, or commanded any forces of the Republic, or commandeered or used violence to any British subjects, and who are willing to lay down their arms at once, and to bind themselves by an oath to abstain from further participation in the war, will be given passes to allow them to return to their homes and will not be made prisoners of war, nor will their property be taken from them."* See Art. 45 of the Hague Convention 1899-07-29.[303] In Bloemfontein, Arthur Barlow, son of the owner and acting editor of *The Friend*, refuses Pretyman's request to assist in the publication of a bilingual publication supporting the British view, as he is not prepared to work for the enemy.

		Lord Roberts establishes a newspaper under military auspices as a propaganda sheet, bearing the name of Barlow's defunct paper.[304] Lord Roberts sends General JPD French with a 1 700-strong 'flying column' in the direction of Ladybrand to intercept the burghers retreating from the southern front. He also orders Lieutenant-General R Pole-Carew south with a strong column consisting mostly of the Guards Brigade, to accept the surrender of burghers at Edenburg. From there, he marches on to join General Clements at Springfontein.[305]
	Northern front	One of Plumer's patrols is attacked at Pitsani-Potlugo and forced to retreat to Lobatsi.[306]
Day 157 Fri **1900-03-16**	Western front	The village of Warrenton is occupied by British troops and Lord Methuen arrives at the destroyed Vaal River bridge. General Du Toit opens up with five or six guns and forces the British to retire beyond artillery range.[307]
	Northern front	Colonel Plumer with 560 men moves to Kanya, Bechuanaland, where he has established a supply base.
	OFS	President Kruger arrives in Kroonstad with a small bodyguard.[308] General Gatacre reaches Springfontein to join Pole-Carew and Clements.
	International	Strathcona's Horse sail from Halifax, Canada.
Day 158 Sat **1900-03-17**	OFS	Republicans, falling back from Colesberg, unite at Thaba Nchu with those retreating from Bethulie and Aliwal North. The united force now numbers about 6 500 men with 800 wagons and 10 000 oxen. The convoy is strung out over a distance of about 40 kilometres.[309] At least 327 soldiers are admitted to hospitals at Bloemfontein suffering from enteric fever, caused mainly by drinking polluted water at Paardeberg.
		THE REORGANISATION OF THE REPUBLICAN FORCES A Great (combined) Republican Council of War is held at Kroonstad. Both Presidents Steyn and Kruger as well as Commandant-General Joubert and Chief Commandant De Wet, General Botha and other leaders attend. On Joubert's proposal, it is decided to uphold the independence of the Republics and to vigorously support their governments. Far-reaching tactical decisions are taken about the future conduct of the war.[310] The measures agreed on, include the following: 1. The establishment of smaller, mobile units, the size of which would be determined by the situation. 2. The abolishment of large wagon convoys and laagers. 3. The establishment of the rank of corporal, and corporalships of about 25 men. 4. The institution of courts martial and the procedures to be followed in case of neglect or misconduct. Disciplinary measures that can include the suspension of officers and other penalties.[311]
Day 159 Sun **1900-03-18**	Cape Colony OFS	**START OF THE FIRST GUERRILLA PHASE OF THE WAR** Lord Kitchener reoccupies Prieska. General Broadwood moves towards Thaba Nchu with the 2nd Cavalry Brigade. Republican scouts under Captain Danie Theron destroy the railway bridge at Glen Siding, north of Bloemfontein.[312] General Piet de Wet sends telegrams to the ZAR Commissariat Committee and to President Kruger, bitterly protesting the fact that he has not yet received any payment for 100 horses sold to the ZAR about five months before. His telegram has an ominous tone. *"It is more than disheartening to fight for a Government under which such injustice*

119

		occurs. I shall no longer ask in fair words for what is lawfully mine, though ready to lay down my life for right. Cost what it may, I demand my lawful price."[313]
Day 160 Mon **1900-03-19**	OFS	Reacting to British proclamations, President MT Steyn issues a counter proclamation, stating that: 1. The Republic of the Orange Free States still exists and its government continues to perform its duties. 2. The proclamation issued by Lord Roberts is null and void. 3. All burghers called up for military service are still obliged to obey such instructions and defaulters will be subject to the full weight of the law. 4. All burghers assisting the enemy in any way, or surrendering without being forced to do so, will be committing treason and will be treated accordingly. 5. Furthermore, it is the duty of all burghers to inform the Republican authorities where acts of high treason are committed by others.[314] British forces occupy Rouxville.[315]
	Cape Colony	Two captured Scandinavian volunteers, CO Johansson and H Petterson-Janek, escape by jumping off the train taking them to Cape Town.
Day 161 Tue **1900-03-20**	OFS	General French's Cavalry occupies Thaba Nchu. A council of war, chaired by President Steyn, adopts De Wet's proposal to abandon wagon laagers which are blamed for Cronje's capture.[317] Newly appointed Combat General De Villebois-Mareuil submits his report on the reorganisation of the 'International Legion' to President Steyn. He proposes to attack the British supply lines with a small mobile force.[318]
	Natal	General Botha announces that there will no longer be any exemptions from commando service and that all Republican burghers are now called up.[319]
Day 162 Wed **1900-03-21**	OFS	Poet and novelist Rudyard Kipling, summoned from Cape Town by Lord Roberts, arrives in Bloemfontein to join the editorial staff of *The Friend*.[320] On General French's orders, Colonel TD Pilcher occupies Newberry's Leeuw River Mills near Tweespruit.
Day 163 Thu **1900-03-22**	OFS	Major-General Clements occupies Philippolis.
	ZAR	Ten days after being fired for being drunk and negligent, Fred Dempsey, alias Desmond, kidnaps the acting state mining engineer, Mr John H Munnik. Dempsey is joined by others and they hold Munnik hostage in a cottage on mine property. Shots are fired and they take £200 from him. They force Munnik to tell them of a secret scheme to blow up the mines. They later release him, he reports his abduction to the police and Dempsey is arrested on charges of kidnapping, robbery, attempted murder and high treason.[321]
	International	The Portuguese government sanctions the passage of British troops and stores via Beira, Mozambique, thereby violating their previous policy of neutrality.
Day 164 Fri **1900-03-23**	Natal	Major-General Sir ERP Woodgate, wounded at Spioenkop on 24 January, dies at Mooi River.[322]
	Cape Colony	Martial law is extended to Gordonia.
	OFS	Four of Theron's Scouts capture four British officers and a soldier at Glen Siding. Colonel TD Pilcher enters Ladybrand, where he arrests the magistrate and Field-cornet Smith. He searches the town for arms and ammunition until he receives reports

		of approaching commandos. After occupying the town for about an hour and a half, the arrival of Commandants Crowther and Fick forces the British to flee with a loss of one wounded and five missing.[323]
		Admissions to military hospitals in Bloemfontein among British soldiers suffering mostly of enteric fever exceed a thousand, while the death rate is climbing.
	Trivia	*Sir Alfred Milner's 46th birthday.*
Day 165 Sat **1900-03-24**	OFS	Commandant-General PJ Joubert plays into British hands by ordering all Republican forces to concentrate on the railway north of Brandfort, rather than attacking Roberts' communications in his rear.[324] Combat General De Villebois-Mareuil leaves for Hoopstad with a 'flying column' of 50 Dutchmen, 25 Frenchmen and 11 Afrikaners, starting his planned offensive operations against the British lines of communications.[325]
	Cape Colony	Sir A Milner in a telegram to Goshen: *"An irreconcilable enemy has tried to extinguish us as a power in South Africa. We must extinguish him. There is absolutely no compromise possible... and ultimate peace between the two white races is perfectly possible. I am sure of that — but possible only under one condition, that there shall be but one flag and one citizenship."*[326]
	Mozambique	'C' Battery of the Royal Canadian Artillery disembarks at Beira, Mozambique. General Carrington leaves Beira for Marandellas, Rhodesia.
	International	A fourth New Zealand contingent sails for South Africa.
Day 166 Sun **1900-03-25**	OFS	At Sand River railway bridge Republican burghers, prepared to continue the struggle, assemble after having been given furlough by Chief Commandant De Wet, thus justifying his confidence in their resilience and commitment to the struggle. Very few burghers decide to accept Roberts' surrender offer. Chief Commandant De Wet moves south to Brandfort. A cavalry reconnaissance expedition is sent from Bloemfontein towards Brandfort. The patrol is lucky to escape with only 10 casualties, as the burgher picket in town cannot get a message to the larger Republican force north of town.[327]
Day 167 Mon **1900-03-26**	OFS	Chief Commandant De Wet and General Tobias Smuts, temporarily in command of the ZAR forces in the Free State in De la Rey's absence, unite near Brandfort. President Steyn visits the burghers retreating from the Southern and Central fronts. He addresses them somewhere north of Ladybrand, inspiring them with new enthusiasm and urging them, despite the poor condition of their horses, to engage the British columns east of Bloemfontein[328] General French returns to Bloemfontein. Lord Roberts proclaims, *"that all persons who, within the territories of the South African Republic and the Orange Free State, shall authorize or be guilty of the wanton destruction or damage, or the councilling, aiding or assisting in the wanton destruction or destruction or damage of public or private properties (such destruction or damage not being justified by the usages of civilized warfare), will be held responsible in their persons and property for all such wanton destruction and damage."*[329]
	ZAR	General De la Rey, on sick-leave, is appointed as Assistant Commandant-General for the Western ZAR.[330]
	Trivia	*CC Froneman's 54th birthday.*

Day 168 Tue 1900-03-27	Western front	**Mafeking siege:** Mafeking suffers the heaviest shelling of the siege.[331]
		Commandant-General Petrus (Piet) Jacobus Joubert dies in Pretoria. Rudyard Kipling writes: *"With those that bred, with those that loosed the strife, He had no part whose hands were clear of gain; But subtle, strong and stubborn, gave his life, To a lost cause, and knew the gift was vain."*[332] General Louis Botha is appointed as Acting Commandant-General and General Schalk W Burger is appointed as Vice-State President of the ZAR.
Comdt.- Gen. PJ Joubert *(National Cultural History Museum)*		Major-General Clements occupies Fauresmith and Jagersfontein.
Day 169 Wed 1900-03-28	OFS	Chief Commandant De Wet leaves Brandfort on a secret expedition with 1 500 men, towards Thaba Nchu and the Bloemfontein Waterworks near Sannaspost, which is, according to available information, guarded by a small British force.[333] Generals Olivier, Lemmer and Grobler detach an 800-man commando with the best horses available to shadow Broadwood's movements at Thaba Nchu. [334] Major-General Brabant occupies Wepener. General JDP French, with about 800 men and 16 fieldguns, joins General Tucker's 6 400-man-strong Infantry Division with six field-guns, at Glen Siding, north of Bloemfontein.[335]
	Northern Cape	At the Fourteen Streams bridge, General SP du Toit, who has been exchanging shells across the Vaal River with the British for several days, concentrates his field-guns and opens a heavy barrage on the British camp. The surprised troops are confused and cannot determine the position of the well-placed Republican artillery. After dark, they move their camp back to Warrenton.[336]
Day 170 Thu 1900-03-29	OFS	**THE FIGHT OF KAREE SIDING** General Tobias Smuts, with a force of about 2 600 men, and Lieutenant-Colonel SPE Trichardt with 11 field-guns are ordered to cover Chief Commandant De Wet's expedition. Neither of them is familiar with the vicinity and they have to wait for guides before taking up their positions. Where they could have easily prevented it, the delay allows the British to cross the river without opposition. In a desperate race for positions near Tafelkop, the burghers reach it first and the British cavalry is repulsed. They have to make a huge detour to work around the Republican flank while the infantry, supported by the artillery, occupy the enemy's attention with assaults on their front. General Chermside's Scottish Borderers, convinced that the Republicans have been cleared out by the overwhelming barrage, are rudely disillusioned when the burghers open up from invisible positions in their front and completely shocked when Trichardt's shells land among them. The British guns are pushed forward with every charge but they remain inefficient in silencing either their counterparts or the enemy riflemen. On their flank Captain Danie Theron and seventeen of his scouts delay General Tucker's vanguard, a unit of about 400 men, for most of the day — even taking the time to capture 100 oxen in the process.[337] The action is inconclusive and General T Smuts returns to Brandfort when, at dusk, the British take heights west of the railway line and threaten their line of retreat.[338] The British lose 30 killed, 155 wounded and five missing in action, while the burghers lose three killed and 18 wounded.[339] Commandant SG Vilonel of Winburg refuses to get rid of 30 ox-wagons accompanying his commando. At a stormy council of war, Chief Commandant De Wet reminds him of the Kroonstad decision and explains that speed is essential for his planned expedition. Vilonel is adamant that his burghers would suffer serious discomfort without their wagon-train.[340]

	ZAR	Mrs JHW de Clercq and 17 ladies of Carolina writes a memorandum to their Commandant, HF Prinsloo, expressing their disgust with the fact that several healthy burghers in their ward, who have had the biggest mouths during peace time, are still, despite the desperate position of the Republic, sitting idle at home. They urge him to immediately arrange for their call-up.[341]
Day 171 Fri **1900-03-30**	ZAR	The late Commandant-General PJ Joubert is buried in Pretoria.[342]
	OFS	Chief Commandant De Wet gives Vilonel a written order to get rid of his wagons, but Vilonel insists that a council of war must be called to revise the Kroonstad decisions and he continues to follow with his wagons tagging along.[343] Major-General Broadwood, commanding about 1 700 men with two horse artillery batteries, is unnerved by reports of Republican forces approaching Thaba Nchu. He presumes that this must be the combined forces of Generals Olivier, Lemmer and Grobler and starts his retirement towards Sannaspost Station. He sends several families of British supporters, who wish to move to Bloemfontein, with his convoy consisting of 92 vehicles under a small escort ahead, while his mounted force covers the rear.[344] Unaware of these developments, Chief Commandant De Wet, planning his attack on the small garrison at the Waterworks, splits his force. He sends his brother, General Piet de Wet, with about 1 700 burghers to cut of the retreat of the British units near Thaba Nchu once Olivier and Lemmer's attack commences and to prevent any unexpected interference from that quarter. With only a force of about 400 without any field-guns, De Wet moves towards Koornspruit Drift on the road to Bloemfontein.[345] At sundown, Vilonel blatantly tells De Wet that he will not obey the council of war's decision and that De Wet must postpone the planned attack until he has had an opportunity to personally reconnoitre the positions his burghers are supposed to occupy. De Wet explodes. Vilonel must either follow orders or he must resign. Vilonel resigns and De Wet appoints Field-cornet Van der Merwe as Acting Commandant until the Winburgers can elect a new commandant. Van der Merwe immediately sends the wagons home and awaits further orders.[346] Broadwood's convoy crosses the Modder River and arrives at the Waterworks near the partially completed railway station at Sannaspost at about midnight. They camp for the rest of the night under the protection of the 200-man garrison protecting the Waterworks, commanded by Major Amphlett and they are only about eight kilometres away from a larger British force waiting for them at Bushman's Kop.[347]
	Western front Black involvement	**Mafeking siege:** A new census conducted by Colonel Baden-Powell records 7 019 black inhabitants — almost 500 fewer than the previous census. Twenty-one blacks are found dead without any relations to bury them. [348]
Day 172 Sat **1900-03-31**	OFS	**THE BATTLE OF SANNASPOST** Amphlett sends out several predawn patrols in all directions, but despite being sniped at, they fail to spot any of De Wet's men and they report that the road to Bushman's Kop is open. One of Lord Roberts' scouts, American Major Frederick Russel 'Hawkeye' Burnham, scouting alone, spots the men waiting in ambush below the banks of the drift but when he tries to warn the convoy by waving a red handkerchief, he only succeeds in attracting burghers' attention, who promptly capture him. In Bloemfontein, Lord Roberts, worried by reports that Generals Olivier and Lemmer's forces are menacing Broadwood's column around Thaba Nchu, orders General Sir Henry Colvile to Bushman's Kop and to cover the convoy's return. At Koornspruit Drift De Wet becomes aware of the changed situation at the Waterworks camp and decides to adjust his plans: rather than a simple raid on Bloemfontein's water supply, he now decides on a classic ambush on a much larger force. At dawn, his brother Piet, acting as beater, opens up with his two Krupps and quickly closes the range to drop his shells into the midst of the convoy wagons. Brigadier-

		General Broadwood, convinced that he is attacked from the northeast by the 5 000 men of Olivier and Lemmer, decides to make a dash for the protection of Lieutenant-Colonel Martyr's force — the advance party of General Colvile's Division — at Bushman's Kop. His convoy quickly inspans and with the civilian carts in front, flees west towards Koornspruit Drift and into the arms of De Wet.
		Disappearing from British view as they descend into the drift, they are met by De Wet, who quietly orders them, *"Dismount. You are prisoners. Go to the wagons"*. Burghers disarm all soldiers, take over the reigns and take the wagons through the ford and up the other bank where the soldiers are placed under guard in a farmhouse, about 400 metres beyond the spruit. One ox-wagon after the other is taken in the same fashion and those approaching the drift are not alarmed as congestion at drifts is a normal occurrence. At about 08:00 the leading mounted men ride down the riverbank and are immediately challenged and ordered to drop their rifles. Isolated cases of resistance are quickly dealt with and two officers reaching for their revolvers are shot down by Commandant Fourie and Captain Gideon Scheepers. When the main force approaches to within a hundred metres, Chief Commandant De Wet sends a captain he has captured to order the troops within range of his burghers's rifles to lay down their arms to avoid unnecessary bloodshed. The captain obeys, but as he nears the approaching soldiers, he shouts a warning and De Wet shoots him down. Most of the troops wheel about and flee as the burghers open fire, trying not to hit those who raise their hands in surrender. The surprise is complete and the British sustain heavy losses. The gunners and crew of 'U' battery are shot down and 'Q' battery loses several horses and seven of the 12 field-guns are abandoned in no man's land. 'Q' battery falls back to the half completed station buildings and come into action at a range of about 1 000 metres but their shells are not effective against the men behind the bank of the spruit. Some burghers leave their positions to subject the field-guns to flanking fire and soon the battery commander, Major Phipps-Hornby, is left with only eight gunners and two noncommissioned officers. The British Army's obsession with their artillery pieces manifests itself again, and volunteers are asked for to save the field-guns. The field-guns are dragged behind the station buildings by hand. Here the surviving artillery horses are hitched and they race away with five field-guns, a single ammunition cart and a limber, across the spruit towards Bushman's Kop under heavy rifle fire.
		The mounted contingent under Colonel Alderson, sent out south-westward by Broadwood to attempt an outflanking movement, is held at bay by De Wet's riflemen positioned on the heights dominating their route. Colvile, on arrival at Bushman's Kop, makes no practical contribution to the column's fate when he, unable to grasp the situation, orders Broadwood to report to him in person. Broadwood cannot oblige and Colvile sends a mounted brigade under Colonel St GC Henry towards Waterval Drift where he expects De Wet to withdraw to. He also decides to wait for a mounted force under French and to launch a sortie to recover the field-guns. However, Chief Commandant De Wet applies 'the tactics of judicious disengagement' decided on at Kroonstad and about noon he orders his men to cross the Modder River and to move eastwards with their prisoners and gains. They destroy the pump installation, offer assistance to the wounded British soldiers in the station buildings and departs southwards with a small escort. Covered by Alderson's mounted troops, Broadwood retires towards Bushman's Kop.[349]
		The British suffer 18 killed, 134 wounded and 426 taken prisoner. They also lose seven field-guns, 96 loaded wagons, 21 other vehicles and a substantial amount of arms and ammunition including two wagon loads of artillery shells. They also capture a supply of dum-dum ammunition and oath of neutrality forms completed by several surrendering Eastern Free State burghers. De Wet loses five burghers killed and 11 wounded.[350] Lieutenant MJ Nix, Dutch military attache with the Republican forces, is fatally wounded by British shrapnel.[351]
	Victoria Cross	Lieutenant FA Maxwell, Indian Staff Corps (Roberts' Light Horse), is recommended

| | | for the Victoria Cross for his efforts in rescuing two of the field-guns and three limbers while under fire. As it is considered that every man of 'Q' Battery, Royal Horse Artillery, has displayed equally conspicuous courage, Roberts decides to invoke Rule 13 of the Warrant of the order and allots four medals — one for officers, one for noncommissioned officers and two for gunners — to be awarded by their peers and comrades. Major EJ Phipps-Hornby, mostly responsible for the recovery of five of the field-guns, Sergeant CEH Parker, Gunner I Lodge and Driver HH Glasock — who has had six horses shot from under him during the attempts to rescue the field-guns — win their recommendations.[352] |
| | Western front | **Mafeking siege:** At Ramatlabama, within sight of Mafeking, Colonel Plumer is attacked by burghers under General Snyman. The British are forced to retire, suffering nine killed, 30 wounded (including Plumer) and 14 missing. Colonel Baden-Powell is devastated by the news that his lifelong friend, Captain 'The Boy' Maclaren , is among the killed, but is later relieved to discover that he is alive and wounded, a prisoner in Snyman's camp.[353] The burghers lose one killed and two slightly wounded. Plumer retires to Sefetile.[354] |

NOTES

JAN 1900 - MARCH 1900 (HAMMER BLOWS)

1. WESSELS, A, Die Anglo-Boereoorlog..., *op cit*, p 10

   BREYTENBACH, *op cit*, vol I, pp 403-7
2. PAKENHAM, *op cit*, p 407
3. BREYTENBACH, *op cit*, vol I, pp 31-33
4. CRESWICKE, *op cit*, vol II, p vii
5. *Ibid*, vol III, p vii
6. BREYTENBACH, *op cit*, vol I, pp 36-44
7. CRESWICKE, *op cit*, vol III, p viii
8. BREYTENBACH, *op cit*, vol II, p 13
9. BREYTENBACH, *op cit*, vol IV, p 4
10. McCRACKEN, *op cit*, p 101
11. BREYTENBACH, *op cit*, vol IV, p 44
12. VAN SCHOOR, De Wet-Annale No 2, p 11
13. BREYTENBACH, *op cit*, vol IV, p 51
14. BREYTENBACH, *op cit*, vol III, pp 17-19
15. *Ibid*, vol III, pp 1-16; AMERY, *op cit*, vol III, pp 176-205
16. CRESWICKE, *op cit*, vol IV
17. WESSELS, A, Die Anglo-Boereoorlog..., *op cit*, p 19
18. BREYTENBACH, *op cit*, vol IV, pp 50-55
19. VAN SCHOOR, De Wet-Annale No 2, p 11
20. WESSELS, Boer War Diary..., *op cit*, p 27
21. VAN RENSBURG, Oorlogsjoernaal..., *op cit*, p 42
22. VAN SCHOOR, De Wet-Annale No 5, p 20
23. BREYTENBACH, *op cit*, vol IV, p 47
24. PLOEGER, *op cit*, p 4:36
25. VAN SCHOOR, De Wet-Annale No 2, p 11
26. CRESWICKE, *op cit*, vol III, p viii
27. BREYTENBACH, *op cit*, vol III, pp 70-71
28. *Ibid*, vol III, pp 77&81
29. BREYTENBACH, *op cit*, vol VI, p 37
30. BREYTENBACH, *op cit*, vol III, p 71
31. DOONER, *op cit*, p 13
32. BREYTENBACH, *op cit*, vol IV, pp 59-60
33. *Ibid*, vol IV, p 60
34. BREYTENBACH, *op cit*, vol III, p 359
35. GRIFFITH, *op cit*, p 228
36. BREYTENBACH, *op cit*, vol III, p 91
37. GRIFFITH, *op cit*, p 228
38. BREYTENBACH, *op cit*, vol III, pp 98-102
39. BREYTENBACH, *op cit*, vol III, p 359
40. GRIFFITH, *op cit*, p 228
41. BREYTENBACH, *op cit*, vol III, p 85
42. *Ibid*, vol III, pp 100-106
43. BELFIELD, The Boer War, p 67
44. BREYTENBACH, *op cit*, vol III, pp 113-120; TODD, *op cit*, p 50
45. BREYTENBACH, *op cit*, vol III, p 360
46. SMIT, Beleg van..., *op cit*, p 204
47. BREYTENBACH, *op cit*, vol III, pp 126-129
48. PEDDLE, Long Cecil..., *op cit*, p 8
49. BREYTENBACH, *op cit*, vol VI, p 33
50. PRETORIUS, Kommandolewe..., p 320
51. BREYTENBACH, *op cit*, vol III, pp 130-147
52. *Ibid*, vol III, p 164
53. *Ibid*, vol III, pp 147-154
54. PEDDLE, Long Cecil..., op cit, p 9
55. PEMBERTON, *op cit*, p 167
56. BREYTENBACH, *op cit*, vol III, pp 149-163
57. *Ibid*, vol III, pp 177-180
58. PEDDLE, Long Cecil..., *op cit*, p 9
59. BREYTENBACH, *op cit*, vol III, pp 182-230 ; PEMBERTON, *op cit*, pp 174-201
60. BELFIELD, The Boer War, pp 72-75
61. KRUGER, *op cit*, pp 188-199; AMERY, *op cit*, vol III, pp 251-295
62. CONRADIE, FW, Met Cronje op die Wesfront, p 106
63. BREYTENBACH, *op cit*, vol III, pp 230-231
64. *Ibid*, vol III, pp 246-26
65. MEINTJES, Anglo-Boer War..., p 59
66. CRESWICKE, *op cit*, vol III, p 132
67. BREYTENBACH, *op cit*, vol III, pp 224-226

68. *Ibid*, vol III, p 256

69. GARDNER, *op cit*, p 161

70. BREYTENBACH, *op cit*, vol II, pp 404-405

71. PLOEGER, *op cit*, p 27:4

72. KRUGER, Good Bye Dolly Gray, *op cit*, p 202

73. BREYTENBACH, *op cit*, vol III, p 240

74. BREYTENBACH, *op cit*, vol II, pp 404-405

75. BREYTENBACH, *op cit*, vol IV, pp 89-98

76. WARWICK, South African War, *op cit*, p 252

77. CRESWICKE, *op cit*, vol III, p 132

78. BREYTENBACH, *op cit*, vol III, p 267

79. WARWICK, South African War, *op cit*, p 317

80. CRESWICKE, *op cit*, vol III, p 134

81. BREYTENBACH, *op cit*, vol III, p 360

82. BREYTENBACH, *op cit*, vol IV, p 128

83. *Ibid*, vol IV, p 130

84. BREYTENBACH, *op cit*, vol III, pp 270-271

85. *Ibid*, vol III, p 282

86. *Ibid*, vol III, pp 288-289

87. BREYTENBACH, *op cit*, vol IV, p 132

88. KRUGER, Good Bye Dolly Gray, *op cit*, p 204

89. BREYTENBACH, *op cit*, vol III, p 286

90. *Ibid*, vol III, pp 290-307

91. *Ibid*, vol III, p 360

92. BREYTENBACH, *op cit*, vol IV, pp 132-134

93. PLOEGER, *op cit*, pp 27-28

94. KRUGER, Good Bye Dolly Gray, *op cit*, p 205

95. BREYTENBACH, *op cit*, vol III, pp 312-319

96. BREYTENBACH, *op cit*, vol II, p 404

97. BREYTENBACH, *op cit*, vol IV, pp 134-135

98. GARDNER, *op cit*, p 162

99. BREYTENBACH, *op cit*, vol III, pp 320-325

100. *Ibid*, vol III, pp 326-327

101. BREYTENBACH, *op cit*, vol II, p 404

102. BREYTENBACH, *op cit*, vol IV, pp 135-138

103. *Ibid*, vol IV, pp 139-140

104. WARWICK, Black people..., *op cit*, p 35

105. PAKENHAM, *op cit*, p 322

106. PEDDLE, Long Cecil..., *op cit*, p 12

107. CHISHOLM, *op cit*, p 193

108. BREYTENBACH, *op cit*, vol III, p 368

109. PEDDLE, Long Cecil..., *op cit*, p 12

110. PAKENHAM, *op cit*, p 322

111. *Ibid*, p 326

112. BREYTENBACH, *op cit*, vol IV, pp 107-125

113. BREYTENBACH, *op cit*, vol IV, pp 165-166

114. BREYTENBACH, *op cit*, vol III, p 366

115. *Ibid*, vol III, pp 386-387 & 389-390

116. BREYTENBACH, *op cit*, vol IV, pp 166-169

117. *Ibid*, vol IV, pp 173-175

118. VAN RENSBURG, Oorlogsjoernaal..., *op cit*, p 67

119. DE SOUZA, *op cit*, p 179

120. BREYTENBACH, *op cit*, vol IV, pp 154-156

121. WARWICK, Black people..., *op cit*, p 26

122. BREYTENBACH, *op cit*, vol IV, p 185

123. *Ibid*, vol IV, pp 178-179

124. SCHOLTZ, Beroemde Suid-Afrikaanse Krygsmanne, p 74

125. DE SOUZA, *op cit*, pp 180-181

126. BREYTENBACH, *op cit*, vol IV, p 156

127. OBERHOLSTER, Oorlogsdagboek ..., p 68

128. BREYTENBACH, *op cit*, vol IV, p 189

129. *Ibid*, vol IV, pp 217-220.

130. BREYTENBACH, *op cit*, vol III, pp 401-406

131. BREYTENBACH, *op cit*, vol IV, pp 159-160

132. *Ibid*, vol IV, pp 214-217

133. PAKENHAM, *op cit*, p 328

134. BREYTENBACH, *op cit*, vol IV, p 228

135. FARWELL, *op cit*, pp 204-205

136. BREYTENBACH, *op cit*, vol IV, pp 232-239

137. *Ibid*, vol IV, p 252

138. *Ibid*, vol IV, p 242

139. *Ibid*, vol IV, pp 247-250

140. BREYTENBACH, *op cit*, vol III, p 412

141. BREYTENBACH, *op cit*, vol IV, pp 247-250

142. PAKENHAM, *op cit*, p 330

143. BREYTENBACH, *op cit*, vol IV, pp 255-263

144. *Ibid*, vol IV, p 264

145. *Ibid*, vol IV, pp 226-229

146. BREYTENBACH, *op cit*, vol III, pp 406-411

147. *Ibid*, vol III, pp 413 & 416

148. CONRADIE, FW, Met Cronje op die Westfront, p 107

149. BREYTENBACH, *op cit*, vol IV, pp 263-269

150. *Ibid*, vol IV, pp 263-285

151. PAKENHAM, *op cit*, p 328

152. GRUNDLINGH, AM, Die 'Hendsoppers' en 'Joiners', p 14
     JOHNSON, Jackdaw Reprint

153. WESSELS, Boer War Diary..., *op cit*, p 29

154. BREYTENBACH, *op cit*, vol III, pp 418-423

155. *Ibid*, vol III, pp 322

156. BREYTENBACH, *op cit*, vol IV, pp 286-312

157. CRESWICKE, *op cit*, vol VI, p 193

158. KRUGER, Good Bye Dolly Gray, *op cit*, p 237

159. BEYTENBACH, *op cit*, vol IV, pp 320-321

160. BREYTENBACH, *op cit*, vol III, pp 431-438

161. BREYTENBACH, *op cit*, vol VI, p 40

162. WULFSOHN, *op cit*, p 19

163. KRUGER, Good Bye Dolly Gray, *op cit*, p 239

164. AMERY, *op cit*, vol III, p 454

165. VAN SCHOOR, De Wet-Annale No 5, p 46

166. BREYTENBACH, *op cit*, vol III, p 442

167. OOSTHUIZEN, *op cit*, p 92

168. KRUGER, Good Bye Dolly Gray, *op cit*, p 242

169. DAVITT, *op cit*, p 393

170. VAN SCHOOR, De Wet-Annale No i-, p 28

171. VAN RENSBURG, Oorlogsjoernaal..., *op cit*, p 83

172. BREYTENBACH, *op cit*, vol IV, p 444

173. BREYTENBACH, *op cit*, vol III, pp 444-450

174. BELFIELD, The Boer War, p 90

175. SLOCUM, Boer War Operations...., *op cit*, pp 33-34

176. VAN RENSBURG, Oorlogsjoernaal..., *op cit*, p 79

177. AMERY, *op cit*, vol III, p 474

178. VAN RENSBURG, Oorlogsjoernaai..., *op cit*, p 82

179. BREYTENBACH, *op cit*, Vol IV, pp 337-347

180. BELFIELD, The Boer War, p 90

181. BREYTENBACH, *op cit*, Vol V, pp 467-472

182. FARWELL, *op cit*, p 230

183. BREYTENBACH, *op cit*, Vol III, p 370

184. SLOCUM, Boer War Operations..., *op cit*, p 34

185. BREYTENBACH, *op cit*, vol IV, p 362

186. SLOCUM, Boer War Operations..., *op cit*, p 35

187. BREYTENBACH, *op cit*, vol III, pp 476-490; AMERY, *op cit*, vol III, pp 515-520

188. *Ibid*, vol III, p 498

189. BREYTENBACH, *op cit*, vol IV, p 446

190. SMIT, Beleg van..., *op cit*, p 231

191. VAN SCHOOR, De Wet-Annale No 1, p 30; BREYTENBACH, *op cit*, vol IV, pp 363-369

192. KRUGER, Good Bye Dolly Gray, *op cit*, p 244

193. BREYTENBACH, *op cit*, vol III, pp 493-495

194. CRESWICKE, *op cit*, vol VI, pp 193

195. BREYTENBACH, *op cit*, vol III, pp 505-506

196. *Ibid*, vol III, pp 507-516

197. *Ibid*, vol III, p 498

198. BREYTENBACH, *op cit*, vol IV, p 457

199. BREYTENBACH, *op cit*, vol V, p 10

200. CRESWICKE, *op cit*, vol IV, p 193

201. BREYTENBACH, *op cit*, vol III, pp 517-522

202. *Ibid*, vol III, p 524

203. *Ibid*, vol III, p 371

204. KRUGER, Good Bye Dolly Gray, *op cit*, p 244

205. SLOCUM, Boer War Operations..., *op cit*, p 35

206. BREYTENBACH, *op cit*, vol IV, p 447

207. PRETORIUS, Kommandolewe..., p 190

208. BREYTENBACH, Kommandant Danie Theron, pp 136-138

209. SCHOLTZ, *op cit*, p 74

210. SLOCUM, *op cit*, p 35

211. *Ibid*, p 35

212. SMIT, Beleg van..., *op cit*, p 231

213. *Ibid*, p 230

214. BREYTENBACH, *op cit*, vol IV, p 449

215. PAKENHAM, *op cit*, p 359

216. BREYTENBACH, *op cit*, vol III, p 524

217. KRUGER, Good Bye Dolly Gray, *op cit*, p 255

218. BREYTENBACH, *op cit*, vol III, p 526-528; AMERY, *op cit*, vol III, pp 532-4

219. SLOCUM, Boer War Operations..., *op cit*, p 36

220. BREYTENBACH, Kommandant Danie Theron, pp 38-40

221. BREYTENBACH, *op cit*, vol IV, p 247

222. VAN SCHOOR, De Wet-Annale No 3, p 16

223. BREYTENBACH, *op cit*, vol IV, p 17

224. BREYTENBACH, *op cit*, vol III, pp 413-414

225. AMERY, *op cit*, vol III, pp 533-535

226. FERREIRA, ... SPE Trichard, p 145

227. BREYTENBACH, *op cit*, vol V, p 10

228. VAN SCHOOR, De Wet-Annale No 1-36; VAN RENSBURG, *op cit*, p. 89

229. BREYTENBACH, *op cit*, vol V, p 17

230. MIDGLEY, *op cit*, p 20

231. CRESWICKE, *op cit*, vol VI, p 193

232. BREYTENBACH, *op cit*, vol III, pp 526-533, 535-567; AMERY, *op cit*, vol III, pp 533-546

233. HOLT, The Boer War, p 205

234. BREYTENBACH, *op cit*, vol V, p 10

235. REITZ, Commando, p 90

236. FARWELL, *op cit*, p 231

237. BREYTENBACH, *op cit*, vol III, p 566

238. GRIFFITH, *op cit*, p 362

239. BREYTENBACH, *op cit*, vol V, p 17

240. OBERHOLZER, Oorlogsdagboek..., p 77; BREYTENBACH, *op cit*, vol V, p 11

241. HATTINGH, Britse Fortifikasies..., p 32

242. BREYTENBACH, *op cit*, vol V, p 232

243. *Ibid*, vol V, p 20

244. FERREIRA, ... SPE Trichard, pp 148-149

245. CHISHOLM, *op cit*, p 215

246. BELFIELD, The Boer War, p 92

247. WULFSOHN, Rustenburg at War, p 45

248. OBERHOLZER, Oorlogsdagboek ..., p 77

249. OOSTHUIZEN, *op cit*, p 87

250. BREYTENBACH, Kommandant Danie Theron, p 144

251. BREYTENBACH, *op cit*, vol V, p 22

252. KANDYBA-FOXCROFT, Russia and the Anglo-Boer War, p 77

253. AMERY, *op cit*, vol III, p 548

254. FERREIRA, ... SPE Trichard, p 149

255. AMERY, *op cit*, vol III, map

256. MIDGLEY, *op cit*, p 61

257. OOSTHUIZEN, *op cit*, p 92

258. OBERHOLZER, Oorlogsdagboek..., p 79

259. *Ibid*, p 77

260. WESSELS, Boer War Diary..., *op cit*, p 31; OOSTHUIZEN, *op cit*, p 93

261. BREYTENBACH, *op cit*, vol V, p 232

262. FERREIRA, Memoirs of General Ben Bouwer, p 56

263. OOSTHUIZEN, *op cit*, p 93

264. BREYTENBACH, *op cit*, vol V, p 23

265. VAN SCHOOR, Bittereinder..., *op cit*, pp 197-198

266. BREYTENBACH, *op cit*, vol V, pp 36-45

267. AMERY, *op cit*, vol III, p 554

268. BREYTENBACH, *op cit*, vol V, p 132

269. FARWELL, *op cit*, p 327

270. BREYTENBACH, *op cit*, vol V, p 326

271. KRUGER, DW, *op cit*, p 22

272. BREYTENBACH, *op cit*, vol V, pp 50-52

273. *Ibid*, vol V, pp 50-52

274. AMERY, *op cit*, vol III, pp 560-569

275. BREYTENBACH, *op cit*, vol V, pp 55-61

276. *Ibid*, vol V, p 132

277. BREYTENBACH, *op cit*, vol V, pp 66-68

278. *Ibid*, vol V, pp 68-72

279. *Ibid*, vol V, p 75

280. MEINTJES, Anglo-Boer War – Pictorial History, p 112

281. BREYTENBACH, *op cit*, vol V, pp 75-93

282. AMERY, *op cit*, vol III, map

283. BREYTENBACH, *op cit*, vol V, p 98

284. *Ibid*, vol V, p 360

285. OBERHOLZER, Oorlogsdagboek..., p 79

286. AMERY, *op cit*, vol III, p 587

287. BREYTENBACH, *op cit*, vol V, p 135

288. AMERY, *op cit*, vol III, p 592

289. FARWELL, *op cit*, p 239; OOSTHUIZEN, *op cit*, p 100

290. WULFSOHN, Rustenburg at war, p 45

291. BREYTENBACH, *op cit,* vol V, pp 97-107

292. WESSELS, Boer War Diary..., *op cit,* p 34

293. BARBARY, The Boer War, *op cit,* p 111

294. BREYTENBACH, *op cit,* vol V, p 113

295. *Ibid*, vol V, p 106

296. AMERY, *op cit,* vol III, map 594

297. BREYTENBACH, *op cit,* vol V, p 123

298. BREYTENBACH, *op cit,* vol V, p 115

299. CRESWICKE, *op cit,* vol IV, p 193

300. BREYTENBACH, *op cit,* vol V, p 116

301. AMERY, *op cit,* vol III, p 593

302. 'SETEMPE', March/April 1998, Article by D Olmesdahl, p 24

303. GRUNDLINGH, AM, Die 'Hendsoppers' en 'Joiners', p 15

304. SPIES, Methods of Barbarism?, p 84

305. BREYTENBACH, *op cit,* vol V, p 137

306. BREYTENBACH, *op cit,* vol VI, p 41

307. BREYTENBACH, *op cit,* vol V, p 356

308. *Ibid*, vol V, p 157

309. AMERY, *op cit,* vol III, pp 593-594

310. FERREIRA, ... SPE Trichard, p 151

311. BREYTENBACH, *op cit,* vol V, pp 164-167

312. BREYTENBACH, Kommandant Danie Theron, p 157

313. DE SOUZA, *op cit,* p 134

314. VAN SCHOOR, Bittereinder..., *op cit,* p 174

315. OOSTHUIZEN, *op cit,* p 102

316. FERREIRA, Krijgsgevangenschap..., p 99

317. VAN SCHOOR, De Wet-Annale No 2, p 80

318. BREYTENBACH, *op cit,* vol V, p 360

319. GRUNDLINGH, AM, Die 'Hendsoppers' en 'Joiners', p 8

320. SPIES, Methods of Barbarism?, p 84

321. CAMMACK, The Rand at War, p 103

322. DOONER, *op cit,* p 431

323. BREYTENBACH, *op cit,* vol V, p 154

324. *Ibid*, vol V, p 47

325. *Ibid*, vol V, p 361

326. PLOEGER, *op cit,* p 8 ; 36

327. BREYTENBACH, *op cit,* vol V, pp 177-179

328. *Ibid*, vol V, p 198

329. PLOEGER, *op cit,* p 27:16

330. FERREIRA, ... SPE Trichard, p 152

331. COMAROFF, The Boer War Diary... Sol Plaatje, p 21

332. MEINTJES, Anglo-Boer War..., p 126

333. BREYTENBACH, *op cit,* vol V, p 186

334. *Ibid*, vol V, p 198

335. *Ibid*, vol V, p 186-7

336. BREYTENBACH, *op cit,* vol V, p 357

337. BREYTENBACH, Kommandant Danie Theron, p 165

338. VAN SCHOOR, De Wet-Annale No 5, p 61

339. BREYTENBACH, *op cit,* vol V, pp 186-191

340. *Ibid*, vol V, pp 192-193

341. *Ibid*, vol V, p 452

342. VAN SCHOOR, De Wet-Annale No 5, p 12

343. BREYTENBACH, *op cit,* vol V, pp 192-193

344. *Ibid*, vol V, p 200

345. *Ibid*, vol V, p 185

346. *Ibid*, vol V, p 193

347. *Ibid*, vol V, p 200

348. PAKENHAM, *op cit,* p 409

349. BREYTENBACH, *op cit,* vol V, pp 200-220; AMERY, *op cit,* vol V, pp 35-51

350. BREYTENBACH, *op cit,* vol V, p 220

351. VAN SCHOOR, De Wet-Annale No 5, p 14

352. CRESWICKE, *op cit,* vol VI, pp 193-194

353. PAKENHAM, *op cit,* p 409

354. MIDGLEY, *op cit,* p 73; BREYTENBACH, *op cit,* vol VI, pp 41-42

APRIL-JUNE 1900

MARCHES AND RETREATS

1900	AUTUMN	APRIL
Day 173 Sun **1900-04-01**	OFS	General French's cavalry division moves to Waterval Drift in support of Broadwood's mauled force, but is unable to make contact with the Republicans under General Piet de Wet who have slipped away eastwards. British doctors arrive with 92 ambulance wagons to recover their wounded in the Sannaspost station buildings. General De Wet moves towards Dewetsdorp, where he plans to obtain dynamite for operations against Lord Roberts' lines of communication south of Bloemfontein. On General Gatacre's instructions, Captain WJ McWhinnie enters Dewetsdorp with about 600 men, mostly Royal Irish Rifles and some mounted infantry. He makes himself very unpopular by demanding food and fodder from the magistrate and billeting his men in the church. Upon receiving information about the occupation of Dewetsdorp, De Wet immediately orders Generals JB Wessels, CC Froneman and AI de Villiers with 2 000 men and three Krupp guns to join him. McWhinnie reports rumours about commandos heading for Dewetsdorp and Lord Roberts, alarmed by De Wet's success at Sannaspost, orders him to move to the railhead near Reddersburg.[1] Combat General De Villebois-Mareuil's small force leaves Hoopstad, planning to skirt around Methuen's force at Boshof and start offensive operations in the enemy's rear. [2]
	Cape Town	Colonel George Gough, sent back to Stellenbosch, commits suicide.[3]
	Western front Black involvement	**Mafeking siege:** A message from Queen Victoria reaches Colonel Baden-Powell in Mafeking: *"I continue watching with confidence and admiration the patient and resolute defence... under your ever resourceful command. VRI."* This and other messages — some of a very frivolous nature — are taken in and out of the besieged town by very brave unknown black runners, who risk being shot as spies if caught by the besiegers. [4]
Day 174 Mon **1900-04-02**	OFS	The Orange Free State Volksraad meets in Kroonstad for its last formal session. In his opening address, President Steyn again states that the war has been thrust upon the OFS by the British government, and that the Orange Free State has no war aims other than the fulfilment of its obligations under its treaty with the ZAR and the defence of its independence. He regrets the recent serious reverses suffered and mourns the death of Commandant-General Joubert, and urges the burghers to greater effort and, if necessary, sacrifice, in honour of those who have already suffered for the cause. Steyn again accuses the British of misuse of the white flag and the disregard of the Red Cross which has been brought to the attention of the neutral powers. He also refers to the Republican peace overtures and the unsuccessful telegram addressed to Lord Salisbury, as well as the intended dispatch of a joint delegation to Europe to plead their cause and to seek intervention to stop the bloodshed.[5] Captain McWhinnie leaves Dewetsdorp, but he is delayed by wet roads and his tired troops progress slowly and rest at Oorlogspoort. De Wet's scouts shadow their movements and he scours the vicinity, commandeering burghers on leave and who have laid down their arms. He orders his approaching reinforcements to swerve towards Reddersburg, while he skirts McWhinnie's sleeping soldiers to take positions further along their route. [6] After a spell of sick leave, General JH de la Rey rejoins his commando south of Brandfort.[7] Major-General EY Brabant's Colonial Division enters Rouxville.
	Western front Black involvement	**Mafeking siege:** After being found guilty and sentenced to death by Colonel Baden-Powell's court of summary jurisdiction for stealing a goat, Jan (alias

		George) Malhombe is executed by a British firing squad at Currie's Post, Mafeking,[8]
	Cape Colony	A mass meeting is held in Cape Town in favour of the annexation of the Republics.[9] A huge banner reads, *"As British subjects assembled in Cape Town, we desire to express our entire concurrence with the refusal of Her Majesty's Ministers to allow the South African Republic and the Orange Free State to retain their independence, and we hereby declare our solemn conviction that the incorporation of those states within the dominions of the QUEEN can alone ensure peace, prosperity, and public freedom throughout SOUTH AFRICA."*[10]
Day 175 Tue **1900-04-03**	OFS	**THE BATTLE OF MOSTERT'S HOEK** (near Reddersburg) The British troops only resume their march after sunrise. At about 10:00, De Villiers' men, tired after their night march and fearing that the British, refreshed after their rest, may outstrip them, open fire on the leading soldiers. Captain McWhinnie orders his men to occupy the heights of Mostert's Hoek where they build stone breastworks. While waiting for reinforcements and field-guns to arrive, De Wet send a message under a flag of truce to the British commanding officer. He states that he has more than 500 men with three Krupp guns — actually he has less than 400 and no artillery — and is expecting further reinforcements. As the British will not be able to maintain themselves, he demands their surrender to avoid unnecessary bloodshed. McWhinnie refuses and opens fire even before the messenger has reached safety. De Wet's men answers and De Villiers charges recklessly across open ground in full view of the enemy to cut off their advance towards Reddersburg, completing their isolation. The burghers, with sustained, accurate rifle fire at remarkably long ranges — ranges at which the British counterfire is completely harmless — inflict mounting casualties despite the well-built British fortifications. General Gatacre, receiving reports of De Wet's presence during the early morning, gathers all available troops and they rush towards Reddersburg, where they are met by five companies Cameron Highlanders, sent by train from Bloemfontein. They advance to within earshot of the battle when they receive a cautionary note from Roberts, advising Gatacre not to engage the enemy, unless he has a 'sufficient force'. They decide not to proceed closer. At about 17:00 De Wet's reinforcements, in the form of the Kroonstad commando and three guns, eventually arrive and come into action. The twilight brings an end to the battle and both sides prepare for the night. The burghers, whose numbers have increased to more than 800, start barbeque fires and slaughter some sheep. The British situation, without sufficient warm clothes and with their water supply dwindling, is more serious.[11]
	Cape Colony	Brigadier-General HH Settle reoccupies Upington in the northern Cape. General PA Cronje, his wife, Colonel Adolf Schiel and about 1 000 Republican prisoners of war sails from Cape Town for St Helena.[12]
	Trivia	*Judge JBM Hertzog's 34th birthday.*
Day 176 Wed **1900-04-04**	OFS	**THE BATTLE OF MOSTERT'S HOEK** At dawn, while the British troops are crowding at the water carts, the Republicans open fire. They rush back to their positions and resume firing. De Wet concentrates some of his burghers to charge the hill. They cut a fence in their front and rush forward until they reach the dead ground at the foot of the hill, where they pause before starting the ascent. When they look up, they see white flags fluttering. Some troops in the vicinity of the field hospital keep on firing and, despite the danger of hitting the hospital, De Wet is forced to order his burghers to eliminate this pocket of resistance. At about noon the battle is over and the burghers disarm the tired and thirsty British soldiers. British casualties amount to 11 killed, 40 wounded and 552 surrendering uninjured, while De Wet loses only three killed and three wounded. They also capture the small convoy and about 500 Lee-Metford rifles.[13]

	International	Major-General Clements arrives at Bloemfontein. Colonel EH Dalgety, commanding the Cape Mounted Rifles, arrives at Wepener.[14] Queen Victoria starts a royal visit to Ireland.[15] The 3rd Queensland Mounted Infantry disembarks at Beira, Portuguese East Africa.
	Trivia	*Prince of Wales is shot at by a 16-year-old anarchist in Brussels, Belgium.*
Day 177 Thu **1900-04-05** *Gen. Georges-Henri Anne Marie Victor Comte de Villebois-Mareuil* *(National Cultural History Museum)*	OFS	**THE BATTLE OF BOSHOF** Combat-General Georges-Henri Anne Marie Victor Comte de Villebois-Mareuil, a former commander in the French Foreign Legion, has recently been appointed as commander of all the Foreign Volunteers fighting with the Republicans. He moves towards Boshof with a force of about 75 foreign volunteers and 11 burghers to attack the railway and disrupt Methuen's supply lines. Due to faulty information and having to rely on unproven guides, his expedition moves very slowly. Lord Methuen, with a force of 750 and four field-guns, surprises him at Tweefontein near Boshof. De Villebois-Mareuil refuses to consider retreating and orders the occupation of two linked koppies. The burghers with him soon realise the hopelessness of the position and fight their way out, while De Villebois-Mareuil gallantly makes a desperate stand. Despite a courageous fight that lasts more than four hours, De Villebois-Mareuil is killed, with a thunderstorm gathering overhead and the charging soldiers about 20 metres away. The survivors surrender after his heroic death and the thunderstorm that could have covered their flight, breaks loose. The Republicans lose seven killed, 11 wounded and 51 captured while Methuen loses three killed and 10 wounded.[16] Colonel Dalgety takes up defensive positions in koppies overlooking Jammersberg Drift, about five kilometres outside Wepener. His force consists of the Cape Mounted Rifles, the CMR Artillery Troop, Brabant's Horse, Driscoll's Scouts, the Kaffrarian Rifles and some Royal Scots — a total of 1 895 men with seven field-guns and six machine guns.[17] Captain John Hassel's American Volunteer Corps have their baptism of fire when they clash with a squadron lancers, south of Brandfort. They keep the enemy at bay for more than three hours until they are reinforced from the Boer laager and succeed in chasing off the lancers.[18]
	St. Helena	The Governor of St Helena, Mr RA Sterndale, issues the following proclamation: *"His Excellency the Governor expresses the hope that the inhabitants will treat the prisoners with that courtesy and consideration which should be extended to all men who have fought bravely in what they considered the cause of their country, and will help in repressing any unseemly demonstration which individuals may exhibit."*[19]
	Trivia	*The American actor Spencer Tracy is born.*
Day 178 Fri **1900-04-06**	OFS	Lord Methuen buries Combat General De Villebois-Mareuil with full military honours at Boshof. One thousand five-hundred men of the Loyal North Lancashires form the guard of honour and Count Pierre de Breda delivers the service in French.[20]
	ZAR	The trial of Dempsey, the man accused of kidnapping the mining engineer JH Munnik, starts in Johannesburg.
Day 179 Sat **1900-04-07**	OFS	Chief Commandant CR de Wet, with about 1 600 men, three field-guns, two pom-poms and two maxims, arrives near Wepener. He sends a spy into town and finds out that the British have received advance notice of his approach and have moved to Jammersberg Drift outside the town.[21]
	ZAR	In an attempt to prevent the burghers from simply leaving their units without per-

	Western front Black involvement	mission, President Steyn institutes a system whereby 10% of the men are granted 10-12 days' furlough on a rotational basis.[22] According to a newspaper report, Lord Roberts has put a reward of £1 000 on Danie Theron's head, dead or alive.[23] **Mafeking siege:** In one of the most savage incidents, Colonel Baden-Powell forces or 'persuades' about 700 Barolong women to attempt a mass exodus at night. They are fired on and turned back by the besiegers and only ten manage to get away. [24]
Day 180 Sun **1900-04-08**	St Helena	A notice (dated 5 April) declares the wharf area of St Helena's main harbour 'out of bounds' in expectation of the arrival of the first Republican prisoners of war, mostly those captured at Paardeberg on board the troopship *Milwaukee*.[25]
Day 181 Mon **1900-04-09**	OFS	**THE BATTLE OF JAMMERSBERG DRIFT** At dawn Chief Commandant De Wet surrounds the British positions and launches his assault from across the Caledon River. Dalgety's southern and south-eastern positions are heavily attacked. The Cape Mounted Riflemen bear the brunt of the attack and Dalgety soon realises where the main thrust of the attack is directed. He reinforces them by transferring troops from elsewhere and they succeed in repulsing De Wet's repeated attacks until dusk silences the battlefield and De Wet's burghers withdraw. Despite their excellent fortifications and the better marksmanship of the Colonial troops, the British lose heavily. They lose 21 killed and 75 wounded, while De Wet suffers seven wounded, of whom three dies of their wounds. [26] Lord Roberts orders General Gatacre home, chiefly because of his dismal performance at the battle of Mostert's Hoek. General Chermside is promoted to command the Third Division in his place.[27]
	Western front	**Mafeking siege:** Due to a stamp shortage, Colonel Baden-Powell authorises the printing of Mafeking siege stamps. Sergeant Goodyear with his bicycle is featured on the one-penny stamp while modestly Colonel Baden-Powell's portrait appears on the three-pence stamp. The stamps are photographically produced on blue paper by Dr D Taylor and some of the sought-after examples are now (1998) valued at R50 000,00 to R55 000,00 each and up to R360 000,00 for a pair with variations. [28]
	Trivia	*Emily Hobhouse's 40th birthday.*
Day 182 Tue **1900-04-10**	OFS	**THE BATTLE OF JAMMERSBERG DRIFT** De Wet is reinforced by the arrival of General Froneman's commando and several burghers from the Rouxville, Dewetsdorp and Wepener districts, called up again after having laid down their arms. His force increases to between 5 000 and 6 000 men. Dalgety spends the day improving his fortifications and correcting the defects in his defence experienced during the previous attack. At 20:00 about 500 burghers launch a night attack, again concentrating on the CMR trenches, but Dalgety's sentries are wide awake. They fall back to their trenches and put up a terrific defence.[29]
	Natal front	The Republican artillery brings seven or eight field-guns into position on the hills on the left bank of the Sundays River. They open up a long-range barrage on the Elandslaagte camp, to which the British long-range guns reply. Shelling continues throughout the day, but with little effect, except that the British camp is moved back a few kilometres.[30]
	International	The Republican deputation consisting of Fischer, Wessels and Wolmarans, arrive in Naples.

Day 183 Wed **1900-04-11**	OFS	**THE BATTLE OF JAMMERSBERG DRIFT** The attack stalls and at about 02:00, the burghers are recalled before Dalgety can get a detachment in position to threaten the Republicans' retirement. Casualties are heavy. The British lose ten killed and 50 wounded while De Wet loses four killed and eight wounded.[31] General Chermside reoccupies Reddersburg.
	Western front	**Mafeking siege:** Besieged Mafeking suffers a heavy bombardment.
	St Helena	General PA Cronje and his wife arrive at St Helena on board the *HMS Doris*, escorting the troopship *Milwaukee* carrying some of the burghers captured with him at Paardeberg.
Day 184 Thu **1900-04-12**	OFS	**Jammersberg Drift siege:** The Republicans attempt another night attack, this time from the north-west. Again the defenders are ready and the attack fails. De Wet's hopes of another quick victory fade and the operation deteriorates into a siege. [32]
	ZAR	The Dempsey trial results in a special hearing brought before ZAR Chief Justice R Gregarowski, seeking a court order to prevent the destruction of the mines. The State Mining Engineer JH Munnik at first declines to give evidence, lest he divulges state secrets. When compelled to continue by the judge, he testifies that, on State Secretary Reitz's instructions, several mines have already been prepared to receive demolition charges. A written affidavit by State Attorney JC Smuts, however, convinces the court that the destruction of the mines is not considered by the government and that foreign delegations have already been informed accordingly.[33]
Day 185 Fri **1900-04-13**	OFS	GOOD FRIDAY Detachments of Lord Methuen's force leave Boshof and march east towards Bultfontein and Brandfort, where they can attack General De la Rey's flank. Field-cornet Diedericks throws his small force of about 100 men across the path of an enemy force of 1 200 foot soldiers and 700 mounted men with an artillery battery. The British clear the path with their field-guns but then they hesitate.[34]
Day 186 Sat **1990-04-14**	OFS	Lord Methuen's troops, convinced that Diedericks' men must be the advance elements of a bigger Republican force, fall back towards Boshof.[35] **Jammersberg Drift siege:** Thirteen troop trains leave Bloemfontein for Bethanie Station, near Reddersburg.
	Cape Colony	Since the end of the first Republican invasion, a cabinet crisis has been threatening in the Cape Colony on the question of rebel trials. The suspension of martial rule implies that these cases are now referred to ordinary courts, but it is impossible to form impartial juries. In an unsolicited letter Mr Chamberlain 'suggests' that special courts be instituted for this purpose.[36]
	Trivia	*The World Exhibition opens in Paris.*
Day 187 Sun **1900-04-15**	OFS	EASTER SUNDAY **Jammersberg Drift siege:** A British column, consisting of Brabant's Colonial Division and elements of Major-General A FitzRoy Hart's division — totalling more than 4 000 men and eight guns — leaves Rouxville for Wepener. General Chermside is ordered to march to Dewetsdorp to prevent the burghers from retiring westwards.
	International	The Republican delegation seeking international intervention, arrives in The Hague.

Day 188 Mon **1900-04-16**	OFS	**Jammersberg Drift siege:** General Froneman, with 600 men, occupies positions at Boesmanskop (about 30 kilometres south of Wepener) to protect De Wet's besiegers from any attack from that direction.
Day 189 Tue **1900-04-17**	Western front	The formation of a 'flying column' under Colonel BT Mahon to relieve Mafeking, is ordered.
Day 190 Wed **1900-04-18**	OFS	**Jammersberg Drift siege:** Generals Rundle and Chermside advance towards Dewetsdorp. President Steyn appoints Christiaan Rudolf de Wet as Commander-in-Chief of all Free State forces.
Day 191 Thu **1900-04-19**	OFS	**Jammersberg Drift siege:** General Rundle, commanding about 12 000 troops, aware of General Piet de Wet somewhere in his front, advances very carefully, covering about 13 kilometres in 24 hours.
	Western front Black involvement	**Mafeking siege:** Angus Hamilton of *The Times*, criticising Baden-Powell's 'leave-here-or-starve-here' policy towards blacks, writes (not for publication): *"There can be no doubt that the drastic principles of economy which Colonel Baden-Powell has been practising in these later days are opposed to... the dignity and liberalism which we profess, and which enter so much into the settlement of native questions in South Africa."*[37]
	Swaziland Black involvement	Commandant MJ van Damm and Major Lombard, sent to confer with the Swazi chief Umbudula, are overpowered by armed Swazi tribesmen and British soldiers on the Swaziland border. Major Lombard is killed and Commandant Van Damm is wounded, captured and later sent to Durban.[38]
Day 192 Fri **1900-04-20**	OFS	**Jammersberg Drift siege:** General Piet de Wet positions about 2 000 burghers with three Krupps and two pom-poms on a range of hills about eight kilometres outside Dewetsdorp. At about 10:00 the burghers on Wakkerstroom Farm open fire on Rundle's advancing soldiers at a range of about 1 200 metres. All efforts by the troops to force the position or to outflank it, fail. Late in the afternoon a determined charge by the Worcestershire Regiment diverts the Republican shelling and rifle fire sufficiently to allow the infantry to retire.[39]
	Victoria Cross	The Victoria Cross is awarded to Lieutenant WHS Nickerson, Royal Army Medical Corps attached to the mounted infantry, for attending to a wounded man while under fire at Wakkerstroom Farm, near Dewetsdorp. Methuen's force, still vacillating near Boshof, sends out a strong yeomanry unit under Major General Douglas. They are attacked at Swartkoppiesfontein by General APJ Cronje's mounted commando. Douglas is unnerved by the vigorous attack, and falls back to Boshof, losing 12 killed, three wounded and eleven taken prisoner — three of whom are wounded and left behind. Two of Cronje's men are wounded.[40]
	Trivia	*Republican scout OJ (Jack) Hindon's 26th birthday.* *PH Kritzinger's 30th birthday.*
Day 193 Sat **1900-04-21**	OFS	**Jammersberg Drift siege:** General Rundle, convinced that he is confronted by more than 6 000 burghers with six field-guns in excellent defensive positions, reports his proposed plans to bypass this force to Lord Roberts in Bloemfontein. The Commander-in-Chief, however, keen to duplicate his coup at Paardeberg, wants to surround all the Republican forces in the south-eastern Free State and cannot allow a large force on the flank of any of his converging columns. He orders Rundle to seek union with French and Pole-Carew before pushing on to Wepener. The battle near Dewetsdorp thus remains a long-range artillery and rifle duel with General Piet de Wet's position remaining intact.[41]
	Western front	At Kimberley General Sir Archibald Hunter is ordered to speed up the formation of a 'flying column' to relieve Mafeking, following a report from Baden-Powell that he can only hold out until 22 May.[42]

Day 194 Sun 1900-04-22	OFS	**Jammersberg Drift siege:** The inconclusive battle between Rundle and Piet de Wet continues south of Dewetsdorp, but it is clear that the British force is too strong to be delayed for too long.
	Victoria Cross	Corporal HC Beet, 1st Battalion, the Nottingham & Derbyshire Regiment (MI), bravely risks his life to fetch water to cool the Maxim machine gun near Wakkerstroom, thereby earning a Victoria Cross.
		At the arrival of Brabant's scouts, some of Froneman's burghers fire prematurely and their excellent defensive positions south of Wepener are betrayed. A long-range rifle duel ensues. Chief Commandant De Wet sends General Olivier with 200 men to reinforce Froneman.[43]
		General Pole-Carew's 11th Division attacks General Lemmer's 400 burghers at Leeuwkop, about 30 kilometres south-east of Bloemfontein. Pole-Carew's infantry division of about 7 800 men is strengthened by about 5 000 mounted troops and has more than 34 field-guns at its disposal. Only Lemmer's excellent use of the terrain prevents him from being surrounded. He inflicts 21 casualties on the enemy for the loss of four wounded burghers, but he is forced to retreat to Dewetsdorp, where he joins General Piet de Wet.[44]
		General Ian Hamilton marches east from the Bloemfontein vicinity. At Bushman's Kop he skirmishes with about 200 burghers who has been detailed to form a mounted guard covering the Waterworks and chases them off.
Day 195 Mon 1900-04-23	OFS	**Jammersberg Drift siege:** General Olivier fights a delaying battle with Brabant's force south of Wepener. Chief Commandant De Wet decides to postpone his planned attack on Colonel Dalgety until the next day.[45]
		General Ian Hamilton reoccupies the Bloemfontein Waterworks at Sannaspost
	Western front	The 10th Division, commanded by Lieutenant-General Sir A Hunter, arrives at Kimberley
Day 196 Tue 1900-04-24	OFS	**Jammersberg Drift siege:** Chief Commandant De Wet, now commanding a besieging force of about 3 000, again attacks Dalgety at Jammersberg Drift. The attack is supported by a fierce bombardment, but Dalgety's colonial troops resist resolutely, despite dwindling supplies of ammunition. The attack is repulsed and De Wet, upon receipt of alarming reports of the vast forces threatening to surround him, decides to abandon the siege.[46]
	ZAR	The Republican position near Warrenton is shelled and General Du Toit asks reinforcements from General APJ Cronje.
		In Johannesburg an explosion at the dynamite factory housed in the Begbie Engineering Workshop, destroys the factory and surrounding houses. The munitions workers, mostly Italians, suspect sabotage by British agents and demand an inquiry.
Day 197 Wed 1900-04-25	OFS	**THE BATTLE OF JAMMERSBERG DRIFT**
		Colonel Dalgety is finally relieved after 16 days. The relieving columns of Major-Generals AF Hart and JP Brabazon enter Wepener. In total the British suffer 33 fatal casualties, 133 wounded and 12 captured. Ten or 11 burghers have died and about 25 have been wounded.[47] More seriously, Chief Commandant De Wet has been distracted from the main purpose of his offensive — the British supply lines. His move into the south-eastern Free State has alerted Roberts, battling an enteric epidemic in Bloemfontein, of his extremely vulnerable position despite his huge numerical superiority. Republican forces retire northwards from Wepener and Dewetsdorp.
		On receiving the news of the reoccupation of Wepener, Lord Roberts orders General French to Thaba Nchu to cut off the Republican retreat.
		General Ian Hamilton, with about 10 000 men, engages General Grobler at Ysternek, near Israel's Poort. Grobler's commando, about 600 men, opens fire at about 14:00 and delays the British advance until dark. The British suffer 27 casualties, including the Canadian Commanding Officer, Lieutenant-Colonel Otter, who is wounded. The Republicans evacuate their position after dark, having suffered one killed and one wounded.[48]

Day 198 Thu **1900-04-26**	OFS	General Ian Hamilton arrives at Thaba Nchu. Chief Commandant CR de Wet, uniting with Generals FA Grobler, Philip Botha and Piet de Wet, passes through Springhaansnek with his convoy.
	International	The Republican delegation has an interview with Mr De Beaufort, the Dutch foreign minister, who cannot commit his country to any diplomatic actions on behalf of the Republican cause.[49] Queen Victoria ends her visit to Ireland.[50]
Day 199 Fri **1900-04-27**	OFS	General French's cavalry joins General Ian Hamilton at Thaba Nchu, too late to trap the retreating Republican convoy. A scouting force occupy Schuinshoogte but is driven off with about 12 casualties during a night attack by a small group of burghers.[51]
	ZAR	General APJ Cronje arrives at Christiana in support of General Du Toit at Fourteen Streams.
	Cape Colony	Cape Prime Minister, WJ Schreiner, answers Chamberlain's suggestion concerning special courts without exposing the serious rift in his Cabinet. Foreign Minister, Dr Te Water, who sees Chamberlain's suggestion as interference and an infringement of civil rights, is willing to compromise on condition that Attorney-General and Justice Minister, Sir Richard Solomon, will support amnesty for rank and file rebels.[52]
	Trivia	*Cape politician Sir JG Sprigg's 70th birthday.*
Day 200 Sat **1900-04-28**	OFS	Using almost all the troops under his command, General French attacks Republican positions at Swartlapberg. He retakes Schuinshoogte and Dickson's cavalry soon moves astride De Wet's route to the north. They ask for reinforcements and await his advance. Gordon's brigade, rushing to assist, moves too fast and runs into intense rifle fire in Springhaansnek. Hamilton's mounted infantry, also keen to reinforce Dickson and corner De Wet, are suddenly attacked from behind by General Olivier's men. The rest of the day is spent by French trying to extricate his units. They lose two killed and 37 wounded and ten men are taken prisoner.[53] *The Times* correspondent, reporting on conditions in the Bloemfontein hospitals, writes, "... men were dying like flies for want of adequate attention... with only a blanket and a thin waterproof sheet... with no beds, no milk and hardly any medicines... with only a few private soldiers to act as 'orderlies'."[54] If this accurately describes the medical attention available to their own soldiers, it bodes ill for any enemy soldier or civilian who is unfortunate enough to be dependant on British medical care.
	Cape Colony	The Cape Cabinet formulates a reply to Chamberlain, proposing a policy of amnesty for rebels, excluding the leaders, referring to the moderate policy adopted after the Canadian Rebellion of 1837-38.[55]
Day 201 Sun **1900-04-29**	OFS	Lord Roberts orders General Ian Hamilton to clear the eastern flank of the Republican line at Houtnek, north-west of Thaba Nchu, and to occupy Jacobsrust, where he is to be heavily reinforced in anticipation of the start of Roberts' march from Bloemfontein. General French sends Rundle's 8th Division against De Wet's positions on Swartlapberg, but this attack also fails. Rundle retreats and De Wet launches a counter-attack, capturing a supply wagon and a water cart, before reinforcements arrive.[56]
Day 202 Mon **1900-04-30**	OFS	**THE BATTLE OF HOUTNEK (TOBABERG)** General Hamilton, moving towards Houtnek with about 5 500 men, about 24 fieldguns and a long convoy, recognises Tobaberg as the key to the Republican position at Houtnek, south-east of Brandfort. At dawn General Philip Botha allows the British

 *Col. EJ Maximov* (War Museum of the Boer Republics)		to cross the Koranna Spruit and at 08:00 he opens up with his two artillery pieces and unleashes long-range rifle fire on the well-deployed troops. The mounted infantry swerve right to pin down the burghers east of the road, the New Zealanders charge ahead to within about 2 000 metres of the pass while most of the infantry head for Tobaberg on their western front. Hamilton's artillery shells the hill, occupied by a small Republican picket. The Russian Colonel EJ Maximov, commanding the remainder of De Villebois Mareuil's International Legion — 150 men consisting of 40 Dutchmen, a few Russians, the Free State German Corps, a few Frenchmen and a couple of Americans — realises the danger and leads his men up the back slope. The Volunteers' attack, using a regular formation, is so correct that the artillery observers mistake them for a well-trained British unit and hesitate long enough to allow them to reach the crest. They open a fierce fusillade on the soldiers, and despite their numbers, launch a counter-attack that stunts Hamilton's attack and thwarts his plans.
	Victoria Cross	Colonel Maximov is wounded twice, but he continues his charge to within 20 metres of the enemy. Captain EB Towse VC, a hero of Magersfontein, earns his second citation for Britain's highest award when he urges a small group forward despite a head wound that costs him his eyesight. The British launch a bayonet charge, but a hail of bullets cuts them down. They try again, but even with substantial reinforcements from below, the Volunteers, supported by accurate Republican shelling and long-range rifle fire from positions further away, repulse all attacks until darkness falls. At about midnight a messenger from General Philip Botha's laager tells the tired and hungry Volunteers to move down the hill for a nice hot meal.[57] Lieutenant-General Tucker, commanding the Seventh Division, launches a disjointed attack at Krantz Kraal. Although he takes the position, the burghers disengage easily and retire without any problems. General De la Rey gathers a group of 250 horsemen to counter a probing expedition by a 2 000 strong mounted force advancing northwards from the Waterworks. By exploiting the half light of twilight and the dusty conditions, General De la Rey bluffs them into believing that they are in danger of being cut off — sending them scurrying back.[58]
	Civilian life	The final issue of *The Friend*, under military auspices, appears in Bloemfontein.[59]
	Western front	The siege of Mafeking enters its two hundredth day.
	ZAR	Demonstrating foreign dynamite factory workers demand the expulsion of all remaining British subjects and the replacement of Commandant Schutte, accused of lax security arrangements, wih a guard under Foreign Volunteer Commandant Ricchiardi. Public pressure and fear of a violent witch-hunt force the government to comply by expelling British subjects and very few are allowed to remain in the ZAR.[60]
	Trivia	*Hawaii officially becomes US territory.*
1900	AUTUMN	**MAY**
Day 203 Tue 1900-05-01	OFS	**THE BATTLE OF HOUTNEK (TOBABERG)** After a few hours' rest, the Foreign Volunteers reoccupy their positions on Tobaberg, only to find that the burghers covering their right flank have abandoned their positions during the night. They bravely continue their defence as the British assault recommences at dawn. They repulse attack after attack while vainly waiting for reinforcements. Mounted troops detached from Generals French and Bruce Hamilton's force left at Waterval's Drift, Israelspoort and the Waterworks, are able to work around the western side of Tobaberg without being noticed by both the Foreigners and De Wet's men at Swartlapberg and Springhaansnek. Almost too late a few burghers notice the 8th Hussars and Maximov's men retreat under heavy shelling, allowing the British to take the hill and thus dominating Houtnek. The seizure of this important position has cost the British 157 casualties, while the Foreign Volunteers lose six killed, including Lieutenants Freiherr von Brachel and Gunther, and 28 wounded, including Colonel Maximov. Ten men are taken prisoner, amongst whom is Cor van Gogh, broth-

		er of the famous painter, who ironically is also to commit suicide while in captivity. [62] General Hart's Fifth Brigade occupies Smithfield.
Day 204 Wed **1900-05-02**	Cape Colony	Mr Chamberlain's response to the Cape cabinet's proposal regarding the granting of amnesty to rebels (excluding leaders), is that it would be unfair to the 'loyalists'. He maintains that all rebels, even those who may claim that they were forced to assist the enemy, must be punished. This splits the Cape cabinet down the centre with Solomon fully agreeing with Chamberlain and Dr Te Water totally rejecting the British 'suggestions' as rape of the so-called self-governing constitution of the Colony.[63]
Day 205 Thu **1900-05-03**	OFS	**THE MARCH TO PRETORIA STARTS** After a period of seven weeks, Lord Roberts leaves Bloemfontein to the strains of the famous marching song *"We are marching to Pretoria "* — which is heard for the first time — to join his main army at Karee Siding. **The Main Army,** starting from Bloemfontein, consists of: **The Central Column**, under Field-Marshal Lord Roberts' personal command, consisting of: The cavalry division (left flank) under Lieutenant-General French: 1st Cavalry Brigade — Col TC Porter 3rd Cavalry Brigade — Brigadier-General JRP Gordon 4th Cavalry Brigade — Major General JBB Dickson **Total** 4 503 men with 3 749 horses. The 1st Mounted Infantry Brigade under Major General ETH Hutton: Four corps of mounted infantry **Total** 4 315 men with 4 508 horses. The 7th Infantry Division under Lieutenant-General C Tucker: 14th Infantry Brigade — Major General JG Maxwell 15th Infantry Brigade — Major General AG Wavell **Total** 7 167 men with 635 horses The 11th Infantry Division under Lieutenant-General R Pole-Carew: 1st Guards Brigade — Major General Inigo Jones 18th Infantry Brigade — Brigadier-General TE Stephenson **Total** 7 805 men with 668 horses **TOTAL** (central force, including corps troops) 24 754 men with 10 252 horses and 66 field-guns. **The Right Column** under Lieutenant-General Ian Hamilton, starting from Thaba Nchu, consists of: 2nd Cavalry Brigade — Brigadier-General RG Broadwood 2nd Brigade Mounted Infantry — Brigadier-General CP Ridley 19th Infantry Brigade — Major General HL Smith-Dorrien 21st Infantry Brigade — Major General Bruce Hamilton **A supporting column,** consisting of the 9th Division commanded by Lieutenant-General HE Colvile and 3rd (Highland) Brigade — Major General HA MacDonald **Total** 18 625 men with 7 595 horses and 48 field-guns. Simultaneously a **Western Force** starts from Kimberley and moves north-eastwards, consisting of: The 1st Infantry Division under Lieutenant-General Lord Methuen: 9th Infantry Brigade — Major General CWH Douglas 20th Infantry Brigade — Major General AH Paget The 10th Infantry Division under Lieutenant-General Sir A Hunter: 5th Infantry Brigade — Major General A FitzRoy Hart 6th Infantry Brigade — Major General G Barton A **Static Formation** is responsible for the line east of Bloemfontein, consisting of: The 3rd Infantry Division under Lieutenant-General Sir HC Chermside: 22nd Infantry Brigade — Major General RE Allen 23rd Infantry Brigade — Major General WG Knox The **Bloemfontein Garrison** forms another static formation: The 6th Infantry Division under Lieutenant-General T Kelly-Kenny: 12th Infantry Brigade — Major General RAP Clements 13th Infantry Brigade — Major General CE Knox A **Back-up Formation** is tasked with advancing from the Orange River, protecting the rear of the main and supporting forces: The 8th Infantry Division under Lieutenant-General Sir HML Rundle. 16th Infantry Brigade — Major General BBD Campbell 17th Infantry Brigade — Major General JE Boyes The **Colonial Division** commanded by Lieutenant-Colonel EH Dalgety (in Brigadier-General EY Brabant's absence) is ordered to move on the eastern flank of the 8th Division.[64]

138

	OFS	At dawn the Republican scouts report the start of Lord Roberts' march to General De la Rey at Brandfort. At about 09:00, from a hill south of the town, they witness the spectacle of an enormous army advancing over a front of more than 25 kilometres. At 10:00 some 300 Heidelbergers gallop out of town and take position on a group of small hills in the front of Major-General Hutton's 8 000 strong force on the British left. They are soon joined by about 150 men of Colonel JYF Blake's Irish Corps and despite the heavy shelling, they open a fierce fusillade on the advancing horde. The British advance hesitates, additional field-guns are brought into action and a mounted force is sent to work around the koppies, forcing the burghers to beat a hasty retreat at about 13:00. On De la Rey's left flank the British run into his brother, 'Klein' (Small) Adriaan de la Rey, recently promoted to Acting Combat General, whose furious counterattack stuns the mounted infantry. Adriaan is wounded during the charge and the momentum is lost. At 16:00, with both flanks crumbling, General De la Rey must use parts of his main force to prevent encircling pincers from cutting off his retreat. At nightfall De la Rey abandons Brandfort, suffering one killed and 17 wounded. The British lose only six killed and 30 wounded. The town's civilians panic and stream northwards as Lord Roberts takes the town.[65]
	Cape Colony	In expectation of encountering determined resistance at heavily defended and fortified positions, like the Pretoria forts, siege guns are landed in Cape Town. The Pretoria forts, however, are unarmed — their 155mm Creusot 'Long Tom' guns having been removed for use on the battlefield.
Day 206 Fri **1900-05-04**	Western front	Mafeking relief column under Colonel Bryan T Mahon, consisting of 1 149 men with four field-guns, two pom-poms and 52 mule wagons, starts from Barkly West. General Sir Archibald Hunter crosses the Vaal River at Windsorton. General Sir Charles Warren, appointed Military Governor of Griqualand West, a region he knows very well, arrives at Orange River Station to take command of what is to be called 'Warren's column'. This is a separate mixed force, less than a brigade strong, ordered to quell the remains of the revolt in Griqualand West.[65]
	OFS	General Ian Hamilton is heavily reinforced by an infantry brigade of Major General Bruce Hamilton, the 2nd Cavalry Brigade from Broadwood's force and 14 additional field-guns. His scouts discover the Republican forces on Tabaksberg and Baviaansberg (Roelofsberg) at dawn and any possibility of a surprise ambush is lost. Generals Grobler and Kolbe put up a desultory defence and when they notice the arrival of Colvile's 9th Division, they retire in the face of Hamilton's huge force. The Republicans lose six men who are taken prisoner and the British report 30 casualties, including Lieutenant-Colonel DSW Ogilvy, Earl of Earlie, who is wounded.[66] General De la Rey orders the destruction of the railway bridge over the Vet River.[67]
	Trivia	*General AF Hart's 56th birthday.*
Day 207 Sat **1900-05-05**	Western front	With fewer than 700 rebels and burghers with a single field-gun, General Du Toit repulses several British advances by General Hunter's troops at Rooidam, south-west of Warrenton. All Du Toit's pleas for reinforcements from General APJ Cronje's force near Boshof fail and when their field-gun is put out of action, they retire northwards. The British lose seven killed and 38 wounded, while 11 burghers are killed, 17 are wounded and three are forced to surrender.[68] General Barton's brigade successfully crosses the Vaal River at Windsorton.[69]
	OFS	**ACTION AT THE VET RIVER** General Grobler falls back to the Vet River where he takes positions on the river bank. He has to retire northwards when he discovers that the British have already crossed the river on his right and some burghers abandon their positions. General Hamilton sends Captain Balfour under a flag of truce into Winburg. While he discusses the surrender of the town with the mayor, the magistrate and several prominent civilians on the market square, General Philip Botha enters the town with about 500 men. He threatens to arrest the British officer despite his white flag, but

	ZAR	realises that the demoralization of the inhabitants makes resistance impossible. Informed that the British are dragging siege guns into position, he and his men furiously gallop out of town. At noon General Hamilton rides into town and the Union Jack is hoisted. [70] President Kruger orders the transfer of burghers who can be spared on the Natal front to the Free State.
Day 208 Sun **1900-05-06**	Western front	General Hunter crosses the Vaal River. General Du Toit's main position at Fourteen Streams is shelled and realising that his position has become untenable with the British already across the river, he retires westwards. General APJ Cronje moves his men to Christiana.[71]
	OFS	**ACTION AT THE VET RIVER** Desertions from the Republican lines are widespread and police sent from Kroonstad by General H Schoeman to force them back, are threatened at gunpoint. General JH de la Rey, now commanding only about 1 000 -1 200 men — almost 1 000 less than he had at Brandfort — spreads his men thinly over a front 20 kilometres long on both sides of the railway line, along the northern bank of the Vet River. The British approach the open veld south of the river over a wide front, supported by artillery and with flanks pushed out on both sides. The six Republican field-guns try valiantly, but cannot make any impression on the widely dispersed troops. During the afternoon a renegade Boer shows Colonel Alderson an unprotected drift on the extreme western flank and they cross the river and threaten the Republicans' right. With Winburg already in British hands, De la Rey is forced to retire. The Republicans lose about ten wounded while about 26 Heidelbergers are captured. They also lose one of their machine guns. The British suffer only one killed, 15 wounded and three missing, presumed dead. The British cross the Vet River and Smaldeel (Theunissen) is occupied.[72]
Day 209 Mon **1900-05-07**	OFS	General De la Rey destroys the bridge over the Doring River at Welgelee Siding. Receiving news that forces under Chief Commandant De Wet retiring from Thaba Nchu, have taken good positions on the Sand River, he abandons his plans of defending the Doring River and falls back to join them. **ACTION AT SAND RIVER BRIDGE** General Hutton, sent to reconnoitre the enemy positions near the Sand River rail bridge, spots a Republican supply convoy south of the river. He immediately despatches troops to cut it off from the ford and capture it. Two groups of burghers charge across the river to cover the wagons and at that moment Commandant-General Botha arrives with 3 000 men, including a few scouts and some Foreign Volunteers. He immediately takes command and orders his two Creusot field-guns into action. Hutton's efforts to bring his own field-guns into action, succeeds only in endangering his own troops, as their shells fall short. All his efforts to approach the wagons are repulsed by the burghers, inspired by the presence of the hero of Colenso and Spioenkop. The wagons are rescued and the British are forced to retire with five casualties. The Republican supreme commanders Botha and De Wet meet at Virginia Siding. Botha starts the preparation of defensive positions along the river banks.
	Western front	Generals Hunter, Barton and Paget join at Fourteen Streams, Griqualand West.
	ZAR	The Volksraad meets for the last time in Pretoria. It is an emotional meeting with many empty chairs in the chamber, as many members are away fighting. The late General JMH Kock's chair is draped in black and General PA Cronje's in the Vierkleur — the four-coloured flag of the Republic.
	Natal front	Captain Ricchiardi raids the coal-mine at Elandslaagte with 20 men of the Italian Corps. They get involved in a furious firefight, but manage to inflict about seven casualties and capture the mine manager, losing only two wounded.[73]

Day 210 Tue **1900-05-08**	OFS	General H Schoeman reports that the arrival of Commandant-General Louis Botha has boosted the Republican morale and hundreds of burghers move south from Kroonstad to reinforce their Sand River positions. Botha's line north of the Sand River is to be about 30 kilometres in length, from Doringberg and Junction Drift on his left, to the heights west of Koppie-alleen on his right.[74] The Republican Irish Brigade destroys the Sand River bridge. The charges go off a bit prematurely and several burghers have to flee from their well-hidden postions near the river bank to avoid falling debris.[75] Major-General Brabant reaches Thaba Nchu
	Natal front	**THE START OF BULLER'S ADVANCE** General Buller finally starts his advance from Ladysmith after two months' inactivity and a drawn-out 'telegraphic controversy' with Roberts in which between 40 and 50 telegrams are exchanged. His force is opposed by about 6 000 burghers, commanded by General Lucas Meyer, after Commandant-General L Botha's departure to the Free State.[76] The **Natal force** commanded by General Sir Redvers Buller VC, starting from Ladysmith, consists of: The cavalry division (no overall commander appointed): 1st Cavalry Brigade — Brigadier-General JF Burn-Murdoch 3rd Cavalry Brigade — Major-General JF Brocklehurst 3rd Mounted Brigade — Major-General Earl of Dundonald The 2nd Infantry Division under Lieutenant-General CF Clery: 2nd Infantry Brigade — Lieutenant-Colonel EOF Hamilton 4th Infantry Brigade — Colonel CD Cooper The 4th Infantry Division under Lieutenant-General the Hon NG Lyttleton: 7th Infantry Brigade — Brigadier-General FW Kitchener 8th Infantry Brigade — Major-General F Howard The 5th Infantry Division under Lieutenant-General HJT Hildyard: 10th Infantry Brigade — JT Coke 11th Infantry Brigade — AS Wynne TOTAL (including corps and support troops) 45 715 men, 11 653 horses with 113 field-guns and 4 naval guns.[78]
	Western front	A special correspondent of the *Manchester Guardian* reports from Colonel Mahon's headquarters at Dry Harts Siding: "*In ten miles we have no fewer than six farmhouses; the wife watched from her sick husband's bedside the burning of her home a hundred yards away. It seems as though a kind of domestic murder were being committed.*"[77] The advance troops of Lieutenant-General Sir F Carrington's Rhodesian Field Force reach Bulawayo, Rhodesia. The force consists of about 4 000 mounted men in two brigades made up mostly of Australians and New Zealanders.
Day 211 Wed **1900-05-09**	Western front	Colonel Mahon's force reaches Vryburg.
	OFS	General De la Rey, disturbed by developments on the Western Transvaal border and worried that the Western Transvalers under his command will desert to protect their farms and families, submits a request to be transferred there. The State President and the Commandant-General immediately agree and De la Rey leaves to take command in the western ZAR.[79] A council of war dismisses a proposal by Wilhelm Mangold to remove all families and livestock, to break all dams and to destroy everything in Roberts' path, leaving the country completely barren — like the Russians had done in the face of Napoleon's advance in 1812. They do, however, take two interesting decisions. They decide to burn the veld in front of the advancing troops to destroy the advantage of the enemy's khaki uniforms. The Commandant-General also orders the transfer of the heavy Creusot 'Long Toms' to the front to counter the British heavy naval guns.

		To improve their mobility, it is decided to experiment by mounting one on a flat car.[80] General Ian Hamilton takes two fords west of Botha's right flank at Blou Drift and De Klerk's Kraal. Some of the Western Australian Mounted Infantry under General Smith-Dorrien's command, finds Junction Drift, on the eastern flank of the Republican line, so weakly held that they occupy it and cross the Sand River. After dark more troops cross and entrench on the north bank while artillery is brought into position.[81]
	Trivia	*Republican scout Captain DJS Theron's 28th birthday.*
Day 213 Fri **1900-05-11**	OFS	**THE BATTLE OF SAND RIVER** With Botha's position already outflanked in two places, almost 30 kilometres apart, the British artillery opens up at 06:00. The 21st Brigade crosses the river and General Ian Hamilton's mounted troops move around the Republican eastern flank. General French sends Generals Porter and Hutton's mounted troops north-eastwards from the drifts he has taken the previous evening, threatening to move around Botha's western flank. A swift move by Wakkerstroom burghers almost suceeds in cutting them off, but they fall back to the stronger force now occupying the heights near Dirksburg Mine. French is forced to attempt wider and wider left hooks, but although he finds the enemy's flank, they furiously prevent any eastward move to cut them off or to roll up their line. On the eastern flank Ian Hamilton's force experiences a similar situation as the burghers rapidly extend their line to prevent them being cut off or surrounded. The strengthening of his flanks, however, weakens Botha's centre and he is forced to make a fighting withdrawal in the face of Roberts' vast superiority. Lord Roberts forces a passage of the Sand River and takes Ventersburg and Ventersburg Station. The British lose at least 23 men killed, 40 wounded and 13 missing, presumed captured. The Republican casualties are heavy as ten are killed and 69, including seven wounded, are taken prisoner.[82]
	Natal front	Sir Redvers Buller halts at Sundays River Drift.
Day 212 Thu **1900-05-10**	Western front	**ASSAULT ON MAFEKING** **Mafeking siege:** With General Kootjie Snyman's blessing, a grandson of President Kruger, Commandant Sarel Eloff, starts his planned assault with 260 volunteers. At 23:00, he moves his men from his camp at Jackal Tree, 10 kilometres south of town, to a starting point in the Molopo River bed. From here he is to launch a determined attack through the Barolong township, assured of the support of a second wave of 500 mounted men under Snyman's orders.[83]
	OFS	The burghers falling back from Sand River, congregate at Boschrand Siding. President Steyn, wearing a bandolier instead of his orange presidential sash, appears among his burghers with a Mauser in his hand. This show of determination does wonders for their morale. Commandant-General Botha is wary of the possibility that Roberts may attempt to pin them down there while sending cavalry on a wide, flanking manoeuvre to encircle Kroonstad. When the British artillery opens up and constantly overshoots their positions, he is convinced that this is the case and orders a withdrawal to Kroonstad. French's cavalry horses are too knocked up to attempt any serious action and he can only send Gordon's cavalry, Henry's mounted infantry and the 8th Battalion mounted infantry to engage General Philip Botha's rearguard.[84] The capital of the Republic of the Orange Free State is transferred to the small town of Heilbron.[85]
	ZAR	About 350 Boer women from Maraisburg and Florida on the Witwatersrand meet in the Irene Hall to discuss ways of helping *"their brave men at the front"*. While some of the more vehement speakers call for the formation of an armed amazon corps, resolutions are adopted offering to replace clerks and other non-combatants with women, *"if by this means a number of young fellows could be sent to the Front, the strains on those now so many months in the field could be relieved"*.[86]

	Natal front	General Buller is at the Waschbank River, 50 kilometres from Ladysmith, on his way to Helpmekaar.[87]
	United Kingdom	At a meeting in Birmingham Mr Chamberlain announces Her Majesty's Goverment's intention to annex the Republics. He adds, "*...after an intervening period of Crown Colony government they should be admitted as soon as it was safe and possible, into the great circle of the self governing colonies of the Empire.*" This confirms President Kruger's accusation at the Bloemfontein Conference in May 1899.
Day 214 Sat 1900-05-12	Western front *Comdt. Sarel Eloff (National Cultural History Museum)* Black involvement	**ASSAULT ON MAFEKING** **Mafeking siege:** Republican forces launch their most determined attack on Mafeking. At 04:00 artillery and rifle fire from the east to distract the garrison, signals the start of Commandant Eloff's attack. The attackers pass Fort Limestone and Fort Hidden Hollow and set fire to several Barolong huts as a signal to Snyman to launch the second wave. Eloff surrounds Baden-Powell's second in command, Colonel Hore, commanding officer of the Protectorate Regiment, and his HQ staff in the old BSAP fort. After a short resistance, the fort surrenders at 05:25. Commandant Eloff takes the 32 occupants prisoner and takes over the fort where he awaits Snyman's attack. Arrogantly Eloff uses the telephone to inform Baden-Powell that he has taken the fort and is within 800 metres of his headquarters. Snyman's supporting attack does not materialise and Commandant Eloff's group is cut off. Baden-Powell is not distracted by the half-hearted Republican diversions in other sectors and by directing the action by telephone, he is soon able to bring heavy countermeasures to bear on the attackers. The armed Barolong actively take part in the action and the burghers outside the fort are driven off or have to fight their way out. Although Baden-Powell cannot shell Eloff's group in the BSAP fort for fear of hitting the British prisoners, a heavy rifle duel continues until dusk, when Eloff surrenders to his former prisoner, Colonel Hore. The Republicans suffer ten killed, 19 wounded and 108 taken prisoner, while the defenders lose four whites and eight blacks killed, and ten whites and ten blacks are wounded.[88]
	OFS	The Republicans decide not to defend Kroonstad and after detailing Colonel Blake's Irish Brigade to destroy a warehouse filled with supplies and the Vals River bridge, they abandon the town. Field Marshal Lord Roberts occupies Kroonstad without resistance. Since his departure from Bloemfontein he has lost 32 killed, 162 wounded and 48 missing. He has also lost the use of 2 880 horses — 2 430 dead and 450 unserviceable.[89]
	ZAR	The first issue of *The Gram*, a publication by British prisoners of war, edited by the Earl of Rosslyn, appears in the officers' camp in the State Model School in Pretoria.
Day 215 Sun 1900-05-13	Western front	General PJ Liebenberg, with 300 men, attempts to head off the relief column. Colonel Mahon beats of his attack at Koedoesrant or Mareetsane, about 60 kilometres from Mafeking. The relief column suffers six killed, 24 wounded and one missing, while two burghers are killed and five are wounded.[90]
	Natal front	In the face of Buller's advance, Piet Retief burghers abandon their positions on the Helpmekaar Hills prematurely, earning themselves the nickname *Piet Retreaters*.[91]
Day 216 Mon 1900-05-14	OFS	The Republicans decide to form a defensive line along the Renoster River. Lord Roberts sends Commandant-General Botha a copy of his proclamation banning the destruction and damage of public and private property.[92]
	Western front	Colonel Plumer is reinforced at Sefetili Village by the Canadian Artillery with four guns and 100 foot-soldiers. They are part of General Carrington's force who has arrived via Beira and Bulawayo and eventually detrained at Outsi Siding. From here they have marched an average of 40 kilometres a day, for four days, to catch up with Plumer.[93]

		Mafeking siege: General De la Rey arrives outside Mafeking and join forces with General Liebenberg at Rietfontein [94]
	Natal front	Telegraphic instructions from Commandant-General Botha on how tactical retirements must be carried out, if necessary, in the discretion of local commanders, are misinterpreted by General Lucas Meyer as a general order to retreat northwards. The Republicans abandon their excellent positions in the Biggarsberg and start a retreat that is to be continued until they reach Laing's Nek.[95] General Buller and Lord Dundonald reach Helpmekaar.
Day 217 Tue **1900-05-15**	Natal front	General Buller and Lord Dundonald enter Dundee and Glencoe is captured by Lyttleton's division.
	Western front	Colonels Mahon and Plumer join forces at Jan Massibi's 32 kilometres west of Mafeking. Their combined force now numbers about 2 000 troops with 14 field-guns.
	ZAR	General Hunter crosses the western border of the ZAR. The honour of being the first unit to enter the ZAR is given to the 2nd Battalion Royal Scots, the last British unit to leave the Transvaal after the armistice in 1881.
	OFS	Lord Methuen advances from Boshof towards Hoopstad. Commandant-General Botha, in a letter to Lord Roberts, confirms the Republicans' strict regulations against wanton destruction, damage and looting of property and the fact that several burghers have been punished in courts of law for such actions. He has, however, not yet heard of anyone punished by the British for similar offences despite the fact that several incidents have been brought to their attention. The barbaric conduct of British troops continues and several reports to this effect have been received from the Vryburg district. If the soldiers reponsible are not punished, the Republics will hold the British government responsible.[96]
	International	The three-man Republican delegation arrives in New York.[97]
Day 218 Wed **1900-05-16**	Western front	**Mafeking siege:** General De la Rey and two of his sons almost fall into British hands when they are challenged by a British picket near Israel's Farm.[98] The combined forces of Colonels Mahon and Plumer are in an action at Israel's Farm. The demoralised burghers retire prematurely, despite Generals De la Rey and Liebenberg's utmost efforts. The burghers lose one killed and eight wounded, while the British suffer about 40 casualties.[99] Major Karri-Davis and eight troopers of the Imperial Light Horse enter Mafeking at about 19:00.[100]
	OFS	All the railway bridges and culverts from the Renoster River to Roodewal Station are dynamited.
	ZAR	General Hunter occupies Christiana, the first ZAR town to be captured.
	Natal front	The railway tunnel at Laing's Nek is blown up and the commandos retreating from the Biggarsberg start preparing defensive positions in the vicinity. Commandant Chris Botha is promoted to Acting Assistant General and ordered eastwards to Doringberg, between Landman and De Jager's Drift on the Buffels River border.[101]
Day 219 Thu **1900-05-17**	Western front Black involvement	**MAFEKING IS RELIEVED** Colonel BT Mahon leaves his overnight position at 00:30 and covers the last 13 kilometres and enters Mafeking at about 03:30.[102] After 216 days the Republican forces abandon their positions and allow the relief column to enter the town and end the siege. During the siege Baden-Powell's forces have lost 67 whites and 25 blacks killed

		in action or died of wounds, 118 whites and 68 blacks wounded, 27 missing, presumed captured and 21 killed in accidents or from other causes. Of the 333 civilians who have died during the siege, only five whites were killed or died of wounds and 32 whites died of disease or illness.[103] Colonel Plumer's Rhodesian Force and Colonel Mahon's Relief Column have had about 166 casualties during the relief operations. The Republicans have lost 64 killed, 105 wounded or injured and 108 captured during the siege and while countering the British relief attemps.[104] No accurate or complete record of black civilian casualties exists.
	United Kingdom	The first 'Mafeking night': In an unprecedented display of public emotions, life in the great cities is brought to a halt as people dance in the street celebrating the news of the relief of Mafeking. The merriment is to continue for another day and night. [105] A new word, 'to MAFFICK', is added to the English language, meaning, *"to celebrate with riotous rejoicings"*.
	OFS	General Ian Hamilton occupies Lindley. The towns of Ladybrand and Clocolan are occupied by Brabant's Colonial Division. Lord Methuen enters Hoopstad.
	Natal front	The retreating Republican commandos in northern Natal start preparing defensive positions at Laing's Nek under the command of General Lucas Meyer. General Buller moves to Dannhauser.
	Trivia	*Lieutenant-Colonel EH Dalgety's 53rd birthday.*
Day 220 Fri **1900-05-18**	OFS	Lord Roberts answers Commandant-General Botha's accusations as follows, *"As the Vryburg district is part of Her Majesty's dominions I am responsible to her Majesty's Government alone for the behaviour of my troops in that district."*[106]
	Natal front	General Buller reoccupies Newcastle. Some of his advance units cross Rorke's Drift and occupy Nqutu in Zululand.

Day 221 Sat **1900-05-19**	**THE OATH OF NEUTRALITY**

THE OATH OF NEUTRALITY
The oath which surrendering burghers is expected to sign, is published in a Government Gazette:

Number ....
I, the undersigned ....
of ....
in the district of ....
Do hereby solemnly make oath and declare that I have handed in and given up all arms and ammunition demanded of me by the British authorities, namely all rifles and rifle ammunition of whatsoever description they may be. And I solemnly swear that I have no rifle or rifle ammunition remaining and that I know of none such being concealed or withheld by anyone whatsoever.
And, I further swear that I will not take up arms against the British Government during the present war, nor will I, at any time, furnish any members of the Republican forces with assistance of any kind, or with information as to the numbers, movements or other details of the British forces that may come to my knowledge. I do further promise and swear to remain quietly at my home until the war is over.
I am aware that if I in any way falsely declared in the premises, or if I break my oath or promise as above set forth, I shall render myself liable to be summarily and severely punished by the British authorities.
I make the above declaration solemnly believing it to be true, so help me God.

...
Before me ....[107]

	OFS	Vrede is proclaimed as the new capital of the Republic of the Orange Free State.[108] The Republican force in the Renoster River positions has increased to between 3 500 and 4 000 men and their morale is improving. Elsewhere, however, in a serious development, without consulting with other officers, General Piet de Wet offers to surrender to General Ian Hamilton with

		his Bethlehem commando, on condition that he will be allowed to return to his farm. According to Lord Roberts' proclamation, Piet de Wet is regarded as a 'leader' and Hamilton cannot guarantee that he will not be deported. De Wet retracts his offer and joins his brother and General Prinsloo in preparations to stop the British advance.[109]
	Natal front	A squadron of Brabant's Horse clash with burghers under General DJE Erasmus. The bloodless skrimish takes place on the historical O'Neill's Farm near Majuba. Buller's advance units reach the Ingogo River, while Buller halts at Newcastle.
	Trivia	*Britian annexes the Tonga Islands.*
Day 222 Sun **1900-05-20**	OFS	When General Hamilton marches out of Lindley, his rearguard is furiously attacked by General Piet de Wet and other Free Staters. The mounted infantry has to fall back to defend the convoy. Piet de Wet charges forward and engages them at short range. A part of the convoy's flanking force, consisting of 40 men, is cut off and forced to surrender when half of their number are either killed or wounded. Some of the British horses stampede and only when Hamilton succeeds in placing his field-guns on high ground, can he extricate his rearguard. In the meantime, the British advance is also surprised when they suddenly draw fire from the burghers on the banks of the Renoster River. When the British 19th Brigade swerves towards Heilbron, the burghers are threatened in their flank and they withdraw, allowing the British to cross the river and camp for the night on the northern bank. The British lose 62 killed and wounded, while 20 are captured unhurt. The Republicans suffer one killed and seven wounded.[110]
	Natal front	**THE FIGHT AT SCHEEPERS NEK** Five squadrons (365 men) of Bethune's mounted infantry with three field-guns leave Nqutu at 10:00. Reports have it that Vryheid is unoccupied and well-stocked with supplies. The mounted infantry, keen to be there first, outstrips the rest of the column and at 15:00, they run into a well-placed ambush at Scheepers Nek, about ten kilometres south-west of Vryheid, ZAR. About 80 men of the Swaziland commando under Commandant Blignaut, allow the charging troops in the front to enter the trap completely before they open fire, at a range of less than 80 metres. Desperate fighting and the arrival of the rest of the column eventually allow the British to disengage and rush back to Nqutu. The British lose 27 killed, 25 wounded, 11 taken prisoner and 29 horses killed. The Republicans capture a machine gun and 26 horses, while losing one burgher killed, one wounded and one captured by the enemy.[111]
	United Kingdom	The London *Daily Telegraph* reports: "*Never have the scenes of irrepressible and irresistible enthusiasm for the relief of Mafeking been equalled in the memory of man or the records of the Empire. Never can they be forgotten by the generation which they have thrilled to the marrow and swept beyond all ordinary limits of nature by the splendid and passionate impulse of national enthusiasm flashed round the world, and making one vast electric circuit of the entire British race. For two whole days and the greater part of three nights throughout the dominions of the QUEEN, the Empire abandoned itself to an outburst of thanksgiving. . . "*[112]
	Trivia	*The second Olympic Games of the modern epoch starts in Paris*
Day 223 Mon **1900-05-21**	Northern Cape	After a few skirmishes, General Sir Charles Warren reoccupies Douglas with about 600 men.
	OFS	The news that their Renoster River positions have been breached, is a great shock to the Republicans. President Steyn is almost isolated at Heilbron and De Wet rushes to his assistance with a Free State commando. They send thier supply wagons northwards and prepare for a hasty retreat with a Creusot 'Long Tom', mounted and heavily sandbagged on a flatcar, ready to cover their rear.[113]
	United Kingdom	*The Morning Leader* reports: "*General French and Pole-Carew at the head of the Guards and 18th Brigade are marching in, burning practically everything on the road.*"[114]

	International	Mr John Hay, the US Secretary of State, receives the Republican delegation in Washington, DC.[115]
Day 224 Tue **1900-05-22**	OFS	**THE MARCH FROM KROONSTAD** After a delay of ten days, Lord Roberts' main army resumes its advance from Kroonstad. The Republican position on the Renoster River north of Koppies finally dissolves and the retreat to Engelbrechtsdrift south of Vereeniging begins. General Hamilton arrives at Heilbron and as there are no suitable defensive positions left and most of their supplies have already moved north, the Republicans fall back to the Vaal River.[116] General Colvile leaves Winburg.
	International	Commandant Haveman, Major Erasmus of the State Artillery and the State Mine Engineer start preparing positions at Klipriviersberg, south of Johannesburg, employing more than 200 black labourers.[117]
		Before the Dukes (Duke of Edinburgh's Own Volunteer Rifles) leave Matjiesfontein for the front, Mr Logan (known as 'the Laird of Matjiesfontein') donates a Maxim machine gun to them, with the following result: *"From Col Spence, Douglas to Hon Logan, Matjesfontein, May 22. Your Maxim was in action yesterday and did excellent work. Much obliged to you for all your kindness to me and the regiment. Hope all well with you."*[118]
	Cape Colony	The Republican delegation meets US President McKinley unofficially. Abraham Fischer acts as spokesman: *"We do think that in coming here we come to a nation that ought to understand our feelings for liberty and freedom: we come to a nation that Great Britain points to as the only nation favourable to it and we say we come to our mutual friend to get at the British public."* The Secretary of State, Mr Hay, hands them a long dissertation on the reasons why the United States cannot deviate from their traditional policy of neutrality.[119] George W Siclen conducts a poll by means of circulars sent to clergy throughout the US. He later publishes his findings as *"American Sentiment, A plebiscite upon the Boer War,"* concluding that the American public overwhelmingly supports the Boer Republics.[120]
	Trivia	*Sir Arthur Conan Doyle's 41st birthday.*
Day 225 Wed **1900-05-23**	OFS	Commandant-General Louis Botha evacuates his positions on the Renoster River and retreats across the Vaal River.
	Natal front	President Kruger loses confidence in General Lucas Meyer when the General objects to the President's instruction that a 'Long Tom' must be place on top of Molskop (Pogwana). Meyer says that it would be difficult to retrieve the gun when they retire. General Lucas Meyer is recalled to Pretoria and General Christiaan Botha is ordered from Vryheid to take command of the burghers on the Natal border.[121]
	Bechuanaland	Having recrossed the border, General A Hunter reaches Vryburg, where he supervises the repair of the railway line to Mafeking.
	Cape Colony	Mr JD Logan, MLC, responds to the telegram from Colonel Spence: *"Exceedingly glad that gun has been of use. Will pay men using it one pound for every rebel they shoot, but will deduct twenty-five per cent for all prisoners taken."*[122]
	ZAR	With Lord Roberts' vanguard only 65 kilometres away, Judge Antonie Kock (son of General JHM Kock killed at Elandslaagte) arrives at the office of Dr FET Krause, the Special Commandant of the Commission for Law and Order in Johannesburg. Judge Kock shows him a warrant signed by State Secretary FW Reitz ordering the destruction of the mines and he demands tools and transport to carry out his instructions. Krause — who has only hours previously been instructed by Commandant-General L Botha personally to protect the mines and to prevent Kock's sabotage attempts — refuses to comply. He warns Kock that he will have him arrested or shot if he persists in his efforts.[123]

Day 226 Thu **1900-05-24**	ZAR	Judge Antonie Kock, having convinced a few of the German-Irish Foreign Volunteer Corps that he has the authority to destroy the mines, orders them to accompany him to the Robertson Mine. Here he finds about 120 000 ounces of unrefined gold worth about half a million pounds which have, contrary to orders, not yet been sent to Pretoria. He immediately (wrongly) assumes that he has uncovered a plot by Krause to hand the gold and the mines intact to the British for personal gain. He rides off with the commando to confront Krause with his suspicions. The confrontation with Krause ends dramatically when Kock draws a revolver, but is overpowered by Krause and Commandant Van Digglen before he can pull the trigger. Kock is arrested and the gold is sent to Pretoria by mule wagon escorted by Detective Burchardt. Kock is later released on Vice-President SW Burgers's orders.[124] A council of war at Vereeniging decides on the confiscation of the property of burghers who refuse to report for commando service.
	Western ZAR	Colonel Baden-Powell occupies Zeerust.
	OFS	General Colvile leaves Ventersburg for Heilbron and Lord Methuen leaves Hoopstad and marches towards Bothaville. General De la Rey, now commanding the forces in the Western Transvaal, is urgently requested to occupy the drifts across the Vaal River on Botha's right. The commandos ordered there, move too slowly and advance units of General French's forces cross the Vaal River at Old Viljoen's Drift, near Parys.[125]
	Cape Colony	Sir Charles Warren leaves Douglas
	Trivia	*JC Smuts' 30th birthday.* *Queen Victoria's 81st birthday.*
Day 227 Fri **1900-05-25**	OFS	General Rundle occupies Senekal. Colonel BE Spragge leaves Kroonstad for Lindley with the 13th Brigade of Imperial Yeomanry consisting of mostly the Irish Yeomanry. They are ordered to head for Lindley, where they are to join Colvile's column.[126] General French's convoy crosses at Lindeque's Drift and swings eastwards along the northern bank of the Vaal River.[127]
Day 228 Sat **1900-05-26**	ZAR	After the repair of the railway has been completed, General Hunter leaves Vryburg for Lichtenburg.
	OFS	General Colvile reaches Lindley and, ignorant of Spragge's orders, he departs for Heilbron without waiting for the Imperial Yeomanry. Colonel Spragge's force arrives about twelve hours late. They draw rifle fire from the surrounding heights and Spragge, with rations for a single day, decides to occupy the town.[128] General Hamilton crosses the Vaal River at Wonderwater Drift (west of present-day Sasolburg) and links up with French. A small party of burghers is brushed aside, but they succeed in destroying the railway bridge across the Vaal River.[129]
	Cape Colony	Sir Charles Warren halts at Faber's Put, a few kilometres south of Campbell.
Day 229 Sun **1900-05-27**	ZAR	**LORD ROBERTS CROSSES THE VAAL RIVER** With the Vaal River fords west of the railway line in British hands, the Republican positions near Vereeniging becomes untenable and they fall back northwards to Klip River Station. Lord Roberts' main army crosses the Vaal River and occupies Vereeniging.[130] French's cavalry, ordered to head north-westwards towards Florida and Roodepoort on the West Rand, are attacked by 300 burghers under Generals Lemmer and Grobler at Van Wyk's Rust and Vlakfontein. The burghers keep up a heavy fusillade and French is forced to bring his horse artillery into action repeatedly, only to find the burghers retreating at one point and harassing him again from the next. His horses are exhausted and when General Ben Viljoen arrives on the scene with three field-guns and a pom-pom, French retires out of range and prepares camp for the night, with the burghers still occupying the high ground astride his route.[131]

Day 230 Mon 1900-05-28	OFS	**THE ORANGE FREE STATE IS ANNEXED**

Lt.-Gen. HM Leslie-Rundle
(War Museum of the Boer Republics)

	OFS	**THE ORANGE FREE STATE IS ANNEXED** The annexation of the Orange Free State is proclaimed by Lord Roberts and back-dated to coincide with the Queen's birthday. (See Art 42 of the Hague Convention 1899-07-29.) The 'new colony' is henceforth to be known as the 'Orange River Colony'. The Liberal politician, John Morley, comments: *"I am sure it is the first time in the history of this country that it has begun its acquisition of the territory of a white community by blotting out, as the Russian censor blots out an obnoxious newspaper article, the sacred word, 'free'."*[132] Lord Methuen arrives at Kroonstad from Bothaville. General Sir H Colvile's rearguard is in action and delayed at Rooipoort, near Vegkop.[133] At Lindley, Colonel Spragge is subjected to long-range sniping. He urgently requests further orders from both General Colvile and General Rundle. He is advised either to catch up with Colvile or to abandon his wagons and retire to Kroonstad, but the message does not reach him.[134] At Senekal, General HM Leslie Rundle decides to assist Spragge by creating a diversion. During the afternoon, leaving a small garrison behind, he marches out of town. His force consists of five battalions and a company of infantry, Driscoll's Scouts and two batteries field artillery — about 4 000 men with 12 field-guns. He bivouacs about eight kilometres outside town and six kilometres from Biddulphsberg. The mountain is occupied by General AJ de Villiers, with about 400 burghers from the eastern Free State with three guns. The yeomanry draw rifle fire and shelling from a field-gun on the slope of the mountain when they scout in that direction.[135]
	ZAR	**THE BATTLE OF KLIPRIVIERSBERG** General French, surprised to find that the enemy have abandoned their positions in his front, crosses the Klip River at Van Wyk's Rust and he pushes on without scouting ahead. His front troops are suddenly subjected to shelling from no less than seven Republican field-guns which have been brought from Mafeking and skillfully positioned by Captain Von Dalwig during the previous night. French's attacks, supported by his horse artillery, pom-poms and machine guns, fail. He is unable to locate the enemy guns and, when reinforcements pushed into the firing line fail to have the desired effect, he is convinced that the Republicans cannot be dislodged by frontal attacks. He pulls back across the Klip River and contents himself by occupying two heights to the east and west of the Potchefstroom/Johannesburg road.[136] President Kruger receives a telegram from President Steyn repeating the Free State's intention to continue the struggle to the end. They will not abandon the struggle voluntarily while the enemy is in their land and expects the ZAR to do the same.[137]
	Northern Cape	**THE ACTION AT KHEIS** Colonel J Adye's column, consisting of about 350 men with four field-guns, surprises a commando made up mostly of Prieska rebels under Chaim David Judelewitz at Kheis.[138] The rebels, reported to be about 400-strong, have formed a laager on the north bank of the river as well as on a wooded island. Most of the rebels get away when the British artillery fires on their own troops, impeding their efforts to cut off the enemy's retreat. The 24-year-old Judelewitz is killed in action. The British lose nine killed and 18 wounded, they capture the laager with women and children and take many prisoners and thousands of head of cattle.[139]
	Natal front	Some of Buller's force moves from Newcastle towards Ingogo and take position south of Mount Prospect. At 15:00, Lieutenant Von Wichmann of the State Artillery opens up with the 'Long Tom' positioned on top of Molskop — the cause of General Meyer's recall to Pretoria. At a range of more than 9 000 metres the shelling is effective and the British are forced to retreat.[140]

Day 231 Tue 1900-05-29	ZAR	**THE BATTLE OF KLIPRIVIERSBERG OR DOORNKOP**

General French's efforts to dislodge the enemy commanded by Von Dalwig with attacks by the 1st and 4th Cavalry Brigades from the heights they have occupied the night before, fail in the face of Von Dalwig's accurate shelling. A Republican force under Generals De la Rey, Oosthuizen and Gravett offers a determined resistance and the outcome is in the balance. At 13:00, however, General Ian Hamilton arrives from Wildebeesfontein. His arrival enables French to pull back his calvary, push Hamilton's troops against the Boer positions and to start a wide flanking move north-westwards. After a brief rest, Hamilton's soldiers, supported by 32 field-guns, start their assault against the heights between Doringkop in the west and the western slopes of Klipriviersberg (in the present-day Soweto). A gap develops as the two brigades diverge and Hamilton pushes in his reserve troops. The rifle fire increases as they approach their objectives and their khaki uniforms become very conspicuous when they enter an area blackened by a veld fire. Lance-corporal J Mackay, 1st Battalion, the Gordon Highlanders, earns his Victoria Cross at Crow's Nest Hill, by repeatedly rushing forward under withering short-range fire to assist wounded comrades.[141] They press on resolutely and fix bayonets for the final charge. To their disappointment, their objective is abandoned before they reach it and, when they push on after a brief rest, they encounter fierce fire from an even stronger position and the attack falters. The British can, however, subject this position to crossfire and their artillery support becomes increasingly more effective. When the wide left hook by French's Cavalry menace the burghers on Doringkop, they retreat and at dusk, the British are in possession of the battlefield while the burghers retreat without being pursued.[142]

On the eastern approaches to Johannesburg, Lord Roberts' main army marches northwards along the Natalspruit, between the present-day townships of Tokoza and Vosloorus. Near Elandsfontein, south of Wadeville, Colonel St GC Henry's Mounted Infantry briefly clashes with Heidelbergers who go home when the British artillery silence their three guns. At Elandsfontein Station, Henry's advance is checked by fierce rifle fire and accurate shelling from the Republican 'Long Tom' mounted on a railway car. When the British artillery concentrate on damaging the railway line behind the train, it steams away, just as a party of Mounted Infantrymen rushes forward to sever the line.

Lord Roberts occupies the important railway junction at Germiston and at Boksburg British troops capture seven locomotives and about 200 railway cars.[143]

The ZAR government decides not to defend Pretoria and Commandant-General Botha is placed in charge of covering the orderly departure of their forces, important officials and supplies from the capital.[144]

	OFS	**THE BATTLE OF BIDDULPHSBERG**

General AJ de Villiers, realising the danger of being outflanked in mountain positions, reinforces his flanks and conceals a small group of 38 burghers in a donga at the foot of the mountain with another small group on the lower slopes in their rear. At 06:00 General Rundle's force starts to move. He orders the yeomanry to demonstrate against the western slopes to keep the enemy pinned down while he moves his main force north-eastwards to attack De Villiers' flank against the northern slope. His artillery comes into action but is ineffective until they concentrate on snipers and a pom-pom near the farmhouse. The pom-pom stops firing and Rundle, believing that it has been wiped out, orders the Grenadier Guards to retrieve it. They recklessly charge ahead, run into the concealed burghers in the donga and are flung back by furious rifle fire at a range

		of less than 150 metres. Three successive charges fail and the pom-pom opens up again and is joined by the rest of the Republican guns. The soldiers go down and their plight becomes desperate as the tall grass catch fire behind them. Several soldiers' uniforms are set alight and the wounded are helplessly caught in the conflagration. The British fall back and De Villiers leads the pursuit in short rushes until he is hit by shell splinters as the British artillery covers the retreat. The British losses amount to 47 killed, 130 wounded and eight missing. The burghers lose one killed and three wounded, including the seriously wounded De Villiers.[145] General Colvile arives at Heilbron and finds out that the supplies he expected to be there, are still at Roodewal siding. **THE BATTLE OF LINDLEY** At Lindley, Lieutenant-Colonel BE Spragge's brigade of Imperial Yeomanry is surrounded by General Piet de Wet. The burghers push closer and the intensity of the rifle fire increases. Although the Yeomanry are well-entrenched and do not suffer serious casualties, Spragge realises that he will not be able to maintain his position if enemy artillery arrives.[146]
	Natal Front	At Laing's Nek, General Christiaan Botha, acting commander in the absence of his brother and General Erasmus, receives a letter from Sir Redvers Buller. General Buller warns him that the Republicans' position is hopeless and that he will be well advised to come to terms.[147] Buller also sends General Hildyard into Utrecht to secure its surrender. Hildyard and the landdrost (magistrate) confer for a considerable time before the landrost hands over a ZAR flag and six rifles as a token of the town's submission. The commandos agree to move out of town and not to return, but they wait in the surrounding hills until Hildyard marches out. They immediately reoccupy the town, tear down the British proclamations and arrest the landrost.[148]
Day 232 Wed **1900-05-30**	ZAR	Generals JDP French and ISM Hamilton occupy Doornkop, the actual koppie beside the farmhouse, where Dr Jameson had raised the white flag five years before. The battles for the approaches to Johannesburg have cost the British 28 killed and 134 wounded, while the Republican casualties are unknown.[149] They occupy Florida and Roodepoort on the western Witwatersrand. In Johannesburg, General Ben Viljoen commandeers all the supplies they need and, accompanied by a large crowd of women, they open a government goods shed and make off with all they can carry.[150] Dr FET Krause, Commandant of Johannesburg, rides out to meet the approaching British forces to arrange the surrender of the city. Dr Krause is concerned that if the burghers in Johannesburg are not allowed to escape, street fighting will break out and many civilians, including women and children, may be caught in the crossfire. Lord Roberts agrees to delay his entry into the city by 24 hours. [151] President Kruger leaves Pretoria for Machadodorp, the newly declared capital of the ZAR. He leaves his invalid wife Gezina behind in their modest house in Church Street. They are never to meet again.[152]
	OFS	At Lindley, a seesaw battle develops between Spragge and Piet de Wet over the possession of a patch of grazing for the British horses and draught animals. A 16-man group of counter-attacking Yeomen are cut off from the main force and is captured. The burghers retain the pasture at dusk.[153] Lord Methuen leaves Kroonstad with the 9th Infantry Brigade, three battalions

		yeomanry and 16 guns, including two pom-poms, to relieve the Imperial Yeomanry at Lindley. As the Free Staters at Biddulphsberg do not have the services of a doctor, the seriously wounded General De Villiers is handed over to the British at Senekal on condition that he will be released on his recovery.[154]
	Northern Cape	**THE FIGHT AT FABER'S PUT** General P de Villiers, with about 600 Griqualand rebels under Commandants Vorster and Venter, attack General Sir C Warren's camp at Faber's Put. A confused, short range battle rages in the half-light of dawn with no overall generalship on either side and every officer engages the enemy firing on his men. The British recover from the initial surprise and their superior firepower wins the day. They lose 23 killed, including Colonel Spence of the DEOVR, and 32 wounded while the rebels lose 38 killed and 50 wounded.[155]
	Bechuanaland	The *Mafeking Mail* publishes a telegram addressed to Colonel Baden-Powell: *"Directors of the BSA Company convey to you an experession of their deep thankfulness at the glorious end of your heroic resistance, and their admiration of the fortitude and pluck displayed by the people of Mafeking. Your stand has saved Rhodesia."*[156]
	United Kingdom	Lady Edward (Violet) Cecil writes to Lord Salisbury on the conditions in Bloemfontein: *"Far more people have been killed by negligence in our hospitals than by Boer bullets... Men are dying by the hundreds who could easily be saved..."*[157]
Day 233 Thu **1900-05-31**	ZAR	Lord Roberts issues a proclamation to the burghers of the ZAR (Proclamation 1 of 1900) proclaiming that, in as far as military operations would allow, British forces would respect the personal rights and property of non-combatants. *"All burghers who have not taken a prominent part in the policy which has led to the war between HM and the S.A.R., or commandeered or used violence to any British subjects, or committted any acts contrary to the usages of civilized warfare, and who are willing to lay down their arms at once, and bind themselves by an oath to abstain from further participation in the war, will be given passes to allow them to return to their homes and will not be made prisoners of war."* See Article 45 of the Hague Convention.[158] Through an oversight, the telegraph wires to the north-eastern Free State have been left intact. President Kruger wires President Steyn that reports reaching him indicates that only a handful of ZAR burghers is willing to continue the struggle. He urges President Steyn to meet him urgently at Machadodorp to discuss future strategies. An hour later President Kruger informs President Steyn that he has convened a council of war. If a negative resolution prevails, he suggests that negotiations with Lord Roberts must start immediately, so that both Republics can lay down their arms 'in protest'.[159] **LORD ROBERTS ENTERS JOHANNESBURG, THE CITY OF GOLD** An unknown soldier, accompanying Robert Pool, makes a sweeping gesture towards the mine dumps and headgear and remarks: *"That's what we're fighting for!"*[160]
	OFS	**THE BATTLE OF LINDLEY** At dawn, the British attempt to recapture the disputed grazing by launching a bayonet charge led by Lord Longford. This battle suddenly ends when the Free Staters open fire with their newly arrived pair of field-guns. Spragge's position worsens when Commandant M Prinsloo arrives just after noon with two addi-

		tional field-guns. When Prinsloo charges the southernmost British-held koppie under cover of his artillery, a corporal panics and raises the white flag. He is immediately shot down by his own comrades, but his lieutenant feels obliged to order cease-fire. The rest of the British positions become untenable and Colonel Spragge cannot sanction further bloodshed.[161] The 13th Battalion of the Imperial Yeomanry, having suffered 25 killed and 55 wounded, surrenders with a total of 464 soldiers to General Piet de Wet outside Lindley.[162] Lord Roberts proclaims martial law in the 'Orange River Colony'. See Article 42 of the Hague Convention 1899-07-29.[163]
	Trivia	*EY Brabant's 61st birthday.*
1900	WINTER	**JUNE**
Day 234 Fri **1900-06-01**	OFS	Lord Methuen arrives at Paardeplaats outside Lindley. He immediately dispatches a strong force, attempting to capture De Wet's convoy and to liberate the British prisoners. A five-hour-long running battle ensues during which the British suffer 26 casualties before returning to reoccupy Lindley. In Bloemfontein, there are 3 968 soldiers in hospitals and the death rate peaks at more than 80 a day. All public buildings, including the Free State Raadsaal and Grey College School, are converted into hospitals. Shortages of supplies, including bedpans, medical and nursing staff, compound the epidemic. Dr Arthur Conan Doyle, working at an improvised hospital in the Bloemfontein Club, estimates that there are between 8 000 and 9 000 cases of enteric fever during Lord Roberts' delay in Bloemfontein. Lord Roberts issues a third proclamation to Republican forces in the field, specifically warning inhabitants of the 'Orange River Colony' that anyone still under arms on 15 June *"will be liable to be dealt with as rebels, and to suffer in person and property accordingly"*. See Article 42 of the Hague Convention 1899-07-29.[164]
	ZAR	A meeting of ZAR military leaders including Botha, De la Rey and Viljoen, disillusioned by the seemingly general demoralisation and the collapse of organized resistance, decides to advise President Kruger that it is time to stop the war. Telegrams to this effect are sent to Presidents Kruger and Steyn.[165]
Day 235 Sat **1900-06-02**	OFS	A supply convoy leaves Roodewal Station for Heilbron with an insufficient escort. **PRESIDENT STEYN ATTACKS THE DEMORALIZED ZAR LEADERSHIP** President Steyn's reply to the demoralized telegrams from President Kruger and the ZAR military leaders, is the most important telegram of the war. He practically accuses the Tranvaalers of cowardice. After they have involved the Free State and the colonial rebels in ruin, he says, they are now ready, as the war reaches their borders, to conclude a selfish and disgraceful peace.[166] The Free State will fight on to the bitter end, even if she must do so alone.[167]
	ZAR	At a council of war in the Chamber of the Second Volksraad in Pretoria, the strongly worded telegram from President Steyn and another from Chief Commandant De Wet stings the ZAR leadership. The Free State's scorn and a fiery speech by Captain Danie Theron, calling everyone considering peace a traitor, carry the day. Commandant-General Botha and General Smuts decide that the honour of the Volk, as well as their personal honours, demand a fight to the death. Talk of surrender is forgotten and the council of war decides on a fighting retreat.[168] They

		decide, however, not to make *"the final stand which Lord Roberts so anxiously longed for and so many Boers expected"*. A proposal to continue the stuggle is unanimously accepted, but a proposal to institute a military government is rejected. Commandant-General Louis Botha proclaims special powers to maintain law and order in Pretoria and he appoints a three-man commission.[169] State Attorney JC Smuts is relieved of his civil duties to allow him to join General De la Rey's commando.
Gen. JC Smuts *(National Cultural History Musum)*	**Victoria Cross**	A British 'flying column' under Major Hunter-Weston, sent to break up the Delagoa railway line in the vicinity of Bronkhorstspruit, runs into a strong Republican force. They manage to extricate themselves with one killed and 13 wounded. Corporal FH Kirby, Royal Engineers, is to be awarded the Victoria Cross for assisting of a soldier whose horse has been shot, and helping him to safety.[170]
	Natal front	General Sir Redvers Buller and General Christiaan Botha meet at O'Neill's Farm, Laing's Nek, on the Natal border. Neither party has authority to make terms, but Buller promises to communicate with Roberts and to suggest terms that would allow the burghers to return to their farms, leaving only their artillery behind. Botha also undertakes to communicate with his government. A three-day armistice is concluded during which no movements will be made by either side.[171]
		The Kosi Bay expedition is abandoned. The planned secret raid through Swaziland on the Komati Poort railway line, is cancelled when it is realised that it has been common knowledge in the cafés and bars of Lourenço Marques for the past month. A detachment of Strathcona's Horse (Canadians) that has been sent under a naval escort to Kosi Bay for this purpose, is recalled.[172]
Day 236 Sun **1900-06-03**	ZAR	Lord Roberts rejects the terms of surrender that Buller has offered to Christiaan Botha and insists on unconditional surrender. Rifles, guns and horses must be handed over, officers are to be kept on parole and an oath undertaking not to take up arms again must be signed. These terms are communicated to Commandant-General Louis Botha.[173]
		Lord Roberts leaves Johannesburg with a force of about 20 000 troops and starts the final leg of his march to Pretoria.
		With less than 3 000 burghers at his disposal, Commandant-General Botha appoints a Committee for Law and Order consisting of prominent Pretoria citizens.[174]
		General Sarel du Toit's commando, arriving from the western front with two Armstrong guns and a pom-pom, occupies a narrow pass on the farm Kalkfontein. Their determined resistance allow most of a Republican convoy to escape and they delay General French's flanking movement for the rest of the day, inflicting nine casualties.[175]
Day 237 Mon **1900-06-04**	OFS	At Swawelkrans (22 kilometres from Heilbron), Chief Commandant CR de Wet comes across a supply convoy consisting of 56 wagons escorted by 160 infantrymen bound for Heilbron. He bluffs the commanding officer into surrendering without bloodshed.[176]
	ZAR	General French occupies Commando Nek (about 32 kilometres west of Pretoria) and Silkaatsnek. General Ian Hamilton is stopped by De la Rey's strong position at Quaggaspoort.
		Commandant-General Louis Botha fights an effective delaying action at Irene and Sesmylspruit against two infantry divisions supported by seven field artillery batteries. The Republican 'Long Tom' mounted on the railway car again does sturdy duty before retiring eastwards. The burghers put up a determined defence, inflicting 51 casualties, with slight own losses. At Irene, Commandant JD Weilbach reportedly tells his men, *"You can stay and fight if you want, I'm going home!"* His Heidelbergers

154

		evacuate their positions prematurely and the rest of the Republicans are forced to fall back.[177] State attorney JC Smuts has a scant force of fewer than 100 men at his disposal with which to keep law and order in the chaotic Pretoria. After days of cajoling and threatening, he finally uses an arrest warrant to convince the directors of the National Bank to hand over coins and gold bullion worth about £500 000 belonging to the government. He also discovers bullion and blank coins worth about £250 000 at the Mint. After meticulously weighing all gold, he prepares a full inventory and dispatches everything by train to Machadodorp while the first British troops enter the suburbs and artillery shells straddle the railway line.[178] At 20:00 Lieutenant Watson of the New South Wales Mounted Rifles, enters Pretoria under a flag of truce and informs Commandant-General Botha that, unless Pretoria surrenders or is declared open, the bombardment will commence at 10:00 the following day.[179]
	Northern Cape	General Warren enters Campbell.
	Trivia	*Sir Garnet J Wolesley's 67th birthday.* *The French artist Auguste Rodin's sculpture 'The Kiss' is publicly exhibited in Paris for the first time.*
Day 238 Tue **1900-06-05**	ZAR	At 14:00, Field-Marshal Lord Frederick Roberts' triumphant entry into Pretoria marks the end of his Great March from Bloemfontein **PRETORIA, CAPITAL OF THE ZAR, IS OCCUPIED** Republican leaders meet at Lewis & Marks' whiskey distillery near Eerstefabrieken. Under the chairmanship of Commandant-General Louis Botha there are five Generals, five Combat Generals, four senior State Artillery officers — 29 officers in all. Almost every officer bemoans the demoralisation and fatigue of their burghers, the weak condition of their animals and the lack of grazing. Botha declares that, unless a new fighting spirit can be imbibed amongst the burghers, they will be forced to lay down their arms and direct their protests to the United States and the European powers. The meeting ends on a slightly more positive note when they decide to defend the chain of hills east of Pretoria.[180]
	Victoria Cross	Sergeant AHL Richardson, Lord Strathcona's Horse (Canadian Forces), is nominated for the Victoria Cross when his small party is attacked by a superior force of the enemy at Wolwespruit, 24 kilometres north of Standerton. Under heavy crossfire, he turns back to rescue a wounded trooper whose horse has been shot.[181]
	OFS	President Steyn arrives in Bethlehem, now declared the new Orange Free State capital.[182]
	Natal front	Commandant-General Louis Botha rejects the terms of surrender offered to his brother, General Chris Botha, by Sir Redvers Buller and revised by Lord Roberts. The armistice on the Natal border is consequently terminated.[183]
	Trivia	*The German liner* Deutschland III *sets a new speed record.*
Day 239 Wed **1900-06-06**	ZAR	Proclamation 2 of 1900: Lord Roberts expands his previous proclamation to allow Boer farmers, in exchange for an oath of neutrality, to return to their farms, unhindered, and to retain all of their livestock. Passes will also be issued to those wanting to move their animals to their winter pastures in the Bushveld.[184] About 3 000 British prisoners of war are released at Waterval about 12 kilometres north of Pretoria. Only about 1 000 prisoners have been evacuated eastwards with the retreating Republican forces.[185]
	Cape Colony	Some Cape Cabinet Ministers advocate the withdrawal of martial law in the areas that have been pacified since the withdrawal of the Republican invaders.
	Natal front	At last, General Buller resumes his march from Newcastle, where the bulk of his army has halted since 18 May.

Day 240 Thu **1900-06-07** *Assistant Field-cornet (later Gen.) CF Beyers* (War Museum of the Boer Republics)	ZAR	Field-Marshal Lord Roberts proposes a meeting with Commandant-General Louis Botha. Commandant-General Botha receives a letter with peace proposals signed by LF de Souza, an ex-chief secretary in the late Commandant-General Joubert's office. The letter includes an offer, allegedly from Lord Roberts, offering Botha and De la Rey parole and permission to reside in a safe place in South Africa, as well as an annual payment of £10 000 each. Botha is insulted by the letter but Roberts' involvement with the drafting of the offer cannot be confirmed.[186] At a council of war held at Vandermerwe Siding, it is decided to take defensive positions along the range of hills stretching from Wonderboom Poort, past Donker Poort, to Tierkloof and beyond. The young Assistant Field-cornet Christiaan F Beyers does a stinging attack on lukewarm and cowardly senior officers. His proposal to have them suspended is too strongly worded for the rest of the officers and is not adopted. It is decided to leave the arrangement of the commandos to the Commandant-General. Every commandant pledges that his men will stand fast and that they will try to make amends for their poor conduct before the fall of Pretoria.[187] Advance units of Roberts' army start out from Pretoria, moving in an easterly direction along the railway line.
	Western ZAR	Lichtenburg is occupied by units under General Hunter. **THE SURRENDER OF KLERKSDORP** Captain H Lambart of General Hunter's force at Hartbeesfontein sends a telegraph to General Andries PJ Cronje (on sick leave) at Klerksdorp requesting a meeting. At 17:00 Captain Lambart, accompanied by Lieutenant Blagden and Corporal Guest, meet General Cronje at the Tivoli Hotel in town. In a brilliant coup of deception and bluff they break the news about the fall of Pretoria of which Cronje is not yet aware, and inform him that a force of 20 000 is about to move to Klerksdorp. Cronje requests time to hold a meeting with his men and Captain Lambart graciously grants permission for such a meeting.[188] General Hunter enters Ventersdorp.
	OFS	**THE BATTLE OF ROODEWAL SIDING** Splitting his forces into three units, Chief Commandant De Wet launches simultaneous attacks on Roberts' communication lines north of Kroonstad. Commandant L Steenekamp with 300 burghers capture the small British camp at Vredefort Road Station without firing a shot, taking 38 prisoners. A troop train carrying about 500 soldiers approaching from the north quickly turns back after a short, sharp exchange of fire. A second force of 300 burghers under Assistant Chief Commandant CC Froneman attacks the 4th Derbyshire Regiment at Renoster River bridge, where, after 36 men are killed and 104 wounded, 486 officers and men surrender. In the main coup of the day, Chief Commandant CR de Wet and 80 men attack two companies — 172 men — guarding a train and supplies at Roodewal Station. De Wet, trying to avoid bloodshed, first attempts a bluff by sending a messenger under a flag of truce informing the British that he has more than a thousand men and four guns. The commanding officer rejects any notion of surrendering but finds the telegraph lines already cut. The British, fortifying themselves behind bales of blankets, clothes and postbags, resist for almost five hours until Froneman arrives with his men and two field-guns. The danger of enemy shelling setting off the ammunition stockpile, forces the soldiers to surrender. The British suffer eight killed and 24 wounded at Roodewal, while De Wet, in all three actions, only lose one burgher killed and four wounded. The total British casualties for the day amount to 45 killed, 123 wounded and 672 taken prisoner. De Wet can only remove between 500 and 600 crates of ammunition (some of which are buried on his own farm for later use). He has to burn the train and other supplies estimated at between £100 000 and £750 000 (according to newspaper reports) in a *"most beautiful"* fireworks display that is visible from as far away as Kroonstad. The

		explosion leaves a crater measuring about 30 metres by 18 metres wide and 6 metres deep. The Republicans also destroy more than 18 kilometres of railway and telegraph lines that will take weeks to repair.[189]
	Cape Colony	General Sir Charles Warren enters Griekwastad.
Day 241 Fri **1900-06-08**	Western ZAR	Completely taken in by Lambart's ruse, General APJ Cronje holds a meeting with his men and about 500 discouraged burghers decide to lay down their arms. Captain Lambart with a total force of 33 men marches in and accepts the surrender of Klerksdorp.[190]
	ZAR	Commandant-General Louis Botha with about 4 000 men, 25 guns and eight pom-poms, start preparing defensive positions from Boekenhoutskloof in the north, across the railway line and south to Diamond Hill and Morskop. His line extends more than 40 kilometres and, mindful of the usual British tactic, Botha strengthens his flanks at the expense of his centre, positioned on the railway line at Pienaarspoort.[191] General French's cavalry starts scouting patrols north-eastwards. The burghers under Generals Douthwaite and Grobler are jittery and fall back until they are rein-forced by General De la Rey. General Ian Hamilton's scouts on the south-eastern flank cause less consternation when they are noticed by General Tobias Smuts' burghers. In the centre, Colonel SPE Trichardt opens long-range artillery fire on the British camp at Silverton, using the train-mounted 'Long Tom'. The British scouting patrols are unable to gain detailed information about the Republican positions.[192]
	Natal front	Generals Chris Botha and Joachim Fourie are caught unawares by General Sir Redvers Buller's move against Botha's Pass. The key position in this sector, Van Wyk's Kop, is defended by a picket of about 25 burghers who are easily pushed off by the South African Light Horse. General Talbot-Coke quickly reinforces their foothold by sending up three infantry battalions and a field battery. Buller's advance against Botha's Pass extends over a 6-kilometre front and is preceded by a heavy 45-minute artillery barrage. The main assault begins at 10:00 and five hours later the British infantry reach the top of the pass. The Republican forces offer no opposition other than rearguard actions and slip away unscathed after setting the grass on fire to cover their movements. Buller enters the Orange Free State after a battle that costs him only 26 casualties, while only four burghers are slightly wounded.[193]
	OFS	A small scouting patrol sent out by De Wet captures 38 infantrymen on their way to Kroonstad. This brings the number of prisoners of war taken by the Republicans in the Free State since 31 May to more than 1 300 men.[194]
	Cape Colony	Cape Prime Minister WP Schreiner consults his parliamentary caucus on the ques-tion of amnesty for rebels. His proposal, to revert to Richard Solomon's suggested special civil courts to try all rebels, but distinguishing between rebel leaders and oth-ers, is defeated by 29 votes to eight.[195]
Day 242 Sat **1900-06-09**	ZAR	Responding to Lord Roberts' invitation to negotiate, a messenger from Louis Botha informs the Field-Marshal: "*Unless you have some new proposals to negotiate, I am ordered by General Botha to state that our leaders decline te meet you.*"[196] The 2nd Battalion Royal Scottish Fusiliers leave Lichtenburg for Potchefstroom.
	Bechuanaland	The first train from the south enters Mafeking.[197]
Day 243 Sun **1900-06-10**	Natal front	In bitterly cold weather, General Chris Botha's small force of about 120 Lydenburg burghers put up a sterling defence at Gansvleikop, at the confluence of the Gansvlei and Klip River, on the Free State side of the Natal border. After a battle lasting the entire afternoon, the burghers abandon their position after dark. The British report six men killed and ten wounded.[198]
	International	A scheme, conceived by ADW Wolmarans of the Republican delegation in Europe,

		proposes offering Russia and France, together or separately, a protectorate over the two Boer Republics. The Russian Foreign Minister replies: *"We know nothing of France's intentions, but in any case, whatever may be our sympathy towards the two republics — the present circumstances appear to us absolutely inopportune for the protectorate, which is the subject of your telegram."*[199]
	Trivia	*JCG Kemp's 28th birthday.*
Day 244 Mon **1900-06-11**	OFS	Chief Commandant CR de Wet fights an hour-long artillery duel with a strong force commanded by Lord Methuen on his own farm Rooipoort and in the Heuningkoppies. De Wet disengages, having inflicted a loss of one man killed and 21 wounded on the enemy. Seven burghers are taken prisoner of war. For some of them, this is the start of an epic journey (See 1901-01-10).[200]
	Natal front	**THE BATTLE OF ALLEMAN'S NEK** At 05:30 Lord Dundonald discovers General Joachim Fourie's burghers preparing trenches on both sides of the Vrede-Volksrust-road where it passes through Alleman's Nek. Dundonald's 3rd Brigade tries to move around the southern flank but, despite their artillery support, they are stopped by well-directed shelling from the four Republican guns and pom-poms. General HJT Hildyard has to postpone his attack on the pass until all the infantry brigades are in position. At 14:30, the British frontal assault starts. The men of the 2nd Infantry Brigade, forming the front ranks, are pinned down in a dry gulley by determined crossfire from the heights. The burghers in their half-completed trenches are subjected to a heavy barrage from four field batteries, four 4,7 inch (120 mm) and four 5,5 kg (12-pounder) naval guns — about 32 guns. The arrival of Major-General Talbot Coke's 10th Infantry Brigade settles the isssue and Fourie's men start falling back. At 17:00 the infantrymen charge the heights commanding the pass, covered by the smoke of the veld fires. Skilful rearguard actions on successive ridges prevent the Cavalry from impeding Fourie's retreat. The British lose 28 killed, and 134 wounded. The Republican casualties are unknown, but at least four burghers are killed.[201]
	Western ZAR	Colonel BT Mahon occupies Potchefstroom. Since 3 May, 27 bridges, 41 culverts and 16 kilometres of track have been repaired on the 426 kilometres of railway line between Bloemfontein and Johannesburg.[202]
	ZAR	**THE BATTLE OF DIAMOND HILL OR DONKERHOEK** Despite the garrisons he has left behind in the key towns and cities along the route of his march and the troops guarding his lines of communications, Field-Marshal Lord Roberts can muster a huge army for his operations east of Pretoria: The **Left Flank**, commanded by Lieutenant-General JDP French: 1st Cavalry Brigade — Colonel TC Porter 4 th Cavalry Brigade — Major General Dickson The 1st Mounted Infantry Brigade under Major General ETH Hutton: Two Corps of Mounted Infantry **Total at least** 1 800 men, 12 guns and 3 pom-poms. The **Central Column**, Lieutenant-general R P le-Carew's 11th Division: 1st Infantry Brigade — Major General IR Jones 18th Infantry Brigade— Brigadier-General TE Stephenson Mounted Infantry Corps — Colonel GC Henry **Total at least** 7 700 men with 30 guns The **Right Flank**, commanded by Lieutenant-General ISM Hamilton: 2nd Cavalry Brigade — Brigadier-General Broadwood 3rd Cavalry Brigade — Brigadier-General J Gordon The 2nd Mounted Infantry Brigade under Brigadier-General CP Ridley: Four Corps of Mounted Infantry 21st Infantry Brigade — Major General BM Hamilton **Total at least** 10 500 men with 32 guns and 6 pom-poms A **Grand total** of at least 20 000 men with 80 guns and 9 pom-poms[203]

Gen. JP Snyman
(National Cultural History Museum)

Gen. RG Broadwood
(War Museum of the Boer Republics)

Plans by Commandant-General Botha and General De la Rey to attack the British are pre-empted when the cavalry troops of Generals French and Hamilton move out at 03:00. Lord Roberts have decided on a fairly conventional battle plan — an infantry demonstration against the centre and flanking moves by his cavalry. French's cavalrymen are allowed to pass the unoccupied Louwsbaken Hill and cross the Krokodilspruit. Just when they think that they have reached the Republican flank, they are met by a fusillade from De la Rey's burghers on the Kameelfontein Heights. General Snyman's burghers start a flanking move of their own, and only by sending Colonel Porter's 1st Brigade in a wide arc, does French avoid the trap from closing. Porter's horse artillery forces Snyman's men to swerve northwards and they occupy the Boekenhoutskloof Heights. French's main force comes under accurate artillery fire from Von Dalwig's well-concealed guns on Krokodilspruit Kop and the assault falters. French's position becomes precarious until about noon, when he succeeds in suppressing the Republican shelling by pushing three batteries into action.

To the south, General Ian Hamilton's move to outflank the Republican position meets a similar fate. Brigadier-General Broadwood's eagerness to reach the Republicans left at Diamond Hill and Morskop, impairs his judgement. He rushes too far ahead and, when he notices Republican guns changing position, he orders his artillery to engage them. They are immediately attacked at close quarters by a small group of burghers. The gunners are hard pressed and have to use case shot to extricate their guns. The Lancers engage the small band and overrun some of them when General Fourie orders the German Corps to their assistance. The Lancers are forced to retire and their commander, Lieutenant-Colonel DSW Ogilvy, tenth Earl of Airlie, of Alyth and Lintherathen, is killed in action.[204] Broadwood's attack is stopped and becomes an artillery duel.

Elsewhere, Major-General Bruce Hamilton's infantry, marching from Garstfontein, pass through Swawelpoort and he orders his advance guard to take Tierpoort. His main force advances across Boschkop and encounters General T Smuts' burghers on Kleinfontein, in front of Diamond Hill. The British assault starts at 14:00, vigorously supported by the siege guns and a field battery. The burghers, cut off from any reinfocements, start to fall back in small groups and at 16:00 the foothills are abandoned. General Ian Hamilton, convinced that the burghers' retreat is a disorganised flight, orders the attack to continue against Donkerhoek itself. The attackers soon run into severe rifle fire and the assault is cancelled as dusk approaches. In the centre, Roberts' demonstrations against Pienaarspoort, supported by two field batteries, two naval guns and two siege guns, succeed in keeping the burghers in their front occupied and uncertain about the objectives of the main attack. The burghers maintain their positions and the 'Long Tom' mounted on the railway car repeatedly dashes forward to answer the British shelling before steaming off again. At twilight, the battlefield falls silent and Lord Roberts returns to Pretoria to consider his next step.[205]

| Day 245 Tue 1900-06-12 | ZAR  *Gen. Ian Hamilton* (War Museum of the Boer Republics) | **THE BATTLE OF DIAMOND HILL OR DONKERHOEK** Only at about 03:00 does Lord Roberts decide to concentrate his main thrust on Donkerhoek in support of General Ian Hamilton's tentative foothold on its foothills. He orders General Pole-Carew to transfer some of his troops, including Inigo Jones' Guards Brigade, a field battery and four heavy guns from the centre, to support a fresh attack in the south. Awaiting these reinforcements, General Hamilton delays his attack until about 12:45 — giving Commandant-General Botha time to scour his line for burghers he can send south to reinforce Generals Tobias Smuts and Fourie. Hamilton's troops, reinforced by Jones' Guards and supported by heavy artillery, move up the face of Diamond Hill in extended order. General Smuts' burghers fall back over the crest to positions further to the rear. When the British reach the top of the hill, they are shocked to find that they are caught in fierce crossfire from the burghers along a dominating rear crest. As these burghers are invisible from the positions in front of the hill, the British artillery, firing blind, cannot effectively support their troops. At 15:00 the ridge of Donkerhoek is also in British hands but the troops cannot make any further headway. It will be suicide to attempt a charge over |

	*Comdt.-Gen. Louis Botha* (National Cultural History Museum) *Gen. Tobias Smuts* (National Cultural History Museum) *Gen. JH de la Rey* (National Cultural History Museum) *Gen. Ben Viljoen* (War Museum of the Boer Republics)	open ground under such deadly crossfire, the soldiers on the top of Diamond Hill can do no more than seek cover. Inigo Jones orders that his 83rd battery be dragged up the slope to dominate the rear slope and other enemy positions. The gun crews suffer heavily but when the guns open up, the Boer rifle fire is almost halved. This is still not enough to allow forward movement and the battle in this sector remains a rifle duel for the rest of the afternoon. The British efforts to move around the Republican southern flank meet with mixed success. The Derbyshires run into Republican trenches and are stopped and forced back. Ridley's Mounted Infantry fares better and forces the burghers in their sector back until Botha pushes General Ben Viljoen's burghers into the firing line. The assault stalls when Ridley's artillery support is distracted by a lone Republican gun shelling the mounted infantry's horses. Although the Republican line is forced back, a stalemate situation develops at the end of the day. In the northern sector General De la Rey improves his position against General French's cavalry as the day wears on. At about 13:00 he is reinforced by Generals Douthwaite and Grobler with two field-guns and two pom-poms. French has to use all his reserve artillery to maintain his position and his situation deteriorates when enemy field-guns force Porter to shift his camp at Doornfontein. At 17:00 De la Rey informs Commandant-General Botha that French has been hemmed in on three sides and is in a very vulnerable postion. De la Rey is convinced that, if reinforced, he can counterattack and capture French. While Botha is preparing to send burghers from the centre, disturbing reports from Smuts and Viljoen reach him and he has to inform the bitterly disappointed De la Rey of the British breakthrough at Diamond Hill and Donkerhoek. As darkness falls, Commandant-General Louis Botha orders his burghers to abandon their positions and they quietly retire to Bronkhorstspruit, leaving the unsuspecting Lord Roberts to make his plans for the next day's battle.[206] The British official accounts give their casualties for the two-day battle as 28 killed, 145 wounded and four missing, while the Republican losses are uncertain, but seem to be 30 killed and wounded with a few taken prisoner.[207] During the battle two burghers, JF de Beer and JS Smit, accompanied by Dr WC Scholtz, meet General Botha with an offer from Lord Roberts to President Kruger that if he surrenders before 20 June, he will not be banished to St Helena. Botha informs them that an interview with President Kruger will serve no purpose and sends them back, refusing General Ben Viljoen's insistence that they must be arrested for treason.[208]
	OFS	President Steyn issues a proclamation, printed at Fouriesburg, refuting Lord Roberts' annexation proclamations. He points out that the Orange Free State government is still in existence and its military forces are still unconquered and thus in terms of Article 42 of the Hague Convention military rule cannot be imposed, etc. The President declares these British proclamations null and void and reaffirms that the people of the Orange Free State are and remain a free and independent nation and refuse to subject themselves to British rule.[209] Near Heilbron, Lord Kitchener receives reports that De Wet is approaching his camp with a raiding party. Kitchener narrowly escapes capture by galloping to safety in his pyjamas.[210]
	Cape Colony	Sir A Milner writes to Prime Minister Schreiner that he, as Governor of the Cape Colony, must have a ministry which can give him unanimous advice and again suggests that the Cape cabinet should be restructured.[211]
	Natal / ZAR	On the Natal front, General Sir R Buller's advance units occupy Volksrust. Since starting from Ladysmith on 7 May Buller's army has covered 288 kilometres in 36 days averaging about 8 kilometres per day. During the same period Lord Roberts' army has advanced about 480 kilometres.[212]

	Natal	Republican forces evacuate their positions at Laing's Nek.
	Rhodesia	General Sir Frederick Carrington's 1st Brigade arrives at Bulawayo, Rhodesia.
Day 246 Wed **1900-06-13**	ZAR	Lord Roberts is astounded to find himself in possession of the battlefield and the burghers well beyond the range of practical pursuit. The train-mounted 'Long Tom' again discourages the probing actions of the British mounted units and Lord Roberts orders French and Hamilton to retire to Sammy Marks' farm, Christinen Hill. Commandant-General Botha is delighted and decides to move on to better defensive positions near Balmoral.[213] President Kruger requests President Steyn to attempt offensive actions against the British rear at Vereeniging or along their lines of communication.
	OFS	President Steyn appoints Reverend Paul H Roux as general to replace the wounded General AJ de Villiers.
	Cape Colony	As the division in the Cape cabinet cannot be resolved, Schreiner's Ministry has no other option but to resign.[214] In his parting letter to Milner he writes: "*I had hoped to steer the ship of the Colony into the port of peace; but as I must hand her over to another pilot, I wish him a good voyage.*"[215]
	Trivia	*The Boxer uprising, aimed against foreigners in China, is launched by the so-called 'Society of Harmonious Fists'.*
Day 247 Thu **1900-06-14**	ZAR	Still not fully recovered from his illness, General Andries PJ Cronje of the Potchefstroom commando, voluntarily lays down his arms at Klerksdorp and signs the oath of neutrality.[216] When the Royal Scots Fusiliers enter Potchefstroom, they hoist a flag with an interesting history: it is the flag hauled down in Pretoria at the end of the Transvaal War of Independence in 1881. It was then buried by loyalists, recovered by Colonel Gildea, taken to England an presented to the regiment.[217] Colonel Baden-Powell and Colonel Plumer accepts the surrender of Rustenburg from Field-cornet Piet Kruger.[218]
	OFS	A Republican attack by 200 men under the newly appointed General PH Roux on a post at Sand River bridge, manned by 730 men under Colonel Capper, is repulsed.[219] The telegraphic communication between Cape Town and Pretoria that has been interrupted since the battle at Roodewal, is restored.[220]
Day 248 Fri **1900-06-15**	OFS	Chief Commandant Christiaan R de Wet's farm Roodepoort, near Koppies, is burned down on Lord Roberts' orders. Lord Roberts states: "*He like all Free Staters now fighting against us, is a rebel and must be treated as such.*" See Article 454 of the Hague Convention 1899-07-29.[221] Chief Commandant De Wet is reported to have written to the field officer who gave the order: "*. . . my house cost me £700 but it will cost you £7 000 000 before I get through with you. . .*"[222]
	ZAR	A Republican council of war held at Balmoral decides to send several commandos to their home districts to rest and reorganize. General Sarel 'Red Bull' Oosthuizen of Krugersdorp is one of the first to leave. The ZAR Executive Council grants the Commandant-General powers to confiscate all livestock, draught animals and horses to prevent them from falling into enemy hands.[223]
Day 249 Sat **1900-06-16**	ZAR	**THE START OF THE SCORCHED EARTH POLICY** Lord Roberts issues a proclamation to Republican forces in the field (Proclamation 5 of 1900). "*Whereas small parties of raiders have recently been doing wanton damage to public property in the O.R.C and the S.A.R. by destroying railway bridges and culverts and cutting the telegraph wires, and whereas such damage cannot be done without the knowledge and*

		connivance of the neighbouring inhabitants, and the principle civil residents in the districts concerned. Now therefore I,... Roberts... warn the said inhabitants and principle civil residents that, whenever public property is destroyed or injured in the manner specified above, they will be held responsible for aiding and abetting the offenders. The houses in the vicinity of the place where the damage is done will be burnt, and the principle civil residents will be made prisoners of war."[224] See Article 45 of the Hague Convention." General Hunter leaves Potchefstroom to take command of General Hamilton's column near Heidelberg.
Day 250 Sun **1900-06-17**	ZAR Black involvement OFS	Steinaecker's Horse, an irregular unit of about 50 mercenaries in British service, using armed black tribesmen and operating from Swaziland, damages a bridge near Kaapmuiden. The rail traffic to Delagoa Bay is interrupted for about 14 days. President MT Steyn appoints Judge JBM Hertzog as a general and puts him in command of the south-western Free State.
Day 251 Mon **1900-06-18**	Cape Colony Western ZAR ZAR	The veteran Cape Progressive Party politician, Sir Gordon Sprigg forms a cabinet, consisting of Sir J Rose-Innes, Sir Pieter Faure, Dr TW Smartt, Mr TL Graham and Mr John Frost. This cabinet is decidedly more imperially inclined than the previous. [225] The nominal state of the parties in the House of Assembly, however, is as follows: Afrikanerbond — 51; Progressive — 43 and the Speaker. Two Progressives (Rhodes and Garrett) are likely to be away for the entire session. There are five absentees from the ranks of the Afikaners — two in prison, two outside the country and one 'mysteriously absent' in the ZAR. Of those present, 41 are Progressives and 46 Afrikaners.[226] Krugersdorp is occupied by Major-General Barton and Colonel Baden-Powell arrives in Pretoria. Commandant-General Botha's plan to reoccupy the abandoned positions at Donkerhoek and Diamond Hill has to be cancelled due to the poor condition of their
Day 252 Tue **1900-06-19**	ZAR Western ZAR Black involvement OFS *Trivia*	General Buller enters Volksrust, the first town in the ZAR to fall into his hands.[228] Proclamation 6 of 1900: Lord Roberts expands on his previous proclamation, announcing that inhabitants in the vicinity of damaged rail or telegraph lines will be collectively held responsible and that prominent citizens will be forced to travel on trains as hostages.[229] See Article 50 of the Hague Convention 1899-07-29. President Kruger orders General HR Lemmer to Rustenburg to prevent the British from seizing all the livestock in that area and *"to do what his hands find to do in support of their great cause".*[230] The hopes of certain Africans, Indians and liberal-minded whites that the harsher Republican laws affecting blacks will be repealed after the British occupation of Bloemfontein and Pretoria, are dashed. The British authorities issue an extraordinary Government Gazette, proclaiming, *"... with a view to the maintenance of order amongst the native population... the provisions of the Pass Law of the South African Republic, will, pending further arrangements, continue in force."*[231] Another convoy dispatched to resupply General Sir HE Colvile (to replace the one taken by De Wet on 4 June) is commanded by Lieutenant-General Lord Methuen. Near Heilbron Chief Commandant De Wet strikes again. Only the arrival of Colvile's naval guns in De Wet's rear saves the convoy. De Wet disengages and retires south to Paardekraal.[232] *HR Lemmer's 51st birthday.*

Day 253 Wed **1900-06-20**	Cape Colony	Rebel leader General P de Villiers and about 30 followers escape, but the rest of his commando surrenders to Sir C Warren with 220 men, 280 horses, 18 wagons and more than 100 000 rounds of ammunition.[233]
	Trivia	*The assassination of the German ambassador in Peking heralds the start of the siege of the international legations.*
Day 255 Fri **1900-06-22**	OFS	Chief Commandant CR de Wet attempts another triple attack on the railway line north of Kroonstad. He cuts the railway line at Serfontein Siding and General Froneman is successful at America Siding, only 13 kilometres north of Kroonstad. An attack by General JH Olivier (Stormberg) at Heuningspruit Siding and the nearby Katbosch post is repulsed. At Katbosch, Captain Radcliffe has carefully entrenched and, after a fight lasting several hours, he only suffers six casualties. At the station, about 400 newly released prisoners under Colonel Bullock, have just arrived from Pretoria. They are poorly armed and are in a very exposed position, but they put up a very determined fight against Olivier's subordinate, Commandant Bosman, and suffer 21 casualties. Both British forces are relieved by a mounted force with field-guns sent from Kroonstad.[234]
	ZAR	General PR Viljoen skirmishes with Buller's advance units near Vankolderskop. They are attacked by superior forces and starts a fighting retreat towards Villiers. General Buller's troops enter Standerton. Eighteen damaged locomotives and 148 railway cars fall into British hands.
Day 256 Sat **1900-06-23**	OFS	General Clements is attacked between Winburg and Senekal by General Roux, but he succeeds in extricating his column and reaches Winburg.
	ZAR	General Hamilton enters Heidelberg after a slight skirmish. General Clery joins Buller at Standerton.
Day 257 Sun **1900-06-24**	*Trivia*	*Lord HH Kitchener's 50th birthday.*
Day 258 Mon **1900-06-25**	OFS	General Clements, suspecting another ambush along his return route to Senekal, sends Colonel Grenfell to attack them from the rear.
	Trivia	*Lord Louis Mountbatten (Batternberg) is born.*
Day 259 Tue **1900-06-26**	OFS	Colonel Grenfell's mounted unit bungles the attack on the suspected ambushers and, they in turn, are surprised at Leliefontein, near Senekal. A part of the Imperial Yeomanry flees all the way to Ventersburg.[235]
	Victoria Cross	Private C Ward, 2nd Battalion, The King's Own Yorkshire Light Infantry, earns a recommendation for the Victoria Cross at Lindley. His small picket is surrounded on three sides by about 500 burghers; all the officers are killed and all but six of the men wounded when Private Ward volunteers to take a message asking for reinforcements to a signalling station about 150 metres away. He reaches the post untouched and delivers his message, but is seriously wounded on the way back. His actions undoubtedly save his comrades and his is to be last VC awarded by Queen Victoria before her death.
Day 260 Wed **1900-06-27**	ZAR	General Sir Archibald Hunter leaves Heidelberg and marches south towards the Orange Free State.
	St Helena	Commandant SJ Eloff, captured after his unsuccessful attack on Mafeking, arrives on St Helena.[236]
	Trivia	*Opening of London Underground Central Line.*

Day 261 Thu **1900-06-28**	South-east ZAR	General Talbot Coke, marching from Volkrust with ten field-guns and Brocklehurst's cavalry protecting his flank, drives off a small enemy party covering his route at Graskop, about 18 kilometres north of Volksrust, but he is unable to proceed to Amersfoort.[237]
	Trivia	*ZAR General GH Gravett's 52nd birthday.*
Day 262 Wed **1900-06-29**	ZAR	General Coke, attempting to advance further, finds his route blocked by a well-entrenched Republican force he estimates to be more than a 1 000 men, and he retires to Volksrust.[238]
Day 263 Sat **1900-06-30**	ZAR	President Kruger orders his railway carriage to be moved to the warmer climate of Waterval-Onder, causing the ZAR government and officials billeted at Waterval-Boven, to commute to and fro daily.
	Official reports **Farm burning:** Official reports record that two buildings have been destroyed by British troops during June.[239]	

NOTES: APRIL 1900 - JUNE 1900 (MARCHES AND RETREATS)

1. BREYTENBACH, *op cit*, vol IV, pp 226-234
2. *Ibid*, vol IV, p 362
3. Pakenham, *op cit*, p 179
4. *Ibid*, p 398
5. WESSELS, Boer War Diary... , p 37 ; VAN SCHOOR, Bittereinder..., p 174
6. BREYTENBACH, *op cit*, vol IV, pp 235-240
7. *Ibid*, vol IV, p 290
8. MIDGLEY, *op cit*, p 150
9. Anglo-Boer War, Northern Cape Publishers – Summary – 9
10. MEINTJES, Anglo-Boer War, A pictorial history, p 139
11. BREYTENBACH, *op cit*, vol IV, pp 240-248
12. Anglo-Boer War, Northern Cape Publishers – Summary – 9
13. BREYTENBACH, *op cit*, vol IV, pp 248-258
14. WESSELS, Boer War Diary..., p 37
15. McCRACKEN, *op cit*, p 74
16. AMERY, *op cit*, vol IV, p; BREYTENBACH, *op cit*, vol IV, pp 367-372
17. AMERY, *op cit*, vol IV, p 57
18. BREYTENBACH, *op cit*, vol IV, p 293
19. FERREIRA, Krijgsgevangenschap..., p 115
20. BREYTENBACH, *op cit*, vol IV, p 373
21. *Ibid*, vol IV, pp 269-270
22. SLOCUM, Boer War Operations..., p 111
23. BREYTENBACH, Kommandant Danie Theron, p 163
24. PAKENHAM, *op cit*, p 410
25. PEMBERTON, Boer War Battles, p 2
26. BREYTENBACH, *op cit*, vol IV, pp 278-280
27. CRESWICKE, vol V, p vii
28. THE SA STAMP COLOUR CATALOGUE 1998, p 8
29. AMERY, *op cit*, vol IV, pp 61-62; BREYTENBACH, *op cit*, vol IV, pp 278-280
30. FERREIRA, Memoirs of Ben Bouwer, p 56; KANDYBA-FOXCROFT, Russia..., *op cit*, p 87
31. BREYTENBACH, *op cit*, vol IV, p 280
32. *Ibid*, vol IV, p 280
33. KRUGER, Krugermiljoene, p 23
34. BREYTENBACH, *op cit*, vol IV, p 382
35. *Ibid*, vol IV, p 382
36. STRYDOM, *op cit*, p 111
37. PAKENHAM, *op cit*, p 408
38. VAN SCHOOR, De Wet-Annale No 2, p 136
39. BREYTENBACH, *op cit*, vol IV, p 302
40. *Ibid*, vol IV, p 383
41. *Ibid*, vol IV, pp 302-303
42. SMIT, Die Beleg van Mafeking, p 258
43. BREYTENBACH, *op cit*, vol IV, p 304
44. *Ibid*, vol IV, pp 308-309
45. *Ibid*, vol IV, p 305
46. *Ibid*, vol IV, p 306
47. AMERY, *op cit*, vol IV, p 63; BREYTENBACH, *op cit*, vol IV, pp 281, 308
48. BREYTENBACH, *op cit*, vol IV, pp 315-316
49. BREYTENBACH, Gedenkalbum..., p 333
50. McCRAKEN, *op cit*, p 79
51. BREYTENBACH, *op cit*, vol IV, p 398
52. STRYDOM, Kaapland en die Tweede Vryheidsoorlog, p 113
53. BREYTENBACH, *op cit*, vol IV, p 398
54. BELFIELD, The Boer War, p 95
55. STRYDOM, *op cit*, p 113
56. BREYTENBACH, *op cit*, vol IV, p 399
57. *Ibid*, vol IV, pp 402-403; AMERY, *op cit*, vol IV, pp 97-99
58. BREYTENBACH, *op cit*, vol IV, p 396
59. SPIES, Methods of Barbarism?, p 84
60. AMERY, *op cit*, vol IV, pp 150-151
61. BREYTENBACH, *op cit*, vol IV, pp 402-409
62. STRYDOM, *op cit*, pp 114-115
63. BELFIELD, The Boer War, pp 157-159
64. BREYTENBACH, *op cit*, vol IV, pp 420-424
65. BELFIELD, The Boer War, p 160
66. BREYTENBACH, *op cit*, vol IV, pp 428-432
67. *Ibid*, vol IV, p 438
68. *Ibid*, vol IV, pp 492-494
69. Anglo-Boer War, Northern Cape Publishers - Summary -9
70. BREYTENBACH, *op cit*, vol IV, pp 432-436

71. *Ibid*, vol IV, pp 494-497
72. *Ibid*, vol IV, pp 437-441
73. *Ibid*, vol IV, pp 460-462
74. *Ibid*, vol VI, p 84
75. *Ibid*, vol IV, p 466
76. *Ibid*, vol IV, p 462
77. AMERY, *op cit*, vol IV, p 167
78. BELFIELD, The Boer War, p 156
79. WESSELS, Egodokumente..., p 146
80. BREYTENBACH, *op cit*, vol IV, p 496
81. *Ibid*, vol IV, pp 464-465
82. *Ibid*, vol IV, p 467
83. *Ibid*, vol IV, pp 466-475
84. VAN DEN BERG, 24 Battles ..., p 60
85. BREYTENBACH, *op cit*, vol IV, pp 475-757; FERREIRA, ... SPE Trichard, p 151
86. AMERY, *op cit*, vol IV, p 122
87. BREYTENBACH, *op cit*, vol IV, p 455
88. AMERY, *op cit*, vol IV, p 195
89. BREYTENBACH, *op cit*, vol VI, pp 48-51; SMIT, *op cit*, p 256
90. BREYTENBACH, *op cit*, vol IV, pp 478-485
91. *Ibid*, vol IV, p 55
92. *Ibid*, vol IV, p 90
93. PLOEGER, *op cit*, pp 27: 16-17
94. MIDGLEY, *op cit*, p 99
95. SMIT, Die Beleg van Mafeking, p 260
96. BREYTENBACH, *op cit*, vol VI, pp 90-94
97. PLOEGER, *op cit*, p 27:17
98. BREYTENBACH, Gedenkalbum.., p 333
99. SMIT, *op cit*, p 264
100. BREYTENBACH, *op cit*, vol IV, p 58
101. SMIT, Die Beleg van Mafeking, p 264
102. BREYTENBACH, *op cit*, vol VI, p 103
103. SMIT, *op cit*, p 264
104. BREYTENBACH, *op cit*, vol VI, pp 59-60
105. MEINTJES, Anglo-Boer War, A pictorial history, p 133
106. PLOEGER, *op cit*, p 27:17
107. AMERY, *op cit*, vol VI, p 575; WOLFSOHN, Rustenburg..., p 78
108. Anglo-Boer War, Northern Cape Publishers – Summary - 11
109. BREYTENBACH, *op cit*, vol IV, p 506
110. *Ibid*, vol IV, p 507
111. BREYTENBACH, *op cit*, vol VI, pp 107-109
112. MEINTJES, Anglo-Boer War, A pictorial history, p 133
113. BREYTENBACH, *op cit*, vol IV, pp 508-512
114. WESSELS, Egodokumente..., p 146
115. BREYTENBACH, Gedenkalbum..., p 383
116. BREYTENBACH, *op cit*, vol IV, p 512
117. *Ibid*, vol IV, p 522
118. CONRADIE, FW, Met Cronje op die Wesfront, p 52
119. BREYTENBACH, Gedenkalbum..., p 383
120. VAN SCHOOR, De Wet-Annale No 2, p 140
121. BREYTENBACH, *op cit*, vol VI, p 122
122. CONRADIE, FW, *op cit*, p 52
123. KRUGER, Krugermiljoene, p 24
124. *Ibid*, p 24
125. BREYTENBACH, *op cit*, vol IV, p 517

126. BREYTENBACH, *op cit*, vol VI, p 212
127. BREYTENBACH, *op cit*, vol IV, p 518
128. BREYTENBACH, *op cit*, vol VI, p 212
129. BREYTENBACH, *op cit*, vol IV, p 518
130. *Ibid*, vol IV, p 519
131. *Ibid*, vol IV, p 526
132. WESSELS, War Diary..., pp 230-231
133. AMERY, *op cit*, vol IV, p 247
134. BREYTENBACH, *op cit*, vol VI, p 213
135. *Ibid*, vol VI, pp 216-217
136. *Ibid*, vol V, pp 528-529
137. *Ibid*, vol V, p 537
138. FARWELL, *op cit*, p 327
139. AMERY, *op cit*, vol IV, pp 227-228
140. BREYTENBACH, *op cit*, vol VI, p 128
141. CRESWICKE, vol IV, p 194
142. BREYTENBACH, *op cit*, vol IV, pp 530-532
143. *Ibid*, vol IV, pp 533-534
144. AMERY, *op cit*, vol IV, p 183
145. BREYTENBACH, *op cit*, vol VI, pp 215-219
146. *Ibid*, vol VI, p 213
147. TODD, Private Tucker's..., p 109
148. *Ibid*, p 109
149. BREYTENBACH, *op cit*, vol IV, p 534
150. *Ibid*, vol IV, p 535
151. MEINTJES, Anglo-Boereoorlog in Beeld, p 135
152. PAKENHAM, *op cit*, p 430
153. BREYTENBACH, *op cit*, vol VI, p 241
154. *Ibid*, vol VI, p 218
155. AMERY, *op cit*, vol IV, p 235
156. WULFSOHN, Rustenburg..., pp 52-53
157. PAKENHAM, *op cit*, p 371
158. GRUNDLINGH, 'Hendsoppers' en..., p 16
159. VAN SCHOOR, De Wet-Annale No 4, p 3
160. PEMBERTON, Boer War Battles, p 17
161. BREYTENBACH, *op cit*, vol VI, p 214; AMERY, *op cit*, vol IV, pp 254-257
162. BREYTENBACH, *op cit*, vol VI, p 215; VAN SCHOOR, De Wet-Annale No 4, p 4
163. VAN SCHOOR, De Wet-Annale No 4, p 9
164. VAN SCHOOR, De Wet-Annale No 4, p 9
165. KRUGER, Krugermiljoene, p 27; BREYTENBACH, *op cit*, vol IV, p 538
166. PAKENHAM, *op cit*, p 412
167. BREYTENBACH, *op cit*, vol IV, p 539
168. PAKENHAM, *op cit*, p 432
169. BREYTENBACH, *op cit*, vol IV, p 541
170. CRESWICKE, vol IV, p 194
171. AMERY, *op cit*, vol IV, p 184
172. AMERY, *op cit*, vol VI, p 90
173. AMERY, *op cit*, vol IV, p 184
174. BREYTENBACH, *op cit*, vol IV, p 542
175. *Ibid*, vol IV, p 544
176. BREYTENBACH, *op cit*, vol VI, pp 219-222
177. AMERY, *op cit*, vol IV, p 158
178. KRUGER, Krugermiljoene, p 27
179. FERREIRA, ... SPE Trichard, p 163
180. BREYTENBACH, *op cit*, vol VI, pp 165-167

181. CRESWICKE, vol VI, p 195

182. Anglo-Boer War, Northern Cape Publishers - Summary - 13

183. AMERY, *op cit*, vol IV, p 184

184. GRUNDLINGH, 'Hendsoppers' en ..., p 16

185. FERREIRA, ... SPE Trichard, p 164

186. GRUNDLINGH, 'Hendsoppers' en..., p 64

187. BREYTENBACH, *op cit*, vol VI, p 174

188. MARX, Klerksdorp, Groeiende Reus, p 35

189. BREYTENBACH, *op cit*, vol VI, pp 222-226;   VAN SCHOOR, De Wet-Annale No 4, pp 5-6

190. MARX, Klerksdorp, Groeiende Reus, p 35

191. BREYTENBACH, *op cit*, vol VI, pp 174-177

192. *Ibid*, vol VI, pp 180-184

193. AMERY, *op cit*, vol IV, p188

194. VAN SCHOOR, De Wet-Annale No 4, p 4

195. STRYDOM, Kaapland en die Tweede Vryheidsoorlog, p115

196. SPIES, Methods of Barbarism?, p 121

197. MIDGLEY, *op cit*, p 102

198. BREYTENBACH, *op cit*, vol IV, p 144

199. KANDYBA-FOXCROFT, Russia..., *op cit*, p88

200. BREYTENBACH, *op cit*, vol VI, p 228

201. BREYTENBACH, *op cit*, vol IV, pp 144-148

202. HATTINGH, Britse Fortifikasies..., p 31

203. BREYTENBACH, *op cit*, vol VI, pp 178-180

204. DOONER, 'Last Post', p 3

205. BREYTENBACH, *op cit*, vol VI, pp 184-192

206. *Ibid*, vol VI, pp 193-203

207. *Ibid*, vol VI, pp 202-203

208. GRUNDLINGH, 'Hendsoppers' en..., p 61

209. VAN SCHOOR, Bittereinder..., p 177

210. TODD, Private Tucker's..., p 114

211. LE MAY, *op cit*, p 70

212. AMERY, *op cit*, vol IV, p 195

213. BREYTENBACH, *op cit*, vol VI, pp 203-205

214. STRYDOM, Kaapland en die Tweede Vryheidsoorlog, p 116

215. LE MAY, *op cit*, p 70

216. BRITS, Diary of National Scout, p 27;   GRUNDLINGH, 'Hendsoppers' en..., p 123

217. AMERY, *op cit*, vol IV, p 225

218. WULFSOHN, Rustenburg..., p 50

219. BREYTENBACH, *op cit*, vol VI, p 231

220. AMERY, *op cit*, vol IV, p 266

221. BREYTENBACH, *op cit*, vol VI, p 230

222. MEINTJES, Anglo-Boereoorlog in Beeld, p 166

223. BREYTENBACH, *op cit*, vol VI, p 270

224. TODD, Private Tucker's..., p 133

225. STRYDOM, Kaapland en die Tweede Vryheidsoorlog, p 117

226. LE MAY, *op cit*, p71

227. BREYTENBACH, *op cit*, Vol VI, p270

228. TODD, Private Tucker's..., p 113

229. GRONUM, *op cit* (2), p 19

230. BREYTENBACH, *op cit*, vol VI, p 242

231. SPIES, Methods of Barbarism?, p 68

232. AMERY, *op cit*, vol IV, p 268

233. Anglo-Boer War, Northern Cape Publishers - Summary - 14

234. AMERY, *op cit*, vol IV, p 268

235. *Ibid*, vol IV, p 301

236. FERREIRA, Krijgsgevangenschap..., p 132

237. AMERY, *op cit*, vol IV, p 400

238. *Ibid*, vol IV, p 400

239. PLOEGER, *op cit*, p 37:8

JULY-DECEMBER 1900

CHANGES

1900	WINTER	JULY
Day 264 Sun **1900-07-01**	ZAR	The burghers defending Utrecht put up a determined fight, but they are forced to retire after killing one soldier and capturing three.
	OFS	Major-General RAP Clements joins Major-General AH Paget at Lindley.
Day 265 Mon **1900-07-02**	ZAR	General Clery arrives at Greylingstad and Utrecht is occupied. Leaving Commandant-General Louis Botha's camp at Balmoral, General De la Rey moves to the western districts of the ZAR, determined to relieve the pressure on the Free Staters and the eastern ZAR. De la Rey, soon to be joined by ex-State Attorney JC Smuts, has been granted extensive powers to virtually become a separate government in the western ZAR [1]
	Trivia	*Maiden flight of an airship built by Count Ferdinand von Zeppelin. Flying at Lake Constance, the powered hydrogen-filled airship named LZ1 reaches a speed of 22,5km/h..*
Day 266 Tue **1900-07-03**	OFS	Major-General Paget is in action on General Piet de Wet's farm Elandsfontein, forcing the Republicans to retire to positions outside Bethlehem.[2]
	Western ZAR	Lord Roberts orders Colonel Baden-Powell to evacuate Rustenburg and to occupy Commando Nek and Silkaatsnek. [3] The British abandon Utrecht on receiving reports of General Grobler's approach. 350 metres of railway line near Greylingstad and almost a kilometre and a half of the Vlaklaagte line are destroyed .[4]
	ZAR	State Secretary FW Reitz sends a telegram via the ZAR consul in Lourenço Marques to the *Sun* in America: "*President and people always desired and still most earnestly desire peace. Condition: complete independence and amnesty Colonials who have fought with us. Otherwise fight bitter end. "*[5]
Day 267 Wed **1900-07-04**	OFS	Major-General Paget is in action at Baken Kop, near Lindley. A well-laid ambush by Republicans is spoiled when one of their field-guns fires prematurely. The British artillery unhitches and comes into action. They are subjected to a fierce bombardment from the hidden Republican field-guns. In the confusion three British field-guns are abandoned in a wheat-field. Danie Theron's scouts eliminate the crew, but they are unable to remove the field-guns in the face of charging reinforcements.[6]
	ZAR	Commandant-General Louis Botha leaves his laager at Balmoral with a strong commando and moves westwards to engage British troops east of Pretoria.
	Trivia	*The American jazz trumpeter and singer Louis 'Satchmo' Armstrong is born.*
Day 268 Thu **1900-07-05**	Western ZAR	After refusing his offer to surrender, General HR Lemmer attacks the small force Methuen has left behind to garrison Rustenburg. Republicans re-enter Rustenburg and take possession of the stores and animals left behind by Baden-Powell. Methuen quickly sends a force under Major Tracey as reinforcement. On their approach, Lemmer abandons the town and decides to occupy Olifantsnek.[7]
	ZAR	Moving from the Pienaar's River area, General FA Grobler takes a British post on a koppie near Waterval, north-east of Pretoria. The British lose three men killed and nine are taken prisoner.
	Trivia	*Cecil John Rhodes' 47th birthday.*

Day 269 Fri **1900-07-06**	Western ZAR	General Lemmer's strategic position in Olifantsnek Pass and his link with General Liebenberg in the Hekpoort Valley force Methuen to return to Rustenburg.[8]
	OFS	Generals Clements and Paget attack Chief Commandant De Wet near Bethlehem with 7 000 - 8 000 troops and 18 field-guns. Their attempt to outflank the Republican right north of the town fails and they are prevented from crossing the river.[9]
Day 270 Sat **1900-07-07**	OFS	Generals AH Paget and RAP Clements resume their assault on the Republican positions around Bethlehem. This time they concentrate on the left flank and bring their full weight to bear on this sector. The Republicans abandon their positions prematurely as news of the approach of another column under General Hunter is received. The Royal Irish take the main position at Wolhuter's Kop and recaptures one of the guns lost at Stormberg. Despite having more than 1 700 mounted troops at their disposal, they do not attempt any pursuit of the retreating Boers. The British losses amount to 107 killed and wounded. Paget and Clements enter Bethlehem and Chief Commandant CR de Wet and his Republicans fall back southwards through Retiefsnek into the Brandwater Basin between Bethlehem and Fouriesburg where they join President Steyn and the Free State government. Fouriesburg becomes the last capital of the Orange Free State.[10] Lieutenant-General Sir A Hunter reaches the village of Reitz.
	ZAR	General ETH Hutton, commanding a strong force of more than 3 000 men with 26 field-guns, is detailed with clearing the country east of Pretoria towards Springs. A part of this force under Colonel BT Mahon is attacked by burghers under Commandant Piet Trichardt and Field-cornet AJ Dercksen on the heights east of Bapsfontein. Efforts by the mounted troops to outflank the attackers are repulsed by a surprise counterattack and Mahon, unable to obtain reinforcements, is compelled to disengage and falls back to Tierpoort — aggressively pursued by the determined burghers. Three burghers are killed and nine wounded and the British casualties total 50.[11] Lord Roberts issues proclamations warning persons against harbouring 'rebels'.
Day 271 Sun **1900-07-08**	ZAR	Commandant Trichardt's force has been reinforced by the Middelburg and Boksburg commandos and several Johannesburgers with a Krupp gun and two machine guns. They plan to push the British back, but at dawn the British open up with all their artillery as well as three siege-guns that arrived during the night. The burghers cannot come within rifle range and an inconclusive artillery duel between the vastly superior British guns and Lieutenant Oosthuizen's Krupp ensues and continues until dark without any side achieving any advantage. [12]
	Trivia	*J Chamberlain's 64th birthday.*
Day 272 Mon **1900-07-09**	ZAR	General Hutton has now deployed his force facing the Republican attacks east of Pretoria over a front of more than 14 kilometres. The burghers are forced to split up into small groups and concentrate on the enemy in front of them. Nowhere are the burghers strong enough to make any impression on the vast British force, but they succeed in repulsing attack after attack.[13]
	Western ZAR	General HR Lemmer reports that he has successfully taken Olifantsnek, chasing off the small garrison stationed there and taking several prisoners.[14] Captain GHM Ritchie of Kitchener's Horse issues a proclamation in Krugersdorp that *"unless the men at present on commando belonging to families in the Town and District of Krugersdorp surrender themselves and hand in their arms to the Imperial Authorities by 20th July, the whole of their property will be confiscated and their families turned out destitute and homeless".*[15]
	OFS	Lieutenant-General Sir A Hunter and Brigadier-General Sir Hector A MacDonald arrive at Bethlehem. Hunter takes over command of all the forces in the north-eastern Free State.

Day 273 Tue **1900-07-10**	OFS	In a letter to Lord Roberts Chief Commandant De Wet protests against the indiscriminate destruction of private property by British troops.[16] *De Basuin*, a short-lived publication of the Free State government, is printed by M Douwes at Fouriesburg. Only three issues, printed on both sides of a single sheet, appear on 10, 17 and 24 July 1900.[17]
	Black involvement	Colonel Lawson reports that De Beer and Van Rooyen's commando, raiding the upper Tugela from the Free State, includes 30 armed Basuto and 20 other armed blacks.[18]
Day 274 Wed **1900-07-11**	Western ZAR	General De la Rey starts his campaign to relieve the pressure on General Botha by reviving the guerrilla struggle in other parts of the ZAR. **THE BATTLE OF SILKAATSNEK** At Silkaatsnek, west of Pretoria, General De la Rey launches a three-pronged attack on the Scots Greys, 'O' Battery and some Lincolns, commanded by Colonel HR Roberts. De la Rey personally leads the frontal assault from the north and sends two groups of 200 men to scale both shoulders of the pass, where the British have placed small pickets. The British are unable to bring their guns to bear or to signal for assistance. Colonel Alexander, stationed about three kilometres south of Commando Nek hears the sounds of battle and he sends out two field-guns and a Maxim to engage the enemy. As soon as they draw retaliatory fire, they withdraw. The burghers surround and capture two of their field-guns, but the British put up a gallant defence that lasts the entire day. Only after dark does a message get through to Colonel Alexander, but they cannot get any confirmation of assistance forthcoming from that direction. They are unable to disengage during the night and Colonel Roberts surrenders the next morning. The British suffer 23 killed, Colonel Roberts and 44 others wounded and 189 (including the wounded) captured. Republican casualties are unknown, but De la Rey's nephew and his adjutant are both killed, two others are seriously wounded and six slightly wounded. The Republicans capture two field-guns, a machine gun, a number of rifles and a supply of ammunition with which De la Rey can rearm several burghers who have returned to duty.[19] **THE ACTION AT DWARSVLEI** General Sarel F Oosthuizen, commanding a group of about 150 burghers armed with rifles of all types but without artillery, ambushes a strong British force at Dwarsvlei, about 11 kilometres from Krugersdorp. The British column, a part of Major-General HL Dorrien-Smith's force, consists of 1 350 men, including Highlanders, Shropshires and Imperial Yeomanry with three field-guns and a machine gun, and is en route to join the Scots Greys at Silkaatsnek. The British field-guns come into action but the fierce rifle fire soon isolates them from their artillery horses and ammunition. Oosthuizen divides his small force in two — one to attack the unlimbered field-guns while the other concentrates on the supply column. The field-guns are in a desperate position and several attempts to bring them to safety fails. Captain DR Younger and Captain WE Gordon, 1st Battalion, the Gordon Highlanders, earns the Victoria Cross (Younger posthumously) for their brave efforts to retrieve the field-guns.[20] A determined counter-attack by the Shropshire Infantry repulses the attack on the supply wagons and they are dragged off westwards. The battle rages all day long and at dusk the burghers launch their final attempt to capture the field-guns. Their charge is repulsed at an incalculable price as General Oosthuizen is seriously wounded. The British abandon their expedition and return to Krugersdorp. The battle costs them four killed and 37 wounded, while the Republicans lose at least two killed and two wounded.[21] North of Pretoria General FA Grobler attacks a mixed force of mounted troops and infantry with artillery support. He forces them back to their camp at Derdepoort, manages to inflict about 40 casualties and he captures 17 troops. Roberts blames his casualties on the fact that many burghers have been seen wearing pieces of British uniform. General French, supported by Generals Hutton and Pilcher, compel Botha's forces to
	Victoria Cross *Gen. FA Grobler* (National Cultural History Museum) ZAR	

		retire from the Tierpoort Hills. British flank attacks by overwhelming forces at Witpoort and Olifantsfontein force the burghers to fall back south-eastwards to Bronkhorstspruit. The British cannot follow up their gains as the attacks at Silkaatsnek and Dwarsvlei force Lord Roberts to order French's cavalry westwards to counter the threat in the Magaliesberg on the other side of Pretoria.[22]
Day 275 Thu **1900-07-12**	ZAR	Generals Chris Botha and Tobias Smuts' attacks on British positions at Paardekop and Sandspruit Stations are repulsed.[23]
	OFS	A court martial at Fouriesburg confirms ex-Commandant SG Vilonel's sentence of five years hard labour for treason.[24]
Day 276 Fri **1900-07-13**	OFS	At a council of war, Chief Commandant De Wet explains the shortcomings of the Republican concentration in the Brandwater Basin and the importance of moving out before they are bottled up. It is decided to divide their forces into three columns: the first, about 2 600 men under De Wet and accompanied by President Steyn, will depart as soon as possible. The second group, about 2 000 men under General Paul Roux, will follow a day later, heading south. The third force, about 500 men under General Crowther, is ordered to seek contact with Hattingh's commandos approaching from Harrismith and to leave together in that direction. Prinsloo, now commanding part of the Bethlehem commando, is ordered to hold the passes and to retire as opportunity offers.[25]
Day 277 Sat **1900-07-14**	OFS Civilian life	President Steyn takes leave of his wife and four children at Fouriesburg, to be reunited only at the end of hostilities. [26] From now on the Free State government is to dispense with the idea of a capital, and they become a government 'in the field'. [27]
	ZAR	A wide-ranging mounted reconnaissance unit skirmishes with Republican pickets near Bronkhorstspruit.
Day 278 Sun **1900-07-15**	OFS	In a sermon in the veld the Reverend Paul Roux (now a general) takes his text from Isaiah 66 verse 8: *"Shall a land be born in one day? Shall a nation be brought forth in one moment?"*[28] Chief Commandant De Wet, President Steyn and members of the Free State government break out of the Brandwater Basin through Slabbert's Nek with about 2 000 men, 400 vehicles and five field-guns.[29] Their column crosses the Bethlehem/Senekal road and passes within three kilometres of Paget's camp at Sebastopol, 14 kilometres west of Bethlehem.[30]
Day 279 Mon **1900-07-16**	OFS	**START OF THE 'FIRST DE WET HUNT'** A two-pronged attack by Generals Paget and Broadwood on Chief Commandant De Wet's rearguard at Witklip north of the Senekal/Bethlehem road is repulsed by accurate Republican shelling. The British lose one killed and eight or nine wounded while one burgher dies and two are wounded.[31]
	ZAR	Three commandos under the newly appointed Combat General Ben Viljoen attack about 4 650 soldiers with 20 field-guns and 4-5 machine guns under General Hutton at Tierpoort, Rietvlei and Olifantsfontein. The burghers are supported by three field-guns and two pom-poms, but they have to charge over open ground. Commandant-General Botha, who observes the Republican charge from a vantage point, later says that he has never seen a braver and more determined Republican attack. The burghers dislodge soldiers from several small round stone defences and sweep the enemy from the heights. Most of the fighting takes place at ranges of less than 100 metres and the heaviest resistance comes from the New Zealanders and Irish Fusiliers at Witpoort on Viljoen's left flank. Field-cornet Christiaan Beyers is prominent in the furious fighting at close quarters and his small group almost takes a British artillery piece before the arrival of large British reinforcements forces the Republicans to call off their attack.

	Western ZAR	The British official casualty reports state a loss of only seven killed, 30 wounded and 24 captured while Viljoen suffers five killed, 13 wounded and two taken prisoner.[32] A culvert on the railway line is blown up near Heidelberg.[33] Lord Methuen reoccupies Rustenburg. This is the third British occupation of the town.
Day 280 Tue **1900-07-17**	ZAR	Lord Roberts informs Commandant-General Louis Botha that families of fighting burghers still living in British occupied territory will be sent to the commandos in the field in the eastern Transvaal. The British Supreme Commander's proclamations guaranteeing the safety of civilians seem to be worthless. [34] An attack on Zuikerbosch post is repulsed
	OFS	Lieutenant-Colonel MO Little, commanding the 3rd Cavalry Brigade of 738 mounted men, is ordered in the direction of Lindley to join the hunt for De Wet.[35] General Paul Roux decides to delay his departure until Crowther has established contact with Commandants FJW Hattingh and CJ de Villiers, commanding the Harrismith and Vrede commandos respectively. These commandos, who have been ordered to accompany Crowther's small group out of the Brandwater Basin, are moving very slowly, reluctant to leave their home districts to the mercy of the approaching British troops. [36]
	Trivia	*RG Kekewich's 46th birthday.*
Day 281 Wed **1900-07-18**	ZAR	A culvert and a section of railway line are blown up near Vlakfontein.[37]
Day 282 Thu **1900-07-19**	Eastern OFS	General Broadwood with about 4 000 troops attacks De Wet's scouts under Captain Danie Theron. A running battle develops with skirmishes at Karroospruit, Palmietfontein and Tierbank near Petrus Steyn. The burghers lose eight killed and the British five killed and 15 wounded. Lieutenant-Colonel Little attacks De Wet's main convoy at Paardeplaats near the Lindley/Kroonstad road. Leaving the main force under the command of his brother Piet, Chief Commandant De Wet tries but fails to surround part of the attackers. The fight is broken off at dusk and the British lose about ten men, while the Republicans suffer five casualties.[38]
	ZAR	Four lengths of railway line are cut, a train is captured and the staff are taken prisoner after the locomotive overturns near Bank Station.[39] Despite Commandant-General Botha's protests, 412 women and children are sent to Van der Merwe Station in open trucks on a cold winter's evening. General Ben Viljoen arranges for them to travel to Barberton.[40]
	International	In a letter to Lord Salisbury, Ludwig Schwennhagen, representing an organization called *Comite pour Mediation dans la guerre Sud-Africaine*, asks the British government to consider a scheme for sending Boers to Brazil.[41]
	Trivia	*The Metro underground railway system is opened in Paris.*
Day 283 Fri **1900-07-20**	OFS	On the farm Blesbokfontein, between Lindley and Heilbron, General Piet de Wet calls his brother, Christiaan, aside and asks him if he seriously thinks that there is any future in continuing the struggle and whether he really plans to carry on fighting. Christiaan loses his temper and shouts: *"Are you mad?"* and stomps off, never to be reconciled with his brother again.[42]
	Eastern OFS	General Hunter, now commanding about 18 500 men with 72 field-guns at various locations within marching distance, starts his operations against the Brandwater Basin. He orders General Bruce Hamilton with about 1 300 men with six field-guns south-east from Bethlehem towards Spitzkrantz, which is held by about 50 burghers.

		Commandants FJW Hattingh and CJ de Villiers, commanding the Harrismith and Vrede commandos respectively, reach Sebastopol Farm, 16 kilometres north-east of Golden Gate. Receiving news of Hamilton's approach, De Villiers immediately moves to reinforce the small Republican force. General Paul Roux has still not started his breakout.[43]
Day 284 Sat **1900-07-21**	ZAR	**LORD ROBERTS' ADVANCE ALONG THE EASTERN LINE BEGINS** Lord Roberts starts his advance from his outposts east of Pretoria, moving eastwards along the Delagoa railway line. The British line east of Pretoria stretches for more than 56 kilometres and Commandant-General Louis Botha cannot do anything else but split his force of about 2 200 men into small groups to render isolated local resistance to the huge army moving eastwards.
	Western ZAR	Lord Methuen, operating in conjunction with General Smith-Dorrien's forces, executes a wide hook, approaching Olifant's Nek from the south. They force Lemmer to abandon Olifant's Nek, but Colonel Baden-Powell is unable to threaten his eastward escape.[44]
	OFS	With flanking forces about five kilometres apart, Chief Commandant De Wet arranges his wagon train (which he calls *"an indescribable burden"*) six abreast and crosses the railway at Serfontein Siding. On De Wet's southern flank Captain Danie Theron cannot resist the temptation of a train slowly puffing up an incline four kilometres north of Heuningspruit Station. Wynand Malan jumps on board the train and disconnects the air brake hose. As the scouts try to disarm the 102 Welsh Fusiliers on board, some shooting breaks out and a burgher is wounded, but the Welsh are soon forced to surrender with four wounded. As the Republican wagon convoy has moved off, the burghers can only loot what they can carry. After placing the wounded under medical care in a railway carriage which they push out of danger, the train is set on fire and destroyed.[45]
	Eastern OFS	Commandant De Villiers' burghers arrive in time to support Blignaut's small group against General Bruce Hamilton's assault. They put up a determined defence, but the eastern summit is taken by British troops at about noon and by nightfall the British field-guns clear the other summit. At a cost of three killed and 27 wounded, the pass dominated by the Spitzkrans position is the first of the Brandwater Basin passes to fall into British hands. [46]
Day 285 Sun **1900-07-22**	Western ZAR	General HL Lemmer attacks 500 Australian Bushmen under Colonel Airey near Selons River, not far from Lichtenburg. The Bushmen are surrounded, their horses are stampeded or shot and they suffer seven killed and 32 wounded. The fighting continues all day long and they are rescued by four parties sent by Baden-Powell from Rustenburg.[47]
	ZAR	Generals Christiaan Botha and Tobias Smuts cannot prevent General Talbot Coke from capturing Graskop, north of Sandspruit Station on the Natal line.
	OFS	General French is ordered to join the hunt for De Wet. Chief Commandant De Wet regroups his forces at Mahemspruit. He congratulates Captain Danie Theron on his coup and promotes him to the rank of commandant.[48]
	Eastern OFS	General Bruce Hamilton repulses a Republican counterattack against Spitzkrans and consolidates his position. General Hunter performs a demonstration in the direction of Spitzkrants and Naauwpoort Nek before swerving west towards Retief's Nek. Prinsloo, guarding this pass, is fooled and sends some burghers towards Naauwpoort Nek.[49]
Day 286 Mon **1900-07-23**	Eastern OFS	**THE BRANDWATER BASIN** General Hunter's operations against the Brandwater passes are delayed when a tremendous storm with drenching rain and snow on the higher slopes stampedes some horses, lashes the troops and turns the roads into a quagmire. His flank attack

		against ridges west of Retief's Nek falters against almost impregnable positions. Several attacks fail and his advance is checked by Prinsloo's weakened force. During the night British scouts discover a high peak about six kilometres east of the pass to be unoccupied. [50] In almost an exact duplicate action, Generals Clements and Paget's forces fail to make headway against formidable positions at Slabbert's Nek. Again the burghers' night-time abandonment of key positions is noticed by scouts and troops are sent up. Elsewhere, General Rundle executes convincing demonstrations against Boers guarding Witnek and Nelspoort while Colonel Dalgety's Colonial Division attacks Moolman's Hoek.[51]
	OFS	General RG Broadwood and Colonel Little unite at Renoster Post. Their combined strength is now about 3 700 men.
	ZAR	Lord Roberts' advance units move towards Middelburg with the Republicans executing a fighting retreat. They subject the troops to heavy rifle fire from every koppie, forcing them to bring their artillery into action, thereby delaying their advance.[52]
	Western ZAR	Lord Roberts orders Lord Methuen to the Potchefstroom area to help subdue the resurgence of guerrilla activities in that district as evidenced by General Liebenberg's attacks on the railway. He leaves Colonel Baden-Powell in command at Rustenburg and Olifant's Nek. General De la Rey clashes with the Queensland Mounted Infantry at the Koster River.
Day 287 Tue **1900-07-24**	Eastern OFS	**THE BRANDWATER BASIN** At Retief's Nek the British occupy the vacant positions during the night and move up all their artillery. They open up a terrific bombardment on Prinsloo's small guard in their mountain positions. At about 15:00 the burghers are in full retreat after hearing the disturbance from Slabbert's Nek, determined not to be caught in a British pincer movement. Both Retief's Nek and Slabbert's Nek passes are captured and as more exits out of the Brandwater Basin fall into British hands, the circumstances of the Free State forces concentrated there become more and more perilous.[53]
	OFS	**THE FLOUR WAGONS SKIRMISH** As Broadwood enters Vredefort, five of De Wet's wagons are leaving loaded with freshly milled flour from the mill. Brigadier-General DP Ridley orders Colonel N Legge, with three to four hundred mounted infantry, to cut off and capture the wagons. De Wet impulsively decides not to abandon his wagons and personally starts a mounted charge over open terrain. He is soon joined by hundreds of his men from various directions, while his field-guns also open up. At Wonderfontein, south of Stinkhoutboom on the Vredefort/Reitzburg road, Broadwood eventually brings all his artillery into action to cover Legge and the mounted infantry's retreat. The battle for the flour wagons costs De Wet five killed and 12 or 14 wounded while the British suffer 39 casualties.[54] Chief Commandant De Wet reaches Reitzburg.
	Western ZAR	Captain Lambart, who has bluffed his way into Klerksdorp, has still not been substantially reinforced. At the approach of Republican forces, he decides not to defend the town. General Liebenberg chases the small British garrison (40 men of the Kimberley Mounted Corps) out and retakes the town.[55]
	ZAR	Lord Roberts leaves Pretoria for Bronkhorstspruit. After a fight on the eastern bank of the Great Olifants River, 16 kilometres south-east of Great Olifants River Station, General French outflanks Commandant-General Botha's 2 200 men and take the station.[56] General Howard captures Rooikoppies, near Amersfoort.
	Victoria Cross	Captain RN Howse, New South Wales Medical Staff Corps (Australian Forces).

Day 288 Wed **1900-07-25**	ZAR	Commandant-General Louis Botha explains to President Kruger that the retreat of the burghers does not imply cowardice or demoralization. "*If we make a stand, I can assure Your Excellency, the war will be over. As soon as we make contact with the enemy's centre, they pull back towards Pretoria and their flanks, about four hours from their centre, rush ahead and at the least delay they will surround us as they did with Cronje. It is already difficult to stay ahead. The enemy advances with its main army and we have about 2 200 to stop them, fight them and to extricate our wagons.*" A tremendous thunderstorm and heavy rains torment both sides during the night. The adverse conditions in the coldest part of the country kills hundreds of draught animals and several British troops die of exposure.[57]
	Eastern ZAR	Lord Roberts reaches Balmoral.
	Eastern OFS	East of Ficksburg, General Rundle's mounted troops capture Commando Nek without opposition while Generals MacDonald and Bruce Hamilton join forces near the present-day Clarens.
	United Kingdom	Referring to the Prime Minister, Lloyd George tells the House of Commons: "*The right honourable gentleman admitted that he had no right to meddle in the affairs of the Transvaal and that there was only one possible justification for it — that our motive was an unselfish one. We have thrown that justification away now... You entered into these two republics for philanthropic purposes and remained to commit burglary... Our critics say you are not going to war for equal rights and to establish fair play, but to get hold of the goldfields.*"[58]
Day 289 Thu **1900-07-26**	ZAR	Lord Roberts and his headquarters staff unexpectedly returns to Pretoria, presumably to arrange replacements for the draught animals killed in the bad weather.
	Eastern OFS	General MacDonald, now commanding more than 3 000 men with about 14 field-guns, attacks General De Villiers and Commandant Haasbroek at Naauwpoort Nek, north of the present-day Clarens. The British steamroller takes the one burgher position after the other and the Republicans can only manage a token rearguard action before falling back. By sunset Naauwpoort Nek, the last major exit from the Brandwater Basin, is blocked. De Villiers falls back towards Golden Gate.[59] In the south General Rundle marches through Commando Nek to Brindisi. On his arrival there, scouts inform him that the Republicans are evacuating Fouriesburg. He immediately asks for volunteers and gallops into the town.[60] General Piet de Wet and his staff lay down their arms at Kroonstad.
	OFS	Chief Commandant CR de Wet, President Steyn and the Free State government move north of Reitzburg and bivouac at Renosterpoort Farm near the Vaal River.[61]
	Trivia	*SG (Manie) Maritz's 24th birthday.*
Day 290 Fri **1900-07-27**	ZAR	Lord Roberts issues Proclamation 9 of 1900. See Article 42 of the Hague Convention 1899-07-29. General ETH Hutton enters and occupies Middelburg without opposition.
	OFS	General Broadwood requests additional reinforcements to corner De Wet and he starts forming a semicircular cordon south of the Vaal River. [62]
	Eastern OFS	In the Brandwater Basin there is uncertainty about who is the commanding officer of the Republican forces in the vicinity. Earlier in the month Marthinus Prinsloo resigned as Chief Commandant of the Free State forces, due to ill health, but he has stayed on as an officer under General Piet de Wet. Meanwhile, President Steyn appointed Reverend Paul Roux as Assistant Chief Commandant, commanding several commandos

	Gen. Marthinus Prinsloo *(War Museum of the Boer Republics)*	in the Brandwater Basin. A council of war is held at Eerste Geluk to solve a leadership crisis between the two. A vote seems to give Prinsloo the majority and he accepts command. Later votes received from commandos stationed further away, give Roux the majority and the confusion persists. The main body of Boers retreat and concentrate at Slaapkrantz, where the roads from Naauwpoort Nek and Golden Gate converge.[63]
	Trivia	*Sir Hamilton Goold-Adams' 42nd birthday*
Day 291 Sat **1900-07-28**	Eastern OFS	General MacDonald sends General Bruce Hamilton in a wide arc to approach Golden Gate from the north. The British, fighting their way deeper into the Brandwater Basin from all directions, converge on the main Republican force at Slaapkrantz Nek. The Republicans make a determined defence, but the weight of British forces, pushing from all sides with a vast superiority in artillery, is overwhelming and at midnight the koppie dominating the entire position is captured.[64]
	ZAR	Lord Roberts occupies Middelburg.
Day 292 Sun **1900-07-29**	Eastern OFS	General Prinsloo sends ex-Commandant Vilonel as an emissary to General Hunter, requesting a four-day armistice. Hunter refuses and insists on unconditional surrender.[65]
	ZAR	Lord Roberts asks Buller to send a division of infantry, with cavalry, to clear the country between the Natal and Delagoa Bay railway lines and then to cover the right flank of the force already in Middelburg.[66]
	Trivia	*King Umberto I of Italy is assassinated in Monza by the anarchist Angelo Bresci.*
Day 293 Mon **1900-07-30** *Gen. Paul Roux* *(National Cultural History Museum)*	Eastern OFS	**EX-CHIEF COMMANDANT PRINSLOO SURRENDERS IN THE BRANDWATER BASIN** In the confusion of the unsolved leadership squabble between himself and Paul Roux, ex-Chief Commandant Prinsloo, who claims to have the most support, surrenders to General Hunter, using the sentenced traitor ex-Commandant Vilonel as a go-between. Some generals, including Froneman, Fourie, Kolbe and Olivier, reject Prinsloo's order to surrender and escape through Golden Gate with about 1 500 men, eight field-guns, a pom-pom and two machine guns. However, by 9 August Prinsloo and three generals (including General Roux, as a matter of honour), nine commandants and 4 314 men have laid down their arms. The British also capture three field-guns, 2 800 cattle, 4 000 sheep, 5 500 horses and two million rifle bullets. The act of surrender takes place at Surrender Hill on the farm Verliesfontein (Loss Fountain), a few kilometres south of the present-day Clarens.[67]
	Western ZAR	Lieutenant-General Lord Methuen's 1st Division arrives at Potchefstroom.[68]
	Eastern ZAR	A British attempt to take Amersfoort is repulsed by General Joachim Fourie and a few hundred burghers. The British lose at least 15 troops killed and a detachment of hussars are almost captured by burghers who suffers no casualties.[69]
Day 294 Tue **1900-07-31**	ZAR	General De la Rey arrests ex-General Schoeman on his farm rear Pretoria for refusing to obey an order to escort a convoy of supply wagons.[70]

OFFICIAL REPORTS

Farm burning:	Three buildings have been destroyed by British troops.[71]
Concentration camps:	A 'refugee camp' has been established at Mafeking.[72]
Communications:	Rail traffic has been disrupted 14 times during June.[73]

1900	WINTER	AUGUST
Day 295 Wed **1900-08-01**	OFS	Major-General AF Hart is sent from Heidelberg, Major-General Sir CE Knox from Kroonstad and Lieutenant-Colonel EH Dalgety is ordered to rush from the Brandwater Basin via Kroonstad to join the hunt for De Wet south of the Vaal River[74]
	ZAR	General Ian Hamilton, commanding a force of about 6 000 men with 26 field-guns, is sent to capture Commando Nek and Silkaatsnek and to cover Baden-Powell's retirement to Pretoria.
	Western ZAR	The small garrison at Schweizer-Reneke is besieged.
	Cape Colony	Milner wires Chamberlain: *"There is thus a considerable and continuous area in both the Orange River Colony and south-western Transvaal, which has temporarily escaped from our control."*[75]
Day 296 Thu **1900-08-02**	OFS	Lord Roberts sends his Chief of Staff, Lord Kitchener, to take overall command of the forces engaged against De Wet.[76] Major-General CE Knox forwards a letter from M Prinsloo to De Wet, informing him of his surrender on 30th July. De Wet explodes when he reads that Prinsloo refers to himself as 'Chief Commandant' — an arrogant presumption to which De Wet vehemently objects.[77]
	ZAR	General Ian Hamilton, having split his force into three columns, attacks the small force of burghers under Field-cornet Coetzee whom De la Rey has left in command at Silkaatsnek. Hamilton, unable to make contact with his column commanded by Colonel Mahon, suspects that they may be in trouble and orders a charge at Coetzee's men. The Argyll & Sutherland Highlanders and Berkshires, supported by 18 field-guns, launch a bayonet charge and the burghers abandon their positions. Mahon's column, which has moved very slowly, is too far away to cut off their retreat. The British suffer 46 casualties.[78]
	Victoria Cross	Private W House, 2nd Battalion, the Royal Berkshire Regiment, Silkaatsnek.
	Western ZAR	General Sir Frederick Carrington arrives at Zeerust where he is reinforced. He now commands about 1 000 men with six field-guns and two pom-poms. He is on his way to Colonel Hore's post at Elands River from where he is to escort a supply convoy waiting there.[79]
	United Kingdom	Mr Chamberlain outlines the system of government he envisages for 'the new colonies'.
	Trivia	*The Shah of Persia is attacked in Paris by the anarchist Salsou.*
Day 297 Fri **1900-08-03**	OFS	**A BREACH OF NEUTRALITY** At 01:20 Captain Danie Theron and his scouts derails a goods train at Holfontein Siding. Two soldiers and the driver are wounded before the train is captured. A special saloon carriage carrying Colonel Stowe, Consul-General of the United States of America, is uncoupled and pushed out of harm's way by the scouts before the train is burned. Stowe is treated with the utmost courtesy and his carriage is not searched when he assures Theron that there are only US consular staff on board. In a clear breach of US neutrality, however, a British intelligence officer, Colonel Lord Algernon G Lennox, carrying important documents from Sir A Milner to Lord Kitchener, is allowed to hide in the carriage, pretending to be a member of Stowe's staff. Theron releases all of his prisoners except four British lieutenants before departing.[80] Lord Kitchener takes command of the forces facing De Wet and the Free State government near Reitzburg on the south bank of the Vaal River. A semicircular cordon of about 11 000 men stretches from the Renoster River in the west to Parys in the east. Across the river Lord Methuen's first division (about 4 500 men) is in a position to complete the circle. [81]

Day 298 Sat **1900-08-04**	Western ZAR	**THE BATTLE OF ELANDS RIVER (BRAKFONTEIN)** General De la Rey, in an action designed to relieve pressure on De Wet's expedition, attacks Colonel CO Hore's garrison at Elands River, the present-day Swartruggens. Colonel Hore, once the prisoner of Commandant Eloff at Mafeking, commands a mixed garrison comprising 299 Australian troops under Major Tunbridge and three units of the Rhodesian Field Force — a force totalling 505 men with an obsolete 7-pounder gun and two machine guns. Their task is to police the area, protect the Pretoria/Mafeking road and to maintain a transmission depot for the supplies moving along this important route. General De la Rey's force, consisting of about 500 burghers from Lichtenburg, Marico and Krugersdorp, commanded by General Lemmer and Commandant Steenkamp with four field-guns, one pom-pom and two machine guns, surrounds the large camp during the night. At dawn they open fire on a detail going down to the river to water the horses. The Republican shelling causes consternation and casualties among the defenders whose outposts are pushed back and especially among the horses and draught animals — some still harnessed to the wagons of the convoy which arrived the previous evening. The colonial troops, most of them facing their baptism of fire, put up a determined defence, causing the attackers to hesitate and the assault becomes an artillery duel with small-arms sniping. For once De la Rey enjoys superiority in artillery and he is happy to use his field-guns at ranges at which the defenders are unable to reply. General Sir F Carrington, informed of the attack, leaves his baggage train and a small guard at the Marico River and presses on with about 650 men and a New Zealand artillery unit with four field-guns and two pom-poms. At dusk the shelling ceases and the garrison uses the opportunity to improve their defences. They dig new trenches and bombproof shelters with any available materials and harness oxen to drag away some of the carcasses of the animals killed by shells. The defenders suffer 32 casualties.[82]
	Trivia	*The Queen Mother is born.*
Day 299 Sun **1900-08-05**	Western ZAR	**THE BATTLE OF ELANDS RIVER (BRAKFONTEIN)** General De la Rey's scouts give him ample warning of General Carrington's approach but he is unable to take more than 75 men out of the firing line surrounding Hore to meet this threat. He sends General HR Lemmer and 40 men to take position on hills commanding the road from the north and takes 30 men, a field-gun and a pom-pom to a position south of Carrington's approach. He also places five members of his staff in bushes directly across his approach with orders not to fire until the enemy is about 200 metres away. At 16:00, only three kilometres from Hore's position, De la Rey's field-guns open up on Carrington's force and moments later the five marksmen open fire, shooting as fast as possible. The fire and shelling are concentrated on Carrington and his staff who turn and retire. De la Rey, on the left, and Lemmer, on the right, immediately start a pursuit and the withdrawal becomes a hasty retreat. Carrington, having suffered only 27 casualties, retreats all the way to the Marico River, pursued by no more than 70 burghers.[83] General Ian Hamilton's force meets Baden-Powell outside Rustenburg. The sounds of battle are audible from the direction of Elands River.
	OFS	After a few days of rest on the farm Renosterpoort between Reitzburg and the Vaal River, Chief Commandant De Wet begins to move his commando across the river at Schoeman's Drift. As some of Chief Commandant De Wet's Free Staters are reluctant to cross into the ZAR, he sends a number of them south to cover a fictional threat. While they are away, he orders their vehicles and personal baggage to be taken across the river. On their return they have little choice but to follow.[84]
	Eastern OFS	Harrismith is occupied without opposition by General Dowling of General Macdonald's force.[85]

Day 300 Mon **1900-08-06**	Western ZAR	Lord Methuen sets off from Potchefstroom with two battalions of mounted yeomanry, two companies of infantry and three sections of artillery to occupy the Vaal River crossings between Scandinavia Drift and Lindeque's Drift, thus closing the trap on De Wet and the OFS government. Another part of his force, almost similar in composition, has been sent towards Parys to close the north-eastern sector of the circle around De Wet. Unfortunately he concentrates his force on Scandinavia Drift, where he arrives about 14:00, to hear that De Wet is crossing at Schoeman's Drift several kilometres to the east. He immediately swerves north-eastwards, towards Tygerpoort, opposite Schoeman's Drift, but his force is exhausted and makes slow progress. In the meantime, near the small hamlet of Venterskroon, only a small part of De Wet's force has crossed the river and they are in a very vulnerable position at the drift and in a narrow corridor between the river and the steep hills overlooking it. [86] **THE BATTLE OF ELANDS RIVER** Pursued for only part of the way by De la Rey and Lemmer's small group, General Carrington retreats to Marico River and Zeerust. He burns his baggage train and surplus supplies and retires towards Mafeking.[87] Baden-Powell, with Mahon's mounted troops, marches towards Hore's camp and reaches the Selons River, almost halfway to Elands River. Hearing shell-fire growing weaker and weaker in a westerly direction, he decides that Carrington must have relieved Hore and that they were falling back to Mafeking. He decides to return to Rustenburg.[88] At Elands River the defenders hang on determinedly and a siege situation ensues with desultory shelling, sniping and night-time sorties to fetch water from the river.
Day 301 Tue **1900-08-07**	Western ZAR	**THE BATTLE OF TYGERPOORT (VENTERSKROON)** The vicinity of Tygerpoort and Venterskroon is characterized by steep, concentric ridges that form part of the geographic phenomenon known as the Vredefort Dome, created by a primordial meteorite strike. During the night Lord Methuen's baggage wagons caught up with his troops and they start their advance against the hills occupied by the Republican rearguard. Chief Commandant De Wet is still in a serious position with part of his force still on the Free State side of the river, covering Kitchener's massive force. His wagon train and field-guns are strung out along the riverbank, heading for the narrow Van Vuurenspoort which can be captured at any moment by troops marching from the Parys side. Methuen's repeated frontal assaults against the rearguard's excellent defensive positions fail. They change their tactic and advance in short rushes, supported by heavy shelling and small-arms fire. De Wet sends about 500 burghers ahead to secure the Van Vuurenskloof Pass and he and his staff rush back with two machine guns and a pom-pom. The rearguard has been forced off the first line of hills to fall back to the next. De Wet's field-guns tries to come into action from a steep, wooded hill, but they find the position unsuitable and the gunners are almost trapped. Captain Danie Theron and 14 of his men arrive, push the approaching yeomanry back with a tremendous fusillade and through a supreme effort they manage to manhandle the field-guns down the hill, losing an ammunition limber in the process. During the afternoon Methuen is reinforced by some Welsh and Scottish Fusiliers diverted from their march towards Parys. At about 14:00 the burghers abandon their positions and Methuen falls back to regroup. De Wet uses the lull to order the last of his men across the river. They rush eastwards and escape through Van Vuurenskloof Pass to safety. To De Wet's relief the British force at Parys does not launch any operations to dispute his passage and he proceeds to Buffelshoek. De Wet's narrow escape costs him four burghers killed and several wounded while Methuen loses three killed and 19 wounded. [89] Lord Roberts receives information that Colonel Hore is still holding out at Elands River but, nevertheless, he orders Ian Hamilton and Baden-Powell to retire towards Pretoria, abandoning the gallant colonials.[90]
	South-eastern ZAR	General Lyttleton attacks Amersfoort with about 11 000 men and 40 guns, advancing

Gen. Sir F Carrington
(War Museum of the Boer Republics)

Chief Comdt. De Wet
(War Museum of the Boer Republics)

		with a front almost 30 kilometres wide. General Chris Botha's few hundred burghers with six guns put up a spirited defence but they are forced to withdraw towards Ermelo. The British suffer 19 casualties while eight burghers are killed and one is missing. Amersfoort is occupied.[91]
	Victoria Cross	Sergeant BTT Lawrence, 17th Lancers, patrol duty.
Day 302 Wed **1900-08-08**	ZAR	At Buffelshoek, a council of war adopts De Wet's proposal to reduce the number of wagons in the convoy. The meeting decides to limit the vehicles to one per 25 men. The surplus vehicles — about 300 of all types — are sent towards Lindeque's Drift from where they are to be taken back to the Free State.[92] De Wet also admonishes Theron's scouts for giving the laager insufficient warning of the approaching enemy.[93]
	ZAR	In Bethlehem, a certain Frans is tried, found guilty, sentenced to death and hanged for raping a white girl.[94]
Day 303 Thu **1900-08-09**	ZAR	Chief Commandant De Wet is again surprised by Lord Methuen because Gideon Scheepers and six of his scouts are involved in a skirmish with a 30-man British patrol and are unable to warn the laager in time. Theron's scouts fight rearguard actions to cover the commando's escape.[95] Some of the wagons De Wet so desperately wants to get rid of, rejoins his force.
	Western ZAR	Ian Hamilton and Baden-Powell evacuate Rustenburg and Olifant's Nek and occupy Commando Drift to attempt to head De Wet off. Generals De la Rey and Smuts enter Rustenburg and the town is under Republican control again.
Day 304 Fri **1900-08-10**	Western ZAR	With Generals Kitchener and Methuen on his heels, Major-General Smith-Dorrien waiting near Bank Station with 1 500 men, Lieutenant-General Ian Hamilton and Major-General Baden-Powell further north with about 9 500 men, Chief Commandant De Wet crosses the Gatsrand. He swerves north-west and crosses the Potchefstroom-Krugerdorp railway line about 5 kilometres south-west of Welverdiend Station. Theron's scouts again form the rearguard and dynamite the railway line in eight different places.[96] General Carrington reaches Mafeking and he narrowly avoids being court-martialled for his inexplicable flight from Elands River (Brakfontein). He later explains his actions to Lord Roberts in Pretoria by declaring that Hore's position is untenable and that he will have to surrender in any case. Roberts is furious and transfers him back to Bulawayo in Rhodesia.[97]
Day 305 Sat **1900-08-11**	South-east ZAR	Lord Dundonald's Mounted Brigade enters Ermelo unopposed. [98]
	Western ZAR	Chief Commandant De Wet meets General Liebenberg near Frederikstad, in the Potchefstroom district.[99]
Day -06 Sun **1900-08-12**	Western ZAR	Chief Commandant De Wet's rearguard fights a running battle with Lord Methuen's force at Modderfontein, west of Ventersdorp. Methuen seizes wagons and prisoners abandoned by the Republicans as well as one of the Armstrong guns captured at Stormberg.[100] Commandant Danie Theron and some of his scouts leave De Wet's force for a well-deserved rest at Mooiriviersoog.[101]
	South-eastern ZAR	General Buller joins Lord Dundonald in Ermelo.
Day 307 Mon **1900-08-13**	ZAR	Chief Commandant De Wet's advance groups and his rearguard become detached during a running battle with their pursuers but they reunite on the banks of the Selons River about 21 kilometres west of Olifantsnek.[102]

THE BATTLE OF ELANDS RIVER One of Colonel Hore's men, having sneaked through the besieger's lines, reaches British lines near Mafeking and confirms that the Australians and Rhodesians are still holding out. Lord Roberts orders Kitchener to divert three brigades from the hunt on De Wet to relieve Colonel Hore. |
| | South-east ZAR | General Tobias Smuts' scouts are involved in a skirmish with Buller's vanguard near Klipstapel on the way to Carolina. |

Day 308 Tue **1900-08-14**	ZAR	De Wet's entire force crosses the unoccupied Olifantsnek Pass near Rustenburg and camps on the banks of the Hex River. **END OF THE 'FIRST DE WET HUNT'** Since 15 July Chief Commandant Christiaan R de Wet's force has covered about 550 kilometres. He has achieved all his objectives: he has captured a train, inflicted losses on the enemy, increased his own numbers and managed to rest some of his burghers for more than a week. He is also well on his way to take President Steyn to consult with the ZAR government, while occupying the attention of about 50 000 British troops.[103] General SF Oosthuizen dies of wounds received at Dwarsvlei on 11-07-1900.[104]
	Eastern ZAR	The Canadians of Strathcona's Horse are the first to enter Carolina. On entering the town, snipers suddenly open fire on the massed troops and a fierce fight ensues between the houses before the burghers escape.
	Civilian life	**PROCLAMATION NO 12 OF 1900** In another proclamation, Lord Roberts announces that personal safety and freedom from molestation are no longer guaranteed, except to burghers who has already taken the oath: *"All burghers who had not taken the oath* (of neutrality) *would be regarded as prisoners of war and transported or otherwise dealt with as I may determine."* And... *"buildings harbouring the enemy would be liable to be razed to the ground."* Families on farms are instructed *"to acquaint Her Majesty's Forces with the presence of the enemy upon their farms,"* failing which... *"they would be regarded as aiding and abetting the enemy."*[105] Burghers who break their oath of neutrality and voluntarily rejoin the commandos, will henceforth be liable to be sentenced to pay a penalty, serve a prison term or be sentenced to death. Furthermore, persons laying down their arms and signing the oath of neutrality after this date, will be treated as prisoners of war and will be liable to be deported. By urging the burghers who have returned home and taken the oath to act as British spies, Roberts essentially forces them to renounce their neutrality.[106] See Articles 44, 45 and 50 of the Hague Convention.
	Trivia	*During what is called the Boxer uprising, combined international forces relieve the besieged embassies in Peking (now Beijing).*
Day 309 Wed **1900-08-15**	ZAR	**ROBERTS' UNION WITH THE NATAL FIELD FORCE IS AT LAST ESTABLISHED** General Buller's scouts meets French's cavalry flank at Twyfelaar, near Carolina. At last, Roberts' planned link-up between his force moving east and the force from Natal, is achieved — too late to exploit the initial Republican demoralisation after the fall of their capitals and too slow to surround Botha's retreating forces along the Eastern line.[107]
	Trivia	*Ex-State Attorney JC Smuts' baby son Kosie dies.*
Day 310 Thu **1900-08-16**	ZAR	**THE BATTLE OF ELANDS RIVER (BRAKFONTEIN)** General De la Rey, satisfied that the diversion caused by his siege of Elands River has succeeded in allowing De Wet to cross Olifantsnek, is convinced that there will not be any further advantage in maintaining the siege. On hearing reports of the approach of superior British forces, he quietly abandons the siege, removes his laager and disperses his burghers allowing Lord Kitchener to relieve Colonel Hore's gallant force. During the 13-day siege, the British have lost 22 killed and 58 wounded while the Republicans have lost four men.[108] The trial of Hans Cordua on charges of parole-breaking and conspiracy to kidnap the British Supreme Commander, Lord Roberts, starts in Pretoria.[109] Cordua has been aided and assisted in his half-baked plans by a South American named Gano — a detective in the pay of the British, who has acted as an *agent provocateur* — who then assists the British in arresting him and giving evidence against him.[110]
	Cape Colony	Martial law is lifted in the Molteno district.

Day 311 Fri 1900-08-17	ZAR	Chief Commandant De Wet and President Steyn arrive at Commando Nek, about three or four hours from Pretoria.[111] Commandant-General Botha sends General Ben Viljoen to inspect their defensive positions at Bothasberg.
Day 312 Sun 1900-08-18	ZAR	Chief Commandant De Wet starts his journey back to the Free State after sending President Steyn, Judge Hertzog and the top Free State officials with a small escort, on their way to the ZAR government.[112] De Wet's small force of about 250 men is again nearly cornered but they escape by using an almost impossible route over the Magaliesberg.
	Trivia	*PD de Wet's 39th birthday*
Day 313 Sun 1900-08-19	Eastern ZAR	On General Ben Viljoen's recommendation, the Republican line of defence is straightened, gaps filled and strategic points reinforced. The Republican line eventually extends over 80 kilometres, all parts are linked by heliograph and plans for mutual support are put in place.[113]
Day 314 Mon 1900-08-20		
Day 315 Tue 1900-08-21	ZAR	**THE BATTLE OF BERGENDAL** Buller's force marches north from Twyfelaar and at Vanwyksvlei, he sends Dundonald's mounted men to secure hills dominating the route he intends following. They are met with sharp rifle fire from General Joachim Fourie's men and have to be reinforced by two mounted brigades, six infantry companies and a field battery. A few burghers lead the 11th Hussars into an ambush and prevent the British from gaining a foothold in the Frischgewaagd Heights. The reinforcements cannot advance and the troops are extricated with difficulty and at 20:00 they are forced to retreat. The burghers lose only three wounded while the British suffer seven killed, three missing, presumed dead, and 26 wounded. General Fourie is ordered to Machadodorp and does not pursue the retreating troops.[114]
	Victoria Cross	Sergeant H Hampton and Corporal HJ Knight, 1st Battalion, the King's Liverpool Regiment, Vanwyksvlei.
Day 316 Wed 1900-08-22	ZAR	**THE BATTLE OF BERGENDAL** Buller and French's men remain at Vanwyksvlei, awaiting the arrival of their baggage train. Major-General Walter Kitchener executes probing attacks to determine the enemy positions but they are repulsed with a loss of ten men.[115] Commandant Danie Theron and ten of his scouts enter the occupied town of Roodepoort. At the station, they loot a few post bags and Henri Slegtkamp places dynamite under the rails.[116]
	Natal	A small group of about 50 burghers under General Grobler, operating in the British rear, attacks about 180 troops near Ingogo Station. The British suffer 13 killed and wounded and two are taken prisoner as the troops flee to Newcastle.[117]
	OFS	Chief Commandant C R de Wet, back in the Free State, sets up his headquarters at Renosterpoort.
	Trivia	*Sir WF Hely-Huchinson's 51st birthday*
Day 317 Thu 1900-08-23	ZAR	**THE BATTLE OF BERGENDAL** General Buller changes his planned route and marches towards Geluk. He finds that his planned bivouac area is dominated by a rocky ridge and launches a two-pronged attack from the west and south to clear the high ground. The western assault proceeds rapidly and the burghers on that side falls back. The southern attack is met with heavy rifle fire and shelling from Captain Alfred von Dalwig's three guns. A field battery

	Victoria Cross	engages the Republican guns but fails to silence them. Late in the afternoon, Captain Alfred von Dalwig is fatally wounded by shrapnel.[118] The western assault's advance is also checked when they move into an area blackened by a veld fire in front of the Heidelberg and Bethal commandos supported by 41 men of the German Corps. A 'Long Tom' in the rear of the burghers' position opens up and the British are caught with limited cover about 500-700 metres from the Republican lines. All efforts to crawl forward are met by heavy salvos. In the failing light, the burghers rush forward and the troops fall back when they are attacked from the flanks and almost cut off. A small group of soldiers make a determined stand, allowing their comrades to escape. Private WE Heaton, 1st Battalion, the King's Liverpool Regiment, is nominated for the Victoria Cross when his unit is cut off in front of British lines and surrounded with dwindling ammunition. He volunteers to take a message through the surrounding enemy to the main force. He succeeds at great personal risk and thus saves his unit.[119] The burghers approach to within 40 metres of the small group, when they are attacked by the reinforcements in closed formation. The burghers inflict heavy casualties on this massed target but they, together with the small rearguard, manage to fall back under the cover of darkness. The British lose 12 killed, 61 wounded and 33 (of whom 11 are wounded) captured. The burghers suffer ten wounded, including Captain Von Dalwig.[120]
Day 318 Fri **1900-08-24**	ZAR	**THE BATTLE OF BERGENDAL** Buller fortifies his force at Geluk and prepares positions for his four heavy guns and 22 other artillery pieces. The burghers are not prepared to attack his strong force in their trenches. They limit their offensive to an artillery battle in which their three guns and 'Long Tom' inflict about 12 casualties. In the centre, Lieutenant-General Sir R Pole-Carew's 11th Division advances along the railway line to Belfast where they come under fire from six Republican guns. They chase off part of the German Corps and take Belfast. The British suffer about 30 casualties on the day. [121]
Day 319 Sat **1900-08-25**	ZAR	**THE BATTLE OF BERGENDAL** Field-Marshal Lord Roberts arrives in Belfast. His combined forces, including that of Pole-Carew, French and Buller, have dug in along a 20-kilometre front, facing Botha's force of about 5 000 men who thinly occupies positions extending more than 80 kilometres. For the first time all four of the State Artillery Creusot 'Long Toms' are together under Botha's command and 32 other artillery pieces, with their dwindling supply of ammunition, are dispersed along his line of defence. Roberts immediately starts to redeploy his force in preparation of his tested tactic of wide flank assaults. He withdraws French's cavalry from their position between Pole-Carew and Buller and orders him to his left flank where he is to clear the Steelpoort Valley, swing east and head for the railway line between Belfast and Machadodorp, behind the Republican main position.[122] Hans Cordua is executed in Pretoria for participating in a 'conspiracy' to kidnap Lord Roberts. President Steyn arrives at Waterval-Onder to meet President Kruger. Chief Commandant De Wet reappears with 246 men at Vanvuurenskloof, on the north bank of the Vaal River.[123]
	ZAR/OFS	Lord Roberts issues instructions for the final mop-up of guerrillas or 'rebels' after the successful completion of his operations along the Delagoa railway line. He plans mobile columns to operate in loosely designated areas to put down open rebellion, removing all horses and forage, collecting cattle and livestock of oath breakers or families whose menfolk are on commando. Commanders are to act against known rebels, organize intelligence agents to glean information of any disaffection and give protection to loyal inhabitants. "...(T)he officer commanding will see that the

		country is so denuded of forage and supplies that no means of subsistence is left for any commando attempting to make any incursions."
		
		His disposition of the 'mobile columns' is as follows:
		The 'Transvaal':
		   1. Northern column commanded by Major General AH Paget based on the Pietersburg railway.
		   2. Commando Nek column commanded by Major General RAP Paget based at Commando Nek.
		   3. Potchefstroom column commanded by Major General AF Hart based on the Potchefstroom railway.
		   4. Western column commanded by Lieutenant-General Lord Methuen based at Mafeking and Zeerust.
		The 'Orange River Colony':
		   1. Eastern district commanded by Lieutenant-General Sir L Rundle based at Vrede and Harrismith.
		   2. Central district commanded by Lieutenant-General Sir A Hunter based at Heilbron and Kroonstad.
		   3. Western district commanded by Major General CE Knox based at Kroonstad.[124]

	Trivia	*German philosopher Friedrich Nietsche dies*
Day 320 Sun **1900-08-26**	ZAR	**THE BATTLE OF BERGENDAL** French moves from near Geluk to Belfast and from there to Bospoort. He pushes the Boksburg commando off Steenkampsberg to Lakenvlei, where his eastward movement is stopped by heavy rifle fire. Receiving French's message that the left flank has been cleared, Pole-Carew moves north, suffering some 35 casualties as they encounter rifle fire and shelling on their right flank while crossing in front of the main Republican position. Buller marches towards Volstruispoort under heavy flank fire from the Heidelbergers. The Bethal burghers occupy positions abandoned by the British and engage Howard's Brigade who forms the rearguard. At Volstruispoort, a well-concealed 'Long Tom ' unleashes a heavy bombardment on the British — at times three or four projectiles are in the air at the same time. All efforts by Buller's two 5-inch (127mm) and two 4,7-inch (120mm) guns to silence the Republican gun, fail. Commandant GH Gravett's Germiston commando maintains a terrific rifle fire on the British troops that lasts all day and they repulse several assaults on their position. In the face of this determined resistance, Buller's advance is slowed to a crawl and they reach Waaikraal, south of Dalmanutha, at dusk, with 48 casualties.[125] Commandant Danie Theron and his scouts storm the Klip River jail south-west of Johannesburg and release 69 prisoners. Most of the prisoners are burghers who have taken the oath of neutrality and they join the commandos. Some of them are to desert later, while the released common criminals just drift away.[126]
	Northern ZAR	Major General Baden-Powell captures Nylstroom.[127]
Day 321 Mon **1900-08-27**	ZAR	**THE BATTLE OF BERGENDAL OR DALMANUTHA** Lord Roberts has decided to launch his main assault against Bergendal Farm and Dalmanutha where General Buller can concentrate about 8 000 men and 38 guns on his sector of the front. General Buller identifies the heights of Bergendal Farm, directly south of the railway line, as the key to the Republican line and decides not to follow Lord Roberts' suggested flank movement but to concentrate his efforts here and thus split the enemy's defence. The heights are occupied by the Krugersdorp commando with a part of the German Corps on their left and the Johannesburg, Germiston, Heidelberg and Bethal commandos further eastwards. An isolated koppie on the west front of the Krugersdorpers occupied by 67 or 74 of the Johannesburg Zuid Afrikaansche Rijdende Politie (South African Mounted Police) or ZARPs under Commandants PR Oosthuizen and S van Lier and Lieutenant WF Pohlman with a single pom-pom, is to bear the brunt of Buller's attention.

	Victoria Cross	At 11:00 the bombardment starts and lyddite and shrapnel rain on the hills with the isolated koppie receiving the most attention. The British guns fire with impunity with a few shells from the 'Long Toms' and Krupps being the only sign of life from the Republican side. Botha's orders to reinforce the Johannesburg police are impractical and are simply ignored by the Krugersdorpers. The bombardment, the heaviest since Vaalkrantz and Pieters, lasts for more than three hours before the two-pronged infantry assault by Colonel Walter Kitchener's brigade starts. The Rifle Brigade approach the koppie from the west and the Inniskilling Fusiliers from the south until, at about 900 metres, the surviving ZARPs open fire and the Germans and Krugersdorpers join in. The astounded infantrymen suffer heavily, are stopped in their tracks and have to take cover. They are rallied by their officers and resume their charge. Twice more they are repulsed by the furious rifle and pom-pom fire. When they reach the foot of the hill, they fix bayonets and, when the bombardment stops, they rush up the rocky slope. The ZARPs return fire until the last possible moment before falling back down the back slope and retiring northwards — most of them on foot as their horses have been killed during the bombardment. The brave Commandant Philip Oosthuizen, who has been seriously wounded, is captured. Lieutenant Pohlman has been killed and 40 of the 74 policemen are dead, wounded or taken prisoner. The British casualties include 13 killed, 103 wounded and four missing. The Republican line has been breached but fatigue and darkness make any further operations impossible. Private AE Durant, 2nd Battalion, the Rifle Brigade, Bergendal. Elsewhere, General French's cavalry skirts the Zuikerbos Kop and Langkloof positions and advance towards the Dullstroom road to link up with General Pole-Carew who is moving northwards along this route. Botha's force retreats towards the Kaapsche Hoop mountains. Since their first attack on the Republican positions on 21 August the British have suffered 385 casualties while the Republicans' casualties amount to 78 men for the same period.[128]
	OFS	Ex-General, now Commandant, JH Olivier makes an unsuccessful attack on Winburg and he is captured with 27 of his burghers. PH Kritzinger is appointed Commandant in his place.[129]
Day 322 Tue **1900-08-28**	Eastern ZAR	Presidents Kruger and Steyn move to Nelspruit — now declared the seat of the ZAR government. At a combined meeting of the Executive Councils of both Republics, President Steyn proposes that the 74-year-old President Kruger be granted six months' leave to further the Republican cause in Europe.[130] The burghers fight delaying actions along the Machadodorp road.
	International	Although pro-Boer demonstrations are banned in St Petersburg for fear of diplomatic complications, demonstrators break through police cordons in a show of enthusiasm occasioned by the arrival of the Republican deputation.[131]
Day 323 Wed **1900-08-29**	ZAR	Generals Buller and French meet at Helvetia, north of Machadodorp.
Day 324 Thu **1900-08-30**	ZAR	General French occupies Waterval-Boven and Waterval-Onder. General Ben Viljoen releases about 2 000 British prisoners of war from the camp at Nooitgedacht and they are received by General Pole-Carew.[132]
	Trivia	*Cape Prime Minister PW Schreiner's 43rd birthday.*
Day 325 Fri **1900-08-31**	ZAR	Commandant Danie Theron captures a train and 30 soldiers at Klip River Station, near the present-day Soweto. The loot includes rifles and ammunition, but especially welcome is the liquor that allows the Hollander members of the Corps to celebrate Queen Wilhelmina's birthday in style.[133]

	Western ZAR	South of Olifantsnek, at Quaggafontein Farm, Colonel Dalgety spots a Republican party scouting the movements of a convoy from Slypsteenkoppie. He spoils De la Rey's planned ambush when he immediately orders his Colonials to attack. The fight lasts all day and Dalgety takes the hill, suffering 14 killed — mostly from the Kaffrarian Rifles — while the burghers lose three men. De la Rey disengages and resumes his shadowing of the convoy, only to find that General Liebenberg has abandoned the ambush positions at a narrow pass on the way to Krugersdorp.[134]
	Trivia	*Queen Wilhelmina's 20th birthday.* *Coca-Cola, first sold in the USA 14 years earlier, is launched in Britain.*

	OFFICIAL REPORTS	
	Farm burning:	Twelve buildings have been destroyed by British troops.[135]
	Concentration camps:	'Refugee camps' have been established at Bloemfontein and Pietermaritzburg.[136]
	Communications:	Fifteen disruptions of rail traffic under British control have been reported during August. [137]

1900	SPRING	**SEPTEMBER**
Day 326 Sat **1900-09-01**	ZAR	**THE ANNEXATION OF THE ZAR** Proclamation 14 of 1900. Lord Roberts destroyed the annexation of the ZAR under the name 'Transvaal Colony'. See Article 42 of the Hague Convention 1899-07-29. Lord Roberts' proclamation of 14 August is extended to include the Orange Free State. He also proclaims that all burghers of the Orange Free State, except those who have been continuously in arms since the annexation, have become British subjects and that any resistance from them will be regarded as rebellion.[138] See Article 42 of the Hague Convention 1899-07-29. [139] WT Stead later publishes the international legal expert Macdonnell's opinion. *"So long as there is an army, however feeble, in the field, so long as large parts of the invaded territory are alternatively gained, lost and regained, there is no talking of conquest or of rebels. If this doctrine was not firmly held, there would be no security for the subjects of a State which had a considerable part of its territory invaded."*[140]
	Victoria Cross	An eight-man scouting party is ambushed by burghers in a narrow gorge near Warmbaths and six are immediately hit. Only the outstanding bravery of two Australians of the Tasmanian Imperial Bushmen, Lieutenant GGE Wylly, rescuing a wounded corporal, and Private JH Bisdee, who assists a wounded officer, allows anyone to escape. The British casualties number six wounded, one of whom is taken prisoner. The Victoria Cross is later awarded to Lieutenant Wylly and Private Bisdee.[141]
	OFS	Commandant Piet Fourie besieges 123 regular soldiers and 30 local volunteers at Ladybrand. Commandant Hertzog sends a burgher under a flag of truce to demand their surrender. The garrison answers that it will be better for all if the burghers will come in and lay down their arms. Fourie, joined by Nieuwoudt and Kritzinger, attack the town, taking it street by street until they are in possession of the town. The garrison, however, retreats to impregnable positions at the foot of Platberg, from where the attackers are unable to shift them.[142]
	Trivia	*General Paul Sanford Lord Methuen's 55th birthday.*
Day 327 Sun **1900-09-02**	Eastern ZAR	General Buller moves north from Helvetia on the Lydenburg road. At Rietfontein on the Crocodile River, south of Lydenburg, the Creusot 'Long Toms' of the ZAR State Artillery fight their last joint action — a long-range artillery duel with Buller's vanguard. Buller decides that the enemy position is too strong for a frontal assault and requests assistance from General Ian Hamilton.[143]

		Lord Roberts writes to Commandant-General Botha, *"... warn all burghers on commando whose families are living in districts occupied by our troops to make timely preparation for receiving and sheltering their families. The expulsion of these families will commence within a few days, a start being now made with those now in Pretoria."*[144]
	ZAR	Commandant Theron's scouts arrive too late to capture a train near Heidelberg.[145]
	OFS	The Republicans position one of their guns in the middle of Ladybrand and opens up an ineffective shelling against the garrison's positions at the foot of Platberg.[146]
Day 328 Mon **1900-09-03**	ZAR	President Kruger issues a counter-proclamation from Nelspruit declaring Lord Roberts' annexation proclamation null and void. *"The people of the Z.A.R. is and stays a free and independent people and refuses to submit to British rule."*[147]
Day 329 Tue **1900-09-04**	ZAR	An extraordinary ZAR Government Gazette is published containing Act no 5 of 1900, allowing for the reorganization of the ZAR forces for the unconventional warfare that is to follow.[148] The reorganization gives more powers to the ZAR Commandant-General and the Free State Chief Commandant. As some commandos are seriously undermanned and have too many officers in relation to the men they command which may lead to confusion and insubordination, it is decided to reconstitute the commandos. Commandos of about 300 men, commanded by a commandant, are to be formed, with a field-cornet for every 100 men and a corporal for every ten men. The appointment of commandants is to be left to the Commandant-General and all surplus commandants and field-cornets are to be reduced to the ranks. For the first time a scale of pay is introduced. The Commandant-General is to receive £20 per day, generals £15, commandants £10, field-cornets £7/6/0 and rank and file burghers £5 per day. Half of the pay is to be given every two months and the rest at the end of the war. (However, no pay was ever to be received.)[149]
	OFS	Commandant Fourie abandons his siege of Ladybrand and leaves for Bothaville where he is to meet Chief Commandant De Wet. The Republicans lose one burgher killed and a woman is wounded. Fourie is content to loot some horses and other supplies. [150]
	Western ZAR *Comdt. Danie Theron* (War Museum of the Boer Republics)	**THE DEATH OF DANIE THERON** In the Gatsrand, Commandant Danie Theron plans an attack on General Hart's column, in combination with General Liebenberg's commando. While scouting alone on a koppie, about 6 kilometres north of the present-day Fochville, trying to find out why Liebenberg is not in his agreed position, he almost collides with seven members of Marshall's Horse. He is forced to fire and kills three and wounds four. He keeps up a terrific volume of fire, presumably trying to give the impression of a far larger force. The column's escort, alerted by the firing, immediately charges the hill. The lone scout continues firing and the column's artillery — six field-guns and a 4,7 inch naval gun — open a heavy barrage on the hill. The legendary Republican hero is killed in an inferno of lyddite and shrapnel.[151] Commandant Dirksen attacks a Canadian post at Pan Station (30 kilometres east of Middelburg), manned by 105 men. The Canadians hold out until they are relieved by Colonel Mahon.
	OFS	General Bruce Hamilton's column arrives in Ladybrand, relieving the tired garrison after a 'siege' lasting five days.
Day 331 Thu **1900-09-06**	Eastern ZAR	General Buller is relieved when part of General Ian Hamilton's force, travelling along the Dullstroom road, arrives in the rear of Botha's position at Rietfontein. The Republicans abandon their positions and Brocklehurst and Dundonald enter Lydenburg.[152] General French occupies Carolina with 5 280 men and 20 guns.

	Northern ZAR	General Paget evacuates Warmbaths and fall back to Pienaar's River Station, 32 kilometres north of Pretoria, now the northernmost post on the railway line.
	Trivia	*ZAR Vice-State President SW Burger's 48th birthday.*
Day 332 Fri **1900-09-07**		
Day 333 Sat **1900-09-08**	Eastern ZAR	General Buller, with 12 000 men and 48 guns at his disposal, attacks General Botha's position at Paardeplaats, near Lydenburg. The British artillery open a heavy bombardment on Botha's 2 000 burghers. At about noon, the two Republican 'Long Toms' withdraw from the pass that is now known as 'Long Tom Pass'. One of their parting shots, fired at about 9 000 metres range, bursts over the Volunteer Company, killing one and wounding 20 with a single shell. Botha evacuates his position and after stiff climbing, the troops reach the crest at 15:30 but cannot prevent the Boer convoy from escaping.[153]
	OFS	The railway line between Leeuwspruit and Vredefort is blown up in five places.
Day 334 Sun **1900-09-09**	Eastern ZAR	General Buller encounters burghers holding ridges in front of Mauchsberg, east of Paardeberg. He launches an infantry assault supported by all his guns. Again the troops reach the summit to see the Republican convoy winding its way down the pass known as The Devil's Knuckles. This time Buller orders pursuit but a skillful rearguard action allows the convoy to escape.[154] Commandant SB Buys is killed in a skirmish with some of Buller's units.[155]
	OFS	General T Kelly-Kenny requests permission from Lord Roberts to establish refugee camps for burghers who surrendered at Bloemfontein and Kroonstad.[156] Major-General Pretyman orders the District Commissioner at Heilbron, *"The farms should not be burnt in a wholesale way but an example made by razing to the ground the farms of men who are known to have harboured the enemy or used them for defensible posts. All stock belonging to burghers who have broken oath without being forced to join a commando should be confiscated leaving enough to support families."*[157]
Day 335 Mon **1900-09-10**	Eastern ZAR	Representatives of the ZAR and the Free State governments meet at Nelspruit. The ZAR Executive allows President Kruger to go to Europe (initially for a period of six months), to prevent the possibility of his falling into British hands and to plead the Republican cause.[158]
Day 336 Tue **1900-09-11**	Portuguese East Africa	**PRESIDENT KRUGER LEAVES THE ZAR** President Kruger and his entourage leave Krokodilpoort by train on his way from Nelspruit to Lourenço Marques, where they arrive the same evening.[159] General Schalk W Burger is appointed as Acting State President in Kruger's absence. President Steyn and the rest of his government start their voyage back to the Free State with an escort of 250 men under Boshof, a light baggage train, plenty of spare horses and £500 000 in gold. They decide against a direct route and head north through the Bushveld.[160]
	Eastern ZAR	Ex-General Schoeman is acquitted on a charge of high treason by a court martial in Barberton.[161]
	Western ZAR	Lord Methuen attacks Commandant Vermaak's laager at Molopo Oog, taking 30 prisoners, 22 wagons and a supply of ammunition, but losing eight men wounded.[162]
Day 337 Wed **1900-09-12**	Eastern ZAR	The first Creusot 'Long Tom' of Adjutant K Roos of the State Artillery is blown up with dynamite near Hectorspruit and the wreckage is thrown into the Crocodile River.[163] General Pole-Carew leaves Waterval-Onder and resumes his march to Komatipoort with Ian Hamilton following the next day.[164]

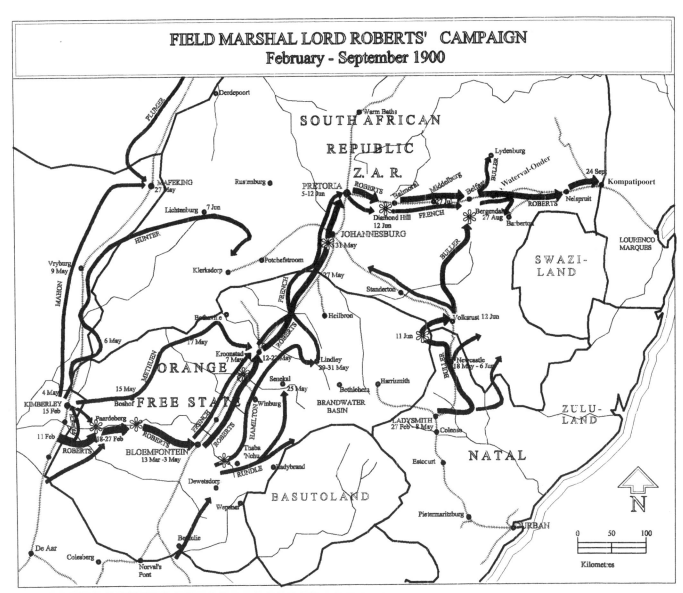

	Portuguese East Africa	The Governor of Portuguese East Africa, JJ Machado, invites President Kruger to stay in the official residence as guest of the Portuguese government. Kruger, highly suspicious of the Portuguese, interprets this as being placed under 'house arrest'.[165]
Day 338 Thu **1900-09-13**	ZAR	Lord Roberts issues a proclamation calling on the Republican forces still in the field to surrender. See Article 42 of the Hague Convention 1899-07-29.
	Eastern ZAR	After a rapid march along very rough roads General French arrives at Barberton and surprises Commandant Opperman, who just manages to escape with the 150 men of the Swaziland commando. The landdrost of Vryheid is captured with £10 000 in gold and notes. Ex-General Schoeman and eighty British prisoners are liberated, about 2 800 Boer refugees and a vast store of supplies fall into British hands.[166]
Day 339 Fri **1900-09-14**	ZAR	Lord Roberts proclaims: "... *the war is degenerating, and has degenerated, into operations carried on in an irresponsible manner by small, and in many cases, insignificant bodies of men. I should be failing my duty to Her Majesty's Government and to Her Majesty's Army in South Africa if I neglected to use every means in my power to bring such irregular warfare to an early conclusion.*" Further he envisages methods that will be "... *ruinous to the country...*" and will bring "... *endless suffering on the burghers and their families... The longer the guerrilla warfare continuous the more vigorously must they be enforced.*"[167] He also declares that no prisoners of war will be released until those Boers who are still in arms have surrendered unconditionally.[168] See Article 42 of the Hague Convention 1899-07-29.

Day 340 Sat 1900-09-15	ZAR	General JDP French sends ex-General Schoeman from Barberton to Pretoria.[169] The body of Commandant Danie Theron is exhumed by his men and later reburied next to that of his late fiancée Hannie Neethling on her father's farm Eikenhof, Klip Rivier.[170]
	International	The Republican deputation in Europe reports on Dr Leyds' interview with Czar Nicholas II: "... *our impression is that the Tsar — like the French Government — might be willing to help us if there was any hope of co-operation from the German Emperor or a less complicated state of affairs in China.*"[171]
Day 341 Sun 1900-09-16	Eastern ZAR	Over the next two days, due to lack of ammunition, twenty-four field-guns of the ZAR State Artillery are blown up by their crews at Hectorspruit and thrown into the Crocodile River.
Day 342 Mon 1900-09-17	Eastern ZAR	Commandant-General Botha, the ZAR government and about 2 000 men leave Hectorspruit, between Kaapmuiden and Komatipoort, and travel north through what is now the Kruger National Park. An advance party sent by General French from Barberton to Avoca siding, finds 50 railway locomotives.[172] President Steyn passes through Pilgrim's Rest on his way to Ohrigstad.[173]
	Western ZAR	South of Lichtenburg Lord Methuen clashes with about 400 burghers under Commandant Tollie de Beer. He pursues the retreating commando and manages to capture 28 prisoners, 26 wagons, a Maxim and one of the guns lost at Colenso.[174]
	OFS/ZAR	A member of the New South Wales Infantry writes: "*From the Vet to Machadodorp, over 3,000 miles, the face of the country is burnt and blackened moss, over which nightly for three months veldt fires have swept and clouds of smoke have hung.*"
	OFS	The railway line between Leeuwspruit and Vredefort is blown up in twenty-one places.
	Trivia	*The Commonwealth of Australia as a federal union of the six colonies, is proclaimed and will come into force on New Year's Day 1901.*
Day 343 Tue 1900-09-18	Eastern ZAR	Brigadier-General Stephenson's Brigade occupies Nelspruit without opposition and Lord Roberts transfers his headquarters here.[175]
Day 344 Wed 1900-09-19	Eastern ZAR	The ZAR government is at Spekboom River, southwest of Ohrigstad.
Day 345 Thu 1900-09-20	Eastern ZAR	General Pole-Carew reaches Kaapmuiden with Henry's Mounted Infantry and the Guards Brigade arriving in the afternoon.[176] Some of the Foreign Volunteers who have fought on the Republican side crosses into Portuguese territory.
Day 346 Fri 1900-09-21	OFS	Chief Commandant De Wet crosses the railway line between Roodewal and Serfontein Siding.
Day 347 Sat 1900-09-22	Western ZAR	With the departure of Commandant Tollie de Beer, the pressure on Schweizer-Reneke is relieved and Colonel Settle enters the town. Lord Methuen is ordered to proceed to Rustenburg to attempt intercepting the returning President Steyn.
	THE START OF THE 'BURGHER' OR 'REFUGEE' CAMPS Major-General JG Maxwell, military governor of the 'Transvaal Colony' announces that "... *camps for burghers who voluntarily surrender are being formed at Pretoria and Bloemfontein*".[177] This signals the start of what was to evolve into the notorious Concentration Camp Policy.	

Day 348 Sun **1900-09-23**	Western ZAR	Major-General RAP Clements is instructed by Lord Roberts that, *"It is absolutely essential to force all the people south of the Magaliesberg to submit and it is not clear that this can only be done by severe measures. You must please have no mercy, and what you cannot bring away you must destroy..."*[178]
	Trivia	CF Beyers' 31st birthday.
Day 349 Mon **1900-09-24**	Eastern ZAR	The vanguard of General Pole-Carew's Division reaches Komatipoort on the eastern ZAR border and finds the bridge into Portuguese territory intact. Lieutenant-Colonel Douglas Haig, Chief Staff Officer of General French, publishes a telegram received from Pretoria, announcing that, *"all burghers taken in arms by us will be treated without exception as prisoners of war and will be deported to St Helena or Ceylon. Burghers who give themselves up voluntarily will not be deported out of South Africa but will be sent down to the Cape Colony or Natal without delay."*[179] Prominent Republican officers JC Breytenbach, DJE Erasmus and DJ Grobler surrender to General Paget and are send to Cape Town as prisoners of war.[180]
Day 350 Tue **1900-09-25**	Eastern ZAR	Generals R Pole-Carew and ISM Hamilton occupy the deserted Komatipoort. Burnt out railway cars form a train almost twelve kilometres long on the Selati line.[181] **THE END OF LORD ROBERTS' MARCH ALONG THE DELAGOA RAILWAY LINE.**
	Portuguese East Africa/ International	A total of 1 004 persons consisting of 849 burghers and boys, 152 women and girls, two coloureds and one black man, cross the border into Portuguese East Africa (Mozambique). Due to lack of suitable facilities, they are later sent to Portugal where they are interned at Caldas da Rainha, Peniche, Alcobaça, Fort de St Gutias de Barra and Tomar until the end of hostilities.[182]
	United Kingdom	The dissolution of the British Parliament marks the start of what is to become known as the 'Khaki election'.
Day 351 Wed **1900-09-26**	Western ZAR	In a malicious act, the Paardekraal Monument near Krugersdorp, commemorating the start of the First War of Independence, is desecrated. During the night, on Lord Roberts' orders, British soldiers remove the stones from the cairn underneath the monument. The stones are packed into flour bags and taken to Johannesburg. They are later taken by train to Durban and thrown into the sea.[183] The desecration of national monuments is a violation of Article 56 of the Hague Convention. The Republicans abandon Rustenburg and General Cunningham's Brigade is the fourth British unit to take the town.
	Eastern ZAR	President Steyn's party, making a big detour on their way back to the Orange Free State, meets General Gert Gravett in Burger's (or Mac-Mac) Pass. He advises them not to delay and to proceed to Pilgrim's Rest.[184] General Buller crosses the Sabie River drift on his way to Burger's Pass beyond which he can see the dust of Botha's convoy trekking north. Gravett skirmishes with Buller's scouts, allowing the important convoys to escape.
Day 352 Thu **1900-09-27**	Eastern ZAR	Lord Dundonald occupies Pilgrim's Rest.
	OFS Concentration camps	Lord Roberts orders Generals A Hunter, L Rundle and Bruce Hamilton to *"clear the whole (Free State) of supplies and inform the burghers that if they choose to listen to De Wet and carry on a guerrilla warfare against us, they and their families will be starved"*. The policy of concentration camps is officially sanctioned by Lord Roberts. See Article 42 of the Hague Convention 1899-07-29.[185]
	Trivia	Louis Botha's 38th birthday.

Day 353 Fri **1900-09-28**	ZAR	A government notice declares that burghers who surrender voluntarily will not be sent out of South Africa. Stock and supplies of men still on commando or of those who have broken their oath will be taken without the issue of receipt and the houses of leaders of bands of snipers will be burned.[186]
	Western ZAR	Lord Methuen clashes with General Lemmer at Bronkhorstfontein. Some of Lemmer's men are reported to be wearing parts of British uniform and march in a regular formation to confuse the enemy. Among other casualties is one British officer, while Lemmer suffers 21 casualties. [187]
	Trivia	*JDP French's 48th birthday.* *Rev Paul H Roux's 33rd birthday.*
Day 354 Sat **1900-09-29**	United Kingdom	The position of Commander-in-Chief at the War Office is offered to Lord Roberts.
	ZAR	Major His Highness Prince Christian Victor Albert Ludwig Ernst Anton, heir of Norway, Duke of Schleswig-Holstein, Stormarn and the Dithmarscher and of Oldenburg, GCB, GCVO, grandson of Queen Victoria and ADC to Lord Roberts, dies of enteric fever at Pretoria.[188]
Day 355 Sun **1900-09-30**	*Trivia*	*General Frederick Sleigh Lord Roberts' 68th birthday.*

OFFICIAL REPORTS

Farm burning:	Ninety-nine buildings have been destroyed by British troops.[189]
Concentration camps:	'Refugee camps' have been established at Kroonstad, Potchefstroom and Vereeniging.[190]
Communications:	Twenty-three disruptions of rail traffic have been reported during September. [191]

1900	SPRING	**OCTOBER**
Day 356 Mon **1900-10-01**	Northern ZAR	General Buller arrives at Kruger's Post. His bivouac is shelled by a 'Long Tom' and two other guns and one soldier is killed and nine others wounded. Attempts to capture the Republican gun in a night attack fails.[192]
	OFS	Chief Commandant De Wet wrecks a train at Wolwehoek and recrosses the railway line.
	International	The International Peace Congress, meeting in Paris, passes resolutions against the annexation of the Republics but tones down a resolution proposed by British delegates calling the British conduct of the war 'criminal'.[193]
Day 357 Tue **1900-10-02**	Northern ZAR	General Buller returns to Nylstroom.
	Trivia	*President MT Steyn's 43rd birthday.* *MK Ghandi's 31st birthday.*
Day 358 Wed **1900-10-03**	ZAR	Scouts Hindon, Slegtkamp, Oosterhuizen and Verstappen join President Steyn at Roossenekal, bringing reports from Chief Commandant De Wet in the Parys vicinity. [194]
	Black involvement	A certain Maplank is executed by firing squad at Lydenburg after being found guilty, the previous day, of raping a white woman.[195]
Day 359 Thu **1900-10-04**	*Trivia*	*General PA Cronje celebrates his 63rd birthday in captivity on St Helena.*
Day 360 Fri **1900-10-05**	Eastern ZAR	A 40-man patrol of Steinaecker's Horse, surprises a burgher force north of Sabie. They fight a running battle, the burghers leave behind rifles, ammunition and a wagon. While camping, the mercenary patrol loses a white man, a black man and a horse to marauding lions.[196]

	Western ZAR	General G Barton sets out on a sweep along the railway line from Krugersdorp to Potchefstroom.[197]
	Trivia	*State Secretary FW Reitz's 56th birthday.*
Day 361 Sat 1900-10-06	ZAR	Commandant-General L Botha issues a proclamation from Roossenekal, warning burghers to disregard disinformation spread by the enemy about the circumstances of President Kruger's departure. The ZAR government still exists and burghers are urged to continue the struggle. He warns them against promises made by the enemy. He points out that surrendering burghers will be sent to St Helena or Ceylon as prisoners of war, thus leaving their property 'between two fires', as it is his intention to act against the property of surrendering burghers. He orders his officers: *"Do everything in your power to prevent the burghers laying down their arms. I will be compelled, if they do not listen to this, to confiscate everything moveable and also to burn their farms."*[198] General Sir Redvers Buller's Natal Field Force is disbanded.
	United Kingdom	A commission is signed separating the Office of High Commissioner in Southern Africa from the Governorship of the Cape Colony, and attaching it to Sir Alfred Milner personally.
	International	President Kruger is denied an audience with Kaizer Wilhelm II.
	Trivia	*Christiaan Botha's 36th birthday.*
Day 362 Sun 1900-10-07	*Trivia*	*Christiaan de Wet's 46th birthday.* *Heinrich Himmler is born in Munich.*
Day 363 Mon 1900-10-08	Eastern OFS	About a hundred burghers enter Ficksburg and after some street fighting, the town police flee to Basutoland.[199]
	ZAR	A detachment of the Rifle Brigade is ambushed while reconnoitring by train along the Natal railway line near Vlakfontein. A commando, led by Hans Botha, opens a terrific fire on the train, wounding seven and killing two before the British are compelled to surrender. [200]
	United Kingdom	Sir Alfred Milner is appointed as Administrator of the 'New Colonies'.
Day 364 Tue 1900-10-09	ZAR	About 300 burghers attack two railway repair parties on the Natal railway near Vlakfontein and the engineers suffer heavily before they are rescued by a column under General Clery.[201]
Day 365 Wed 1900-10-10	Eastern ZAR	Three soldiers are killed and 15 injured when a train derails on a diversion near Kaapmuiden.[202]
	Trivia	*State President SJP Kruger's 75th birthday.*
Day 366 Thu 1900-10-11	Cape Colony	**THE WAR ENTERS ITS SECOND YEAR** Martial law is withdrawn from the Steynsburg and Britstown districts.
	Trivia	*JH de la Rey's 52nd birthday.*
Day 367 Fri 1900-10-12	ZAR	While fighting a rearguard action against overwhelming odds at Witpoort, in the Mapogsgronden, General HG Gravett is fatally wounded by shrapnel, next to one of the Republicans' last field-guns.[203] General French commences his march from Machadodorp to Heidelberg.
	Western ZAR	Chief Commandant De Wet receives a request for assistance from General Liebenberg who is threatened by General Barton's operations in the Gatsrand.[204]
	Cape Colony	Indemnity and Special Tribunals Act, 1900, is promulgated in the Cape Colony

Day 368 Sat **1900-10-13**	Eastern ZAR	The ZAR government is at Boschhoek, south-west of Lydenburg. Colonel Mahon is attacked by General Tobias Smuts at Geluk, near Bergendal.
	Victoria Cross	Major ED Brown of the 14th Hussars earns a commendation for the Victoria Cross at Geduld when he rescues a sergeant whose horse has been shot. He also holds the horse of another officer, allowing him to mount, while under heavy fire.[205]
	Western ZAR	Colonel Settle arrives in Christiana with 1 350 infantry, 600 mounted men and 10 guns.
Day 369 Sun **1900-10-14**	United Kingdom Civilian life	**THE KHAKI ELECTION** The last of the British election results are announced. The final results are: Unionist-Conservatives 402 Liberals 186 Irish Nationalists 82 Lord Salisbury's 1895 Parliamentary majority of 152 is reduced by 18 seats to 134. In actual votes cast, the majority is much smaller, being 2 428 492 (54%) for the Unionists and 2 105 518 (46%) for the opposition parties. In the new cabinet, Chamberlain keeps the portfolio of Colonial Secretary, Lord Lansdowne is appointed as Foreign Secretary and is succeeded as Secretary for War by St John Brodrick. The young Winston Churchill, benefitting from the publication of his exploits in South Africa, is elected as the member for Oldham.[206]
	Western ZAR	Colonel HH Settle enters Bloemhof with a 2 000-man column and takes 50 prisoners. He is soon promoted to Brigadier-General.
Day 370 Mon **1900-10-15**	ZAR	Sir Alfred Milner arrives in Pretoria.[207] The German government requests Dr Leyds to cancel his proposed visit to Germany, as his presence would not be welcome in Berlin *"on account of possible wrong interpretations"*.[208]
Day 371 Tue **1900-10-16**	OFS	Republican forces under General JBM Hertzog attack Jagersfontein. The town is defended by two companies of Seaforth Highlanders with two guns and 100 Town Guard and police. About 25 burghers sneaks into the town and open fire on the reserve troops. They release all the prisoners in the jail and retire, having inflicted about 24 casualties (killed and wounded) on the garrison.[209]
Day 372 Wed **1900-10-17**	ZAR Civilian life	Commandant-General Botha protests Lord Roberts' conduct of the war, *"I regret to note that the barbarous actions of Your Excellency's troops, such as the blowing up and destruction of private dwellings and the removal of all food from the families of fighting burghers... have not only met with Your Excellency's approval, but are done on Your Excellency's special instructions. This spirit of revenge against burghers who are merely doing their duty according to law, may be regarded as civilised warfare by Your Excellency, but certainly not by me. I am obliged to bring to Your Excellency's notice the fact that I have resolved to carry on the war in the same humane manner as hitherto, but should I be compelled by Your Excellency's action to take reprisals, then the responsibility therefore will rest with Your Excellency."*[210]
	Western ZAR	Lord Methuen clashes with Commandant Tollie de Beer near Schweizer-Reneke.
Day 373 Thu **1900-10-18**	Eastern ZAR	The second Creusot 'Long Tom' of Sergeant-Major D Cox is dynamited by its crew three kilometres east of Heanertsburg and the wreckage is thrown into the Letaba River.[211]
	Western ZAR	General French reaches Ermelo. He is constantly harassed by snipers and short, sharp hit-and-run engagements. General Barton, operating north of Potchefstroom, is reinforced by about 500 troopers with two pom-poms. This brings his force to about 3 000 men with seven guns, including a 120mm naval gun and three pom-poms.
	Northern ZAR	General Ben Viljoen reaches Pietersburg where Commandant-General Louis Botha, the ZAR government and President Steyn discuss the future conduct of the war.

	OFS	Republican forces under Commandant Gideon Scheepers attack Philippolis with 60 burghers. The town is defended by 11 policemen and 30 armed civilians who refuse to surrender and put up a plucky defence.[212]
Day 374 Fri **1900-10-19**	ZAR	Chief Commandant De Wet executes a feint towards Tygerfontein, crosses the Vaal River and enters the ZAR to assist General Liebenberg who has been shadowing General Barton's force north of Potchefstroom.
	OFS	General JBM Hertzog's force attacks Fauresmith. The defenders, consisting of 117 Seaforth Highlanders, 20 Imperial Yeomanry and a Town Guard of 17 men, fortify themselves on a koppie outside town and hold out until the Boers retire in the evening, having inflicted nine casualties. [213]
	Natal/ZAR	General Hildyard is appointed to the command of Natal and South-eastern Transvaal.
	Western ZAR	W Robinson is shot for treason by General Liebenberg's commando.[214]
Day 375 Sat **1900-10-20**	Western ZAR *Gen. G Barton* *(War Museum of the Boer Republics)*	**THE BATTLE OF FREDERIKSTAD** Chief Commandant De Wet and General Liebenberg unite and, now numbering about 1 500 men with two Krupps and two pom-poms, they start taking positions on all sides of General Barton's camp at Frederikstad (20 kilometres north of Potchefstroom). Barton immediately signals for reinforcements and he recalls his patrols. A returning patrol of infantry and mounted troops is suddenly attacked in the flank by burghers charging through a narrow gap between two hills. The mounted men panic and head for camp, leaving the infantrymen in the lurch. Only with great difficulty and some loss do they make a fighting retreat to Barton's main position. The burghers press closer, complete the encirclement and sustain a constant long-range fusillade until twilight. [215]
	Victoria Cross	Lieutenant AC Doxat, 3rd Battalion, Imperial Yeomanry, leads a small party reconnoitring a hill held by more than 100 burghers near Zeerust. They approach to about 300 metres when they come under severe fire, forcing them to retire. Lieutenant Doxat notices a trooper who has lost his horse. He gallops back, under fierce fire, and brings the man to safety on the back of his own horse, thus earning the Victoria Cross. [216]
	Eastern ZAR	General French occupies Bethal.
	Portuguese East Africa	President Kruger and his party board the *Gelderland*, a Dutch battleship sent by Queen Wilhelmina to take them to Europe.
Day 376 Sun **1900-10-21**	Western ZAR	**THE BATTLE OF FREDERIKSTAD** During the night, General G Barton abandons his camp at the railway station, leaving only his hospital and disperses his troops on two hills, virtually splitting his force in two. He places the Welsh Fusiliers with five guns on Gun Hill, north-east of the station, the Scots Fusiliers on a long hill to the south-west. The rest of his men is thinly spread out in between. Barton is under the impression that De Wet is being pursued by a British force and he takes no offensive actions. He resigns himself to taking defensive positions and waiting for reinforcements.[217]
	OFS	The British decide to punish the civilians of Jagersfontein for aiding the commando that entered the town the previous week. Just as the inhabitants of Jagersfontein are preparing to go to church, the British authorities act. One hundred and twenty eight persons, including 70 children and Mrs Hertzog, wife of the General, and her son Albert, who has been visiting her sister, are rounded up. They are instructed to prepare for a long voyage, given a little time to get ready and are taken to Edenburg in an armed convoy.[218]
Day 377 Mon **1900-10-22**	Western ZAR	**THE BATTLE OF FREDERIKSTAD** Barton's 4,7inch (120mm) naval gun scores a direct hit on a Republican pom-pom, killing the crew.[219]

	ZAR	Lord Roberts, reacting to Botha's protests about the British conduct of the war, states that as the Boers are now waging a guerrilla war "... *which I shall be compelled to repress by those exceptional methods which civilised nations have at all times found it obligatory to use under like circumstances*".[220]
	OFS	Republican forces under General JBM Hertzog attack Luckhoff.
Day 378 Tue **1900-10-23**	Western ZAR	**THE BATTLE OF FREDERIKSTAD** The burghers push their ramparts to within 400 metres of South Hill. They fire through the British loopholes silhouetted against the sky-line, inflicting several casualties.[221]
	OFS Civilian life	Lieutenant-General A Hunter destroys the town of Bothaville, burning at least 48 houses but sparing the church and a few public buildings. The official justification for this act is only given as, "*Laying waste country used as base by enemy.*"[222]
Day 379 Wed **1900-10-24**	Western ZAR *Gen. PJ Liebenberg* *(National Cultural History Museum)*	**THE BATTLE OF FREDERIKSTAD** Chief Commandant De Wet realises that Barton's reinforcements are approaching and he and General Liebenberg decide to force the issue. De Wet has noticed that the besieged force relies on water from a small dam near the railway bridge. He orders Liebenberg and Froneman to furnish 200 volunteers to occupy positions dominating the dam. He is convinced that, if the British can be denied water, they will be forced to surrender. The planned positions are about 1 000 metres removed from the Republican lines and the men will be virtually without support and will only be able to fall back safely after dark.[223] Lord Methuen attacks General HR Lemmer at Kruis River and, after a spirited pursuit, manages to capture about 40 burghers and 21 wagons.[224]
	OFS	The small Philippolis garrison under magistrate Gostling is relieved by Barker's force after a seven-day 'siege'.
	Cape Colony	General Sir R Buller sails from Cape Town for England.
Day 380 Thu **1900-10-25**	Western ZAR *Capt. SA Cilliers* *(National History Museum)*	**THE BATTLE OF FREDERIKSTAD** Only about half of the burghers ordered to occupy the exposed position at the railway bridge between Frederikstad and Gun Hill musters. The men bravely decide to carry on nevertheless. They move out during the night and, leaving their horses about two kilometres away, they make their way to the bridge where they dig in. Shortly after daybreak the expected mule train approaches to fetch water and to water some horses. The blacks tending the horses turn and run when ordered to surrender and they are shot down. Barton initially thinks that only a few snipers are involved and sends a company to deal with them, but when they are repeatedly repulsed, he launches a full-scale two-pronged attack, using five companies, against the isolated burghers. Elsewhere De Wet directs his attack at Barton's main positions. Barton comes under fierce fire and is hard pressed until reinforcements led by Colonel HT Hicks start arriving from Welverdiend Station, where they have detrained. The burghers near the railway bridge put up a stubborn resistance, but with their ammunition running low, they are forced to make a fast retreat over open veld towards the river and are mown down by artillery firing from high ground. In the confusion some burghers put up white flags while others continue firing. Liebenberg retires towards Klerksdorp while De Wet heads back to the Free State. The burghers suffer heavily — losing about 80 killed, wounded and captured. Among the wounded is Captain Cilliers of the OFS Signal Corps, a grandson of the Voortrekker leader. In retaliation for the alleged abuse of the white

	OFS	flag, the British prevent a Republican doctor from attending to the wounded.[225] Seventy men of General JBM Hertzog's commando attacks Jacobsdal, defended by 45 Cape Town Highlanders and eight policemen. They sneak into town and at 03:00 they open fire on the troops' tents pitched on the market square, killing 14 and wounding 13 of the 34 troops billeted under canvas. The rest of the troops hold out until relieved by a force from Modder River.[226] At Damplaas, near Boshof, Commandant Badenhorst liberates two elderly burghers from the 30-man British patrol who has captured them.[227]
	Gen. JBM Hertzog *(War Museum of the Boer Republics)* International	The *Gelderland* with President Kruger and his party arrives at Dar-es-Salaam.[228]
	Trivia	*Sir NG Lyttelton's 55th birthday.*
Day 381 Fri **1900-10-26**	ZAR	General French reaches Heidelberg. He reports armed blacks amongst the Republican forces harassing him between Barberton and Heidelberg. During the preceding fortnight he has suffered about 100 casualties and lost 320 horses, 1 230 oxen and 55 wagons while taking only nine burghers prisoner and accepting 49 voluntary surrenders.[229] General Gerhardus Hendrik Gravett dies at Roossenekal from shrapnel wounds sustained at Witpoort, Mapochsgronden, on 12 October.
	OFS	General CE Knox and Colonel Le Gallais head for Tygerpoort and Reitzburg to head off De Wet.
	Southern OFS	The Koffiefontein garrison, made up of miners and policemen under the command of Captain Robertson, repulse a Republican attack led by General JBM Hertzog. A 'siege' ensues and a local entrepreneur, emulating Baden-Powell, promptly prints 'siege money', mostly to be sold to collectors.
Day 382 Sat **1900-10-27**	ZAR	Republican leaders, including President Steyn, Commandant-General Botha and Generals De la Rey and Smuts, meet for a council of war at Cyferfontein in the Magaliesberg, about 120 kilometres west of Pretoria. It is decided to concentrate for an attack on the Rand mines and to invade the Cape Colony.[230]
	OFS/ZAR	Pursued by columns under General Knox and Colonel Le Gallais, De Wet is prevented from crossing the Vaal River at Schoeman's Drift and is blocked at Buffelshoek. He crosses by moonlight at Rensburg Drift, near Parys, and is surprised by Colonel Le Gallais' Australians. They open up on the Republican laager in the riverbed with a pom-pom and a field battery. A Republican ammunition wagon explodes and the burghers speed off in all directions. De Wet loses two field-guns and eight wagons and suffers 24 casualties. Le Gallais wastes time crossing the river and De Wet gets away cleanly, aided by a violent thunderstorm.[231]
Day 383 Sun **1900-10-28**	ZAR	Sir A Milner protests the military's actions in a letter to Chamberlain. Punitive measures against the usages of war, he says, can be justified; but the *indiscriminate burning of all houses in a particular neighbourhood, simply to make it untenable by the enemy... To that, I object, thinking it (1) barbarous, and (2) ineffectual.*[232]
	International	The *Gelderland* with President Kruger and his party leaves Dar-es-Salaam.[233]
Day 384 Mon **1900-10-29**	OFS	Chief Commandant De Wet outspans at Winkel Drift on the Renoster River. He sends Froneman on to Bothaville and he proceeds to Ventersdorp with a small escort to meet President Steyn.
Day 385 Tue **1900-10-30**	ZAR	Burghers TC Lombard, PS Fourie and JA Basson are executed after being found guilty by a British court martial. After surrendering during the battle of Frederikstad, they picked up their rifles and resumed firing, killing a British officer.[234] ZAR government leaves Boschhoek, south-west of Lydenburg.

	Cape Colony	The women and children from Jagersfontein, joined by a similar group from Fauresmith, are housed in iron shanties on the race-course outside Port Elizabeth.[235]
Day 386 Wed **1900-10-31**	ZAR	President Steyn and Chief Commandant De Wet meet at Bulskop, south of Ventersdorp. The President's reports on the dire situation in the eastern ZAR convince them that an invasion of the Cape Colony is now necessary to relieve pressure on the ZAR and Commandant-General Botha.[236]
	Eastern ZAR	**START OF THE SECOND REPUBLICAN (GUERRILLA) OFFENSIVE** The ZAR government is at Draaikraal, east of Roossenekal.
	OFFICIAL REPORTS **Farm burning:** **Concentration camps:** **Communications:**	One-hundred and eighty-nine buildings have been destroyed by British troops. [237] A 'refugee camp' has been established at Port Elizabeth.[238] The railway lines have been cut 32 times during October.[239]
1900	SPRING	**NOVEMBER**
Day 387 Thu **1900-11-01**	OFS	Major-General Bruce Hamilton destroys Ventersburg, burning most of the houses and buildings.[240] C Pienaar is hanged in Bloemfontein after being found guilty of murder and being an accessory after murder.[241]
	Eastern ZAR	Major General Smith-Dorrien and Colonel Spens start a night march from Belfast in the direction of Vanwyksvlei.
Day 388 Fri **1900-11-02**	Eastern ZAR	Battered by a raging blizzard, Major General Smith-Dorrien decides to abandon his operation and orders his force to retire to Belfast. At Vanwyksvlei Republican forces attack the retreating British and Canadians. Lieutenant Chalmers displays conspicuous bravery by sacrificing his life in rescuing his superior officer. The troops extricate themselves with 17 casualties.[242]
	International	President Kruger and his party arrive at Djibouti in French-Somaliland.[243]
Day 389 Sat **1900-11-03**	Western ZAR	President Steyn and Chief Commandant De Wet address burghers on the market square of Klerksdorp. President Steyn says: *"Proclamation! What does the Boer care for a British Proclamation? The British military authorities are at their wit's end what to do. They issue proclamation after proclamation, one contradicting the other, and no one can understand them! They must not think they can conquer the republics by proclamation."*[244]
	OFS	After a 'siege' lasting nine days, Koffiefontein is relieved by a force led by Colonel Sir Charles Parsons. General JBM Hertzog's commando withdraws.
Day 390 Sun **1900-11-04**		
Day 391 Mon **1900-11-05**	OFS	As Colonel Le Gallais approaches the ruins of Bothaville with three companies mounted infantry, two companies imperial yeomanry, a few Australian Bushmen and four guns, they are fired on by De Wet's guns on the south bank of the Vals River. The British send two companies across the river to attack the Boer flanks, but it is soon too dark to continue and they cannot do more than establish pickets on the south bank. The rest of the force camps on the town square. De Wet's scouts see the smoke rising from their fires and relax. The laager outspans at Doornkraal Farm about eight kilometres south of the river.[245] Lieutenant-General Hunter succeeds General Kelly-Kenny as commander in Bloemfontein.

Day 392 Tue **1900-11-06**	OFS	**THE BATTLE OF BOTHAVILLE OR DOORNKRAAL** Colonel Le Gallais leave Bothaville at 04:00 and a company of mounted infantry stumbles on the sleeping Boer picket and captures them without firing a shot. Realising that De Wet's force must be close, they send for reinforcements and gallop on and at 05:30, they discover the sleeping laager at Doornkraal. They dismount and open fire at less than 300 metres. The surprise is complete. Panic-stricken the burghers mount and gallop off, leaving behind their field-guns and about 130 of their comrades whose horses have stampeded. These burghers take cover behind a low garden wall and furiously return fire. Two of the British field-guns arrive, their lead horses are immediately killed, they unlimber and promptly come into action. Some of the mounted infantry occupy a sheep kraal as more troops and field-guns arrive. Le Gallais sends urgent messages for reinforcements when he notices that De Wet has rallied the fleeing burghers who are returning to attack the British left flank. Le Gallais and Ross enter the deserted farmhouse and they are shot through the windows by the burghers behind the garden wall 120 metres away — Le Gallais falls mortally wounded. General CE Knox's force, encamped about 12 kilometres north of Bothaville, hears Le Gallais guns go into action and Colonel De Lisle gallops to their assistance, followed by all available men. Arriving on the scene, he finds De Wet's counterattack developing on three sides. He immediately takes command and orders turning movements by strong forces against the attacking burghers who are soon forced to fall back. At about 09:00 he orders a bayonet charge against the isolated survivors behind the garden wall by the 5th Mounted Infantry and about 80 West Australians. The burghers surrender. Chief Commandant De Wet and President Steyn have escaped with most of their men, but the Republicans suffers heavily — 17 are killed, 17 wounded and 97 unwounded are taken captive. Six field-guns, including two taken at Colenso and Sannah's Post, a pom-pom and a machine gun are captured and although their ammunition has almost been exhausted, De Wet is left without any artillery. The British lose 38 killed and wounded, including the brave Le Gallais, who expires at 20:30.[246]
	Eastern ZAR	Major General Smith-Dorrien again marches eastwards from Belfast.
	Trivia	*Operetta composer Sir Arthur Sullivan dies.*
Day 393 Wed **1900-11-07**	ZAR **Victoria Cross**	**THE BATTLE OF LELIEFONTEIN** At Witkloof, southeast of Belfast, a small commando under General J Fourie attacks Major General Smith-Dorrien's force consisting of 1 400 men and six field-guns. Smith-Dorrien again orders retreat and his Canadian rearguard is almost cut off at Leliefontein on the Komati River. Only the extreme bravery of Sergeant EG Holland, Lieutenant RW Turner and Lieutenant HZC Cockburn, Royal Canadian Dragoons, succeeds in repulsing a determined Republican attempt to seize the Canadian field-guns. The burghers charge, firing from the saddle and their assault is stopped within 70 metres of the guns. General Fourie and Commandant H Prinsloo, both from Carolina, are killed while another Republican general, General J Grobler, is wounded.[247] The Canadian Dragoons suffer 31 casualties out of the 95 men engaged.[248]
	United Kingdom	St John Brodrick sends a telegram to Lord Roberts: *"Severe methods are inevitable, and in their ultimate result humane as tending to bring the war to a close."*[249]
Day 394 Thu **1900-11-08**	ZAR	Major General Smith-Dorrien fights rearguard actions as he retreats to Belfast.
Day 395 Fri **1900-11-09**		
Day 396 Sat **1900-11-10**	OFS Civilian life	General Bruce Hamilton reports that Ventersburg has been partially destroyed (1900-11-01) and supplies have been removed due to repeated attacks on the railway line in

	OFS	the vicinity. The town will not be resupplied by the British and the Republican commandants will have to furnish the inhabitants with supplies unless they want them to perish. For this act David Lloyd George later refers to Hamilton as *"... a brute and a disgrace to the uniform he wears"*.[250] Chief Commandant De Wet and President Steyn with 200 men cross and destroy the railway line near Doornspruit.[251]
	Western ZAR	Lord Methuen fights an inconclusive action with General HR Lemmer at Wonderfontein, near Klein Marico, and 40 burghers are killed or captured.
Day 397 Sun **1900-11-11**	Western ZAR	Lord Methuen returns to Lichtenburg.
Day 398 Mon **1900-11-12**	Cape Colony	There are now between 300 and 400 women and children in the camp for 'undesirables' outside Port Elizabeth. A lay preacher, who has been allowed to hold a church service there, reports that their circumstances are unacceptable. Some are housed in tents and are not allowed to use spirit lamps or petroleum stoves (for fear of fire).[252]
Day 399 Tue **1900-11-13**	OFS	Recovering from his defeat at Bothaville, Chief Commandant De Wet has again mustered 1 500 men from the Winburg, Harrismith and Kroonstad districts. He is joined by General Philip Botha and Commandants Lategan, Theron and Haasbroek. With only a single field-gun he starts moving south from Doornberg, near Winburg, on his mission to invade the Cape Colony.
	ZAR	The ZAR government leaves Draaikraal, east of Roossenekal.
Day 400 Wed **1900-11-14**	OFS	Chief Commandant De Wet's force passes Korannaberg, heading south.
	ZAR	The ZAR government arrives at Steelpoort River, near Tautesberg.
Day 401 Thu **1900-11-15**	International	The *Gelderland* arrives at Port Said.[253]
Day 402 Fri **1900-11-16**	OFS	**THE START OF THE 'SECOND DE WET HUNT'** Skirting the Bloemfontein-Thaba Nchu defensive line, Chief Commandant De Wet sends General Philip Botha to attack two of the small fortified posts forming a chain of defensive positions about 2 000 metres apart while he forces a passage through Springhaansnek.[254]
	Western ZAR	Major-General CWH Douglas clashes with General PJ Liebenberg of the Potchefstroom commando near Klerksdorp. The burghers withdraw, allowing Generals Barton and Douglas to occupy Klerksdorp. They arrest several persons and take ten horses, three mules and 270 head of cattle.[255]
	Trivia	*Kaizer Wilhelm II is attacked by a woman wielding an axe, but is not hurt.*
Day 403 Sat **1900-11-17**		
Day 404 Sun **1900-11-18**	OFS	Chief Commandant De Wet reconnoitres the British positions around Dewetsdorp.
	Civilian life	Preparing to leave South Africa, Field-Marshal Lord Roberts issues his last 'scorched earth' instruction: *"All cattle and foodstuffs are to be removed from all farms; if that is found to be impossible, they are to be destroyed, whether the owner is present or not."* See Articles 45, 50 and 52 of the Hague Convention 1899-07-29.[256]
Day 405 Mon **1900-11-19**	ZAR	General Ben Viljoen and Commandant Chris Muller attack Balmoral and Wilge River Stations. An outlying post near Balmoral is captured with a loss of 43 men to the British but the attacks fail in their main objectives.[257]

	Western ZAR	The Queensland Mounted Infantry is involved in skirmishes with forces under Generals Erasmus and Viljoen at Rhenosterkop near the Olifants River. Lord Methuen arrives back in Zeerust.
Day 406 Tue **1900-11-20**	OFS	The pursuit of Chief Commandant De Wet starts in earnest when General CE Knox arrives at Edenburg Station. He detrains his force of about 800 men and takes overall command of columns under Colonels Pilcher, Herbert and Barker.
	Cape Colony Black involvement	Bezuidenhout invades the Maclear district with 53 men and engages Captain H Elliot and 300 black levies at Gatberg, near Ugie. Captain Elliot, son of Chief Magistrate Sir Henry Elliot, is killed and the burghers withdraw with a loss of six men.[258]
	Ceylon	Prisoner of war L Bredenhamer is killed by a guard while trying to escape from Diyatalawa camp.[259]
Day 407 Wed **1900-11-21**	OFS	**THE BATTLE OF DEWETSDORP** Major WG Massey is in command of the garrison consisting of three companies of the Gloucester Regiment, one of the Highland Light Infantry, 50 mounted infantry, a few police and other soldiers totalling about 450 men with two guns and a Maxim. He has positioned his main force on the heights west of town with a smaller force on the eastern side. Chief Commandant Christiaan R de Wet, with Lategan and Philip Botha, attack from three sides, taking one defensive post after the other.[260]
	Natal	The first burghers from the Harrismith district arrive at Pietermaritzburg to be housed in a camp for 'refugees and undesirables'.[261]
Day 408 Thu **1900-11-22**	OFS	**THE BATTLE OF DEWETSDORP** Approaching from the east, Field-cornet Wessel Wessels surrounds and captures an isolated post on Lonely Hill and the British are also soon forced to abandon their post called Crow's Nest. The Republicans can now approach the main eastern position along a donga and the Highlanders abandon this strongpoint and fall back to the main position to the west. Here, the trenches are overcrowded and efforts to extend their positions are hampered by a shortage of picks and shovels.[262]
	Victoria Cross	Private CT Kennedy, 1st Battalion, the Highland Light Infantry, Dewetsdorp
	Trivia	*A partial eclipse of the sun is visible in the northern Free State.*[263]
Day 409 Fri **1900-11-23**	OFS	**THE BATTLE OF DEWETSDORP** A Gloucester trench north of town is taken after some resistance and the burghers can now direct plunging fire into the main position. On the eastern side, the Republican Krupp opens fire from Lonely Hill and, as the day progresses, the defenders' supply of water and ammunition becomes critical. At 16:00, a junior officer in an isolated gun pit raises the white flag but it is immediately ordered down. Soon afterwards on an absurd report that the burghers are murdering the wounded it is raised again and Dewetsdorp, named after his father, is captured by Chief Commandant CR de Wet. British losses amount to 14 killed, 52 wounded, 30 slightly wounded and 384 taken prisoner.[264] Lieutenant Boyle of the Orange River Colony police is captured, court-martialled for treason by De Wet and acquitted.[265] March Phillipps, an officer serving under Colonel Rimington, writes from Frankfort, *"Farm-burning goes merrily on, and our course through the country is marked as in prehistoric ages by pillars of smoke by day and fire by night. We usually burn from six to a dozen farms a day; these being about all that in this sparsely-inhabited country we encounter. I do not gather that any special reason or cause is alleged or proved against the farms burnt... Anyway, we find*

		that one reason or another generally covers pretty nearly every farm we come to, and so to save trouble we burn the lot without enquiry..."[266]
	Eastern ZAR	The town of Dullstroom is razed to the ground by Major-General Smith-Dorrien, leaving only the church standing.[267]
	Cape Colony	Lieutenant Leopold Neumeyer of the Orange River Colony police, responsible for the burning and plundering of Boer farms in the southern Free State, is ambushed and killed at Stolzkraal, north of Aliwal North, allegedly on Scheepers and Fouchee's orders. His companion, Van Aswegen, escapes with a bullet through his hat.[268]
	International	President SJP Kruger disembarks at Marseilles and receives a tumultuous welcome. [269]
Day 410 Sat **1900-11-24**	OFS	A relieving column under Colonels Barker and Herbert arrives outside Dewetsdorp but, finding the burghers firmly entrenched, can do no more than open up ineffectual long-range firing.[270]
	Cape Colony Civilian life	An article, based on a report from Heidelberg, accusing General French of shelling a farmhouse, appears in the Cape magazine, *Ons Land*. When informed that there are women and children in the house, French is reported to say, *"I don't care. Shoot the beggars. Afrikanerdom must be wiped off the earth."* It is reported that five field-guns shelled and destroyed the house and no assistance was rendered to the inhabitants. The editor FS Malan is arrested and subsequently sentenced to a year's imprisonment for criminal libel.[271]
Day 411 Sun **1900-11-25**	OFS	Chief Commandant De Wet leaves a small rearguard as a blind and, taking his prisoners with him, abandons Dewetsdorp, continuing his march southwards.[272]
	ZAR	Sir Alfred Milner leaves Pretoria for Bloemfontein. At Kroonstad, the train is stopped as the line has been cut at Ventersburg Road.[273]
	International	President Kruger arrives in Paris to an even bigger welcome and is visited by the French President, M. Emile Loubet.[274]
Day 412 Mon **1900-11-26**		
Day 413 Tue **1900-11-27**	OFS	General Knox's advance units clash with Chief Commandant De Wet's rearguard at Helvetia between Dewetsdorp and Smithfield, very near to Leeukop, the birthplace of General De Wet.
	ZAR	Sir A Milner's departure for Cape Town is delayed by a 'blow-up on the line near Kaffir River'.[275]
Day 414 Wed **1900-11-28**	OFS	General Knox arrives at Smithfield.
Day 415 Thu **1900-11-29**	Eastern ZAR	**BATTLE OF RENOSTERKOP** In the last set-piece battle of the war, General B Viljoen's entrenched position manned by about 2 000 men 24 kilometres north of Bronkhorstspruit is attacked by Major-General Paget with about 2 500 troops and at least nine field-guns. Paget's orthodox attack, which starts at about 04:00, entails a strong frontal infantry assault on Viljoen's main position, supported by artillery, with his mounted troops attempting outflanking moves on the left and right. Both flank attacks fail and despite repeated charges, the infantry attack is stopped. At 07:30 Paget's entire line has become static and the troops are ordered to entrench. At 19:00 Commandant Chris Muller launches a vicious counter-attack on the New Zealanders, but he is repulsed after a battle lasting about an hour. Viljoen abandons his positions in the dark, losing

		two men killed and 22 wounded, against 15 killed and 72 wounded on the British side.[276]
	ZAR	Ex-General Schoeman, detained after being found in the company of members of the Transvaal Constabulary, is again acquitted on a charge of high treason by a court martial in Nylstroom. It is decided to keep him in detention in the Pietersburg jail.[277] **LORD KITCHENER SUCCEEDS LORD ROBERTS AS COMMANDER-IN-CHIEF IN SOUTH AFRICA**
	OFS	Captain Pretorius joins Chief Commandant De Wet's column with two hundred men from Fauresmith and Philipolis.
Day 416 Fri **1900-11-30**	OFS	Chief Commandant De Wet is joined by General Piet Fourie and Captain Gideon Scheepers. He now commands about 2 500 well-mounted men with several spare horses. General Knox, marching along the Caledon River, has lost touch with De Wet's column.[278]
	ZAR	The ZAR government reaches Paardeplaats, near Tautesberg.
	Trivia	*Winston LS Churchill's 26th birthday.*
	OFFICIAL REPORTS **Farm burning:** Two-hundred and twenty-six buildings have been destroyed by British troops.[279] **Concentration camps:** 'Refugee camps' have been established at Harrismith and Standerton.[280] **Communications:** The railway lines have been cut 30 times during November.[281]		
1900	SUMMER	**DECEMBER**
Day 417 Sat **1900-12-01**	OFS	General Knox and Colonels Pilcher and Barker enter Bethulie.
	Western ZAR	Lord Methuen issues an order banning Mrs Nonnie de la Rey from coming within ten miles (16 kilometres) of Lichtenburg. She loads a wagon, harnesses a spider, takes her children, three black servants, a few cows, sheep and chickens, leaves their farm Elandsfontein, and she starts wandering. Never captured, she is to roam about in the veld for the next nineteen months.[282] A convoy containing some Christmas delicacies for Rustenburg and other smaller garrisons in the region, leaves Pretoria.[283] Lord Kitchener orders General RAP Clements to operate in the Hekpoort Valley between the Witwatersrand and the Magaliesberg, north of Krugersdorp.[284]
	Cape Town	Sir Alfred Milner arrives in Cape Town.
Day 418 Sun **1900-12-02**	OFS	Chief Commandant De Wet engages Colonel Herbert at Goede Hoop, between Smithfield and Bethulie. General Knox immediately sends reinforcements and De Wet breaks off and heads towards Carmel where he is joined by Hertzog's commando.[285]
	South-east ZAR	
	International	The Utrecht garrison skirmishes with about 200 burghers outside town.
Day 419 Mon **1900-12-03**	Western ZAR	**THE BATTLE OF BUFFELSPOORT OR VANWYKSPRUIT** (2,5 kilometres west of Mooinooi) A 138-wagon convoy bound for Rustenburg is commanded by Colonel Woolridge-Gordon with a detachment of West Yorkshires and two guns. General De la Rey, well-

202

		informed on its route and movements, plans an attack, in conjunction with General JC Smuts and Commandant FJ Boshoff, on the convoy as it enters the narrow Buffels-poort. He splits his force into three parts to approach the rendezvous position from different directions. Contrary to usual practice, the convoy has pushed on during the night to avoid a possible ambush in the Buffelspoortnek. At 03:00, General Smuts, the first to arrive, finds, to his dismay, that the convoy has proceeded beyond the planned point of attack and that Woolridge-Gordon has wisely positioned soldiers in two positions on higher ground covering the pass' exit and another in a donga covering the road in their rear. An attempt to dislodge some of the soldiers is met with concentrated fire and De la Rey is forced to change his plans. Sticking to his main aim — the capture of the convoy — he decides to keep the soldiers in the hills pinned down and to concentrate his main force against the troops guarding the wagons. At 13:00 the donga is overrun and the convoy is in Republican hands. General De la Rey orders Boshoff's men to remove as many wagons as they can, while the rest of the burghers attempt to force Woolridge-Gordon to surrender. The troops on the lower hill resist furiously with their guns firing grape at point-blank range but the higher hill is stormed and taken at 16:00. De la Rey decides to call it a day as his burghers are increasingly distracted by the prospect of looting the wagons rather than concentrating on fighting the enemy. They remove what they can, set fire to the rest and move off before reinforcements can arrive. The British lose 18 killed, 46 wounded and 54 taken prisoner, while De la Rey suffers 'light' casualties — two killed and seven wounded — and captures 138 supply wagons and 1 832 oxen.[287] General Clements leaves Krugersdorp but he is too late to influence events at Buffelspoort.
	ZAR	Commandant-General Botha issues a circular instructing officers and landdrosts to compile lists of burghers in their areas who have surrendered their arms to the enemy and have taken the oath of neutrality. These burghers are to be called up again and, on refusal, they must be sent to the nearest jail for punishment according to law. Their moveable property must be taken and a proper inventory must be made. Care must be taken that sufficient livelihood is left for the wife and family. All passes or permits issued by the enemy must be returned by burghers who have again taken up arms. He also issues an 'oath of neutrality counter-oath' for burghers who are taking up arms again: *"Form of oath* *I, the undersigned burgher of the South African Republic, declare under oath that the oath of neutrality taken by me, in the hands of the enemy, was taken without the sanction of my military officers, and I consider the same null and void.* *Louis Botha* *Commandant-General."*[288]
Day 420 Tue **1900-12-04**	OFS	General De Wet has shaken off his pursuers and, in pouring rain, he moves to Kareefontein on the Caledon River.
	United Kingdom	St John Brodrick, Secretary of War, sends a telegram to Lord Kitchener: *"Statements are freely circulated here asserting that burning of farms has taken place on an enormous scale. According to one version, a third of the whole number of farms has been destroyed. Could you supply us with any information on this point?"*[289]
Day 421 Wed **1900-12-05**	OFS	Rain and flooded drifts on the Orange River force Chief Commandant De Wet to abandon his projected raid into the Cape Colony. He orders Hertzog, Kritzinger and Scheepers to invade the eastern and midland districts of the Cape Colony with smaller detachments.
Day 422 Thu **1900-12-06**	South-east ZAR	The Wakkerstroom garrison is shelled by a single gun and a pom-pom in a bombardment that lasts almost an hour.

	Cape Colony	The Worcester Congress, organised by the Afrikanerbond and Cape Afrikaners, adopts resolutions demanding an end to the war, the retention of independence by the Republics, the right of the people of the Colony to manage their own affairs and expressing grave disapproval of Milner's policies.[290]
Day 423 Fri **1900-12-07**	Northern ZAR	General CF Beyers leaves Warmbaths and marches south-westwards.
	OFS	Chief Commandant De Wet's scouts are driven off by 40 members of the Highland Light Infantry guarding the post at Kommissie Bridge on the Caledon River. De Wet brings the guns he has captured at Dewetsdorp into action but the valiant group rejects his offer to surrender and they keep up their determined defence. De Wet retires and crosses the river elsewhere. The flooded river runs deep and his guns are completely submerged. [291]
	United Kingdom	Mr Chamberlain expounds his planned future policy with regard to 'the new colonies' in the House of Commons.
Day 424 Sat **1900-12-08**	Western ZAR	General Clements makes camp at Nooitgedacht at the foot of a sheer 300 metre-high cliff, guarding the mouth of a narrow gorge.
	Cape Colony Black involvement	Alfred Malapi is executed by a British firing squad in Aliwal North for spying. According to a British intelligence officer, Malapi *dressed exactly like one of our men, Khaki coat, breeches, puttees, and an army cap*". It seems as if he has masqueraded as a labourer in British service for months while supplying Republican forces with information.[292]
Day 425 Sun **1900-12-09**	Western ZAR	General HR Lemmer is wounded in action at Varkfontein between Lichtenburg and Marico during an attack on a convoy heading for Lichtenburg with an escort commanded by Lieutenant-Colonel Money.[293]
Day 426 Mon **1900-12-10**	OFS	Chief Commandant De Wet rests his men at Helvetia, between Smithfield and Dewetsdorp.
	ZAR	Meyer de Kock, an ordinary burgher but a prominent local leader and official before the war, lays down his arms in the Belfast district.[294]
Day 427 Tue **1900-12-11**	South-eastern ZAR	General Chris Botha, commanding about 1 000 burghers, begins his planned attack on the Vryheid garrison consisting of the Lancaster Regiment, some mounted infantry, two guns and a Maxim — about 900 men. With only a small force stationed in town, the main British positions are on the flat top of Lancaster Hill and an adjoining lower plateau. During the evening, the burghers approaching from the north overwhelm and capture a 20-men outpost without firing a shot. They stealthily start creeping up the slopes of the hill.[295]
	Western ZAR	General Beyers reaches Bethanie, north-west of Brits.
	Cape Colony	After visiting his son's grave near Colenso, Lord Roberts sails from Cape Town on board *HMS Canada* for England. He sends the following telegram to Queen Victoria: "*I have just made over command of Your Majesty's Army in South Africa to Lord Kitchener, in whose judgement, discretion and valour I have the greatest confidence.*"[296] Sir Alfred Milner rejects all the resolutions adopted at the Worcester Congress.[297]
Day 428 Wed **1900-12-12**	South-eastern ZAR	**THE ATTACK ON VRYHEID** At 02:15 the Republicans open fire on the mounted infantry on the lower plateau, stampeding their horses and causing utter confusion. At 03:30 the burghers attack Lancaster Hill from three sides but they fail to gain a foothold on the crest. A furious fight for the possession of three strongpoints lasts until about 07:00 when the burgers start their retreat. The garrison lose nine killed, 20 wounded and 30 missing, presumed captured.[298]

	Western ZAR	General Beyers makes a rapid night march along a rarely used wagon track, crosses the Magaliesberg and meets General De la Rey at Boschfontein, about six kilometres west of Nooitgedacht. Together, they command about 2 500 men with five field-guns. They ride out to a hill from where they reconnoitre Clements' camp and finalise their plan of attack.[299]
	OFS	General Knox with Colonels Baker, Williams and White pursues De Wet's column north of Helvetia, but he easily outdistances them.
	Civilian life	Mr Gideon de Wet, a prominent resident of Rouxville, is sentenced to two years' imprisonment by a British court martial because he, having taken the oath of neutrality, takes a neutral stand and refuses to give information to the British forces. See Article 44 of the Hague Convention.[300]
		Sir D Barbour is commissioned to head an inquiry into the finances of the ' Transvaal' and 'O.R.C.'
Day 429 Thu **1900-12-13**	ZAR	**THE BATTLE OF NOOITGEDACHT**

On the farm Nooitgedacht, at the foot of the Magaliesberg range, Major-General RAP Clements, recently joined by Colonel Legge, commands about 2 000 men and ten field-guns. He has placed pickets in small fortified positions forming a three-kilometre perimeter on the high mountains above his camp on both sides of the gorge. In the valley, he has positioned his guns and defences in a three-kilometre radius semicircle around the mouth of the gorge, with small pickets on isolated outposts at various distances from his camp. The strongest is on a prominence called Yeomanry Hill, about 3 kilometres south-east of the camp.

General De la Rey's plan of attack calls for General CF Beyers to clear the British positions on the mountain with about 1 000 burghers, while De la Rey and Smuts, exercising independent command for the first time, will attack the main position with about 700 men.

The nature of the terrain to be covered makes it difficult to estimate the time needed by the different groups to reach their starting points. De la Rey's plans go slightly awry when his left flank under Commandant Badenhorst gains contact with the enemy outposts at about 03:30 — earlier than expected. He immediately attacks but draws fire from all sides. Both sides suffer casualties — Colonel Legge is among the first to fall — and Badenhorst is repulsed. On the mountain, the sentries are alerted by the shooting and they open fire on Krause's approaching burghers. At sunrise, Krause, on Beyers' right, starts the attack against the emplacements on the western mountain and his yelling burghers charge forward. Covering each other's advances with heavy rifle fire, Krause and Commandant MP van Staden systematically overrun the positions on the western ridge. They pour fire into the retreating troops below and support Commandants Kemp and Marais in their assault on the eastern side of the gorge. At about 07:00 the troops there also surrender and the summit is in Republican hands; the defenders suffering 97 killed or wounded. Sergeant DD Farmer, 1st Battalion, the Queen's Own Cameron Highlanders, with fifteen men, going to the assistance of the embattled pickets on the ridge, come under heavy fire. Two are killed and five are wounded, including Lieutenant Sandilands. Without hesitation, Sergeant Farmer goes to his assistance, carrying him to safety before returning to the firing line until taken prisoner. For this courageous act, he is to receive the Victoria Cross.[301]

Directing fire from the ridge, Beyers forces the major part of Clements' force to flee, enabling De la Rey to take the camp. De la Rey and Smuts, however, their line of attack having been altered by Badenhorst's early setback, are not in position to prevent Clements' retreat. Smuts is too late and Clements, leaving behind most of his supplies, reach Yeomanry Hill under the covering fire of the Yeomanry and Yorkshire Light Infantry. Again, the burghers, anxious not to lose out on the looting, are half-hearted in their pursuit of the fleeing British and are soon back at the camp to share in the booty. General Broadwood's force, less than 20 kilometres away on the northern side of the

Comdt. MP van Staden
(National Cultural History Museum)

Victoria Cross

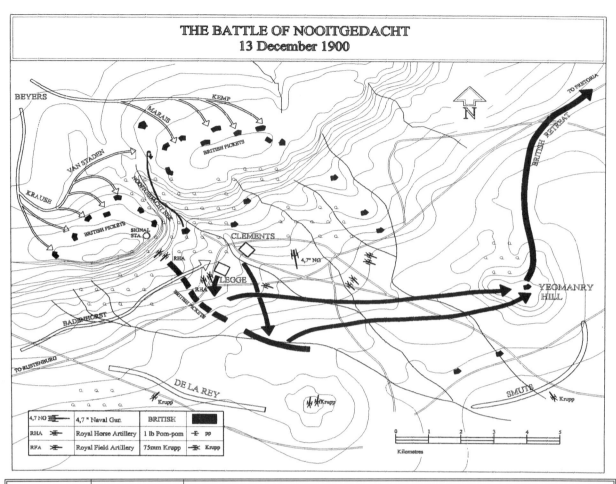

		mountain range, can hear the firing but they are put at ease when a Republican heliographist, using captured equipment, signals: *All's well, no assistance needed.*
The British casualties — the heaviest they have suffered since arriving in the Transvaal — include 109 killed, 186 wounded and 368 taken prisoner, while the Republicans lose 32 killed and 46 wounded. They also take 70 laden wagons, 200 tents, ammunition of all types, 700 horses and mules, and about 500 head of cattle. When he discovers that one of the wagons is carrying liquor, General De la Rey presents it to his prisoners and is astonished when they crowd around him, singing *For he's a jolly good fellow.*[302]
	OFS	Commandant PH Kritzinger overwhelms a party of 250 Brabant's Horse at Koesberg, near Zastron, killing or wounding 20 and taking 100 prisoners.
	United Kingdom	Mr Tim Healy, Irish MP, tells the House of Commons that *"all the British can offer the Boers is 'the pleasure' of a black magistrate, a black policeman, an English official and a band in Potchefstroom garrison playing 'God save the Queen', to remind them of old times".*[303]
	'UITSCHUDDEN'
With no facilities to detain prisoners of war, the Republicans resort to the practice of *'uitschudden'* — 'shaking out' — stripping prisoners of their uniforms and sending them back to their camp in shirt and socks or even stark naked. The British deem this to be robbery and contrary to the rules of war. The wearing of khaki by the Boers is to lead to tragic incidents in which British troops mistake the enemy for their comrades and are attacked before the mistake is realised. The Republicans, however, defend their actions by the fact that as their supplies are being cut off by the British and even the civilian clothes they have left at home have been burnt, they are forced to obtain clothes by any other means. They maintain that khaki material has been generally available before the war and that only the wearing of insignia and badges constitute the unlawful acts referred to in the Hague Convention. Confusion in the veld is also increased by the British soldiers who have discarded the pith helmets which they wore at the start of the war in favour of the slouch hats as worn by the Boers.[304]	

Day 430 Fri **1900-12-14**	Western ZAR	General Clements' battered force reaches Rietfontein, below Silkaatsnek.
	OFS	**BREAKTHROUGH AT SPRINGHAANSNEK** Chief Commandant De Wet and President Steyn decide to escape through Springhaansnek, about 24 kilometres east of Thaba Nchu. Again confronted by the fortified posts between Thaba Nchu and the Basotholand border, General Michal Prinsloo and his Bethlehem commando bravely attack two posts east of Thaba Nchu and delay an approaching column commanded by Colonel Byng. This diversion costs about eight burghers but has the desired effect. General Piet Fourie heads the main convoy and Chief Commandant De Wet the rearguard as they rush through the neck. They feint towards Thaba Phatshwa and then double back and turn north leaving the British in confusion. The burghers lose eight men killed, 17 wounded and 33 captured. Commandant Haasbroek and his small party are cut off but later break through the fortified line near the Waterworks to join the main force some days later.[305]
	Black involvement	A black newspaper in Natal *Ipepa lo Hlanga* notes the inconsistency of British political principles when applied to whites and blacks: *"What is the matter at issue between the Boers and the English (?)— one thing only — the English want a voice in the government of the Transvaal — the very thing they refuse to give us here."*
Day 431 Sat **1900-12-15**	*Trivia*	*Field-chaplain JD Kestell's 46th birthday.*
Day 432 Sun **1900-12-16**	ZAR	The Day of the Covenant is celebrated with church services and speeches by Generals De la Rey and Beyers. A cairn is erected on Schimmelkop, Buffelsfontein, south of Noupoort in the western ZAR.
	Cape Colony	**THE START OF THE SECOND REPUBLICAN INVASION OF THE CAPE COLONY** Commandant PH Kritzinger, with Captain Gideon J Scheepers as his second-in-command, Willem D Fouchee as one of his officers, and 200 men enter the Cape Colony near Norvalspont. On the same night, General JBM Hertzog crosses the Orange River at Sand Drift, near Petrusville, with a well-supplied force of about 1 200 men.[306]
Day 433 Mon **1900-12-17**	OFS	Having shrugged off his pursuers, General De Wet passes north of Korannaberg on his way to Clocolan.[307] **END OF THE 'SECOND DE WET HUNT'**
	Cape Colony	General JBM Hertzog occupies Philipstown and captures a number of horses. Sir A Milner is surprised by Hertzog's invasion and he writes to Chamberlain: *"I learned this morning that a second invasion had taken place. Where this body comes from I cannot even surmise."* On the fact that Hertzog's commando seems to be avoiding contact with British forces, he comments, *"Their obvious policy is to rush forward avoiding encounters."*[308]
Day 434 Tue **1900-12-18**	Cape Colony	General Hertzog crosses the railway line at Houtkraal, north of De Aar.[309]
Day 435 Wed **1900-12-19**	Western ZAR	**SKIRMISH AT HEKPOORT** General Clements shells a decoy group of burghers on Vaalkop. Three commandos under General De la Rey fall back systematically to lure him into a well-laid trap at Hekpoort. Just before closing the trap a report is received that General French and a huge mounted force are approaching, and the Republicans have to abandon their

	OFS Civilian life Concentration camps	ambush and retire under intense rifle fire and shelling.[310] Lord Kitchener telegraphs Lieutenant Sir Leslie Rundle, at Harrismith: *"From experience and on the advice of Boer prisoners desirous of bringing the war to a close, it has been found that by removing all men, women and children left on farms, to camps in our lines and by allowing those Boers who voluntarily surrender to live in these laagers an excellent effect is produced and many Boers surrender and the consequent failure of constant supplies from the farms greatly interfere with Boer Guerrilla operations. The Commander in Chief therefore wishes General officers Commanding and Officers Commanding Columns to carry out this policy and establish camps on the railway. All natives on farms should also be brought in. A Confidential Circular is being sent to you."*[311]
Day 436 Thu **1900-12-20**	Western ZAR	Generals De la Rey and Beyers part company — De la Rey moving west and Beyers to the north-west.
	Civilian life Concentration camps	A proclamation issued by Lord Kitchener in Pretoria, states: *"It is hereby notified to all Burghers that if, after this date, they voluntarily surrender they will be allowed to live with their families in Government Laagers until such time as the Guerrilla Warfare now being carried on will admit of their returning safely to their homes. All stock and property brought in at the time of surrender of such Burghers will be respected and paid for, if requisitioned by Military Authorities."*[312]
	Cape Colony	Martial law is again proclaimed in the northern Cape Colony.
Day 437 Fri **1900-12-21**	ZAR Civilian life Concentration camps Black involvement	In a memorandum to general officers, Lord Kitchener points out the advantages of bringing into the camps *"all men, women and children and natives from the Districts which the enemy's band persistently occupy"*. This will be *"the most effective method of limiting the endurance of the Guerrillas...* *The women and children brought in should be divided in two categories, viz.: 1st. Refugees, and the families of Neutrals, non-combatants, and surrendered Burghers. 2nd. Those whose husbands, fathers and sons are on Commando. The preference in accommodation, etc. should of course be given to the first class.* *With regard to natives, it is not intended to clear... locations, but only such (blacks) and their stock as are on Boer farms."*[313] See Articles 44, 45 and 50 of the Hague Convention.
	ZAR	The inaugural meeting of the Burgher Peace Committee is held in Pretoria and ex-Generals APJ Cronje, Piet de Wet, Mr Meyer de Kock and others are elected to the leadership and subcommittees.[314] Lord Kitchener discusses his proposed policies with this group: *"He was about to form Burgher Camps at centres on the railway, and would then collect all men, women and children of the various districts. Stock and (blacks) from the farms would also be brought in."*[315]
Day 438 Sat **1900-12-22**	Cape Colony	Commandant Nieuwoudt enters Britstown unopposed, after the town's garrison, consisting of 15 soldiers and seven policemen, flees on his approach.[316]
	United Kingdom	More reinforcements are ordered out to South Africa.
Day 439 Sun **1900-12-23**	Cape Colony	General Hertzog joins Commandant Nieuwoudt at Britstown.
Day 440 Mon **1900-12-24**	ZAR	Colonel SPE Trichard's corps captures a train loaded with supplies and Christmas presents destined for the garrisons at Middelburg and Lydenburg at Uitkyk Station.[317] Commandant Buys is attacked on the Rietvlei Hills near Vlakfontein. The burghers turn the tables on the 13th Hussars and the Rifle Brigade, who are forced to retreat steadily under heavy fire in a running battle that lasts until nightfall.[318]

	Black involvement	A certain Sekota is hanged at Barberton after being found guilty by a British court martial of *"secretly and treacherously endeavouring to obtain information regarding British forces"* and for cattle theft.[319]
	Cape Colony	General Hertzog leaves Britstown and moves to Dr Smartt's farm, Houwater, 32 kilometres to the north-west. Lord Kitchener arrives at Noupoort to organize the expulsion of the invading Republican commandos from Cape Colony.
Day 441 Tue **1900-12-25**	South-east ZAR	CHRISTMAS — the second Christmas of the war **THE ATTACK ON UTRECHT** About 300 local burghers and a few foreign volunteers attack the 673-men strong Utrecht garrison but the British have been forewarned and easily repulse the attack. Three Russian volunteers, Captains Petrov, Duplov and Leo Pokrowsky, are killed in action.[320]
	Cape Colony	A British force under Brigadier-General HH Settle reoccupies Britstown.
Day 442 Wed **1900-12-26**	Southeast ZAR	BOXING DAY Commandant Buys attacks the South Rand mine, near Greylingstad. A part of Lieutenant-Colonel Colvile's column is attacked and the baggage train is especially hard pressed. A part of the guard is cut off and has to surrender. The main column arrives and the burghers are forced to retreat, leaving some of their prisoners behind. The British lose 11 killed, 44 wounded and 19 taken prisoner.[321]
	ZAR	General PR Viljoen's commando attacks the New Kleinfontein mine on the East Rand and inflicts £200 000 worth of damage.[322]
	Cape Colony	Brigadier-General HH Settle attacks General Hertzog at Houwater but is repulsed. Hertzog retires north-westwards in the direction of Prieska but his ambulance under Dr Ramsbottom falls into British hands and is sent to Bloemfontein, contrary to the customs of war.[323]
Day 443 Thu **1900-12-27**	Western ZAR	JAB de Beer and PC de Bruin are captured, tried and found guilty of treason and shot by De la Rey's commando at Lapfontein, near Klerksdorp. HC Boshoff is reprieved because of his youth.
	ZAR	Sir A Milner writes on his proposed immigration plans, *"... on the political side, I attach the greatest importance of all to the increase of the British population... If, ten years hence, there are three men of British race to two of Dutch, the country will be safe and prosperous...We not only want a majority of British, but we want a fair margin...* *Next to the composition of the population, the thing that matters most is education... in the new Colonies the case will be easier to deal with, provided we make English the language of the higher education. Dutch should only be used to teach English, and English to teach everything else."*[324]
	Cape Colony	General Hertzog enters Vosburg unopposed, after the small Town Guard surrenders. Martial law is extended to Beaufort West and Carnavon.
Day 444 Fri **1900-12-28**	ZAR	On Meyer de Kock's proposal, the Burgher Peace Committee elects 24 surrendered burghers to be sent to the Republican lines with pamphlets to try and convince fighting burghers of the hopelessness of their cause and to entice them to surrender.[325]
Day 445 Sat **1900-12-29**	Eastern ZAR	**THE BATTLE OF HELVETIA** General Ben Viljoen, assisted by Commandants Muller and Viljoen, launches a two-pronged night attack on a British force of 350 men under the command of Major Cotton near Helvetia, about 10 kilometres north of Machadodorp. The well-fortified British positions are spread along four koppies and form part of the fortified line between Lydenburg and the Delagoa line. Viljoen's forces totalling about 580 attack at

	 *Comdt. CH Muller* (War Museum of the Boer Republics)	03:30 and achieve a total surprise. Muller attacks Gun Hill, the main position and takes it. Major Cotton is wounded and the British, with the exception of a small force on King's Kopje is forced to surrender. The British artillery on Swartkoppies attempt to support their comrades but their shelling is not effective. British losses amount to 11 killed, 29 wounded and 253 captured, while the Republicans suffer 'light' casualties, capture the 'Lady Roberts', a 4,7 inch (120mm) naval gun and burn all the supplies they cannot remove.[326]
Day 446 Sun 1900-12-30		
Day 447 Mon 1900-12-31	**OFFICIAL REPORTS** Farm burning: Concentration camps: Communications:	Six buildings have been destroyed by British troops.[327] 'Refugee camps' have been established at Edenburg, Irene, Johannesburg and Renoster River.[328] The railway lines have been cut 21 times during December.[329]

NOTES:

JULY 1900 – DECEMBER 1900 (CHANGES)

1. VAN SCHOOR, De Wet-Annale No 4, p 21
2. *Ibid*, De Wet-Annale No 4, p 12
3. AMERY, *op cit*, vol, IV, p 348
4. SPIES, Methods of Barbarism?, p 106
5. PLOEGER, *op cit*, p 34:29
6. AMERY, *op cit*, vol IV, pp 305-306
7. *Ibid*, vol IV, p 348
8. *Ibid*, vol IV, p 348
9. *Ibid*, vol IV, p 308
10. AMERY, *op cit*, vol IV, pp 308-309
    VAN SCHOOR, De Wet-Annale No 4, p 12
    WESSELS, Egodokumente..., p 27
11. BREYTENBACH, *op cit*, vol VI, pp 276-277
12. *Ibid*, vol VI, p 276
13. *Ibid*, vol VI, pp 277-278
14. *Ibid*, vol VI, p 255
15. MEINTJES, Anglo-Boereoorlog in Beeld, p 143
16. PLOEGER, *op cit*, p 4, 28:17
17. VAN SCHOOR, De Wet-Annale No 8, p 11
18. WARWICK, Black people..., *op cit*, p 26
19. BREYTENBACH, *op cit*, vol VI, pp 256-260; AMERY, *op cit*, vol IV, p 349
20. CRESWICKE, vol VI, p 195
21. BREYTENBACH, *op cit*, vol VI, pp 261-263
22. *Ibid*, vol VI, pp 279-280
23. *Ibid*, vol VI, p 298
24. VAN SCHOOR, De Wet-Annale No 8, p 11
25. AMERY, *op cit*, vol IV, p 316
26. VAN SCHOOR, De Wet-Annale No 8, p 37
27. PRETORIUS, The Anglo-Boer War, p 28
28. *Ibid*, p 42
29. VAN SCHOOR, De Wet-Annale No 4, p 22
30. WESSELS, Egodokumente..., p 33
31. VAN SCHOOR, De Wet-Annale No 4, pp 32-36
32. BREYTENBACH, *op cit*, vol VI, pp 280-281
33. SPIES, Methods of Barbarism?, p 106
34. *Ibid*, pp 128-131
35. WESSELS, Egodokumente..., p 34
36. AMERY, *op cit*, vol IV, p 325
37. SPIES, Methods of Barbarism?, p 106
38. VAN SCHOOR, De Wet-Annale No 4, pp 43-52
39. SPIES, Methods of Barbarism?, p 106
40. *Ibid*, pp 128-231
41. *Ibid*, p 236
42. VAN SCHOOR, De Wet-Annale No 4, p 52
43. AMERY, *op cit*, vol IV, pp 324-325
44. *Ibid*, vol IV, p 356
45. VAN SCHOOR, De Wet-Annale No 4, pp 61-64
46. AMERY, *op cit*, vol IV, p 327
47. *Ibid*, vol IV, p 357
48. VAN SCHOOR, De Wet-Annale No 4, p 66
49. AMERY, *op cit*, vol IV, p 328
50. *Ibid*, vol IV, pp 327-327
51. *Ibid*, vol IV, pp 330-332
52. BREYTENBACH, *op cit*, vol VI, p 287
53. AMERY, *op cit*, vol IV, pp 330-332
54. VAN SCHOOR, De Wet-Annale No 4, pp 73-77
55. BRITS, Diary of a National Scout, p 101; MARX, *op cit*, p 35
56. BREYTENBACH, *op cit*, vol VI, p 288
57. *Ibid*, vol VI, pp 288-289
58. PAKENHAM, *op cit*, p 314
59. AMERY, *op cit*, vol IV, pp 334-335
60. *Ibid*, vol IV, p 332
61. VAN SCHOOR, De Wet-Annale No 4, pp 52&77
62. WESSELS, Egodokumente..., p 40
63. AMERY, *op cit*, vol IV, pp 337-339
64. *Ibid*, vol IV, pp 337-339
65. *Ibid*, vol IV, p 339
66. TODD, Private Tucker's..., p 123

67.	AMERY, *op cit*, vol IV, pp 339-341
68.	WESSELS, Egodokumente..., p 40
69.	BREYTENBACH, *op cit*, vol VI, pp 302-303
70.	GRUNDLINGH, 'Hendsoppers'..., p 64
71.	PLOEGER, *op cit*, pp 37:8
72.	*Ibid*, p 41:23
73.	HATTINGH, Britse Fortifikasies..., p 140
74.	VAN SCHOOR, De Wet-Annale No 4, p 82
75.	*Ibid*, De Wet-Annale No 4, p 79
76.	VAN SCHOOR, De Wet-Annale No 4, p 83
77.	WESSELS, Egodokumente..., pp 41-42
78.	AMERY, *op cit*, vol IV, p 360
79.	VAN DEN BERG, 24 Battles and Battlefields..., p 75
80.	VAN SCHOOR, De Wet-Annale No 4, pp 108-109
81.	WESSELS, Egodokumente..., pp 40-44
82.	VAN DEN BERG, 24 Battles and Battlefields..., p 74-75
83.	*Ibid*, pp 76-77
84.	*Ibid*, pp 64-67
85.	Boer War Album, Cape Publishers Summary..., p 20
86.	VAN DEN BERG, 24 Battles and Battlefields..., pp 64-67
87.	*Ibid*, p 77
88.	AMERY, *op cit*, vol IV, p 261
89.	VAN DEN BERG, 24 Battles and Battlefields..., p 68-72
90.	AMERY, *op cit*, vol IV, p 361
91.	BREYTENBACH, *op cit*, vol VI, pp 302-307
92.	WESSELS, Egodokumente..., p 46
93.	SCHOLTZ, Beroemde Suid-Afrikaanse Krygsmanne, p 97
94.	SPIES, Methods of Barbarism?, pp 71
95.	SCHOLTZ, Beroemde Suid-Afrikaanse Krygsmanne, p 97
96.	*Ibid*, p 97
97.	VAN DEN BERG, 24 Battles and Battlefields..., p 77
98.	BREYTENBACH, *op cit*, vol VI, p 310
99.	VAN SCHOOR, De Wet-Annale No 2, p 108
100.	WESSELS, Egodokumente..., p 49
101.	SCHOLTZ, Beroemde Suid-Afrikaanse Krygsmanne, p 97
102.	WESSELS, Egodokumente..., p 49
103.	VAN SCHOOR, De Wet-Annale No 4, p 198
104.	*Ibid*, De Wet-Annale No 2, p 114
105.	GRONUM, *op cit*, (2)p 20
106.	GRUNDLINGH, 'Hendsoppers'..., pp 44-45
107.	AMERY, *op cit*, vol IV, p 439
108.	VAN DEN BERG, 24 Battles and Battlefields..., pp 78-79
109.	SPIES, Methods of Barbarism?, pp 78-79
110.	AMERY, *op cit*, vol VI, p 594
111.	VAN SCHOOR, De Wet-Annale No 2, p 115
112.	*Ibid*, De Wet-Annale No 2, p 115
113.	BREYTENBACH, *op cit*, vol VI, p 319
114.	*Ibid*, vol VI, p 320
115.	BREYTENBACH, *op cit*, vol VI, p 321
116.	SCHOLTZ, Beroemde Suid-Afrikaanse Krygsmanne, p 97
117.	BREYTENBACH, *op cit*, vol VI, p 31
118.	VAN SCHOOR, De Wet-Annale No 2, p 131
119.	CRESWICKE, vol VI, p 195
120.	BREYTENBACH, *op cit*, vol VI, pp 321-324
121.	*Ibid*, vol VI, pp 325-326

122.	*Ibid*, vol VI, pp 326-327
123.	VAN SCHOOR, De Wet-Annale No 4, pp 195-196
124.	AMERY, *op cit*, vol IV, pp 448-449
125.	BREYTENBACH, *op cit*, vol VI, pp 327-331
126.	SCHOLTZ, Beroemde Suid-Afrikaanse Krygsmanne, p 98
127.	AMERY, *op cit*, vol IV, p 479
128.	AMERY, *op cit*, vol IV, pp 452-456
	BREYTENBACH *op cit*, vol VI, pp 331-345
129.	McDONALD, In die skaduwee van die dood, p 24
130.	VAN SCHOOR, De Wet-Annale No 4, p 196
131.	KANDYBA-FOXCROFT, Russia..., *op cit*, p 89
132.	AMERY, *op cit*, vol IV, p 457
133.	SCHOLTZ, Beroemde Suid-Afrikaanse Krygsmanne, p 98
134.	WULFSOHN, Rustenburg at War, p 109
135.	PLOEGER, *op cit*, p 37:8
136.	*Ibid*, p 41:23
137.	HATTINGH, Britse Fortifikasies..., p 140
138.	LE MAY, *op cit*, p 53
139.	GRONUM, *op cit*, (2), p 20
140.	PLOEGER, *op cit*, p 13:41
141.	CRESWICKE, vol VI, pp 195-196
142.	McDONALD, In die skaduwee van die dood, pp 24-25
143.	FERREIRA, ... SPE Trichard, p 172; AMERY, *op cit*, vol IV, pp 461-462
144.	WESSELS, Egodokumente..., p 150
145.	SCHOLTZ, Beroemde Suid-Afrikaanse Krygsmanne, p 98
146.	McDONALD, In die skaduwee van die dood, pp 24-25
147.	GRONUM, *op cit*, (2) p 17
148.	BREYTENBACH, *op cit*, vol VI, p 346
149.	AMERY, *op cit*, vol IV, p 477
150.	McDONALD, In die skaduwee van die dood, pp 25-27
151.	BREYTENBACH, Kommandant Danie Theron, pp 220-223
152.	AMERY, *op cit*, vol IV, pp 462-463
153.	*Ibid*, vol IV, pp 465-466
154.	*Ibid*, vol IV, pp 467-468
155.	FERREIRA, ... SPE Trichard, p 173
156.	PLOEGER, *op cit*, pp 14-22
157.	*Ibid*, p 29:10
158.	OBERHOLSTER, Dagboek... HC Bredell, p 29
159.	*Ibid*, p 9
160.	AMERY, *op cit*, vol IV, p 477
161.	GRUNDLINGH, 'Hendsoppers'..., p 64
162.	Boer-War Album, Sum-21
163.	PRETORIUS, Kommandolewe..., p 38
164.	AMERY, *op cit*, vol IV p 480
165.	OBERHOLSTER, Dagboek... HC Bredell, p 11
166.	AMERY, *op cit*, vol IV, pp 471-472
167.	GRONUM, *op cit*, (2) p 30
168.	LE MAY, *op cit*, p 87
169.	GRUNDLINGH, 'Hendsoppers'..., p 64
170.	BREYTENBACH, Kommandant Danie Theron, p 227
171.	KANDYBA-FOXCROFT, Russia..., *op cit*, p 90
172.	Boer-War Album, Sum-20
173.	AMERY, *op cit*, vol VI, p 479
174.	AMERY, *op cit*, vol V, p 56
175.	PLOEGER, *op cit*, p 29:8

176. Boer-War Album, Sum-18
177. *Ibid*, Sum-21
178. SPIES, Methods of Barbarism?, p 122
179. MEINTJES, Anglo-Boereoorlog in Beeld, p 148
180. PLOEGER, *op cit*, p 29:9
181. Boer-War Album, Sum-21
182. FERREIRA, ... SPE Trichard, p 172
183. SPIES, Methods of Barbarism?, pp 123-124
184. FERREIRA, Memoirs of General Ben Bouwer, p 72
185. AMERY, *op cit*, vol V, p 8
186. AMERY, *op cit*, vol IV, p 493
187. *Ibid*, vol IV, pp 56-57
188. DOONER, Last Post, p 340; VAN SCHOOR, De Wet-Annale No 2, p 131
189. PLOEGER, *op cit*, p 37:8
190. *Ibid*, p 41:23
191. HATTINGH, Britse Fortifikasies..., p 140
192. AMERY, *op cit*, vol IV, p 480
193. *Ibid*, vol IV, p 500
194. VAN ZYL, Die Helde-album..., p 171
195. SPIES, Methods of barbarism?, p 71
196. Boer-War Album Sum-21
197. VAN DEN BERG, 24 Battles and Battlefields..., p at 87
198. GRONUM, *op cit*, (2) p 33; FARWELL, *op cit*, p 383
199. Boer-War Album, Sum-21
200. TODD, Private Tucker's..., p 136
201. AMERY, *op cit*, vol V, p 52
202. Boer-War Album, Sum-22
203. VAN ZYL, Die Helde-album..., p 169
204. AMERY, *op cit*, vol IV, p 9
205. CRESWICKE, vol VI, p 196
206. HOLT, The Boer War, p 251; KRUGER, Good-bye Dolly Gray, p 372
207. Boer-War Album Sum-22
208. KANDYBA-FOXCROFT, *op cit*, p 78
209. AMERY, *op cit*, vol V, p 25
210. PLOEGER, *op cit*, p 28:16
211. PRETORIUS, Kommandolewe..., p 38
212. AMERY, *op cit*, vol V, p 24
213. *Ibid*, vol V, p 24
214. BRITS, Diary of a National Scout, p 16
215. AMERY, *op cit*, vol V, p 10
216. CRESWICKE, vol VI, p 196
217. AMERY, *op cit*, vol V, p 11
218. PLOEGER, *op cit*, p 15:5-6
219. AMERY, *op cit*, vol V, p 11
220. GRONUM, *op cit*, (2) p 33
221. AMERY, *op cit*, vol V, p 11
222. WESSELS, War Diary of..., p 89; GRONUM, *op cit*, (2) p 22
223. VAN DEN BERG, 24 Battles and Battlefields..., p 91
224. AMERY, *op cit*, vol V, p 57
225. VAN DEN BERG, 24 Battles and Battlefields..., pp 91-92
226. AMERY, *op cit*, vol V, pp 25-26
227. VAN ZYL, Die Helde-album..., p 97
228. OBERHOLSTER, Dagboek..., HC Bredell, p 11
229. AMERY, *op cit*, vol V, p 49
230. SMUTS, *op cit*, p 122

231. AMERY, *op cit*, vol V, p 14; BRITS, Diary of a National Scout, p 23
232. LE MAY, *op cit*, p 90
233. OBERHOLSTER, Dagboek... HC Bredell, p 11
234. SPIES, Methods of Barbarism?, p 71
235. PLOEGER, *op cit*, p 15:6
236. BRITS, Diary of a National Scout, p 21
237. PLOEGER, *op cit*, p 37:8
238. *Ibid*, p 41:24
239. FARWELL, *op cit*, p 326
240. BREYTENBACH, Gedenkalbum.., p 450
241. SPIES, Methods of Barbarism?, p 71
242. AMEY, *op cit*, vol V, pp 50-51
243. OBERHOLSTER, Dagboek... HC Bredell, p 12
244. WALLACE, Unofficial Dispatches of the Anglo-Boer War, p 305
245. AMERY, *op cit*, vol V, p 15
246. *Ibid*, vol V, pp 16-20
247. VAN ZYL, Die Helde-album, p 171
248. AMERY, *op cit*, vol V, p 51
249. LE MAY, *op cit*, p 90
250. PAKENHAM, *op cit*, pp 504-505
251. GRONUM, *op cit*, (2) p 27
252. PLOEGER, *op cit*, p 15:9
253. OBERHOLSTER, Dagboek... HC Bredell, p 12
254. AMERY, *op cit*, vol V, p 28
255. MARX, Klerskdorp..., p 35
256. AMERY, *op cit*, Vol IV, p 493
257. AMERY, *op cit*, Vol V, p 61
258. WARWICK, Black people..., *op cit*, p 124
259. VAN SCHOOR, Bannelinge, p 5
260. AMERY, *op cit*, vol V, pp 30-31
261. PLOEGER, *op cit*, p 15:3
262. AMERY, *op cit*, vol V, pp 31-32
263. WESSELS, War Diary of..., p 84
264. AMERY, *op cit*, vol V, pp 31-32
265. DOONER, 'Last Post' ... p 35
266. LE MAY, *op cit*, p 89
267. PLOEGER, *op cit*, p 30:20
268. OOSTHUIZEN, Rebelle van die Stormberge, p 146
269. OBERHOLSTER, Dagboek... HC Bredell, p 14
270. AMERY, *op cit*, vol V, p 33
271. VAN REENEN, Emily Hobhouse..., p 444
272. AMERY, *op cit*, vol V, p 33
273. HEADLAM, *op cit*, vol II, p 156
274. OBERHOLSTER, Dagboek... HC Bredell, p 14
275. HEADLAM, *op cit*, vol II, p 156
276. AMERY, *op cit*, vol V p 63
277. GRUNDLINGH, 'Hendsoppers'..., p 64
278. AMERY, *op cit*, vol V, p 34
279. PLOEGER, *op cit*, p 38:7
280. *Ibid*, p 41:23
281. FARWELL, *op cit*, p 326
282. SCHOLTZ, Beroemde Suid-Afrikaanse Krygsmanne, p 126
283. VAN DEN BERG, *op cit*, p 98
284. *Ibid*, p 104
285. NIENABER, Gedenkboek Generaal JBM Hertzog, p 84

286. OBERHOLSTER, Dagboek... HC Bredell, p 14

287. VAN DEN BERG, *op cit*, pp 97-100

288. DAVITT, *op cit*, p 587

289. PLOEGER, *op cit*, p 30:7

290. HEADLAM, *op cit*, vol II, p 176

291. AMERY, *op cit*, vol V, pp 37-38

292. PRETORIUS, Kommandolewe..., p 318

293. AMERY, *op cit*, vol V, p 116; FERREIRA; Memoirs of General Ben Bouwer, p 87

294. GRUNDLINGH, 'Hendsoppers'..., p 84

295. AMERY, *op cit*, vol V, p 117

296. FARWELL, *op cit*, p 318; TODD, Private Tucker's..., p 157

297. HEADLAM, *op cit*, vol II, p 176

298. AMERY, *op cit*, vol V, pp 117-118

299. AMERY, *op cit*, vol V, p 98; VAN DEN BERG, *op cit*, p 107

300. GRUNDLINGH, 'Hendsoppers'..., p 46

301. CRESWICKE, vol VI, *op cit* p 196

302. WESSELS, Anglo-Boereoorlog... oorsig, p 40;
AMERY, *op cit*, vol V, pp 99-108; VAN DEN BERG, *op cit*. pp 102-111

303. McCRACKEN, The Irish Pro-Boers, p 106

304. HOLT, The Boer War, pp 276-277

305. AMERY, *op cit*, vol V, pp 41-42

306. WESSELS, Anglo-Boereoorlog... oorsig, pp 36-37

307. VAN SCHOOR, De Wet-Annale No 7, p 57

308. NIENABER, *op cit*, p 85

309. *Ibid*, p 85

310. VAN ZYL, Die Helde-album, pp 187-189

311. PLOEGER, *op cit*, p 15:33

312. GRONUM, *op cit*, (2) p 38

313. GRONUM, *op cit*, (2) p 40

314. GRUNDLINGH, 'Hendsoppers'..., p 90

315. PLOEGER, *op cit*, p 15:28

316. VAN SCHOOR, De Wet-Annale No 7, p 58

317. FERREIRA, ... SPE Trichard, p 179

318. TODD, Private Tucker's..., pp 163-165

319. SPIES, Methods of Barbarism?, p 71

320. AMERY, *op cit*, vol V, p 118; KANDYBA-FOXCROFT,
op cit, p 236

321. TODD, Private Tucker's..., p 167

322. SPIES, Methods of Barbarism?, p 173

323. VAN SCHOOR, De Wet-Annale No 7, p 59

324. KEMP, Pad van die Veroweraar, pp 74&80

325. GRUNDLINGH, 'Hendsoppers'..., p 91

326. AMERY, *op cit*, vol V, pp 121-122
WESSELS, Anglo-Boereoorlog... oorsig, p 42

327. PLOEGER, *op cit*, p 37:8

328. *Ibid*, p 41:23

329. FARWELL, *op cit*, p 326

JANUARY - JUNE 1901

GUERRILLA

1900	SUMMER	JANUARY
Day 448 Tue 1901-01-01		NEW YEAR'S DAY— the REAL first day of the new century.
	Cape Colony	The Colonial Defence Force is called out in the Cape Colony.
	Trivia	*The Commonwealth of Australia is established with Edmund Barton as first Prime Minister.*
Day 449 Wed 1901-01-02	Western ZAR	**THE SKIRMISH AT CYFERFONTEIN** A mobile column of about 2 000 men under General Babington runs into a small group of General De la Rey's burghers near Cyferfontein. They are actually part of a force of about 700 burghers, the main force being concealed in a fold of the ground covered by long grass. De la Rey skilfully leads the attacking troop of charging Imperial Light Horse into a trap. Before they can be extricated, the ILH lose two officers and 46 men killed or wounded and about 70 of their horses are also killed. The burghers retire north-westwards before Babington can regroup.[1]
	OFS	ORC police Lieutenant Cecil Boyle, a prisoner of war captured after the battle of Dewetsdorp and acquitted on a charge of treason, is shot on General Philip Botha's orders by Barend Cilliers.[2]
	United Kingdom	Lord Roberts arrives at East Cowes, and is immediately taken to the Queen at Osborne House where he is made a Knight of the Garter.
Day 450 Thu 1901-01-03		
Day 451 Thu 1901-01-04	OFS	At Kromspruit, near Lindley, General Philip Botha's commando attacks the Commander-in-Chief's Bodyguard, a 154-man select unit under Colonel Laing. Laing and 12 men are killed, 33 are wounded and the rest are taken prisoner.
	Trivia	*General Chris Muller's birthday.*
Day 452 Fri 1901-01-05	Eastern ZAR	A council of war held on the farm Hoedspruit, against the Bothasberg, decides on an extensive, general attack against the railway line.[3]
Day 453 Sat 1901-01-06	Eastern ZAR	Starting at midnight, the Republican forces launch a general attack along 60 kilometres of the Delagoa railway line between Wonderfontein and Machadodorp.
	OFS	JJ Morgendaal, a Boer who laid down arms and is acting as a volunteer peace emissary, has been captured on his way to see Chief Commandant De Wet, and appears before a court martial in the Heilbron district. The court martial decides to refer the case to a higher court.[4]
Day 454 Sun 1901-01-07	Eastern ZAR	**THE ATTACK ON BELFAST AND THE DELAGOA RAILWAY LINE** Aided by thick mist Republican forces launch attacks on Belfast and other stations along the Delagoa railway line. The main attack is aimed against Belfast, where General Smith-Dorrien is in command of 1 200 infantrymen, 280 lancers and 130 mounted infantrymen holding a 20-kilometre perimeter. General Ben Viljoen's attack, commanded by Chris Muller, is centred on the important post at Monument Hill, north of the town, which is held by Captain Fosbury with 83 men of the Irish Regiment. Viljoen himself is ready to launch a direct assault on the town once Muller's attack succeeds, while General Chris Botha and Wolmarans' men attack from the south and west respectively. Muller achieves complete surprise and overwhelms

	Victoria Cross	Fosbury's well-fortified post after close hand-to-hand combat using fists and rifle-butts. Fosbury is killed and 39 of his men are killed or wounded. Private J Barrie, 1st Battalion, the Royal Irish Regiment, earns the Victoria Cross (posthumously) for disabling their machine gun before it falls into enemy hands. In the west a small post at the colliery is taken, but posts to the south resist fiercely. All Smith-Dorrien's reserves are committed and the outcome is in the balance. The darkness and fog prevent Viljoen from ascertaining the progress in other sectors and he calls off his attack. Elsewhere the attacks against the small garrisons at Pan, Wonderfontein, Nooitgedacht and Wildfontein stations are not pressed home. The fog allows the burghers to approach to within close range and inflict casualties, but at 01:30 the attacks peter out and the attackers withdraw. The British suffer 24 killed, 78 wounded and 70 captured.[5]
	Cape Colony Black involvement	Sir Alfred Milner receives a deputation, representing more than 100 000 of Her Majesty's 'coloured' subjects in the Western Province. They rejoice at the incorporation of the Republics into the Empire, *"because we feel that only under the British flag and British protection can the coloured people obtain justice, equality and freedom"*. They trust that everything will be done in those colonies to secure liberty and freedom for all civilized people, and that every opportunity will be given to the uncivilized to raise their status. Milner replies that he *"thoroughly agreed that it was not race or colour, but civilization, which was the test of a man's capacity for political rights".[6]* Martial law is extended to western districts of Cape Colony.
	Trivia	*Sir Redvers H Buller's 62nd birthday.*
Day 455 Mon **1901-01-08**	Northern ZAR	Three members of the ZAR government meet at Pietersburg.
	OFS	The peace emissary Morgendaal and his father-in-law, A Wessels, are taken to Chief Commandant De Wet and General Froneman's commando on the farm Nobelsfontein, near Kroonstad.[7]
Day 456 Tue **1901-01-09**	OFS	Near Heilbron one of De Wet's black scouts reports the approach of a British patrol and the laager is thrown into turmoil in their haste to inspan and get away. Prisoner Morgendaal, maybe sensing imminent rescue, refuses to obey General Froneman's order to help with the harnessing of a vehicle. After repeating the order several times, Froneman loses his temper and lashes out at him with a sjambok which Morgendaal yanks out of his hands. A furious De Wet shouts, *"Shoot the m....r f....r (moerneuker)!"* Froneman shoots and Morgendaal is seriously wounded.[8]
	Western ZAR	Schweizer-Reneke is relieved.
Day 457 Wed **1901-01-10**	ZAR	The 80-year-old ex-President Pretorius returns from an exploratory mission to Louis Botha on Kitchener's request. He reports, *"As soon as Botha saw me, he abused me for carrying messages for the British. He said, 'Had it been anyone else I would have shot him.' He added, 'Tell Lord Kitchener if he wants to send any messages to me to send them with a soldier with a white flag which we will respect, but if he sends any by Boers we will shoot them whoever they are. Tell him we don't want messages and we don't want peace. We want our independence and we will fight till we get it. Tell him he has the railways but we have the country. We take a convoy or a train and do not want anything, and it is no use asking for peace.' "[9]*
	Pres. MW Pretorius (National Cultural Histor Museum)	
	OFS	Morgendaal's father-in-law, A Wessels, is found guilty of treason and sentenced to death by a court martial chaired by Chief Commandant De Wet. A petition for clemency is addressed to President Steyn.
	Cape Colony Black involvement	A Free State commando under Commandant Charles Nieuwoudt occupies Calvinia and he appoints his field-cornet, Van der Merwe, as magistrate. A group of Coloureds stone the commando as they enter town and 45-year-old Abraham Esau, described as

	International	*"the most poisonous Hottentot in Calvinia"*, is immediately imprisoned. Esau is a local Coloured leader and blacksmith, who has previously offered to organise the 'Calvinia Native Levy', but was refused arms by the British intelligence agent and the magistrate of Clanwilliam. In an effort to win support of local farmers, Niewoudt and Van der Merwe launch a reign of terror, especially against local Coloureds and black farm workers accused by their employers of the 'crimes' of 'disrespect' and 'laziness'.[10] Five Republican prisoners of war escape from the prison ship *Catalonia* in the harbour of Colombia, Ceylon, and swim to the Russian ship *Gherson* that eventually takes them to the Crimea. The five, Steyn, Hausner, Botha and two Steytler brothers, travel via St Petersburg and Berlin to Utrecht in the Netherlands, where they meet President Kruger. From here they travel on board a German ship to German South West Africa, from where they make their way overland to rejoin the commandos near Doornrivier during August 1901. Their adventure since their capture at Heuningkoppies is to take almost a year and they are to travel almost 32 000 kilometres.[11]
	Trivia	*Oil is discovered at Beaumont, Texas, USA.*
Day 458 Thu **1901-01-11**		
Day 459 Fri **1901-01-12**	ZAR	General CF Beyers audaciously attacks Kaalfontein and Zuurfontein (now Kempton Park) between Johannesburg and Pretoria and crosses the railway line.[12]
Day 460 Sat **1901-01-13**		
Day 461 Mon **1901-01-14**	OFS	In a proclamation President Steyn and Chief Commandant De Wet protest the numerous violations of the Geneva and Hague Conventions such as waging war against women and children; the capturing of ambulances and medical staff; the destruction of property; the misuse of the white flag as well as the arming of 'natives' and the libellous propaganda against the Republics. Although they will never stoop to waging war against women and children, unless British forces stop the destruction, they are ready to retaliate against the property of British subjects during the present Republican invasion of the Cape Colony.[13]
Day 462 Tue **1901-01-15**	United Kingdom	A letter from *"a British officer now serving at the front"* is published in the Dublin *Freeman's Journal.* The letter describes Lord Kitchener's military operations to capture De Wet during 1900: *"Lord Kitchener, having as he thought, caged his enemy, sent secret instructions to the troops to take no prisoners; that is, if the Boers surrounded on all sides found themselves unable to resist and hoist the white flag as a token of surrender, they are to be shot down to the last man."*[14]
Day 463 Wed **1901-01-16**	Western ZAR	Six prisoners are tried and sentenced to death for treason by Lemmer's commando. Three others are fined and sent over the Bechuanaland border.[15]
	Trivia	*ISM Hamilton's 48th birthday.*
Day 464 Thu **1901-01-17**	Eastern ZAR	Captains Trichard and Hindon capture two trains between Brugspruit and Balmoral.[16] Commandant Beyers's men raid the racecourse near Johannesburg, taking 1 700 head of cattle.[17]
	Cape Colony	Martial law is extended to the whole of Cape Colony except ports and 'native' territories.

	United Kingdom	Sir Douglas Powell, a famous heart and lung specialist, is summoned to Osborne after the Queen is thought to have suffered a heart attack [18]
	Trivia	*The ZAR independence day (Sand River Convention 1852).* *D Lloyd-George's 38th birthday.*
Day 465 Fri **1901-01-18**	ZAR	Pursuing British troops recover 500 head of cattle that have strayed from the herd taken by Beyers' men.[19]
	United Kingdom	The letter from *"a British officer now serving at the front,"* is republished in *The Times*.[20]
Day 466 Sat **1901-01-19**	OFS	JJ Morgendaal dies of the wound he received ten days earlier.[21]
	Western ZAR	General HR Lemmer is killed in action at Rietfontein between Lichtenburg and Marico while engaging about 300 British soldiers with 23 burghers. He is succeeded by Commandant Vermaas.[22]
	Cape Colony	General Hertzog arrives at Vanrhynsdorp.[23]
	United Kingdom	*The Times* reports that the SA Conciliation Committee has drawn Lord Roberts' attention to the letter and has stressed the importance of having it immediately refuted or contradicted. No such contradiction is received.[24] Kaizer Wilhelm II visits his ailing grandmother, Queen Victoria.
	Trivia	*JJ Cheere Emmet's 34th birthday (General L Botha's brother-in-law).*
Day 467 Sun **1901-01-20**		
Day 468 Mon **1901-01-21**	Concentration camps	Emily Hobhouse obtains a letter of authorization to visit *"any Refugee camp in the T.V. (Transvaal) or the O.R.C. if the Military will allow it"*. Lord Kitchener, however, disallows visits north of Bloemfontein.[25]
	Cape Colony	Milner telegraphs Chamberlain, *"I am all for the most forbearing and generous treatment of the Boers when they are once completely beaten — if only because that is the sole means of absorbing and ultimately getting rid of them as a separate, exclusive race... But with their primitive and political conditions can go on merrily for a long time... just as low types of animal organisms will long survive injuries which would kill organisms of a higher type outright. They die too, in the long run, but it takes time... cruel as it may sound, there is nothing for it but to wear them out."*[26]
Day 469 Tue **1901-01-22**	Eastern ZAR	Peace envoy Meyer de Kock, attempting to distribute peace pamphlets and to address burghers in the Belfast district, is arrested for treason by General Ben Viljoen.[27]
	Cape Colony	Milner, referring to the latest Republican invasion of the Cape Colony, writes, *"These marches of the enemy... cannot affect the ultimate issue of the war but they keep a good many of our men employed, tire them out and their horses, inflict a considerable amount of injury upon the country and certainly damage very greatly the prestige of its government."*[28]
	International	President Kruger arrives at Utrecht from The Hague. He sends Queen Victoria a *"respectful message of sympathy"*, but she is unconscious and is never to know.[29]
	United Kingdom	**QUEEN VICTORIA DIES** At 18:20, Queen Victoria dies at Osborne House on the Isle of Wight. Her last words are, *"What has been happening in South Africa these last few days?"*

Day 470 Wed **1901-01-23**	Western ZAR	General Cunningham is attacked by Commandant FJ Potgieter at Middelfontein, about 11 kilometres from Olifantsnek. After a fierce battle Potgieter's Wolmaransstad commando retires in the face of a bayonet charge by the Worcester Regiment. The exhausted British troops make camp in an untenable position, surrounded by rocky hills.[30]
	Cape Colony	General Hertzog, on learning of the death of Queen Victoria, allows the resident magistrate of Vanrhynsdorp to fly the Union Jack half-mast.[31]
Day 471 Thu **1901-01-24**	Western ZAR	At Middelfontein, General De la Rey attacks Cunningham's force and captures a mounted infantry picket. His burghers fire into the badly positioned camp from all directions and only the arrival of reinforcements under General Babington from Ventersdorp saves Cunningham's force from complete defeat. The burghers withdraw with six killed and 19 wounded while Cunningham has lost 54 men killed and wounded over the two days.[32]
	OFS Concentration camps	Emily Hobhouse visits the Bloemfontein concentration camp and is appalled at the conditions. She decides to visit as many camps as possible. (Due to limited time and resources she does not visit the camp for blacks, although she urges the Guild of Loyal Women to do so.)[33]
	Cape Colony	Boer prisoners in the Green Point prisoner of war camp suspend *all amusements* until after the Queen's funeral, as a token of respect to her memory.[34]
	United Kingdom	The accession of King Edward VII is proclaimed.[35]
Day 472 Fri **1901-01-25**	OFS	**THE MEETING AT DOORNBERG** The Free State leaders, including Generals Fourie and Froneman, Commandants Prinsloo, Haasbroek, De Vos, Van der Merwe, Ross, Wessels, Kolbe and Theron, assemble at Doornberg, north of Winburg. Because his term as president has expired, Steyn is re-elected (until such time as regular elections can be held, in holy respect of the constitution, he is sworn in as Vice-State President) and the executive council is nominated[36] Chief Commandant De Wet reorganises the Free State forces by creating seven regions, each commanded by a general given the rank of assistant commandant-general. The regions west of the railway line are to be commanded by Generals Hertzog and Badenhorst, while the eastern regions are put under the command of Generals Hattingh, Michal Prinsloo, Wessels, Froneman and Piet Fourie. Each of the regions is subdivided into three to six districts, each commanded by a commandant.[37]
Day 473 Sat **1901-01-26**	ZAR	The South African Constabulary is established under the Command of Major-General Baden-Powell. Members are mostly drawn from Colonial troops already serving with the British forces. The unit, now about 1 000 men strong, is named to reinforce the notion that the nature of operations has now changed to policing actions only.
	Western ZAR	General Liebenberg captures a water cart on its way to fetch water from a stream for the British post at Modderfontein at the junction of the Krugersdorp/Vereeniging and Potchefstroom/Johannesburg roads.[38]
Day 474 Sun **1901-01-27**	OFS	**START OF 'THE THIRD (OR GREAT) DE WET HUNT'** Chief Commandant De Wet starts his second invasion of the Cape Colony with 2 200 men, a single field-gun and a pom-pom. He is spotted by British columns as he crosses the Smaldeel (Theunissen)/Winburg branch railway and the pursuit begins with General Bruce Hamilton from Ventersburg and General Knox from Leeuwkop in the south.
	ZAR	**START OF GENERAL FRENCH'S DRIVE IN THE EASTERN ZAR** Under Major-General JDP French's overall command five large columns prepare to

		drive the Republican forces against the Swaziland and Zululand borders and force them to surrender. Brigadier-General Alderson, with about 2 000 men, eight field-guns and a pom-pom, starts from Mooiplaats, east of Pretoria; Lieutenant-Colonel E Knox, with about 1 800 men, seven field-guns and two pom-poms, starts from Bapsfontein; Lieutenant-Colonel Allenby, with about 1 800 men, six field-guns and two pom-poms, starts from Putfontein; Lieutenant-Colonel Pultney, with about 1 800 men, seven fieldguns and two pom-poms, and the Natal officer, Brigadier-General Dartnell with about 2 600 men, four field-guns, a naval gun and two pom-poms, start from Springs. Together with headquarter units and support troops, the total force consists of about 21 000 men, 11 500 horses, 9 000 mules and 58 field-guns and pom-poms using two railway lines for their supplies.[39]
	Trivia	*Kaizer William II's 42nd birthday.* *Giuseppe Verdi, opera composer, dies.*
Day 475 Mon **1901-01-28**	OFS	The columns of Paget and Plumer, about to join French's drive, are transferred south in preparation for protecting the Cape Colony against De Wet's invasion. Observation posts are set up along the south bank of the Orange River and Lieutenant-General Lyttelton moves from the eastern ZAR to take command of the forces concentrating at Noupoort.[40]
	ZAR	French's drive maintains its line and marches about 24 kilometres and encamps on a line from Witklipbank to Leeufontein.[41] Richard Solomon, previously the Cape Attorney-General and a member of WP Schreiner's ministry, is appointed as legal advisor to the 'Transvaal' administration.[42]
	Victoria Cross	Farrier Sergeant-Major WJ Hardham, 4th New Zealand Contingent, during guerrilla warfare.
Day 476 Tue **1901-01-29**	Western ZAR	**THE BATTLE OF MODDERFONTEIN** (the present Hillshaven, south of Westonaria) Generals Smuts and Liebenberg reconnoitre the British post at Modderfontein, manned by 109 South Wales Borderers with two field-guns, under Captain Casson, at Modderfontein on the Gatsrand. A supply convoy from Krugersdorp, escorted by 108 men of the Oxfordshire Yeomanry under Captain H Magniac, arrives and Casson sends an escort to accompany the convoy over the last few kilometres to the camp. The convoy is harassed by Field-cornet Breytenbach's men — on their way to reinforce Smuts and Liebenberg. Smuts, in overall command of about 30 burghers with two field-guns, allow the convoy to enter the camp and finalise his plans for the attack. During the night the camp is surrounded and the guns are positioned.[43]
	ZAR	Generals Beyers and Kemp slip past General French's line and damage the railway line between Springs and Brakpan. They cut a field telegraph cable and start fires at two mines near Benoni.[44]
	Eastern ZAR	Peace envoy Meyer de Kock is found guilty of treason and sentenced to death by a special military court at Roossenekal, with Magistrate G Joubert presiding.[45]
	OFS	General Knox and Colonel Pilcher attacks Chief Commandant De Wet at Tabaksberg and engage him all day long as his big column moves south. The Boer rearguard keeps them at bay and launch a counterattack after dark, capturing a British pom-pom. The British suffer 43 casualties.[46]
Day 477 Wed **1901-01-30**	OFS	General Bruce Hamilton, planning to forestall De Wet along the Thaba Nchu/Ladybrand chain of posts, is delayed by a traffic block on the railway line and reaches Sannaspost. Chief Commandant De Wet outdistances Knox and he crosses the line at Israel's Poort, west of Thaba Nchu.[47]

	Western ZAR	**THE BATTLE OF MODDERFONTEIN** The burghers tighten their stranglehold on the surrounded camp, but their progress is slow and accurate shelling from the British field-guns silences both Republican field-guns with heavy casualties among the gunners. By late afternoon, however, most of the outposts have been taken with the defenders falling back to their main position on the hill.[48]
	South-eastern ZAR	Pushing panic-stricken groups of old men, women and children, crowded in wagons and preceded by huge flocks of livestock in front of them, French's drive enters the south-eastern ZAR.[49]
	Trivia	*OFS independence day (Bloemfontein Convention 1854).*
Day 478 Thu **1901-01-31**	Western ZAR	**THE BATTLE OF MODDERFONTEIN** Generals Smuts and Liebenberg decide to force the issue with a night attack. Their approach from the south-west is covered by a heavy downpour and they take one post after the other and at 04:30 the last position is taken with hardly a shot being fired. The lack of resistance is ascribed to the fact that the British, unable to obtain water from the spruit, have quelled their thirst with the Scotch that arrived with the last convoy. The British casualties are 26 killed and wounded with the rest surrendering. The Republican casualties are unknown.[50]
	ZAR	Mrs Sybella Margaretha (Isie) Smuts is considered to be 'undesirable' by the British military authorities in Pretoria. She is sent to Pietermaritzburg, where she is placed under house arrest, despite her pleas to be sent to a concentration camp like other Boer women.
	Trivia	*BD Bouwer's 26th birthday.* *Anton Chekhov's play 'Three Sisters' opens in Moscow.*
	OFFICIAL REPORTS **Farm burning:** **Concentration camps:** **Communications:**	No official return of the number of buildings destroyed by British troops is available. 'Refugee camps' have been established at Aliwal North, Brandfort, Elandsfontein, Heidelberg, Howick, Kimberley, Klerksdorp, Viljoensdrift, Waterval North and Winburg.[51] The railway lines have been cut 16 times during January.[52]
1901-02-00	SUMMER	**FEBRUARY**
Day 479 Fri **1901-02-01**	South-eastern ZAR	Colonels Pultney and Allenby clash with the rearguard of a Republican force armed with five field-guns and a pom-pom.[53]
	Trivia	*The American film star Clark Gable is born.*
Day 480 Sat **1901-02-02**	Western ZAR	**THE BRITISH ATTACK ON MODDERFONTEIN** Brigadier-General Cunningham, with about 2 600 men, attacks General Smuts' position at Modderfontein. General Smuts, now occupying the captured British post with 1 500 burghers and two field-guns, easily repulses the frontal assault and 800 mounted troops trying to work around his right flank, are also pushed back. Cunningham withdraws with 40 casualties.[54] Lord Methuen leaves Taung and starts on a march towards Klerksdorp.
	Trivia	*Queen Victoria's funeral.*
Day 481 Sun **1901-02-03**	South-eastern ZAR	Lieutenant-Colonel Campbell, with about 1 200 men, five field-guns and a pom-pom, sets out from Middelburg and Major-General Smith-Dorrien, with 3 300 men, 10 field-guns and two pom-poms, sets out from Wonderfontein Station, and march south to extend French's line eastwards. When night falls, the seven British columns form a 100-kilometre arc facing Ermelo.[55]

	OFS	Major (Sir Hamilton) Goold-Adams, the Administrator of British-Bechuanaland, takes over the administration of the 'Orange River Colony' from General Pretyman.[56]
	Cape Colony	General JBM Hertzog leaves Vanrhynsdorp and heads north-eastwards to join up with Chief Commandant De Wet's invasion force.[57]
	International	On St Helena Commandant SJ Eloff and four burghers are arrested for trying to buy a small boat from fishermen in a half-baked escape attempt.[58]
	Trivia	*71st birthday of Lord RATG Cecil, Marquis of Salisbury.*
Day 482 Mon **1901-02-04**	South-eastern ZAR	A 20-kilometre-wide gap develops between the columns of Campbell and Smith-Dorrien. General Chris Botha ambushes a troop of hussars and about 300 burghers slip though the net on the other side, between Campbell and Alderson.[59]
	Western ZAR	Brigadier-General Cunningham abandons his attempts to recapture Modderfontein and retires to Roodepoort.[60]
	Cape Colony Black involvement	**REPUBLICAN ATROCITY** Abraham Esau, the Calvinia Coloured leader imprisoned by Nieuwoudt and Van der Merwe, has been tortured and humiliated over a period of weeks. He is sentenced to 25 lashes, administered by Nieuwoudt personally. He collapses and is kicked, smeared with dung and even stoned by members of the commando. He is eventually placed in leg-irons and dragged between two horses about a kilometre out of town, where he is shot. The perpetrator alleges that Esau has attacked him with a knife. A British newspaper later reports: *"He has suffered cruel martyrdom for no worse crime than loyalty to the British."*[61]
	OFS Black involvement	General Froneman instructs his burghers that in future captured blacks will not be shot, but taken across the Basutoland border. Blacks accused of molesting women will, however, be shot if found guilty.[62]
Day 483 Tue **1901-02-05**	OFS	General Froneman, executing a feint to divert attention from De Wet's advance, wrecks and loots a goods train at Pompie Station, capturing some of General Bruce Hamilton's baggage.[63]
	South-eastern ZAR	General French's line contracts as the columns converge on Ermelo. General Smith-Dorrien arrives at Lake Chrissie and makes camp at Bothwell, a small hamlet on the northern shore. Commandant-General Louis Botha, with about 2 000 burghers, marching north-eastwards from Ermelo, passes through the British line west of the lake and turns east to attack the Bothwell camp from the north-west.[64]
Day 484 Wed **1901-02-06**	ZAR	**THE ACTION AT LAKE CHRISSIE** At 02:50, in pitch darkness, Botha's men open a furious fire on the Yorkshire's pickets on the north-western perimeter of the Bothwell camp. Although the sentries are alert and ready, the mounted infantry's horses stampede and throw the camp into turmoil. The burghers turn back the horses and, their movements covered by the frightened animals, charge in and overwhelm several of the sentry posts. Supporting units, rushing to reinforce the outposts, are also cut to pieces. The burghers, however, cannot gain a foothold on the slopes and are unable to open direct fire on the main camp which is situated on a plateau. As the initial surprise wears off and the British recover, Botha realises that no further advantage is to be gained and at 04:30 he orders retreat. Smith-Dorrien plans a pursuit, but the thick morning mist covers the Boer retreat. The mounted infantry picks up the trail, but Botha succeeds in reaching safety in the rear of the driving columns. The Republicans suffers about 80 casualties, including Field-cornet Spruyt, and the British about 70. About 300 horses are killed or missing

	Victoria Cross	after the stampede and Smith-Dorrien's mounted units are crippled.[65] Sergeant WW Traynor, 2nd Battalion, West Yorkshire Regiment, Bothwell Camp, near Lake Chrissie. Lieutenant-Colonel Pulteney enters the almost deserted Ermelo.
	Cape Colony	AP Cartwright, editor of the *South African News*, republishes *The Times* letter under the heading: *"How we are waging war / A dreadful disclosure / by a British officer in command / Lord Kitchener's secret instruction as conveyed by a leading general./ Are prisoners being shot?"* Cape Attorney-General Rose Innes telegraphs Kitchener for verification of the charges which are promptly denied. Cartwright publishes the denial prominently, but is nevertheless charged and subsequently sentenced to one year's imprisonment.[66] In a letter to Chamberlain Milner writes: *"... It is no use denying that the last half-year has been one of retrogression. Seven months ago this Colony was quiet, at least as far as the Orange River... Even a considerable portion of the Transvaal... Today the scene is completely changed."*[67]
	Trivia	*In Paris public telephones are introduced at railway stations.*
Day 485 Thu **1901-02-07**	South-eastern ZAR	Chief Commandant French starts the second phase of his drive. He re-extends his columns and resume his drive south-eastwards.
	OFS	Chief Commandant De Wet crosses the railway line between Springfontein and Jagersfontein and heads for Philippolis.
	United Kingdom	The War Office decides to send 30 000 additional mounted troops to South Africa. Chamberlain warns Milner: *"... if some progress is not made before long I think public dissatisfaction may become serious and threaten the existence of the Government in spite of its enormous majority."*[68]
	Trivia	*Queen Wilhelmina marries Count Hendrik van Melckenburg-Schwerin. Sir Charles Warren's 61st birthday.*
Day 486 Fri **1901-02-08**	South-eastern ZAR	Brigadier-General Dartnell occupies Amersfoort.
	ZAR	Mrs Annie Botha receives permission from Lord Kitchener to visit her husband. At a previous interview with Kitchener she has protested against her treatment by the occupying forces in Pretoria. Her husband's bank account has been frozen on British orders, forcing her to live on an allowance of only £15 a month.[69]
Day 487 Sat **1901-02-09**	Eastern ZAR	Despite pleas for clemency by some burghers, peace envoy Meyer de Kock's death sentence is confirmed by Acting State President SW Burger, in consultation with the Executive Council.[70]
	St Helena	MT Goddefroy (19) is killed while trying to escape from a prisoner of war camp on St Helena.[71]
	Trivia	*General RAP Clements' 46th birthday. Dr LS Jameson's 48th birthday.*
Day 488 Sun **1901-02-10**	OFS/ Cape Colony	Chief Commandant De Wet crosses the Orange River at Sand Drift with about 2 000 men and enters the Cape Colony. He is accompanied by ex-State Artillery Captain (now Commandant) Wynand C Malan and Corporal Salomon (Manie) G Maritz.
	South-eastern ZAR	General Smith-Dorrien marches north-eastwards from his Bothwell camp and his mounted infantry overtakes an enemy convoy, capturing about 50 wagons and 30 burghers.[72]

	United Kingdom	Lord Raglan, Under-Secretary of State for War, dispels the rumour that General Sir Evelyn Wood intends going to South Africa or that a peace commission is being contemplated after King Edward has used his personal influence on part of the Cabinet. It is intimated that the last words of Queen Victoria to her successor have a bearing in this direction. *"The report as to a peace commission is false from beginning to end,"* Lord Raglan says. *"The policy of the Government is the opposite of what would prompt such a step. Troops, not peace commissioners, are going to South Africa."*[73]
Day 489 Mon 1901-02-11	OFS/ Cape Colony	The weather worsens. Heavy rains turn rivers into raging torrents and roads into muddy streams. Chief Commandant De Wet's force is weakened when Commandants Prinsloo, Van Tonder, De Vos and 800 burghers refuse to leave the Free State.[74]
	Bermuda	The Republican prisoners of war on Bermuda refuse to listen to peace envoys Mr CL Botha, Mr JW (later Sir John) Wessels and ex-General P de Wet (Chief Commandant CR de Wet's brother) sent by Kitchener to persuade prisoners to sign the oath of allegiance. The envoys are booed and hissed out of the camps and as a result the prisoners' issue of jam is stopped.[75]
Day 490 Tue 1901-02-12	OFS/ Cape Colony	Generals Hamilton and Knox, covering about 110 kilometres in forced marches, arrive at Sand Drift at 07:00, about 15 hours too late. Colonel Plumer, marching from Colesberg, makes contact with Chief Commandant De Wet's invaders north of Hamelsfontein. De Wet swerves away from Philipstown towards Hondeblafs River. Commandant Malan and Corporal Maritz, with 24 men, are cut off from the main force and they decide to operate independently.[76] The Queensland Mounted Infantry is in action at Zwartkoppie.
	South-eastern ZAR	Commandant Pulteney is stopped by a Republican rearguard on the Welgevonden ridges, between Amersfoort and Amsterdam. A determined cavalry charge by Rimington's force dislodges them and about 30 burghers are killed or captured.[77]
	Eastern ZAR	Peace envoy Meyer de Kock is executed by a Republican firing squad near Belfast.[78]
	Western ZAR	Lord Methuen, marching from Taung, arrives at Wolmaransstad.[79]
Day 491 Wed 1901-02-13	Cape Colony	Chief Commandant De Wet shrugs off his pursuers, but has to abandon about 200 horses.
	ZAR	Captains Trichard and Slegtkamp capture a train they call the 'Sugar Train', because of its cargo of sweets, near Brugspruit.[80] Lord Kitchener proposes an interview with Commandant-General Louis Botha to discuss peace.
Day 492 Thu 1901-02-14	Cape Colony	After a night of drenching rain, Colonel HCO Plumer attacks Chief Comandant CR de Wet's outspanned convoy at Wolvekuil, near Philipstown. The New Zealanders and Australians lose 23 men in a reckless charge and De Wet disengages during a heavy downpour, abandoning some of his vehicles.[81]
	Eastern ZAR	General Smith-Dorrien reaches Amsterdam.
	Western ZAR	After an abortive expedition by three columns — 1 800 men and nine field-guns — from Belfast, Machadodorp and Lydenburg against Viljoen's base at Windhoek, General Walter Kitchener retreats with 15 casualties.[82]
Day 493 Fri 1901-02-15	Cape Colony	Chief Commandant CR de Wet crosses the railway line at Bartman's Siding, but he loses most of his vehicles when they get stuck in mud at a flooded drift.[83] Colonel Plumer has been shrugged off and De Wet heads for Strydenburg where he hopes to be united with Hertzog.[84]

Day 494 Sat **1901-02-16**	Cape Colony	Lord Kitchener arrives at De Aar to take personal command of the operations against Chief Commandant De Wet's invasion force in the northern Cape Colony.[85] From Hopetown to Victoria West, over a front of about 250 kilometres, he arranges 15 columns, each roughly 1 000 men strong, ready to advance at right angles with De Wet's expected route. Plans are put in place to leapfrog fresh units into the chase, using the railway.[86] General Bruce Hamilton and Bethune's columns are detailed to head for Britstown to intercept Hertzog's commando. Hertzog splits his force and sends Commandant Brand towards Britstown for supplies while he heads for Strydenburg.[87]
	ZAR	Generals Beyers and Kemp cross the railway line between Kaalfontein and Irene on their way to the western ZAR[88]
Day 495 Sun **1901-02-17**	Cape Colony	Colonel Plumer clashes with De Wet's rearguard under Commandant Haasbroek at Gouwspan and they retire towards Gelukspoort.[89] Commandant Brand heads north from Britstown.
	Western ZAR	Lord Methuen receives reports that Celliers and Liebenberg are in the Hartebeesfontein area and he immediately starts a wide sweep to the north of the town.[90]
Day 496 Mon **1901-02-18**	Cape Colony	Colonel Plumer, after pursuing De Wet for nine days without rest, is forced to fall back for supplies. Chief Commandant De Wet laagers at Vroupan, 24 kilometres ahead of Plumer's tired column. De Wet's mobility is improved when he captures about 200 horses near Hopetown and he can get some of his walking men in the saddle again.[91] General Bruce Hamilton reaches Britstown and follows Brand's commando.
	Western ZAR	**THE BATTLE OF HARTEBEESFONTEIN** Lieutenant-Colonel S von Donop captures Celliers' unprotected laager at Brakpan, north of Hartebeesfontein, and takes 40 prisoners. Methuen's main force, now about 900 strong, engages the Republicans, also reinforced during the night, in a strong position on the Cyferfontein ridge, just north of town. The burghers, consisting of a combined force under Generals Du Toit (Wolmaransstad), Cilliers (Lichtenburg) and Liebenberg (Potchefstroom), easily repulse Methuen's attack. At about 11:00 the Republicans counterattack but also fail to make an impression. They retire during the afternoon, leaving 18 dead on the battlefield. Lord Methuen's casualties are 49 killed and wounded.[92]
	South-eastern ZAR	General Knox and Colonel Pulteney occupy Piet Retief, completing the second phase of French's drive. Seven columns have ended their wheeling movement and they now form a 60-kilometre line along the Swaziland border. The plan to corner large Republican forces here and to force them to surrender, ends in failure.[93]
Day 497 Tue **1901-02-19**	Cape Colony	With his pursuers about 15 kilometres behind him, De Wet reaches the banks of the flooded Brak River, about 16 kilometres east of Prieska. Unable to proceed and realising that his present circumstances will not gain him any recruits, he decides to abandon his invasion.[94] He immediately doubles back and General Knox, Plumer's relief column, who has decided to take a short cut westwards to head him off, loses touch completely.[95]
	Western ZAR	Lieutenant-General Lord Methuen arrives at Klerksdorp. The Republicans disperse and De la Rey, Smuts and Cilliers move north-westwards, in the direction of Lichtenburg.[96]
	South-eastern ZAR	Heavy rain causes serious floods and General French's supply arrangements break down and four of his columns are running out of supplies, having been on half rations for the last few days. Foraging parties are sent out in all directions, burning farms and looting for supplies. Hundreds of burghers surrender, large quantities of rifles and ammunition are discovered and seven field-guns, buried by their crews, are dug up.[97]

Day 498 Wed 1901-02-20	Cape Colony	General Knox reaches the flooded Brak River and heads off in the wrong direction.[98]
Day 499 Thu 1901-02-21	Cape Colony	Chief Commandant De Wet marches north towards the Orange River and rests at Blaauwkop. A small party of Plumer's Australian Scouts notices his movements and manages to inform Knox, who turns back to take up the chase again.[99]
Day 500 Fri 1901-02-22	Cape Colony	General Hertzog and Commandant Brand are reunited at Zwingelpan, 20 kilometres west of Strydenburg.[100]
	ZAR	Mrs Annie Botha returns to Pretoria with a letter from her husband to Lord Kitchener. After consultation with his government, Commandant-General Louis Botha agrees to a meeting with Kitchener.[101]
	Trivia	*RSS Baden-Powell's 44th birthday.*
Day 501 Sat 1901-02-23	Cape Colony	Colonel Plumer, resupplied, rejoins the hunt for De Wet. The invaders are vigorously pursued by Australian troops who are travelling light and are regularly relieved by fresh units. De Wet maintains his lead, but about 20 kilometres north-west of Hopetown, Victorian Imperial Bushmen overtake his rearguard and they abandon a 15-pounder field-gun and a pom-pom. Darkness ends the pursuit and De Wet increases the gap, but his scouts report a force from Kimberley blocking his advance.[102] General Hertzog enters Strydenburg and his men loot what they can carry.
	Western ZAR	Their sentences confirmed by Generals De la Rey and Smuts, traitors R McLachlan, JDP Theunissen, A Ahrens, R Boyd and C Matthysen (an ex-ZARP) are executed by Lemmer's commando near Wolmaransstad. C Theunissen is reprieved and taken across the Bechuanaland border.[103]
Day 502 Sun 1901-02-24	Cape Colony	Chief Commandant De Wet skirts around Hopetown and the mobile posts barring his progress. He crosses the railway south of Orange River Station.[104] After a short rest he continues and arrives on the banks of the Orange River during the afternoon. His scouts report that Lombard, Visser's and Glade Drifts are impassable.[105]
	Victoria Cross	Hamilton's scouts overwhelm a picket of six Boers on a koppie, near Strydenburg. In fierce hand-to-hand combat Corporal JJ Clements, Rimington's Guides, kills three with his revolver and he later receives the Victoria Cross.[106]
Day 503 Mon 1901-02-25	Cape Colony	The Kimberley column mistakes Plumer's New Zealanders for the enemy and a lively skirmish results which lasts almost half an hour before the blunder is realised. The exhausted and starving columns of Plumer and Knox converge on Hopetown.[107] General Hertzog crosses the railway line between Potfontein and Poupan Siding, dynamiting the track before proceeding.[108]
	Concentration camps	A former member of the Free State Volksraad, HS Viljoen, and five other prisoners are set free from Green Point Camp near Cape Town. They are sent to visit Free State concentration camps with the intention of influencing the women in the camps to persuade their husbands to lay down their arms. They meet with very little success.[109]
	ZAR	In Johannesburg two accused, named Captain and George, are tried for attempted murder, rape and robbery.[110]
Day 504 Tue 1901-02-26	Mozambique	The Portuguese ship *Benguella* leaves Delagoa Bay en route for Lisbon with about 700 Republican internees on board.[111]
	Trivia	*Two leaders of the Boxer Rebellion, Chi-hsui and Hsu-cheng-yu, are executed in Peking (Beijing).*

Day 505 Wed **1901-02-27**	Cape Colony	With three columns converging on them, Generals De Wet and Hertzog join forces at Sand Drift. Two young burghers brave the swirling waters and make it across with a tremendous effort. The drift is impassable. They continue along the river bank, testing one drift after the other. At the most crucial stage of the hunt all the columns ordered to corner De Wet's force against the river, are late in starting and De Wet passes through the flimsy cordon Colonel Byng has thrown across his path at Seekoei River, north of Colesberg.[112]
	Concentration camps ZAR	Discriminatory food rations — 1st class rations for the families of 'hands-uppers' and 2nd class rations for the families of fighting burghers or those who refuse to work for the British — are discontinued in the 'Transvaal' concentration camps.
	Trivia	*JNH Grobler's 37th birthday (commandant of Ermelo).*
Day 506 Thu **1901-02-28**	Cape Colony / OFS	Chief Commandant De Wet and General Hertzog capture a seven-man picket and arrive at Bothasdrift, 25 kilometres west of Norvalspont. This is the fifteenth ford they have attempted to cross during the previous nine days. With bated breath the burghers watch as a few men guide their horses into the strong current and with a bit of effort make it across. A mad rush follows and the men charge through and return to Free State soil. The burghers are elated and swear never to cross the infernal river again.[113] During the previous 74 days General Hertzog has covered more than 1 600 kilometres. He has captured more than 1 000 horses, but due to a lack of weapons and supplies, he has been unsuccessful in starting a rebellion in the Cape Colony.[114]
	ZAR	**THE MIDDELBURG CONFERENCE** Supreme Commander Lord Kitchener and Commandant-General Louis Botha meet at Middelburg to discuss terms. After a 'cordial' five-hour meeting, the conditions they promise to submit to their governments, include the following: 1. General amnesty for Republicans including rebels (except for temporary disfranchisement). 2. The speedy return of all prisoners of war. 3. Self-government to be granted as soon as possible. 4. Payment of Republicans' commandeering debts up to £1 000 000. 5. Church property, the orphans' funds and other public trusts to be respected. 6. Teaching of both languages to be allowed in schools. 7. Assistance to farmers and compensation for their losses to be granted. 8. No special war taxes to be levied. 9. Certain farmers to be licenced to have firearms. 10. The question of black political rights to be postponed until after the granting of self-government. Lord Kitchener comments to Lord Roberts, now Commander-in-Chief at the War Office: *"They evidently do not like their women being brought in and I think it has made them more anxious for peace."*[115]
	South-eastern ZAR	Colonel Henry leaves Amsterdam and executes a fast dash into Swaziland. He captures a Republican convoy, takes about 100 prisoners and some cattle.[116]
	Cape Colony	Sir Alfred Milner leaves Cape Town for Johannesburg to take up his duties as administrator of 'the new colonies.'
	OFFICIAL REPORTS	
	Farm burning:	No official report of buildings destroyed by British troops is available. British military authorities admit that 634 buildings have been destroyed by British troops since June 1900.[118]
	Concentration camps:	'Refugee camps' have been established at Kromellenboog, Middelburg, Norvalspont, Springfontein, Volksrust and Vredefort Road.[117]
	Communications:	The railway lines have been cut 30 times during February.[119]

1901-	AUTUMN	**MARCH**

1901-03-00	**THE BLOCKHOUSE LINES** The large-scale construction of fortified lines starts along railway lines to form 'paddocks' in an effort to protect the railway lines and to limit the mobility of the guerrillas. This huge undertaking starts off with substantial multi-storey masonry blockhouses at railway stations and bridges, and is systematically extended, later using the largely prefabricated corrugated iron forts designed by Major SR Rice, Royal Engineers. The first lines run along the main railway lines from Norvalspont to Pretoria (660 km), Orange River Station to Mafeking (840 km), Klerksdorp to Springs (250 km), Newcastle to Johannesburg (280 km) and Pretoria to Komatipoort (450 km).[120]

Day 507 Fri **1901-03-01**	Concentration camps	The 'refugee' camps in the 'Orange River and Transvaal Colonies' are transferred to civil control under Sir Alfred Milner.
	OFS	Chief Commandant De Wet reaches Philippolis. On the same day the commandos split up and disperse. De Wet and President Steyn move north, with no more than a bodyguard.[121]
	Western ZAR	Brigadier-General Cunningham and Colonel Shekleton, ordered to clear the area of Kemp's commando, start a sweep from Krugersdorp along the Witwatersrand, towards General Babington's position at Noupoort.[122]
Day 508 Sat **1901-03-02**	Western ZAR	At Dwarsvlei General Kemp dodges the approaching British by escaping along the most dangerous route. He moves his commando through a valley, less than five kilometres wide and overlooked by Babington's positions. His audacity pays off, he evades his pursuers and moves north with 400 men to join De la Rey.[123] **THE ATTACK ON LICHTENBURG** General De la Rey has summoned his commandos to a rendezvous north of Lichtenburg where he issues his orders for the attack on the garrison. General Celliers with Commandants Vermaas and Lemmer is to attack from the west, General Smuts and Commandant Du Toit from the east and General Liebenberg and his Potchefstroom burghers from the north. Although De la Rey has about 1 200 men at his disposal, the assault on the town is to be made by 300-400 men. The planned three-pronged attack makes co-ordination of the utmost importance and the burghers assemble at Zoetmelksvlei, about ten kilometres west of town, where they dismount to approach the town on foot.[124]
	Cape Colony	H van Heerden, a loyal Colonial farmer, is arrested after the tracks of a commando have been found on his farm. He is wounded when his escort is attacked on their way to Cradock. While being cared for by his family, he is tried for treason (assisting a commando) and sentenced to death in his absence. Returning to his farm, British troops drag him from his bed and execute him by firing squad on his farm, Sewefontein, near Cradock.
Day 509 Sun **1901-03-03**	OFS	**The Middelburg Conference:** On Milner's insistence Lord Kitchener meets him in Bloemfontein to discuss the Middelburg proposals before transmitting them to London. Kitchener privately pleads with Milner to allow amnesty for the rebels, as he realises that it is *"obviously a point of honour for the Boers"*. Milner is adamant that rebels fighting on the Republican side, are traitors.[125] Sir A Milner writes to Lady Edward Cecil, *"Have had two hours with Kitchener. We don't see eye to eye, as might be expected. He is fearfully sick of the war, sees no possible credit in the continuance of it and is, I think, rather disposed to go far in making things easy for the enemy. I feel that every concession we make now means more trouble hereafter. At the same time it is not easy, with people sensibly weakening at home and your General (Kitchener) on the spot desperately anxious to come to terms, to insist on all that you personally consider important, I foresee that I shall be driven to compromise — a thing I loathe."* [126]

		Plumer and Bethune arrive at Philippolis to find that De Wet has left 24 hours previously.
	Western ZAR	**THE ATTACK ON LICHTENBURG** The British garrison at Lichtenburg consists of about 620 men with two field-guns and is commanded by Lieutenant-Colonel CGC Money. He has turned the market square in the middle of town into a fortified redoubt with strong pickets in sangars positioned on the outskirts of the town. His task is made somewhat easier by almost impassable marshlands situated around the town to the east, south and west. De la Rey's meticulous plans are wrecked when General Liebenberg decides, without consulting anyone, that a charge on horseback is asked for. At 03:15 he charges, the pickets are alerted and he is repulsed. With all the sentries now wide awake, Smuts' men, approaching from the east, are noticed while they are still struggling to get through the marsh. They draw fire from the nearest sangar and retreat in confusion. The attack from the west fares better and they reach the outskirts, isolate the sangars they encounter and start to make their way to the town centre. Early in the attack, however, both General Celliers and Commandant Lemmer are wounded and Field-cornet Blignaut of Marico is killed, and the assault starts to falter. Only Commandant Vermaas, fighting furiously, reaches the British main position with 34 men. De la Rey has to send in his own men to protect Vermaas' flanks. The burghers, without food or water, are pinned down by machine gun fire. An afternoon shower brings relief and they manage to hold on until nightfall. At 17:30 a two-hour armistice to permit the removal of dead and wounded is agreed on. Firing resumes on expiry, but De la Rey withdraws during the night, having lost at least 14 killed and 38 wounded (including General Celliers and Commandant Lemmer). The British casualties amount to about 18 killed and 24 wounded.[127]
	Victoria Cross	Lieutenant FB Dugdale, 5th Royal Irish Lancers, near Derby.
Day 510 Mon **1901-03-04**	Western ZAR	At Lichtenburg some of the retreating burghers are still in the marsh when the sun comes up and they have to hide there all day long before escaping after dark.[128]
	OFS Concentration camps	Brigadier-General Plumer is in action with Fourie and Brand at Zuurfontein and the burghers turn eastwards. De Wet arrives at Fauresmith.[129] Miss Emily Hobhouse visits the Springfontein concentration camp.[130]
	Trivia	*President McKinley is inaugurated as the 25th US president.*
Day 511 Tue **1901-03-05**	OFS	Arriving north of the Riet River, Bethune gives up the chase, leaving only Plumer still doggedly following De Wet.[131]
Day 512 Wed **1901-03-06**	ZAR	**THE MIDDELBURG CONFERENCE** Milner receives the amended peace proposals from Chamberlain for transmission to Commandant-General Botha. The amendments include the following: 1. Cape rebel leaders will be subject to courts-martial. 2. Repatriation of prisoners of war will happen 'as soon as practical'. 3. The question of future self-government is referred to as 'a privilege' and is phrased in vaguer terms. 4. The £1-million payment is re-termed as 'an act of grace' and is heavily qualified. 5. The assistance to farmers will be a repayable loan and will be subject to the recipient swearing an oath of allegiance to the King. 6. The use of Dutch in school will be allowed only when requested by the parents. 7. Black franchise will be similar to that in the Cape Colony.

	OFS	Chief Commandant De Wet crosses the Modder River at Abraham's Kraal, extending his lead on his pursuers.[132] General Philip Botha is killed in action near Ventersburg.[133]
	Concentration camps	Discriminatory food rations are also discontinued in the 'Orange River Colony' camps.
Day 513 Thu **1901-03-07**		
Day 514 Fri **1901-03-08**	OFS	Chief Commandant De Wet swerves east and crosses the railway line between Brandfort and Smaldeel (Theunissen).[134]
	Concentration camps	Miss Emily Hobhouse visits the Norvalspont concentration camp.[135]
Day 515 Sat **1901-03-09**	Cape Colony	K Nienaber, P Nienaber and J Niewhoudt are executed after being found guilty of assisting in the derailment of a train at Taaibosch, near De Aar. (A subsequent trial in June 1902 finds a witness guilty of perjury.)
	Portuguese East Africa	The Portuguese ship *Zaire* sails from Lourenço Marques for Lisbon with 89 burghers, 56 women and 172 children, bound for internment in Portugal.[136]
Day 516 Sun **1901-03-10**	Cape Colony	A rebel commando enters Aberdeen and releases the prisoners from the jail.[137]
Day 517 Mon **1901-03-11**	OFS	**END OF 'THE THIRD (OR GREAT) DE WET DRIVE'** Chief Commandant De Wet arrives back in the Senekal district and disperses the last of his burghers. On the same day Colonel Plumer leads his weary troops into Brandfort.[138] During the last 43 days, constantly pursued, De Wet's commando has covered about 1 300 kilometres.[139] His successful escape influences Botha's decision on the negotiations with Kitchener.
	ZAR	The first of the new type of prefabricated blockhouses is erected on Gun Hill near Middelburg, ZAR.[140]
	Western ZAR	Babington and Shekleton join forces at Ventersdorp.
Day 518 Tue **1901-03-12**	Concentration camps	Miss Emily Hobhouse visits the Kimberley concentration camp.[141]
	Trivia	*US businessman Andrew Carnegie provides 2,5 million dollars to start the public library system.*
Day 519 Wed **1901-03-13**	*Trivia*	*HCO Plumer's 44th birthday.*
Day 520 Thu **1901-03-14**		
Day 521 Fri **1901-03-15**	Northern ZAR	Colonel Park, operating from Lydenburg, captures a small Republican laager at Kruger's Post, taking 35 prisoners.[142]
	OFS	Circular No 31 titled *Clearing of Orange River Colony* is issued by Adjutant-General WF Kelly on orders from Lord Kitchener, and states: 1. All families on farms, with their livestock, must be brought to the nearest railway station. 2. All vehicles unsuitable for use by the military, must be used for the transport of the civilians. 3. The number of personal possessions that the families can take with them, will be

		determined by the availability of transport. Tarpaulins and materials that can be used as shelters, must be removed. 4. Where supplies are found, part must be given to the family and the black farm workers, part can be confiscated by the military, and the rest must be destroyed. 5. All crops must be destroyed and fodder must be confiscated or destroyed. 6. All livestock and horses must be removed. 7. All baking ovens and furniture must be destroyed.[143]
Day 522 Sat **1901-03-16**	ZAR United Kingdom	**THE MIDDELBURG CONFERENCE** Commandant-General Botha rejects Kitchener's peace terms, as amended by Milner, Chamberlain and the British government. He writes: *"Your Excellency can hardly feel surprised that I did not feel at liberty to recommend the terms expressed in this letter to the serious consideration of my Government. Let me add to the present that my Government and the commanding officers here about me, quite agree with my views of the case."*[144] In a letter addressed to his burghers, Botha writes: *"Virtually, Lord Kitchener's letter contains nothing more, but rather less than what the British Government will be obliged to do should our cause go wrong... The cause is not yet lost and since nothing worse than this can befall us, it is well worthwhile to fight on... The spirit of Lord Kitchener's letter makes it very plain to you that the British Government desires nothing less than the destruction of our Afrikaner people."* He exhorts his men to put their trust in God *"who in His own time and in His own way will surely send deliverance"*.[145] Kitchener is bitterly disappointed and writes to Brodrick: *"Milner's view (on Cape rebels) may be strictly just, but, to my mind, they are vindictive... We are now carrying on the war to put two or three hundred Dutchmen in prison at the end of it. It seems to me absurd."*[146] However, J Chamberlain writes to St J Brodrick: *"I am rather relieved by Botha's reply. I feared the results of a long negotiation. I hope Kitchener is ready for a vigorous attack upon him."*[147]
Day 523 Sun **1901-03-17**	United Kingdom	Winston Churchill, who has recently made his maiden speech in the House of Commons, writes to Milner: *"... although every act of justice or generosity towards the Boers will be regarded by the Loyalists as a personal insult to themselves, you must not shut your eyes to the feeling in this country. The intellect of the nation is piling up on the other side: the strength of the Government cannot be measured by its large majorities. Thousands of voices silenced by the warlike shouts of the crowd these many months will be heard again when peace is restored."*[148]
Day 524 Mon **1901-03-18**		
Day 525 Tue **1901-03-19**	Cape Colony Black involvement	Commandant Gideon Scheepers executes two armed Coloureds of a group that has fired at his commando from a farmhouse near Jansenville. He releases two loyal Cape farmers and ten other Coloureds.[149]
Day 526 Wed **1901-03-20**	Northern ZAR	The State Secretary, Mr FW Reitz, authorises the postmaster of Pietersburg to print postage stamps. A small supply is printed on the presses of *De Zoutpansberg Wachter* and the issued stamps are initialled by Mr JT deV Smit.[150]
Day 527 Thu **1901-03-21**	ZAR Black involvement	Acting President SW Burger, referring to the correspondence between Botha and Kitchener, wites to President Steyn: *"There is no mention of terms that meet us in any way, therefore I keep to the decision to surrender unconditionally if this must happen, which I trust God forbid."*[151] A British missionary, Canon Farmer, accuses General Smuts of having committed an atrocity against members of his flock at Modderfontein at the end of January.[152] Smuts' commando is at Paardeplaats, on his way to join De la Rey and Kemp near Hartebeesfontein.[153]

Day 528 Fri 1901-03-22	Western ZAR	**THE ACTION AT GEDULD** A party of British scouts, investigating reports of De la Rey's laager being in the vicinity, is sent to Geduld, north of Hartbeesfontein. They are almost drawn into a trap and take cover in a kraal. A force of about 250 members of the Imperial Light Horse with one pom-pom, under the command of Major CJ Briggs, is sent to extricate the scouts. At about 07:30 the British are attacked by about 400 burghers with three guns, commanded by General JH de la Rey. De la Rey's men attack on horseback, firing from the saddle and the ILH escape in the nick of time. A running battle develops with Smuts joining in and the three squadrons are subjected to long-range sniping. The British fight their way through to Hartbeesfontein, losing two officers and five others killed and 13 men wounded. The Republicans lose at least one man killed while General Smuts is slightly wounded.[154]
Day 529 Sat 1901-03-23	*Trivia*	*Sir Alfred Milner's 47th birthday.*
Day 530 Sun 1901-03-24	Western ZAR	**THE ACTION AT WILDFONTEIN** Babington's Mounted Infantry overwhelms a small picket forming part of De la Rey and Kemp's rearguard. A running battle with De la Rey's convoy ensues. In a determined pursuit across the farms of Wildfontein and Kafferskraal, near Ventersdorp, he is forced to leave his guns and some of his vehicles behind. The British keep up their chase and take 140 prisoners and 77 wagons and carts, losing only nine soldiers in the process. British soldiers recapture two of Long's Armstrong guns, captured at Colenso, together with a Maxim-Nordenfeldt and six machine guns.[155]
Day 531 Mon 1901-03-25	Natal Black involvement	The British military authorities declare martial law in the Zululand districts north of the Tugela.
Day 532 Tue 1901-03-26	Northern ZAR	Brigadier-General HCO Plumer, commanding a compact force of about 1 300 mounted rifles, a small detachment of engineers, 8 field-guns and a pom-pom, leaves Pretoria for operations in the northern ZAR. One of the units accompanying him is the Bushveld Carbineers, a new corps that have been raised by Mr Levi, a British supporter and the proprietor of a hotel at Pienaar's River.[156]
	South-eastern ZAR	General French, his supply problems alleviated and now commanding a reduced force with a fighting strength of about 13 000, completes his arrangements for the final phase of his operation. His force, extending over almost 200 kilometres, lines two sides of the triangle formed by Vryheid, Piet Retief and Langdraai Drift on the Pongola River, near the Swaziland border. The other side of the triangle is formed by the Zululand border. In desperation, the British army is deliberately manoeuvring to force the Zulus to fight their war.[157]
	Natal Black involvement	General Hildyard informs the Natal Prime Minister Mr AH Hime as follows, "*After consultation with French at Vryheid the following arrangements have been made: a selected party have been sent under Bottomly, with Struben and Loxton, to assist General French's operations by informing the Zulus that they should oppose entry of Boers into Zululand by encouraging them to resist any invasion by force... Colonel Bottomley is instructed to inform magistrates or other officials in Zululand that he is acting in conjunction with force under General French.*" The Zulus in the Nqutu and Nkandla districts are issued with 100 rifles and ammunition.
	Cape Colony	Miss Emily Hobhouse addresses an audience of Cape Afrikaners in Cape Town.[158]
	Trivia	*CC Froneman's 55th birthday.*
Day 533 Wed 1901-03-27	South-eastern ZAR	General French starts the last phase of his drive, but the difficult country slows his progress.

Day 534 Thu **1901-03-28**	Northern ZAR	Brigadier-General Plumer arrives at Pienaar's River Station, about 60 kilometres north of Pretoria.
	Portugal	The Portuguese ship *Benguella* lands at Alcantara, Lisbon, with its cargo of about 700 Republican internees. Five Republicans have died en route and have been buried at sea.[159]
Day 535 Fri **1901-03-29**		
Day 536 Sat **1901-03-30**	South-eastern ZAR	The broken nature of the terrain prevents French's columns from maintaining mutual contact and they form bases from which they launch mounted forays.[160]
	Northern ZAR	Plumer arrives at Warmbaths.
Day 537 Sun **1901-03-31**	South-eastern ZAR	Brigadier-General Dartnell clashes with Commandant Cheere Emmett (Louis Botha's brother-in-law) at Smaldeel and captures about 20 prisoners and 20 wagons.[161]
	Trivia	*Seventy-two 'revolutionaries' are arrested in Russia after recent riots.*
	OFFICIAL REPORTS **Communications:**	The railway lines have been cut 18 times during March.[162]
1901	AUTUMN	**APRIL**
Day 538 Mon **1901-04-01**	ZAR	Brigadier-General Plumer occupies Nylstroom.
	OFS	**Middelburg Conference:** Chief Commandant CR de Wet issues a circular to his burghers, declaring that the majority of the people will not accept Kitchener's proposals, even if their government does, and that it is useless to examine them, *"as the only object for which we are fighting is the independence of our Republics"*. Nothing short of it will put an end to the conflict.[163]
	Portugal	The Portuguese ship *Zaire* lands at Lisbon, with its cargo of Republican men, women and children to be interned in Portugal. Three internees have died en route and have been buried at sea.[164]
Day 539 Tue **1901-04-02**	ZAR	Lord Kitchener gives permission for the establishment of a Cattle Ranger Corps to look after government cattle in the Pretoria area. They are later to be employed in bringing in looted cattle and will receive some of the loot as payment.[165]
Day 540 Wed **1901-04-03**	Natal Black involvement	The Natal Prime Minister AH Hime complains to General Hildyard that Colonel Bottomley is exceeding his instructions by using Zulu warriors on cattle-looting expeditions in the south-eastern districts of the ZAR.
	Cape Colony	Commandant Van Reenen, with 300 burghers, returns to the Free State but Kritzinger, Scheepers, Fouchee and Malan remain in the Cape Colony to continue guerrilla activities.[166]
	Trivia	*JBM Hertzog's 35th birthday.*
Day 541 Thu **1901-04-04**	Natal Black involvement	Colonel Bottomley writes a letter to King Dinizulu, ordering him to arm: *"Under authority from Gen. French Commanding... Forces in S.E. Transvaal I hereby authorise Zulu Chief Dinizula (sic) to arm all his followers and to protect the Zulu Border from Invasion by the Boers. He will not cross with any armed party, but he may employ his men to scout and drive cattle in the Transvaal — the men to be unarmed. He will capture Boer stock and hand same over to me or my representative. He will understand that he is acting in cooperation with the British Forces in S.E. Transvaal and he and his followers to do no act which is contrary to civilized warfare."*

Day 542 Fri **1901-04-05**	ZAR	GOOD FRIDAY The ZAR Government leaves Perdeplaats, near Tautesberg, to join Commandant-General Botha near Ermelo.
Day 543 Sat **1901-04-06**	South-eastern ZAR	General Grobelaar doubles back towards Vryheid. He evades a hastily prepared trap and slips through between the tired troops of Generals Knox and Dartnell.[167]
	ZAR	The ZAR government, travelling south, crosses the Delagoa railway line near Pan Station, between Middelburg and Wonderfontein.
	Cape Colony	Commandant Gideon Scheepers captures a detachment of 75 men at Zeekoeigat, near Cradock. Miss Emily Hobhouse returns to Kimberley.[168]
	International	President Kruger and his party move to Hilversum, where they are again welcomed by thousands.[169]
Day 544 Sun **1901-04-07**	South-eastern ZAR	EASTER SUNDAY Republican commandos under Chris Botha, Opperman, Mears and Emmett escape northwards crossing the British line between Piet Retief and Jagd Drift and they threaten Smith-Dorrien's supply line from Wakkerstroom.[170]
	Northern ZAR	General CF Beyers, with 500 burghers and a 'Long Tom', evacuates Pietersburg, removing all the stores they can transport.[171]
	ZAR	Lieutenant-General Sir Bindon Blood, newly appointed to take command of all the troops on the eastern line of communications, arrives at Middelburg to carry out operations against General Ben Viljoen.[172]
	Cape Colony	When a deputation of rebels from the Northern Cape requests officers to lead a new rebellion in the Brandvlei area, Commandant WC Malan sends Salmon Maritz, his corporalship of ten men, including the Marquis Robert de Kersuason, a French Volunteer and former member of Theron's Scouting Corps, and six Coloureds after-riders to go to their assistance.[173]
Day 545 Mon **1901-04-08**	Northern ZAR	EASTER MONDAY Brigadier-General Plumer occupies Pietersburg. A schoolmaster, the sole defender of the town, hides in long grass and accounts for two officers and a trooper before he throws down his rifle and surrenders. He is immediately bayonetted to death.[175] The British capture a large quantity of stores, two locomotives and 36 trucks. They destroy four steam mills and the presses of the *Zoutpansberg Wachter*.[176]
Day 546 Tue **1901-04-09**	Natal Black involvement	The Zulu army marches back to Nongoma. Two Zulus have been killed in confrontations with Boer cattle guards and about 48 000 head of cattle have been looted. The expedition has been terminated by Bottomley because feeding the 6 000-man Zulu Army is a problem and some of the Zulus have been looting stock from Zulu kraals.
	South-eastern ZAR	The ZAR government is at Spitzkop, south-east of Ermelo.
	Concentration camps	Miss Emily Hobhouse visits the Mafeking concentration camp. [176]
	Trivia	*Emily Hobhouse's 41st birthday.*
Day 547 Wed **1901-04-10**	Northern OFS	Major-General E Locke Elliot, Divisional Commander at Kroonstad, now the headquarters of the Northern District, commences the first drive in the northern Free State. Planning to clear the area west of the railway line between Kroonstad and the Vaal River, he employs three columns, commanded by Broadwood, Bethune and De Lisle, marching in parallel lines northwards towards the Vaal.[177]
	OFS	Colonel Monro, participating in forays by mounted columns operating from Dewetsdorp, surrounds and captures 83 burghers under Commandant Bressler at Rietspruit Farm after a long chase.[178]

233

Day 548 Thu 1901-04-11	Eastern ZAR	A train is wrecked near Witbank.
Day 549 Fri 1901-04-12	Cape Colony	The expiration of the Cape Indemnity Act. The jurisdiction of the special commissions to try rebels under the Treason Act of 1900 expires.
	Concentration camps	Emily Hobhouse witnesses the clearing of Warrenton and the dispatch of people in open coal trucks.[179]
Day 550 Sat 1901-04-13	Eastern ZAR	A train is wrecked near Machadodorp.
	Cape Colony Concentration camps	Emily Hobhouse returns to Kimberley, witnessing the arrival of the people removed from Warrenton at the Kimberley camp, where there are only 25 tents available for 240 people.[180]
Day 551 Sun 1901-04-14	ZAR	**THE ACTION AT GOEDVOORUITZICHT** Receiving reliable information, Babington executes a night march and, at dawn, he pounces on General Smuts' laager at Goedvooruitzicht. The 500 to 600 burghers, commanded by Commandant Wolmarans in Smuts' absence, are completely taken by surprise when Sir Henry Rawlinson's mounted men charge the laager. They can only manage an ineffective counter-attack before the British artillery drives them off. The British capture the laager and take a 12-pounder gun captured at Silkaatsnek and a pom-pom. The Republicans lose six killed, ten wounded and 23 taken prisoner, while on the British side three are wounded.[181]
	South-eastern ZAR	**THE END OF THE DRIVE IN THE SOUTH-EASTERN ZAR** General Smith-Dorrien, his supply lines threatened by the burghers who have slipped through the British lines, abandons Piet Retief and marches north towards the Delagoa railway line. This signals the end of the first great drive of the guerrilla phase of the war. The British estimate that 1 332 burghers have been eliminated — 362 killed or wounded, 233 captured and 730 have surrendered voluntarily. This estimate is almost certainly too high and may include many old men, children and non-combatants. Not one officer of note has been captured. They have also captured 11 guns, 2 300 vehicles, 272 000 rounds of rifle ammunition, 7 000-8 000 horses and mules and large quantities of livestock. No official return of British losses is available.[182]
	North-eastern ZAR	**THE DRIVE IN THE NORTH-EASTERN ZAR** In an ambitious operation encompassing a huge, wild part of the country, the British start a drive in the north-eastern ZAR. Colonel Plumer leaves Pietersburg and marches south, towards the Olifants River. At the same time, Lieutenant-General Bindon Blood's columns commence their advance, marching northwards from the Delagoa railway line against Viljoen and Muller in the Dullstroom vicinity. Bindon Blood is in overall command of four columns under Major General Beatson, Lieutenant-Colonel GE Benson, Lieutenant-Colonel Pulteney and Lieutenant-Colonel Douglas, starting from Middelburg, Belfast and Machadodorp. Another two columns under Lieutenant-Colonels Park and Walter Kitchener start from Lydenburg, moving northwards and eastwards respectively. The force totals about 11 000 rifles and 31 guns.[183]
	Trivia	*Actors of the New York Academy of Music are arrested for wearing costumes on Sunday.*
Day 552 Mon 1901-04-15	North-eastern ZAR	Brigadier-General Plumer splits his force south of the Strydpoort Mountains and heads for various drifts in the Olifants River.
Day 553 Tue 1901-04-16	North-eastern ZAR	Generals Ben Viljoen and Chris Muller have gathered about 1 100 burghers in the vicinity of Roossenekal, Mapochsgronden and Dullstroom. General Douglas, who has marched along the Lydenburg road before swinging first eastwards and then southwards, is approaching Dullstroom from the north. General Viljoen, fully aware of his movements, sends Muller with 400 burghers to attack him from the rear near Palmietfontein. Viljoen with about 500 men and Commandant Taute simultaneously

		attack from both flanks. A sharp action results in which Muller is slightly wounded, before the Republicans disengage and move back to Mapochsgronden.
	Northern ZAR	Further north, at Rietfontein, north-east of Lydenburg, the third State Artillery Creusot 'Long Tom' gun is blown up by Lieutenant D Erasmus and his crew.[184]
	Eastern ZAR	The ZAR government is at Rietspruit, near Ermelo.
Day 554 Wed **1901-04-17**	North-eastern ZAR	Lieutenant-Colonel Pulteney enters Dullstroom from the south.[185]
Day 555 Thu **1901-04-18**	North-eastern ZAR	For the first time, Chancellor of the Exchequer Sir Michael Hicks Beach's budget proposals anticipate a higher revenue from direct than indirect taxes. Personal income tax is increased by 2d to 14d in the £.
Day 556 Fri **1901-04-19**	Eastern ZAR	The ZAR government is at Beginderlijn, south of Ermelo.
Day 557 Sat **1901-04-20**	North-eastern ZAR	General Beatson moves to Leeufontein and Colonel Benson to Blinkwater, completing, with the rest of the southern columns, an almost continuous line to Dullstroom. About 200 Boksburgers surrender at Blinkwater.
	North-eastern OFS	The columns of Broadwood, Bethune and De Lisle, having turned eastwards on reaching the Vaal River, converge on the Vredefort road. The towns of Parys and Vredefort and many outlying farms have been cleared of inhabitants and supplies but no contact has been made with any of the commandos in the district.[186]
	Trivia	*PH Kritzinger's 31st birthday.* *Republican scout OJ (Jack) Hindon's 27th birthday.*
Day 558 Sun **1901-04-21**	Eastern ZAR	The ZAR government is at Vyfhoek, north of Amersfoort.[187]
	OFS Concentration camps	Miss Emily Hobhouse arrives in Bloemfontein.
Day 559 Mon **1901-04-22**	North-eastern ZAR	Brigadier-General Plumer completes his occupation of the Olifants River drifts, but the river is passable almost at any point and his arrangements are not as effective as he imagines. General Ben Viljoen moves eastwards and crosses the Olifants River south of Beatson's post at Crocodile Drift. Lieutenant-Colonel Pulteney captures Roossenekal where he accepts the surrender of the magistrate and 60 burghers.[188]
	Western ZAR	**THE ACTION AT PLATBERG** A Republican commando attacks a convoy, escorted by 400 men with two guns, at Platberg, near Klerksdorp. The burghers launch a three-pronged attack, with two parties attacking from the Lapfontein hills and another from Platberg. The escort put up a gallant defence, one small party preventing the attackers from crossing the Schoonspruit. Another group sacrifices themselves by attacking a group of burghers who were in a position to threaten the guns. They heroically keep up a determined fusillade to their last bullet before surrendering, allowing the guns and the convoy to escape. The British lose two killed, three wounded and eight taken prisoner, while the Republicans lose one killed and one wounded.[189]
	OFS	Sir Hamilton Goold-Adams, Assistant-Administrator of the 'Orange River Colony', writes, *"I have come upon case after case where men who have taken the oath of neutrality are ... expected to report to us, work for us and even to fight in our ranks."*[190]
	Cape Colony	Lord Kitchener publishes an important notice to warn *"all subjects of His Majesty and*

		all persons residing in the Cape Colony who shall in the districts thereof in which Martial Law prevails, be actively in arms against His Majesty, or who shall directly incite others to take up arms against Him, or who shall actively aid or assist the enemy or commit any overt act by which the safety of His Majesty's forces or subjects is endangered shall immediately on arrest be tried by Court Martial convened by my authority and shall on conviction be liable to the severest penalties of the law".[191]
Day 560 Tue **1901-04-23**	North-eastern ZAR	General Viljoen feints northwards before turning towards Bronkhorstspruit.
	Eastern ZAR	The ZAR government returns to Rietspruit, near Ermelo.
	OFS	Sir Alfred Milner refuses to issue a permit to Emily Hobhouse authorising her to travel north of Bloemfontein.[192]
Day 561 Wed **1901-04-24**	North-eastern ZAR	General Viljoen feints eastwards and passes north of Rhenosterkop before turning south towards the Delagoa railway line. With their main quarry outside the net, the British columns carry out raids in all directions, burning farms and looting livestock.
	Trivia	*For the next month, until 1901-05-25, a comet, known only as 'The Great Comet of 1901', is visible over most of South Africa. It is looked upon as an omen by all parties and all kinds of meanings are attached to it.*[193] *NPJJ (Siener or 'Seer') van Rensburg, a psychic attached to General De la Rey's staff, however, never offers any interpretations to his dreams or any other phenomena.*
Day 562 Thu **1901-04-25**		
Day 563 Fri **1901-04-26**	North-eastern ZAR	Forty-seven burghers surrender at Klipdam, about 20 kilometres north of Pietersburg.[194]
Day 564 Sat **1901-04-27**	Trivia	*Cape politician sir JG Sprigg's 71st birthday.*
Day 565 Sun **1901-04-28**		
Day 566 Mon **1901-04-29**	Eastern OFS	General Rundle, commanding a force of about 2 600 men with seven guns and a huge ox-wagon convoy, leaves Bethlehem on an expedition against 700 burghers under Commandants Rautenbach and Steyn in the Brandwater Basin. A more unwieldy force against mobile guerrillas in one of the most difficult parts of the country can hardly be imagined.[195] A column under Lieutenant-Colonel Pilcher destroys the town of Reitz, leaving a single house, that of the Justice of the Peace, standing. A trooper of the Imperial Yeomanry later writes: *"We had some good fun at Reitz — we burnt the place so that you would not know it. We broke all the grates, pans, etc., and the furniture. I think that the pianos got the worst of it. We turned them upside down, picked the notes to pieces, and then threw them out the window."*[196]
	Southern OFS	Commandant PH Kritzinger captures a supply train near Molteno and re-enters the Free State near Bethulie.[197]
Day 567 Tue **1901-04-30**	Eastern OFS	The ZAR State Artillery's fourth and last Creusot 'Long Tom', that of Lieutenant H Du Toit, is dynamited by its crew before falling into British hands at Bergplaas, also known as Houtbosberg or Feesberg, 46 kilometres east of Pietersburg (13 kilometres north of Haenertsburg). According to Viljoen this happened only 200 metres from the charging enemy. This is most likely the gun known as 'the Jew,' which had been damaged at Ladysmith, was repaired and then used at Kimberley during the last days of the siege.[198]

		OFFICIAL REPORTS
		Communications: Railway lines have been cut 18 times during April.[199]
1901	AUTUMN	**MAY**
Day 568 Wed **1901-05-01**	North-eastern ZAR	**THE END OF THE DRIVE IN THE NORTH-EASTERN ZAR** General Bindon Blood's columns in the north-eastern ZAR are withdrawn. This huge operation cannot be called an unqualified success. The British claim to have captured 1 100 burghers. As the main Republican forces in the area — those under General Viljoen, General Muller and Commandant Taute have escaped — it must be accepted that a large number of old men, children and non-combatants must be included in their figures. A Long Tom, the 4,7 inch naval gun taken at Helvetia, a Krupp, an Armstrong, two pom-poms and two machine guns — all out of ammunition and destroyed by their crews — fall into British hands, along with only 540 rifles, a supply of rifle ammunition, 247 horses, 611 vehicles and large quantities of livestock.[200]
	Western ZAR	**METHUEN'S DRIVE IN THE WESTERN ZAR** All available troops have been sent to Mafeking by rail and, with Babington at Syferkuil, Rawlinson at Brakspruit, Dixon at Tafelkop and a strong force under Lieutenant-Colonel Ingouville-Williams at Klerksdorp, Lord Methuen starts an operation to clear the Lichtenburg-Ventersdorp-Klerksdorp triangle.[201]
	Cape Colony	Fresh instructions are issued to martial law administrators in the Cape Colony.
Day 569 Thu **1901-05-02**	Eastern ZAR	The ZAR government is at Vlakfontein, east of Ermelo. Without having made contact with the enemy, General Rundle's heavy convoy reaches Fouriesburg.[202]
Day 570 Fri **1901-05-03**	Western ZAR	Lord Methuen arrives at Lichtenburg.
	Eastern ZAR	The ZAR government is at Klipbank, near Ermelo.
Day 571 Sat **1901-05-04**	Cape Colony	Miss Emily Hobhouse arrives in Cape Town.[203]
	Trivia	*General AF Hart's 57th birthday.*
Day 572 Sun **1901-05-05**	Western ZAR	General Liebenberg crosses the Schoonspruit, eluding Rawlinson's column.
Day 573 Mon **1901-05-06**	Western ZAR	Lord Methuen's columns converge on the deserted Hartebeesfontein without a single burgher in the trap. The net result of his drive is a single gun abandoned by General Celliers' Lichtenburg commando. Methuen contents himself by burning the supplies found in the village and planning a combined sweep westwards.
	Cape Colony	Commandant Willem D Fouchee crosses the railway line at Reynier Siding between Stormberg and Burgersdorp with 250 men.[204]
	United Kingdom	Although the Imperial government originally demanded £4 000 as compensation for the widow Edgar (see 23 December 1899), in correspondence from Milner to Chamberlain, she is no longer considered *"a very deserving person".*
Day 574 Tue **1901-05-07**	ZAR	Some of the gold-mines on the Witwatersrand are allowed to resume operations on a small scale.
	North-eastern OFS	Major-General EL Elliot commences another drive in the north-eastern Free State. With the columns of Eustace Knox and Rimington acting as stopper groups on the Vaal River, Elliot, commanding the columns of Bethune, De Lisle and Lowe, starts

		from the Villiers-Frankfort-Tafelkop line and marches eastwards, heading for the town of Vrede.[205]
	Cape Town	Miss Emily Hobhouse leaves for Britain after an extended fact-finding tour of the concentration camps.[206]
	Trivia	*American film star Gary Cooper is born.*
Day 575 Wed **1901-05-08**	Cape Colony	Sir Alfred Milner leaves Cape Town for England on board the *Saxon*.
Day 576 Thu **1901-05-09**	Western ZAR	Lord Methuen, marching along a broad front towards Schweizer-Reneke, Bloemhof and Wolmaransstad, changes his mind and swings northwards, towards Biesiesvlei and the Great Hart's River.[207]
Day 577 Fri **1901-05-10**	Eastern ZAR	**THE MEETING AT DE EMIGRATIE** A ZAR council of war, consisting of Commandant-General L Botha, Generals JC Smuts, C Botha and B Viljoen and members of the ZAR government meet at De Emigratie between Ermelo and Wakkerstroom. The ZAR leadership falters again. Without consulting President Steyn and the Free State government, the meeting decides on renewed peace negotiations. President Kruger is to be involved through a telegraphic connection that Kitchener will make available to Smuts, who will act as a go-between.[208]
Day 578 Sat **1901-05-11**	Western ZAR	Lord Methuen abandons his drive, having taken less than 100 prisoners. The British columns withdraw: Methuen and Rawlinson to the Kimberley-Mafeking railway, Babington and Ingouville-Williams to Klerksdorp and Dixon to his entrenched camp at Noupoort, south of the Magaliesberg.[209]
	Eastern ZAR	The ZAR government is at De Emigratie, south-east of Ermelo.
Day 579 Sun **1901-05-12**	Eastern ZAR	The ZAR government is at Mooiplaats, near Ermelo.
	Western Cape	Maritz ambushes two detachments of the Calvinia District Mounted Troops at Melkboschfontein and captures both, taking substantial supplies and ammunition.[210]
Day 580 Mon **1901-05-13**	Western Cape Colony	At Nelskop, not far from Brandvlei, on the road to Klawervlei, Major HS Jeudwine captures 16 members of a patrol Maritz has stationed there, as well as 20 vehicles and about 7 000 head of stock. On the same day, Maritz captures 30 members of a 75-man patrol of Calvinia troops at Lekkeroog.[211] General Grobler is killed in action.[212]
	United Kingdom	British Prime Minister, the Marquis of Salisbury, attacks Irish Home Rule in the House of Commons. (See Milner's proposals at Bloemfontein on 2 June, 1899.)
Day 581 Tue **1901-05-14**		
Day 582 Wed **1901-05-15**	OFS	**PRESIDENT STEYN ADMONISHES HIS NORTHERN ALLIES** President Steyn receives a letter, dated 10 May and signed by State Secretary FW Reitz, setting out the ZAR's perception of the present state of the war. The dwindling numbers of fighting men, the lack of ammunition and supplies, concern about the leadership's ability to inspire, and despair about the Republican deputation's efforts to achieve any kind of foreign intervention, convince them that it is time to re-open

		peace negotiations with Kitchener.[213]
		"The hint awoke an explosion of wrath in the Free State President... he returned an indignant reply, bitterly denouncing the decision already taken and... the idea of an armistice. He argued that all the evils that oppressed the Transvaal weighed equally on his own country, where surrenders, hardships and difficulties had left the spirit of the people unshaken. He reminded the Transvalers that the Free State had staked its existence in order to help them, that for them to weaken now was to betray not only their allies but the Colonial rebels."[214]
		"If the South African Republic now leaves the Orange Free State and the Colonials in the lurch, that will be the death-blow to the South African people. What trust can we then ever have in one another?... To think of surrendering at this time... would be suicide, in which I certainly do not wish to take part... Stand fast, man! Trust in God, there lies our strength."[215]
		Miss Emily Hobhouse writes to Mrs Steyn, describing her second visit to the Springfontein concentration camp: *"I broke my journey at Springfontein. There, to my horror, still massed on the railway siding, I found the same unfortunate people whom I had seen when passing north 10 days previously — their condition beggars description; the picture photographed on my mind can never fade..."[216]*
	United Kingdom	Lord Kitchener's financial adviser, G Fleetwood Wilson, passes a suggestion from Major Karri Davis (a close friend of Rhodes) on to the Secretary of War, St J Brodrick. Apparently, Davis has *"reason to believe"* that the French government will support a proposal to establish a Boer colony on Madagascar. He believes that the scheme has the approval of *"many persons of influence"* in South Africa, who have come to the conclusion that *"a certain class of Boer"* will never settle under British rule.[217]
Day 583 Thu **1901-05-16**	**Victoria Cross**	Lieutenant FW Bell, West Australian Mounted Infantry, Brakpan.
	Cape Colony	Commandant Kritzinger enters the Cape Colony for the second time and concentrates his efforts in the Zuurberg.
Day 584 Fri **1901-05-17**	Eastern ZAR	The ZAR government evades the columns of Colonels Bullock and Grey and returns to Spitzkop, 40 kilometres south-east of Ermelo.[218]
	ZAR	Civil administration is instituted in Johannesburg.
Day 585 Sat **1901-05-18**	**Victoria Cross**	Lieutenant GHB Coulson, 1st Battalion, the King's Own Scottish Borderers, Lambrechtfontein.
Day 586 Sun **1901-05-19**	North-eastern OFS	Major-General Elliot, on Kitchener's orders to continue to the Natal border after reaching Vrede, reaches Botha's Pass. He turns around and converges on Witkoppies, about 40 kilometres to the west. About 400 burghers scatter on his approach and Elliot has to send his exhausted columns off in different directions to resupply.[219]
	Western ZAR	In Potchefstroom, the 82-year-old MW Pretorius, first President of the ZAR, dies of pneumonia, after having been questioned by British officers for more than two hours outside his home, three nights previously.
Day 587 Mon **1901-05-20**		
Day 588 Tue **1901-05-21**	Cape Colony	In Rooskloof, east of Noupoort, Commandant Lategan attacks a column of about 250 men under Lieutenant-Colonel EMS Crabbe. In an inconclusive action Lategan captures a number of horses.[220]
	Trivia	*Sir Arthur Conan Doyle's 42nd birthday.* *The racing yacht* Shamrock II *with King Edward VII on board, is wrecked at the Isle of Wight — no one is hurt.*

Day 590 Thu **1901-05-23**	Western ZAR	Receiving reports that General De la Rey is on his way to confer with the Free State leaders, the columns of Methuen, Rawlinson and Ingouville-Williams start another drive in the southern part of the western ZAR.[221]
Day 591 Fri **1901-05-24**	Western ZAR	In the only success of their drive, Ingouville-Williams' column locates and attacks Commandant Van Rensburg's laager at Leeudoorns. The New South Wales troopers launch a spirited charge and capture 28 burghers and 47 vehicles.[222]
	United Kingdom	Miss Emily Hobhouse arrives at Southampton.[223] On the same day Sir Alfred Milner also arrives at Southampton. He is taken by train to London where he is met by almost the full cabinet and Lord Roberts. He rides in an open landau with Lord Salisbury and Chamberlain to Marlborough House where he is received by the King and made a peer. Since he has no landed estate, he takes the name of Baron Milner of St James' and Cape Town.[224] In the House of Commons Lloyd-George pleads for the humane treatment of non-combatants in South Africa. The Minister of War, St J Brodrick, counters: *"No doubt there were hardships. But war is war."* Lloyd-George interjects, *"But you should not make it on women and children."*[225]
	Trivia	*JC Smuts' 31st birthday.*
Day 592 Sat **1901-05-25**	South-eastern ZAR	**THE ACTION AT MOOIFONTEIN** At Mooifontein, between Bethal and Standerton, General Ben Viljoen attacks a British column of about 150 wagons containing sick, wounded, prisoners and Boer families, escorted by about 850 men with two field-guns, commanded by Colonel Gallwey. General Viljoen, assisted by Commandant W Mears, attacks the front and the rear of the convoy simultaneously and a running battle follows that rages over 15 kilometres. The unwieldy, slow-moving convoy, accompanied by thousands of looted livestock, manages to repulse the burghers' repeated attacks — even an attack with horsemen firing from the saddle, charging through the smoke of a grass fire. The convoy suffers 45 casualties and the attackers about 30.[226]
	Western ZAR	With General De la Rey away and the British columns occupied in the southern part of the ZAR, General Kemp quietly musters a commando at Swartruggens.[227]
Day 593 Sun **1901-05-26**	Western ZAR	PENTECOST (Whit Sunday) Brigadier-General HG Dixon, with 430 mounted men, 800 infantrymen, seven field-guns and a pom-pom, sets out from his entrenched camp at Noupoort to raid farms to the west of his position.[228]
	Eastern ZAR	The ZAR government is at Isihlele River, south of Amsterdam.
	ZAR	Ex-General Hendrik Schoeman dies in Pretoria when a lyddite shell he used as an ashtray in his home, explodes. This is seen by many as *"the judgement of the Almighty for having surrendered"*.[229]
Day 594 Mon **1901-05-27**	Western ZAR	Informed about Dixon's raid, General Kemp moves his force of about 400 burghers under Commandants Van Deventer, Claassens and Oosthuizen to Waterval, between Koster and the present-day Derby.[230]
	OFS	General De la Rey, Chief Commandant De Wet and President Steyn meet near Reitz.[231]
Day 595 Tue **1901-05-28**	Western ZAR	Dixon's scouts skirmish with those of General Kemp and the British make camp at Vlakfontein (the present-day Derby), between Ventersdorp and Rustenburg.[232]
	Natal Black involvement	King Dinizulu refuses British instructions to take up arms. Colonel Bottomley warns the king that, under martial law, he is obliged to follow orders or face banishment.
	Cape Colony	At Jamestown Commandant Van Reenen sends a letter to magistrate Kidwell, demanding the peaceful surrender of the town.[233]

Day 596 Wed 1901-05-29	Western ZAR	**THE BATTLE OF VLAKFONTEIN** Continuing his farm-burning operation and scouring the area, looking for hidden arms caches, Brigadier-General Dixon leaves his camp at Vlakfontein (the present-day Derby). Marching westwards, he splits his force of about 1 230 troops, seven field-guns and a pom-pom into three roughly equal sections. While he commands the central column moving along the valley, the other column moves along ridges on both sides, covering his flanks. Before reaching Kemp's position on high ground commanding both the valley and the ridges, Dixon decides to head back towards Elandsfontein to investigate reports of arms hidden on that farm. The wheeling movement turns the southern flanking force's advance screen into a weak rearguard. Observing the British moves from his commanding position, Kemp, expecting an attack, is baffled, but soon realises that he has an opportunity to attack. He redeploys his men and at about noon he attacks. He opens with a diversionary attack on the northern force and then falls upon the southern force's rear. The soldiers converge and try to withdraw under the cover of the smoke of a veld fire they have started. However their tactic 'backfires' and in what is to become a typical mounted charge, General Kemp and about 500 burghers gallop through the smoke and they charge the rearguard and the field-guns. After a brief stand at their field-guns, another charge by Commandant Van Deventer forces them to flee. The two captured guns are quickly turned on the fleeing troops and Dixon's main force in the valley. The confusion of battle affects both sides. Out of visual contact at the crucial stage of the Republican attack, Dixon only realises what is happening when he is shelled from the direction of his flanking force. To the north, the burghers of Kemp's original diversion, not realising that the field-guns are now in Boer hands, open up on their own men. Dixon recovers quickly and launches a strong counterattack. Kemp, realising that it will be as difficult for him to hold his position on the captured ridge as it had been for the British, decides to withdraw. With the field-guns' ammunition expended and without horses to remove them, he abandons the field-guns to be retaken by the British. At twilight both sides remove their dead and wounded under flags of truce. Dixon withdraws to Noupoort, having suffered at least 49 killed and 129 wounded while the Republican loss is uncertain, but at least seven are killed and two of the wounded succumb later.[234]
	Black involvement	During the Republican withdrawal, an after-rider, known only as Windvoël, performs a heroic deed when he rushes to the aid of a burgher who has trouble mounting a stubborn horse. Under a hail of bullets he helps the burgher into the saddle and he covers his retreat, dismounting several times to shoot at the pursuers until the two of them reach safety.[235]
Day 597 Thu 1901-05-30	Eastern ZAR	General Rundle leaves the Brandwater Basin through Golden Gate after a completely unsuccessful operation during which a single burgher has been captured. Rundle has spent the best part of the month destroying supplies and mills and removing wagons, stock and horses.[236]
Day 598 Fri 1901-05-31	North-eastern OFS	Major-General EL Elliot regroups his columns at Vrede.[237]
		OFFICIAL REPORTS **Gold mining:** On the Witwatersrand 150 of the 6 000 gold stamps are back in production and the monthly gold production is 7 400 ounces or about 2,5% of pre-war production.[238] **Communications:** The railway lines have been cut 12 times during May.[239]

LORD KITCHENER'S ARMY

During May 1901 the army at Kitchener's disposal reaches its peak strength of about 240 000 men with 100 heavy guns, 420 horse and field-guns and 60 pom-poms, made up as follows:

Mounted forces:

Cavalry	Approximately	14 000
Mounted Infantry	Appoximately	12 000
Imperial Yeomanry	Approximately	17 000
Overseas Colonials	Approximately	5 500
South African Constabulary	Approximately	7 500
Subtotal :		80 000

Infantry forces:

Regulars	Approximately	85 000
Militia	Approximately	20 000
Subtotal :		105 000

Other forces:

Artillery	Approximately	13 000
Engineers	Approximately	4 000
Medical corps, Service corps & support troops	Approximately	11 500
Local defence forces	Approximately	26 500
Subtotal:		55 000
GRAND TOTAL	Approximately	240 000 men[240]

1900	WINTER	JUNE
Day 599 Sat **1901-06-01**	Cape Colony	Commandant Kritzinger, with 50 burghers, attacks the town guard sentries outside Jamestown.[241]
Day 600 Sun **1901-06-02**	Cape Colony	After fighting in the streets of the town, the Jamestown town guard surrenders unconditionally. Magistrate Kidwell, the commanding officer, offers to sign an oath of neutrality on condition that Kritzinger and Lotter do not execute two armed blacks. (Surprisingly, after the commandos leave, Kidwell decides to honour his oath and loses his rank and position.) The British lose four soldiers killed, five wounded and 130 captured, while Kritzinger loses one burgher killed in action.[242]
Day 601 Mon **1901-06-03**	OFS	Major-General Elliot leaves Vrede, heading for Kroonstad via Reitz and Lindley.[243]
Day 602 Tue **1901-06-04**	United Kingdom	The War Minister, St John Brodrick, grants Emily Hobhouse an interview.[244] She reports, *"I had pleaded hard; the vision of the camps and the suffering women was vivid, and I feel myself the mediator between them and the powers of England."*[245]
	International	Tsar Nicholas II approaches King Edward VII personally, expressing a desire that the war should end, but his attempt to achieve peace fails.[246]
	Trivia	*Sir Garnet J Wolesley's 68th birthday.*
Day 603 Wed **1901-06-05**	United Kingdom	At a banquet in honour of Cape politicians Sauer and Merriman, Mr Courtney declares that the annexation of the Republics as *"a wrong and a blunder"*. He states that it will be the policy of the Liberal Party to *"temper, if not to abrogate it"*. At a meeting in the Queen's Hall, chaired by Mr Labouchere, the ZAR colours are worn, the Union Jack hissed at and a member who uncovers his head at the mention of the King, is ejected.[247]
Day 604 Thu **1901-06-06**	OFS	**THE BATTLE OF GRASPAN** Major Sladen, with about 600 men, executes a night march and at dawn he attacks a women's laager, protected by about 100 old men. At Graspan, near the town of Reitz, the British soon overwhelm the laager, capturing about 120 vehicles of all description and 45 of the defenders, chasing off the rest. About eight kilometres away, General De la Rey and President Steyn, preparing for their journey to the Eastern Transvaal to confer with the ZAR government, are tak-

		ing their leave of Chief Commandant De Wet, when the news from Graspan arrives. As it is of the utmost importance to save their horses for the long trip ahead, they can do no more than send General Piet Fourie and Commandant Davel to the rescue with about 200 men. At noon, after reconnoitring the position, Davel attacks from the east. The British advance line, who at first takes the approaching horsemen for Bethune's column, is driven back with considerable loss. They retire through the line of parked wagons, forcing the burghers' fire to slacken, careful not to hit the women and children in the laager. Thus covered by the laager, they fall back and take position in a cluster of black farm labourers' huts and an adjoining cattle kraal. The burghers recapture the wagons and start moving off with some of them. A fierce fight, with excellent sharp-shooting from the Republicans, rages for four hours with both sides suffering severe-ly. At 15:00 Colonel Le Lisle arrives and the burghers retire. The convoy, which has not gone far, is retaken along with 40 of the prisoners. Sladen has lost 26 killed and 25 wounded and the burghers 17 killed and 20 wounded.[248] After the battle President Steyn, accompanied by Chief Commandant De Wet and Generals De la Rey and Hertzog with about 30 burghers, leaves to consult with the ZAR government in the eastern Transvaal.[249]
	Eastern ZAR	The ZAR government slips through between the columns of Colonel Bullock and Brigadier-General Plumer and arrives at Piet Retief.[250] Brigadier-General Beatson leaves Brugspruit Station on a drive towards Bethal.
	Cape Colony	In the Zuurberg Commandant Van Reenen is surprised by Colonel Wyndham's 17th Lancers and 23 men are taken prisoner.[251]
Day 605 Fri **1901-06-07**		
Day 606 Sat **1901-06-08**	Eastern ZAR	The ZAR government is at St Helena, between Piet Retief and Amersfoort.
Day 607 Sun **1901-06-09**	Eastern ZAR	The ZAR government is at Langkloof, east of Amersfoort.
Day -608 Mon **1901-06-10**	Eastern ZAR	Brigadier-General Beatson arrives at the confluence of the Steenkoolspruit and the Olifants River and detaches his left wing to investigate reports of a small Boer laager, about 40 kilometres to the east.[252]
	Cape Colony	FA Marais is hanged at Middelburg for treason and attempted murder.
	Trivia	*JCG Kemp's 29th birthday.*
Day 609 Tue **1901-06-11**	ZAR	NT Venter and PR Krause are executed by firing squad in Pretoria after being found guilty of attempted assassination, breaking the oath of neutrality and illegal posses-sion of arms.[253]
Day 610 Wed **1901-06-12**	Eastern ZAR	**THE BATTLE OF WILMANSRUST** Brigadier-General Beatson's left wing, about 350 men of the 5th Victorian Mounted Rifles under Major Morris, encamps at Wilmansrust, between Middelburg and Er-melo. Their sentry posts are badly planned and at 19:30 General Muller and 120 local men, guided by the farm owner, sneak past the sentries without being challenged. They charge the camp and overruns it, shooting down about 50 men. Major Morris is captured before he can rally any resistance, Captain Watson is killed and Captain Dyson, commanding the pom-poms, is wounded. The Australians lose 15 killed and 42 wounded. Almost all the others are captured and two pom-poms are seized. Republican losses are 'insignificant'. Due to a lack of facilities, Muller has to release

	Cape Colony	his prisoners before moving on. [254] The ZAR government returns to De Emigratie, south-east of Ermelo. Commandant Kritzinger issues a proclamation ruling that only those black and Coloured spies, who voluntarily and acting on their own give information to British forces, will henceforth be shot. Other local inhabitants who give information about the movements of commandos will be subject to fines of fifty pounds or three months imprisonment.
	Trivia	*The Cuban convention virtually makes Cuba a protectorate of the US, on condition that the US troops withdraw.*
Day 611 Thu **1901-06-13**	Eastern ZAR	Brigadier-General Beatson, commanding officer of the column mauled at Wilmansrust, musters the Australians and calls them *"a lot of waster, and white-livered curs"* and, seeing an Australian officer making notes, *"You can add 'dogs' too."* The Australians mutiny and refuse to march under him. Three of the leaders are arrested, court-martialled for mutiny and desertion. They are found guilty and sentenced to death by a summary court-martial. (Kitchener commutes the sentence to three years imprisonment and, when pressed by the Australian government, the British government grants a full pardon.)[255]
	ZAR	At the time of the occupation of Pretoria by the British a year ago, about 75% of Indians in the area have been living in the town. The military authority, with the approval of the High Commissioner, now publishes regulations authorising their removal, with the exception of those of *known respectability*, to a location outside the town. The same course is recommended for Johannesburg.[256]
	Black involvement	The British authorities decide to retain the South African Republican laws prohibiting 'non-whites' from walking on pavements or riding in cabs other than those marked 'Natives only'. They charge several Indians with these 'offences'.[257]
Day 612 Fri **1901-06-14**	Eastern ZAR	The ZAR government is at Van Oudtshoornstroom, near Ermelo.
	United Kingdom	**'METHODS OF BARBARISM'** Speaking at a dinner given by the National Reform Union, Sir Henry Campbell-Bannerman, the Liberal leader of the opposition, says, *"A phrase often used is that 'war is war'. But when one comes to ask about it, one is told that no war is going on — that is not war. When is a war not a war? When it is carried on by methods of barbarism in South Africa."*[258]
Day 613 Sat **1901-06-15**	ZAR	The Department of Native Refugees is established in the 'Transvaal Colony'. The ZAR government is at Kranspoort, north-west of Ermelo.
	Victoria Cross	Sergeant J Rogers, SA Constabulary, near Thaba Nchu.
	Cape Colony	JP Coetzee is executed at Cradock by hanging.
Day 614 Sun **1901-06-16**	Eastern ZAR	The ZAR government is at Kalbasfontein, north-east of Bethal.
Day 615 Mon **1901-06-17**	United Kingdom Concentration camps	David Lloyd-George condemns the concentration camps in South Africa: *"By every rule of civilised war we were bound to treat the women and children as non-combatants... We want to make loyal British subjects of these people. Is this the way to do it? Brave men will forget injuries to themselves much more readily than they will insults, indignities, and wrongs to their women and children... When children are being treated this way and dying, we are simply ranging the deepest passions of the human heart against British rule in Africa."* He warns, *"A barrier of dead children's bodies will rise between the British and Boer races in South Africa."*[259]

		William Redmond pleads, *"I ask you to put an end to these camps of hell... in the name of God and for the sake of Christianity, I ask you to abolish that system and restore these people to the comforts and decencies of ordinary civilised life."*[260] The War Office informs Kitchener that the fact of rebellion alone does not justify the death penalty, which should be confined to those who have *"committed outrages or attacked trains, or can be convicted of sniping or similar murderous proceedings..."* He is also told that it is preferable to shoot, rather than hang, rebels.[261]
	Eastern ZAR	The ZAR government is at Yzervarkfontein, north-west of Bethal.
Day 616 Tue 1901-06-18	Eastern ZAR	The ZAR government is at Driefontein, south of Middelburg.
	United Kingdom Concentration camps	Miss Hobhouse's report appears under the title, *"To the S.A. Distress Fund, Report of a visit to the camps of women and children in the Cape and Orange River Colonies, by Emily Hobhouse."*[262] Summarising the reasons for the high fatality rate, she writes, *"Numbers crowded into small tents: some sick, some dying, occasionally a dead one among them; scanty rations dealt out raw; lack of fuel to cook them; lack of water for drinking, for cooking, for washing; lack of soap, brushes and other instruments of personal cleanliness; lack of bedding or of beds to keep the body off the bare earth; lack of clothing for warmth and in many cases for decency..."*[263] Her conclusion is that the whole system is cruel and should be abolished.[264]
Day 617 Wed 1901-06-19	Eastern ZAR	The ZAR government is at Rietspruit, south of Witbank.
	OFS	President Steyn appoints Judge JBM Hertzog as general and as chief commandant of the south-western Free State districts.[265]
Day 618 Thu 1901-06-20	Eastern ZAR	**THE WATERVAL MEETING** Both the Republican governments and their military leaders, including President Steyn, Acting President Burger, General Botha, Chief Commander De Wet, Generals De la Rey, Smuts, Viljoen and Hertzog, meet at Waterval, near Standerton. A telegram received from President Kruger, in answer to Reitz's communication of 10 May, urges his burghers to continue the struggle.[266] President Steyn seriously admonishes his allies for their unilateral decisions taken at De Emigratie (on 10 May). He states, *"Make peace, if you will. I shall not."*[267] It is decided to continue the struggle and to issue a proclamation to this effect. They resolve that *"... no peace will be made, no peace conditions will be accepted whereby our independence and separate national existence or the interests of our Colonial brothers will be surrendered, and that the war will be energetically continued with the adoption of all measures which are calculated to maintain that independence and those interests".*[268] General JH de la Rey is ordered to prepare a well-supplied commando for an invasion of the Cape Colony under General Smuts to relieve pressure on the Republics.
	Cape Colony	PW Kloppert is executed at Burgersdorp by hanging.
Day 619 Fri 1901-06-21	ZAR	In a letter to St John Brodrick, Secretary of War, Lord Kitchener declares, *"It was a mistake to regard the Boers as a civilized race which could ever be an asset to the British Empire: they are uncivilized Africander savages with a thin white veneer..."* who, even if conquered, will revolt again *"... when we are least prepared for it."* He asks the Cabinet to endorse a scheme that will allow the permanent banishment of all Boers who at any time have fought against Britain, as well as their families.[269] He continues, *"We have now got more than half the Boer population either as prisoner of war, or in our refugee camps. I would advise that they should not be allowed to return. I think we should start a scheme for settling them elsewhere, and SA will then be safe, and there will be room for the British to colonize..."* He suggests the Fiji Islands in the South Pacific.

	Cape Colony	As an alternative he suggests that the trick may be to divide and rule, *"... have them hate each other more than they hate the British"*.[270] In an audacious raid, a commando enters Krugersdorp and makes off with 700 head of cattle and 1 000 sheep.[271] Commandant Kritzinger captures a detachment of the Midland Mounted Rifles near Maraisburg (now Hofmeyr).
Day 620 Sat **1901-06-22**	OFS	In a handbill published at Villiers, President Steyn announces a day of general thanksgiving for 8 August, to be followed by a day of atonement and prayer on 9 August. This action has its origins at the Waterval meeting and is extended to both republics.[272]
Day 621 Sun **1901-06-23**	ZAR	The ZAR government is at Strehla, north of present-day Leandra.
Day 622 Mon **1901-06-24**	*Trivia*	*The 19-year-old Pablo Picasso from Barcelona, impresses critics with his first exhibition in Paris. The works exhibited includes 'The Harlequin and his Companion'.* *Lord HH Kitchener's 51st birthday.*

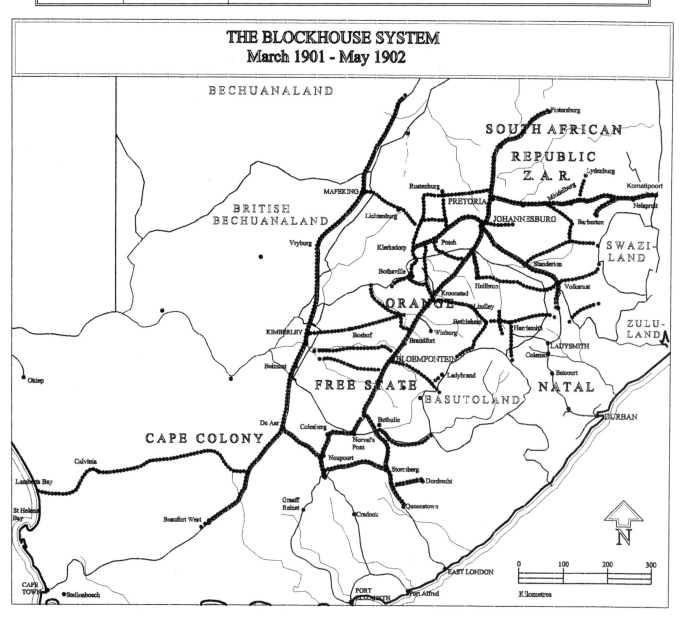

Day 623 Tue **1901-06-25**		
Day 624 Wed **1901-06-26**	Eastern ZAR	Republicans attack and take two blockhouses along the Delagoa railway line, losing three burghers. General Viljoen crosses the railway line between Balmoral and Brugspruit. He suffers more losses when an armoured train arrives on the scene and his burghers are caught in its searchlight. His force is cut in two and they have to take cover on both sides of the railway line.[273]
	Concentration camps	Lord Kitchener, in a telegram to Milner, *"I fear there is little doubt the war will now go on for considerable time unless stronger measures are taken... Under the circumstances I strongly urge sending away wives and families and settling them somewhere else. Some such unexpected measure on our part is in my opinion essential to bring war to a rapid end."*[274]
	Trivia	*The luxury liner* Lusitania *is wrecked off Newfoundland — 350 survivors are rescued.*
Day 625 Thu **1901-06-27**	Eastern ZAR *Capt. Jack Hindon* *(National Cultural History Museum)*	Captain Jack Hindon, a scout with General Viljoen's commando, takes revenge for the rough treatment they have suffered the previous night, by wrecking an armoured train with a contact mine placed on the tracks near Uitkyk Station.
	United Kingdom	The War Department promises to look into Miss Hobhouse's suggestions. regarding improvements to the concentration camps.[275]
Day 626 Fri **1901-06-28**	Eastern ZAR	The ZAR government is at Kromdraai, north of Leandra. Since 7 June 1900 railway traffic has been interrupted 255 times, while the figure for the month of June stands at eight.[276]
Day 627 Sat **1901-06-29**	OFS Black involvement	In a report to Chief Commandant De Wet, Commandant S Haasbroek, commanding the Winburg commando, reports that they shoot armed blacks, captured with British columns, *"almost weekly"*.[277]
Day 628 Sun **1901-06-30**	**OFFICIAL REPORTS:**	

Blockhouse lines: Fortified lines along the main railway lines have been almost completed, and are subsequently to be upgraded and strengthened with barbed wire entanglements, trenches and additional forts at closer and closer intervals.

The following blockhouse lines have been completed:

Cape Colony — from De Aar to Orange River (110 km), De Aar to Noupoort (110 km), Middelburg to Norval's Pont (125 km), Middelburg to Stormberg (130 km) and from Stormberg to Bethulie (90 km).[278]

Concentration camps: The official camp population is 85 410 for the white camps and the deaths reported for June are 777.

Black involvement: The official camp population of the black camps is 32 360 and the deaths are not shown in official returns.[279]

NOTES:

JANUARY 1901 – JUNE 1901 (GUERRILLA)

1. WULFSOHN, Rustenburg at War, p 154 BRITS; Diary of a National Scout, p 36
2. DOONER, 'Last Post'..., p 35
3. FERREIRA, ... SPE Trichard, p 181
4. GRUNDLINGH, 'Hendsopper'..., p 102
5. AMERY, *op cit*, vol V, pp 123-125
6. HEADLAM, *op cit*, vol II, p 225
7. GRUNDLINGH, 'Hendsoppers'..., p 102
8. *Ibid*, p 103
9. MAY, Music of the Guns, pp 159-160
10. SAUNDERS, Reader's Digest Illustrated History of SA ..., p 258
11. PANORAMA magazine, Sept 1989, pp 10-15
12. OBERHOLSTER, Oorlogsdagboek..., p 195
13. VAN SCHOOR, Bittereinder..., pp 178-180
14. VAN REENEN, Emily Hobhouse..., p 478
15. BRITS, Diary of a National Scout, p 36
16. FERREIRA, ... SPE Trichard, p 182
17. DAVITT, *op cit*, p 478
18. COULTER, Queen Victoria, p 184
19. DAVITT, *op cit*, p 478
20. VAN REENEN, Emily Hobhouse..., p 478
21. GRUNDLINGH, 'Hendsoppers'..., p 103
22. BRITS, Diary of a National Scout, pp 13&26
23. NIENABER, Gedenkboek Generaal JBM Hertzog, p 86
24. VAN REENEN, Emily Hobhouse..., p 478
25. *Ibid*, p 43
26. GRONUM, *op cit*, (2) p 44
27. GRUNDLINGH, 'Hendsoppers'..., p 96
28. HEADLAM, *op cit*, vol II, p 196
29. OBERHOLSTER, Dagboek... HC Bredell, p 15
    COULTER, Queen Victoria, p 209
30. WULFSOHN, Rustenburg at War, p 154
31. NIENABER, *op cit*, p 86
32. WULFSOHN, Rustenburg at War, p 154
33. VAN REENEN, Emily Hobhouse..., pp 48-448
34. COULTER, Queen Victoria, p 199
35. *Ibid*, p 140
36. AMERY, *op cit*, vol V, pp 132-133
37. *Ibid*, p 235
38. VAN DEN BERG, *op cit*, p 112
39. AMERY, *op cit*, vol V, pp 159-161
40. *Ibid*, pp 134-135
41. *Ibid*, p 163
42. SPIES, Methods of Barbarism?, p 70
43. VAN DEN BERG, *op cit*, pp 112-113
44. OBERHOLSTER, Oorlogsdagboek..., p 200
45. GRUNDLINGH, 'Hendsoppers'..., p 96
46. AMERY, *op cit*, vol V, p 133
47. *Ibid*, p 133
48. VAN DEN BERG, 24 Battles..., p 113
49. AMERY, *op cit*, vol V, p 164
50. VAN DEN BERG, *op cit*, pp 113-114; AMERY, *op cit*, vol V, p 115

51. FARWELL, *op cit*, p 326
52. PLOEGER, *op cit*, p 41:24-25
53. AMERY, *op cit*, vol V, p 164
54. *Ibid*, p 115
55. *Ibid*, p 164
56. HEADLAM, *op cit*, vol II, p 236
57. NIENABER, *op cit*, p 87
58. FERREIRA, Krijgsgevangenschap..., p 159
59. AMERY, *op cit*, vol V, p 165
60. *Ibid*, p 115
61. SAUNDERS, Reader's Digest Illustrated History of SA..., p 258
62. PRETORIUS, Kommandolewe..., p 269
63. AMERY, *op cit*, vol V, p 136
64. *Ibid*, pp 166-167
65. *Ibid*, pp 167-169
66. VAN REENEN, Emily Hobhouse..., p 478
67. McCORD, JJ, South African Struggle, p 289
68. LE MAY, *op cit*, p 125
69. SPIES, Methods of Barbarism?, p 208
70. GRUNDLINGH, 'Hendsoppers'..., p 96
71. VAN SCHOOR, Die Bannelinge..., p 13
72. AMERY, *op cit*, vol V, pp 171-172
73. COULTER, Queen Victoria, p 355
74. AMERY, *op cit*, vol V, p 137
75. VAN SCHOOR, De Wet-annale, No 8, pp 52-53
76. PRELLER, Scheepers se dagboek..., p 147
77. AMERY, *op cit*, vol V, p 172
78. GRUNDLINGH, 'Hendsoppers'..., p 96
79. AMERY, *op cit*, vol V, p 220
80. FERREIRA, ... SPE Trichard, p 183
81. AMERY, *op cit*, vol V, p 138
82. *Ibid*, vol V, p 199
83. *Ibid*, vol V, p141
84. *Ibid*, vol V, p 141
85. WESSELS, Anglo-Boereoorlog ... oorsig, p 38
86. AMERY, *op cit*, vol V, pp 139-140
87. *Ibid*, vol V, p 146
88. OBERHOLSTER, Oorlogsdagboek..., p 225
89. AMERY, *op cit*, vol V, p 141
90. *Ibid*, vol V, 220
91. *Ibid*, vol V, p 142
92. BRITS, Diary of a National Scout, p 37; AMERY, *op cit*, vol V, pp 220-221
93. AMERY, *op cit*, vol V, p 173
94. WESSELS, Anglo-Boereoorlog... oorsig, p 38
95. AMERY, *op cit*, vol V, p 142
96. *Ibid*, vol V, p 221
97. *Ibid*, vol V, pp 176-177
98. *Ibid*, vol V, p 142
99. *Ibid*, vol V, p 143
100. *Ibid*, vol V, p 146
101. SPIES, Methods of Barbarism?, pp 208-209

102.	AMERY, *op cit*, vol V, p 144	156.	*Ibid*, vol V, p 201
103.	BRITS, Diary of a National Scout, p 39	157.	*Ibid*, vol V, p 178
104.	AMERY, *op cit*, vol V, p 144	158.	VAN REENEN, Emily Hobhouse..., p 97
105.	*Ibid*, vol V, p 148	159.	WESSELS, Egodokumente..., p 111
106.	*Ibid*, vol V, p 147	160.	AMERY, *op cit*, vol V, p 179
107.	*Ibid*, vol V, p 144	161.	*Ibid*, vol V, p 179
108.	*Ibid*, vol V, p 147	162.	FARWELL, *op cit*, p 326
109.	VAN SCHOOR, De Wet-annale, No 8, p 63	163.	HEADLAM, *op cit*, vol II, p 214
110.	SPIES, Methods of Barbarism?, p 71	164.	WESSELS, Egodokumente..., p 95
111.	WESSELS, Egodokumente..., p 107	165.	GRUNDLINGH, 'Hendsoppers'..., p 186
112.	AMERY, *op cit*, vol V, pp 150-152	166.	AMERY, *op cit*, vol V, p 241
113.	*Ibid*, vol V, p 152	167.	*Ibid*, vol V, p 180
114.	NIENABER, *op cit*, p 87	168.	VAN REENEN, Emily Hobhouse..., p 99
115.	SPIES, Methods of Barbarism?, p 209	169.	OBERHOLSTER, Dagboek... HC Bredell, p 16
116.	AMERY, *op cit*, vol V, p 117	170.	AMERY, *op cit*, vol V, p 180
117.	FARWELL, *op cit*, p 326	171.	*Ibid*, vol V, p 203
118.	PLOEGER, *op cit*, p 37:8	172.	*Ibid*, vol V, p 200
119.	*Ibid*, p 41:24	173.	PRELLER, Scheepers..., p 147; WESSELS, Egodokumente..., p 58
120.	HATTINGH, Britse Fortifikasies..., p 61	174.	WITTON, Scapegoats of the Empire, p 43
121.	VAN SCHOOR, De Wet-annale, No 7, p 61	175.	AMERY, *op cit*, vol V, p 203
122.	AMERY, *op cit*, vol V, p 221	176.	VAN REENEN, Emily Hobhouse..., p 99
123.	*Ibid*, vol V, p 221	177.	AMERY, *op cit*, vol V, p 238
124.	VAN DEN BERG, 24 Battles..., p 117	178.	*Ibid*, vol V, pp 238-239
125.	SPIES, Methods of Barbarism?, p 136	179.	VAN REENEN, Emily Hobhouse..., p 103
126.	McCORD, JJ, South African Struggle, p 290	180.	*Ibid*, p 103
127.	WESSELS, War Diary..., p 97; VAN DEN BERG, *op cit*, pp 116-118	181.	AMERY, *op cit*, vol V, p 228
	AMERY, *op cit*, vol V, pp 222-223	182.	*Ibid*, vol V, pp 180-181
128.	VAN DEN BERG, *op cit*, p 118	183.	*Ibid*, vol V, pp 206-209
129.	AMERY, *op cit*, vol V, p 153	184.	PRETORIUS, Kommandolewe..., p 38
130.	VAN REENEN, Emily Hobhouse..., p 80	185.	AMERY, *op cit*, vol V, p 210
131.	AMERY, *op cit*, vol V, p 153	186.	AMERY, *op cit*, vol V, p 238
132.	AMERY, *op cit*, vol V, p 153	187.	VAN REENEN, Emily Hobhouse..., p 107
133.	VAN SCHOOR, De Wet-annale, No 2, p 80	188.	AMERY, *op cit*, vol V, p 214
134.	AMERY, *op cit*, vol V, p 153	189.	*Ibid*, vol V, p 229
135.	VAN REENEN, Emily Hobhouse..., p 84	190.	GRUNDLINGH, 'Hendsoppers'..., p 47
136.	WESSELS, Egodokumente..., p 95	191.	MEINTJES, Anglo-Boereoorlog in Beeld, p 173
137.	DAVITT, *op cit*, p 488	192.	VAN REENEN, Emily Hobhouse..., p 109
138.	AMERY, *op cit*, vol V, p 153	193.	OBERHOLSTER, Oorlogsdagboek..., p 239
139.	WESSELS, Anglo-Boereoorlog... oorsig, p 38	194.	AMERY, *op cit*, vol V, p 216
140.	HATTINGH, Britse Fortifikasies..., p 50	195.	*Ibid*, vol V, p 241
141.	VAN REENEN, Emily Hobhouse..., p 88	196.	PLOEGER, *op cit*, p 31:32-33
142.	AMERY, *op cit*, vol V, p 199	197.	AMERY, *op cit*, Vol V, p 245
143.	WESSELS, Egodokumente..., p 158	198.	PRETORIUS, Kommandolewe..., p 38
144.	PLOEGER, *op cit*, p 34:3	199.	FARWELL, *op cit*, p 326
145.	AMERY, *op cit*, vol V, p 193	200.	AMERY, *op cit*, p 326
146.	SPIES, Methods of Barbarism?, p 136	201.	*Ibid*, vol V, p 231
147.	*Ibid*, p 210	202.	*Ibid*, vol V, p 241
148.	LE MAY, *op cit*, p 112	203.	VAN REENEN, Emily Hobhouse..., p 114
149.	PRETORIUS, Kommandolewe..., p 245	204.	OOSTHUIZEN, Rebelle van die Stormberge, p 147
150.	THE SA COLOUR STAMP CATALOGUE 1998, p 33	205.	AMERY, *op cit*, vol V, p 287
151.	PLOEGER, *op cit*, p 34:4	206.	VAN REENEN, Emily Hobhouse..., p 114
152.	PAKENHAM, *op cit*, p 573	207.	AMERY, *op cit*, vol V, p 233
153.	AMERY, *op cit*, vol V, p 224	208.	GRONUM, *op cit*, (2) p 6
154.	WESSELS, War Diary..., p 100; AMERY, *op cit*, vol V, p 225	209.	AMERY, *op cit*, vol V, pp 233, 279
155.	AMERY, *op cit*, vol V, p 226	210.	WESSELS, Egodokumente..., p 64

211. *Ibid*, p 64

212. Zuid-Afrikaanse Verjaardagboek

213. VAN SCHOOR, Bittereinder aan die woord, pp 210-211

214. AMERY, *op cit*, vol V, p 278

215. SMUTS Selections 1, pp 321-322

216. WESSELS, Egodokumente..., p 164

217. SPIES, Methods of Barbarism?, p 236

218. AMERY, *op cit*, vol V, p 294

219. AMERY, *op cit*, vol V, p 288

220. VAN SCHOOR, De Wet-annale, No 7, p 63

221. AMERY, *op cit*, vol V, p 280

222. *Ibid*, vol V, p 280

223. VAN REENEN, Emily Hobhouse..., p 115

224. HEADLAM, *op cit*, vol II, p 248

225. BREYTENBACH, Gedenkalbum..., p 1b 409

226. AMERY, *op cit*, vol V, p 293

227. *Ibid*, vol V, p 280

228. *Ibid*, vol V, p 280

229. GRUNDLINGH, 'Hendsoppers'..., p 119

230. VAN DEN BERG, 24 Battles..., p 119

231. AMERY, *op cit*, vol V, p 285

232. VAN DEN BERG, 24 Battles..., p 119

233. OOSTHUIZEN, Rebelle van die Stormberge, p 148

234. VAN DEN BERG, *op cit*, pp 19-122; AMERY, *op cit*, vol V, pp 281-284

235. PRETORIUS, Kommandolewe..., p 321

236. AMERY, *op cit*, vol V, p 241

237. *Ibid*, vol V, p 288

238. PAKENHAM, *op cit*, p 555

239. FARWELL, *op cit*, p 326

240. AMERY, *op cit*, vol V, pp 246-250

241. OOSTHUIZEN, Rebelle van die Stormberge, p 148

242. *Ibid*, p 148

243. AMERY, *op cit*, vol V, p 288

244. VAN REENEN, Emily Hobhouse..., p 122

245. BREYTENBACH, Gedenkalbum ..., p 412

246. KANDYBA-FOXCROFT, Russia..., *op cit*, p 80

247. HEADLAM, *op cit*, vol II, p 252

248. AMERY, *op cit*, vol V, pp 288-289

249. VAN SCHOOR, Bittereinder..., p 214

250. AMERY, *op cit*, vol V, p 294

251. *Ibid*, vol V, p 310

252. *Ibid*, vol V, p 295

253. SPIES, Methods of Barbarism?, p 71

254. AMERY, *op cit*, vol V, pp 295-296

VAN SCHOOR, De Wet-annale, No 7, pp 74, 76

255. KRUGER, Good-bye Dolly Gray, p 435

256. SPIES, Methods of Barbarism?, p 68

257. *Ibid*, p 68

258. HOLT, The Boer War, p 269

259. MEINTJES, Anglo-Boer War... Pictorial..., p 168; PAKENHAM, *op cit*, p 500

260. BREYTENBACH, Gedenkalbum..., p 410

261. LE MAY, *op cit*, pp 100-101

262. VAN REENEN, Emily Hobhouse..., p 460

263. WESSELS, Egodokumente..., p 162

264. PAKENHAM, *op cit*, p 508

265. NIENABER, *op cit*, p 84

266. GRONUM, *op cit*, (2) p 7

267. VAN SCHOOR, Bittereinder ..., p 215

268. SMUTS Selections 1, p 403

269. GRONUM, *op cit*, (2) pp 7/8

270. SPIES, Methods of Barbarism?, p 135

271. WESSELS, War Diary..., p 123

272. VAN SCHOOR, Bittereinder..., p 180

273. AMERY, *op cit*, vol V, p 299; FERREIRA, ... SPE Trichard, p 191

274. GRONUM, *op cit*, (2) p 90

275. BREYTENBACH, Gedenkalbum..., p 412

276. FARWELL, *op cit*, p 326

277. PRETORIUS, Kommandolewe..., p 295

278. AMERY, *op cit*, vol V, map

279. WARWICK, Black People..., p 151

JULY – DECEMBER 1901		
ATTRITION		
1901	WINTER	JULY
Day 629 Mon **1901-07-01**		
Day 630 Tue **1901-07-02**	Northern ZAR	Six unarmed prisoners (later called the Geyser group) are murdered by members of the Bushveld Carbineers in the Spelonken area, near Fort Edward, not far from Louis Trichardt.[1]
	United Kingdom	An account by Private Victor Swift of the East Kent Imperial Yeomanry, serving in the Free State, is published in the Times: *We burn every farm we come across, and are living like fighting-cocks. We think it a bad day if we haven't a couple of chickens and a suckling pig apiece. It's funny to see us with bayonets chasing the pigs round the farm-yard. I have an appetite like a wolf. We went to Vrede next, and after a day's rest left that place in a shocking state. We killed thousands of sheep, and put them in every house. The stench in a week will be horrible. It is to prevent the Boers from returning.*[2]
Day 631 Wed **1901-07-03**	OFS	A general council of war meets at Spijtfontein, the farm of ex-General Piet de Wet, between Lindley and Reitz. With President Steyn presiding, the case against Barend Cilliers, accused of the murder of Lieutenant Cecil Boyle, is heard. The accused is acquitted. The court finds that, on 2 January 1901, Cilliers had received a direct order from General Philip Botha to shoot the prisoner. General Botha has subsequently been killed in action on 06-03-1901.[3]
	ZAR	The ZAR government is at Wildebeestfontein, north of present-day Evander.
	Victoria Cross	Lieutenant WJ English, 2nd Scottish Horse, Vlakfontein.
Day 632 Thu **1901-07-04**	Northern ZAR	General CF Beyers captures a troop train near Naboomspruit, killing nine soldiers.[4] Trooper Van Buuren, a member of the Bushveld Carbineers, is taken on a two-man patrol by Lieutenant Harry 'Breaker' Morant of the same unit, after Van Buuren has objected to the shooting of prisoners. Morant returns alone.[5]
	Eastern ZAR	The ZAR government is at Kaffirskraal, west of Bethal.
	ZAR	In a letter to Milner, Lord Kitchener describes *"a new system of kraaling the Boers up into areas".*[6]
	Victoria Cross	Private HG Camdon, 18th Hussars, Springboklaagte.
	Trivia	A *civil government with WH Taft as governor-general, is proclaimed in the Philippines. Amnesty is offered to rebels taking an oath of allegiance to the US.*
Day 633 Fri **1901-07-05**	ZAR	After some excellent scouting, General Kemp simultaneously attacks several Witwatersrand towns. Seventy burghers attack Florida and 200 men under Kemp enter Roodepoort. After a brisk engagement in the streets and manoeuvres around the mine-dumps, the station building is set alight and Kemp retires with a few looted horses.[7] Commandant-General Botha receives a telegraph from President Kruger urging him to continue fighting. The ZAR government is at Eerstegeluk, about five kilometres east of Bethal.
	Trivia	*CJ Rhodes' 48th birthday.*

Day 634 Sat 1901-07-06	OFS	President Steyn and the Free State government, with their small bodyguard commanded by Commandant Davel, elude a British drive in the north-eastern Free State, commanded by Lieutenant-General EL Elliot. Four columns commanded by Colonels Broadwood, Lowe, Bethune and De Lisle sweep along the left bank of the Wilge River in parallel lines. On the left flank, Colonel De Lisle's column sweeps through the deserted town of Reitz.[8]
	Eastern ZAR	The ZAR government moves via Rietfontein to Onverwacht, south of Kriel.
Day 635 Sun 1901-07-07		
Day 636 Mon 1901-07-08	*Trivia*	*Joseph Chamberlain's 65th birthday.*
Day 637 Tue 1901-07-09	OFS	Hearing that the enemy has missed a supply of maize in Reitz, President Steyn and the Free State government decide to head there. They arrive to find the maize destroyed and the town ransacked.[9]
	Cape Colony	'Long Cecil', the gun designed and manufactured during the siege, is taken from Kimberley by train to Cape Town to be exhibited during the visit of the Duke and Duchess of Cornwall (later HM King George V and Queen Mary).[10]
Day 638 Wed 1901-07-10	OFS	President Steyn's party occupies the partially destroyed house of the Resident Justice of the Peace, Mr Rossouw. The President plays cards in a tent pitched in the garden until late. He decides to sleep there with Generals Cronje and Wessels, while his secretaries move into the house.[11] General Elliot orders General Broadwood, with 400 men and a pom-pom, to double back towards Reitz.
Day 639 Thu 1901-07-11	OFS Black involvement	**THE OFS GOVERNMENT IS CAPTURED** With dawn approaching, General Broadwood rushing towards Reitz, decides to gallop into the village rather than surround it. He achieves complete surprise. In the confusion President Steyn's Griqua groom and manservant, Jan Ruiter, who is making coffee in the predawn, immediately wakes the President. They rush to the stable and, borrowing a saddle, he helps the President mount up. With soldiers everywhere, Ruiter mounts another horse and they gallop away. A soldier yells an order to halt and shoots at the fleeing figures. Ruiter dismounts and distracts the soldier, allowing the President — without hat or coat — to escape into the darkness. The complete Free State Executive Council, State Secretary Brain, Generals Cronje and Wessels, PG Steyn (the President's brother), the President's secretaries and Commandant Davel and the President's bodyguard are captured — 29 in all. All the government papers and £11 500 in notes and sovereigns fall into British hands. Broadwood sends his prisoners to Heilbron and rejoins the drive. Ruiter is left behind with the other blacks — to rejoin his famous employer as soon as possible.[12]
Day 640 Fri 1901-07-12	OFS	A commando under Alberts and Strydom captures a British post south of the Vaal, seizing an old seven-pounder gun and inflicting 12 casualties.[13]
Day 641 Sat 1901-07-13	Cape Colony	JP Coetzee is executed in Cradock and all male adults are ordered to attend.[14] Commandant PH Kritzinger issues his 'Stormberg Proclamation', declaring that the November 1899 Free State Annexation Proclamation is still in force and that the north-eastern Cape is Free State territory.[15]
Day 642 Sun 1901-07-14	Cape Colony	General French drives Scheepers out of the Camdeboo Mountains. Major Moore, with a detachment of Connaught Rangers, defeats Myburgh at Zuurvlakte and captures his laager.

Day 643 Mon 1901-07-15	Western ZAR	General Smuts, preparing his invasion, sends Commandants Van Deventer, Kirsten and Bouwer ahead, arranging to rendezvous near Hoopstad.[16]
	Black involvement	General Kemp protests to Kitchener that in many instances the war is fought *"contrary to civilized warfare on account of it being carried on in a great measure with (blacks)".*[17]
	Bechuanaland Concentration camps	Dr K Franks, the camp doctor at the Mafeking refugee camp reports that the camp is *"overwhelmed"* by 1 270 women and children brought in after sweeps on the western ZAR. Lack of facilities adds to the hardships encountered by the new arrivals.[18]
Day 644 Tue 1901-07-16	OFS	Lieutenant-General EL Elliot's drive ends on the railway line. At the cost of only three casualties, the drive has resulted in three burghers killed and wounded, 61 prisoners, 7 000 horses, 7 000 cattle, 6 000 rounds of ammunition and 300 vehicles captured.[19]
	United Kingdom Concentration camps	**THE LADIES COMMISSION** The Colonial Office announces the appointment of a Ladies Commission to investigate the concentration camps in South Africa. The commission, whose members are reputed to be impartial, is made up as follows: – Chairlady Mrs Millicent G Fawcett, who has recently criticized Miss Hobhouse in the *Westminister Gazette.* – Dr Jane Waterson, daughter of a British general, who recently wrote against *"the hysterical whining going on in England"* while *"we feed and pamper people who had not even the grace to say thank you for the care bestowed on them".* – Lady Anne Knox, wife of gGeneral Knox, who is presently serving in South Africa. – Nursing sister Katherine Brereton, who have served in a Yeomanry Hospital in South Africa. – Miss Lucy Deane, a government factory inspector and expert on child welfare, – Dr the Hon Ella Scarlett, a medical doctor. One of the doctors is to marry a concentration camp official before the end of their tour.[20]
Day 645 Wed 1901-07-17	Western ZAR	A small party of Imperial Yeomanry, attempting to surprise a group of burghers (but only succeeding in capturing some cattle) is attacked by Kemp's commando at Wildfontein, near Ventersdorp. Lieutenant CD Kimber, son of the Lord Mayor of London, is killed while attempting to rescue a wounded soldier.[21]
	Blockhouse lines	In a letter to St John Brodrick, Secretary of War Lord Kitchener writes, *"Let me recommend the blockhouse system; I have no doubt it would have an excellent effect in parliament; you pin your adversary down to certain areas."*[22]
	Cape Colony	Commandant Fouchee, joined by Commandant Myburgh and 170 men, clashes with a force of 220 Connaught Rangers commanded by Major Moore, at Zuurvlakte, between Aliwal North and Jamestown. Moore launches a sharp attack and manages to capture Myburgh's laager. Fouchee and Myburgh counter-attack and inflict about 30 casualties but Moore holds out until dark when he is reinforced by Lovat's Scouts and Monro's column.[23] Lord Milner writes to Mr Haldane in connection with the Cape constitutional crisis, *"All I contend for is that we should fearlessly go on governing without Parliamentary authority, as long as the meeting of Parliament is at all likely to lead to a prolongation of the war or fresh disturbances. We cannot afford to repeat the scandals of the Session of 1900."*[24]
	Trivia	*RG Kekewich's 47th birthday.*
Day 646 Thu 1901-07-18	ZAR	The ZAR government arrives at Zwakfontein from Onverwacht.
	Cape Colony	**THE FIRST DRIVE IN THE CAPE COLONY** Under the overall command of General French, the columns of Lund, Wyndham, Doran, Scobell and Crew are deployed along the Beaufort West-Graaff-Reinet line and march north.

Day 647 Fri 1901-07-19		
Day 648 Sat 1901-07-20	Cape Colony	Commandant Hendrik Lategan and Field-cornet Neser are both slightly wounded in a skirmish with a strong force under Colonel Scobell at Tweefontein in the Graaff-Reinet district.
	ZAR	General CJ Spruyt is killed in action while attempting to cross the railway line between Val Station and Vlaklaagte on his way to invade Natal.[25] At Paardekop, in the Gatsrand, near Vereeniging, General Smuts and a small party are surprised in their sleep. His black orderly, Kleinbooi, is shot and killed but General Smuts manages to get away by shouting orders in English and stealing away on bare feet. He later retrieves all the documents he has had to leave behind in the dark.[26]
	United Kingdom	Commenting on confiscation of property and banishment of families, St J Brodrick writes to Kitchener: *"Hitherto the effects of severity have not been all we could have hoped. Those who knew SA best expected the same results from farm-burning as are now claimed for confiscation — but we were led quite wrong in this.* *"If confiscation did not lead to surrender, we should be worse off than ever — for every man still out would have every motive against surrender and Europe would be needlessly scandalised.* *"Your other suggestion of sending the Boer women to St Helena, etc., and telling their husbands that they will never return, seems difficult to work out. We cannot permanently keep 16,000 men in ring fences and they are not a marketable commodity in other lands..."*[27] On the question of public executions, Kitchener replies: *"When two prisoners were quietly executed here in gaol, the Dutch people refused absolutely to believe that they had been executed and insisted that they had been quietly removed."*[28]
	Trivia	*President Kruger's wife, Gezina, dies in Pretoria.*
Day 649 Sun 1901-07-21	Swaziland Black involvement	**THE BURNING OF BREMERSDORP** (Manzini, Swaziland) Reacting to complaints from Swazi Queen Regent Labotsibeni, ruling on behalf of the young Sobhuza II, concerning the conduct of Steinaecker's Horse, Commandant-General Botha sends Tobias Smuts to attack Bremersdorp (Manzini). Members of Steinaecker's irregular unit of about 50 mercenaries, employing about 300 Tonga tribesmen, have been tasked to seal the ZAR/Mozambique border. They, however, *"spend at least as much time looting Swazi homesteads, ransacking abandoned white property and gunrunning as they did resisting the Boers"*. They have imprisoned Prince Mancibane on suspicion of 'having Boer sympathies'. Assistant Commandant-General Smuts surrounds and quickly overpowers the mercenaries, taking 41 prisoners before burning down the town.[29]
	ZAR/OFS	**THE START OF SMUTS' RAID** At Lindeque's Drift, Colonel Garratt engages General JC Smuts and Commandant TFJ Dreyer. Smuts withdraws and moves westwards. He skirts along the north bank of the Vaal, avoiding the seven British columns sweeping the area and the cordon Colonel Western from Klerksdorp is forming along the river. General Smuts' advance parties under Commandants Van Deventer, Kirsten and Bouwer arrive at the planned rendezvous at Grootvlei, about 20 kilometres east of Hoopstad.[30]

254

	Cape Colony	Commandant PH Kritzinger attacks Colonel E Crabbe at Jakkalsfontein, 32 kilometres south-west of Cradock. Three hundred horses are stampeded and Crabbe has to fight on foot until making his way to the railway after dark. About 150 men of Commandant Lategan's commando are surprised at dawn by 90 Cape Mounted Rifles under Colonel Lukin at Tweefontein, north of Graaff-Reinet. In a two-hour battle the bewildered commando is dispersed, leaving behind 11 men who are captured. The Cape Mounted Rifles lose one killed and four wounded and also take about 105 horses and saddles. After this action Lategan is forced to retire to Philippolis to regroup.[31] A supply train is attacked, captured and burned about 12 kilometres north of Beaufort West. Three soldiers are killed and 18 wounded.[32]
Day 650 Mon **1901-07-22**		
Day 651 Tue **1901-07-23**	United Kingdom	Lord Milner is presented with the freedom of the city of London at the Guildhall.
Day 652 Wed **1901-07-24**	Western ZAR	Lieutenant-General Elliot's sweep along the Vaal River reaches Klerksdorp and he joins Fetherstonehaugh's four columns.
	Cape Colony	HL Jacobs and AC Jooste are executed for treason by firing squad at Kenhardt. In Somerset East, C Claassen, described as 'poor in spirit' and unable to follow the proceedings, is sentenced to death and hanged for treason. He has been charged with acting as a horse guard for an invading commando.
Day 653 Thu **1901-07-25**	United Kingdom	Since 25 June, Emily Hobhouse has addressed 26 public meetings on the concentration camps, raising money to improve conditions.[33]
Day 654 Fri **1901-07-26**	ZAR	A farmhouse in the Middelburg district, belonging to Lieutenant-Colonel SPE Trichard of the State Artillery, is destroyed with dynamite.[34]
	United Kingdom Concentration camps	Emily Hobhouse again writes to Brodrick asking for reasons for the War Department's refusal to include her in the Ladies' Commission. If she cannot go, *"it was due to myself to convey to all interested that the failure to do so was due to the Government"*.[35] Lord Roberts, now Chief of the Army, receives a letter from Kitchener regarding the banishment of Boer families: *"If I could threaten them with being all permanently banished from the country they would, I believe, give in. I do not expect this will be allowed, but a little bluff now would finish the war..."*[36]
	Trivia	*SG (Manie) Maritz's 25th birthday.*
Day 655 Sat **1901-07-27**	OFS Black involvement	Chief Commandant De Wet, operating in the Bethlehem district, issues instructions to Commandant Willem D Fouchee in the Eastern Cape Colony to summarily execute any armed blacks they capture.[37]
	ZAR Black involvement	Prisoners taken on 1901-07-21 at Bremersdorp by General Tobias Smuts are tried and sentenced by a summary court martial. Traitor Joubert and five or six armed

		blacks are sentenced to death and executed.
	United Kingdom Concentration camps	St J Brodrick replies to Emily Hobhouse's letter, *"The only consideration in the selection of ladies to visit the Concentration Camps, beyond their special capacity for such work, was that they should be, so far as is possible, removed from the suspicion of partiality to the system adopted or the reverse."*[38]
	Trivia	*Sir H Goold-Adams' 43rd birthday.*
Day 656 Sun 1901-07-28	ZAR/OFS	General Smuts and Commandant Dreyer skirt around Western's cordon south of Klerksdorp and they join Commandants Van Deventer, Kirsten and Bouwer at Grootvlei, near Hoopstad.
		THE DRIVE IN THE NORTH-WESTERN FREE STATE Lord Kitchener, hoping to corner Smuts, starts a huge drive from the Vaal River towards the line of posts manned by the SA Constabulary west of Bloemfontein. Lieutenant-General Elliot, commanding the drive, arranges his columns as follows: on the left, De Lisle starts from the confluence of the Ysterspruit and the Vaal, west of the present-day Orkney, and on the right, Rawlinson is at Reitzburg. In between are the columns of Lowe, Broadwood and Owen. Garrat follows behind the left flank as a 'sweeper' and on the right, Henry fulfils the same function. 'Stopper' columns are also stationed all along the railway line from Kroonstad to the Vet River. Not counting the static elements, Elliot has more than 15 000 troops at his disposal. Inside the trap are about six small local commandos and General Smuts with about 340 men.[39]
Day 657 Mon 1901-07-29	Cape Colony	**THE SECOND CAPE DRIVE** As all the Republican commandos in the area of the first Cape drive have broken through and escaped, a second drive in the Cape Colony starts. This time three additional columns under Atherton, Alexander and Kavanagh join in — making it ten in all. They start from the Victoria Road Station-Stormberg junction line and march south — this time in columns rather than in line abreast.[40]
	Eastern ZAR	General Walter Kitchener attacks General Muller near Blaauwbank and inflicts a loss of 30 men, a few vehicles and about 30 horses. One of the pom-poms lost at Wilmansrust is recaptured.[41]
	South-east ZAR	Colonel Benson leaves Wonderfontein for operations in the Carolina and Ermelo districts. Using Colonel Woolls-Sampson as his intelligence officer and employing many black scouts and surrendered Boers, he is to specialise in night marches and dawn attacks based on excellent information.[42]
Day 658 Tue 1901-07-30	Eastern ZAR	General W Kitchener again attacks Viljoen's commando under General Muller at Crocodile Drift, near Middelburg. Muller is seriously challenged before he succeeds in disengaging and he slips away from Kitchener's superior force.[43]
Day 659 Wed 1901-07-31	Cape Colony	Edgar Wallace writes the first of a series of articles under the banner *"Has Kitchener failed?"* His articles are highly critical of Lord Kitchener and he blames his 'lenient policies' towards rebels and disloyal Cape Dutch for the second invasion of the Cape Colony and the prolongation of the war.[44]
		Commandant PH Kritzinger, confirming his 'Stormberg Proclamation', informs Lord Kitchener that he will execute any blacks employed by the British army, falling into his hands, whether armed or not.

		OFFICIAL REPORTS
	Concentration camps:	The officially recorded camp population is 93 940 for the white camps and the deaths for July stands at 1 412.
	Black involvement:	The camp population in the black camps is 37 472 and 256 have died in the Free State camps during the month, while in the Transvaal deaths are not yet recorded.[45]
	Communications:	The railway lines have been reportedly cut four times during July.[46]

1901	WINTER	AUGUST
Day 660 Thu **1901-08-01**	ZAR	Sir G Lagden, formerly Resident Commissioner in Basutoland, is appointed as the Commissioner of Native Affairs in the Transvaal.
	OFS	General Smuts is surprised and attacked by 200 of De Lisle's South Australians at Grootvlei, east of Hoopstad. Smuts' invasion force lose six burghers killed, 12 captured and some horses taken by the enemy.[47] The activities of the Department of Native Refugees are extended to the 'Orange River Colony'.
	United Kingdom	The British Parliament votes an additional £12 500 00 for munitions.
Day 661 Fri **1901-08-02**	ZAR/OFS	General JC Smuts sets out from Koppieskraal Drift on the Vaal River with 340 ZAR burghers moving south-west to invade the Cape Colony.
	United Kingdom Black involvement	Mr J Chamberlain tells the House of Commons, *"The reason we have not employed natives is not because we do not think they... might fairly be placed in the field even against civilized nations, but because, in the peculiar circumstances of South Africa, we believe it would be bad policy."*[48]
Day 662 Sat **1901-08-03**	OFS	General Smuts' force dodges back and — safely behind Elliot's driving line — he splits his force. Van Deventer heads east towards the railway line while Smuts continues south in the wake of the British columns.[49] At Koot Krause's farm he finds a sheep kraal that the British have filled with sheep and then blew up with dynamite, leaving most sheep only mangled.[50]
	Cape Colony	The invading commandos again evade French's drive and he again reverses the direction and extends his forces along the Beaufort West-Pearston-Cathcart line and they march north.[51]
Day 663 Sun **1901-08-04**	Western ZAR	Lord Methuen destroys the village of Schweizer-Reneke, burning every building, leaving only the church standing.[52]
Day 664 Mon **1901-08-05**	South-eastern ZAR	After a long night march, Colonel Benson attacks and captures a Boer laager at Tweefontein. The ZAR government arrives at Uitkomst between Bethal and Ermelo via Graspan and Vaalbank.
Day 665 Tue **1901-08-06**	Eastern ZAR	The remnants of the notorious Steinaecker's Horse, led by Captain Francis, are surrounded by 100 men under General Viljoen in a fort at M'piaanstat. During the charge seven burghers are killed and 12 wounded. Captain Francis is killed and 20 of his white mercenaries are captured and several of the armed blacks in their employ are executed.[53]
	United Kingdom	The British Parliament votes a grant-in-aid of £6 500 000 to the 'Transvaal Colony' and the 'Orange River Colony'.

Day 666 Wed **1901-08-07**	ZAR	**LORD KITCHENER'S BANISHMENT PROCLAMATION** Lord Kitchener publishes the most famous of what the Boers call, his 'paper bombs', *"All Commandants, Field-cornets and Leaders of armed bands, being Burghers of the late Republics, still engaged in resisting HM's forces... and all members of the Governments... shall, unless they surrender before September 15th next, be permanently banished from South Africa; the cost of the maintenance of (their) families shall be recoverable from such burghers and shall be a charge upon their property moveable and immovable in the two Colonies."*[54]
	OFS	A party of burghers under Commandant Alberts attacks and captures a blockhouse near Brandfort, inflicting a loss of seven killed and several wounded.[55] General JC Smuts reports on the devastation in the Free State, *"Dams everywhere full of rotting animals; water undrinkable. Veld covered with slaughtered herds of sheep and goats, cattle and horses. The horror passes description. But the saddest sight of all is the large number of little lambs, staggering from hunger and thirst round the corpses of their dead or mangled mothers. I have never seen anything more heartrendering or heard anything more piteous than their bleating in this war of horrors. Surely such outrages on man and nature must move to certain doom."*[56]
	Cape Colony	Commandant Manie Maritz attacks Vanrhynsdorp. Two British soldiers die and 29 members of the Western Province Mounted Rifles are captured while many vehicles including three laden supply wagons are taken by Maritz who leaves almost immediately.[57]
Day 667 Thu **1901-08-08**	OFS	Commandants JL van Deventer and BD Bouwer cross the railway line between Brandfort en Eensgevonden, on their way to Zastron where they are to wait for General Smuts.[58]
Day 668 Fri **1901-08-09**	Eastern ZAR	The ZAR government has been at Uitgezocht since 1901-08-06.
Day 669 Sat **1901-08-10**	OFS	Lieutenant-General EL Elliot's 'drive' in the western Free State ends on the Modder River. The operation, during which the capture of at least half the OFS forces has been envisaged, results in 814 vehicles, 186 000 sheep and 21 000 cattle seized or destroyed. Only 17 burghers have been killed or wounded and 259 are captured but there are very few fighting men amongst them. The commandos get away unscathed but very few non-combatant families are left on the destroyed farms.[59]
	ZAR	The ZAR government is at Klipbank.
	Cape Colony	Commandant Hans Lötter's commando captures a party of General French's scouts at Bethesda Road.
	United Kingdom	Lord Milner leaves England to return to South Africa.
Day 670 Sun **1901-08-11**	ZAR	The ZAR government is at Compies River.
	Northern ZAR	F Visser, an unarmed and wounded prisoner of war, is murdered by members of the Bushveld Carbineers.[60]
Day 671 Mon **1901-08-12**		
Day 672 Tue **1901-08-13**	Cape Colony	Colonel Gorringe clashes with Commandant PH Kritzinger's commando between Steynsburg and Venterstad.
	South-eastern ZAR	The ZAR government is at Schimmelhoek, east of Ermelo.

"...slaughtered herds of sheep and goats..."
(War Museum of the Boer Republics)

	Victoria Cross	Sergeant-Major A Young, Cape Police, South African Forces, Ruiterskraal.
	Natal	The Duke and Duchess of Cornwall and York (the future George V and his wife) arrive in Durban for a quick royal visit to Natal.
Day 673 Wed **1901-08-14**	Cape Colony	Commandant Kritzinger returns to the Free State, crossing the Orange River near Venterstad.[61]
Day 674 Thu **1901-08-15**	OFS	**PRESIDENT STEYN'S REACTION TO KITCHENER'S BANISHMENT ORDER** President Steyn, encouraged by *"the not unfriendly tone"* of the document, decides to answer in some detail to Lord Kitchener's Banishment Proclamation. He refers to the Jameson Raid that openly confirmed the traitorous intentions of the Uitlanders whose yearning for voting rights supposedly is the cause of the war. He points to the leniency granted to the leaders and their release on the occasion of *"some frivolity"* (actually the Queen's Jubilee), the irregularities around the Parliamentary Commission of Inquiry and the default in payment of the agreed damages to the ZAR. He carries on summarising the repeated British interference in the ZAR's internal affairs, the continual revision of demands and the fact, recently admitted by Lord Lansdowne, that the ZAR's ultimatum merely pre-empted the British one by a matter of days. *"We did not draw the sword, but only parried the sword already at our throats ... Acting in self-defence — one of the holiest of rights of man — to maintain our existence."* Discussing the present state of the war, and Kitchener's view of the hopeless position of the Boers, Steyn disagrees, pointing out that their position is actually much better than a year ago. The commandos are fighting all across the Cape Colony and except for the cities, the bigger towns and the railways, the OFS and the ZAR are under Republican control. *"May I be permitted to say that your Excellency's jurisdiction is limited to the range of your Excellency's guns?"* Reacting to Kitchener's threats, *"Our country is ruined; our hearths and homes wrecked; our cattle are looted or killed by the thousand; our women are made prisoners, insulted, and carried away by armed* (blacks); *and many hundreds have already given their lives for the freedom of the fatherland. Can we now — when it is merely a question of banishment — shrink from our duty?* *"If it is a crime to struggle in self-defence and if such crime must be punished, His Majesty's Government can be satisfied with the destruction of our land, the chastisement of our women and children and the general wretchedness brought by this war. It is in Your Excellency's power, more than in any other power on earth to end this and to return this unfortunate region to its previous happiness... but we are not asking for magnanimity, we demand justice."*[62] South of Springfontein, Commandant Kritzinger crosses the railway line between two blockhouses. He has devised an effective technique to deal with this obstacle: arriving at a level crossing, he sends a single man to open the gates. Then the rest of his commando gallops across in single file, with wide intervals. If a man is hit or unhorsed, the man following picks him up and the gallop continues. Despite heavy fire and the approach of two armoured trains, 12 horses fall but 150 men get away unscathed and head for Zastron.[63]
	South-eastern ZAR	Colonel Benson executes another night march followed by a dawn attack at Koppie Alleen, bringing his tally to 60 burghers captured along with several wagons.[64]
	Natal	The Royal couple embark for Cape Town.
Day 675 Fri **1901-08-16**	Eastern ZAR	General Muller ambushes and routs General Walter Kitchener's 19th Hussars at Vrieskraal (Fourieskraal), near the Elands River. Five Hussars are killed and 26 captured before they can be extricated.[65] General De la Rey protests the British mistreatment of women and children.[66]

Day 676 Sat **1901-08-17**	Eastern ZAR	At Delport, south of Amsterdam, the ZAR Executive Council instructs Commandant-General Louis Botha to investigate and, if necessary, punish Assistant Commandant-General Tobias Smuts for the burning of Bremersdorp, because his actions were, in their opinion, not according to the 'customs of civilized warfare'.[67] The SA Constabulary captures a Boer laager near Middelburg.
	Cape Colony	The Duke and Duchess of Cornwall arrive in Cape Town on board the *Ophir*.
	United Kingdom	As an expression of imperialist sentiment, the Royal Titles Act adds the words *"and of the British Dominions beyond the Sea"* to Edward VII's title.
Day 677 Sun **1901-08-18**	OFS	Lord Kitchener orders a drive against Froneman and Haasbroek. Elliot arranges four columns between Glen Station and Ladybrand on the Basutoland border. Columns under Barker and Pine-Coffin operate from Winburg, and Spens, Rimington and Wilson from Senekal.[68]
	Trivia	*PD de Wet's 40th birthday.*
Day 678 Mon **1901-08-19**	Cape Colony	At Graaff-Reinet, PJ Fourie, J van Rensburg and LFS Pfeiffer are executed by firing squad for treason and the murder of British troops.
Day 679 Tue **1901-08-20**	ZAR	A party of SA Constabulary and Morley's Scouts under Captain Woods stumbles on a concentration of about 200 Boers about 32 kilometres south of Bronkhorstspruit Station. Woods orders an immediate attack, throwing the startled Republicans into confusion. Twenty-three are killed, a large number are wounded and 11 are taken prisoner. The Boers rally and counter-attack. They regain their prisoners and take a few from Woods, who is forced to flee towards the railway line.[69]
	Concentration camps Western ZAR	Colonel EC Ingouville-Williams' column transports General De la Rey's mother to the Klerksdorp concentration camp. A member of the Cape Mounted Rifles notes in his diary: *"She is 84 years old. I gave her some milk, jam, soup, etc. as she cannot eat hard tack and they have nothing else. We do not treat them as we ought to."*[70]
Day 680 Wed **1901-08-21**	OFS	General Smuts crosses the railway line near Edenburg and travels east towards Zastron.
	Trivia	*The Cadillac car company is formed in Detroit, Michigan, USA.*
Day 681 Thu **1901-08-22**	ZAR	RC Upton is executed by firing squad in Pretoria for spying.[71]
	Trivia	*Sir WF Hely-Huchinson's 52nd birthday.*
Day 682 Fri **1901-08-23**	Northern ZAR	A group of eight surrendered prisoners of war are shot by the Bushveld Carbineers. On the same day, a German missionary, Reverend CA Daniel Heese, is murdered because he may have witnessed the atrocity.[72]
	Cape Colony	The royal couple embarks at Simon's Town for Canada and the next leg of their royal tour. Among the many an varied gifts they have received during their visit, the most valuable is a parcel of diamonds, 700 stones weighing 261,5 carats, worth £14 000.
Day 683 Sat **1901-08-24**		

Day 684 Sun **1901-08-25**	OFS	President Steyn, Chief Commandant de Wet and Commandant-General Botha determine to continue fighting. In a letter addressed to Commandant Kritzinger and all other Free State commandants, President Steyn outlines a plan to transform Cape rebels into a third party in the conflict against Great Britain and to seek recognition for them as co-belligerents in accordance with the customs of war. As such, the execution of rebels would be illegal and Britain would be forced to treat captured rebels as prisoners of war. Until such time as they are a strong enough force, the two Republics have assigned General De la Rey as Acting Officer Commanding of the Cape Forces. Steyn further reaffirms both Republics' commitment not to consider any peace that does not fully recognise the rights and interests of their Colonial brothers.[73]
	Eastern OFS	Colonel Lowry Cole raids Munnik Hertzog's laager at Liebenberg's Pan and takes 14 prisoners.
	Cape Colony	In terms of martial law regulations, the veteran Cape politician, John X Merriman, is confined to his farm near Stellenbosch by a group of armed soldiers.[74]
Day 685 Mon **1901-08-26**	Cape Colony	D Olewagen and J Nel are executed by firing squad for treason because they acted as horse guards for an invading commando.
	Trivia	*US cyclist Robert Walthour sets a time of 1 minute 37,4 seconds in a one-mile bicycle race.*
Day 686 Tue **1901-08-27**	OFS	General JC Smuts joins Commandants JL van Deventer and B Bouwer at Zastron for the invasion of the Cape Colony. Overtaken near Reddersburg, first by Rawlinson, losing 30 captured, and later by Damant losing another four, the invading convoy has been reduced to about 200 men.[75] This small group is surrounded by the columns of Colonel Lord Basing and Damant at Smithfield, Rawlinson at Bastards Drift on the Caledon River, Thorneycroft and Pilcher near Rouxville and Fitzroy Hart on the south bank of the Orange River, strung out between Bethulie and the Basutoland border.[76]
	Cape Colony	Lord Milner arrives back in Cape Town. The Cape Ministry produce a list of complaints to substantiate their opinion that the manner in which martial law is administered is aggravating the conditions in the Cape Colony and that district commandants are acting outside their authority.[77]
	Black involvement	John Tengo Jabavu's newspaper, *Imvo Zabantsundu*, is banned under martial law regulations, only to appear again on 1902-10-08, after the ban has seriously impoverished its owner, editor and staff.
Day 687 Mon **1901-08-28**	Eastern ZAR	The main house and outbuildings on Commandant-General L Botha's farm *Waterval* are dynamited and burned by British columns.[78] After ten days at Delport, the ZAR government arrives at Athole, west of Amsterdam.
Day 688 Thu **1901-08-29**	Cape Colony	The Cape Ministry formally refuses to accede to Kitchener's request that martial law be extended to the Cape ports.[79] 'Long Cecil' returns to Kimberley.[80]
Day 689 Fri **1901-08-30**	*Trivia*	*Cape Prime Minister WP Schreiner's 44th birthday.* *NPJJ (Siener) van Rensburg's 37th birthday.*
Day 690 Sat **1901-08-31**	ZAR	Commandant-General Botha demotes Assistant Commandant-General Tobias Smuts because of his actions at Bremersdorp. He serves the rest of the war as an ordinary burgher.[81] Republicans wreck a train between Waterval and Hammanskraal. Scout Jack Hindon's men line the banks of the cutting, call on the survivors to surrender, and when refused, they open fire on the derailed carriages. Hindon seizes ammunition, dyna-

		mite and food supplies and estimates British casualties at 40, including Lieutenant-Colonel CFS Vandeleur, who is shot and killed. Lord Kitchener later states that the casualties include one officer, 13 men, one civilian and two natives killed and four officers, 20 men and one woman wounded.[82] This is the fourth railway interruption, due to guerrilla action, for the month.
	South-eastern ZAR	Colonel Benson launches another night attack at Kromdraai.
	Cape Colony	Guided by a Cape Afrikaner, Lieutenant-Colonel T Capper with about 700 men, surprises Commandant Maritz's commando at Brandwacht, 56 kilometres east of Calvinia. The commando escapes, losing only three wounded. A few stragglers are taken prisoner and about 50 ponies are captured.[83]
	OFFICIAL REPORTS **Concentration camps:** **Black involvement:** **Blockhouse lines:**	The officially recorded camp population for white camps is 105 347 and the camp fatalities for August stand at 1 878. The camp population in black camps is 53 154 and 575 deaths are recorded for August.[84] The following blockhouse lines have been completed: ZAR — From Frederikstad to Olifantsnek (85 km) and between Naauwpoort (south-west of Rustenburg) and Pretoria (95 km). Cape Colony — From Bethulie (OFS) to Herschel (110 km).
1901	SPRING	**SEPTEMBER**
Day 691 Sun **1901-09-01**	OFS	At the critical moment, Kitchener orders Hart to keep the enemy north of the Orange River. Hart immediately calls his mobile force to Driefontein Drift, about 25 kilometres east of Aliwal North, to transfer them to the north bank.[85]
	Western ZAR	The British have formed a cordon consisting of six columns in an effort to corner General Kemp. The columns of Allenby, Kekewich, Hickie, Williams, Gilbert Hamilton and Methuen surround his lair at Roodewal in the Swartruggens. Kemp slips through between Methuen and Hickie, leaving behind about 180 unmounted burghers.[86]
	Trivia	*General Paul Sanford Lord Methuen's 56th birthday.*
Day 692 Mon **1901-09-02**	Cape Colony	Lord Milner leaves Cape Town for East London, from where he proceeds to Bloemfontein with his staff. This circuitous route is taken because of the security situation in the Cape Colony.
Day 693 Tue **1901-09-03**	Cape Colony Black involvement	**SMUTS ENTERS THE CAPE COLONY** General Smuts, with about 250 men, invades the Cape Colony through Kiba Drift at Klaarwater near Kafferkop in the Herschel area and has to fight all night long against armed blacks. Three burghers are killed and, when their bodies are later retrieved, they are found to have been dreadfully mutilated for 'muti' (tribal medicine).[87]
	ZAR	Lord Kitchener writes to Commandant-General Botha that, in his opinion, the destruction of railway and telegraph lines, as presently carried out by the Boers, are no longer acceptable military acts. As the Boers have no intention of holding the communication or of preventing the advance of their enemy, it can only be defined as *"marauding of the worst form"*. He threatens with unspecified steps and orders lists of prospective hostages to be compiled.[88]
Day 694 Wed **1901-09-04**	OFS	General Fitzroy Hart completes the transfer of his troops to the north bank of the Orange River, only to hear that Smuts has crossed about 20 kilometres upstream.[89]
	ZAR	Lord Kitchener issues formal instructions regarding civilians travelling on trains. Every train, conveying passengers or troops, running on the northern line will henceforth carry two prominent burghers of the 'late South African Republic'.[90]

	Natal	General Lyttleton is appointed as Commander of HM's forces in Natal with General Hildyard as his Second in Command.
	Cape Colony	F Troy, a Swede from Johannesburg, H J Veenstra and J van Vuuren are executed for treason by firing squad at Colesberg.
Day 695 Thu **1901-09-05**	Cape Colony	**LÖTTER'S COMMANDO IS CAPTURED** Commandant CJ (Hans) Lötter and part of his commando are surprised by a force under Colonel HJ Scobell at Bouwershoek, near Cradock. Scobell approaches the sleeping laager under the cover of a rainstorm and, despite a desperate fight, the commando is forced to surrender. The Republicans lose at least 14 killed and more than 100 captured, including about 50 wounded. Lötter is one of the wounded. The British casualties amount to about 20. General JC Smuts reaches the Stormberg Mountains.[91]
	Western ZAR	**THE ACTION AT RHENOSTERFONTEIN** General LAS Lemmer, assisted by General Kemp, attacks Lord Methuen in thick bush at Rhenosterfontein (at the site of the present-day Marico Dam). The convoy is seriously threatened by the determined attack but, on discovering that there are women and children in the camp, the commando disengages. They inflict 40 casualties and capture 20 soldiers and 18 horses. General Lemmer is wounded for the second time during the war.[92]
	Northern ZAR	Lieutenant Hannam and members of the Bushveld Carbineers fire on wagons with women and children who offer no resistance. Despite their pleas, two children are killed and a girl is wounded.[93]
Day 696 Fri **1901-09-06**	*Trivia*	*US President McKinley is shot by an anarchist named Leon Czolgosz.* *Sir A Hunter's 45th birthday.* *ZAR Acting State President SW Burger's 49th birthday.*
Day 697 Sat **1901-09-07**	Northern ZAR	Two burghers and a young boy are allegedly murdered after surrendering to the Bushveld Carbineers.[94]
	South-eastern ZAR	Commandant-General L Botha leaves Blaauwkop, 19 kilometres east of Ermelo with almost 1 000 men, starting his planned second invasion of Natal.[95]
	Cape Colony	In a narrow defile, Moordenaarspoort, near Dordrecht, General Smuts and a small scouting party are ambushed by a force commanded by Lieutenant KH Jackson. J Neethling and the two Adendorf brothers are killed and Smuts, who has a narrow escape as his horse is shot from under him, is the only one to escape unharmed.[96]
	Trivia	*The Boxer rebellion ends in the Peking Treaty that also demands indemnity to be paid to the great powers.* *Sir Henry Campbell-Bannerman's 65th birthday.*
Day 698 Sun **1901-09-08**	South-eastern ZAR	General Walter Kitchener and Colonel WP Campbell leave Wonderfontein Station and march south towards Ermelo.
	Trivia	*HF Verwoerd, future South African Prime Minister and architect of apartheid, is born in the Netherlands.*
Day 699 Mon **1901-09-09**	South-eastern ZAR	Colonel Colvile marches eastwards from Standerton towards Amsterdam and Colonel Garrat moves east from Wakkerstroom.
	Cape Colony	Martial law is extended to the Cape ports.
	Trivia	*French painter Henri de Toulouse-Lautrec dies in Paris.*

Day 700 Tue **1901-09-10**	South-eastern ZAR	Colonel Benson attacks a Boer laager at Pullen's Hope, near Carolina.
	Cape Colony	The youngest Boer commandant, the 19-year-old Commandant Piet van der Merwe is killed in action at Driefontein at the foot of the Swartberg Mountains, when he and 30 burghers are attacked by about 700 troops under Colonel Crabbe. Only three burghers escape.[97]
Day 701 Wed **1901-09-11**	ZAR	Lord Milner arrives in Johannesburg and writes to Mrs Montefiore, *"At the liberal computation there are not more than 6 000 Boers still in arms against us. They are ill-mounted, ill-clad, ill-armed, the most wretched objects conceivable and constantly on the run. Still they keep on, deluded by the persistent lying of their leaders, and it may take a long time yet to catch them in twenties and thirties. It is a miserable business.*[98] *"The state of the country is horrible, death and devastation everywhere, as the continuance of this wretched and senseless guerrilla warfare has forced the military to sweep the country from end to end. The Orange River Colony is virtually a desert, almost the whole population living in refugee camps along the railway line."*[99]
	Cape Colony	A certain Mrs Brooks and nine young girls appear in court in Maraisburg (now Hofmeyr), on charges relating to the brief visit of a Republican commando to the town. Legal argument centres on whether they sang the Republican anthems and whether the men they kissed were related to them or not. Two of the girls are acquitted, but Mrs Brooks and seven girls, one aged 15, two 16, three 17 and a nineteen-year-old are sentenced to 30 days in jail.[100]
Day 702 Thu **1901-09-12**	Cape Colony	General Smuts' commando, consisting of about 200 men, is completely surrounded by superior British forces in the vicinity of Penhoek Pass, but, in a fight lasting from 11:00 to 22:00, they succeed in breaking out. They cross the Sterkstroom-Indwe railway line at Hasleton and the line between East London and Dordrecht at Putterskraal, destroying it in passing.[101] In Graaff-Reinet, five teenage Cape rebels (part of Lötter's commando) are condemned to death for treason. Lord Kitchener later reduces the sentences of H van Meynen (14), J du Plessis (16), SC Schoeman (17), JJ Lötter (17) and CJH van Heerden (19) to prison terms and corporal punishment.[102]
	ZAR	Towards the end of August more than fifty suspects have been arrested in Pretoria. One of them, Cornelius Broeksma, an ex-public prosecutor, is put on trial for breaking his oath of neutrality and high treason. Correspondence found in his house indicates that he has been trying to communicate with Republican generals in the field and trying to smuggle 'anti-British propaganda' to Europe.[103] Vice-President Schalk Burger and the ZAR government leave Athole after a stay of 15 days.
	Eastern ZAR	Commandant-General Botha leaves Rooikraal for Luneberg.
Day 703 Fri **1901-09-13**	Concentration camps Natal	The Merebank Refugee Camp is established near Durban in an attempt to reduce the camp population in the Republics. Its most famous inmates are to be Mrs De Wet and her children.[104]
	Cape Colony	After men and horses of his commando have been trekking and fighting for 40 hours without eating or resting, General Smuts crosses the East London railway line near Putterskraal and arrives at the Klaas Smits River.[105]
Day 704 Sat **1901-09-14**	Eastern ZAR South-eastern ZAR	The ZAR government is at Marydale, north of Amsterdam. Commandant-General Botha arrives at Frischgewaagd, east of Paulpietersburg.
	OFS	Colonel Rimington, emulating Benson's intelligence gathering methods and night marches, captures a small laager at Anderkant.

	Cape Colony	General Smuts laagers at Wildschutberg.
	Trivia	*Vice-president Roosevelt becomes the 26th President of the USA.*
Day 705 Sun **1901-09-15**	South-eastern ZAR	Colonel Benson, continuing his night operations in the Carolina district, attacks Tweefontein.
	Northern ZAR	Fifteen members of the Bushveld Carbineers send a petition to Colonel Hall of the Royal Artillery, requesting a full and impartial inquiry into the alleged atrocities perpetrated by members of their unit.[106]
	OFS	Surrounded by several columns under General Charles Knox, Commandants Kritzinger and Brand are united in the Zastron district.
	Natal	The columns of Colonels Gough and Stewart are sent to the Natal border at De Jager's Drift.
Day 706 Mon **1901-09-16**	South-eastern ZAR	Colonel Benson repeats his night attacks, this time against Middeldrift, near Carolina.
	Natal	Colonel Gough is ordered to clear the road and escort a supply column from Vryheid to Dundee.
	Cape Colony	Commandant WH Lategan enters the Cape Colony, divides his commando into small units and with only 14 men he moves on to Murraysburg (Hofmeyr).[107] A small party of Grenadier Guards receives accurate information that Commandant Wynand C Malan is sleeping at Visserskraal on the De Aar/Noupoort line, near Hanover. They decide to attack, exploiting a very wild and stormy night to approach the sleeping commando, but they make a complete hash of it. They mistake a raging spruit for the road and have to spend half the night in the cold and wet. Eight of the men lose their way and disappear. At dawn they abandon their plan. On their return to camp, they sight five burghers and immediately give chase only to find themselves ambushed. A running battle develops until Malan orders a charge. One officer and three men are killed and the rest surrenders.[108]
Day 707 Tue **1901-09-17**	OFS	Commandants Kritzinger and Brand splits up and General Knox loses contact. Kritzinger moves south towards the Orange River and Brand heads north towards the Bloemfontein/Thaba Nchu line of blockhouses.[109]
	ZAR/Natal	**THE BATTLE OF BLOOD RIVER'S POORT** Commandant-General Botha leaves Frischgewaagd and moves to Blood River's Poort, west of Vryheid. Colonel Gough's scouts report Botha's men in the pass and he first decides to seek contact with Stewart's force and to wait until dark before clearing the pass. However, when he notices offsaddled Boer horses turned out to graze, he decides to execute a flank movement and surprise the unwary Boer sentries. Just as his attacking mounted infantry is closing on their objective, 500 Republicans gallop out of the pass in close formation. They cross the British front, wheel round and attack the British from the right flank and the rear. The mounted infantry, widely extended, cannot rally fast enough and in ten minutes it is all over. Stewart's force is too far away to assist and they fall back with part of the convoy to avoid being surrounded. Gough's force loses 44 killed and wounded. The remaining 241 soldiers are taken prisoner and two field-guns are captured.[110]
	Victoria Cross	Lieutenant LAE Price-Davies, the King's Royal Rifle Corps, is nominated for the Victoria Cross for firing on the attackers with his revolver until hit.
		BOTHA'S INVASION OF NATAL Commandant-General Botha and General Cheere Emmett join forces and now have about 2 000 men. In very bad weather they proceed southwards to invade Natal.[111]

	Cape Colony	**THE ACTION AT MODDERFONTEIN** General JC Smuts surprises a squadron of 17th Lancers at Modderfontein, in the Elandsrivierpoort, between Tarkastad and Cradock, and captures two field-guns. The British suffer four officers and 28 men killed and 51 wounded, including Captain VS Sandman and Lord George Crespigny Brabazon Vivian. The remaining 50 men are taken prisoner. When another squadron of lancers appears on the scene, Smuts retires, leaving his prisoners behind and destroying the field-guns that they cannot remove.[112]
Day 708 Wed **1901-09-18**	OFS	The drive against General Froneman and Commandant Haasbroek ends in failure after Haasbroek has slipped through Spens' fingers.
	Eastern ZAR	A Republican laager is attacked by Colonel Benson at Middeldrift, on the uMpuluzi River, south-east of Carolina. He captures 54 prisoners, 240 horses, several wagons and some cattle.[113]
	Natal	The columns of Stewart and Allenby reach De Jager's Drift and Pulteney blocks Staal Drift to prevent Botha's planned invasion.
Day 709 Thu **1901-09-19**	OFS	**THE ACTION AT SLANGFONTEIN** After crossing the Bloemfontein/Thaba Nchu fortified line from the south, General George Brand comes across a farm-burning party of 200 mounted infantry and SA Constabulary with two field-guns sent out from Boesman's Kop by General Tucker who is stationed at Bloemfontein. Taken completely by surprise in the already devastated region at Slangfontein, near Sannah's Post, Commandant J Ackermann quickly captures all 200 men, two field-guns, a large quantity of ammunition and more than 200 horses.[114]
Day 710 Fri **1901-09-20**	Southern OFS	**THE ACTION AT QUAGGAFONTEIN** Commandant PH Kritzinger, with about 70 men, surprises about 100 of Lovat's Scouts under Colonel Andrew Murray in their camp at Quaggafontein, near Herschel-Zastron. Murray, his brother and 48 others are among those killed and wounded. The rest and a single field-gun are captured.[115]
	Western ZAR	Colonel Kekewich leaves Naauwpoort for operations in the Magaliesberg Mountains. His column consists of about 800 infantrymen, 560 cavalry men, three field-guns and a pom-pom.[116]
	ZAR	The ZAR government is at Bellskop on the Swaziland border.
Day 711 Sat **1901-09-21**	ZAR	The ZAR government is at Nerston on the Swaziland border.
Day 712 Sun **1901-09-22**	OFS	Colonel Rimington executes a night march and captures a small laager at the confluence of the Wilge and Vaal Rivers.
Day 713 Mon **1901-09-23**	ZAR/Natal	Allenby's column moves to Vant's Drift on the ZAR/Natal border.
	Trivia	*CF Beyers' 32nd birthday.*
Day 714 Tue **1901-09-24**	Cape Colony	General Smuts reaches the Katberg Mountains in the vicinity of Fort Beaufort.[117]
	Natal/Zululand	Commandant-General Louis Botha arrives at Babanango, on the Zululand border, with about 2 000 men. He decides to attack two small British fortified posts on the Zululand border. He dispatches his brother Chris with about 1 400 men towards Fort Itala, his brother-in-law Cheere Emmet towards Fort Prospect, while he stays behind at Babanango with a small reserve. Colonel Spens blocks Rorke's Drift.[118]
	ZAR	The ZAR government returns to Athole, west of Amsterdam.

Day 715 Wed **1901-09-25**	Natal/Zululand	**THE ATTACK ON FORT ITALA** The post at Fort Itala is defended by about 300 mounted infantrymen commanded by Major Chapman. Its defences consist of trenches between 50 and 100 metres apart, commanding a clear field of fire up to a range of about 600 metres, with a detached post, defended by about 80 men, on the summit of the steep Mount Itala, about two kilometres away. Just after midnight General Chris Botha starts his attack, but the defenders, forewarned by Zulu scouts, are alert and opens a heavy fusillade. The burghers soon surround and overwhelm the small party on the mountain. The main assault on the British camp at the fort starts at about 02:00, with Chris Botha attacking from the side of the mountain, Opperman from the south-east and Potgieter and Scholtz from the north. In bright moonlight, the defenders are able to use their guns to good effect and at 04:00 the attack peters out. At dawn the burghers renew their attack and as the light improves, life becomes impossible for the gun crews and they cease firing. Firing continues all day long, but Chris Botha is unable to persuade his men to charge across the open ground dominated by the defenders' rifles. At 19:00, with ammunition running out on both sides, the burghers retire. Botha reports that he has suffered a loss of 18 killed, including both Potgieter and Scholtz, and 40 wounded, including Opperman. The British have lost about 81 killed and wounded, including Chapman and his second in command Captain Butler who are both wounded. Chapman, almost out of ammunition and with no prospect of being reinforced, quietly evacuates his post and retires to Nkandhla.[119]
	Vicitoria Cross	Driver FH Bradley, 69th Battery, Royal Field Artillery, Fort Itala. In the meantime, Emmet is approaching his objective at Fort Prospect.
	Southern ZAR	Captain RDC Miers of the South African Constabulary is shot and killed near Heidelberg while attempting to entice Field-cornet Salmon van As to surrender. It is later alleged that he has been shot under a flag of truce and Van As is accused of committing a war crime.[120]
	Trivia	*Britain annexes the Ashanti Kingdom in West Africa as part of the Gold Coast Colony.*
Day 716 Thu **1901-09-26**	Natal/Zululand	**THE ATTACK ON FORT PROSPECT** Fort Prospect, about 15 kilometres east of Itala, is defended by about 80 men under Captain Rowley of the Dorsetshire Regiment. The fort is well situated with strong defences that can support each other. Emmet and Grobler complete the encirclement during the early hours of the morning and the attack begins at 04:15. The attackers approach to within 20 metres of the trenches, but at dawn the British machine gun opens up and the attackers are forced to fall back. Another fierce attack is launched at 09:30, but the defenders gallantly repel them. A party of Zulu policemen under Sergeant Gumbi, outside the British lines at the time of the first attack, fights their way through Emmet's lines to share in the defence. The burghers spend the rest of the day sniping at the British positions and retire at about 18:30 having suffered about 30 casualties. Thanks to the excellent defences Rowley loses only nine men.[121]
	Black involvement	
	Cape Colony	Sixteen-year-old Rochelle de Villiers, son of the mayor of Aberdeen, is sentenced to a week in jail in terms of martial law regulations, for galloping down the main street of the town.[122]
Day 717 Fri **1901-09-27**	Natal/Zululand	After *"a fine march"'* of about 80 kilometres in 24 hours, General Bruce Hamilton, with 1 600 cavalry, reaches Itala, only to find that Chapman has been safely in Nkandlha for 17 hours.[123]
	Trivia	*Louis Botha's 39th birthday.*
Day 718 Sat **1901-09-28**	OFS	Commandant Dreyer and nine burghers are captured at Jammersberg Drift.
	International	A cartoon by Jean Veber entitled *L 'Impudique Albion,* appears on the back cover of

		L 'Assiette au Beurre. It depicts Edward's face superimposed on Albion's buttocks. Most editions are circulated before the Paris police acts and orders it to be changed. The cencored version features a blue polka dot petticoat over the offending anatomy.
	Trivia	JDP French's 49th birthday. PH Roux's 34th birthday
Day 719 Sun **1901-09-29**	Natal/Zululand	General Chris Botha captures a convoy of 30 wagons escorted by a few Zulu policemen near Melmoth.
	Western ZAR	Colonel Kekewich's column camps at Moedwil on the bank of the Selons River, between Zeerust and Rustenburg. He sends an empty convoy with prisoners and 'refugees' with an escort towards Naauwpoort, thereby reducing his force to about 930 men. General De la Rey, whose scouts have stalked the column for a week, quietly concentrates about 1 000 men at Buffelshoek, about 16 kilometres away. His force includes the commandos of General Kemp and the men under Commandants Van Heerden, Steenekamp and Boshoff.[124] A proclamation is issued providing for the sale of the property belonging to Boers still in the field.
	ZAR	Tjaart AP Kruger, a son of President Kruger and reputedly the chief of the Transvaal Secret Service, dies.[125]
Day 720 Mon **1901-09-30**	Western ZAR	**THE BATTLE OF MOEDWIL** Colonel Kekewich concentrates the major part of his force astride the ford along the east bank of the river with smaller pickets in a semicircle to the north and north-east, more to the east and south and a stronger picket in an old kraal about 500 metres south-west of the drift. Having just 'swept' the region, he believes that there are no enemy forces of any consequence in the vicinity. De la Rey leaves his men at Dwarsspruit, 11 kilometres away, and does his final assessment of the British positions. He decides on a surprise frontal assault from the west on Kekewich's line along the river. In bright moonlight De la Rey arranges his men: the main thrust against the river is entrusted to Kemp's men with smaller forces working around the northern and southern flanks while he forms a reserve with 36 men of the Johannesburg police on a hill about 3 000 metres west of the camp. At 04:30 his left flank under Steenekamp clashes with a small dawn patrol by the yeomanry, sweeps them aside and breaks through the picket line, rolling them up to both sides. On the right flank Field-cornets Fourie and Coetzee also reach their objectives. Kemp's main assault overruns the pickets on the bank of the river and pours a heavy fire into the camp which is silhouetted against the dawning sky. Complete surprise is achieved, the horses stampede and the camp is in turmoil. As the light improves, Kekewich is able to restore some semblance of order. A new skirmish line is formed between the camp and the river and the field-guns and pom-poms open up, but they are soon silenced by accurate rifle fire. A British counter-attack develops against Steenekamp's men who are rapidly moving northwards fuelling rumours that a Boer attack on the British rear is imminent. Elements of the Scottish Horse and yeomanry launch a counter-attack on Kemp's left flank. With his line already stretched thinly and his ammunition running low, Kemp, unable to reply should the British shelling resume, is concerned that his line of retreat may be threatened. At 06:15 he orders his commandants to withdraw.[126] Piet Schuil and two burghers, sent to the British lines under a flag of truce, are fired on. Schuil, a foreign volunteer, tears the white flag from his rifle and returns fire while his companions escape. (He is later captured, charged with abuse of the white flag and sentenced to death.)[127]

	Victoria Cross	The British lose 56 killed, 131 wounded (including Kekewich), 327 horses and hundreds of draught animals. The Republicans suffer at least nine killed, including the brave Commandant Boshoff, 33 wounded and three (including one of the wounded) captured. After the battle, De la Rey sends in his ambulance to recover the bodies of the four burghers killed and the three wounded who had to be left behind. To his horror, the ambulance returns with seven bodies, three whose skulls are crushed and with obvious other bruises and lacerations to their bodies. Private W Bees, 1st Battalion, the Derbyshire Regiment, is to receive the Victoria Cross for his gallantry in fetching water from the river for the wounded under short-range enemy fire.
	ZAR	Cornelius Broeksma is executed by firing squad in Johannesburg after having been found guilty of breaking the oath of neutrality, inciting others to do the same and high treason. A fund is started in Holland for his family and for this purpose a postcard with a picture of himself and his family is sold, bearing the inscription: *"Cornelius Broeksma, hero and martyr in pity's cause. Shot by the English on 30th September, 1901, because he refused to be silent about the cruel suffering in the women's camps."*[128]
	Cape Colony	General Smuts and 70 of his men are incapacitated after eating a wild fruit known as 'Hottentots Bread'.[129]
	Trivia	*Field-Marshal Frederick Sleigh Lord Roberts' 68th birthday.*

OFFICIAL REPORTS	
Concentration camps:	The officially recorded camp population of the white camps is 109 418 and the monthly deaths for September stand at 2 411.
Black involvement:	The camp population in the black camps is 65 589 and 728 deaths are recorded.[130]
Blockhouse line:	OFS — The blockhouse line between Koppies in the Free State and Potchefstroom (80 km) is completed.
Communications:	Only two railway interruptions due to enemy action are recorded during September.[131]

1901	SPRING	**OCTOBER**
Day 721 Tue **1901-10-01**	Northern ZAR	General CF Beyers forces a British unit to surrender on the farm Pruisen, south of Potgietersrust, but three burghers, including the brave Lieutenant Du Toit of the Soutpansberg Police, are killed.[132]
	South-east ZAR	Commandant-General Botha's burghers, returning from their expedition towards Natal, skirmish with Walter Kitchener's column at Vaalkrans Nek
	Cape Colony	General Smuts' commando is in the Addo Forest, near Uitenhage.
	United Kingdom	Miss Emily Hobhouse again urges the Minister of War, *"in the name of the little children whom I have watched suffer and die"* to implement improvements in the concentration camps.[133]
Day 722 Wed **1901-10-02**	ZAR	Lord Methuen leaves Mafeking with two columns, heading for Zeerust. Piet Schuil, a foreign volunteer, sentenced to death for abuse of the white flag, is executed by a British firing squad near Ratsagae's Kraal, west of Rustenburg.[134]
	Cape Colony	General Smuts crosses the railway line between Port Elizabeth and Graaff-Reinet.
	Trivia	*The Vickers company launches Britain's first submarine.* *OFS President MT Steyn's 44th birthday.* *MK Ghandi's 32nd birthday.*

Day 723 Thu **1901-10-03**	OFS	Colonel Rimington scores another success, this time at Oploop, against Commandant Buys' commando, who has been chased into the Free State by Colonel Rawlinson.
	South-eastern ZAR	General Botha clashes with Colonel Garrat's men at Geluk.
	Cape Colony	General Smuts' commando attacks Colonel Gorringe's column in a narrow valley in the Zuurberg Mountains. Three of Smuts' scouts are captured near Bayville (Kirkwood) and executed for wearing khaki.[135]
Day 724 Fri **1901-10-04**	Cape Colony	General Smuts sends Commandant Bouwer with a small commando to operate independently in the Graaff-Reinet district.[136]
Day 725 Sat **1901-10-05**	South-eastern ZAR	Commandant-General Louis Botha crosses the Bivane River between Wakkerstroom and Piet Retief.
	Cape Colony	After a meeting in the Kabouka's Gorge, General Smuts decides to split his commando, putting Commandant JL van Deventer and JRF Kirsten in command of a separate force.[137]
	Trivia	*FW Reitz's 57th birthday.*
Day 726 Sun **1901-10-06**	South-eastern ZAR	Commandant-General Louis Botha skirmishes with Colvile's patrols at Yorkshire Farm.[138] Abandoning his wagons, he crosses the Pondwana Mountains and escapes to the north.
	Cape Colony	General Smuts clashes with the defence forces of Alexandria and Grahamstown and takes both camps. Commandant Bouwer routs the Somerset East Defence Force at Springvale and resupplies both commandos.[139]
	Trivia	*Christiaan Botha's 37th birthday.*
Day 727 Mon **1901-10-07**	ZAR	The Pretoria Commissioner of Police does not regard the 'prominent persons' selected as hostages on trains, as persons of any great consequence. He adds, *"I think it quite possible that many of the marauding Boers in the field would be glad of an opportunity to blow them up for having surrendered, if for no other reason.* *"I therefore submit that prisoners of war — in batches — would be more suitable for this purpose."*[140]
	Cape Colony	JH Roux (18) is executed by firing squad in Graaff-Reinet for treason.
	Trivia	*CR de Wet's 47th birthday.*
Day 728 Mon **1901-10-08**	South-eastern ZAR	Commandant-General Louis Botha reaches Piet Retief.
	Cape Colony	Martial law is extended to the Cape ports and now includes the Cape Town, Wynberg, Simonstown, Port Elizabeth and East London districts.[143]
	International	Two Dutch volunteers held as prisoners of war on St Helena, HA de Haas and H Mulder, are picked up by *HMS Doris* while trying to reach a supply ship in a small boat.[142]
Day 729 Wed **1901-10-09** .		
Day 730 Thu **1901-10-10**	Cape Colony	General Smuts crosses the railway line between Klipplaat and Graaff-Reinet.
	United Kingdom	In the course of an after-dinner speech, Sir Redvers Bullers explains how he *"suggested"*

		surrender in his telegram after Colenso as a *"cover"* to protect General White: *"I was in command in Natal, and it was my duty to give my subordinate some assistance, some lead, something that in the event of his determining to surrender he would be able to produce and say, Well, Sir Redvers Buller agreed."* This 'extraordinary pronouncement' leads to a cabinet decision relieving him of his command at Aldershot and he is put on half-pay. [143]
	Trivia	*State President SJP Kruger's 76th birthday.*
Day 731 Fri **1901-10-11** *Comdt. Gideon Scheepers* *(National Cultural Histoy Museum)*	Cape Colony	**THE WAR ENTERS ITS THIRD YEAR** Commandant JC (Hans) Lötter, his Field-cornets Kruger, Schoeman and Breedt and his Adjutant Wolfaardt, are sentenced to death for treason at Middelburg. **SCHEEPERS IS TAKEN PRISONER** Commandant Gideon Scheepers is captured near Blood River Station, in the Prince Albert district, while incapacitated by fever. The seriously ill Scheepers is taken to the British military hospital at Matjiesfontein. Commandant SW Pypers takes over command of his commando.
	Bechuanaland	At Vryburg, JWG Jansen and Rautenbach are executed by hanging for horse theft.
	South-east ZAR	Commandant-General Botha joins Acting State President SW Burger and the ZAR government at Athole, near Amsterdam, near the Swaziland border.
	Trivia	*JH De la Rey's 53rd birthday.*
Day 732 Sat **1901-10-12**	Cape Colony	Commandant Manie Maritz is in action with the Colonial Light Horse near Hoedjesbaai.[144] Commandant JC (Hans) Lötter (26) is executed by firing squad in Middelburg, with the adult male inhabitants of the town forced to witness. Olive Schreiner writes: 　*"Lötter rests well; he sleeps the quiet sleep,* 　*which nevermore the blast of trump can break,* 　*or yell of hate can disturb.* 　*He has escaped from out the tangled web,* 　*which men call life into the grand simplicity of death."* J Schoeman is executed by firing squad in Tarkastad.
Day 733 Sun **1901-10-13**	Western ZAR	Colonel Kekewich, having recovered from the wounds he received at Moedwil, resumes command of his column and marches from Rustenburg towards Swartruggens to cooperate with Lord Methuen.
	South-eastern ZAR	Ex-General Tobias Smuts attacks a British column at Geluk.[145]
	Cape Colony	Commandant Jaap van Deventer and Commandant JRF Kirsten clash with the Somerset East Defence Force and some Cape Mounted Rifles at Doringbosch, in the Aberdeen district, taking 210 prisoner and capturing 220 horses.[146] JA Baxter, grandson of an English minister working in Johannesburg before the war, has volunteered and joined the Klerksdorp Commando. He becomes detached from Smuts' commando and is captured by Colonel Scobell and executed in Aberdeen by firing squad, for wearing a British uniform.[147]
Day 734 Mon **1901-10-14**	ZAR	Lord Methuen reaches Zeerust on his way to Lindleyspoort.[149] St J Brodrick inquires from Lord Kitchener *"whether there is any truth in the reports that looting corps have been formed in South Africa, composed of men who find all their own equipment except guns and ammunition but receive no pay, remunerating themselves by selling stock, etc. which they capture"*.[150]

	Cape Colony	A Martial Law Board is established in the Cape Colony. A permanent board, representing the civil and military administrations, under the chairmanship of Mr Mitchell, is established to inquire into all grievances under martial law.[151]
Day 735 Tue **1901-10-15**	ZAR	Replying in a letter to Brodrick, Lord Kitchener denies the existence of 'burgher corps' in British service who are rewarded in looted cattle.[152] Kitchener's report to Brodrick is interspersed with resentment and despair: *"Extermination... is a long and very tiring business... they seem as fanatically disposed to continue the war as ever, and I fear it can only end by our catching all or almost all of them. It is hard work for our men... if you think that someone else could do better out here, I hope you will not hesitate to for a moment in replacing me. I try all I can but it is not like the Soudan and disappointments are frequent..."*[153]
	Cape Colony	Commandant Jaap van Deventer overwhelms and captures 157 men of the Somerset East District Mounted Troops at Doornbosh.[154] PJ Wolfaardt is executed by firing squad at Middelburg.
	Natal Colony	A farewell function is organised at the Congress Hall in Durban for Mohandas K Ghandi, who is returning to India where he anticipates to win a leadership position in the Indian nationalist movement.[155]
Day 736 Wed **1901-10-16**	Cape Colony	Scheepers' commando, now commanded by Pypers, joins hands with General Smuts' force. General Hertzog's commando reaches Saldanha Bay.[156]
	Trivia	*Booker T Washington, a black teacher, dines with President Roosevelt at the White House.*
Day 737 Thu **1901-10-17**	ZAR	After a stay of three weeks at Athole, the ZAR government moves to Mooiplaats, between Lake Chrissie and Breyten.
	Cape Colony	W Kruger and DC Breedt are executed by firing squad at Cradock.
Day 738 Fri **1901-10-18**	South-east ZAR	Commandant-General Botha and the ZAR government are at Bankkop near Ermelo.
	Cape Colony	General Smuts crosses the Swartberg Mountains.
Day 739 Sat **1901-10-19**	OFS	The first of eleven issues of the *Staats Courant van den Oranjevrijstaat* is printed on a press hidden in a cave near Fouriesburg.[157]
	Cape Colony	Gideon Scheepers is transferred to the hospital at Beaufort West.[158]
Day 740 Sun **1901-10-20**	Western ZAR	One of Lord Methuen's columns, a convoy from Mafeking to Zeerust escorted by 1 000 troops with five field-guns and two pom-poms, commanded by Lieutenant-Colonel SB von Donop, makes camp at Rondavelskraal, near the present-day Twyfelspoort Station.[159]
	Northern ZAR	Three Republican laagers are captured near Nylstroom.
Day 741 Mon **1901-10-21**	Western ZAR	Lord Methuen and Kekewich join forces at Lindleyspoort.[160]
	Cape Colony	Commandant Manie Maritz reaches Darling, about 60 kilometres from Cape Town — the furthest penetration of Republican forces into the Cape Colony.[161] Attacking at daybreak, Colonel Lukin surprises Commandant Van Deventer at Steilhoogte, on the Sundays River. The Republicans lose one killed and one wounded, while ten are captured.[162]
Day 742 Tue **1901-10-22**	ZAR	After executing a night march, Colonel Benson surprises a Republican laager at Klippoortjie and takes 37 prisoners.[163]

Day 743 Wed 1901-10-23		
Day 744 Thu 1901-10-24	Western ZAR	**THE BATTLE OF KLEINFONTEIN (near the present-day Groot-Marico)** Lieutenant-Colonel SB von Donop's convoy sets out for Zeerust with Yeomanry on both flanks, a pom-pom in the vanguard, the infantry with about 100 wagons in the middle and the field-guns travelling with the rear. At about 07:00, at Kleinfontein or Driefontein, as the convoy is passing a clump of beech trees, a small group of burghers under General Lemmer is sighted to the front and the pom-pom is brought into action. Simultaneously, General Kemp, with about 500 burghers in three successive lines, attacks along the entire length of the convoy. Their charge, centred on the wagons, cuts right through the column, drives the Yeomanry into the clump of trees. While some of the burghers attempt to remove as many of the captured wagons, the rest wheel towards the column's rear and they attack the guns, overrun and capture them. Kemp is unable to remove the guns, as their teams have been shot down. De la Rey's burghers, who are supposed to attack from the rear, have lagged too far behind and at 09:00, with the British rallying in the bush and preparing to counter-attack, Kemp disengages. The British lose about 30 killed, 54 wounded, 15 wagons, and 300 horses and mules before the Republicans break off the fight with about 20 killed and 31 wounded (including Commandant Oosthuizen).
	South-eastern ZAR	Commandant-General L Botha and the ZAR government are at Schimmelhoek, 32 kilometres east of Ermelo.
	Eastern ZAR	General Ben Viljoen attacks the blockhouse line near Badfontein.
	Trivia	*The Eastman Kodak Company is formed in New Jersey, following the success of the $1-Brownie camera they launched the previous year.*
Day 745 Fri 1901-10-25	Eastern ZAR	**THE ACTION AT SCHIMMELHOEK** On receiving information from black scouts that Commandant-General L Botha and the ZAR government are at Schimmelhoek, 32 kilometres east of Ermelo, Colonels Rimington and Sir H Rawlinson with 2 000 men and eight guns are sent in pursuit. The British force stumbles on General Chris Botha's 300 men and the ensuing firing alerts Louis Botha, allowing him to make a narrow escape with the small party with him, including his eleven-year-old son. He leaves behind his hat and a bag of correspondence. The ZAR government, who is actually on the neighbouring farm, also gets away after the British columns are led on a wild-goose chase by Commandant Opperman.[164] Vice-President Schalk Burgher and the ZAR government arrive safely at Klipstapel west of Breyten.
	Cape Colony	Seven or eight commandos consisting mainly of rebels, hold a council of war at Kloudskraal near Calvinia. SG (Manie) Maritz is appointed as Acting Assistant Chief-Commandant and separate operational areas are allocated to the different commandos.[165]
	Natal	Lord Milner arrives, unheralded, at Pietermaritzburg for a long overdue visit to Natal, Britain's 'most loyal' colony.
	United Kingdom	Joseph Chamberlain delivers an anti-German speech at Edinburgh.
	Trivia	*Sir NG Lyttelton's 56th birthday.*
Day 746 Sat 1901-10-26	ZAR	Colonel Benson skirmishes with a small party of burghers at Rietkuil on the Steenkoolspruit.[168] As the commandos in the Bethal district have become wise to Benson's night attack tactics, his success rate declines and he contents himself with 'ordinary clearing work' — burning farms and herding women, children, old men and other

	Western ZAR	non-combatants with their livestock and vehicles.[167] The ZAR government is at Kranspoort, north-west of Ermelo To counter the dynamiting of trains, Major-General Wilson orders leading inhabitants of Klerksdorp and Potchefstroom 'with pro-Boer tendencies' to travel in a truck in front of the locomotive until further orders.[168]
Day 747 Sun **1901-10-27**	Cape Colony	Emily Hobhouse arrives in Table Bay on board the SS *Avondale Castle*, but she is refused permission to go ashore by Colonel H Cooper, the Military Commandant of Cape Town.[169]
Day 748 Mon **1901-10-28**	Natal	Lord Milner receives an enthusiastic welcome in Durban. In an address he says: *"I wish I could have congratulated you on the fact that not only Natal but all South Africa was at rest. But I have come to the conclusion that it is no use waiting till the war is over. In a formal sense it may never be over, but may just slowly burn itself out, as it is doing now ... but it would be a great mistake to allow these circumstances to prevent our gradually resuming our normal life, and gradually restarting in the conquered territories not only industry, but even to some extent agriculture."*[70]
	Trivia	*In the United States, 34 die in race riots sparked by a black teacher dining at the White House.*
Day 749 Tue **1901-10-29**	ZAR	Lieutenant-Colonel GE Benson, moving from Middelburg towards the railway at Bethal with the result of his clearing operations — 50 prisoners and 'a great many non-combatants' — camps at Swakfontein, 20 kilometres west of Bethal. His force consists of about 1 000 mounted men and 650 infantrymen with four field-guns, two pom-poms, 350 vehicles, including 120 ox-wagons, a total of about 2 100 men.[171]
	Cape Colony	General Manie Maritz captures a 20-wagon convoy between Lambert's Bay and Clanwilliam.
	United Kingdom	Reverend John Knox Little states, *"Among the unexampled efforts of kindness and leniency made throughout this war for the benefit of the enemy, none have surpassed the formation of the Concentration Camps."*[172]
	Trivia	*President McKinley's killer Czolgosz is executed on the new Westinghouse electric chair.*
Day 750 Wed **1901-10-30**	Eastern ZAR	**BATTLE OF BAKENLAAGTE** (about 30 km north-west of Bethal) Lieutenant-Colonel Benson's column, starting at 04:30 , is harassed by small groups of burghers under Grobler and Opperman pressing his rearguard. The road across the undulating terrain is slippery after the recent rain and the column starts to straggle and the distance between the vanguard and the rearguard widens. At about 09:00 the passage of a drift causes more delays and the head of the column halts at Nooitgedacht Farm. Benson pushes out a strong rearguard and flanking detachments supported by two guns on a rise between his rear and the parked convoy. A cold driving rain begins to fall and the Republicans, exploiting the adverse conditions, increase their fire, forcing the rearguard to fall back in stages. At about noon, Commandant-General Louis Botha arrives with about 400 men. He confers with Grobler and Opperman and takes overall command of the Boer force — now numbering about 1 200 men. He sends small groups in wide arcs to attack the protecting screens on all sides and, at 14:15, he orders a charge by about 800 horsemen against the rearguard. The British retreat and a race towards the two guns on Gun Hill develops, with the charging burghers rapidly gaining. Most of the soldiers reach the hill, where Benson has positioned himself, but several infantry detachments are overwhelmed. Dropping a few men to round up their prisoners, the charge continues until the burghers reach the foot of the hill. They dismount and using anthills as cover, they press on up the hill.

		Several officers including Colonel Benson are wounded or killed, and with reinforcement made impossible by Botha's flanking groups, the situation on the hill becomes desperate. A brave quartermaster-sergeant reaches the back of their position and toss boxes of cartridges to the doomed troops. Benson is wounded again and after another fifteen minutes, the Republicans surge forward and take the hill. They swing the guns around and open fire on the laager. Botha orders a cease-fire and they do not follow up their success with an attack on the main camp at Nooitgedacht Farm for fear of injury to Boer women and children in the camp. British losses amount to at least 66 killed, 165 wounded (including the fatally wounded Benson) and 120 captured, while two guns are removed by the attackers. Republican losses amount to fewer than 100.[173]
Day 751 Thu **1901-10-31**	ZAR	The ZAR government is at Brakfontein, south-east of Bethal.
	Cape Colony	General Smuts fights a tough skirmish against Colonel CTM Kavanagh at Tygershoek, and crosses the main railway line at Constable Station between Matjiesfontein and Touws River. Despite letters of protest to Lord Alfred Milner, Sir Walter Hely-Hutchinson and Lord Ripon, Emily Hobhouse, although unwell, is forced to undergo a medical examination. She is eventually wrapped in a shawl and physically carried off the *Avondale Castle*. She is taken aboard the *Roslin Castle* for deportation under martial law regulations.[174]
	OFFICIAL REPORTS **Concentration camps:** **Black involvement:** **Blockhouse lines:**	**Black October** The officially recorded camp population of white camps is 113 506 and the deaths for October stand at 3 156. The population of black camps is 75 950 and 1 327 deaths are recorded for the month.[175] The following blockhouse lines have been completed: Cape Colony — Between Herschel and Basutoland border (50km). OFS — From Kroonstad via Lace-mine to Potchefstroom railway (110 km), and between Wolwehoek and Frankfort (70 km). ZAR — From Ventersdorp to the Frederikstad/Olifantsnek line (30 km), from Pretoria to Nylstroom (220 km) and between Wakkerstroom and the Swaziland border (90 km).[176]
1901	SPRING	**NOVEMBER**
Day 752 Fri **1901-11-01**	Cape Colony	Miss Emily Hobhouse, under deportation orders on board the *Roslin Castle*, writes to Lord Kitchener, *"Your brutality has triumphed over my weakness and sickness.* *You have forgotten so to be a patriot as not to forget that you are a gentleman.* *I hope that in future you will exercise greater width of judgement in the exercise of your high office. To carry out orders such as these is a degradation both to the office and the manhood of your soldiers. I feel ashamed to own you as a fellow-countryman."* And to Lord Milner, *"Your brutal orders have been carried out and thus I hope you will be satisfied.* *Your narrow incompetency to see the real issues of this great struggle is leading you to such acts as this and many others, straining your own name and the reputation of England.* *You have lost us the heart of a fine people; beware lest that is but the prelude to the loss of their country too."*[177] Colonel Kekewich captures Commandant Alberts' laager.
Day 753 Sat **1901-11-02**	South-eastern ZAR	Benson's battered laager at Bakenlaagte is relieved by the columns of Colonels Barter and Gilbert Hamilton arriving from Standerton.

	ZAR	In Johannesburg, a certain DG Wernick is executed by firing squad for high treason, breaking the oath of neutrality and inciting others to do the same.[178]
	OFS	President Steyn issues a proclamation lowering the Free State conscription age to 14 years.[179]
Day 754 Sun **1901-11-03**		
Day 755 Mon **1901-11-04**	ZAR	The ZAR government arrives at Roodepoort, west of Ermelo.
Day 756 Tue **1901-11-05**	ZAR	Lord Kitchener's exasperation is evident in a secret cable to Roberts: *"... the strong rumours current everywhere that I am to be relieved of my command... Perhaps a new commander might be able to do something more than I can do to hasten the end of the war."*[180]
Day 757 Wed **1901-11-06**	OFS	**KITCHENER'S DRIVE IN THE NORTH-EASTERN OFS** Lord Kitchener, hoping to clear the area inside the quadrangle formed by Winburg, Heilbron, Standerton and Harrismith, starts a concentric drive in the north-eastern Free State. He employs more than 15 000 men in 14 columns, starting at various towns and obeying a strict timetable. They march at a predetermined pace to flush the commandos out over this huge area. The aim is to surround them at Paardehoek, 40 kilometres south of Frankfort and 25 kilometres north of the town of Reitz.[181]
	ZAR	Lord Milner arrives back in Johannesburg.
Day 758 Thu **1901-11-07**	Natal Colony	The Governor of Natal informs St J Brodrick that Mrs (President) Steyn, Mrs (General Paul) Roux, Mrs (Chief Commandant CR) De Wet, Mrs (Vice-President Schalk) Burger and Mrs (General JBM) Hertzog, the last four all presently in Natal, are to be sent to a port, other than a British port, outside South Africa.[182]
	ZAR	Sir Ian Hamilton is appointed as Chief of Staff to Lord Kitchener. Lord Milner, referring to the concentration camps, writes to Chamberlain, *"I did not originate this plan, but as we have gone so far with it, I fear that a change now might only involve us in fresh and greater evils."*[183]
	Civilian life	The first sitting of the Rand Water Supply Commission takes place.
Day 759 Fri **1901-11-08**	Cape Colony	On General Maritz's orders, Commandant Jan Theron, a second cousin of Danie Theron and his successor as commander of Theron's Scouts, attacks Piketberg during the early morning. The town is defended by Major Pilson with 86 officers and men behind well-planned and well-constructed fortifications. The defenders lose three killed and about five wounded but repulse the attack inflicting three killed and seven wounded.[184]
Day 760 Sat **1901-11-09**	Cape Colony	The combined commandos of Commandant Van Deventer and Commandant Neser attack the 5th Lancers under Lieutenant-Colonel Callwell near Voëlfontein. The British lose 16 killed and 30 captured.[185]
Day 761 Sun **1901-11-10**		
Day 762 Mon **1901-11-11**	ZAR	General Du Toit's laager is captured at Doornhoek.
Day 763 Tue **1901-11-12**	OFS	The concentric drive ends at Paardehoek, an isolated group of hills about 40 kilometres south of Frankfort, without a single burgher in the trap. As the commandos simply avoid the marching columns who have to march in almost straight lines to keep to the timetable, the success of this effort is limited to 34 burghers killed and

		wounded and 86 captured. The loot, however, includes 10 000 head of cattle, 200 wagons and an unknown number of farms are burned and their crops destroyed.[186]
	ZAR	The ZAR government is at Tafelkop, near Ermelo.
	Cape Colony	Field-cornet Casparus Hildebrand, originally a member of Smuts' invasion force, is killed in action 16 kilometres east of Darling. His grave is accepted as the closest to Cape Town of all burghers killed in action during the war.[187] N van Wyk is executed by firing squad at Colesberg. At Tarkastad, PW van Heerden, with very poor eyesight, is executed by firing squad for treason and attempted murder.
Day 764 Wed **1901-11-13**	OFS	Chief Commandant De Wet meets President Steyn at Blydschap, near Reitz. Since the capture of the Free State Executive Council at Reitz in July, the President with his bodyguard, commanded by Van Niekerk from Ficksburg, has been wandering about in the north-eastern Free State, rarely sleeping in a house or at the same place on two successive nights and regularly in the saddle at about 02:00.[188]
Day 765 Thu **1901-11-14**	Cape Colony	General Smuts is in action against the Prince of Wales' Light Horse at Vaalfontein.[189] The captured Gideon Scheepers, still seriously ill, is put on a train to be transferred to Graaff-Reinet. At Noupoort, his situation deteriorates and he is taken to the local military hospital.[190]
	ZAR	The ZAR government moves to Kranspan, south of Lake Chrissie.
Day 766 Fri **1901-11-15**	ZAR	In his 'General Review of the Situation in the Two New Colonies', Lord Milner reports to Chamberlain, *"Terrible as have been the ravages of war and destruction of agricultural capital which is now pretty well complete, the great fact remains that the Transvaal possesses an amount of mineral wealth virtually unaffected by the war which will ensure the prosperity of South Africa for the next fifty years... and humanly speaking for ever."*[191]
	Concentration camps	On the concentration camps, he comments, *"... even if the war were to come to an end tomorrow, it would not be possible to let the people in the concentration camps go back to their former homes. They would only starve there. The country is, for the most part, a desert..."*[192]
	Cape Colony	General Smuts again clashes with the Prince of Wales' Light Horse, this time at Brandkraal.[193]
Day 767 Sat **1901-11-16**	ZAR	General Bruce Hamilton commences operations in the eastern Transvaal.
	Concentration camps	On being questioned by Brodrick on his motivations for proposing the deportation of prominent Boer women, Kitchener cancels his orders. He complains, *"in view of immense burden imposed on country by war, sentimental considerations ought not be allowed to interfere with measures which seem necessary to use on the spot to check machinations of enemy and hasten the end. It is difficult for us to make use of discretion if steps taken under it are liable to be thus checked. Result is to give impression of weakness, which cannot but produce bad effect."*[194]
	Trivia	*In New York, the French driver Henri Fournier sets a new automobile speed record by covering one mile in 52 seconds — 69,2 miles per hour or 110,8 kph.*
Day 768 Sun **1901-11-17**		
Day 769 Mon **1901-11-18**	Cape Colony	Since his unsuccessful attack on Piketberg ten days before, Commandant Jan Theron has been pursued by the columns of Crabbe, Capper, Kavanagh and Wormald. He crosses the Great Berg River near Bridgetown and escapes.[195]

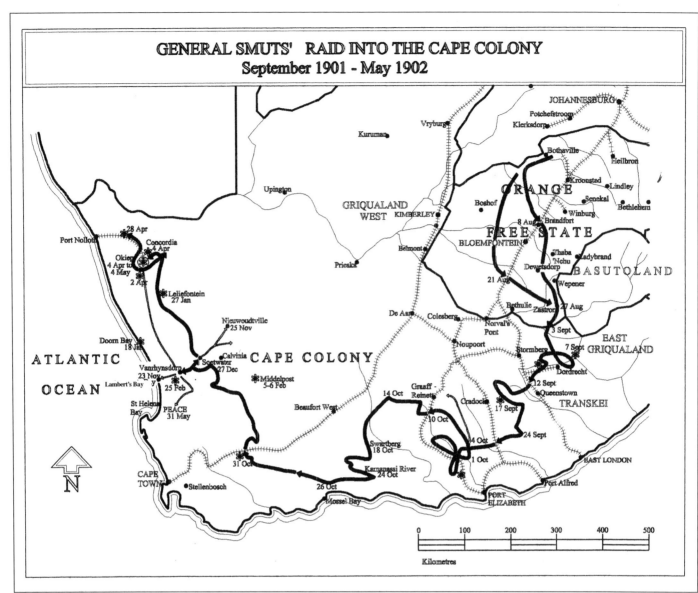

		Colonel Harry Scobell captures Stoffel Myburgh's commando at Koningskroon, near Jamestown. That night, one of the rebels, Piet Bester, an ex-Cape policeman, is sentenced to death by a summary court martial at Dordrecht. As regulations demand that rebels must be executed in public, he is taken to a farmhouse, where Johanna Coetzer, a midwife and herbalist, has been caring for a few pregnant women. She is furious when she realises that they want the women to witness this despicable act. The officers relent, and take Bester to a nearby gorge. He refuses to be blindfolded and faces the firing squad. The soldiers cannot shoot and the prisoner is tied to a chair, turned round and shot in the back.[196]
Day 770 Tue **1901-11-19**		
Day 771 Wed **1901-11-20**	Cape Colony	After successfully attacking a British post guarded by 50 men near Villiers, Commandant Buys is captured by Colonel Rimington near the Vaal River.[197]
Day 772 Thu **1901-11-21**	ZAR Concentration camps	Referring to a 'scorched earth' raid, Acting State-President SW Burger and State Secretary FW Reitz address a protest to the Marquis of Salisbury, the British Prime Minister: *"This removal took place in the most uncivilized and barbarous manner, while such action is... in conflict with all the up to the present acknowledged rules of civilised warfare. The fam-*

		ilies were put out of their houses under compulsion, and in many instances by means of force... (the houses) were destroyed and burnt with everything in them... and these families among them were many aged ones, pregnant women, and children of very tender years, were removed in open trolleys (exposed) for weeks to rain, severe cold wind and terrible heat, privations to which they were not accustomed, with the result that many of them became very ill, and some of them died shortly after their arrival in the women's camps." The vehicles were also overloaded, accidents happened and they were exposed to being caught in crossfire in case of military action. *"The persons removed were in many instances exposed to insults and ill-treatment by (Blacks) in the service of your troops as well as by soldiers... British mounted troops have not hesitated in driving them for miles before their horses, old women, little children, and mothers with sucklings to their breasts..."*[198]
Day 773 Fri 1901-11-22	Cape Colony	Commandant Naude crosses the Orange River at Sand Drift to join Smuts in the western Cape Colony.
	Concentration camps	At the Boschhoek concentration camp for Blacks, about 1 700 inmates, mostly Basuto, hold a protest meeting. They state that when they have been brought into the camps they have been promised that they will be paid for all their stock taken by the British, for all their grain destroyed and that they will be fed and looked after.
	Black involvement	They are also unhappy because *"... they receive no rations while the Boers who are the cause of the war are fed in the refugee camps free of charge... they who are the 'Children of the Government' are made to pay".*[199]
Day 774 Sat 1901-11-23	Concentration camps Black involvement	Two inmates of the Heuningspruit concentration camp for blacks, Daniel Marome and GJ Oliphant, complain to Goold-Adams, *"We have to work hard all day long but the only food we can get is mealies and mealie meal, and this is not supplied to us free, but we have to purchase same with our own money.* *"Meat we are still not able to get at any price, nor are we allowed to buy anything at the shops at Honingspruit...* *"We humbly request Your Honour to do something for us otherwise we will all perish of hunger for we have no money to keep on buying food."* Oliphant is described by the resident magistrate at Kroonstad, *"He is one of those highly educated Natives who evidently does not use his advantages in the right direction, but is a source of trouble and annoyance to all who have dealings with him."*[200]
	Eastern ZAR	The ZAR government is at Smithfield, near Lake Chrissie.
	Cape Colony	General Smuts and Commandant Bouwer arrive at Vanrhynsdorp. WH Louw is executed by firing squad at Colesberg.
	Victoria Cross	Lieutenant LC Maygar, 5th Victoria Mounted Rifles, Geelhoutboom.
Day 775 Sun 1901-11-24		
Day 776 Mon 1901-11-25	ZAR	Daniel van Schalkwyk is found guilty and sentenced to death by a military court at Krugersdorp. He has been charged with picking up his rifle after having surrendered, and shooting a trooper of the SA Constabulary near Hartebeesthoek on 15 November.[201]
	Cape Colony	General Smuts arrives at Nieuwoudtville.
	International	The offer of a further Canadian contingent is accepted by the War Office.
Day 777 Tue 1901-11-26	Eastern ZAR	Commandant D Joubert is captured. The ZAR government arrives at Twyfelaar, east of Carolina, and remains here for almost a month.

Day 778 Wed **1901-11-27**		A committee is appointed to inquire into the working of the gold law.
Day 779 Thu **1901-11-28**	OFS	President Steyn and Chief Commandant De Wet concentrate several commandos for a council of war at Blydschap, between Lindley and Reitz. Colonel MF Rimington, chasing a women's laager, receives incorrect information about De Wet's whereabouts from a traitor. He and Colonel Wilson, march to Spytfontein, nine kilometres from Blydschap, with a force of 2 100 men and nine field-guns.[202]
	Cape Colony Black involvement	The combined commandos of Malan, Maritz, Lategan and Van Deventer surround a remount depot at Tonteldooskolk (85 kilometres north-east of Calvinia) guarded by 87 men of the Western Province Mounted Rifles and about 175 Coloureds of the Bushmanland Borderers. The attack is bravely repulsed, the WPMR losing two killed, three wounded and three captured. Although the commandos capture 300 horses, the main object of the attack, they cannot take the depot and the action degenerates into a 'siege'.[203]
Day 780 Fri **1901-11-29**	OFS	**THE ACTION AT SPYTFONTEIN** Colonel Rimington, unable to locate De Wet, resumes his pursuit of the women's laager. His rearguard is suddenly attacked by 500 men under the command of General Michael Prinsloo, assisted by Hattingh and Commandant Manie Botha. Rimington takes defensive action and digs in at Victorie Spruit. Realising that De Wet will make a concentrated attack the next morning, and remembering Benson's defeat at Bakenlaagte, Rimington abandons his position during the night and falls back to Heilbron, 25 kilometres away, leaving his supplies behind.[204]
Day 781 Sat **1901-11-30**	*Trivia*	*The first hearing aid, designed by Miller Reese Hutchinson, is introduced in America. Winston LS Churchill's 27th birthday.*

OFFICIAL REPORTS

Gold-mining: On the Witwatersrand 600 of the 6 000 gold stamps are back in production and the monthly gold production is 32 000 ounces or about 10,7% of prewar production.[205]

Farm burning: British columns have completely or partially destroyed 436 farms.

Concentration camps: The officially recorded camp population of the white camps is 117 974 and the deaths for November are 2 807.

Black involvement: The population of the black camps is 85 114 and 2 312 deaths are recorded for the month.[206]

Blockhouse lines: The following blockhouse lines have been completed:
Cape Colony — between Stormberg and Queenstown (150 km).
Natal — between Dundee and Vryheid (50 km).[207]

1901	SUMMER	**DECEMBER**
Day 782 Sun **1901-12-01**	Concentration camps	Fully aware of the state of devastation in the Republics, Lord Milner approves a letter that Kitchener sends to London, with identical copies to Burger, Steyn and De Wet. In the letter he informs them that as they have complained about the treatment of the women and children in the camps, he must assume that they themselves are in a position to provide for them. He therefore offers to allow all families in the camps who are willing to leave, to be sent out to the commandos, as soon as he has been informed where they can be handed over.[208]
	Cape Colony	Changes to the administration of martial law in Cape Colony are announced.

Day 783 Mon **1901-12-02**	*Trivia*	*The US Supreme Court rules that Puerto Ricans are not US citizens.*
Day 784 Tue **1901-12-03**	South-eastern ZAR	The ZAR government, covered by a bodyguard of 200 men commanded by Commandant Joubert, breaks through the fortified line close to Dalmanutha Station. Despite heavy fire from two blockhouses they escape, suffering only two burghers wounded and losing ten horses. [209] *FG Gatacre's 58th birthday.*
Day 785 Wed **1901-12-04**	Eastern ZAR	General Bruce Hamilton, using a Boer traitor named Lange, and employing the tactics devised by Benson and Woolls-Sampson, surprises Commandant-General Botha's laager at Oshoek on the Swaziland border, near Ermelo. About 100 burghers and some supplies are captured.[210]
	Concentration camps	Lord Milner comments on the high death rate in the Free State concentration camps: *"The theory that, all the weakly children being dead, the rate would fall off, it is not so far borne out by the facts. I take it the strong ones must be dying now and that they will all be dead by the spring of 1903!* *"Only I shall not be there to see as the continuance of the present state of affairs for another two or three months will undoubtedly blow us all out of the water.* *"I say this quite calmly and 'objectively'. It is impossible not to see that, however blameless we may be in the matter, we shall not be able to make anybody think so. And I cannot avoid an uncomfortable feeling that there must be some way to make the thing a little less awfully bad if one could only think of it."*[211]
Day 786 Thu **1901-12-05**	Cape Colony	General Malan ends the 'siege' of Tonteldooskolk and moves off. Soon afterwards the British abandon the post. It is later used by General Maritz as a temporary headquarters.[212]
Day 787 Fri **1901-12-06**	South-eastern ZAR	Commandant-General Botha, having rallied his burghers, doubles back and surprises the pursuing force of Brigadier-General Plumer at Kalkoenskraal. Botha breaks through and gets away before Plumer can launch a counter-strike.[213]
Day 788 Sat **1901-12-07**	ZAR Concentration camps	In a letter to Mr Chamberlain, Lord Milner writes, *"... The black spot — the one very black spot — in the picture is the frightful mortality in the Concentration Camps... while a hundred explanations may be offered and a hundred excuses made, they do not really amount to an adequate defence... It was not until 6 weeks or 2 months ago that it dawned on me personally (I cannot speak for others), that the enormous mortality was not incidental to the first formation of the camps and the sudden inrush of thousands of people already starving, but was going to continue. The fact that it continues is no doubt a condemnation of the camp system. The whole thing, I think now, has been a mistake."*[214]
	ESTABLISHMENT OF THE NATIONAL SCOUTS CORPS The corps of National Scouts is inaugurated (see Lord Kitchener's message to Brodrick on 21 June). This unit consists of burghers who surrendered and are willing to take up arms on the British side. Various local burgher corps, including Morley's Scouts, the Kroonstad Burgher Scouts, Beddy's Scouts, the Lydenburg Volunteer Burgher Scouts, the Lebombo Scouts, the Cattle Ranger Corps, the Vereeniging Burgher Corps and others are amalgamated into a single force.[215] Ex-Generals Piet de Wet and Andries Cronje assume leadership roles, convinced that they are fulfilling their duty and saving their country by attempting to accelerate the end of the war.	
Day 789 Sun **1901-12-08**	OFS	A combined operation with Generals Elliot, Broadwood and Colonel Byng, moving from Kroonstad, and Colonels Rimington, Damant and Wilson from Heilbron and Frankfort, start an elaborate drive, making sudden changes of direction in an attempt to corner De Wet between Kroonstad and Wolwehoek Station.

	ZAR Concentration camps	Chief Commandant De Wet clashes with General Broadwood at Quaggafontein, near Lindley, and avoids the net.[216] Commenting on the concentration camps, Lord Milner writes to Lord Haldane, *"I am sorry to say I fear... that the whole thing has been a sad fiasco. We attempted an impossibility — and certainly I should never have touched the thing if, when the 'concentration' first began, I could have foreseen that the soldiers meant to sweep the whole population of the country higgledy piggledy into a couple of dozen camps...* *"Things will improve, but it will always remain a bad business, the one thing, as far as I am concerned, in which I feel that the abuse so freely heaped upon us for everything, we have done and not done is not without some foundation."*[217]
Day 790 Mon **1901-12-09**	Cape Colony	The captured Commandant Gideon Scheepers arrives at Graaff-Reinet, where he is held in the civilian jail.[218]
Day 791 Tue **1901-12-10**	Western ZAR Black involvement	General Kemp launches a punitive expedition against Chief Linchwe and his armed Tswana tribesmen who have attacked a women's laager at Holfontein where two burghers have been killed and four other persons, including a young girl, wounded. Linchwe also 'annexed' a part of the ZAR, declaring the Elands River his border with the 'Transvaal'. Kemp returns with 7 000 cattle and 8 000 sheep and goats which are distributed amongst black tribal chiefs who are on friendly terms with the ZAR.[219]
	Eastern ZAR	General Bruce Hamilton, commanding a 2 000-man force under Colonels Rawlinson and Ingouville-Williams, swoops on General Piet Viljoen's Bethal commando at Trigaardtsfontein. The burghers lose 131 men and a quantity of supplies.[220]
	OFS Concentration camps	President Steyn replies to Lord Kitchener's letter about releasing the women and children: *"Now as if the martyrdom of the women and children were not sufficient, Your Excellency makes a proposal which you know, if accepted by us, would result in making the lives of those poor innocent victims intolerable. For Your Excellency knows and His Majesty's Government knows, or ought to know, that there is hardly a single house in the Orange Free State that is not burnt or destroyed, that all the furniture and especially the bedding and clothing of the women and children have been burnt or have been looted by His Majesty's troops. If then we should take back our women they would be exposed to the weather under the open sky... However gladly (sic) therefore every father and husband would be to have his relatives near him, we must on account of the above-mentioned reasons emphatically refuse to receive them... I am convinced that it will again be proclaimed to the whole world that the Boers refuse to take back their women, and therefore I expect that Your Excellency as an honourable man will publish the reasons for our refusal..."*[221]
	Trivia	*The first Nobel prizes are awarded in Oslo.* *Mr G Marconi makes the first transatlantic radio transmission from Cornwall to Newfoundland.*
Day 792 Wed **1901-12-11**	Concentration camps	In his reply to the British Commander-in-Chief's letter, Chief Commandant De Wet says, *"I positively refuse to receive the families until such time as the war will be ended, and we shall be able to vindicate our right by presenting our claims for the unlawful removal of and the insults done to our families as well as indemnification on account of the uncivilized deed committed by England by the removal of the families..."*[222]
	Cape Colony	General HH Settle succeeds General Wynne as Commanding Officer of the Cape Colony.

Day 793 Thu **1901-12-12**	ZAR	General Bruce Hamilton, using the same troops he used on 10 December, overruns General Piet Viljoen's laager at Witkrans, this time killing 16 burghers, capturing 70 and retaking one of the field-guns lost at Bakenlaagte.[223]
	Natal Black involvement	Lord Milner writes to the Dean of Pietermaritzburg, "*One thing which appears to me quite evident is, that a distinction must be drawn in the case of the Natives between personal and political rights. A political equality of white and black is impossible, though I do think that in any South African Parliament the interests of the blacks should be specially represented. Perhaps this could be best done by white men, not elected but nominated for that particular purpose. The Imperial Government might reserve a right of such nomination at any rate at first. As regards personal rights, I hold that those of the Natives should be just as clearly defined, and just as sacred as those of the white men. I do not, however, think that they need always be, ought always to be the same.*"[224]
	United Kingdom Concentration camps	**THE FAWCETT REPORT** The report of the Ladies (or Fawcett) Commission is completed on this day, but is only published during February 1902. The commission is highly critical of the camps and their administration, but cannot recommend the immediate closure of the camps "*... to turn 100 000 people now being fed in the concentration camps out on the veldt to take care of themselves would be a cruelty; it would be turning them out to starvation. Even if peace were declared tomorrow, Great Britain must continue to supply the camp people with the necessaries of life for some months to come. If they were scattered over the country, what is now sufficiently difficult would become impossible...*"[225]
Day 794 Fri **1901-12-13**	OFS	When Lieutenant-General Elliot and General Broadwood's drive ends on the railway line between Kroonstad and Wolwehoek, there is not a single burgher in the net.[226]
	Western ZAR	Lord Methuen captures one of Commandant Potgieter's laagers in the Makwassie hills.
Day 795 Sat **1901-12-14**	International	New Zealand offers 1 000 additional men for service in South Africa.
Day 796 Sun **1901-12-15**	OFS	Colonel Colenbrander captures Commandant Badenhorst. Commandant PH Kritzinger crosses the Orange River at Sand Drift and enters the Cape Colony for the third time.
	Trivia	*Free State field-chaplain JD Kestell's 47th birthday.*
Day 797 Mon **1901-12-16**	OFS	President Steyn, Chief Commandant De Wet and the north-eastern Free State commandos celebrate the Day of the Covenant at Kaffir Kop, near Lindley.[227] Commandant Sarel Haasbroek is killed in action during an attack on a convoy commanded by Major Marshall near Senekal.[228] Brigadier-General Edward Hamilton, responsible for the construction of the fortified line between Frankfort and Tafelkop, reports that his small covering force is repeatedly clashing with enemy parties and that, unless reinforced, he will be unable to continue. [229]
	Western ZAR	Lord Methuen captures another of Commandant Potgieter's laagers in the Makwassie hills, bringing his tally to 36 burghers and more than 100 vehicles captured.[230]
	Cape Colony	**COMMANDANT KRITZINGER IS CAPTURED** Constantly pursued by the 5th Lancers and other units for a hundred and twenty kilometres in the Great Karoo during the hot season, Commandant PH Kritzinger, losing ponies all the way, flings his commando across the De Aar/Noupoort block-

283

		house line. They cross near Hanover Road Station, charging between two forts about 800 metres apart, in bright daylight. Unbelievably all the mounted burghers cross without casualties and they are well across before Lieutenant Bolding is wounded. Kritzinger, who was with the lead group who cut the wire, waits until all his men are clear when he sees one of his men trying to cross on foot. With bravery *"worthy of a VC"*, Kritzinger immediately charges back through the crossfire and is seriously wounded. His adjutants take him to the nearest station and summon a British ambulance.[231] At Graaff-Reinet Commandant Gideon Scheepers is informed of the charges against him. Despite being a ZAR burgher and thus technically a prisoner of war, he is charged under martial law and is to be tried by a court martial. He is charged with 30 counts of murder, seven of arson, mistreatment of prisoners and the 'barbaric' treatment of blacks.[232]
	United Kingdom	Lord Rosebery, speaking at Chesterfield, urges the government to show *"a more accommodating tempe"*. He gives his reasons why the war must be brought to an end: *"(1) ... it is an open sore through which is oozing much of our strength. (2) ... it weakens our international position and reduces to a standpoint in international politics very different from what we are accustomed to occupy. (3) ... it stops all domestic reforms, and (4) ... it adjourns and embitters the ultimate settlement of South Africa".*[233]
	Trivia	*Dingaan's Day (Day of the Covenant).*
Day 798 Tue **1901-12-17**	OFS	Kitchener orders Rimington and Damant to reinforce Brigadier-General Edward Hamilton's fort-building party near Tafelkop.
	ZAR	The Johannesburg Stock Exchange reopens.
Day 799 Wed **1901-12-18**	OFS	**THE ACTION AT TYGERKLOOF** Chief Commandant De Wet, immediately returning to the area just 'swept', is determined to attack one of the returning columns. At Tygerkloof Spruit, not far from Harrismith, he divides his force of about 550 men into two sections to ambush a British force that he estimates at between 600 and 700 strong. The force under General Dartnell, assisted by Colonels Briggs and McKenzie, is, however, about 1 200 strong with two field-guns and two pom-poms. Dartnell, furthermore, has been forewarned by a Boer traitor. When the signal to attack is given by De Wet's pom-pom, only half of his burghers obey and the attack fails. A Republican attack from the rear is also repulsed and the burghers disengage. De Wet loses two killed and nine wounded while inflicting 18 casualties. General Dartnell is reinforced by Colonel Campbell with 400 men and three guns from Bethlehem, but declines to counterattack.[234]
	Victoria Cross	The Victoria Cross is awarded to Surgeon-Captain TJ Crean of the Imperial Light Horse for gallantry in attending the wounded.
	Eastern ZAR	Lord Kitchener orders Colonel Urmston from Belfast and Colonel Park from Lydenburg to launch an attempt to capture the ZAR government, now under the protection of General Muller's commando.[235] The ZAR government arrives at Windhoek, west of Dullstroom, after crossing the eastern railway line east of Belfast.[236]
	Cape Colony	Commandant Gideon Scheepers' trial begins at Graaff-Reinet. [237]
	United Kingdom	At a meeting in Birmingham's town hall, David Lloyd George is prevented from speaking by a huge mob spurred on by four brass bands playing patriotic music. Opportunist vendors are selling half-bricks at *"three a penny, to throw at Lloyd George"*, and he has to escape disguised as a policeman. The mob breaks more than 1 200 win-

	Gold mining International	dows and pushes into the hall. The police, reinforced by members from neighbouring towns, read the Riot Act before launching a baton charge in which one man is killed and 40 have to be hospitalised. [238] An agreement is concluded with the Portuguese authorities for the recruiting of black mine workers in their territory.
Day 800 Thu **1901-12-19**	Black involvement	General Smuts announces changes to the policy regarding armed blacks, with specific instructions that all prisoners of war must receive correct treatment and that trials can only be held by officers with the rank of field-cornet or higher. Death sentences will apply only in cases of 'secret' or covert spying within commandos' areas of operation.[239]
	South-eastern ZAR	Commandant Coen Brits ambushes Major Bridgeford with his battalion of 214 men of the 14th Mounted Infantry at Holland, 28 kilometres south of Ermelo. Only 63 soldiers escape, while 117 are captured and 33 officers and men are killed and wounded.[240]
	Eastern ZAR	General Chris Muller and Colonel SPE Trichard ambush Colonel CW Park at Elandspruit, near Dullstroom, allowing the ZAR government to escape. The British suffer 37 casualties, while the Republicans lose five killed and about 20 wounded.[241]
	International	*De Strever,* a camp paper and mouthpiece of a Christian organisation, appears in the Boer prisoner of war camp on St Helena.
Day 801 Fri **1901-12-20**	OFS *Gen. Wessel J Wessels* *(National Cultural History Museum)* **Victoria Cross** ZAR Black involvement	**THE ACTION AT TAFELKOP** Colonels Rimington and Damant are sent to assist General Edward Hamilton, who is being harassed by General Wessel Wessels and Commandants Ross and De Kock with 300 burghers while constructing blockhouse forts between Frankfort and Vrede. Damant's force of 500 men on Tafelkop is completely fooled by Wessels, who assumes a typical British cavalry formation with his burghers. When the British realise their mistake, the Republicans disappear into a small ravine, dismount and attack the hill on foot. A bloody fight ensues, the gunners are wiped out and two field-guns and pom-poms are taken but cannot be removed as the gun teams have been shot. When Rimington and other reinforcements arrive, the Republicans disengage and escape with 20 casualties. The British loss amounts to 33 killed and 45 wounded.[242] The Victoria Cross is awarded to Shoeing-smith AE Ind, Royal Horse Artillery. Major GJ de Lotbiniere, Commissioner for Native Affairs, writes to Major General Maxwell, "*In fact in many cases, well to do natives are now absolutely destitute through no fault of their own. Nor can they understand why the British should rob them of everything*".[243] Lord Milner writes to Mr Chamberlain about the pro-Boers in England, "*It is quite ludicrous the way all their interest seems to centre in the enemy — never for a moment do they consider our friends, or even those Boers who have come over to us. It is only the desperadoes still in the field, whose cause they espouse, and the fewer these latter become, the more wildly anxious are their British sympathisers to give away everybody else for their sakes. Just now, I see, the pro Boers are all screaming for 'terms of peace'. The one thing they seem to care about is that the enemy should not be simply conquered, but should be able hereafter to say that they have not been, and should manage somehow to worry us into concessions fraught with future embarrassment...* "*There are only two things which can placate the extreme Boers, one is the restoration*

		of their absolute independence, the other the enslavement of the native. The one thing which might possibly reconcile them to British rule, would be a native policy, the direct opposite to any we could adopt. As for the moderate section, it is not by any promises we make now, but what we actually do hereafter, that we can win or alienate them." [244]
Day 802 Sat **1901-12-21**	OFS	One of Rundle's columns, about 500 men with a single field-gun and a pom-pom, under Major FA Williams, has been detailed to cover the construction of the block-house line near Tradouw and Mooimeisiesfontein, about 30 kilometres east of Bethlehem. They clash with a small party of burghers and Williams encamps on Groenkop, an isolated hill dominating the landscape. [245]
	Cape Colony	A bystander who greets Commandant Gideon Scheepers on his way to the court-house, is fined with £5 or 14 days' imprisonment. [246]
Day 803 Sun **1901-12-22**	OFS	Chief Commandant De Wet and his staff reconnoitre the construction of the block-house line east of Bethlehem. Two of his officers spot some horses and capture them, shooting the black horse guard. This draws the attention of the gunners on the sum-mit of Groenkop who immediately let off a few rounds on the party rounding up the horses, thereby betraying their position on the hill. [247]
	Western ZAR	General Celliers attacks a yeomanry unit near Lichtenburg, inflicting 33 casualties killed and wounded and capturing 40. About a hundred horses and a supply of ammunition are also taken. [248]
	United Kingdom	On Peace Sunday, Dr Charles Aked, a Baptist minister in Liverpool protests: *"Great Britain cannot win the battles without resorting to the last despicable cowardice of the most loathsome cur on earth — the act of striking a brave man's heart through his wife's hon-our and his child's life. The cowardly war has been conducted by methods of barbarism... the concentration camps have been Murder Camps.* [249] *"We shall lose South Africa. We have created a race hatred. In the heat of which every link with the old Cape Colony will melt... The ancestors of these men broke the power of Spain; their children may yet break us. And I tremble for my fatherland when I think of the fact that God is just."* [250] Dr Aked is followed home by a large crowd and they smash the windows of his house.
	International	A Republican prisoner of war, A Smorenburg, attempts to escape from St Helena by having himself nailed shut in a crate and loaded onto the mail ship *Goth*. He is dis-covered on the high sea and is later sent back via Gibraltar. [251]
Day 804 Mon **1901-12-23**	Eastern ZAR	General Chris Botha, with about 400 burghers, fights a running battle with Brigadier-Generals Pulteney and Plumer among the northern foothill of the Randberg and the burghers escape with little loss. [252]
	Cape Colony	Between Clanwilliam and Calvinia Lieutenant-Colonels Crabbe and Wyndham suc-ceed in repulsing an attack that turns into a running battle lasting for two days. The convoy they are escorting is untouched, mainly through the fine efforts of the 16th Lancers, who lose two killed and 13 wounded. [253]
	OFS	The Kroonstad/Lindley blockhouse line (75 kilometres) is completed.
Day 805 Tue **1901-12-24**	OFS	General Rundle, with a small escort, encamps at Mooimeisiesfontein, about five kilometres from Groenkop. In bright moonlight Chief Commandant De Wet, with about 1 000 men, approach-es Groenkop from the north-west. [254]

	North-eastern Cape	Drunken British soldiers desecrate and destroy the 'Taalmonument' in Burgersdorp, erected to commemorate legislation passed in 1882 giving equal status to Dutch and English in the Cape Colony.[255]
Day 806 Wed **1901-12-25**	OFS	CHRISTMAS — the third Christmas of the war **THE BATTLE OF GROENKOP, TWEEFONTEIN OR KRISMISKOP** De Wet leaves his horses and pom-pom with about 100 men at the foot of the hill and silently, on stockinged feet, they start to climb the hill. At 02:00, after a brief rest just below the summit, Chief Commandant De Wet shouts, *"Burghers! Storm!"*, and they swarm over the crest, overwhelming the sleeping pickets. They take the higher positions and unleash murderous fire on the tented camp. The surprise is complete. Several soldiers are hit in their tents. The horses stampede and about a third of the British soldiers flee down the hill in their night-clothes. Some officers vainly try to establish some resistance, but within a few minutes it is all over. The burghers, barefoot and dressed in rags, loot with enthusiasm — thoroughly enjoying their Christmas fare. At least 57 British soldiers are killed (the bodies of 25 blacks are later found on the battlefield), 84 are wounded and about 200 soldiers (including the wounded) fall into De Wet's hands. On the Republican side 14 men die and 30 are wounded. Two soldiers of a patrol sent from Rundle's camp to investigate, are also captured and Rundle's contribution to the battle is a few shells falling among the wagons as they are removed by the victors. Contrary to their custom, De Wet takes the unwounded prisoners with him to put them across the Basutoland border a few days later.[256]
Day 807 Thu **1901-12-26**	OFS	BOXING DAY De Wet's force vanishes. Lieutenant-General Elliot's column leaves Lindley and marches towards Reitz, but the British have lost contact completely and no pursuit is attempted.
	Trivia	*The Uganda railway between Mombasa and Lake Victoria is completed.*
Day 808 Fri **1901-12-27**	Eastern ZAR	Commandant Coenraad Brits is surrounded by two columns commanded by Colonel Spens.
	Cape Colony	**GENERAL SMUTS REORGANISES HIS FORCE** On General Smuts' instructions about 16 commandos and roving bands, consisting of a total of about 3 000 men, mostly rebels, meet at Soetwater, between Calvinia and Nieuwoudtville. To spread operations over a wider area, the commandos are divided into three groups, each commanded by a combat general with Smuts in overall command. General JL van Deventer will command the southern districts, General SG Maritz the copper-mining districts of Namaqualand and General WC Malan will take command of the Midland districts.[257]
	International	The Anglo-German alliance negotiations break down, principally because of Chamberlain's Edinburgh speech in October.
	Trivia	*Film and singing star Marlene Dietrich is born as Magdalena von Losch.*
Day 809 Sat **1901-12-28**	ZAR	The Royal Horse Artillery and the Royal Field Artillery in South Africa are organized into a mounted infantry corps. In a letter to Lord Roberts, a disheartened Lord Kitchener writes: *"As long as De Wet is out I can see no end to the war. If we can only manage to catch him, I believe all others are heartily sick of it."*[258]
	Eastern ZAR	Commandant Coenraad Brits wriggles out of the cordon thrown around him by

	OFS *Gen. Michael Prinsloo* *(National Cultural History Museum)* Cape Colony Black involvement	Colonel Spens, losing 31 men who are taken prisoner. Brits splits his force in two, one crossing the Natal railway at Platrand and the other moving off to join Botha on the upper Vaal River.[259] With De Wet away to report to President Steyn, his commando, now commanded by General Michael Prinsloo, is spotted by Elliot's scouts as they cross the Liebenbergsvlei. Elliot, with about 2 000 men at his disposal, orders an immediate pursuit, but Prinsloo, with the field-guns taken at Groenkop, takes up strong positions on the high ground dominating Armstrong's Drift. Elliot's pursuit is stopped and Prinsloo slips away after dark.[260] Ex-Field-cornet A Reyneke and L Brink are executed in Mafeking by hanging. Five burghers, captured in June, have been sentenced to death for wiping out a small black settlement from where they have been fired on while passing by. Three of the burghers are later reprieved, and their sentences are reduced to life sentences by the governor of the Cape Colony.[261]
Day 810 Sun **1901-12-29**	ZAR	General Bruce Hamilton captures General Erasmus near Ermelo.
Day 811 Mon **1901-12-30**	ZAR	In army orders published on this date, the name of the unit known as the Bushveld Carbineers, is changed to the 'Pietersburg Light Horse' — thus transferring a very black military record to a unit with a South African name. The order is backdated to 1 December 1901.[262]
Day 812 Tue **1901-12-31**	OFS	General Michael Prinsloo is involved in a skirmish with the Scots Greys at Bronkhorstspruit Farm. The British lose five killed and 13 wounded.[263]
	OFFICIAL REPORTS **Gold mining:** **Blockhouse lines:** **Farm burning:** **Concentration camps:** **Black involvement:**	**OFFICIAL REPORTS** On the Witwatersrand 953 or 15,9% of the gold stamps are back in production and the monthly gold production is 53 000 ounces or about 17,7% of pre-war production.[264] The following blockhouse lines have been completed: Cape Colony — from Beaufort West via Victoria Road to De Aar (230 km) and between Stormberg and Dordrecht (60 km). OFS — between Allisonskop (Natal) and Harrismith (100 km) and between Frankfort and Tafelkop (40 km with 47 blockhouses). ZAR — between Klerksdorp and Ventersdorp (150 km), Nylstroom and Pietersburg (190 km) and between Standerton and Ermelo (90 km with 131 blockhouses).[265] British columns have completely or partially destroyed 23 farms and one black village (kraal).[266] The officially recorded camp population of the white camps is 117 017 and the deaths for December stand at 2 380. The population of the black camps is 89 407 while the deaths peak at 2 831 during December.[267] The monthly reports show that 149 men have disappeared from camps in the Transvaal and 136 from Free State camps. (The following month, 117 more abscond.) The Native Refugee Department speculates that many of the deserters have joined Boer commandos.[268]

NOTES:

JULY 1901 - DECEMBER 1901 (ATTRITION)

1. PLOEGER, *op cit*, p 33:20
2. WESSELS, Egodokumente...., p. 156
3. AMERY, *op cit*, vol V, p 300
4. DAVITT, *op cit*, p 510
5. PLOEGER, *op cit*, p 33:20
6. HATTINGH, Britse Fortifikasies..., p 136
7. GRONUM, *op cit*, (2) p 15
8. AMERY, *op cit*, vol V, p. 300
9. VAN SCHOOR, De Wet-annale, No 3, p 24
10. PEDDLE, Long Cecil..., p 13
11. VAN SCHOOR, De Wet-annale, No 3, p 24
12. AMERY, *op cit*, vol V, p 301;
    VAN SCHOOR, Bittereinder..., pp 183-186;
    VAN SCHOOR, De Wet-annale, No 3, pp 24-26
13. DAVITT, *op cit*, p 510
14. MEINTJES, Anglo-Boereoorlog in Beeld, p174
15. OOSTHUIZEN, Rebelle van die Stormberge, p 181
16. AMERY, *op cit*, vol V, p 302
17. WARWICK, South African War..., p 196
18. GRONUM, *op cit*, (2) p 16
19. AMERY, *op cit*, vol V, pp 301-302
20. FARWELL, *op cit*, p 411; VAN REENEN, Emily Hobhouse..., p 461
21. DOONER, 'Last Post', p 203
22. HATTINGH, Britse Fortifikasies..., p 136
23. AMERY, *op cit*, vol V, p 314
24. HEADLAM, *op cit*, vol II, p 272
25. VAN ZYL, Helde-album..., p 329
26. SPIES & NATTRASS, Jan Smuts, Memoirs..., p 201
27. SPIES, Methods of Barbarism?, p 237
28. *Ibid*, p 240
29. WARWICK, Black People..., p 107
30. AMERY, op cit, vol V, p 302
31. VAN SCHOOR, De Wet-annale, No 7, pp 64-67
32. DAVITT, *op cit*, p 511
33. BREYTENBACH, Gedenkalbum..., p 413
34. PLOEGER, *op cit*, p 32:18
35. VAN REENEN, Emily Hobhouse..., p 461
36. SPIES, Methods of Barbarism?, p 237
37. PRETORIUS, Kommandolewe..., p 295
38. VAN REENEN, Emily Hobhouse..., pp 461-462
39. AMERY, *op cit*, vol V, pp 306-307
40. *Ibid*, vol V, pp 315-316
41. GRONUM, *op cit*, p 39
42. AMERY, *op cit*, vol V, p 330
43. GRONUM, *op cit*, (2) p 39
44. WALLACE, Unofficial Dispatches, p 276
45. WARWICK, Black People..., p 151
46. FARWELL, *op cit*, p 326
47. FERREIRA, Memoirs of Ben Bouwer, p 136;
    AMERY, *op cit*, vol V, p 308
48. WARWICK, South African War..., p 194
49. AMERY, *op cit*, vol V, p 308
50. SMUTS, *op cit*, p 134
51. AMERY, *op cit*, vol V, p 316
52. WESSELS, War Diary..., p 131
53. GRONUM, *op cit*, (2) p 38
54. BRITS, Diary of a National Scout, p 65
55. DAVITT, *op cit*, p 513
56. WESSELS, Egodokumente..., p 157
57. *Ibid*, p 72
58. FERREIRA, Memoirs of Ben Bouwer, p 141
59. AMERY, *op cit*, vol V, p 304
60. PLOEGER, *op cit*, p 33:20
61. McDONALD, In die Skaduwee van die Dood, p 82
62. FARWELL, *op cit*, p 340; VAN SCHOOR, Bittereinder, pp 187-194
63. AMERY, *op cit*, vol V, p 317;
    McDONALD, *op cit*, p 83
64. AMERY, *op cit*, vol V, p 330
65. *Ibid*, vol V, p 328
66. ZUID-AFRIKAANS VERJAARDAGBOEK
67. WARWICK, Black People..., p 107
68. AMERY, *op cit*, vol V, p 324
69. *Ibid*, vol V, p 331
70. WESSELS, War Diary..., p 136
71. SPIES, Methods of Barbarism?, p 72
72. PLOEGER, *op cit*, p 33:20
73. VAN SCHOOR, De Wet-annale, No 7, pp 101-102
74. BREYTENBACH, Gedenkalbum..., p 481
75. AMERY, *op cit*, vol V, p 309
76. *Ibid*, vol V, p 318
77. LE MAY, *op cit*, p 117
78. ELOFF, Oorlogsdagboekie..., p 3
79. LE MAY, *op cit*, p 117
80. PEDDLE, Long Cecil..., p 13
81. FARWELL, *op cit*, p 326
82. DOONER, 'Last Post', p 394
    SPIES, Methods of Barbarism?, p 240
83. WESSELS, Egodokumente..., p 74
84. WARWICK, Black People..., p 151
85. AMERY, *op cit*, vol V, p 391
86. WESSELS, War Diary..., p 139
87. FERREIRA, Memoirs of Ben Bouwer, p 150
88. SPIES, Methods of Barbarism?, p 241
89. AMERY, *op cit*, vol V, p 319
90. SPIES, Methods of Barbarism?, p 241
91. WESSELS, War Diary..., p 140
92. GRONUM, *op cit*, (2) p 17
93. PLOEGER, *op cit*, p 33:20
94. *Ibid*, p 33:20
95. AMERY, *op cit*, vol V, p 335

96. FERREIRA, Memoirs of Ben Bouwer, pp 152-153

97. VAN ZYL, Helde-album..., p 329

98. LE MAY, *op cit*, p 125

99. McCORD, South African Struggle, p 297

100. SCHEEPERS, Kaapland... die Tweede Vryheidsoorlog, pp 219-220

101. VAN ZYL, Helde-album..., p 345

102. KRIEL, Rondom die Anglo-Boereoorlog, p 106

103. KRUGER, Good-Bye Dolly Gray, p 441

104. BRITS, Diary of a National Scout, p 99

105. VAN ZYL, Helde-album..., p 345

106. PLOEGER, *op cit*, p 33:20

107. VAN ZYL, Helde-album... p 321

108. AMERY, *op cit*, vol V, pp 389-390

109. *Ibid*, vol V, p 385

110. *Ibid*, vol V, pp 339-340

111. GRONUM, *op cit*, (2) p 27

112. AMERY, *op cit*, vol V, pp 149; 388

113. ZUID-AFRIKAANS VERJAARDAGBOEK

114. GRONUM, *op cit*, (2) p 50

115. AMERY, *op cit*, vol V, p 387

116. *Ibid*, vol V, p 377

117. FERREIRA, Memoirs of Ben Bouwer, p 165

118. AMERY, *op cit*, vol V, pp 343-344

119. *Ibid*, vol V, pp 347-348

120. VAN SCHOOR, De Wet-annale, No 7, pp 69-74

121. AMERY, *op cit*, vol V, p 349

122. BREYTENBACH, Gedenkalbum, p 480

123. AMERY, *op cit*, vol V, p 350

124. AMERY, *op cit*, vol V, pp 378-379

125. VAN SCHOOR, De Wet-annale No 7, p 33

126. VAN DEN BERG, 24 Battles..., pp 125-12

127. WESSELS, War Diary..., p 148

128. KRUGER, Good-bye Dolly Gray, p 441

129. FERREIRA, Memoirs of Ben Bouwer, p 170

130. WARWICK, Black People..., p 151

131. FARWELL, *op cit*, p 326

132. VAN ZYL, Helde album..., p 301

133. BREYTENBACH, Gedenkalbum, p 465

134. WESSELS, War Diary..., p 146

135. VAN ZYL, Helde-album..., p 345

136. PRELLER, Scheepers se dagboek..., p 204

137. FERREIRA, Memoirs of Ben Bouwer, p 177

138. ZUID-AFRIKAANS VERJAARDAGBOEK

139. VAN ZYL, Helde-album..., p 345

140. SPIES, Methods of Barbarism?, p 242

141. WESSELS, Egodokumente..., p 75

142. FERREIRA, Krijgsgevangenschap..., p 174

143. LE MAY, *op cit*, p 123

144. BREYTENBACH, Gedenkalbum.., p 236

145. ZUID-AFRIKAANS VERJAARDAGBOEK

146. VAN ZYL, Helde-album..., p 347

147. BRITS, Diary of a National Scout, p 25

148. WESSELS, Egodokumente..., p 76

149. OBERHOLSTER, Oorlogsdagboek..., p 302

150. GRUNDLINGH, 'Hendsoppers'..., p 187

151. AMERY, *op cit*, vol V, p 395

152. GRUNDLINGH, 'Hendsoppers'..., p, 190

153. PAKENHAM, *op cit*, p 535

154. AMERY, *op cit*, vol V, p 395

155. SAUNDERS, Reader's Digest Illustrated History of SA, pp 274-275

156. ZUID-AFRIKAANS VERJAARDAGBOEK

157. VAN SCHOOR, De Wet-annale, No 8, p 11

158. PRELLER, Scheepers se dagboek, p 78

159. VAN DEN BERG, 24 Battles..., p 131

160. OBERHOLSTER, Oorlogsdagboek..., p 302

161. BREYTENBACH, Gedenkalbum..., p 236

162. PRELLER, Scheepers se dagboek..., p 205

163. AMERY, *op cit*, vol V, p 364

164. GRONUM, *op cit* (2) p 30

165. VAN SCHOOR, De Wet-annale, No 7, p 73

166. ZUID-AFRIKAANS VERJAARDAGBOEK

167. AMERY, *op cit*, vol V, p 365

168. SPIES, Methods of Barbarism?, p 243

169. VAN REENEN, Emily Hobhouse..., pp 139-144

170. HEADLAM, *op cit*, vol II, pp 286-287

171. AMERY, *op cit*, vol V, p 364

172. BREYTENBACH, Gedenkalbum..., p 414

173. AMERY, *op cit*, vol V, pp 366-374

174. VAN REENEN, Emily Hobhouse..., pp 145-150

175. WARWICK, Black People..., p 151

176. AMERY, *op cit*, vol V, map

177. VAN REENEN, Emily Hobhouse..., p 151

178. SPIES, Methods of Barbarism?, p 72

179. ZUID-AFRIKAANS VERJAARDAGBOEK

180. PAKENHAM, *op cit*, p 535

181. GRONUM, *op cit*, (2) p 51

182. SPIES, Methods of Barbarism?, p 274

183. KEMP, Pad van die Veroweraar, p 65

184. WESSELS, Egodokumente..., p 79

185. AMERY, *op cit*, vol V, p 543

186. GRONUM, *op cit*, (2) p 52

187. GRONUM, *op cit*, (2) p 11

188. AMERY, *op cit*, vol V, p 417

189. BREYTENBACH, Gedenkalbum..., p 239

190. PRELLER, Scheepers se dagboek..., p 79

191. HEADLAM, *op cit*, vol II, p 299

192. SPIES, Methods of Barbarism?, p 259

193. BREYTENBACH, Gedenkalbum..., p 239

194. SPIES, Methods of Barbarism?, pp 274-275

195. WESSELS, Egodokumente..., p 53

196. OOSTHUIZEN, Rebelle van die Stormberge, p 160

197. AMERY, *op cit*, vol V, p 419

198. PLOEGER, *op cit*, pp 44:21,22

199. SPIES, Methods of Barbarism?, p 263

200. *Ibid*, p 263

201. MEINTJIES, Anglo-Boereoorlog in Beeld, p 179

202. GRONUM, *op cit,* (2) p 52

203. VAN SCHOOR, De Wet-annale No 7, p 89

204. GRONUM, *op cit,* (2) p 52

205. PAKENHAM, *op cit,* p 555

206. WARWICK, Black People..., p 151

207. AMERY, *op cit,* vol V, map

208. SPIES, Methods of Barbarism?, p 258

209. AMERY, *op cit,* vol V, p 451

210. *Ibid,* vol V, pp 451-453

211. LE MAY, *op cit,* p 109

212. VAN SCHOOR, De Wet-annale No 7, p 89

213. AMERY, *op cit,* vol V, p 454

214. HEADLAM, *op cit,* vol II, p 229

215. GRUNDLINGH, 'Hendsoppers'..., pp 187-188

216. AMERY, *op cit,* vol V, pp 422-423

217. HEADLAM, *op cit,* vol II, pp 230-231

218. PRELLER, Scheepers se dagboek..., p 84

219. GRONUM, *op cit* (2) p 25

220. AMERY, *op cit,* vol V, p 454

221. SPIES, Methods of Barbarism?, p 259

222. *Ibid,* p 260

223. AMERY, *op cit,* vol V, p 454

224. HEADLAM, *op cit,* vol II, p 314

225. SPIES, Methods of Barbarism?, p 258

226. GRONUM, *op cit,* (2) p 54

227. DAVITT, *op cit,* p 540

228. *Ibid,* p 540

229. AMERY, *op cit,* vol V, p 423

230. GRONUM, *op cit,* (2) p 26

231. McDONALD, In die Skaduwee van die Dood, pp 90-93

232. PRELLER, Scheepers se dagboek..., p 88

233. LE MAY, *op cit,* p 128

234. GRONUM, *op cit,* (2) p 54

235. GRONUM, *op cit,* (2) p 41

236. AMERY, *op cit,* vol V, map

237. PRELLER, Scheepers se dagboek, p 88

238. HOLT, The Boer War, p 281;

   KRUGER, Good-bye Dolly Gray, p 456

239. PRETORIUS, Kommandolewe..., p 295

240. GRONUM, *op cit,* (2) p 37

241. AMERY, *op cit,* vol V, pp 464-465

242. *Ibid,* vol V, pp 424-427

243. PLOEGER, *op cit,* pp 43-37

244. HEADLAM, *op cit,* Vol II, p 291

245. AMERY, *op cit,* vol V, p 433

246. PRELLER, Scheepers se dagboek..., p 91

247. KRUGER, Good-bye Dolly Gray, p 468

248. GRONUM, *op cit,* (2) p 25

249. GRONUM, *op cit,* (2) p 144

250. McCORD, JJ, South African Struggle, p 327

251. FERREIRA, Krijgsgevangenschap..., p 176

252. AMERY, *op cit,* vol V, p 456

253. WESSELS, Egodokumente..., p 80

254. AMERY, *op cit,* vol V, p 437

255. MEINTJES, Stormberg..., p 178

256. AMERY, *op cit,* vol V, pp 437-445

257. VAN SCHOOR, De Wet-annale, No 7, p 89

   FERREIRA, Memoirs of Ben Bouwer, p 224

258. SPIES, Methods of Barbarism?, p 360

259. AMERY, *op cit,* vol V, p 456

260. *Ibid,* vol V, p 445

261. VAN ZYL, Helde-album..., p 133

262. PLOEGER, *op cit,* p 33:34;

   AMERY, *op cit,* vol V, p 461

263. AMERY, *op cit,* vol V, p 461

264. PAKENKAM, *op cit,* p 555

265. HATTINGH, *op cit,* pp 78-79

266. PLOEGER, *op cit,* p 33:40

267. WARWICK, Black people..., p 151

268. *Ibid,* p 157

JANUARY-JUNE 1902

THE BITTER END

War would end if the dead could return.
— Stanley Baldwin

1902	SUMMER	**JANUARY**
Day 813 Wed **1902-01-01**	ZAR Black involvement	NEW YEAR'S DAY A mine-workers strike on the Rand, protesting against the reduction in wages from the pre-war level of 49/9 to 30/- to 35/- per month, turns violent. Two strikers are killed and a number wounded. Forty-two are arrested and later sentenced to prison terms of up to 12 months.[1]
	Cape Colony	General Hertzog's commando is at Witwater, near Carnarvon.
	Trivia	*El Greco art exhibition opens in Madrid.*
Day 814 Thu **1902-01-02**		About 950 ex-burghers have joined the National Scouts while many more are acting as guides or scouts attached to British columns. Their pay, up to 2s 6d per day and a half share of confiscated livestock, is increased to 5s a day.[2]
Day 815 Fri **1902-01-03**	Eastern ZAR	Brigadier-General Plumer's column marches from Beginderlyn. Twenty-eight New Zealanders, forming his advance guard, are captured by General Chris Botha's men at Aasvogelkrantz, near the Swaziland border.[3]
Day 816 Sat **1902-01-04**	Eastern ZAR	**AMBUSH AT BANKKOP** At Bankkop, Onverwacht, east of Ermelo, Brigadier-General Plumer's column suffers another setback when another one of his advance screens is lured into an ambush. A mixed mounted force of Britons and Australians under Major JM Vallentin impetuously gallops after a group of about 25 burghers, when the trap, set by about 300 burghers under General JD Opperman, slams shut. The soldiers resist desperately but most of the officers, including Vallentin, are killed and when Opperman's men receive further reinforcements, the fight is over. The victors just have time to gather their spoils and melt away before Plumer's main force appears. The British lose 20 killed and 45 are wounded, while 70 men, several horses and a pompom are taken. Republican losses are 'slight', but Opperman, one of Botha's bravest officers, is killed.[45]
	Cape Colony Black involvement	In a letter to WT Stead, General JC Smuts explains his views on black policy: *"The peculiar situation of a small white community in the midst of the very large and rapidly increasing coloured races and the danger which in consequence threatens this small white community and with it civilization itself in South Africa, have led to... a special tacit understanding which forbids the white races to appeal for assistance to the coloured races in their mutual disputes... otherwise the coloured races must become the arbiters in disputes between the whites and in the long run the predominating factor or 'casting vote' in South Africa. That this would soon cause South Africa to relapse into barbarism must be evident to everybody."[6]* On the destruction of the Republics he writes, *"The condition of the two South African Republics in every truth baffles decription... The civilian population are herded into the camps where under the beneficent shadow of the British flag they perish in far greater numbers than combatants fall on the battle-fields of South Africa."*

		Refering to the results of the 'drives', he says, *"... the long lists of monthly captures by Lord Kitchener comprise almost purely those elements which the Boer forces can very well miss now, and shew a dimunition in our numbers which is not in any way a proportionate reduction in our fighting strength."* Those who remain in the field are *"... the men of invincible hope in the future and childlike faith in God — truly a select band, the like of whom I fondly think, is not to be found in the wide world today".*[7]
	Trivia	*General Chris Muller's birthday.*
Day 817 Sun **1902-01-05**		
Day 818 Mon **1902-01-06**	Eastern ZAR	The ZAR government leaves Paardeplaats, south-west of Roossenekal, after a stay of three weeks.
Day 819 Tue **1902-01-07**	Eastern ZAR	The ZAR government is at Windhoek, west of Dullstroom.
Day 820 Wed **1902-01-08**	ZAR	Lord Milner is the guest speaker at a banquet given by the Johannesburg Town Council, the Chamber of Mines and the Chamber of Commerce. He says: *"A great Johannesburg means a British Transvaal. A British Transvaal will turn the scale in favour of a British South Africa, and a British South Africa may go a long way to consolidate the British Empire."*[8]
Day 821 Thu **1902-01-09**	ZAR	Lord Kitchener retracts his previous statements regarding the existence of 'looting corps': *"The plain facts regarding these corps are as follows: The whole of the cattle of surrendered Burghers were confiscated by the Boers still in the field. It is only occasionally that cattle captured by our troops can be identified as the private property of... surrendered Burghers. In order to surrender, the men in this... category have been forced to sacrifice their stock, and it seemed only just that they should have an opportunity afforded them of recovering it from the irreconcilables who have seized it. I am particularly anxious to give them this opportunity, inasmuch as those farmers who are willing to accept British rule, and are eagerly waiting for peace, realise that they will have the utmost difficulty in replacing the cattle they possessed before the war... I therefore authorised the formation of those Forces which the enemy, and pro-Boers who hold them in particular horror, have sometimes held up to opprobrium under the designation of Looting Corps. I need hardly say that this name is entirely misleading."*[9]
Day 822 Fri **1902-01-10**	OFS	Chief Commandant De Wet and President Steyn meet at Leeukuil.
	Eastern ZAR	General Bruce Hamilton, in association with Wooll-Sampson's black scouts, executes a night raid against a Boer laager at Witbank, 35 kilometres northwest of Ermelo. Ex-State Artillery officers Major Wolmarans and Captain Wolmarans are captured, together with 42 burghers.[10]
	United Kingdom	The War Office decides to raise fresh volunteer companies for South Africa.
	International	The German Chancellor Von Bulow delivers a speech considered to be 'hostile to Britain' in the Reichstag, Berlin.
Day 823 Sat **1902-01-11**	OFS	Chief Commandant De Wet leaves to visit the Bethlehem, Kroonstad and Heilbron commandos.
	Black involvement	Major GJ de Lotbiniere, Commissioner for Native Affairs, writes: *"I am convinced it is in the interest of the British Government to make the natives loyal and happy, and*

		that it will never do to send them back to their kraals without giving them some cattle, both for the sake of their health, which will suffer greatly unless they have stock, and also in the interest of the agricultural industry of the country, to be resumed on the cessation of hostilities... Promises have been made to these natives, and, unless they are faithfully adhered to, we shall place ourselves in a false light with all the farm natives of both colonies."[11]
Day 824 Sun 1902-01-12	OFS	Chief Commandant De Wet and Major General Elliot clash at Liebenbergsvlei near Bethlehem.
	Eastern ZAR	Another night raid by General Bruce Hamilton at Kaffirstad, near Witbank, results in the taking of 32 prisoners.
	Cape Colony	Lieutenant I Liebenberg, a Free Stater, is executed by hanging at Aliwal North. After a very controversial trial, he has been found guilty of the 'murder' of Lieutenant L Neumeyer (23 Nov 1900).[12]
Day 825 Mon 1902-01-13		
Day 826 Tue 1902-01-14	Northern Cape Colony	Major Whitehead is attacked by Combat General Edwin Conroy at Doornfontein, near Griquatown. The British report 24 casualties, including Whitehead, who is killed.[13]
Day 827 Wed 1902-01-15		
Day 828 Thu 1902-01-16	Northern ZAR	A court-martial, chaired by Lieutenant-Colonel Denny to investigate the atrocities by the Bushveld Carbineers, is convened in Pietersburg. The accused are Major RW Lenehan and Lieutenants HH Morant, Picton (British), PJ Handcock and GR Witton.[14]
	Eastern ZAR	General Ben Viljoen leaves his base at Pilgrim's Rest to visit the ZAR government at Mapogsgronden near Roossenekal.
	United Kingdom	The British Parliament reopens and Campbell-Bannerman attacks the government on its conduct of the war in South Africa. He demands answers to the following questions: whether or not the policy of farm burning is continuing; how many executions were carried out under martial law in the Cape Colony; how many times civilians were forced to watch executions and why the Cape Parliament has not yet reopened its session. He also wants to know everything that has been committed in England's name in South Africa and what the chances of peace in the near future are.[15]
	Trivia	ISM Hamilton's 49th birthday.
Day 829 Fri 1902-01-17	Cape Colony	In Graaff-Reinet, Commandant Gideon Scheepers is found guilty and condemned to death.
	Trivia	ZAR independence day (Sand River Convention 1852). Lloyd George's 39th birthday.
Day 830 Sat 1902-01-18	Eastern ZAR	Hamilton's columns capture 27 burghers at Spitskop, about 40 kilometres southeast of Ermelo.
	Cape Colony Comdt. Gideon Scheepers (War Museum of the Boer Republics)	**GIDEON SCHEEPERS IS EXECUTED** Commandant Gideon Scheepers is shot by firing squad at Graaff-Reinet. His request to be shot by a regular British unit is honoured but his request to be buried in a coffin, not. He is bound to a chair and forced to wear a blindfold. His body is

		dropped into a grave and slaked lime is poured over it. To avoid the creation of a 'martyr's grave', his body is secretly exhumed at night and reburied in the bed of the Sundays River.[16]

Scheepers shot by firing squad
(War Museum of the Boer Republics)

A NAVAL ACTION

At Doorn Bay, a Republican commando, commanded by General Bouwer, fires on *HMS Partridge*, *"spoiling his* (sic) *paint"*. The warship shells the dunes, weighs anchor and steams out of the bay. Bouwer is uncertain whether or not to claim a naval victory.[17]

	Black involvement Concentration camps	Major De Lotbiniere, in charge of the Native Refugee Department, writes that supplying workers to the army *"formed the basis on which our system was founded"*. The department's mobilisation of black labour is very successful — not really surprising, considering the incentives offered: those in service and their families can buy mealies at a halfpence per lb, or 7/6 a bag, while those who do not accept employment have to pay double, or 1d per lb and 18/- or more per bag. By the end of 1901, when the death rate peaks, more than 6 000 accept employment in the army. This figure grows to more than 13 000 in April 1902.[18]
	Trivia	*A US commission appointed by President Roosevelt chooses Panama as the site for a canal, giving rise to the palindrome: 'A man, a plan, a canal, Panama.'*
Day 831 Sun **1902-01-19**	*Trivia*	*JJ Cheere Emmet's 35th birthday (Commandant-General L Botha's brother-in-law).*
Day 832 Mon **1902-01-20**	United Kingdom	Continuing the parliamentary debate, AJ Balfour states: *"Farm burning is not given up in those cases where farm burning is a military necessity... And when those circumstances arise I hope and believe our generals will not shrink even from that necessity, painful as it must necessarily be.* *"We do mean to subjugate the Boers — subjugation means conquering; we do mean to conquer them. We do mean to annex them, we do mean to incorporate them within the Empire... The Boers say... 'We are not going to surrender our independence.' We say: 'You are going to', and there the matter stands. And until one of those parties is subjugated the war is to go on, and we do not mean to be subjugated."*[19]
Day 833 Tue **1902-01-21**	Western ZAR	A British force of about 250 from Lichtenburg harasses General De la Rey's hospital at Leliesdal, near the present-day Coligny. General Cilliers and Commandant Viljoen (of the Marico scouts) arrive at the scene and the British flee, pursued by the burghers, firing from the saddle. The British suffer 80 killed, wounded and captured, while a single burgher is killed.[20]
	Eastern ZAR	The ZAR government decides not to accompany General Ben Viljoen to Pilgrim's Rest and remains at Oshoek, south-west of Lydenburg as Viljoen's party departs.[21]
Day 834 Wed **1902-01-22**	Northern ZAR Concentration camps	In an audacious exploit, General Beyers and about 300 men seize the concentration camp at Pietersburg and take the camp superintendent and his staff prisoner.[22]
	Eastern ZAR	The ZAR government is at Grady's Farm, west of Dullstroom.[23]
Day 835 Thu **1902-01-23**	Northern ZAR Concentration camps	After an all-night party with wives, friends and family, General Beyers' men release their prisoners unharmed and leave in the morning. About 150 surrendered burghers held in the camp join Beyers, but four desert soon afterwards and return to captivity.[24]
Day 836 Fri **1902-01-24**	Northern ZAR	Forewarned by the returned burghers, the British garrison is in prepared positions and repulses Beyers' attack on Pietersburg carried out by only 75 men on open ground. The burghers can only loot a few livestock before retreating.[25]

	Eastern ZAR	In another night raid General Bruce Hamilton's columns capture 12 burghers at Boschmansfontein.
Day 837 Sat **1902-01-25**	Eastern ZAR Black involvement	**GENERAL BEN VILJOEN IS CAPTURED** General Ben Viljoen is captured and two of his staff are killed in an ambush near Lydenberg. A black scout named Wildebeest is later to receive payment of £5 for the information leading to Viljoen's capture. General Chris Muller takes over command in the northern operational area while Viljoen's brother, Willem, takes over his commando.[26] Brigadier-Generals Plumer and Pulteney execute a drive in the mountains north-east of Wakkerstroom. They take 34 prisoners and force 30 towards the blockhouse line where they are seized by other units.[27]
	Cape Colony	FE Davies, previously of Nesbitt's Horse, is executed for desertion and treason by the British at Somerset East.[28]
	International	**THE DUTCH OFFER TO MEDIATE** An offer of mediation from the Dutch government is sent by the Dutch Prime Minister, Dr Abrahan Kuyper, to Lord Lansdowne, the British Foreign Secretary.[29]
		THE 'VELDPOND' During this period the ZAR government experiences reluctance from blacks in the eastern Transvaal to accept government notes. Mr PJ Kloppers, in charge of 'the State Mint in the Veld' at Pilgrim's Rest, is ordered to use the refined gold brought from Pretoria to strike gold coins. After several experiments, he and his assistants, using the facilities of the Pilgrim's Rest Gold Mining Company, succeed in striking coins that are known as 'Veldponde'. Eventually 986 coins are struck. The 1997 value of these rare coins ranges between R30 000 and R150 000.[30]
Day 838 Sun **1902-01-26**	Eastern ZAR	Ex-State Artillery Captain De Jager and 86 burghers are captured while six are killed by one of Hamilton's columns at Nelspan, about ten kilometres west of Ermelo.[31]
Day 839 Mon **1902-01-27**	Cape Colony Black involvement	**THE LELIEFONTEIN INCIDENT** General Manie Maritz and eight of his men enter the Leliefontein Mission Station, near Garies. While they are explaining to the inhabitants that, if they remain neutral, they will be left in peace, they are suddenly attacked by the inhabitants who attempt to capture them. Maritz and his party, only lightly armed, escape after desperate hand-to-hand fighting during which Maritz hurls an opponent against the church building with astounding force.[32] The remnants of Kritzinger's commando, now reduced to only about 50 men under Louis Wessels, derail and burn a loaded cargo train between Middelburg and Cradock.[33]
	Trivia	*Kaizer Wilhelm II's 43rd birthday.*
Day 840 Tue **1902-01-28**	Cape Colony Black involvement	The furious General Manie Maritz launches a retaliatory attack on Leliefontein, during which 35 Coloureds are killed. The rest of the community is dispersed, a thousand bags of cereal are confiscated, 500 cattle and 3 000 sheep are taken and sent to Bushmanland. The attack meets with deep disapproval from General Smuts.[34]
	Northern ZAR	Lieutenants Morant, Handcock and Witton of the Bushveld Carbineers are found guilty by a court martial and they are sentenced to death at

		Pietersburg for various atrocities (including the shooting of unarmed prisoners) committed from July to September east of Pietersburg. Major Lenehan is reprimanded.[34]
Day 841 Wed **1902-01-29**	United Kingdom	The British government refuses the Dutch government's offer of mediation. Lord Lansdowne tells the Dutch: *"The quickest and most satisfactory means of arranging a settlement would be by direct communication between the leaders of the Boer Forces in South Africa and the Commander-in-Chief of His Majesty's Forces."*[35]
Day 842 Thu **1902-01-30**	Cape Colony	Colonel Crabbe, with a mixed force of about 500 men, is ordered to move towards Fraserburg to clear the road for a 100-donkey-wagon convoy leaving Beaufort West, escorted by Major Crofton with 100 West Yorks and 150 District Mounted troops.[36]
	Trivia	*OFS independence day (Bloemfontein Convention 1854).*
Day 843 Fri **1902-01-31**	Trivia	*BD Bouwer's 27th birthday.*

OFFICIAL REPORTS

Gold mining:	On the Witwatersrand 1 057 or 17,6 % of the gold stamps are back in production and the monthly gold production is 70 000 ounces or about 23,3 % of peak pre-war production.[37]
Concentration camps:	The officially reported camp population of the white camps is 114 376 and the deaths for January are 1 805.
Black involvement:	The population of the black camps is 97 986 and 2 534 deaths are recorded.
Farm burning:	British columns have partially or completely destroyed 47 farms and 14 black huts.[38]
Blockhouse lines:	The following blockhouse lines have been completed: Cape Colony — From Lambert's Bay to Clanwilliam (53 blockhouses over 55 km) and between Carnarvon and Victoria Road (112 blockhouses and three posts over 128 km).[39] OFS — From Bloemfontein to Thaba Nchu (42 forts covering about 64 km), from Ficksburg via Bethlehem to Harrismith (200 km) and between Tafelkop and Botha's Pass (100 km). ZAR — From Ventersdorp to Tafelkop (40 km), from Carolina to Wonderfontein (55 blockhouses about 700 m apart covering 40 km) and between Machadodorp and Lydenburg (72 km with 55 blockhouses).[40]

1902	SUMMER	**FEBRUARY**
Day 844 Sat **1902-02-01**	Cape Colony	Commandants Van Reenen and Smit attack Colonel Crabbe's column, but they are easily repulsed.
	Trivia	*The binding of women's feet in China is banned by imperial decree.*
Day 845 Sun **1902-02-02**	OFS	Major the Earl of Munster Lord Tewkesbury is accidentally killed at Lace Mine between Viljoenskroon and Kroonstad.[41]
	Cape Colony	General Wynand Malan combines with the commandos of Hugo, Pyper, Lategan and Smit. They attack Crabbe's column and a running fight develops. Crabbe suffers 21 casualties and encamps at Waterval Farm. They prepare sangars, but realise that it is not a very defensible position. Malan allows a doctor to proceed to Fraserburg with the British wounded.[42]

Day 846 Mon **1902-02-03**	OFS	Commandant W Mears and Captain Muller are ordered by De Wet to join him at Elandskop, 32 kilometres north-east of Lindley. Commandant Mears, with 200 men, runs into Colonel Garrat's screen consisting of 200 New Zealanders and 100 Queenslanders, at Roodekraal near Reitz. [43] The Republican rearguard disengages prematurely. Garrat launches flank attacks and a part of Mears' force is overwhelmed. Captain Muller, with 13 artillerists and burghers, is forced to surrender on the farm Fanny's Home near Liebenbergsvlei. He also loses two field-guns (captured at Tweefontein) and a pom-pom while Garrat loses two men.[44]
	Cape Colony	Just after midnight Major Crabbe and his men leave Waterval, sneak through the Boer lines and reach Rietfontein at dawn — only to find that they are again surrounded. Crabbe's rations are giving out and messengers sent to get assistance from Fraserburg, fail to get through. However, Malan's humanitarian gesture backfires when the doctor in charge of the wounded informs the garrison at Fraserburg of Crabbe's plight.[45] In the meantime Crofton's donkey convoy entrenches at Uitspanningsfontein, about 16 kilometres away.
	Trivia	*Lord RATG Cecil Salisbury's 72nd birthday.*
Day 847 Tue **1902-02-04**	OFS	**LORD KITCHENER'S NEW MODEL DRIVES** Brigadier-General Rimington's orders are typical of the night-time arrangements and indicate the meticulous planning that goes into these operations: "1. *Every man from the Brigadier to the last native to be on duty and act as sentry for one-third of the night.* 2. Front Line — *Each squadron to be allotted a length of front, to be covered by entrenched pickets of six men, 50 to 100 yards apart; two men to constitute a double sentry; four to sleep close beside them. Guns loaded with case to be posted in front line... Transport, artillery vehicles and all horses to be in small laagers, handy to their units.* 3. Rear Line — *A thin line of rear pickets, each of six men, 500 yards in rear of front line: two pickets to a mile. If attacked, to fall back on the laagers.* 4. Sham Front Line — *A sham line of pickets to be taken up by daylight, a mile or two in front of the real line, and evacuated after dark; fires to be burning along it. The two real lines to be selected by daylight but on no account to be occupied till after dark.* 5. Cover and Obstacles — *Advantage to be taken of natural cover and obstacles, such as dongas, spruits and wire fences. Wire entanglements to be used where feasible.* 6. Lights — *After dark no fires or smoking and only whispered talking. Cooking to be done only at midday halt, and as much sleep as possible to be taken then too.* 7. Subterfuges — *Tricks of every sort to deceive enemy as to strength and position of the real front line. Eg. (a) supports to be loudly called for when a picket is attacked; (b) gaps to be left in the smouldering fires of sham front line, opposite strong-points in the real front line.*"[46]
	Cape Colony	Columns commanded by Capper and Lund rush from Sutherland and towards the evening all pressure on Crabbe is relieved as the Boers disappear. The British assume that, with the exception of Commandant Smit who heads towards Crofton's position at Uitspanningsfontein, all the other commandos retreat northwards. Major Crofton has prepared sangars on two koppies dominating the 150 wagons of his donkey convoy at Uitspanningsfontein. A reconnaissance patrol of 25 members of the District Mounted Troops is captured by the enemy, leaving

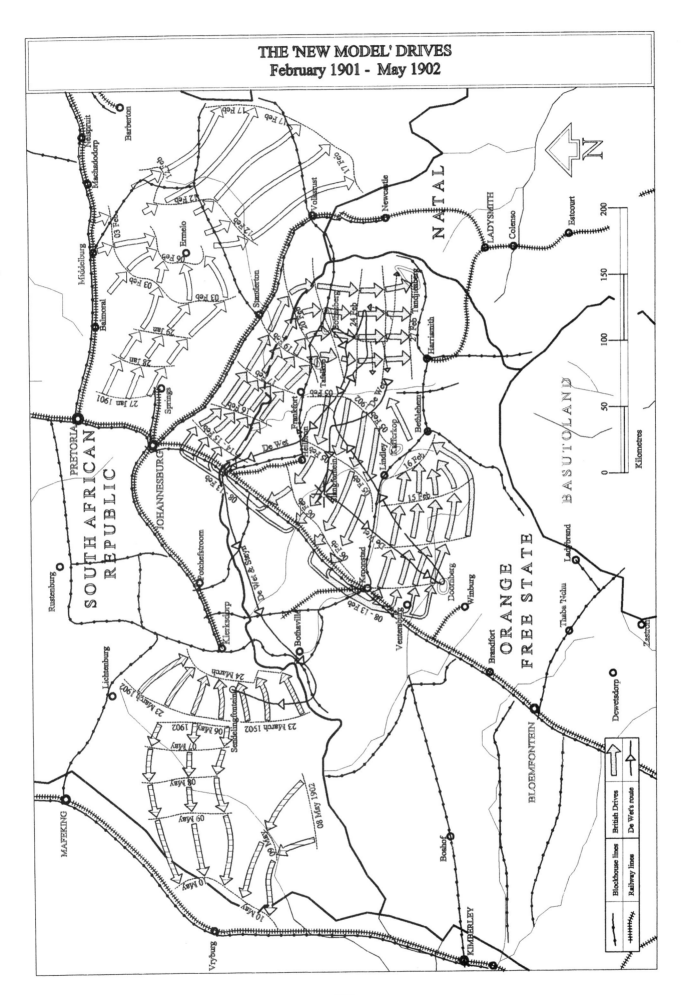

		Crofton with only about 125 soldiers to defend his laager. At 14:00, Smit opens a tentative attack.
	Trivia	*The US aviator Charles Lindbergh is born.*
Day 848 Wed **1902-02-05**	OFS	Chief Commandant CR de Wet concentrates his commandos at Slangfontein.[47]
	Western ZAR	**THE ACTION AT GRUISFONTEIN** Guided by National Scouts, part of Colonels Kekewich and Hickie's force, consisting of 634 men with a pom-pom, under Major HP Leader, surprises a laager of Commandant Sarel Alberts at Gruisfontein, 24 kilometres east of Lichtenburg. The Republicans lose eight men killed, at least ten wounded and between 100 and 132 captured, including Commandant Alberts, while the British lose only eight wounded. The commando's horses bolt and are later rounded up by Kemp's men enabling him to remount some of the almost 1 000 horseless burghers in his laager. As dismounted men are practically of no use in guerrilla operations, the recaptured horses almost make up for the loss of Alberts' men in terms of fighting strength.[48]
	Cape Colony	**THE ACTION AT UITSPANNINGSFONTEIN** Soon after midnight, the events of the last few days become clear. With Crabbe's force pinned down and the relieving columns of Capper and Lund taken on a wild-goose chase, Malan swings round and joins Smit's attack on Uitspanningsfontein, near Fraserburg. The sangars are taken piecemeal and despite a determined defence by the wounded Major Crofton — which costs him his life — the convoy is taken, looted and burned. The British lose 13 killed, 41 wounded and the rest taken prisoner. Crabbe, now trying to resume his original role to assist the convoy and assuming that he only has to contend with Smit's commando, approaches Uitspanningsfontein. He is too late to save the convoy and almost shares Crofton's fate when he is furiously set upon by Malan's combined force. Capper and Lund are sent for again and save the retreating column. Crabbe suffers 31 casualties.[49] **THE ATTACK AT MIDDELPOST** A convoy under the command of Lieutenant-Colonel WRB Doran is left vulnerable when the columns of Crabbe and Lund rush to assist Crofton and Crabbe. Unwisely, Doran rushes off to attack Geldenhuys' small rebel laager. General Van Deventer, with only 25 men, seizes the opportunity and attacks the convoy at Middelpost, between Sutherland and Calvinia.[50] F du Rand is executed by firing squad at Cradock.
Day 849 Thu **1902-02-06**	OFS	Aimed at cornering Chief Commandant CR de Wet, the first of Lord Kitchener's 'new model drives' starts in the north-eastern Free State. About 9 000 men start off from the Liebenbergsvlei River between Frankfort and Kafferkop along a line of approximately 87 kilometres. (This means a theoretical average spacing of one man every ten metres.)[51] The Kroonstad/Wolwehoek line is reinforced by the 2nd Seaforth Highlanders and patrolled by four armoured trains, while the Wolwehoek/Heilbron line is strengthened by the 2nd Leinster Regiment and three armoured trains. In round figures, the cordon is thus made up of about 17 000 men, 300 blockhouses and seven armoured trains.[52]

	Cape Colony	General Smuts arrives with reinforcements for Van Deventer's attack at Middelpost and the British are driven out of their defensive positions. One hundred and thirty wagons are captured and destroyed and 400 horses and mules are taken. The British lose nine killed and 22 wounded, while four burghers are killed and ten are wounded.[53]
Day 850 Fri 1902-02-07	OFS	Chief Commandant De Wet, with 700 men, moves south and breaks through the blockhouse line between Kroonstad and Lindley, west of Doornkloof. Commandants Van Coller and Van der Merwe break through the Imperial Light Horse at Jagersrust and cross the Heilbron/Frankfort blockhouse line with about 300 men. [54]
	Trivia	*Sir Charles Warren's 62nd birthday.*
Day 851 Sat 1902-02-08	OFS	The 'new model drive' in the Free State results in 286 Republicans killed, wounded or captured. As De Wet reports at least two instances of boys aged nine and 12 forcibly taken from their parents during this 'drive', it is unlikely that the 286 reported captured refer to 'real fighting men'. [55]
	Western ZAR	Commandant Potgieter is attacked near Wolmaransstad by Lord Methuen and 36 of his men are taken prisoner. Lord Methuen leaves General JC Barker in command of the garrison at Klerksdorp while he moves to Vryburg to attend to administrative business and to spend a few days with his wife, Lady Methuen, who has arrived for a short visit. Lieutenant-Colonel SB von Donop, who has been left in charge of operations in the area, occupies Wolmaransstad from where he conducts farm-burning operations.[56]
	Victoria Cross	Surgeon-Captain A Martin-Leake, South African Constabulary, Vlakfontein.
Day 852 Sun 1902-02-09	OFS	Chief Commandant CR de Wet breaks through the blockhouse line at Palmietfontein, losing one burgher killed and four wounded. A boy of ten is also killed and a boy aged 11 is wounded. These children have joined family members in De Wet's force to avoid being rounded up in the scorched earth drives.[57]
	Eastern ZAR	The ZAR government leaves Grady's Farm.[58]
	Trivia	*Dr LS Jameson's 49th birthday.*
Day 853 Mon 1902-02-10	OFS	Chief Commandant CR de Wet arrives back at Elandskop.[59]
	Eastern ZAR	The ZAR government is at Witpoort, south of Roossenekal.[60]
	Cape Colony	General BD Bouwer attacks a convoy consisting of about 1 500 men under the command of Colonels CTM Kavanagh, GP Wyndham and Haig, at Aties, between Calvinia and Clanwilliam. A running battle develops until the British make a stand at Doorn River bridge, where they repulse Bouwer's attack.[61]
Day 854 Tue 1902-02-11	Western ZAR	Lieutenant-Colonel SB von Donop dispatches a resupply column from Wolmaransstad to Klerksdorp.
	Eastern ZAR	The ZAR government is at Bothasberg, north-west of Stofberg.[62]
Day 855 Wed 1902-02-12	Eastern ZAR	The ZAR government is at Bothasberg.[63]
	ZAR	The 28th Company of the Mounted Infantry is ambushed at Klip River. A

		British force, about 320-strong, commanded by Major Dowell, is lured into a trap by 'fleeing' burghers and ambushed by about 250 burghers under Generals Alberts and Grobler. The British lose ten killed and 50 wounded.[64]
	Western ZAR	Lord and Lady Methuen give a ball at the Palace Hotel, Klerksdorp, and he escorts her to Johannesburg the following day, from where she returns to Corsham, in Wiltshire.[65]
Day 856 Thu **1902-02-13**	OFS	**THE SECOND OFS DRIVE** The second 'new model drive' against De Wet in the north-eastern Free State commences. The first phase entails a sweep between the Natal railway, the Natalspruit/Brandfort line and the Harrismith/Winburg line. This time Kitchener employs about 30 000 troops.[66] The columns of Elliot, Marshall, Holmes, Lawley and Du Cane are lined up from Kroonstad to Doornberg and they march towards the Lindley/Bethlehem line.
	Eastern ZAR	Commandant-General L Botha and about 500 men skirt the Wakkerstroom/Piet Retief blockhouse line by darting through southern Swaziland to the mountains east of Vryheid.[67] The ZAR government is at Langkloof on the Olifants River. [68]
Day 857 Fri **1902-02-14**	Cape Colony	At Krantz, near Vredendal, General Bouwer's commando is surprised in their sleep as a result of information given to the British by L Colyn, who deserted from his commando the previous evening. The attackers are mostly of the 10th Hussars, commanded by Colonel CTM Kavanagh. Seventeen burghers and rebels are killed or wounded and nine, including Bouwer's brother, are captured. [69] JF Geldenhuis is executed by firing squad at Graaff-Reinet.
	St Helena	HJ Bantjes is shot and killed by a guard while trying to escape from the prisoner of war camp.[70]
Day 858 Sat **1902-02-15**	OFS	The six columns reach the Lindley/Bethlehem line. During the first part of the drive only about ten burghers have been taken prisoner.
	Trivia	*Berlin's first underground railway is opened.*
Day 859 Sun **1902-02-16**	OFS	The second phase of the Free State drive starts between the Natal railway line and the Wolwehoek/Heilbron/Frankfort line.[71]
Day 860 Mon **1902-02-17**	Cape Colony	Stephenson starts a short drive in the Victoria West/Williston area, using the columns of B Doran, Capper, Crabbe, Bentinck Lund and Wormald.[72] On its way to Malan's operational area in the midlands, an advance party of his commando clashes at Oorlogsfontein (50 kilometres south of Victoria West) with a column under Lieutenant-Colonel Doran whom they mistake for a Boer force. Judge HJ Hugo, Free State judge-in-the-field promoted to the rank of Commandant, is fatally wounded.[73] Judge Kock is captured in the Cape Colony. Commandant H Badenhorst routs Colonel Henry's column from Kimberley at Wasberg. [74]
	Eastern ZAR	The ZAR government leaves Langkloof. [75]
	St Helena	A 24-year-old Italian volunteer, J Balderacchi, succeeds in escaping from St Helena by swimming to a Spanish ship, the *Nautilus*, which later takes him to Spain.[76]
Day 861 Tue **1902-02-18**	Western ZAR	Lieutenant-Colonel SB von Donop's resupply column returns to

	ZAR	Wolmaransstad from Klerksdorp. General De la Rey's scouts closely monitors the convoy's movements. Using about 60 'fleeing' burghers as a decoy, Commandant Grobler and General Alberts lead about 400 members of the Dragoon Guards and Scots Greys under General Gilbert Hamilton into a trap at Klippan, south of Nigel. The British lose ten wounded and about 50 captured.[77]
	OFS	Chief Commandant De Wet and President Steyn are at Rondebosch, north-east of Reitz [78] Brigadier-General Rimington, Keir, Wilson and Damant start a pivoting movement at Tafelkop, while Barker and Lieutenant-General EL Elliot arrive at the Wilge River. [79]
Day 862 Wed **1902-02-19**	OFS	The construction of the last of 86 blockhouses, about 900 metres apart, completes the Vals River line.[80]
Day 863 Thu **1902-02-20**	ZAR Black involvement	Colonel CW Park, commanding three columns, accompanied by about 300 National Scouts and a commando of armed blacks, surprise General Chris H Muller in the Bothasberg, about 60 kilometres north-east of Middelburg. Although the ZAR government, their real quarry, has already left the area, 153 burghers of Colonel Trichard's commando are taken prisoner and at least two are killed.[81]
	Western ZAR	Colonel SB von Donop's convoy camps at Rondavelskraal near Twyfelpoort Station.
Day 864 Fri **1902-02-21**	OFS	Most of the northern Free State commandos under Wessel Wessels, Manie Botha and Alec Ross break through the line. Chief Commandant De Wet and President Steyn cross the Wilge River as Lieutenant-General Elliot occupies the fords behind them. There are now about 3 000 burghers including the Harrismith men inside the cordon formed by about 30 000 soldiers.[82]
	Cape Colony	General Malan, Commandant Fouchee and Commandant Myburgh enter the midland districts of Cape Colony. South of Noblesfontein, General Malan and 150 men dynamite the railway line as they cross it and immobilise two armoured trains.[83]
Day 865 Sat **1902-02-22**	OFS	General Alberts, Commander Manie Botha and Jan Meyer joins Chief Commandant De Wet at Brakfontein. A detachment of ORC volunteers under Vilonel captures seven burghers near Winburg.[84]
	Eastern ZAR	Grobler's commando is captured near Lake Chrissie.
	Cape Colony	The short drive ends at the Victoria West/Williston blockhouse line, but the commandos easily break through the widely spaced forts. [85]
	Trivia	*RSS Baden-Powell's 45th birthday.*
Day 866 Sun **1902-02-23**	OFS	**ACTION AT LANGVERWACHT (OR KALKKRANS)** Chief Commandant De Wet, using a selected force commanded by Ross, Manie Botha and Alberts, as a battering ram, recklessly charges through a line of New Zealanders under the command of Lieutenant-Colonel FS Garratt. They force a gap enabling President Steyn and the convoy to escape across the Holspruit at Kalkkrans. Jan Meyer and the Harrismith men swerve east and attack Colonel Byng's line. They are repulsed and flee south. Six hundred of

		the best men break through, leaving 14 dead and taking about 20 wounded with them, along with a group of refugees. The New Zealanders lose 23 killed and 49 wounded. Several of the smaller groups also break through the line but Chief Commandant De Wet's son Kotie and about 400 burghers are captured.[86]
	Western ZAR	When General De la Rey's scouts inform him that Von Donop's column has left Wolmaransstad, he immediately concentrates his men. He has at his disposal 250 Lichtenburg and Marico burghers under General Celliers at Jakkalsfontein, between Wolmaransstad and Klerksdorp; 250 Klerksdorp and Potchefstroom men under General Liebenberg and 200 men of the Pretoria and Krugersdorp commandos under General Kemp, both in separate laagers in the vicinity of Hartbeesfontein.[87] Colonel SB Von Donop's convoy — a train of about 160 wagons — is escorted by a force of about 700 men, commanded by Lieutenant-Colonel WC Anderson, made up of 230 Imperial Yeomanry, 225 Northumberland Fusiliers, 80 men of Paget's Horse and 60 other mounted men with two field-guns, a pom-pom and a machine gun. They make an overnight stop at Kareeboomspruit, about a third of the way to Klerksdorp.[88]
	Cape Colony	Commandant Louis Wessels reaches Williston.
Day 867 Mon **1902-02-24**	Western ZAR	Von Donop's convoy is closely shadowed by Boer scouts as they move towards their next overnight stop at Ysterspruit, about 20 kilometres from Klerksdorp. Almost at their destination, Anderson allows the 80 men of Paget's Horse to proceed to Klerksdorp. In the meantime, General De la Rey finalizes his planned ambush: Liebenberg's men are to take cover in bushes and shrubs forming a line across the road while Kemp is to attack the convoy in the left flank and General Celliers the rear. [89]
	OFS	Commandant Mentz and the Heilbron burghers break through the British cordon at Waaiwater.
Day 868 Tue **1902-02-25**	Western ZAR	**THE BATTLE OF YSTERSPRUIT** (about 16 kilometres south-west of Klerksdorp) At about 01:00, in dark and wet conditions, General De la Rey's men are in position. A British sentry becomes aware of Kemp's men moving in the dark and alerts Colonel Anderson. He decides to move on immediately and at 04:30, while it is still dark, the convoy comes into motion. Anderson places his guns, a company of infantry and some of the Yeomanry in the vanguard, a company of infantry on either flank and the rearguard is made up of another company of infantry and the rest of the Yeomanry. A thick morning mist resulting from the previous evening's rain limits the visibility to a few metres. About 30 minutes after starting — where the terrain begins to slope towards the Jagdspruit — the advance guard approaches to within 20 yards of the thicket when Liebenberg's burghers open up. Anderson quickly orders a defensive formation and the first attack by Liebenberg and Kemp is repulsed. Liebenberg's second attack also fails and when the British guns open up, his men scurry back to the thicket. The Boer officers resort to using their sjamboks to rally their men and the success of the ambush is in the balance when General Cilliers — who has lagged too far behind because of the convoy's early start — suddenly appears in the British rear. Cilliers, with only about 100 men, firing from the saddle, charges through the rearguard and pierces the British defence. Kemp's burghers renew their attack and Liebenberg's men overwhelm the van-

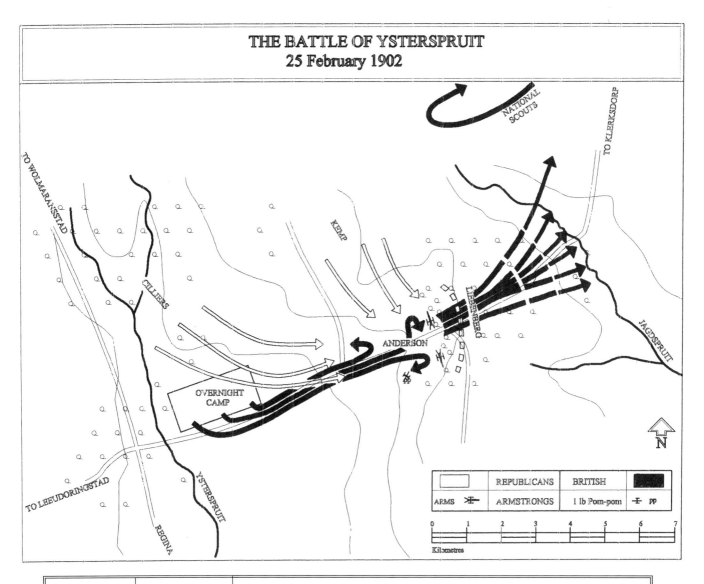

guard and take the guns. They swing the guns around but can only fire a single shot at the fleeing horsemen and vehicles before the pursuing burghers are among them. British resistance collapses. Careful to avoid a repeat of what has happened at Kleinfontein, the burghers remove the rifle bolts of the surrendering soldiers before rushing towards the wagons which are bunched up at the Jagdspruit. The battle has lasted less than 100 minutes. About 150 of the mounted Yeomanry dash past the stuck and overturned wagons and do not look around before reaching Klerksdorp. The garrison commander tries to organise a counter-attack with about 250 horsemen, including about 80 National Scouts and some artillerists. When they run into Kemp's men, they think it wiser to return to camp and report the complete disaster.

The British lose 55 men killed, about 270 captured, including 130 wounded. The convoy's 156 wagons, 1 500 mules, two guns, pom-pom, 2 000 rifles and half-a-million rounds of ammunition fall into De la Rey's hands. His casualties amount to 12 dead and 42 wounded.

Later, when the British ambulances under Dr Laing arrive, General De la Rey gives him two wagons to take the seriously wounded to Klerksdorp. In return, he supplies Dr Von Rennenkampf, De la Rey's doctor, with some surgical instruments. The burghers move off with their booty, taking the British prisoners and walking wounded with them. (They are later put across the Bechuanaland border at Madibogo, between Mafeking and Vryburg.)[90]

	Northern ZAR	The death sentences of Lieutenants Harry 'Breaker' Morant and Peter J Handcock of the Bushveld Carbineers, found guilty by a court-martial at Pietersburg, are confirmed by Kitchener, while that of Lieutenant George Witton is changed to life imprisonment. (He is released in November 1904 and his book *Scapegoats of the Empire* is published in 1907.) Major Lenehan and Lieutenant Picton are reprimanded, cashiered and deported, eventually to return to Australia.[91]
	Cape Colony	General Smuts, uniting with the commandos of Bouwer, Van Deventer, Theron, Neser and Naude, attacks the Cape Police at Windhoek, south of Vredendal. They succeed in taking the British positions and they kill one soldier, wound seven and capture 80 together with 100 horses and 25 wagons. It is, however, an expensive victory, because Smuts loses four officers, eight burghers killed and ten wounded, including General BD Bouwer.[92] General Smuts is forced to abandon his plan to invade the Western Cape and decides to concentrate on the north-western Cape.[93] The traitor Lambert Colyn is captured, tried, condemned to death for treason and executed by General Smuts' commando near Aties.
	International	General Ben Viljoen arrives as a prisoner of war at St Helena on board the *Britannic*.

THE PRISONER OF WAR CAMPS

About 27 000 Boer prisoners of war are in British hands at the end of the war of whom about 24 000 are deported to camps that have been established in several isolated parts of the British Empire. Separate camps have been formed for 'irreconcilables' or 'undesirables' and for prisoners who have taken the oath of allegiance.

South Africa: Tin Town (Ladysmith), Bellevue (Simon's Town), Green Point (Cape Town), Umbilo (Durban). Several anchored ships are also used as temporary prisons.

Bermuda: Burt's and Hawkin's Islands (penal camps and Cape rebels), Darrel's Island, Hinson's Island (children), Port's Island (hospital camp), Tucker's Island (oath takers), Morgan's Island and Long Island.

St Helena: Broadbottom, Deadwood No 1, Deadwood No 2 (oath takers), Fort High Knoll (penal camp), Jamestown (parole camp) and a RAMC hospital camp.

Ceylon: Diyatalawa, Ragama (penal camp), Mount Lavinia (sanatorium), Hambantota and Urugasmanhandiya (oath takers).

India: Abbottabad, Ahmednagar, Amritsar (Fort Govindgarh penal camp), Bellary, Bhim Tal, Dagshai (parole camp), Kaity-Nilgiris, Kakool, Muree Hills, Satara (parole camp), Shahjahanpur, Sialkot, Solon, Trichinopoly, Umballa, Upper Topa and Wellington.

Of the 577 burghers who died as prisoners of war, 77 died on board ship, 171 on St Helena, 156 on Ceylon, 31 on Bermuda and 142 in India.[94]

Day 869 Wed **1902-02-26**	Western ZAR	Colonel Kekewich, with about 1 500 men, rushes from Hartbeesfontein towards Wolmaransstad to cut off De la Rey's retreat but he is too late and De la Rey disappears.
	OFS	The drive in the eastern Free State ends on the Elands River Bridge/Van Reenen's Pass line, heavily reinforced for this purpose. De Wet and some 600 burghers escape again but he suffers serious losses with about 50 killed and 778 captured along with 25 000 head of cattle and 200 vehicles. This is the biggest haul of captured burghers since Prinsloo's surrender in the

	Bermuda	Brandwater Basin and includes Commandant Jan Meyer and 571 members of the Harrismith commando, who are captured near Tandjiesberg.[95] A 16-year-old prisoner of war, FH Bosch, is fatally wounded while 'trying to escape' on Tucker's Island, Bermuda.[96]
Day 870 Thu **1902-02-27**	ZAR	**MORANT AND HANDCOCK ARE EXECUTED** The death sentences of Lieutenants Morant and Handcock of the Bushveld Carbineers found guilty of various atrocities, including the murder of unarmed prisoners of war and civilians, are carried out by firing squad in the old prison in Pretoria.[97] On the same day both the oldest and youngest prisoners of war to be deported, are captured at Dwaalspruit. They are Gideon J van Zyl of Vrede, 78 years old, and Johannes van Heerden of Heidelberg, only seven years old.[98]
	Trivia	*JNH Grobler's 38th birthday (Commandant of Ermelo).* *US novelist John Steinbeck is born.*
Day 871 Fri **1902-02-28**	Eastern ZAR	The ZAR government is at Zwartfontein, south-west of Groblersdal.[99]
	OFFICIAL REPORTS	
	Gold mining:	On the Witwatersrand 1 540 or 25,7% of the gold stamps are back in production and the monthly gold production is 81 000 ounces or about 27% of peak pre-war production.[100]
	Concentration camps:	The officially reported camp population of the white camps is 114 311 and the monthly deaths for February are 682
	Black involvement:	The population in the black camps is 101 344 and 1 466 deaths are recorded.[101]
	Farm burning:	British columns have completely or partially destroyed 85 farms.[102]
	Blockhouse lines:	The following blockhouse lines have been completed: OFS — Between Lindley and Bethlehem (60 km), Lace Mine and the confluence of the Vals and Vaal Rivers (47 blockhouses about 1 450 m apart, covering about 60 km) and between Thaba Nchu and the Basutoland border (37 blockhouses covering about 67 km). ZAR — Between Lichtenburg and Ventersdorp (60 km), Tafelkop to Naauwpoort, south of Rustenburg (60 km), between Volksrust and Wakkerstroom (25 km) and between Ermelo and Carolina (55 km).[103] Only a single interruption of railway traffic is officially reported for February.[104]
1902	AUTUMN	**MARCH**
Day 872 Sat **1902-03-01**	ZAR	General Kemp and Commandant Wolmarans liberate a women's laager captured by the British.
	Eastern ZAR	The ZAR government is at Stroomwater, west of the present-day Loskop Dam.[105]
	Natal	The Natal territory is enlarged by the addition of the Utrecht, Vryheid and part of the Wakkerstroom districts.[106]
Day 873 Sun **1902-03-01**	Western ZAR	Lord Methuen marches from Vryburg with a motley column consisting of whatever troops he can scrape together in that area. His force of about 1 500

		men is scraped together from 14 units and include irregular Colonial levies, fresh Yeomanry drafts, an armed Coloured Cape Special Police unit and a few National Scouts. Only 800 are mounted men and they are accompanied by four guns, two pom-poms and 85 wagons — hardly a 'flying column'. At the same time, part of Kekewich's flying column, 1 500 men under Colonel Grenfell, set out from Klerksdorp to rendezvous with Methuen at Rooirandjesfontein, about 27 kilometres south of Lichtenburg. Methuen, keen to avenge his defeat at Ysterspruit, plans not only to block De la Rey's northward movement, but to force him back towards the Vaal River, into the arms of a third force, that of Colonel Rochford who have occupied Wolmaransstad.[107]
	International	The oldest deported Republican burgher to die in an overseas prisoner-of-war camp, 74-year-old Arnoldus Mauritz Meiring, of Parys near Heilbron, dies of bronchitis on St Helena.[108]
Day 874 Mon **1902-03-03**	OFS	The Orange River Colony Volunteers, a unit consisting of burghers who surrendered, is formed with ex-General Piet de Wet as commanding officer. This unit is never to have more than 448 members.[109]
Day 875 Tue **1902-03-04**	United Kingdom Concentration camps	**THE FAWCETT REPORT** The long-awaited report of the Ladies or Fawcett Commission Report on the concentration camps is discussed in the House of Commons. They conclude that there are three causes of the high death rate: *"1. The insanitary condition of the country caused by the war.* *2. Causes within the control of the inmates.* *3. Causes within the control of the administration."*[110] The Opposition tables the following motion: *"This House deplores the great mortality in the concentration camps formed in the execution of the policy of clearing the country."* Chamberlain replies: *"The camps were not formed in the execution of the policy of clearing the country... it was* (the Boers) *who forced us upon this terrible alternative. We had to take care of them and there was absolutely no other way than to bring them into camp... if Gen Botha would allow them to observe the oath of neutrality... Botha refused that offer. Kitchener... offered... that if the Boers would take the charge of their women and children, they were all at liberty to leave the camps, and would be delivered at any point appointed. You may take what view you please of that action. Some people say it was admirable and heroic. Others say it was cruel and selfish; but never before has one belligerent Power endeavoured to bring another belligerent Power to submission by refusing to allow exit of the women and children from a besieged city but never before has one belligerent tried to work on the feelings of the other by exposing its own women and children to death and famine, to suffering and disease. They* (the Boers) *it was who forced us upon this terrible alternative and forced us to make provisions suddenly for this immense additions to the burdens of the country. Now let me say that never in the whole history of the world as far as we know it, have there been such gigantic efforts made by any nation to minimise the horrors of war."* When brought to the vote, the Opposition motion is defeated by 230 votes against 119.[111]
	Trivia	*The American Automobile Association is founded.*
Day 876 Wed **1902-03-05**	Western ZAR	Lord Methuen's scratch force is at Baberspan, still about 55 kilometres from his proposed rendezvous with Grenfell at Rooirandjesfontein.[112]
	OFS	President Steyn and Chief Commandant De Wet leave the north-eastern Free State to meet with General De la Rey.

	Trivia	*French miners strike, calling for an eight-hour working day.*
Day 877 Thu **1902-03-06**  *'Siener' van Rensburg* (War Museum of the Boer Republics)	Western ZAR	Lord Methuen crosses the Great Harts River at its confluence with the Klein Harts. Part of De la Rey's force, General Van Zijl's Griqualand West rebels, skirmishes with Methuen's rearguard, causing a near panic among the inexperienced Yeomanry and Colonials. Methuen decides to camp at Tweebosch.[113] The Cape Police contingent terrorises the women, loots the house, destroys the orchard and prepares to burn the farmhouse until Methuen personally intervenes to prevent it. The clairvoyant 'Siener' van Rensburg tells General de la Rey of his vision: A furious red bull charges down a hill, but the closer he comes, the more his head sags and his horns droop. At last, the bull turns back with broken horns and limps with a broken foreleg.[114]
	South-western ZAR	The ZAR government leaves Stroomwater.[115]
Day 878 Fri **1902-03-07**  *Lord Methuen* (War Museum of the Boer Republics)	Western ZAR	**THE BATTLE OF TWEEBOSCH OR DE KLIPDRIFT** (near Sannieshof) Lord Methuen divides his force into three columns. At 03:00, the ox-wagon convoy starts off, escorted by the Cape Police, two companies of Yeomanry, 300 infantrymen of the Northumberland Fusiliers and the North Lancashire Regiment and Lieutenant Venning's guns. The main column starts an hour later, escorted by the Coloured men of the Cape Special Police, Ashburner's Light Horse with two pom-poms and with Dennison's Scouts; the Diamond Fields Horse and Lieutenant Nesham's guns form the rearguard. At 05:00, when the vanguard reaches De Klipdrift on the Great Harts River, General Van Zijl's burghers open fire on the rearguard. Nesham's guns and one of the pom-poms wheel round and open fire but the rest of the rearguard panics. Half an hour later, the ox wagons are ordered to halt and at 06:00, General De la Rey, supported by the burghers of Celliers and Wolmarans, starts his main strike against Methuen's right. In three or more consecutive, well-extended lines, the burghers bear down on the entire length of the column from the south or right rear. The leading lines charge to within accurate rifle range, dismount and pour a deadly fire into the strung-out British force. The rear line of burghers remains mounted and, firing from the saddle, they charge past their dismounted comrades, through the demoralised British infantry, attacking the mounted troops before they can either rally or escape across the river. The only serious resistance comes from Nesham's gunners who put up a stern fight until the mule teams pulling the ammunition wagons and the gun crews are shot down. Lieutenant Nesham refuses offers to surrender and is shot down. Elsewhere, Lieutenant Venning's battery suffers the same fate until he falls, mortally wounded. At 09:30 Lord Methuen is hit in the thigh. He dismounts, his horse is hit and falls on him, breaking his leg. Colonel Townsend, his medical officer, splints his leg and is also hit. General Kemp, tasked with executing a right hook to cut off the fleeing enemy at the river, is outstripped by the rapidly fleeing troops. A small group returns fire from a stone kraal until Republican gunners open up with the Armstrongs captured at Ysterspruit. At 10:00 the battle is over. The British lose 68 killed, 121 wounded and 872 taken prisoner (including Lord Methuen and the other wounded). De la Rey loses eight killed, including his adjutant, and 26 wounded. A dark blot mars De la Rey's brilliant victory when 11 of the armed black prisoners responsible for misconduct at the farmhouse are taken to the neighbouring farm Gunsteling, forced to dig a mass grave, blindfolded and summarily executed.[116]

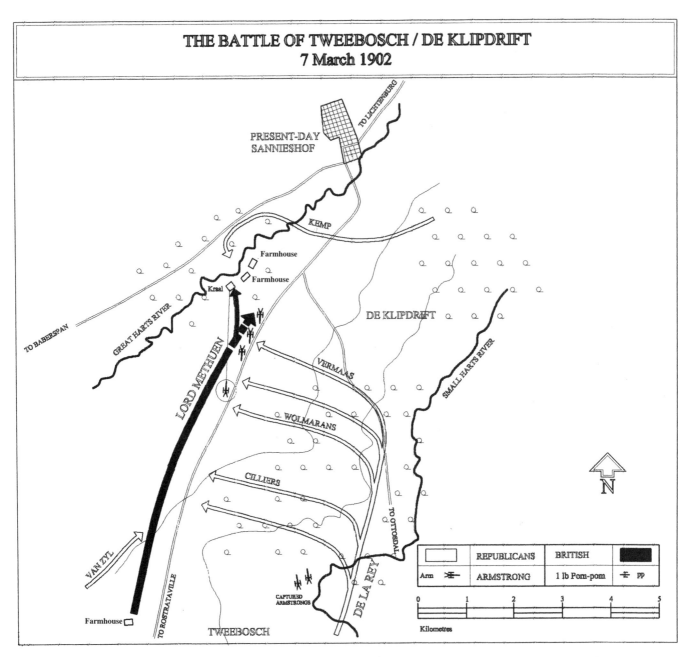

	Cape Colony	Commandant PH Kritzinger's trial begins at Graaff-Reinet. He is charged with four counts of murder involving the deaths of six blacks on various dates and at various localities.[117]
Day 879 Sat 1902-03-08	Western ZAR	Amid protests from several of his men, General De la Rey magnanimously decides to release Lord Methuen as soon as his wounds have been treated. De la Rey also arranges that a telegram be sent to Lady Methuen, expressing his concern about her husband's condition. After being served a fried chicken dish prepared by Mrs Nonnie de la Rey, Lord Methuen, attended by a doctor and a few others, is sent to Klerksdorp. Soon after their departure De la Rey is forced by a majority decision to reverse his instructions, and messengers overtake Methuen's party at Oorbietjesfontein, about 29 kilometres from Klerksdorp. They are taken to Gestoptefontein. Lord Kitchener collapses after receiving the news about Lord Methuen. He refuses food for 36 hours, allowing only his ADC, the young Captain Frank Maxwell, to comfort him.[118]

Day 880 Sun 1902-03-09	Western ZAR	At a meeting De la Rey convinces the burghers that it will be in the best interest of their cause to release Lord Methuen, and he is again allowed to proceed to Klerksdorp. Later Methuen orders the spring wagon in which he has been transported to be returned to De la Rey, loaded with foodstuffs and a new rifle to replace the one used as a splint to set his leg.[119]
Day 881 Mon 1902-03-10	Cape Colony	Commandant Rudolph of General Malan's commando is seriously wounded in a skirmish near Richmond and has to be left behind.[120]
	North-eastern OFS	A drive in the north-eastern Free State ends on the Kroonstad/Wolwehoek/Lindley line and yields only about 100 prisoners. Commandant FE Mentz's commando is unscathed as it crosses between two blockhouses, destroying the barbed-wire entanglements.[121]
Day 882 Tue 1902-03-11	Cape Colony	General Wynand Malan appoints the 25-year-old Carel van Heerden in Rudolph's position.[122]
	Eastern ZAR	The ZAR government is at Witnek, east of Rust de Winter.[123]
Day 883 Wed 1902-03-12		
Day 884 Thu 1902-03-13	*Trivia*	*HCO Plumer's 45th birthday.*
Day 885 Fri 1902-03-14	Eastern ZAR	The ZAR government returns to Witnek.[124]
Day 886 Sat 1902-03-15	Natal	General Cheere Emmett, Commandant-General Louis Botha's brother-in-law, is captured by General Bruce Hamilton near Vryheid.
	Western ZAR	President Steyn and Chief Commandant De Wet enter the Transvaal near Commando Drift, south-east of Makwassie.
Day 887 Sun 1902-03-16		
Day 888 Mon 1902-03-17	Western ZAR	President Steyn and Chief Commandant De Wet arrive at General De la Rey's laager at Zendelingsfontein between Klerksdorp and Wolmaransstad. President Steyn has his eyes examined by De la Rey's physician, Dr J von Rennenkampf, but his treatment seems to be ineffective.[125]
Day 889 Tue 1902-03-18		
Day 890 Wed 1902-03-19	ZAR	Sir J Maxwell relinquishes the military governorship of Pretoria.
Day 891 Thu 1902-03-20	United Kingdom Black involvement	In the House of Commons David Lloyd George suggests that there are as many as 30 000 armed blacks in British military employ in South Africa.
	Northern ZAR	General CF Beyers besieges a British force of about 550 men at Fort Hendrina.[126]
	North-eastern OFS	The Fourth 'New Model Drive' in the Free State starts in the area between the Heilbron/Frankfort/Botha's Pass-line and the Lindley/Bethlehem/Harrismith line, moving from west to east.[127] The columns of Rimington, Nixon, Garratt, Elliot and Barker participate — about 14 000 men.

Day 892 Fri **1902-03-21**	Eastern ZAR	The ZAR government leaves Witnek and, without prior consultation with their ally, requests a safe conduct from the British to confer with the Free State government.
Day 893 Sat **1902-03-22**	Eastern ZAR	The ZAR government enters the British lines at Balmoral en route to the peace talks.
	United Kingdom	Lady Methuen, having received De la Rey's telegram while still on board, arrives at Southampton and immediately boards another ship to return to South Africa.[128]
Day 894 Sun **1902-03-23**	ZAR	The ZAR government arrives in Pretoria on its way to Kroonstad to consult with Free State leaders. Commandant MW Myburgh is appointed as general commanding the Utrecht and Vryheid commandos, succeeding the recently captured General Cheere Emmet.[129]
	Western ZAR	Siener van Rensburg has a vision of the veld covered by thousands of meerkats wearing leggings. He urges De la Rey to move his camp from Doornbult.[130]
	North-eastern OFS	The fourth Free State drive reaches Liebenbergsvlei. There are no captures worth mentioning, but Nixon discovers three Krupp guns sunk in the Renoster River.
	Natal Black Involvement	General Bruce Hamilton orders King Dinizulu with a Zulu army of 250 warriors to accompany him on a sortie into the Vryheid district to loot Boer cattle. A local chief Sikhobobo joins his march.
	India	Prisoner of war W Hoffman is shot and killed while trying to escape from a hospital at Bellary, India.[131]
	Trivia	*Lord Alfred Milner's 48th birthday.*
Day 895 Mon **1902-03-24** *Pres. MT Steyn* (*War Museum of the Boer Republics*)	Western ZAR	The British concentrate about 16 000 troops, divided into 15 columns, for a one-day 'umbrella-like' drive against De la Rey's commandos. Rushing out from Klerksdorp in a rapid straight march without transport or field-guns, the columns spread out at the ordered position, wheel round and sweep back in extended order. General De la Rey, with President Steyn in his care, slips out of the net easily. When the columns of Walter Kitchener pass within earshot of his laager, General Kemp saddles up and follows them. He watches them deploy and then slips around their flank. General Liebenberg has a much closer shave. His commando is spotted early in the morning and a determined chase ensues. He is forced to abandon his wagons and field-guns at Buisfontein, north-east of Hartbeesfontein. The tired British encamp for the night and gaps form in the drive line. In drenching rain Liebenberg's tired men slip through near Renosterberghoek, south of Hartbeesfontein.[132]
	North-eastern OFS	A part of the huge army executing the drive loses their way in a driving storm and they arrive at the junction of the Wilge River and the Holspruit to find themselves completely cut off behind impassable fords.
	Concentration camps	Mr HR Fox Bourne, Secretary of the Aborigines Protection Society, after being made aware by Emily Hobhouse of the fact that the Fawcett Commis-

	Black involvement	sion ignored the plight of blacks in the concentration camps, writes to Chamberlain. He requests that such inquiries should be instituted by the British government *"as should secure for the natives who are detained no less care and humanity than are now prescribed for the Boer refugees"*. On this request Sir Montagu Ommaney, the permanent Under-Secretary at the Colonial Office, is later to record that it seems undesirable *"to trouble Lord Milner... merely to satisfy this busybody"*.[133]
Day 896 Tue 1902-03-25	Western ZAR	The one-day drive results in eight burghers killed and 165 taken prisoner. Three British field-guns, two pom-poms, about 100 wagons and carts, including those abandoned by General Liebenberg, fall into British hands, as well as 1 700 horses and cattle.[134]
Day 897 Wed 1902-03-26	Cape Colony	**CJ RHODES DIES** Mr Cecil John Rhodes (49) dies in his cottage at Muizenberg where he has been cared for by his faithful friend, Dr Jameson. His last words are reputed to be, *"So little done, so much to do."* One of the richest and most powerful men in the world, his personal estate is to exceed £4 000 000 by a handsome margin.
	ZAR/Natal Black involvement	The cattle looting expedition commanded by General Bruce Hamilton, King Dinizulu and Chief Sikhobobo, arrives back in Vryheid. Two Boers have been killed, one taken prisoner and thousands of Boer cattle have been looted. The King and his army are ordered to return to the royal kraal with 100 mangy cattle as a gift. Chief Sikhobobo and his impi remain at the Vryheid railway station for fear of Boer reprisals.
	North-eastern OFS	Almost the entire army participating in the eastern Free State drive, except Gordon's column, is cut off without supplies by the swollen rivers.
	Trivia	*CC Froneman's 56th birthday.*
Day 898 Thu 1902-03-27	Cape Colony	'Long Cecil', the gun manufactured in Kimberley during the siege, is sent to Cape Town to serve as the gun carriage in Rhodes' funeral procession to the Cape Town railway station and again from the Bulawayo station to Rhodes' final resting place in the Matopo Hills. For this part of the journey it is pulled at first by mules and for the final stage by twelve gleaming black oxen.[135]
	Western ZAR	President Steyn, while in General De la Rey's operational area near Roodewal, receives a letter from Acting State President SW Burger at Kroonstad: *"I include copies of correspondence between ourselves and Lord Kitchener the result of which the Executive Council and I have travelled here to meet Your Excellency.* *"We understand that lord Kitchener has sent, or intend to send the same to Your Excellency but do not know your present whereabouts... I thus also include a copy of His Excellency's letter addressed to Your Excellency.* *"We will remain here until we receive notice of a time and place at which we can meet with Your Excellency..."*[136] The furious President Steyn is thus confronted with proposed negotiations already a *fait accompli*, and to maintain Republican unanimity in the face of the enemy, he is obliged to support the ZAR government's actions. Major-General Walter Kitchener, having concentrated about 16 000 troops

		in the central part of the western ZAR, confers with his group commanders at Klerksdorp. Leaving Rochfort on the Vaal River, it is decided that Kekewich is to move to Middelbult, Kitchener to Driekuil and Rawlinson to Renosterspruit. Entrenched camps are to be formed at these locations from where patrols are to be sent to seek contact with the enemy.[137]
Day 899 Fri **1902-03-28**	Western ZAR Northern ZAR	GOOD FRIDAY Kekewich leaves Vaalbank and marches to Middelbult, south of Gerdau, between Sannieshof and Coligny. Colonel JW Collenbrander, with a strong force from Pietersburg, forces General Beyers to abandon his siege of Fort Hendrina and retreat.[138]
Day 900 Sat **1902-03-29**	Western ZAR United Kingdom	General Walter Kitchener leaves Klerksdorp and marches via Rietvlei towards Driekuil. Lord Salisbury tells Chamberlain that Sir Michael Hicks Beach, the Chancellor of the Exchequer, has asked that, if any peace proposals are received, the Cabinet should be summoned to consider them *"at whatever inconvenience"*, before a reply is sent. His uneasiness about the cost of continuing the war is compounded by the King, who *"talks at length of the war emulating the Thirty Years' War in Germany"*. Chamberlain resents this interference: *"... the King with his Coronation* (postponed until the end of hostilities) *and Beach with his Budget are both too eager for Peace of a sort. I have spoken several times to the King and thought each time that I had satisfied him that while we were all most anxious to finish the war, nothing would be more dangerous for the country and for his own popularity than that any responsible person should appear ready to sacrifice essential points and show weakness at this stage.* *"I have an idea that the Rosebery clique and perhaps Rosebery himself have been assuring him that an honourable peace was possible if only we were rid of Milner — and perhaps — of the Colonial Secretary."*[139]
Day 901 Sun **1902-03-30**	Western ZAR Eastern ZAR	EASTER SUNDAY General Walter Kitchener splits his force at Rietvlei, sending Lowe ahead to Driekuil to start preparing their entrenched camp. He orders Cookson and Keir to reconnoitre westwards along the Brakspruit.[140] A serious railway accident near Barberton causes loss of life amongst members of the 2nd Hampshire Regiment.
Day 902 Mon **1902-03-31**	Western ZAR	EASTER MONDAY **THE BATTLE OF BOSCHBULT** (27 kilometres from Ottosdal on the Delareyville road) The two British columns, about 1 800 men strong with four field-guns, under Lieutenant-Colonels Cookson and Keir, with Cookson in command, leaves camp at 02:00. They move along the Brakspruit with Damant's Horse and the Canadian Mounted Rifles leading. At about 10:00, they pick up the tracks of a party of horsemen and Damant's Horse follow at a stiff pace towards Boschbult with the Canadians waiting for the transport. Suddenly their quarry who has reached support, turns round and the British draw fire from the front, as well as from both sides of the spruit. Cookson immediately orders his force to form camp at Boschbult's two homesteads, on the bank of the Brakspruit. The British dig in and form a screen of mounted men in a semicircle towards the north. General De la Rey's men are encamped at Roodewal, the neighbouring farm. The burghers, commanded by Generals Liebenberg, Kemp, Du Toit and Celliers, are quickly reinforced to a strength of about 2 000. At 13:30,

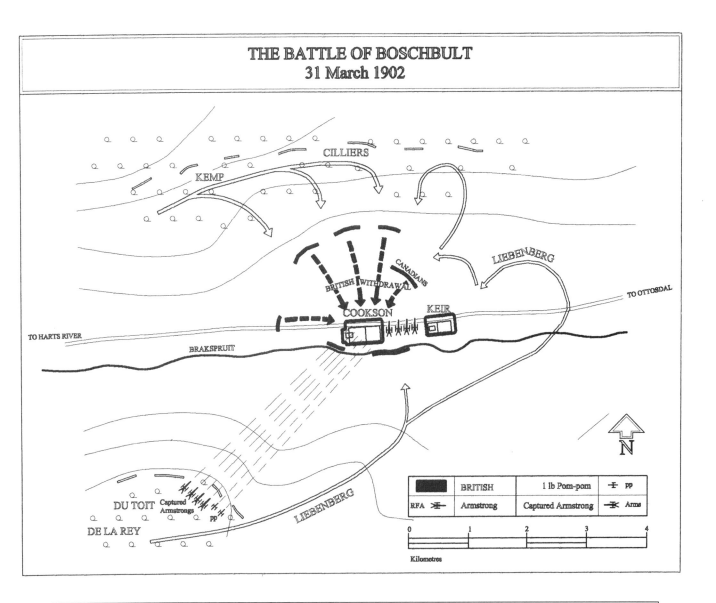

Kemp and Celliers' horsemen emerge from the thicket on the north bank and advance at a walking pace in an extended line. At the same time their artillery, four field-guns and a pom-pom, open up from a scrub-covered rise to the south-west. They immediately score hits on the concentrated target around the farmhouses, while the British artillery make no impression on the thin line of advancing horsemen. The mule drivers panic and in their attempts to get away, the mules stampede, causing confusion in the camp and upsetting part of Cookson's mounted screen. Trying to exploit the disarray on the eastern side, Liebenberg, galloping from the Republican field-guns, crosses the spruit upstream of the British position, swings left and launches a spirited attack from the north-east. He is repulsed and falls back northwards to join Kemp and Celliers' line. At about 15:30 Cookson orders his screens to fall back on the main position which has been completely fortified. Their retreat signals a general Republican charge in all sectors, but the British resist furiously from their strengthened positions. General De la Rey arrives late on the battlefield and assesses the situation. Convinced that little can be gained by further charges, he calls off the attack at 17:00 and the burghers disappear. Kitchener sends Lowe's column from Driekuil, but they meet bewildered fleeing stragglers and mule drivers and when

		they hear the firing diminishing, they are convinced that Cookson has been overrun and they return to their camp. The British lose 27 killed, about 70 wounded, 100 taken prisoner and about 400 horses and mules killed, while the Republicans suffer six killed and about 15 wounded.[141]
	OFFICIAL REPORTS **Gold mining:** **Blockhouse lines:** **Farm burning:** **Concentration camps:** **Black involvement:**	On the Witwatersrand 1 760 or 29,3 % of the gold stamps are back in production and the monthly gold production is 104 000 ounces or about 34,6% of peak pre-war production.[142] The following blockhouse lines have been completed: ZAR — Between Mafeking and Lichtenburg (65 km) 400 blockhouses have been erected within six weeks. OFS — A blockhouse branch line between the Bloemfontein/Basutoland line and Ladybrand (30 km).[143] British columns have partially or completely destroyed 52 farms.[144] The officially reported camp population of the white camps is 114 508 and the deaths for March are 402. The population of the black camps is 101 299 and 972 deaths are recorded.[145]
1902	AUTUMN	**APRIL**
Day 903 Tue **1902-04-01**	ZAR	**THE FIGHT AT BOSCHMAN'S KOP** Colonel RT Lawley and Lieutenant-Colonel HD Fanshawe with 312 of the Queen's Bays, guided by 40 National Scouts, attempt a night raid on the commandos of Generals Piet Viljoen and JJ Alberts at Boschman's Kop, about 29 kilometres south-east of Springs in the Johannesburg/Pretoria 'protected zone'. The Scouts are able to lead the attackers past the pickets and the Republicans are surprised, but they recover quickly and about 100 launch a mounted charge at the attackers, firing from the saddle. The British suffer 77 casualties including one National Scout while the Republicans lose about 33 men, mostly wounded.[146]
	Western ZAR	A mounted force of about 1 000 relieves Colonel Cookson at Boschbult and escorts the battered unit back to General Walter Kitchener's base at Driekuil.[147] Colonel Kekewich, assisted by Woolls-Sampson's scouts, executes a raid towards the confluence of the Great and Little Harts Rivers, near Barberspan. They arrive empty-handed and return to Middelbult.
	Cape Colony	**THE ATTACK ON SPRINGBOK** At about 01:00, Generals SG Maritz, Van Deventer and BD Bouwer attack the forts at Springbok (then Springbokfontein). Van Deventer takes one blockhouse at about 07:00, Maritz another at about 08:00, but the third bravely holds out.[148]
Day 904 Wed **1902-04-02**	Cape Colony	At 02:00 the last fort at Springbok capitulates due to lack of water and the obvious futility of continuing resistance. The defenders lose their commander, Lieutenant RJ Steward, and another volunteer killed while two are wounded. The attackers suffer light casualties with maybe three wounded.[149]
	North-eastern OFS	Commandant Manie Botha breaks through the drive line by evading White's New Zealanders in the ravines of the Wilge River.
	International	The youngest deported Republican to die in overseas prisoner-of-war

316

		camps, David Matthys Jacobs, eight years old, of Schoongesicht, Vrede, dies of measles in Bellary Camp in India.[150]
Day 905 Thu 1902-04-03	Cape Colony	Generals Smuts, Van Deventer and Bouwer find the village of Nababeep deserted. General Van Deventer stays behind, occupying the town.[151]
	Trivia	*JBM Hertzog's 36th birthday.*
Day 906 Fri 1902-04-04	Cape Colony	About 10 kilometres north-east of Okiep, Generals Smuts, Maritz, Bouwer and 25 burghers reconnoitre the village of Concordia from a nearby koppie. On an impulse General Smuts sends a burgher under a flag of truce to demand the surrender of the town. To their surprise he returns with a letter expressing their willingness to comply, on condition that private property will be respected and that the mines will not be interfered with. Smuts accepts and the 250-man garrison lay down their arms. [152] Kitchener's Director of Military Intelligence reports, *"The surrender of Concordia strikes me as being the most disgraceful affair of the war."*[153] **THE SIEGE OF OKIEP** General Smuts demands the surrender of Okiep, but is curtly rejected by Colonel WAD Shelton, the Commandant of British forces in Namaqualand. Smuts surrounds the town and the siege of Okiep begins.[154] Okiep's defences consist of 15 strong blockhouses, skilfully positioned around the eight-kilometre-long perimeter. The defenders consist of 44 men of the Warwickshire Militia, 12 of the Cape Garrison Artillery, 206 white miners and 661 Coloureds — a total of 923 men with a 9-pounder gun and a machine gun.[155]
	International	Commandant FS Alleman and ex-Mining Commissioner JL van der Merwe visit President Kruger in Utrecht, the Netherlands. At the end of 1901 they have been sent via German South West Africa to report to the President about the situation in South Africa.[156]
Day 907 Sat 1902-04-05	Western ZAR	President Steyn agrees to meet the ZAR government at Klerksdorp. He receives a safe conduct pass from Lord Kitchener, allowing himself and members of the Free State government to travel there.[157]
	OFS	The fourth drive in the north-eastern Free State ends against the Drakensberg foothills with 86 burghers killed or captured and huge herds of livestock taken.[158]
Day 908 Sun 1902-04-06	Western ZAR	Colonels Kekewich and Rawlinson, acting on information supplied by Woolls-Sampson's scouts, carry out a night raid towards Baberspan. The information turns out to be false and they again return to Middelbult.
	Cape Colony	Commandant PH Kritzinger is acquitted on all charges of murder and is made a prisoner of war.[159]
Day 909 Mon 1902-04-07	Western ZAR	Lieutenant-General Sir Ian Hamilton, Lord Kitchener's Chief of Staff, arrives at Klerksdorp to take command of the operations against De la Rey. President Steyn, accompanied by members of his government and General De la Rey, leaves the farm Weltevreden on their way to Klerksdorp.[160] General De la Rey leaves General JCG Kemp in command of the Western Transvaal commandos with a final warning to avoid contact with the enemy, if possible.[161]

Day 910 Tue **1902-04-08**	Western ZAR	Lieutenant-General Hamilton arrives at Walter Kitchener's camp at Drie-kuil, between Ottosdal and Delareyville. Rawlinson urges Hamilton to use the opportunity offered by De la Rey and Steyn's absence, calling it a *"good time to smash up their subordinates"*. Hamilton agrees, writing to Churchill, *"Once more all my fortunes on the die!"*[162]
	Northern ZAR	Colonel JW Colenbrander, a mercenary known as 'the White Scourge', commanding Kitchener's Fighting Scouts, attacks General Beyers from three sides in Malepspoort near Pietersburg. General Beyers is wounded in the leg and Mauritz Dommisse and Hendrik Mentz take over command.
	Eastern ZAR Black involvement	Commandant Groenewald is killed by black tribesmen while trying to obtain grain sorghum for his men.[163]
	OFS	At the Hartenbosch farms near Bultfontein, General CCJ Badenhorst captures a detachment of 200 men sent out against him by Colonel Ternan.[164] Two blockhouses at Steenkampskop near Fouriesburg are captured, 150 metres of barbed-wire entanglement are removed and 21 guards are captured or wounded.[165]

Day 911 Wed
1902-04-09
	Peace talks
	Western ZAR
		THE KLERKSDORP CONFERENCE
		The Republican governments meet at Klerksdorp to discuss the correspondence between the Netherlands and the United Kingdom and the possibility of peace negotiations.
		The two delegations are made up as follows:
		
		The ZAR delegation: The OFS delegation:
		  Acting State President SW Burger President MT Steyn
		  State Secretary FW Reitz Acting State Secretary
		  Commandant-General L Botha WJC Brebner,
		  General JH de la Rey Chief Commandant CR de Wet,
		  Ex-General LJ Meyer General CH Olivier
		  D van Velden (secretary) Judge (Gen) JBM Hertzog
		  N de Wet Reverend JD Kestell (secretary)
		  GC Krogh BJ du Plessis
		  L Jacobsz
		  J Ferreira[166]
		The residential arrangements are such that the Free State delegation is billeted in the old town, while the ZAR delegation resides in the new town. They only meet during actual negotiations in the 'tent of assembly', pitched for this purpose on the banks of the Schoonspruit running through the town.[167]
		Colonel Kekewich marches to Noodshulp, on the Little Harts River, and Rawlinson to Driekuil, where he meets Lieutenant-General Ian Hamilton.

	Northern ZAR	Colonel JW Colenbrander forces Commandant Mentz to retreat with 20 killed and wounded and 108 taken prisoner.[168]
	Cape Colony	**Okiep siege:** The besiegers attack forts around Okiep, but are repulsed. General Ben Bouwer receives a head wound.[169]
	United Kingdom	Colonial Secretary Chamberlain sends a cable to Lord Milner: *"Although I am firmly convinced that we must fight this business out to a finish, I am disappointed that the results have not been conclusive and more quickly attained ... Personally I believe, as I always have done, that anything short of unconditional surrender will be most dangerous and may lead to further trouble; but this is not the opinion of everyone, and unless the issue was clear and supported by strong argument, we could be seriously attacked if we allow the negotiations to go off*

		on what could with any show of reason be alleged to be insufficient cause." Referring to Methuen's defeat, he writes: *"We are to a certain extent discredited abroad by these constant failures, and the pressure both financial and otherwise in consequence of the prolongation of the struggle is very great. I suppose no civilian can understand why 200 000 men and a million and a half a week are required to put an end to the resistance of 8 000 farmers who probably do not possess £10 apiece."*[170]
	Trivia	*Emily Hobhouse's 42nd birthday.*
Day 912 Thu **1902-04-10**	Western ZAR	Lieutenant-General Ian Hamilton, commanding about 11 000 men, plans a semi-circular drive, sweeping south along the Harts River and then along the Vaal towards Klerksdorp. Kekewich's columns (under Von Donop, himself and Grenfell) are to form the right with Rawlinson in the centre and W Kitchener on the left. Deviating from the normal procedures for 'new model drives', Hamilton orders the columns to march in close order. Rawlinson deploys his line between Oshoek and Doornpan with W Kitchener from there to Klipdrift, south of Ottosdal. Kekewich, however, does not receive a crucial message and while his other columns proceed, he arrives at Bospan, in Rawlinson's rear, leaving a gap between Von Donop and Grenfell. He realises the mistake and marches west towards Roodewal in an attempt to get closer to his correct position and close the gap on the right. General Kemp, in command of the commandos of Lemmer, Du Toit, Liebenberg, Celliers and Potgieter, has about 2 600 burghers at his disposal. During the afternoon he orders a demonstration against the left of the British line, hoping to draw troops away from the Roodewal gap where he plans to attack. The demonstration is too transparent and fails to impress Hamilton sufficiently to change the disposition of his forces.[171]
	Cape Colony	**Okiep siege:** The attacks on the Okiep forts are resumed, this time by throwing home-made dynamite bombs at them, but still without success.[172]
Day 913 Fri **1902-04-11**	Western ZAR	**THE BATTLE OF ROODEWAL** During the night Grenfell becomes aware of the gap between himself and Von Donop and just after midnight he moves west to close it up. About five kilometres south-west of Kekewich's columns, in a slight fold in the ground, General Kemp forms up his commandos. For once Boer scouting is deficient and Kemp's plans are based on the British positions as they have been before dark the previous evening. A line of about 800 burghers is formed with General Liebenberg on the right, Commandant Potgieter in the centre and General Celliers on the left. Another 500 men under Generals Lemmer and Du Toit gather on the extreme left flank, beyond the Brak River, ready to move around Von Donop's front. At about 07:00 Kekewich's columns continue their westward movement with Von Donop's mounted men leading. Although the order is rearranged, Kekewich's columns, still marching in close order, have re-established contact with each other and the opportunity that Kemp has gambled on, has passed. Soon after starting out Von Donop's screen notices a strong mounted force on the left horizon, moving parallel to them at a leisurely pace. They assume it to be part of Rawlinson's screen and do not find anything unusual as the horsemen approach closer at a steady pace, now forming three or four files seemingly stretching from horizon to horizon. At about 07:15 the approaching riders stop about 600 metres away and seem to dress their line before proceeding through a maize field at a steady trot. Von Donop sends about 60 mounted infantrymen

THE BATTLE OF ROODEWAL
11 April 1902

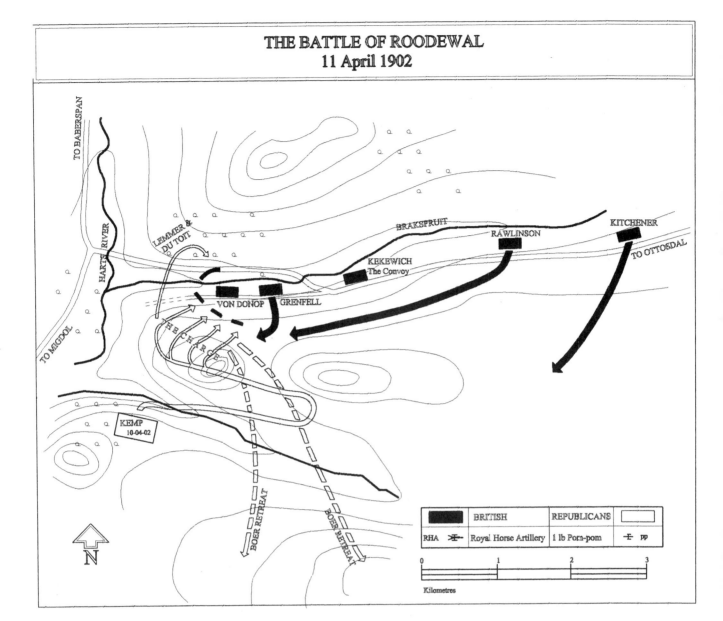

with a pom-pom to reinforce the left flank of his advance screen. When they suddenly draw fire from the approaching horsemen, they panic and fall back all the way to Grenfell's column who is just coming into view over a slight rise some kilometres to the rear. Kemp's view is obstructed by the tall maize plants and he does not realise that he is attacking a force four times his number. His line has also approached too close to the British to be recalled. His only option now is to launch a bold attack on Von Donop before the British can recover from the initial surprise. The burghers charge, firing from the saddle. Von Donop's screen falls back in panic and flees through Grenfell's own screen. An officer rushes back, shouting, *"They are Boers, all those men are Boers!"* Grenfell quickly deploys his field-guns and they open fire at a range of 1 000 metres. He also sends men forward to support Von Donop, who is now also attacked in the front by Lemmer and Du Toit's men sweeping across the Brakspruit.

The main attack progresses to within 600 metres and, realising that there is no possibility of outflanking the extended British position, they start to bunch up. The burghers, shouting and shooting, charges in an irregular solid line at a determined pace with the tall figure of Commandant Potgieter, conspicuous in his blue shirt, in the centre. With 1 500 rifles and six field-guns tearing into them, they sweep

		nearer and nearer. Gaps appear as ponies tumble, but only at about 275 metres does the attack begin to falter. Potgieter carries on with an ever-dwindling band until he is hit — about 60 metres from the British lines. Rawlinson's troops arrive and Kemp retires. It is about 08:00. Hamilton orders an immediate general pursuit, but his plans entails wide sweeping movements and it takes another hour and a half before the troops are under way. Kemp has gained a head start and abandons his field-guns. The chase continues over almost 30 kilometres until it is abandoned at 14:30. The troops return with the captured guns and about 30 prisoners. Despite the heroic charge, the battle has been a complete disaster for the Republicans. They lose the brave Commandant FJ Potgieter and 42 others killed, 50 wounded, of whom 40 fall into enemy hands, and 36 unwounded burghers captured. The British suffer about 12 killed and 75 wounded.
	Cape Colony	**Okiep siege:** General JC Smuts sends a letter to Colonel WAD Shelton, the officer commanding the Okiep garrison, suggesting the removal of non-combatants to a place of safety south of the town. Shelton replies that, after consulting the inhabitants, they have elected to remain in town.[173]
Day 914 Sat **1902-04-12**	Peace talks ZAR	**THE MEETING IN PRETORIA** The Republican leaders meet Lord Kitchener in Pretoria. The Republicans submit a document with the following proposals: 1. The conclusion of an enduring treaty of friendship. Arrangements on customs, post, telegraph and railway union and franchise agreements. 2. The demolition of the Republican forts in Pretoria and Johannesburg. (See Milner's demands dated 4 September 1899.) 3. The appointment of arbitrators for future disputes. 4. Equal rights for Dutch and English. 5. Mutual amnesty.[174] Kitchener is astonished: *"Must I understand from what you say that you wish to retain your independence?"* *"Yes,"* President Steyn answers, *"the people must not lose their self-respect."*[175] Kitchener replies that there can be no possible question of men, who have fought so well in the field, losing their self-respect by facing the inevitable.[176] The Republicans point out that, according to the constitutions of the Republics, they are not capable of making or considering any proposals concerning their independence. Where the independence or the Republics is involved, THE PEOPLE will have to be consulted.[177]
	South-eastern ZAR	General Bruce Hamilton starts a drive from the line between Carolina and the Great Olifant's Station. The columns of Park, Williams, Spens, Allenby, Stewart, Wing and Mackenzie sweep south towards the Natal railway line between Standerton and Val Station.[178]
	Western ZAR	Twelve members of the 8th New Zealand Contingent are killed when a troop train slams into a goods train and derails at Machavie between Klerksdorp and Potchefstroom.[179]
	Cape Colony	**Okiep siege:** General Smuts attacks Okiep, but is repulsed.
Day 915 Sun **1902-04-13**	Peace talks ZAR	At the peace negotiations, the argument now revolves around who will constitute 'the people' (die volk). The Republican argument is that those who have taken the oath of neutrality are, according to British proclamations, essentially

321

		prisoners of war on parole and thus 'civilly dead'. Furthermore, the National Scouts and others serving the British, and those who have sworn an oath of allegiance to His Majesty, can no longer be regarded as 'burghers' and will be deemed to be represented by the British negotiators. Acceptance of this argument will prevent the British from pitting brother against brother to achieve their aims and will essentially sideline those whom the British expected to play a meaningful role during negotiations and in the leadership of the new colonies after the war.[180]
	Cape Colony	**Okiep siege:** A special force formed to curb Generals Smuts and Maritz's activities around Springbok and Okiep, embarks on two transport ships at Cape Town to sail for Port Nolloth.
	Black involvement	In answer to a question by St John Brodrick, Lord Kitchener admits providing firearms to 2 496 Africans and 2 693 Coloureds in the Cape Colony and to 4 618 Africans in Natal, the Free State and the ZAR A total of 10 053 — this seems to be a gross underestimate.[181]
	Trivia	*A new car speed record of 148 km/h (74 mph) is set in France.*
Day 916 Mon **1902-04-14**	Peace talks	A second meeting of the Republican peace delegates is attended by Lord Alfred Milner. On the same day he cables Chamberlain: *"Personally I distrust all negotiations, and should regard the future with more hope if the war was ended by a continuation of captures and surrenders, which despite our constantly recurring mishaps, continue to take place at a satisfactory rate."*[182] President Steyn cannot believe that Lord Milner is serious in suggesting that the Republican prisoners of war must also be consulted. *"How can the prisoners-of-war be consulted? — they are civilly dead. To mention one practical difficulty; suppose the prisoners should decide that the war should be continued, and the burghers on commando that it should not — what then?"*[183]
	ZAR	General Bruce Hamilton's drive south of Middelburg arrives on the Natal railway line between Standerton and Val Station, yielding 134 prisoners.[184]
	Cape Colony	Commandant Jan H Theron, Danie Theron's successor as commander of Theron's Scouts, dies of gastric fever in the Calvinia district.[185]
Day 917 Tue **1902-04-15**	Northern ZAR	Colonel JW Colenbrander again attacks General Beyers in the Wolkberg, but is repulsed with 'heavy' casualties, the Kitchener's Fighting Scouts losing 48 men in an ambush.[186]
	Western ZAR	Under the overall command of General Ian Hamilton, the columns of Kekewich, Rawlinson, Rochfort and Walter Kitchener perform a one-day sweep towards Klerksdorp and take a disappointing total of 64 prisoners.[187]
Day 918 Wed **1902-04-16**	United Kingdom	The British government replies by cable that it cannot *"entertain any proposals based on the continued independence of the former Republics which have been formally annexed to the British Crown"*.[188] Lord Kitchener communicates this information to the Republican delegates.[189]
	Peace talks	Chamberlain informs Milner and Kitchener: *"We have just asked Parliament for means to prosecute the war on the present scale for another year, and there is no doubt that the funds will be voted."*

		He also insists that any agreement with the Boers must not take the form of a bilateral 'treaty', but must simply be a document signed by the Boer leaders committing themselves, the burghers and the prisoners of war to surrender.[190]
Day 919 Thu 1902-04-17	Peace talks ZAR	At the peace talks, the British decide to allow a national convention of Republican delegates—30 from each Republic— to meet at Vereeniging to decide whether or not to continue the struggle. Hereby the British recognise the fighting burghers to be the sole representatives of inhabitants of 'the new colonies', condemning those who accepted, obeyed, supported or served them to virtual impotency in the future of South Africa.[191] The British undertake that, from 11 May, they will not attack commandos whose leaders are attending the conference, provided these commandos stay within their operational areas.[192]
Day 920 Fri 1902-04-18	Peace talks	The Republican leaders leave Pretoria to consult with the fighting commandos in the field.
	South-eastern ZAR	General Bruce Hamilton starts another drive in the south-eastern ZAR. The columns of Mackenzie, Spens, Garratt, Nixon, Rimington and Lawley drives from a line between Waterval Station and Nigel Mine northwards. Park and Wing are to reinforce the line of constabulary posts on the right flank. Commandant Alberts doubles around the night-picket line and dashes south with 500 men. He forces the blockhouse line near Heidelberg and rests in the Suikerbosrand before moving on to the Free State.[193]
	OFS	Vilonel's ORC Volunteers capture a single burgher near the present-day Marquard. When the rest of the burghers counterattack, Vilonel turns and only the speed of the racehorse he rides allows him to escape. His ORC Volunteers lose two killed and five captured. Three of those captured are subsequently sentenced to death by a court martial, chaired by General CC Froneman, and are executed at Kafferskraal between Senekal and Ficksburg.[194]
Day 921 Sat 1902-04-19		
Day 922 Sun 1902-04-20	South-eastern ZAR	General Bruce Hamilton's drive reaches the Delagoa railway line with nothing to show for the effort.
	Trivia	*P H Kritzinger's 32nd birthday.* *Republican scout OJ (Jack) Hindon's 28th birthday.*
Day 923 Mon 1902-04-21	Peace talks ZAR	Lord Milner, realising the inconsequential position of the surrendered burghers and the National Scouts in the negotiations, state: *"Of course, it is the vice of all negotiations with the men who have stuck out, that it, to some extent gives away the men who have already come in."*[195]
	Cape Colony	**Okiep siege:** The cannon built by Maritz's men outside Okiep blows itself to pieces, and they immediately start on a new one.[196]
Day 924 Tue 1902-04-22	Cape Colony	**Okiep siege:** The new Okiep cannon also explodes.[197]
Day 925 Wed 1902-04-23	Natal Black involvement	During a meeting held in the Vryheid district to elect delegates to the peace conference, Commandant-General Botha orders General MW Meyer to burn Zulu kraals in the district in reprisal for the looting of Boer cattle by the expedition under General Bruce Hamilton, King Dinizulu and Chief Sikhobobo.

	Cape Colony	**Okiep siege:** Outside Okiep two British officers arrive under a flag of truce with a despatch, from Colonel Haig addressed to General Smuts concerning the peace talks. General Smuts is summoned to join the planned peace talks at Vereeniging, not as an elected representative, but as legal adviser.[198]
Day 926 Thu **1902-04-24**	Peace talks	The first of the special meetings with burghers in the field are convened to discuss the question of peace, and to elect delegates to the proposed peace conference.
Day 927 Fri **1902-04-25**	Cape Colony	General Smuts enters the British lines under a flag of truce. His party boards a train for Port Nolloth where a ship is waiting to take him to Simon's Town. He is joined by Tottie Krige and Deneys Reitz.[199] Not familiar with British ranks, Reitz elects to be Smuts' orderly, but soon finds out that orderlies are not treated as officers. He is immediately promoted to the more suitable rank of chief of staff.[200]
	South Africa	British intelligence reports put the number of surrendered ex-burghers now in British service at 3 963.[201]
Day 928 Sat **1902-04-26**	Cape Colony	**Okiep siege:** A part of the Okiep relief column, under Lieutenant-Colonel CE Callwell, makes a reconnaissance against the besiegers, but they are forced to fall
Day 929 Sun **1902-04-27**	Bermuda	The sixteen-year-old FH Bosch dies after being wounded by a guard while attempting to escape from the prisoner of war camp on Bermuda.[203]
	Trivia	*Cape politician Sir JG Sprigg's 72nd birthday*
Day 930 Mon **1902-04-28**	Cape Colony	**Okiep siege:** General Maritz's besieging forces challenge the Okiep garrison to a football match, which, although considered, is eventually declined. An attack by a relief column is beaten off by the besiegers. The relief column carries out a strong reconnaissance against Van Deventer at Steinkopf, but they are forced to fall back to Klipfontein, losing four killed and three wounded. On the Boer side six burghers are killed and some 15 wounded.[204]
	OFS	Commandant KD Coetzee is killed in a skirmish with about 15 Coloured scouts at Rooikop, between Bloemfontein and Dewetsdorp.[205]
	Natal	The Oliviershoek/Allison's Kop blockhouse line, consisting of 25 blockhouses, 22,4 kilometres of wire entanglements and trenches is completed as a countermeasure against the repeated Republican attacks from the Witzieshoek area into northern Natal.[206]
	Trivia	*British troops undertake a punitive expedition against Muhammed Abdallah Hassan (the 'Mad Mullah') in Somalia, East Africa. It is considered to sent a unit of National Scouts as a South African contingent.*
Day 931 Tue **1902-04-29**	South Africa	There are now 1 125 ex-burghers in the National Scouts and 385 in the Orange River Colony Volunteers, and a total of 9 963 ex-burghers have now taken up arms against their own people by joining enemy units.[207]
Day 932 Wed **1902-04-30**	**OFFICIAL REPORTS**	
	Gold mining:	On the Witwatersrand 2 095 or about 35% of the gold stamps are back in production and the monthly gold production is 120 000 ounces or about 40,0% of peak pre-war production.[208]
	Farm burning:	British columns have completely or partially destroyed 158 farms and an unknown number of black villages (kraals).
	Blockhouses:	The following blockhouse lines have been completed:

		ZAR — From Mareetsane to near Lichtenburg (65 km) and between Ermelo and the Swaziland border (90 km). Cape Colony — From Calvinia via Williston to Carnarvon (233 km). OFS — From Kimberley via Boshof to Smaldeel (the present-day Theunissen) (180 km) and between Bloemhof and Hoopstad (40 km). The blockhouse lines are now approaching their final form and extent. About 8 000 forts and blockhouses have been erected at an estimated total cost of about £1 000 000 to the British taxpayer.[209]
	Concentration camps:	The officially reported population of the white camps is 112 733 and the death toll for April stands at 298.
	Black involvement:	The population of the black camps is 108 386 and 630 deaths are recorded.[210]
1902	AUTUMN	**MAY**
Day 933 Thu **1902-05-01**	OFS	The last 'drives' in the north-eastern Free State start.
	Natal Black involvement	On orders issued by Commandant-General Botha on 23 April, a Boer commando under Field-cornet J Potgieter burns several Zulu villages, loots cattle and grain and force the inhabitants to flee to Vryheid where they camp near the railway station.
	Cape Colony	**Okiep siege:** A train truck loaded with dynamite is pushed towards Okiep, but it ignites too soon and explodes harmlessly.[211]
Day 934 Fri **1902-05-02**	*Trivia*	*In Pennsylvania, USA, 200 000 miners strike, calling for union recognition and pay rises.*
Day 935 Sat **1902-05-03**	Natal Black involvement	AJ Shepstone, son of Theophilus Shepstone — the man responsible for both the annexation of the Transvaal in 1877 and the events that led to the Anglo-Zulu War — has been appointed as magistrate at Vryheid by the British authorities. He visits Chief Sikhobobo at the Vryheid railway station in the company of members of the British Military Intelligence Department. He is later to contend that the purpose of his visit is to count the Zulu women and children for the provision of rations. On the same day he warns Mr JC Pretorius that he expects the Zulus to attack a group of Boers at Holkrantz.
	OFS	The last of 11 issues of the *Staats Courant van den Oranjevrijstaat* is printed on a press hidden in a cave near Fouriesburg.[212]
	Cape Colony	Commandant Willem Fouchee, with only 40 men, attacks a British force at The Willows, near Middelburg.[213]
Day 936 Sun **1902-05-04**	Natal OFS	General Smuts, travelling from Simon's Town to Vereeniging on a British train, is met by Lord Kitchener at Kroonstad.
	Cape Colony	**Okiep siege:** The siege of Okiep is raised after the arrival of Colonel H Cooper and his relief column.[214]
	Trivia	*General AF Hart's 58th birthday.*
Day 937 Mon **1902-05-05**	ZAR Civilian Life	Forty 'leading citizens' of the Witwatersrand, led by Percy Fitzpatrick, appeal to Milner that only the unconditional surrender of the Boers be accepted: *"... we feel bound to say that in our judgement the conceding of any conditions at all — entirely apart from the principles in them — is undesirable and impolitic, and the granting of terms which would form a kind of convention is absolutely inadmissible... a granting of conditions will erect into a party within the colony a particularly resolute and hostile body of men deeming themselves entitled by treaty to special rights; will give to this party much prestige; and will*

		place the men who are still in the field... in a position morally, if not materially, superior to those burghers who surrendered..."[215]
Day 938 Tue **1902-05-06**	Black involvement Natal	**THE HOLKRANTZ MASSACRE** Qulusi-Zulu chief Sikhobobo takes an impi to recover cattle allegedly raided from him by Field-cornet Potgieter, against whom he is known to have a personal vendetta, resulting from cattle raids and reprisals. The 300-strong impi armed with firearms and assegais, overwhelms Field-cornet Potgieter's sleeping 70-man commando in a cave. Fifty-six burghers are murdered and their bodies mutilated, while 52 Zulus are killed and 48 wounded. Boer survivors are convinced that the attack was instigated by the British. This incident is to have a profound influence on the peace negotiations [216]
	OFS	A fast-moving one-day drive is carried out by troops travelling light without wagons or artillery. They march from the Heilbron line south to the Kroonstad/Lindley line and take 143 prisoners, but about 600 get away.[217]
Day 939 Wed **1902-05-07**	ZAR Western ZAR	An armoured train is involved in a serious accident near Pretoria. General Ian Hamilton is in overall command of about 17 000 troops executing the final drive in the western ZAR. They march westwards, attempting to drive the commandos against the Vryburg/Mafeking fortified line and its blockhouses and forts manned by 4 000 guards. During this drive the British also use six armoured trains.[218]
Day 940 Thu **1902-05-08**	Eastern ZAR	A combined force of British soldiers and armed blacks attempts to surround General CH Muller's commando, commanded in his absence (while underway to the peace conference) by Colonel Trichard, near Belfast. The attackers are repulsed, but the Republicans lose one burgher in this attack which they consider a despicable act.[219]
Day 941 Fri **1902-05-09**		
Day 942 Sat **1902-05-10**	OFS	Last drives in the north-eastern Free State end. Commandant Manie Botha, a nephew of General Louis Botha, is captured in the Brandwater Basin.
	Cape Colony	A petition for the suspension of the Cape constitution is presented to Sir W Hely-Hutchinson by members of the Cape legislature.
Day 943 Sun **1902-05-11**	Western ZAR	General Ian Hamilton's last drive in the western Transvaal ends. The drive results in one burgher killed, 363 taken prisoner as well as 236 wagons and carts, 326 horses, 95 mules, 20 donkeys, 3 600 head of cattle and 13 000 sheep captured.[220] Temporary General AJG (Klein Adriaan) De la Rey, an elder brother of General De la Rey, is captured near Vryburg. As the peace negotiations are nearing, he is permitted to join his wife in the concentration camp at Merebank in Natal. Four of his 16 children have died in the Klerksdorp concentration camp.[221] On this day the suspension of British attacks on those commandos whose leaders are delegated to the peace talks comes into effect.
Day 944 Mon **1902-05-12**	ZAR	In a letter to his wife Isie, General Smuts writes: *"Nothing will however deter me from doing my duty, for I do not regard the favour either of my friends or my enemies but shall ever strive to do my duty, to retain my own self-respect and sense of personal rectitude and — last not least — the goodwill and respect of her who is the last thing left me in this life. A man may lose his possessions, even his home and country, but he may yet remain a citizen of that larger and higher kingdom whose limits are the conscience and aspirations of humanity."*[222]

Day 945 Tue **1902-05-13**		
Day 946 Wed **1902-05-14**		
Day 947 Thu **1902-05-15**	Peace talks ZAR	**THE OPENING OF THE VEREENIGING CONFERENCE** The sixty Republican delegates elect General CF Beyers as chairman and for the next three days situation reports from the different operational areas are heard.[223] General Kemp is unshakable: *"As far as I am concerned, unless relief comes, I will fight on till I die."*[224] Commandant-General Louis Botha senses a hopelessness in their situation. He reports that his commandos have to provide for 2 540 destitute families. Food supplies are exhausted, the 'black' question is becoming more serious, the condition of the women is pitiable, the number of men is dwindling, their horses are giving out. *"We must face the fact that things are not at a standstill; we are slipping back every moment."*[225]
Day 948 Fri **1902-05-16**	Peace talks ZAR	Vice-President Schalk Burger argues that it would be criminal to continue fighting until everything is destroyed and everyone killed, if they are convinced that the struggle is hopeless. State Secretary FW Reitz says, *"We might offer to surrender Witwatersrand and Swaziland; we might also relinquish our rights to a foreign policy; we might even accede to an English Protectorate. If France has been able to do without Alsace and Lorraine, surely we can do without the goldfields. What benefit have they ever done us? Did the money they brought ever do us any good? No! Rather it did us harm. It was the gold which caused the war. It is then actually to our advantage to cede the goldfields, and moreover by so doing we shall be rid of a very troublesome part of our population."*[229] General Koos De la Rey does not believe in the possibility of foreign intervention and he feels that it is time to negotiate with the British. *"So far as I myself am concerned, I cannot think of laying down my arms."* He is, however, shocked by the conditions elsewhere and is not convinced that the war can be continued. *"There has been talk of fighting to the bitter end. But has the bitter end already come? Each man must answer that question for himself. You must remember that everything has been sacrificed — cattle, goods, money, wife and child. Our men are going about naked and our women have nothing but clothes made of skins to wear. Is this not the bitter end?"*[27] De la Rey is convinced that Britain would never agree to Reitz's proposal to cede the goldfields, lest it will confirm that she had gone to war only for possession of the mines.[228] Chief Commandant Christiaan de Wet is determined: *"Persevere. We have everything to lose, but we have not yet lost it."* They must not give up any territory, not even the goldfields. The war is an act of faith. *"... For me, this is a war of religion and thus I can only consider the great principles involved. Circumstances are to me just obstacles to be cleared out of the road... At all costs let us continue fighting."*[229]
	Natal	Mr Seddon, Prime Minister of New Zealand, arrives in Durban.
	United Kingdom	Speaking on the execution of Morant and Handcock, Swift MacNeill, an opposition member, states in the House of Commons that *"it was pretty clear that, unless these men had had the misfortune to come into contact with a German missionary, they would have enjoyed immunity from punishment. But the death of the Rev Dr Heese made it a serious matter and the Government, well aware that the German authorities would press the question home, found it necessary to bring the men to trial..."*[230]
Day 949 Sat **1902-05-17**	Peace talks	The Assembly passes two resolutions: Firstly, empowering the two governments to conclude peace on the basis of Reitz's proposals and secondly to appoint a negotiat-

327

		ing commission, consisting of Generals Louis Botha and JH de la Rey with State Attorney (General) JC Smuts for the ZAR; Judge (General) JBM Hertzog and Chief Commandant CR de Wet for the Orange Free State.[231] If their draft document based on Reitz's proposals is rejected, they are empowered to negotiate at large, with the proviso that any document which they agree on must be submitted to the Assembly for ratification.[232]
Day 950 Sun **1902-05-18**	Peace talks ZAR	The elected negotiators leave Vereeniging to confer with Lord Milner and Lord Kitchener in Pretoria.
	Cape Colony	In a combined night attack with General Wynand Malan, Commandant CP van Heerden and two others are wounded in an audacious but senseless attack on Aberdeen (Van Heerden's hometown) to steal 35 horses. Commandant Van Heerden falls in front of the impressive church and has to be left behind. After his death, his naked body is exhibited to the town's inhabitants.[233]
Day 951 Mon **1902-05-19**	Peace talks ZAR	The Boer negotiators hand Lord Kitchener the following letter: *"Your Excellencies,* *With a view to finally concluding the existing hostilities, and being fully empowered by the Government of the two Republics, we have the honour to propose the following points — in addition to the conditions already offered in the negotiations of April last — as a basis for negotiations:* *(a) We are prepared to cede our independence as regards our foreign relations.* *(b) We wish to retain self-government in our country, under British supervision.* *(c) We are prepared to cede a part of our territory.* *Should your Excellencies be prepared to negotiate on this basis, then the above-mentioned points can be elaborated."*[234] These proposals are rejected as His Majesty's Government cannot entertain any proposals based on the continued independence of the former Republics. Lord Milner again presents the Middelburg proposals as *"the utmost concessions that the British Government is able to grant".*[235] The peace conference is almost deadlocked over the wording of a surrender document submitted by Milner, which would have the effect that the Boers recognise the annexation proclamations of 24 May and 1 September 1900. This would imply that they have been rebels against a lawful authority since that date. Sensing De Wet's uncompromising stand, Kitcheners proposes that the military members withdraw, leaving Milner, assisted by Sir Richard Solomon, Smuts and Hertzog to draft a schedule. The Boer peace delegation insists on a bipartite document signed by both parties, thus winning a diplomatic victory.[236]
	Cape Colony	Commandant Fouchee and General Malan attack and capture a few British troops at Marais Siding.[237]
Day 952 Tue **1902-05-20**	Peace talks	The status of the fighting burghers presently negotiating with the British is confirmed by a preamble to the surrender terms drafted by the subcommittee. The document recognizes them as *"acting as the Government of the South African Republic"* and *"acting as the Government of the Orange Free State,"* essentially negating the premature annexation of the republics, almost two years previously. In return, the preamble expects the burghers to recognise King Edward VII as *"their lawful sovereign".*[238]
Day 953 Wed **1902-05-21**	Peace talks United Kingdom	Lord Milner complains to Chamberlain that negotiations have *"taken a turn for the worse"* and that he finds himself *"in a weak position, as Kitchener does not always support me even in the presence of Boers... He does not care what he gives away."* He begs the Cabinet to postpone replying if Kitchener sends them *"strange proposals".*[239]

		The preliminary draft proposals drawn up by the subcommittee are submitted to the full negotiating teams. During the negotiations, while Smuts is locked in an intense argument with Milner, Kitchener suddenly interrupts. He asks Smuts to join him for a stroll. Once outside, he says, *"Look here, Smuts, there is something on my mind that I want to tell you. I can only give it to you as my opinion, but I believe in two years' time a Liberal government will be in power. And if a Liberal government comes into power it will grant you a constitution for South Africa."* *"This is a very important pronouncement,"* Smuts replies, *"if one could be sure of this it would make a great difference."*[240] The proposed peace proposals are sent to London and are better received than Milner has expected. Milner denounces the terms in a 'private and confidential' telegram to Chamberlain, especially the *"detestable Clause 11"* dealing with the payment of £3 000 000 as resettlement aid and to cover the Republic's war debts.[241]
	ZAR	Mr Seddon, the New Zealand Prime Minister, arrives in Pretoria.
Day 954 Thu **1902-05-22**	Peace talks United Kingdom	Mr Chamberlain, obviously keen not to jeopardise the negotiations on detail, wires Milner: *"There should be some argument more cogent than the money cost to justify risking failure on this point. Can you supply it, and would go so far as to wreck agreement at this stage upon this question?"*[242] The Cabinet discusses the new terms and finds them *"an improvement"* on the Middelburg proposals, especially the introduction. Chamberlain queries the clause concerning the native political rights, but Milner replies, *"While averse in principle to all pledges, there is much to be said for leaving question of political rights of natives to be settled by colonists themselves."* The Cabinet accedes and the undefined postponement of Black rights makes *"a mockery of Chamberlain's claim that one of Britain's war aims was to improve the status of Africans"*.[243]
	Trivia	*Sir Arthur Conan Doyle's 43rd birthday.*
Day 955 Fri **1902-05-23**		
Day 956 Sat **1902-05-24**	ZAR	General Sir Ian Hamilton is invited to Smuts' birthday party. He later writes to Churchill: *"I sat between Botha and De la Rey. On Botha's right was De Wet: on De la Rey's left sat Smuts. I had the most enchanting evening, and never wish to eat my dinner in better company."*[244]
	Trivia	*JC Smuts' 32nd birthday.*
Day 957 Sun **1902-05-25**		
Day 958 Mon **1902-05-26**		
Day 959 Tue **1902-05-27**	Peace talks	The peace proposals, as approved by the British Cabinet, are wired to Lord Milner and Lord Kitchener.[245]
	Cape Colony	Combining forces with Fouchee, General Wynand Malan attacks Sheldon Station, near Jansenville. Malan is seriously wounded while herding the captured horses and falls into British hands.[246]
Day 960 Wed **1902-05-28**	Peace talks	Kitchener wires Brodrick, hoping that *"if my telegrams are published in a Blue Book or elsewhere you will kindly see that they are carefully edited so that they do not show any divergence of views between Lord Milner and myself. Of course, I do not mind the vital necessity of subject of clause 11 being put down to me if it is advisable."*[250]

		THE FINAL PROPOSALS Lord Alfred Milner and Lord Horatio Kitchener submit the final draft as agreed to by the British government, to the Boer negotiators. Milner calls it absolutely final and the Republican Peace Commission must either accept or reject it before midnight on 31 May. General Smuts immediately deletes 'ACT OF SURRENDER' on the title page and replaces it with 'ACT OF PEACE'. The ten articles are: 1. The burghers are to lay down arms and acknowledge the King as their lawful sovereign. 2. All prisoners and internees are to be returned on making the same acknowledgement. 3. Burghers who lay down arms are not to lose personal liberty or property. 4. No legal prosecution of burghers to be instituted except specific cases for war crimes. 5. Dutch is to be taught at schools where parents desire it and will be admitted in law courts. 6. Burghers are permitted to own licenced rifles for personal protection. 7. Military administration is to be followed by civil, and subsequently by self-government 'as soon as circumstances permit'. 8. The issue of 'Native Franchise' is not to be finalised before after the granting of self-government. 9. There is to be no special war tax. 10. (Including the original clause 11.) District commissions are to be set up to assist resettlement, provide necessities lost in the war and to honour Republican bank or promissory notes. For this purpose, a free gift of £3 000 000 is to be provided by the British government, as well as loans on 'liberal terms'.[248] On the question of amnesty, it is confirmed that a general amnesty will be granted to all burghers with the exception of three cases where the British contend that war crimes have been committed. The cases specified refer to Field-cornet Salmon van As, accused of shooting Captain Miers under a flag of truce; Barend Cilliers, accused of killing Lieutenant Boyle, and that of a certain Muller, details of which cannot be traced. No clause on amnesty for rebels is included in the final proposals. A statement issued by the Cape government confirms that rebels will be disenfranchised for life (later to be reduced to five years) and though leaders will be put on trial, none will be executed. Natal insists that the law will take its course.[249] At 19:00, the Boer negotiators board a train at Pretoria Station and return to Vereeniging
	Cape Colony	Dr Smartt resigns from Cape Ministry to support the suspension of the constitution movement. The blockhouse line between Clanwilliam and Calvinia (200 km) in the Cape Colony is completed.[250]
Day 961 Thu **1902-05-29**	Peace talks	At Vereeniging, the returned negotiators submit the final terms, the best they have been able to obtain, to the Republican delegates. The Assembly is now faced with three choices: 1. they can refuse to sign the peace terms and simply surrender unconditionally; 2. they can decide to continue fighting, or, 3. they can accept the British proposals. The essential issue, however, is no longer the continuation of the war, but unity or division between the two Republics. In a final plea, President Steyn, the ultimate bitter-ender, suggests that there may be a fourth choice, *"to insist upon our cause being decided in Europe by persons empowered, and sent thither by us."* As he is too ill to take any further part in the struggle, he decides that he probably has no right to speak fur-

		ther. He transfers the presidency of the Free State to Chief Commandant De Wet. Steyn is too weak to leave his tent, suffering from double vision and pain in the legs that makes walking impossible. (Modern medical opinion is that he suffered either from *myasthenia gravis* or botulism, probably as a result of eating spoiled sausage.)[259]
Day 962 Fri **1902-05-30**	Peace talks	Acting President Burger announces President Steyn's resignation to the Assembly and, on behalf of the ZAR government, he hands De Wet a sum of money for the use of Steyn, who is destitute. This draws *"the heart of the Free Stater closer to that of the Transvaler than before".*[252] Steyn leaves for Krugersdorp to receive medical treatment from Dr WJ van der Merwe.[256] Commandant-General Botha discloses the figures obtained from Kitchener, indicating the full extent of Republican losses — 20 000 dead in the concentration camps, 3 800 killed in action and 31 600 taken prisoner. (See 'The Butcher's Bill' addendum.)[254] Acting President Schalk Burger continues the proceedings saying: " *... it is my holy duty to stop this struggle now that it has become hopeless, and not to allow one more man to be shot and not to allow the innocent, helpless women and children to remain any longer in their misery in the plaque-stricken concentration camps...*"[255] General JC Smuts states: "*... if we view the matter from a military standpoint, if we consider it only as a military matter, then I must admit we can still go on with the struggle. We are still an unvanquished military force... But we are not here as an army, but as a people; we have not only a military question, but also a national matter to deal with...*"[256] He continues: "*...one and all, we represent the Afrikaner nation, and not only those who are now in the field, but those who rest beneath the soil, and those yet unborn who shall succeed us. From the prisons, the camps, the grave, the veld, and from the womb of the future, that nation cries out to us to make a wise decision now...*"[257] To continue the war would be "*to sacrifice the Afrikaner nation itself on the altar of independence".*[258] By the end of the day, 21 Transvalers and nine Free Staters have participated in the debate. Twenty of the Transvalers are in favour of accepting the proposals, one in favour of stopping the war but surrenderring unconditionally. Of the Free Staters, Hertzog is undecided, another wants to surrender unconditionally and the remainder are for continuing the war.[259]
	OFFICIAL REPORTS **Farm burning:** **Concentration camps:** **Black involvement:**	British columns have completey or partially destroyed 152 farms. British military authorities officially admit to completely or partially destroying at least 953 farms and an unknown number of black settlements and huts.[260] The officially reported camp population of the white camps is 116 572 and the deaths for May are 196. Black concentration camp population in the 66 black camps reach 115 700, of which 60 004 are in Free State camps and 55 969 in the ZAR. 523 deaths are recorded for the month.[261] The total recorded deaths are calculated at a minimum of 14 154 (more than 1 in 10) with an average death rate of 350 per thousand per annum, peaking at 436 per thousand per annum in certain Free State camps. Eighty-one percent of the fatalities are children.
Day 963 Sat **1902-05-31** *Lord Kitchener* *(War Museum of the Boer Republics)*	Peace talks	**THE FINAL DAY** Early in the morning, Botha and De la Rey visit De Wet in his tent. No record exists of this meeting but it can be assumed that the Transvalers stress the importance of unity. The two delegations meet separately before assembling for the last time. A declaration, drafted by Smuts and Hertzog, sets out the Republicans' reasons for laying down their arms: 1. The devastation of the country by the enemy — the burning of farms and villages and the exhaustion of supplies necessary for the support of their families and the continuation of the war.

Gen. JC Smuts
(National Cultural History Museum)

Gen. Schalk Burger
(National Cultural History Museum)

Gen. JH de la Rey
(National Cultural History Museum)

Comdt.-Gen. Louis Botha
(National Cultural History Museum)

Sir Alfred Milner
(War Museum of the Boer Republics)

Gen. JBM Hertzog
(War Museum of the Boer Republics)

2. The suffering and deaths of the women and children in the concentration camps.
3. The fact that blacks, armed by the British, are participating in the war and committing atrocities.
4. The proclamations which threaten confiscation of fighting burghers' property.
5. The inability of the commandos to take the prisoners they capture out of the conflict.
6. The fact that the struggling remnant of the Volk, constituting only a small minority, is practically in a state of famine and deprivation, and that — against the overwhelming might of the enemy — ultimate victory can no longer reasonably be expected.[262]

It concludes: *"This Assembly expresses its confidence that the conditions called into being by accepting the proposal of His Majesty's Government may soon be so improved that our Nation will attain the enjoyment of those privileges which it considers itself justly entitled to claim."*

This is *"the manifesto of a people unbeaten in battle, but worn down by attrition"*.[263]

When the peace proposals are finally brought to the vote, 54 delegates are in favour of accepting and six against.[64] Three Transvalers (General JCG Kemp, Commandant JJ Alberts and burgher JF Naude) and three Free Staters (General CCJ Badenhorst, Commandant AJ Bester and Commandant CA van Niekerk) vote in the minority.[265]

Acting President Schalk Burger solemnly concludes: *"We are standing at the grave of the two Republics. Much yet remains to be done, although we shall not be able to do it in the official capacities which we have formerly occupied. Let us not draw our hands back from the work which is our duty to accomplish. Let us ask God to guide us, and to show us how we shall be enabled to keep our nation together. We must be ready to forgive and forget whenever we meet our brethren. That part of our nation which has proved unfaithful we must not reject."*[266]

THE TREATY OF VEREENIGING IS SIGNED

The final peace conditions are signed by both parties at 23:05 at Melrose House, Pretoria.

For His Majesty's government:
Lord Horatio H Kitchener of Khartoum and Lord Alfred Milner

For the ZAR:
Acting State President SW Burger, State Secretary FW Reitz, Commandant-General Louis Botha, Generals JH de la Rey, LJ Meyer and JC Krogh.

For the OFS:
Acting State President (Chief Commandant) CR de Wet, State Secretary WJC Brebner, Judge (General) JBM Hertzog and JH Olivier.

During the next few weeks the bitter-enders and prisoners of war are asked to sign the following declaration:

"I... (name and home address) ... adhere to the terms of the agreement signed at Pretoria on 31 May 1902, between my late Government and the representatives of His Majesty's Government. I acknowledge myself to be a subject of King Edward VII and I promise to own allegiance to him, his heirs, and successors according to law."[267]

A total of 21 256 burghers and 3 437 Colonial rebels are to lay down their arms — 6 455 in the Orange Free State; 11 166 in the Transvaal and 3 635 burghers in the Cape Colony. A few irreconcilables cross the Orange River into German South-West Africa.[268]

NOTES:

JANUARY – JUNE 1902 (THE BITTER END)

1. WARWICK, Black people..., p 173
2. PRETORIUS, Kommandolewe... p 73
3. AMERY, *op cit*, vol V, p 456
4. AMERY, *op cit*, vol V, p 456-458; ELOFF, Oorlogsdagboekie..., p 19
5. AMERY, *op cit*, vol V, p 457
6. WARWICK, South African War..., p 194
7. PLOEGER, *op cit*, pp 27-34
8. McCORD, JJ, South African Struggle, p 320
9. GRUNDLINGH, 'Hendsoppers'..., p 187-188
10. AMERY, *op cit*, vol V, p 458
11. PLOEGER, *op cit*, pp 37-43
12. OOSTHUIZEN, Rebelle van die Stormberge, p 162
13. DAVITT, *op cit*, p 546
14. PLOEGER, *op cit*, pp 30-33
15. GRONUM, *op cit*, (2) p 165
16. PRELLER, Scheepers se dagboek..., pp 45-49
17. FERREIRA, Memoirs of Ben Bouwer, p 233
18. WARWICK, Black people..., p 150
19. GRONUM, *op cit*, (2) p 165
20. GRONUM, *op cit*, (2) p 25
21. AMERY, *op cit*, vol V, map
22. VAN ZYL, Die Helde-album..., p 395
23. AMERY, *op cit*, Vol V, map
24. VAN ZYL, Die Helde-album..., p 395
25. *Ibid*, p 395
26. VAN ZYL, Die Helde-album..., p 395; AMERY, *op cit*, vol V, p 465
27. AMERY, *op cit*, vol V, p 459
28. GRUNDLINGH, 'Hendsoppers'..., p 193
29. GRONUM, *op cit*, (2) p 112
30. THE COIN REPORT vol 1, No 4, Issue 4
31. AMERY, *op cit*, vol V, p 458
32. WARWICK, Black people..., p 122
33. AMERY, *op cit*, vol V, p 544
34. PLOEGER, *op cit*, p 33:31
35. FARWELL, *op cit*, p 429
36. AMERY, *op cit*, vol V, p 546
37. PAKENHAM, *op cit*, p 55
38. PLOEGER, *op cit*, p 33:41
39. HATTINGH, Britse fortifikasies..., p 85
40. AMERY, *op cit*, vol V, map
41. DOONER, 'Last Post', p 276
42. AMERY, *op cit*, vol V, pp 546-547
43. GRONUM, *op cit*, (2) p 61
44. VAN ZYL, Die Helde-album..., p 375
45. AMERY, *op cit*, vol V, p 547
46. KRUGER, Good-bye Dolly Gray, p 472
47. GRONUM, *op cit*, (2) p 61
48. WESSELS, War Diary ..., p 169
49. AMERY, *op cit*, vol V, p 548
50. *Ibid*, vol V, p 548
51. WESSELS, War Diary..., p 171
52. AMERY, *op cit*, vol V, p 478; HATTINGH, Britse fortifikasies..., p 115
53. AMERY, *op cit*, vol V, pp 548-549
54. *Ibid*, vol V, pp 479-480
55. WESSELS, War Diary..., p 171
56. VAN DEN BERG, 24 Battles..., p 136
57. GRONUM, *op cit* , (2) p 70
58. AMERY, *op cit*, vol V, map
59. GRONUM, *op cit* (2), p 70
60. AMERY, *op cit*, vol V, map
61. FERREIRA, Memoirs of Ben Bouwer, pp 238-239
62. AMERY, *op cit*, vol V, map
63. *Ibid*, vol V, map
64. DAVITT, *op cit*, pp 556-557
65. ORFORT, Unpublished manuscript
66. WESSELS, War Diary..., p 173; HATTINGH, Britse fortifikasies..., p 117
67. ELOFF, Oorlogsdagboekie..., p 29
68. AMERY, *op cit*, vol V, map
69. VAN SCHOOR, De Wet-annale No 7, p 94
70. VAN SCHOOR, Die Bannelinge..., p 12
71. HATTINGH, Britse fortifikasies...., p 117
72. *Ibid*, p 121
73. AMERY, *op cit*, vol V, p 546
74. VAN ZYL, Die Helde-album..., p 381
75. AMERY, *op cit*, vol V, map
76. FERREIRA, Krijsgevangenschap..., p 177
77. DAVITT, *op cit*, p 557
78. GRONUM, *op cit*, (2) p 71
79. *Ibid*, (2) p 79
80. HATTINGH, Britse fortifikasies..., p 77
81. GRUNDLINGH, 'Hendsoppers'..., p 214
82. AMERY, *op cit*, vol V, p 487
83. AMERY, *op cit*, vol V, p 549
84. GRUNDLINGH, 'Hendsoppers'..., p 216
85. HATTINGH, Britse fortifikasies..., p 121
86. AMERY, *op cit*, vol V, pp 489-490; HATTINGH, *op cit*, p 117
87. VAN DEN BERG, 24 Battles..., p 137
88. AMERY, *op cit*, vol V, p 497
89. VAN DEN BERG, 24 Battles..., pp 137-138
90. *Ibid*, pp 138-141
91. WITTON, Scapegoats of the Empire, p 150; PLOEGER, *op cit*, pp 31-33
92. AMERY, *op cit*, vol V, p 549
93. WESSELS, Die Anglo-Boereoorlog... Oorsig..., p 39
94. VAN SCHOOR, Die Bannelinge..., Pamphlet.
95. AMERY, *op cit*, vol V, p 491; OBERHOLSTER, Dagboek... HC Bredell, p 62; WESSELS, War Diary...., p 173; HATTINGH, *op cit*, p 117
96. VAN SCHOOR, De Wet-annale No 8, p 93
97. WITTON, Scapegoats..., p 153
98. VAN SCHOOR, Die Bannelinge..., p 2
99. AMERY, *op cit*, vol V, map
100. PAKENHAM, *op cit*, p 555
101. WARWICK, Black people..., 151
102. PLOEGER, *op cit*, p 33:41
103. AMERY, *op cit*, vol V, map

104. HATTINGH, Britse fortifikasies..., p 140

105. AMERY, *op cit*, vol V, map

106. VAN ZYL, Die Helde-album..., p 397

107. VAN DEN BERG, 24 Battles ..., pp 144-145

108. VAN SCHOOR, Die Bannelinge..., p 13

109. GRUNDLINGH, 'Hensoppers'... p 219

110. LE MAY, *op cit*, p 108

111. GRONUM, *op cit* (2), pp 174-178

112. VAN DEN BERG, 24 Battles..., p 145

113. *Ibid*, pp 145-146

114. VAN DEN BERG, 24 Battles..., p 144

115. AMERY, *op cit*, vol V, map

116. VAN DEN BERG, 24 Battles..., pp 144-154

117. McDONALD, In die Skaduwee van die Dood, pp 102-106

118. WESSELS, War Diary..., p 176

119. *Ibid*, p 176

120. VAN ZYL, Die Helde-album..., p 359

121. HATTINGH, Britse fortifikasies..., p 118

122. VAN ZYL, Die Helde-album..., p 359

123. AMERY, *op cit*, vol V, map

124. AMERY, *op cit*, vol V, map

125. FERREIRA, ... SPE Trichard, p 207

126. VAN ZYL, Die Helde-album..., p 365

127. HATTINGH, Britse fortifikasies..., p 118

128. ORFORD, Unpublished manuscript

129. VAN ZYL, Die Helde-album..., p 391

130. VAN DEN BERG, 24 Battles..., p 145

131. VAN SCHOOR, Die Bannelinge..., p 9

132. AMERY, *op cit*, vol V, pp 512-517

133. SPIES, Methods of Barbarism?, p 264

134. WESSELS, War Diary..., p 182

135. PEDDLE, *op cit*, p 13

136. GRONUM, *op cit,* (2) p 112

137. AMERY, *op cit*, vol V, pp 518-519

138. VAN ZYL, Die Helde-album..., p 395

139. LE MAY, *op cit,* p 130

140. AMERY, *op cit,* vol V, p 519

141. VAN DEN BERG, *op cit*..., pp 157-161; AMERY, *op cit*, vol V, pp 520-524

142. PAKENHAM, *op cit*, p 555

143. HATTINGH, Britse fortifikasies..., p 86

144. PLOEGER, *op cit*, pp 33-42

145. WARWICK, Black people..., p 151

146. GRUNDLINGH, 'Hendsoppers'..., p 209; KRUGER, Goodbye Dolly Gray, p 491

147. GRONUM, *op cit,* (2), p 111

148. FERREIRA, Memoirs of Ben Bouwer, p 266

149. *Ibid*, p 266

150. VAN SCHOOR, Die Bannelinge..., p 9

151. FERREIRA, Memoirs of Ben Bouwer, p 266

152. *Ibid,* p 272

153. SMUTS, *op cit*, p 144

154. FERREIRA, Memoirs of Ben Bouwer, p 272

155. AMERY, *op cit*, vol V, p 551

156. FERREIRA, Memoirs of Ben Bouwer, p 228

157. GRONUM, *op cit,* (2) p 113

158. HATTINGH, Britse fortifikasies..., p 119

159. McDONALD, In die Skaduwee van die Dood, p 106

160. GRONUM, *op cit* (1), p 113

161. AMERY, *op cit*, vol V, p 529

162. FARWELL, *op cit,* p 557

163. FERREIRA, ... SPE Trichard, p 205

164. AMERY, *op cit*, vol V, p 556

165. HATTINGH, Britse fortifikasies..., p 90

166. AMERY, *op cit,* vol V, pp 526-527

167. GRONUM, *op cit.* (1) p 113

168. AMERY, *op cit*, vol V, p 558; VAN ZYL, Die Helde-album..., p 395

169. FERREIRA, Memoirs of Ben Bouwer, p 272

170. LE MAY, *op cit,* p 130

171. AMERY, *op cit,* vol V, pp 528-530

172. FERREIRA, Memoirs of Ben Bouwer, p 272

173. *Ibid,* p 270

174. FERREIRA, ... SPE Trichard, p 208

175. KRUGER, Good-bye Dolly Gray, p 492

176. HEADLAM, *op cit*, vol II, p 331

177. SPIES, Methods of Barbarism?, p 381

178. AMERY, *op cit*, vol V, p 561

179. KLERKSDORP GRAVEYARD

180. SPIES, Methods of Barbarism?, p 282

181. GRONUM, *op cit,* (1) p 120

182. *Ibid,* (1) p 116

183. SPIES, Methods of Barbarism?, p 282

184. AMERY, *op cit,* vol V, p 561

185. FERREIRA, Memoirs of Ben Bouwer, p 222

186. VAN ZYL, Die Helde-album..., p 395

187. WESSELS, War Diary..., p 190

188. AMERY, *op cit,* vol V, p 565

189. FERREIRA, ...SPE Trichard, p 208

190. GRONUM, *op cit* (2), p 198

191. WESSELS, War Diary..., p 192

192. *Ibid,* p 192

193. AMERY, *op cit*, vol V, pp 561-562

194. GRUNDLINGH, 'Hendsoppers'..., p 216

195. SPIES, Methods of Barbarism?, p 283

196. FERREIRA, Memoirs of Ben Bouwer, p 276

197. *Ibid,* p 276

198. *Ibid,* p 267

199. *Ibid,* p 277

200. REITZ, Commando..., pp 316-317

201. GRUNDLINGH, 'Hensoppers'..., p 167

202. FERREIRA, Memoirs of Ben Bouwer, p 278

203. VAN SCHOOR, Die Bannelinge.., p 4

204. FERREIRA, Memoirs of Ben Bouwer, p 279

205. VAN ZYL, Die Helde-album..., p 385

206. HATTINGH, Britse fortifikasies..., p 88

207. PRETORIUS, Anglo-Boer War, p 73

208. PAKENHAM, *op cit*, p 555

209. HATTINGH, Britse fortifikasies..., p 61

210. WARWICK, Black people..., p 151

211. FERREIRA, Memoirs of Ben Bouwer, p 281

212. VAN SCHOOR, De Wet-annale No 8, p 11

213. VAN ZYL, Die Helde-album..., p 363

214. FERREIRA, Memoirs of Ben Bouwer, p 282

215. LE MAY, *op cit*, pp 140-141

216. WARWICK, Black people..., pp 90-93

217. HATTINGH, Britse fortifikasies..., p 119

218. WESSELS, War Diary..., p 194

219. FERREIRA, ... SPE Trichard, p 206

220. WESSELS, War Diary..., p 197

221. SPIES & NATTRASS, *op cit*, p 180

222. SMUTS, *op cit*, pp 155-156

223. GRONUM, *op cit*, (2) p 127

224. FARWELL, *op cit*, p 433

225. *Ibid*, p 434

226. DE WET, Three Year's War, p 350

227. SPIES, Methods of Barbarism?, p 285

228. LE MAY, *op cit*, p 144

229. FARWELL, *op cit*, p 435; LE MAY, *op cit*, p 145

230. SPIES, Methods of Barbarism?, p 276

231. PAKENHAM, *op cit*, p 563

232. LE MAY, *op cit*, p 145

233. VAN ZYL, Die Helde-album..., p 363

234. DE WET, Three Year's War, p 366

235. FARWELL, *op cit*, p 435

236. GRONUM, *op cit*, (2) p 202

237. VAN ZYL, Die Helde-album ..., p 363

238. PAKENHAM, *op cit*, p 562

239. *Ibid*, p 564

240. FARWELL, *op cit*, p 436

241. *Ibid, op cit*, p 346

242. PAKENHAM, *op cit*, p 564

243. *Ibid, op cit*, p 565

244. *Ibid, op cit*, p 561

245. *Ibid, op cit*, p 565

246. VAN ZYL, Die Helde-album..., p 363

247. LE MAY, *op cit*, p 148

248. FARWELL, *op cit*, p 436

249. KRUGER, Good-bye Dolly Gray, p 500

250. HATTINGH, Britse fortifikasies..., p 69

251. FARWELL, *op cit*, p 436

252. LE MAY, *op cit*, pp 150-151

253. GRONUM, *op cit*, (2) p 199

254. LE MAY, *op cit*, p 151

255. SPIES, Methods of Barbarism?, p 290

256. *Ibid*, p 292

257. LE MAY, *op cit*, p 151

258. SAUNDERS, Reader's Digest Illustrated History of SA..., p 260

259. LE MAY, *op cit*, p 152

260. PLOEGER, *op cit*, pp 33-42

261. WARWICK, Black people..., p 151

262. SPIES, Methods of Barbarism?, p 284

263. LE MAY, *op cit*, p 153

264. FARWELL, *op cit*, p 436

265. LE MAY, *op cit*, p 153

266. SAUNDERS, Reader's Digest Illustrated History of SA..., p 260; AMERY, *op cit*, vol V, p 606

267. FARWELL, *op cit*, p 441

268. *Ibid*, p 440

AND THEN ...

The tumult and the shouting dies;
The Captains and the Kings depart;
Still stands thine ancient sacrifice,
An humble and a contrite heart.
Lord God of Hosts, be with us yet,
Lest we forget — lest we forget!
                    — Rudyard Kipling (1865 — 1936)

The Republics ceased to exist and passed into history.

The shooting and burning stopped. The burghers laid down their arms, the prisoners of war came home, the survivors left the concentration camps and they all went home to.... nothing.

Most of the soldiers went home with their loot, leaving behind an Imperial garrison of 20 000 men — and the hurt and bitterness.

Lord Kitchener hastily invested his £50 000 victory grant voted by Parliament in South African gold shares and left for England (with a hoard of looted works of art). He did not become the Viceroy of India. The King was finally crowned. Generals Botha, De Wet and De la Rey left for Europe to raise funds for the widows and orphans and Chamberlain visited South Africa.

The Transvaal and Orange River Colony were inaugurated as Crown Colonies with Lord Milner as High Commissioner. The man whom most of the Afrikaners had held responsible for bringing about the war was now charged with managing the peace. Milner gathered a group of brilliant young men known as his 'Kindergarten' to administer Britain's latest acquisitions. The repatriation and reconstruction process started. Claims for compensation in terms of the peace agreement were initially handled by a Military Compensation Board — a strange arrangement, empowering soldiers to decide the fortunes of their former enemies. The claims of hands-uppers, collaborators and National Scouts enjoyed preference. Milner instituted a Central Judicial Commission to finalize the claims. Seventeen months after the war the only claims settled were those of hands-uppers, collaborators and National Scouts. When the burghers' claims were finally paid out, they received no more than two shillings in the pound plus £25 each. The hands-uppers and National Scouts were ostracized as traitors by Afrikaner society and were paid off and forgotten by their former allies.

Gold production remained lower than pre-war figures. Most of the black workers rejected the lower wages and the capitalists' new labour contracts. They stayed in their tribal areas and refused to return to the Rand. The black farm workers lingered in the concentration camps. Their own livestock had been destroyed, their previous employers had been ruined and were in no position to fetch them and bring them home. Some of them also believed the promises of a better life under British rule and others feared reprisals for having been forced to serve the British. The close relationship that existed on the farms for generations and the cameraderie that had them joining their masters on the battlefield or keeping the farms going while their masters were away on commando, had been effectively destroyed. The status of tribal leaders that had formed the basis of black and white co-existence in the Republics, was removed. A black rebellion in Zululand was ruthlessly suppressed and King Dinizulu was imprisoned. The blacks protested their treatment at the Peace negotiations with several deputations to London that resulted in nothing but led to the formation of the African Native National Congress — the forerunner of the African National Congress.

Milner's British immigration plan failed. His anglicization policy in education was countered by the 'Christian National Education' movement's private schools. Afrikaner national consciousness reawakened and gave birth first to a cultural and then to a political revival.

Chamberlain resigned the Colonial Secretaryship which was offered to Milner, but he declined.

President Kruger died in Clarens, Switzerland, and his body was brought home to Pretoria for a huge funeral attended by his mourning nation. A month later a new Afrikaner political body, the 'Het Volk' ('The People') party was formed in the Transvaal under Botha and Smuts' leadership.

Then came Milner's biggest blunder. Desperate to improve gold production, he acceded to the mine owners' constant pleas for cheap labour. He advocated and engineered the 'Chinese Labour Ordinance' and started recruiting Chinese to work in the mines.

Lord Salisbury was succeeded by Balfour who, in turn, was swept out of office by Campbell-Bannerman's victory in the British election. When Milner sanctioned flogging as a punishment on the mines, the allegations that Britain had instituted slavery in South Africa became a burning issue in the British election and throughout the Empire.

Milner had become a political millstone. He resigned and left South Africa.

Campbell-Bannerman kept his promise and granted self-government first to the Transvaal and then to the Orange River Colony. Botha's 'Het Volk' swept to victory in the Transvaal and was soon followed by the success of Hertzog and De Wet's 'Orangia Unie' (Orange Union) in the Free State. Botha sent the Chinese home.

Lord Selborne became Governor of the Transvaal and a memorandum prepared by him led to the National Convention of the British Territories in South Africa. Although the map boded ill for the future with the inclusion of certain areas annexed by the British, such as Zululand, Transkei, Pondoland and British Bechuanaland, and the exclusion of others, like Basutoland, Swaziland and the Bechuanaland Protectorate, the Union of South Africa was established on 31 May 1910 — the eighth anniversary of the Treaty of Vereeniging. The Boers may have lost the war but they won the peace.

Louis Botha became the first Prime Minister of the Union. His South African Party won the first national elections but soon afterwards a split with Hertzog led to the formation of the National Party.

The pistol shot in Sarajevo started the First World War. Ironically, the British defeats during the Anglo-Boer War and the military lessons learned against the Boers were to save the British Empire. The Army was reformed, artillery was upgraded and the value of accurate rifle fire and of taking cover were to be decisive in the war that stalled along an almost static front formed by the final development of De la Rey's trenches.

In the Free State and Western Transvaal, it seemed to many that the time had come to wipe the humiliation of Vereeniging off the slate and to wrestle back their lost independence. Fiery speeches were held and when Botha donned khaki and decided to support the British war effort by invading German South-West Africa, the Rebellion broke out. Before he could show his hand, De la Rey was accidentally shot and killed at a police roadblock meant for a notorious gang of bank robbers. De Wet took to the veld again, Maritz crossed into German territory and attacked Upington. Kemp took his followers on an epic trek from the Western Transvaal, across the arid northern Cape to the border with German South-West Africa. Beyers drowned in the Vaal River while trying to escape from government troops who, only days before had honoured him as their Commandant-General. De Wet lost his son and was captured — by an Afrikaner. The Rebellion, which threatened to become a civil war, was quickly brought under control, the leaders imprisoned and Botha did his imperial duty by invading and conquering the German colony. South African troops also served in German East Africa, Palestine and Europe, where their heroic stand at Delville Wood won them the admiration of friend and foe.

After the war, Botha and Smuts pleaded for reconciliation between the white races and, almost unconsciously, Afrikaner bitterness focused on a common 'peril' — the rapidly increasing black majority. Franchise — the pretext of the war and all its suffering — again became a bogey. The inevitability of numbers compelled several Afrikaner thinkers to question democracy as an appropriate political system for the country. During the Great Strike of 1922, some flirted with the Red Flag that confronted both the capitalist mine owners (still the Uitlanders in their collective memory) and the threat of blacks taking over 'white' jobs. Many Afrikaners who left their farms and sought their future in mining and industry, lost their jobs during the Great Depression and those who struggled on trying to rebuild their destroyed farms were devastated by the Great Drought of 1933. Known as 'poor whites', they became like beggars in their own country, travelling like nomads from job to job, only to find themselves competing with blacks, who were willing to work for less.

It was hardly surprising that some of the young intelligentsia who, during the brief boom in the twenties, had been sent to study in Europe, returned, inflamed by the policies that saw the re-emergence of Germany. Like in Germany, massive public works projects, including road and dam building schemes, created jobs for whites and restored their pride. The 'Broederbond', an organization devoted to the economic development of the Afrikaner, played a major role in uniting and mobilizing whatever funds were available to create Afrikaner financial institutions that could compete in a market dominated by firms linked to mining capital or British-based conglomerates.

Afrikaner nationalism was fuelled by 'cultural' and propaganda campaigns that culminated in the patriotic ardour that surrounded the symbolic ox-wagon trek from all corners of the country, commemorating the Great Trek a century before. The 'Volk' was bombarded by 'new' accounts of their pioneer sagas and Boer War exploits written by skilled propagandists. A new Afrikaner mythology was created, stressing their role as a 'chosen people' on the Dark Continent, their racial superiority and resurrecting the bitterness of the war. Almost all references to black participation in the war and the common suffering endured, were purged.

Democracy was ridiculed and, with the emergence of several uniformed paramilitary 'cultural' organizations, the Afrikaner hesitated close to National Socialism.

The Second World War again saw white South Africa divided. Smuts led the country into the war on the side of Britain and took the rank of Field-Marshal in the Allied Forces. His remarkable intellect made him invaluable to the Allied cause and a major figure in the international politics of the postwar New World — but estranged him from the Afrikaner, who had developed serious reservations about foreigners and Uitlanders. Soon after the war, he and the South African Party lost the election and the 'Age of the Generals' came to a close.

The National Party came to power with the assistance of several organizations that have dispensed with their pre-war trappings but not their ideologies. Gradually the racial mores of the country's rulers from the first white settlement, pursued by British Colonial policies and given a special vehement edge by the Anglo-Boer War and subsequent events, were written into the laws of the country. And then, they went further... A spate of laws followed: the rights of blacks, already limited, were reduced and eventually almost completely scrapped. The Afrikaner and the blacks with whom they had so much in common through a shared country, history and suffering, were pushed further and further apart until they became adversaries. South Africa was no longer the home of the heroes who took on the might of the British Empire, it was the country who gave a new word to the world — apartheid.

International postwar politics brought new issues to the already complicated South African scene. The new world order, the threat of communism, the rise of African nationalism and the decolonisation of Africa all had a direct bearing on the country and its future. Then Britain indicated a solution: to avoid the domination of a minority by a majority, both India and Palestine were partitioned, with the acquiescence of the international community, along borders which were no more than lines drawn on paper. Led by Verwoerd, a Hollander who came to the country just after the Anglo-Boer War, Afrikaner thinkers furiously started drawing maps. By moving people against their wishes, they started doing what had been done to them, forgetting the bitterness it had brought. But, before they were ready, the international climate had changed. The international community, led by the ex-colonial powers and Britain, who had granted independence to Lesotho, Swaziland, Botswana and others, was no longer prepared to consider splitting apart what they had been instrumental in in forcing together. So, South Africa rejected Britain and left the Commonwealth. They had stood alone before and thought they could do it again. A long-treasured dream came true when, at last, on the 59th anniversary of Vereeniging, the Republic was resurrected. They rejected the international community and formed a laager.

With the Anglo-Boer War relegated to the past, the power of a rising nationalism and the fiery emotions that can be kindled by withholding the franchise were forgotten — so too were the horrors of war, the cruel ruthlessness necessary to win a guerrilla war and how a war can be won and a peace lost.

Lord God of Hosts, be with us yet,
Lest we forget — lest we forget!

ANGLO-BOER WAR RIFLES
A COMPARISON

MARTINI-HENRI 11,4 mm calibre single-shot rifle (falling block action)
Country of Origin: Great Britain (1871)
Length: 1,265 m   Barrel length: 0,825 m   Mass: 3,86 kg
Muzzle velocity: ± 400 m/sec   Max. Sight adjustment: 1 280 m (1 400 yds)

Quantity available:
Z.A.R.   32 756
O.F.S.   12 335   TOTAL   45 091
Britain   Unknown

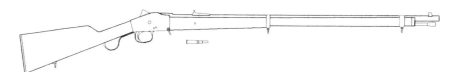

GUEDES 8 mm calibre single-shot rifle (falling block action)
Country of Origin: Portugal / Austria (1885)
Length: 1,210 m   Barrel length: 0,810 m   Mass: 4,10 kg
Muzzle velocity: ± 533 m/sec   Max. Sight adjustment: 2 000 m

Quantity available:
Z.A.R.   6 055
O.F.S.   1 450   TOTAL   7 505
Britain   None

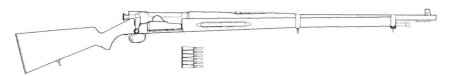

KRAG-JÖRGENSEN 6,5 mm calibre bolt action rifle
Country of Origin: Norway (1889)
Length: 1,267 m   Barrel length: 0,762 m   Mass: 4,25 kg
Muzzle velocity: ± 700 m/sec   Max. Sight adjustment: 2 000 m
Magazine: 5 round fixed horizontal magazine

Quantity available:
Z.A.R.   351
O.F.S.   None   TOTAL   351
Britain   None

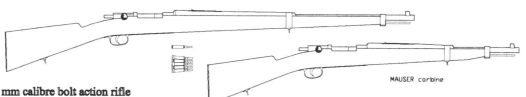

MAUSER carbine

MAUSER 7 mm calibre bolt action rifle
Country of Origin: Germany (1895)
Length: 1,235 m   Barrel length: 0,738 m   Mass: 4,00 kg
Muzzle velocity: ± 728 m/sec   Max. Sight adjustment: 2 000 m
Magazine: 5 round fixed magazine -- cartridges in loading clips

Quantity available:
Z.A.R.   35 850
O.F.S.   9 525   TOTAL   45 375
Britain   None

LEE-METFORD (.303) 7,9 mm calibre bolt action rifle
Country of Origin: Great Britain (1895)
Length: 1,266 m   Barrel length: 0,767 m   Mass: 4,63 kg
Muzzle velocity: ± 628 m/sec   Max. Sight adjustment: 1 830 m (2 000 yds)
Magazine: 10 round detachable magazine

Quantity available:
Z.A.R.   2 430
O.F.S.   None   TOTAL   2 430
Britain   Unknown

LATEGAN, F.V., Die Boer se Roer   SMITH, W.H.B. Small Arms of the World   BESTER, Ron, Boer Rifles and Carbines of the Anglo-Boer War

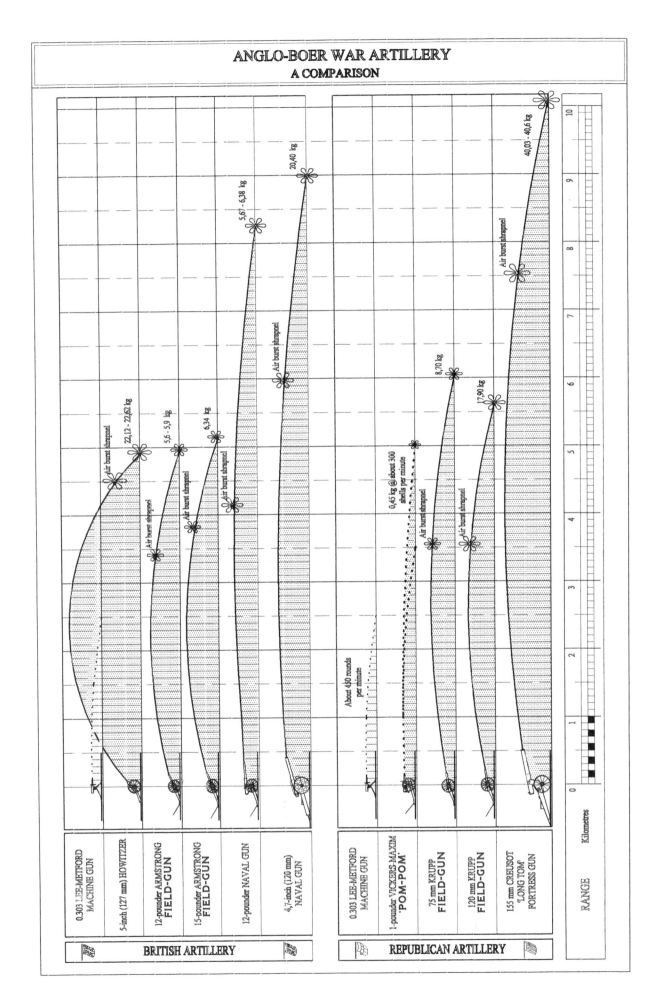

A RECKONING
THE BALANCE SHEET

THE REPUBLICS			THE BRITISH EMPIRE

AREAS [1]

The 'Zuid Afrikaansche Republiek' (Z.A.R.)	288 000 sq km	244 000 sq km	The United Kingdom and Northern Ireland
The Orange Free State (O.F.S.)	130 500 sq km	688 200 sq km	The Cape Colony (excl. Bechuanaland)
		91 000 sq km	Natal
TOTAL	418 500 sq km	1 023 800 sq km	TOTAL

POPULATIONS [2]

The 'Zuid Afrikaansche Republiek' (Whites)	approx 300 000	approx 45 500 000	The United Kingdom and Northern Ireland
The Orange Free State (Whites)	approx 145 000	approx 579 000	The Cape Colony (excl. Bechuanaland)
		approx 97 000	Natal
Blacks	(Unknown)	(Unknown)	Blacks
TOTAL (Whites)	approx 445 000	approx 46 176 000	TOTAL (Whites)

TOTAL NUMBER OF COMBATANTS EMPLOYED

The 'Zuid-Afrikaansche Republiek' [3]	25 411		The United Kingdom and Northern Ireland :
Z.A.R. Artillery, Signal Corps, etc.	733	256 340	Regulars (including Reserves)
Police	1 545	45 566	Militia
		36 353	Yeomanry
The Orange Free State	14 834	19 853	Volunteers
O.F.S. Artillery, Signal Corps, etc.	approx 490	7 273	South African Constabulary
Police	150		Colonials:
Mixed detachments from both states	8 925	16 378	Australians
Cape Rebels	3 635 - 7 000	6 416	New Zealanders
Foreign Volunteers [4]	2 120	7 289	Canadians
		840	Other Colonies
		52 414	South Africans (the largest contingent)
Blacks (Approx 7 000 to 9 000 — mostly used as auxiliaries and thus non-combatants)	(Unknown)	(Unknown)	Blacks (Officially 10 053 — probably more than 30 000)
TOTAL Approx	55 000 - 58 000	448 000	TOTAL [5]

EXPENDITURE

The 'Zuid Afrikaansche Republiek'	(Unknown)		The United Kingdom and Northern Ireland:
The Orange Free State	(Unknown)	£ 214 000 000	Military Budget Votes (±£1 500 000/week)
		3 000 000	Grant to Burghers (Peace Treaty)
		2 000 000	Grant to British subjects & others
		2 000 000	Protected Ex-Burgher Fund (Handsuppers and National Scouts)
		(Unknown)	Cape Colony (excl. Bechuanaland) & Natal
		(Unknown)	Other Colonies
TOTAL	(Unknown)	221 000 000	TOTAL (At least) [6]

OTHER LOSSES

Both Republics:		(Unknown)	The United Kingdom and Northern Ireland:
Approximately 30,000 farms and farmhouses damaged, plundered or destroyed. [7]	(Unknown)	(Unknown)	Other British Colonies South African Colonies
An unknown number of town houses, mills, huts, tribal vilages and other buildings damaged or destroyed.	(Unknown)	(Unknown)	Houses and property damaged or destroyed Claims submitted: [10]
Millions of sheep, cattle and horses as well as an incalculable tonnage of produce destroyed.	(Unknown)	£ 55 900	The Cape Colony (excl. Bechuanaland)
Claims submitted: [8]		£ 92 800	Natal
The 'Zuid Afrikaansche Republiek'	£ 4 900 000		
(Only £ 640 000 paid out)			
The Orange Free State	£ 6 000 000		
(Only £ 1 160 00 paid out)			
Blacks [9]	£ 661 000		
(Only £ 112 500 paid out)			
TOTAL (At least)	£ 11 561 000	£ 148 7000	TOTAL (At least)

A RECKONING
THE BUTCHER'S BILL

	REPUBLICAN CASUALTIES [11]				BRITISH & IMPERIAL CASUALTIES [12]	

DEATHS
SOUTH AFRICAN OPERATIONAL DEATHS

Killed in action	}	3 937	A	5 774	Killed in action
Died of wounds	}		B	2 018	Died of wounds
Accidental deaths		157	C	798	Accidental deaths
Foreign volunteers in Republican service		53	D		
Blacks in Republican Service		(Unknown)	E	(Unknown)	Blacks in British Service
TOTAL		4 147		8 590	TOTAL

OTHER FATALITIES

Died of disease	924	F	13 250	Died of disease
Prisoners who died in captivity in SA camps	541	G	102	Prisoners who died in captivity
Prisoners who died in captivity overseas	577	H	508	Soldiers who died after being invalided home
TOTAL	2 042		13 860	TOTAL
TOTAL Republican War Deaths (At least)	6 189		22 450	TOTAL Imperial War Deaths

OTHER CASUALTIES

Wounded	(Unknown)	I	8 517	Wounded	— Invalids sent home
Prisoners of war parolled and in SA camps	Approx 3 000	J	65 936	Sick	— Invalids sent home
Prisoners of war deported overseas	25 555	K	108	Missing and prisoners	
(Including 783 boys under 16			466	Not specified	
and 1 025 men over 60) [13]					
TOTAL Other Casualties	At least 27 000		75 027	TOTAL Other casualties	
TOTAL REPUBLICAN CASUALTIES	At least		97 477	TOTAL IMPERIAL CASUALTIES	

CIVILIAN FATALITIES [14]

CONCENTRATION CAMPS			WHITE CAMPS		BLACK CAMPS	IMPERIAL CIVILIAN CASUALTIES	
Children (under 16)			22 074	L	Approx 11 500	(Unknown)	Children
Women (over 16)		4 177					
Men (over 16)		155					
Men (over 60)		1 421					
Adults (Total)			5 753	M	Approx 2 600	(Unknown)	Adults
TOTAL			27 827		At least 14 100	(Unknown)	
TOTAL WHITE REPUBLICAN DEATHS			34 116			(Unknown)	
TOTAL REPUBLICAN CIVILIAN DEATHS					At least 42 081		

TOTAL COST IN HUMAN LIVES   At Least 70 720 Men, Women and Children

REPUBLICANS	OPERATIONAL DEATHS	A&B
	DIED OF DISEASE	F
	OTHER FATALITIES	G&H
BRITISH	OPERATIONAL DEATHS	C B A
	DIED OF DISEASE	F
	OTHER FATALITIES	G&H
CIVILIANS	WHITE CAMPS	L M
	BLACK CAMPS	L M ESTIMATED

Scale: 0, 5,000, 10,000, 15,000, 20,000, 25,000

NOTES:
1. BELFIELD, The Boer War, p 165.
2. Ibid, pp 165-166
3. SLOCUM, Boer War Operations, pp 101-104
4. BREYTENBACH, Die ... Tweede Vryheidsoorlog, Vol I, p68
   PAKENHAM, The Boer War, p 572
5. AMERY, Times History ...Vol VI, p 279
6. Ibid, Vol VI, p 607
7. PLOEGER, Lotgevalle van ..., p 3813
8. PLOEGER, op cit, p 3839
9. PAKENHAM, op cit, p 573
10. PLOEGER, op cit, p 3746
11. MEINTJES, Anglo-Boer Wa- ..., p 383
12. AMERY, op cit, Vol VII, p 25
13. DAVITT, The Boer Fight ..., p 584
14. MEINTJES, op cit, p 383

THE CONCENTRATION CAMPS
THE INNOCENTS

CAMPS FOR WHITES[1]

TRANSVAAL CAMPS
1. Balmoral
2. Belfast
3. Heidelberg
4. Irene
5. Klerksdorp
6. Krugersdorp
7. Middelburg
8. Standerton
9. Vereeniging
10. Volksrust
11. Barberton
12. Johannesburg
13. Nylstroom
14. Pietersburg
15. Potchefstroom
16. De Jagersdrift (Temporary)
17. V d Hofendrift (Temporary)
18. Meintjeskop (National Scouts)

CAPE COLONY AND BRITISH BECHUANALAND
1. Kimberley
2. Aliwal North
3. East London
4. Kabusi
5. Norval's Pont
6. Port Elizabeth
7. Uitenhage
8. Mafeking
9. Vryburg

FREE STATE CAMPS
1. Harrismith
2. Heilbron
3. Vredefort Road
4. Winburg
5. Bethulie
6. Bloemfontein
7. Brandfort
8. Kroonstad
9. Orange River
10. Springfontein
11. Kromellenboog (Temporary)
12. Ladybrand (Temporary)

NATAL
1. Colenso
2. Eshowe
3. Howick
4. Jacobs
5. Isipingo
6. Ladysmith
7. Mooi River
8. Merebank
9. Pietersmaritzburg
10. Pinetown
11. Wentworth

CAMPS FOR BLACKS[2]

TRANSVAAL CAMPS
1. Balmoral
2. Belfast
3. Heidelberg
4. Irene
5. Klerksdorp
6. Krugersdorp
7. Middelburg
8. Standerton
9. Vereeniging
10. Volksrust
11. Bantjes
12. Bezuidenhout's Valley
13. Boksburg
14. Brakpan
15. Bronkhorstspruit
16. Brugspruit
17. Elandshoek
18. Elandsrivier
19. Frederikstad
20. Greylingstad
21. Groot Olifants River
22. Koekemoer
23. Klipriviersberg
24. Klip River
25. Meyerton
26. Natalspruit
27. Nelspruit
28. Nigel
29. Olifantsfontein
30. Paardekop
31. Platrand
32. Rietfontein West
33. Springs
34. V d Merwe Station
35. Witkop
36. Wilgerivier

FREE STATE CAMPS
1. Harrismith
2. Heilbron
3. Vredefort Road
4. Winburg
5. Allemans Siding
6. America Siding
7. Boschrand
8. Eensgevonden
9. Geneva
10. Holfontein
11. Honingspruit
12. Houtenbek
13. Koppies
14. Rooiwal
15. Rietspruit
16. Smaldeel
17. Serfontein
18. Thaba Nchu
19. Taaibosch
20. Vet River
21. Virginia
22. Ventersburg Road
23. Welgelegen
24. Wolwehoek

CAPE COLONY AND BRITISH BECHUANALAND
(Administered by the O.R.C.)
1. Kimberley
2. Orange River
3. Taungs
4. Dryharts

TOTAL NUMBER of CAMPS	50	**TOTAL NUMBER of CAMPS**	64

DATE		CAMP POPULATION	DEATHS	DATE		CAMP POPULATION	DEATHS
1901	June	85 410	777	1901	June	32 360	-
	July	93 940	1 412		July	37 472	256
	Aug	105 347	1 878		Aug	53 154	575
	Sept	109 418	2 411		Sept	65 589	728
	Oct	113 506	3 156		Oct	75 950	1 327
	Nov	117 974	2 807		Nov	85 114	2 312
	Dec	117 017	2 380		Dec	89 407	2 831
1902	Jan	114 376	1 805	1902	Jan	97 986	2 534
	Feb	114 311	628		Feb	101 344	1 466
	March	111 508	402		March	101 299	972
	April	112 733	298		April	108 386	630
	May	116 572	196		May	115 700	523
TOTAL	(OFFICIAL)		18 150	**TOTAL**	(OFFICIAL)		14 154[4]
LATER CALCULATED TO BE			27 927[3]	**ESTIMATED TO EXCEED**			18 000

NOTES:
1 PLOEGER, Lotgevalle van ..., p 41:23
2 WARWICK, Black People ..., p 154
3 MEINTJES, Anglo-Boer War ... p 383
4 WARWICK, op cit, p 151

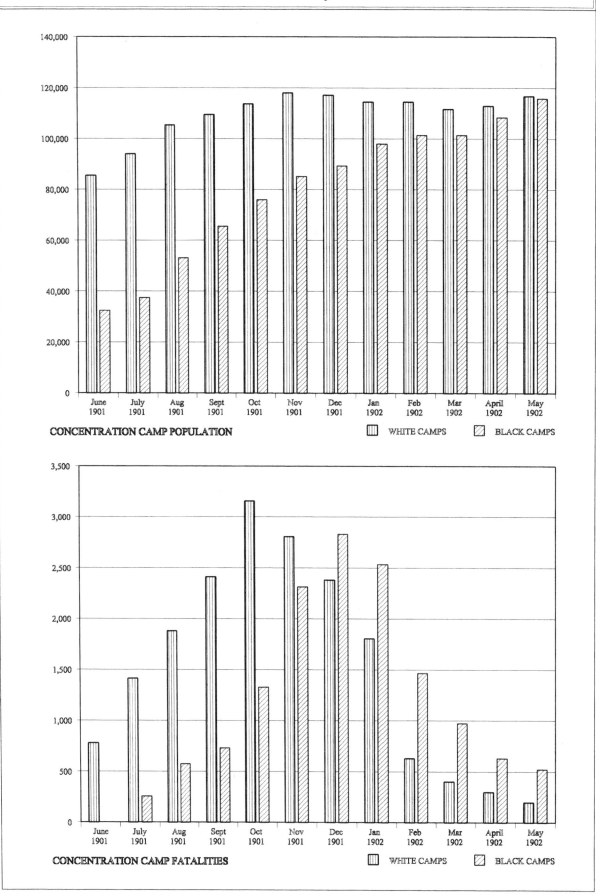

BIBLIOGRAPHY

AMERY, LCMS (ed.), The Times History of the War in South Africa 1899-1902, 7 vols. Sampson, Low & Marston, London, 1900-9.

ANDRIESEN, WF, Gedenkboek van die Oorlog in Zuid-Afrika. Amsterdam, 1904.

BARBARY, J, The Boer War. London, 1971.

BARNARD, Dr DJ, Genl. Louis Botha op die Natalse front 1899-1900. Cape Town, 1970.

BELFIELD, E, The Boer War. London, 1975.

BENBOW, CH, Boer Prisoners of War in Bermuda. Hamilton, Bermuda, 1994.

BREYTENBACH, JH, Die Geskiedenis van die Tweede Vryheidsoorlog in Suid-Afrika 1899-1902, 6 vols. The Government Printer, Pretoria, 1969-98.

BREYTENBACH, JH, Gedenkalbum van die Tweede Vryheidsoorlog. Cape Town, 1949.

BREYTENBACH, JH, Kommandant Danie Theron. Cape Town, 1950.

BRITS, JP (ed.), Diary of a National Scout, P.J. du Toit, 1900-1902. HSRC, Pretoria, 1974.

CALDWELL, TC (ed.), The Anglo-Boer War — Why was it fought? Who was responsible? Lexington, Mass., 1968.

CAMMACK, D, The Rand at War 1899-1902. London, 1990.

CHISHOLM, R, Ladysmith. Braamfontein, Johannesburg, 1979.

COIN REPORT (THE). Vol I, No 5, 1998.

COMAROFF, JL (ed.), The Boer War diary of Sol. T. Plaatje, COIN REPORT (THE). Vol I, No 5, 1998 an African at Mafeking. Johannesburg 1973.

CONRADIE, FD, Met Cronjé op die Wesfront. Cape Town, 1943

COULTER, J and COOPER, JA, Queen Victoria. Ontario, 1901.

CRESWICKE, L, South Africa and the Transvaal War (6 vols). TC & EC Jack, London, 1901.

DAVIDSON, A and FILATOVA, I, The Russians and the Anglo-Boer War 1899-1902. Cape Town, 1998.

DAVITT, M, The Boer Fight for Freedom. Funk & Wagnell, 1902, Reprint Scripta Africana, Pretoria, 1988.

DE JONG, C (ed.), Skandinawiërs in die Tweede Anglo-Boere-Oorlog. Amsterdam, 1984.

DE SOUZA, CWL, No Charge for Delivery. Cape Town, 1969.

DE WET, CR, De Strijd tusschen Boer en Brit. Amsterdam, 1902.

DE WET, CR, Three Year's War (reprint 1985). New York, 1902.

DOONER, MG, The 'Last Post', (reprint 1980). Suffolk, 1980.

DOYLE, ARTHUR CONAN, The Great Boer War. Struik (reprint), Cape Town, 1976.

DU PLESSIS, Ph J, Oomblikke van Spanning op Kommando. Cape town, 1942.

DUXBURY, GR, Die slag van Magersfontein 11 Desember 1899. Johannesburg, 1975.

ELOFF, CC (ed), Oorlogsdagboekie van H.S. Oosterhagen, Januarie-Junie 1902. HSRC, Pretoria, 1976.

FARWELL, B, The Great Boer War, Harper and Row. New York, 1976.

FERREIRA, OJO (ed.), Geschiedenis, Werken en Streven van SPE Trichard – door hemselve beschreven. HSRC, Pretoria, 1975.

FERREIRA, OJO (ed.), Krijgsgevangenschap van LC Ruijssenaars. HSRC, Pretoria, 1977.

GARDNER, B, The Lion's Cage. London, 1969.

GREENWALL, R, Artists and Illustrators of the Anglo-Boer War. Cape Town, 1992.

GRIFFITH, K, Thank God We Kept the Flag Flying. London, 1974

GROENEWALD, C, Bannelinge oor die oseaan, Boerekrygsgevangenes 1899-1902. Pretoria, 1992.

GRONUM, MA, Die Bittereinders, Junie 1901-Mei 1902. Cape Town, 1974.

GRONUM, MA, Die Engelse Oorlog, 1899-1902. Cape Town, 1972.

GRONUM, MA, Die Ontplooiing van die Engelse Oorlog, 1899-1900. Cape Town, 1977

GRUNDLINGH, AM, Die 'Hendsoppers' en die 'Joiners': die rasionaal en verskynsel van verraad. Pretoria, 1979.

GUEST, HM, Incidents in the Western Transvaal. Klerksdorp, 1902.

HANCOCK, WK, Smuts – The Sanguine Years 1870 - 1919. Cambridge, 1962.

HANCOCK, WK and VAN DER POEL (eds.), Selections for the Smuts Papers. Cambridge, 1969.

HATTINGH, J and WESSELS, A, Britse fortifikasies in die Anglo Boereoorlog (1899-1902). Bloemfontein, 1997.

HEADLAM, C, The Milner Papers, 2 vols. London, 1933.

HILLEGAS, HC, With the Boer Forces. London, 1900. (reprint Johannesburg, 1987).

HOLT, Edgar, The Boer War. London, 1958.

JOHNSON, D, The Anglo-Boer War, a collection of contemporary documents compiled by... Jackdaw Publications, London.

JORDAAN, G. Hoe zij stierven: medelingen aangaande het einde dergenen aan wien gedurende den laasten oorlog, in den Kaap-Kolonie, het doodvonnis voltrokken is. Burgersdorp, S.A.

KANDYBA-FOXCROFT, E, Russia and the Anglo-Boer War, 1899-1902. Roodepoort, 1981.

KEMP, JCG, Die Pad van die Veroweraar. Cape Town, 1942.

KEMP, JCG, Vir Vryheid en Reg. Cape Town, 1942.

KESTELL, JD, Through Shot and Flame. London, 1903.

KRIEL, C and DE VILLIERS, J, Rondom die Anglo-Boereoorlog 1899-1902. Perskor, Johannesburg, 1979.

KRUGER, DW, Die Krugermiljoene. Johannesburg, 1979.

KRUGER, R, Good-Bye Dolly Gray: a history of the Boer War. London, 1964.

LEE, Emanoel CG, To the Bitter End. Middlesex, England, 1985.

LE MAY, GHL, British Supremacy in South Africa 1899-1907. London, 1965.

LE RICHE, PJ (auth.) and FERREIRA, OJO (ed.), Memoirs of Ben Bouwer. Pretoria, 1980.

MALAN, J, Die Boere-offisiere van die Tweede Vryheidsoorlog 1899-1902. Pretoria, 1990.

MARX, Roelf (ed.), Klerksdorp, Groeiende Reus 1837-1987. Klerksdorp, 1987.

MAY, JM, Music of the Guns. Based on two journals of the Boer War. London, 1970.

McCORD, Capt. JJ, South African Struggle. Pretoria, 1952.

McCRACKEN, DP, The Irish Pro-Boers. Johannesburg, 1989.

McDONALD, RD, In die skaduwee van die dood. Cape Town, 1943.

MEINTJES, J, Anglo-Boereoorlog in Beeld. Cape Town, 1976.

MEINTJES, J, Anglo-Boer War, A pictorial history. Cape Town, 1976.

MEINTJES, J, Stormberg: a lost opportunity. Cape Town, 1969.

MEINTJES, J, Sword in the sand: the life and death of Gideon Scheepers. Cape Town, 1969.

MEINTJES, J, The Commandant-General. Cape Town, 1971.

MIDGLEY, JF, Petticoat in Mafeking. Cape Town, 1974.

MULLER, Prof. CFJ, 500 Years – A History of South Africa. Pretoria, 1984.

NIENABER, PJ (ed.), Gedenkboek Generaal JBM Hertzog. Johannesburg, 1965.

OBERHOLSTER, AG (ed.), Dagboek van H.C. Bredell 1900-1904. Pretoria, 1972.

OBERHOLSTER, AG (ed.), Oorlogsdagboek van Jan F.E. Celliers 1899-1902. Pretoria, 1978.

OOSTHUIZEN, AV, Rebelle van die Stormberge. Pretoria, 1994.

OOSTHUIZEN, P, Boer War Memorabilia. Edmonton, 1987.

ORFORD, J, Unpublished manuscript.

PAKENHAM, T, The Boer War. Weidenfeld and Nicholson, London, 1979.

PEDDLE, Col. DE, Long Cecil, the story of the Gun made during the Siege of Kimberley, 15 October 1899 to 15 February 1900. Johannesburg, 1997.

PEMBERTON, WB, Battles of the Boer War. London, 1964.

PIETERSE, HCJ, Oorlogsavonture van Genl. Wynand Malan. Cape Town, 1946.

PLOEGER, Dr J, Die Lotgevalle van die Burgerlike Bevolking gedurende die Anglo-Boereoorlog, 1899-1902, (5 vols.). State Archive Service, Pretoria, 1990.

PORTER, AN, The origins of the South African War – Joseph Chamberlain and the Diplomacy of Imperialism 1895-99. Manchester, 1980.

POTTINGER, B, The Foreign Volunteers. They fought for the Boers. Scripta Africana, Pietermaritzburg, 1986.

PRELLER, GS, Scheepers se dagboek en die stryd in Kaapland (1 Okt. 1901 - 18 Jan. 1902). Cape Town, 1940.

PRELLER, GS, Talana: die Driegeneraalslag by Dundee met lewenskets van Genl. Danie Erasmus. Cape Town, 1942.

PRESTON, A, Pictorial History of South Africa. London, 1995.

PRETORIUS, F, Die eerste dryfjag op hoofkomdt. C.R. de Wet. Christiaan de Wet-annale 4, Okt. 1976, pp. 1 - 220.

PRETORIUS, F, Kommandolewe tydens die Anglo-Boer-oorlog. Cape Town, 1991.

SAUNDERS, C, et al (ed.), Reader's Digest Illustrated History of South Africa – The Real Story. Cape Town, 1988.

SCHOLTZ, GD, Generaal Christiaan Frederik Beyers. Johannesburg, 1941.

SCHOLTZ, L, Beroemde Suid-Afrikaanse Krygsmanne. Cape Town, 1984.

'SETEMPE Magazine, March/April 1998.

SLOCUM, Capt. SLH and REICHMANN, Capt. C, Boer War Operations in South Africa, 1899-1901. Washington, 1901 (reprint Johannesburg, 1987).

SMIT, AP and MARÉ L (eds.), Die beleg van Mafeking: Dagboek van Abraham Stafleu. Pretoria, 1985.

SPIES, SB and NATRASS, G (ed.), Jan Smuts – Memoirs of the Boer War. Johannesburg, 1994.

SPIES, SB, Methods of Barbarism? Human & Rousseau. Pretoria, 1976.

STRYDOM, CJS, Kaapland en die Tweede Vryheidsoorlog. Cape Town, 1943; The Anglo-Boer War 1899-1902, An Album... Northern Cape Publishers, S.A.

TAITZ, J, The War Memoirs of Commandant Ludwig Krause, 1899-1900. Cape Town, 1996.

THE ANGLO-BOER WAR 1899-1900, An Album. Northern Cape Publishers, no date.

TODD, P and FORDHAM, D (ed.), Private Tucker's Boer War Diary. London, 1980.

VAN DEN BERG, Prof. GN, 24 Battles and Battle-fields of the North-West Province. Potchefstroom, 1996.

VAN DER MERWE, JCK, Met God, Sambok en Mauser; Die taktiese waardering van . . . Nooitgedacht. Pretoria, 1986.

VAN REENEN, R (ed.), Emily Hobhouse, Boer War Letters. Cape Town, 1984.

VAN RENSBURG, T, (ed.), Oorlogsjoernaal van S.J. Burger, 1899-1902, HSRC. Pretoria, 1977.

VAN SCHOOR, MCE (ed.), 'n Bittereinder aan die Woord, Marthinus Theunis Steyn. Bloemfontein, 1997.

VAN SCHOOR, MCE (ed.), Die Bannelinge – Anglo-Boerekrygsgevangenes 1899-1902 – 'n Gedenkbrosjure. Bloemfontein, 1983.

VAN SCHOOR, MCE (ed.), Christiaan de Wet-Annale Nommer 1. Bloemfontein, October 1972.

VAN SCHOOR, MCE (ed.), Christiaan de Wet-Annale Nommer 2. Bloemfontein, October 1973.

VAN SCHOOR, MCE (ed.), Christiaan de Wet-Annale Nommer 3. Bloemfontein, October 1975.

VAN SCHOOR, MCE (ed.), Christiaan de Wet-Annale Nommer 4. Bloemfontein, October 1976.

VAN SCHOOR, MCE (ed.), Christiaan de Wet-Annale Nommer 5. Bloemfontein, October 1978.

VAN SCHOOR, MCE (ed.), Christiaan de Wet-Annale Nommer 6. Bloemfontein, October 1984.

VAN SCHOOR, MCE (ed.), Christiaan de Wet-Annale Nommer 7. Bloemfontein, March 1988.

VAN SCHOOR, MCE (ed.), Christiaan de Wet-Annale Nommer 8. Bloemfontein, November 1990.

VAN ZYL, PHS, Die Helde-album van ons Vryheidstryd. Johannesburg, 1944.

VILJOEN, B, My Reminiscences of the Anglo-Boer War. London, 1902.

WALLACE, Edgar, Unofficial Dispatches. Cape Town, 1975.

WARWICK, P, Black people and the South-African War, 1899-1902. Cambridge, 1983.

WARWICK, P (ed.), The South African War – The Anglo-Boer War 1899-1902. Harlow Essex, 1980.

WATERS, WHH, and DU CANE, H (transl.), The German Official Account of the War in South Africa. London, 1904 (reprint Johannesburg, 1986)

WESSELS, A (ed.), Anglo-Boer War Diary of Herbert Gwynne Howell. Pretoria, 1986.

WESSELS, A, Die Anglo-Boereoorlog 1899-1902. 'n Oorsig van die militêre verloop van die stryd. Bloemfontein, 1991.

WESSELS, A (ed.), Egodokumente – Persoonlike ervaringe uit die Anglo-Boereoorlog. Bloemfontein, 1993.

WITTON, Lieut. GEORGE, Scapegoats of the Empire. Melbourne, 1982.

WOODS, F (ed.), Young Winston's Wars. London, 1972.

WULFSOHN, LIONEL, Rustenburg at War. Rustenburg, 1992.

ZUID-AFRIKAANS VERJAARDAGBOEK, Zuid-Afrikaanse Vrouwe-Federasie, no date.

Index

A

Aberdeen 328
Abrahamskraal (Driefontein), Battle of 115, 116
Ackermann, Comdt. J 266
Acton Homes 84, 86
Adye, Col. J 113, 115, 149
Aked, Dr C 286
Alberts, Comdt. JJ 29, 252, 258, 275, 316, 323, 331
Alberts, Comdt. Sarel 300, 302, 303, 323
Alberts, Field-cornet 46
Albrecht, Maj. FWR 59, 61, 62, 94, 98, 100, 102-104
Alderson, Brig. EAH 90, 124, 219, 221
Alexander, Col. 256
Aliwal North 51, 53, 117, 119, 220, 294
Alleman's Nek, Battle of 158
Allen, Gen. RE 138
Allenby, Col. EHH 219, 220, 262, 266, 321
America Siding 163
Anderson, Col. WC 304
Aties 301, 306

B

Babington, Gen. JM 94, 95, 214, 218, 227, 229, 231, 234, 237, 238
Baden-Powell, Col. (Gen.) RSS 22, 38, 40, 43, 44, 50, 54, 75, 79, 84, 95, 107, 111, 123, 125, 129, 132, 134, 143, 144, 147, 152, 161, 162, 218, 225, 303
Badenhorst, Comdt. (Gen.) CJJ 196, 205, 218, 318, 331
Badenhorst, Comdt. H 302
Baken Kop 167
Bakenlaagte, Battle of 274
Bankkop, Ambush at 292
Balmoral 167, 174, 199, 216, 247, 312
Barberton 171, 187-189, 196, 209, 314
Barker, Gen. JC 301, 303, 311
Barton, Col. (Gen.) G 38, 59, 65, 70-72, 104, 111, 138-140, 162, 192-195, 199
Beatson, Gen. SB 234, 235, 243, 244
Beit, A 12
Belfast 284, 326
Belfast, Attack on 214
Belmont, Battle of 57
Benson, Maj. (Col.) GE 67, 234, 235, 256, 257, 259, 262, 264-266, 272-275, 280, 281
Bergendal (Dalmanutha), Battle of 181-183
Bester, Rebel P 278
Bethlehem 167, 168, 170, 171, 179, 236, 255, 284, 286, 293, 294, 297, 302, 307, 311
Beyers, (Gen.) CF 156, 170, 187, 190, 204, 205, 207, 208, 216, 217, 219, 224, 233, 251, 269, 295, 311, 314, 318, 322, 327
Biddulphsberg, Battle of 149, 150, 152
Blignaut, Comdt. JSF 172
Blockhouse lines 227, 229, 247, 253, 258, 259, 262, 265, 269, 273, 275, 280, 281, 283, 285, 286, 288, 296, 297, 300-303, 307, 311, 316-318, 323-326, 330
Bloemfontein 38, 45, 54, 55, 59, 82, 90, 91, 99, 100, 109, 113-123, 129-131, 133-138, 143, 155, 158, 162, 185, 187, 189, 197, 199, 201, 209, 217, 218, 227, 235, 236, 238, 256, 262, 265, 266, 297, 316, 324
Bloemfontein, Plague of 119, 121, 135, 136, 152, 153
Bloemfontein, Occupation of 118
Blood River's Poort, Battle of 265
Blood, Gen. Sir Bindon 233, 234, 237
Boschbult, Battle of 314, 316
Boschman's Kop, Fight at 316
Boshof 117, 129, 131, 133, 134, 139, 144, 187, 196
Boshof, Battle of 131
Boshoff, Comdt. FJ 202, 268, 269
Botha's Pass 157, 297, 311
Botha, Comdt. HNW 280, 303, 316, 326
Botha, Gen. C 70, 74, 144, 147, 150, 154, 155, 157, 170, 172, 179, 192, 204, 214, 221, 233, 238, 267, 268, 270, 273, 286, 292
Botha, Gen. L 29, 40, 48, 57, 62, 64, 65, 70, 73, Promotion 54, 62
Botha, Comdt.-Gen. L 80, 82, 83, 85-87, 89-93, 101, 106, 110, 112, 113, 119, 120, 122, 140-145, 147, 150, 153-155, 160-162, 167, 169-174, 180-182, 184, 186, 187, 189, 190, 192, 193, 195-197, 202, 203, 215, 221, 223, 225, 226, 228-230, 233, 238, 245, 251,

254, 260-265 Invades Natal 265, 266, 269, 270-274, 281, 288, 302, 308, 311, 318, 323, 325, 327-329, 331, 332
Botha, Gen. PR 103, 107, 136, 137, 139, 142, 199, 200, 214, 229, 251
Bothaville 186, 195-197, 199
Bothaville (Doornkraal), Battle of 198
Bouwer, Comdt. BD 90, 253, 254, 256, 258, 261, 270, 279, 295, 297, 301, 302, 306, 316-318
Boyes, Gen. JE 138
Boyle, Lt. C 200
Brabant, Gen. EY 51, 89, 101, 114, 116, 117, 122, 129, 133, 135, 138, 141, 145
Brain, TP 252
Brand, Comdt. (Gen.) GA 224, 225, 228, 265, 266
Brandwater Basin 168, 170-176, 306, 326
Brebner, WJC 318, 332
Bremersdorp, The Burning of 254, 255, 260, 261
Bridgeford, Maj. 285
Briggs, Col. 284
Brits, Comdt. (Gen.) C 285, 287
Broadwood, Brig. RG 95, 100, 106, 119, 122-124, 129, 138, 139, 158, 170, 171, 173, 174, 205, 235, 252, 256, 281-283
Brocklehurst, Gen. JF 51, 141, 163, 186
Brodrick, St J 193, 198, 203, 230, 240, 242, 245, 253-256, 271, 272, 276, 277, 281, 322, 329
Broeksma, C 264, 269
Brynbella Hill 57
Buffelspoort (Vanwykspruit), Battle of 202
Buller, Gen. Sir R 32, 41, 49, 51, 57, 59, 64, 65, 67, 69-73, 82, 83, 85-87, 89-95, 97-99, 103, 104, 106, 108-113, 141-146, 149, 150, 154, 155, 157, 160, 162, 163, 175, 179-187, 190-192, 195, 215, 270
Bullock, Col. GM 239, 243
Bunu, King 70
Burger, SW (Gen.) (Vice-Pres.) 17, 26, 29, 38, 60, 62, 89-91, 122, 263, 264, 271, 278, 280, 313, 318, 327, 331, 332
Burgher Peace Committee 208, 209
Burn-Murdoch, Brig. JF 141
Bushveld Carbineers 251, 258, 260, 263, 265, 288, 294
Butler, Gen. Sir W 10, 12, 18-20, 23
Byng, Col. JHG 207, 226, 281, 303

C

Callwell, Col. 276, 324
Calvinia 215, 221, 238, 300, 301, 322, 325, 330
Campbell, Gen. BBD 138, 220, 221
Campbell, Col. WP 263, 284
Campbell-Bannerman, Sir H 12, 244, 294
Capper, Col. T 262, 277, 298, 300, 302
Carleton, Col. FRC 47-49
Carrington, Gen. Sir F 121, 141, 143, 161, 176-179
Carter's Ridge, Attack on 60, 62
Cavendish-Bentinck, Lord C 40
Cecil, Lord E 40
Celliers, Gen. JG 286, 295, 304, 309, 314, 319
Chamberlain, J 9, 11, 13, 15, 16, 18-31, 34; Crisis 9, 11, 15, 16, 19, 23-25, 27-29, 34; Anti-German speech 63, 83, 92, 133, 136, 138, 143, 168, 176, 193, 196, 204, 207, 217, 222, 228, 230, 237, 240, 252, 257, 273, 276, 277, 281, 285, 287, 308, 313, 314, 318, 322, 328, 329
Chemside, Gen. Sir HC 95, 104, 106, 122, 132-134, 138
Christain Victor Albert, Prince 191
Churchill, WS 41, 54, 64, 69, 74, 75, 193, 202, 230, 280, 318, 329
Cilliers, Barend 214, 251, 330
Cingolo, Battle of 99-101, 103
Clements, Gen. RAP 94, 95, 98, 104, 106, 109, 112, 114, 116, 118-120, 122, 131, 138, 163, 167, 168, 173, 183, 190, 202, 204, 205, 207, 222
Clery, Gen. CF 59, 84, 85, 87, 141, 163, 141, 163, 167, 192
Coetzee, Comdt. KD 324
Coke, Gen. JT 86-89, 106, 141, 157, 158, 163, 172
Cole, Col. L 261
Colesberg 49, 53, 55, 70, 79-83, 90, 94, 98, 104, 110, 112, 114-116, 118, 119
Colenbrander, Col. JW 314, 318, 322

Colvile, Col 209, 263
Colvile, Gen. Sir HE 53, 61, 62, 64, 96, 102, 115, 123, 124, 138, 147, 149, 162
Colyn, L 302, 306
Commando Nek 167, 169, 174, 176, 181, 183
Communications 90, 104, 121, 154, 167, 169, 174-176, 181, 183, 185, 191, 197, 202, 210, 220, 226, 232, 233, 237, 241, 257, 262, 269
Conan Doyle, Dr A 73, 239, 329
Concentration camps 175, 185, 187, 189-191, 197, 202, 208, 210, 217-220, 225-229, 233-235, 238, 244, 245, 247, 253, 255-257, 260, 262, 264, 269, 274-283, 286, 288, 295, 297, 307, 308, 312, 316, 325, 326, 331
Concordia 317
Conroy, Comdt. EA 294
Cookson, Col. 314-316
Cooper, Col. H 325
Cordua, Hans 180, 182
Crabbe, Col. EMS 239, 255, 264, 277, 286, 297, 298, 300, 302
Crofton, Maj. 297, 298, 300
Cronje, Gen. APJ 29, 94, 134-136, 139, 140, 156, 157, 161, 208, 281
Cronje, Gen. PA 38, 39, 41-43, 49, 51, 55, 60, 62, 67, 86, 89, 90, 92, 95, 97-107, 109-111, 115, 120, 130, 133, 140, 174, 191
Cronje, PA (OFS) 46, 82, 83, 89, 252
Crowther, Comdt. (Gen.) 31, 121, 170, 171
Cunningham, Gen. GG 190, 218, 220, 221, 227, 262, 273, 280, 286, 287
Cyferfontein, Council of War 196
Cyferfontein Skirmish at 214

D

Dalgety, Col. EH 75, 76, 101, 131-133, 135, 138, 145, 173, 176, 185
Damant, Col. JH 261, 281, 284, 285, 303, 314
Davel, Comdt. OAI 243, 252
Davies, 'Karri' 11, 81, 144, 238
Davitt, M 19, 46
De Aar 38, 51, 63, 101, 113, 224, 229, 247, 265, 283, 288
De Beer, Comdt. Tollie JF 29, 100, 102, 103, 189, 193
De Emigratie, Meeting at 238
De Jager, Z 81
De Kock, Meyer 204, 208, 209, 217, 219, 222, 223
De la Rey, Gen. JH 29, 39, 41, 43, 44, 46, 47, 54, 58-64, 82, 104, 106, 109, 116, 117, 121, 129, 133, 137, 139-141, 144, 147, 150, 153, 154, 157, 158, 160, 167, 169, 173, 175-180, 185, 192, 196, 202, 205, 207-209, 214, 218, 224, 225, 227, 228, 230, 231, 236, 240, 242, 245, 259-261, 268, 269, 271, 273, 295, 303-306, 308-314, 317, 318, 327-329, 331, 332
De Lisle, Col. H de B 233, 235, 237, 243, 252, 256, 257
De Lotbiniere, Maj. GJ 285, 293, 295
De Villebois-Mareuil, (Col.) Gen. 116, 120, 121, 129, 131
De Villiers, Comdt. (Gen.) 31, 42, 45, 51
De Villiers, Comdt. (Gen.) CJ 80, 81, 171, 172, 174
De Villiers Field-cornet 81
De Villiers, Gen. AJ 129, 130, 149, 150, 152, 161
De Villiers, Gen. P 152, 163
De Wet, Comdt. M 114
De Wet, (Gen.) Chief Comdt. CR 42, 45, 48, 49, 65, 92, 94, 95, 97, 99, 100, 103, 104, 106, 107, 109, 110, 115-124, 129-137, 140, 146, 153, 154, 156-158, 160-163, 168-170, First Hunt 170-174, 176-180, 180-182, 186, 189-192, 194-199, Second Hunt 199-205, 207, 214-216; Proclamations 216, 232; Third Hunt 218, 219, 221-229; 240, 243, 245, 247, 255, 261, 270, 277, 280-284, 286-288, 293, 294, 298, 300-303, 306, 308, 311, 318, 327-329, 331, 332
De Wet, Gen. PD 80, 104, 119, 123, 129, 134-136, 145, 146, 150, 151, 153, 167, 171, 174, 181, 208, 223, 251, 260, 281, 308
De Wet, Gideon 205
De Wet, Scout A 91
Du Toit, Gen. SP 98, 119, 122, 135, 136, 139, 140, 154, 224, 227, 276, 314, 319, 320
Delegation, Republican 118, 129, 133, 136, 144, 147, 157
Derby, Lord 11
Derdepoort, Atrocity at 58, 60, 62, 63, 75

Dewetsdorp 129, 132-135, 199, 201, 204, 324
Dewetsdorp, Battle of 200, 201
Diamond Hill (Donkerhoek), Battle of 157-160, 162
Dickson, Gen. JBB 136, 138, 158
Dinizulu, King 232, 240, 312, 313, 323
Dixon, Brig. HG 237, 238, 240, 241
Doornberg, Meeting at 218
Doran, Col. WRB 253, 300, 302
Dordrecht 63, 75, 76, 80, 82, 101, 104, 114
Douglas 79, 146, 147
Douglas, Gen. CWH 95, 134, 138, 199, 234
Douthwaite, Comdt. (Gen) 157, 160
Drives, 'New Model' 298, 300-302, 306, 311-313, 316, 317, 319, 325, 326
Du Plooy, Comdt. 31, 54, 65, 66
Dullstroom 234, 235, 284, 285, 293, 295
Dundee 28, 42-47
Dundonald, Gen. Earl of 65, 70, 72, 82-84, 86, 96, 98, 101, 112, 141, 144, 158, 179, 181, 186, 190
Dwarsvlei, Action at 169, 170, 180

E
Eekstein 14
Edgar Incident 10-12, 19, 237
Edward VII, King 218, 223, 239, 242, 260, 268
Elandslaagte 42, 47, 92
Elandslaagte, Battle of 44, 47, 49
Election, 'Khaki' 190, 193
Elliot, Gen. EL 233, 237, 239, 241, 242, 252, 253, 255-258, 260, 281, 283, 287, 288, 294, 302, 303, 311
Elliot, Sir H 65, 200
Eloff, Comdt. SJ 142, 143, 163, 221
Emmet, Comdt. JJC 84, 232, 233, 265-267, 295, 311, 312
Enslin (Graspan) Battle of 59
Enslin, Attack on 64
Erasmus, Comdt. JLP 200
Erasmus, Gen. D 29, 40, 42, 43
Erasmus, Gen. DJE 146, 150, 190, 288
Erasmus, Lt. D 235
Esau, Abraham 215, 221
Evans, E 10, 12

F
Faber's Put, Battle of 148, 152
Farm burning 91, 175, 185, 187, 191, 192, 197, 199-203, 208, 210, 220, 226, 251, 254, 255, 257, 258, 261, 266, 273, 277, 280, 288, 294, 295, 297, 301, 307, 309, 316, 331
Fawcett, Mrs MG 253, 283, 308, 312
Ferreira, Gen. IS 82, 100, 102-104
Fetherstonehaugh, Col. 255
Giddes, GV 9, 14, 15
Fischer, A 20, 21, 110, 118, 132, 147
Fitzclarence, Capt. C 47, 75
Fitzpatrick, P 12-14, 57, 61, 325
Forestier-Walker, Gen. Sir FWEF 23, 38
Fort Itala, Attack on 267
Fort Prospect, Attack on 267
Fouchee, Comdt. WD 201, 207, 303, 325, 328, 329
Fourie, (Comdt.) Gen. Piet 124, 175, 185, 186, 202, 207, 218, 228, 243
Fourie, Gen. Joachim 157-159, 175, 181, 198
Fouriesburg 168-170, 174, 237, 272, 318, 325
Franchise issue 12-16, 18, 19, 21-25, 45
Frederikstad 262, 275
Frederikstad Battle of 194-196
French, Gen. JDP 43, 44, 47, 48, 50, 56, 65, 76, 79-81, 90, 94, 95, 97, 98, 100, 102, 106, 115-117, 119-122, 124, 139, 134-138, 142, 146-151, 154, 157, 158, 161, 169, 170, 172, 173, 180-184, 186, 188-194, 196, 201, 207, 218-222, 224, 231, 232, 252, 253, 257, 258, 268, 271
Frere 54, 64, 65
Froneman, Gen. CC 100, 104, 121, 129, 132, 134, 135, 156, 163, 175, 195, 196, 215, 218, 221, 231, 260, 266, 313, 323

G
Game Tree Fort, Attack on 75
Garrat, Col. 263, 298, 303, 311, 323
Gatacre, Gen. Sir W 80, 104, 107, 114, 116-119, 129, 130, 132
Geduld, Action at 231
Ghandi, MK 85, 191, 272
Goedvooruitzicht, Action at 234
Gold mining 9, 30, 31, 52, 74, 115, 120, 174, 237, 241,

277, 280, 285, 288, 292, 293, 297, 307, 316, 317, 324, 327
Goold-Adams, Sir H 40, 221, 235, 256, 279
Gordon, Brig. JRP 95, 136, 138, 142, 158, 208, 313
Gough, Col. G 38, 52, 59, 129, 265
Graskop, Action at 80, 81
Graspan, Battle of 242
Gravett, Gen. GH 150, 163, 183, 190, 192, 196
Greene, Sir W Conyngham 13, 22-24, 34, 38
Gregarowski, Judge R 11
Grenfell, Col. HM 163, 308, 319, 320
Greylingstad 167, 209
Grimwood, Col. GG 47, 48
Grobler, Comdt. HS 29
Grobler, Comdt. (Gen.) JNH 29, 167, 181, 198, 226, 267, 274, 302, 303, 307
Grobler, Comdt. SP 49
Grobler, Gen. ER 38, 53
Grobler, Gen. FA 38, 43, 45, 53, 55, 104, 109, 110, 112, 118, 122, 123, 135, 136, 139, 148, 157, 160, 167, 169, 187, 238
Groenkop, Tweefontein (Krismiskop), Battle of 286, 287
Gruisfontein, Action at 300
Gumbold 51
Gun Hill, Sortie against 64

H
Haasbroek, Comdt. SF 174, 199, 207, 218, 224, 247, 260, 266, 283
Haig, Col. D 190, 301, 324
Hamilton, Gen. ISM 44, 47, 48, 50, 80, 81, 83, 135, 136, 138-140, 142, 145-148, 150, 154, 157-159, 161-163, 176-179, 185-187, 190, 216, 276, 294, 317-319, 321, 322, 326, 329
Hamilton, Col. EOF 141, 283, 284
Hamilton, Col. Gilbert 262, 275, 283-285, 303
Hamilton, Gen. BM 137-139, 158, 159, 171, 172, 174, 175, 186, 190, 197, 198, 218, 219, 221, 223-225, 267, 277, 281-283, 288, 293, 294, 296, 311-313, 321-323
Handcock, Lt. PJ 296, 306, 307, 327
Hannay, Col. OC 97, 99, 100, 102, 103
Harcourt, Sir WV 12, 31
Hart's Hill, Battle of 106-109
Hart, Gen. A Fitzroy 65, 70, 72, 85, 104, 106-108, 133, 135, 138, 176, 183, 186, 237, 261, 262, 325
Hartbeesfontein 224, 230, 237, 304, 306, 312
Hattingh, Comdt. (Gen.) FJW 80, 170-172, 218, 280
Heidelberg 162, 163, 171, 176, 183, 186, 192, 196, 201, 220
Heilbron 171, 183, 187, 214, 215, 252, 276, 280, 281, 293, 300-302, 304, 308, 311, 326
Hekpoort, Skirmish at 207
Helvetia, Battle of 209
Helvetia (OFS) 201, 204, 205
Hely-Hutchinson, Sir W 326
Henry, Col. St GC 142, 150, 158, 189, 226
Hertzog, Judge (Gen.) JBM 116, 130, 162, 181, 193-197, 202, 203, 207-209, 217, 218, 221, 223-226, 232, 243, 245, 272, 292, 317, 318, 328, 331, 332
Hertzog, Comdt. JA Munnik 185, 261
Hickie, Col. 262, 300
Hicks Beach, Sir M 235, 314
Hicks, Col. HT 195
Hildyard, Gen. HJT 55, 57, 59, 65, 70-72, 92, 101, 103, 141, 150, 158, 194, 231, 232, 263
Hindon, Scout OJ 191, 216, 235, 247, 261, 323
Hlangwane Hill 64, 65, 70, 72, 83, 96, 99, 106, 111
Hlangwane, Battle of 99, 104, 106
Hobhouse, Emily 47, 217, 218, 228, 229, 231, 233-238, 240, 242, 245, 247, 253, 255, 256, 269, 274, 275, 312, 319
Hofmeyer, JH 16, 21
Holkrantz Massacre 326
Hoopstad 129, 144, 145, 147, 253, 254, 256, 257, 325
Hore, Col. CO 143, 176-180
Horses, Procurement of 40
Houtnek (Tobaberg), Battle of 136, 137
Houwater, Fight at 115
Howard, Gen. F 141, 173, 183
Hugo, Judge HJ 297, 302
Hunt, Col. HV 65
Hunter, Gen. Sir A 134, 135, 138-140, 144, 147, 148, 156, 162, 163, 168, 171, 172, 175, 183, 190, 195, 197
Hutton, Gen. ETH 95, 138-140, 142, 158, 168-170, 174

I, J
Ingouville-Williams, Col. EC 237, 238, 240, 260, 262, 282, 321
Jabavu, JT 46, 53, 261
Jameson, Dr LS 10, 11, 13, 18, 41, 50, 95, 301, 313
Jamestown 116, 240, 242, 253, 278
Jammersberg Drift, Siege 131, 132-135
Jeudwine, Maj. HS 238
Johannesburg 38, 40, 42, 44, 54, 55, 80, 90, 94, 115, 131, 135, 147, 149-152, 154, 158, 183, 190, 210, 216, 218, 225-227, 239, 244, 263, 264, 269, 271, 276, 284, 293, 302, 316, 321
Jones, Const. B 10, 12, 14
Jones, (Lt.) Digby 80, 81
Jones, Gen. Inigo 138, 158-160
Jooste, Scout Koos 90, 91
Joubert, Comdt. D 54-56, 279
Joubert, Comdt. J 70, 72, 281
Joubert, Comdt.-Gen. PJ 12, 15, 19, 20, 29, 38-40, 42, 43, 45, 46, 48, 51, 53, 58, 59, 62, 63, 79, 83, 85, 90, 91, 112-114, 116, 118, 119, 121-123, 129
Joubert, Hendrina 81
Joubert, Peace efforts 19, 29
Judelewitz, Comdt. CD 115, 149

K
Karee Siding, Action at 122
Kavanagh, Col. CTM 256, 275, 277, 301, 302
Keeromskop, Action at 97
Keir, Col. 303, 314
Kekewich, Col. RG 26, 38, 41, 51, 52, 90, 95, 98, 100, 101, 171, 253, 262, 266, 268, 269, 271, 272, 275, 300, 306, 307, 314, 316-319, 322
Kelly-Kenny, Gen. T 63, 89, 95, 99, 101, 102, 115, 116, 138, 187, 197
Kemp, Comdt. (Gen.) JCG 29, 89, 205, 219, 224, 227, 230, 231, 240, 241, 243, 251, 253, 262, 263, 268, 273, 282
Kestell, Rev. JD 81, 283, 318
Khama, Chief 43
Kimberley 26, 30, 35, 38, 41, 43, 99, 106, 252, 261, 220, 225, 229, 233, 234, 236, 238, 252, 261, 302, 313, 325
Kimberley, Siege 41, 45-47, 50-52, 54, 55, 60, 62, 75, 82, 84-86, 89, 90, 94, 95, 97-99
Kirsten, Comdt. JRF 253, 254, 256, 270, 271
Kitchener's Army 242
Kitchener's Koppie 102, 104, 106, 107
Kitchener, Brig. FW 85, 111, 141, 181, 184, 223, 234, 256, 259, 263, 269, 312-314, 316, 318, 319, 322
Kitchener, Drives 256, 260, 276
Kitchener, Gen. Lord HH 73-76, 82, 94, 95, 99, 101-104, 106, 119, 160, 163, 176, 178-180, 202-204, 208, 209, 215-217, 222-227, 229, 230, 232, 238, 239, 242, 244-247, 251, 253-256, 260-262, 264, 271, 272, 275-277, 280-282, 284, 287, 293, 298, 300, 302, 306, 308, 310, 313, 317, 321, 322, 325, 328-332
Kitchener, Proclamations 208, 229, 235, 238, 258, 259, 262
Kitchener, Becomes C-in-C 202
Kleinfontein/Driefontein, Battle of 273
Klerksdorp 156, 157, 161, 173, 195, 197, 199, 209, 220, 224, 227, 235, 237, 238, 254-256, 260, 271, 274, 288, 301-305, 308, 310-312, 314, 317, 319, 321, 322, 326
Klerksdorp Conference 318
Klip Drift, Breakthrough at 97, 98
Klip River (ZAR) 183, 184, 301
Klip River Dam 83, 84, 91, 92, 95, 96, 106, 109
Klipriviersberg, Battle of 147, 149, 150
Knox, Col. E 43, 48, 219, 237
Knox, Gen. CE 95, 102, 103, 138, 176, 183, 196, 198, 200-202, 205, 218, 219, 223-225, 233, 253, 265
Knox, Gen. WG 138
Kock, Gen. JHM 39, 43-45, 49, 50
Kock, Judge A 12, 147, 302
Koedoesberg, Battle of 91, 92, 94, 95
Koffiefontein 196, 197
Kolbe, Gen. WJ 98, 175, 218
Kraaipan, Battle of 39
Krause, Comdt. LE 205, 208
Krause, Dr FET 83, 147, 151
Kritzinger, Comdt. PH 184, 185, 203, 206, 207, 232, 235, 236, 239, 242, 244, 246, 252, 255, 256, 258, 259, 261, 265, 266, 283, 296, 310, 317, 323
Kroonstad 117, 119, 129, 140-143, 147-149, 151, 156, 157, 163, 171, 174, 176, 183, 187, 191, 199, 201, 215, 233, 242, 256, 275, 279, 281, 283, 286, 293, 297, 300-302, 311-313, 325, 326

349

Kroonstad, Council of War 119, 122-124
'Kruger Single 9', Coin 50
Kruger, Concessions 12, 14, 18, 19, 21, 26
Kruger, Demoralized 152, 153
Kruger, In exile 187, 188, 192, 194, 196, 197, 201, 202
Kruger, Inspiration 105, 112, 113, 115
Kruger, Pres. SJP 11, 12, 15-19, 21, 29, 34, 84, 91, 97,
113-115, 119, 140, 142, 143, 147, 149, 151, 153,
160-163, 174, 182, 184, 187, 192, 216, 217, 233,
238, 245, 251, 254, 268, 271, 317
Kruger, Proclamation 186
Krugersdorp 161, 162, 168, 169, 177, 185, 190, 192,
202, 218, 219, 227, 246, 279, 304, 331
Kuruman 79
Kuruman, Siege 53, 56, 64, 73, 75
Kuyper, Dr A 296

L

Labotsebeni, Queen Regent 70, 254
Labram, George 75, 84, 95
Ladies Commission 253, 308
Ladybrand 185, 186
Ladysmith 28, 35, 43, 45-47, 50, 54, 236, 306
Ladysmith, Siege 50-52, 55, 60, 64-66, 73-75, 79, 80,
82-84, 91, 92, 96, 106, 109, 112, 113
Lagden, Sir G 31, 257
Laing, Col. 214
Lake Chrissie, Action at 221
Langverwacht (Kalkkrans), Action at 303
Lansdowne, Lord 69, 193, 259, 296, 297
Lategan, Comdt. (Gen.) H 199, 200, 239, 254, 255,
265, 280, 297
Lawley, Col. RT 302, 316, 323
Le Gallais, Col. PWJ 196-198
Leliefontein, Battle of 198
Leliefontein, Incident 296
Lemmer, Gen. HR 109, 135, 148, 162, 167, 168, 172,
177, 178, 191, 195, 199, 204, 216, 217
Lemmer, Gen. LAS 109, 115, 116, 118, 122-124, 225,
227, 263, 273, 319, 320
Lennox, Col. Lord AG 176
Leyds, Dr WJ 15, 23, 63, 189, 193
Lichtenburg 217, 224, 237, 286, 295, 300, 304, 307,
308, 316, 325
Lichtenburg, Attack on 227, 228
Liebenberg, Gen. PJ 89-91, 100, 112, 114, 115, 143,
144, 168, 173, 179, 185, 186, 192, 194, 195, 199,
218, 219, 224, 227, 228, 237, 304, 312-314, 319
Linchwe, Chief 282
Lindley 167, 171, 214, 242, 251, 280, 282, 283, 286,
287, 298, 301, 302, 307, 311, 326
Lindley, Battle of 146, 148-153, 163
Little, Col. MO 171, 173
Lloyd George, D 83, 93, 174, 199, 284, 294, 311
Lombaard, Field-cornet 10, 14, 55
Long, Col. CJ 53, 70-72
Lötter, Comdt. JC 242, 258, 263, 264, 271
Lubbe, Comdt. D 55, 59, 75, 103
Lyttelton, Gen. NG 65, 85, 87, 89, 92, 98, 100, 101,
104, 111, 141, 144, 178, 219, 263

M

MacDonald, Gen. HA 91, 92, 94, 95, 103, 138, 168,
174, 175, 177
Machadodorp 151, 152, 155, 181, 182, 184, 189, 192,
209, 214, 223, 234
Mafeking 30, 31, 38, 39, 134, 144-147, 149, 152, 157,
163, 175, 177-179, 183, 227, 233, 237, 238, 253,
269, 272, 288, 305, 316, 326
Mafeking, Siege 40-47, 49-52, 54, 64, 66, 70, 75, 79, 82,
84, 95, 106, 109, 111, 113, 117, 122, 123, 125, 129,
132-134, 137, 139, 142-144
Magersfontein, Battle of 64, 66, 67, 69
Mahon, Col. BT 134, 139, 141, 143-145, 158, 168, 176,
178, 186, 193
Malan, Comdt. (Gen.) WC 172, 222, 223, 232, 233,
265, 280, 281, 287, 297, 298, 300, 302, 303, 311,
328, 329
Malan, PJ 84, 91, 92, 96, 106
Mangold, Dr GA 62
Marcum, CE 50
Maritz, Gen. SG (Manie) 222, 223, 233, 238, 255, 258,
262, 271-274, 276, 280, 281, 287, 296, 316, 317,
322-324
Marwick, JS 31
Maximov, Col. EJ 137

Maxwell, Gen. JG 138, 189, 285, 311
McWhinnie, Capt. WJ 129, 130
Mears, Comdt. W 233, 240, 298
Mentz, Comdt. FE 304, 311
Methuen, Gen. Lord PS 25, 53, 56-62, 64-67, 69, 94-
96, 117, 119, 129, 131, 133, 134, 138, 144, 145, 147,
149, 151, 153, 158, 162, 167, 168, 171-173, 175,
176, 178, 179, 183, 187, 189, 191, 193, 195, 199,
200, 202, 220, 223, 224, 237, 238, 240, 257, 262,
263, 269, 271, 272, 283, 301, 302, 307-312, 319
Meyer, Comdt. Jan 303, 307
Meyer, Gen. LJ 29, 40, 42, 43, 46, 65, 91, 92, 100, 113,
141, 144, 145, 147, 149, 318, 332
Meyer, Gen. MW 323
Middelburg 168, 173-175, 186, 208, 220, 226, 229, 233,
234, 243, 245, 247, 255, 256, 260, 274, 303, 322
Middelburg Conference 226-228, 230, 328, 329
Middelburg, CC 296, 325
Middelfontein 218
Middelpost, Attack at 300
Miers, Capt. RDC 267
Milner, Becomes a Lord 240
Milner, Belligerent actions 9, 14, 15, 17-19, 21-26, 28,
29
Milner, Sir (Lord) A 9, 12-25, 27-29, 31, 83, 121, 160,
161, 176, 192, 193, 196, 201, 202, 204, 207, 209,
214, 217, 222, 226-228, 230, 231, 236-238, 240, 247,
251, 253, 255, 258, 261, 262, 264, 273-277, 280-283,
285, 293, 312-314, 318, 321-323, 325, 328-330, 332
Mobilization, British 32
Mobilization, Republican 28-31
Modder River (Tweeriviere), Battle of 59, 61
Modderfontein, Action at 266
Modderfontein, Battle of 219-221, 230
Modderspruit, Battle of 48
Moedwil, Battle of 268, 271
Molala, Chief 41, 46
Molteno 65, 66, 80, 107
Money, Col. CGC 38, 204, 228
Monepenny, WF 12, 13, 15
Monro, Col. 233, 253
Monte Cristo, Battle of 99, 103, 104
Montmorency, Capt. R de 76, 108, 117
Montshiwa, Chief 52, 82
Morant, Lt. HH 251, 294, 296, 306, 307, 327
Morgendaal, JJ 214, 215, 217
Mostert's Hoek, Battle of 130, 132
Muller, Comdt. (Gen.) CH 199, 201, 209, 214, 234,
237, 243, 256, 259, 284, 285, 293, 296, 303, 326
Murray, Col. A 266, 330
Myburgh, Gen. MW 252, 253, 278, 303, 312

N

National Scouts Corps 281, 292, 300, 303, 305, 307,
316, 322-324
Naude, Comdt. CD 279, 306
Neser, Comdt. JP 254, 276, 306
Nicholas, II, Tsar 17, 189, 242
Nicholson's Nek, Battle of 48
Nieuwoudt, Comdt. C 215, 221
Nieuwoudt, Comdt. (Gen.) TK 185, 208
Nooitgedacht, Battle of 204, 205, 208
Norval's Pont 114, 116, 118, 226, 227, 229, 247

O

OFS government 19, 20, 26-28, 101, 117, 252, 318, 332
Oath of Allegiance 306, 322, 328, 330, 332
Oath of Neutrality 118, 124, 145, 155, 161, 180, 182,
183, 187, 191, 202, 203, 205, 223, 235, 242, 243,
308, 322
Oath of Neutrality, Counter-oath 203
Okiep, Siege of 317-319, 321-325
Olifant's Nek 167, 168, 172, 173, 179, 180, 185, 218
Olifant's River 234, 235, 243, 302, 321
Olivier, Chief Comdt. JH 38, 51, 53, 55, 56, 58, 63, 65,
66, 79, 80, 113, 122, 123, 135, 136, 163, 175, 184
Olivier, Gen. CH 318, 332
Oosthuizen, Comdt. PR 183, 184, 240, 273
Oosthuizen, Gen. S 150, 161, 169, 180, 240
Opperman, Comdt. D 84, 87-89
Orange River 109, 112, 115, 117, 118, 138, 139, 176,
203, 207, 219, 222, 225, 227, 247, 259, 262, 265,
279, 332
Orange River Colony Volunteers 303, 308, 323, 324
Otter, Col. 49

P

Paardeberg, Battle of 101, 102, 104-107, 109, 110, 119
Paardekraal Monument 190
Paget, Gen. AH 138, 140, 167, 168, 170, 173, 183, 187,
190, 201, 219, 304
Park, Col. CW 81, 229, 234, 284, 285, 303, 321, 323
Peace overtures 114
Perrin, CH 50
Perrin, J 50
Petition 10, 12-14, 17, 214, 215
Phillips, L 11, 13
Pieter's Hill, Battle of 106, 110, 111
Pilcher, Col. TD 79, 120, 169, 200, 202, 219, 236, 261
Pine-Coffin, Col. 260
Plaatje, Sol T 49
Platberg, Action at 235, 236
Platrand (Wagon Hill), Battle of 79, 80, 82
Plumer, Col. HCO 35, 38, 46, 49, 50, 63, 75, 76, 83, 97,
106, 109, 115, 116, 118, 119, 125, 219, 223-225, 228,
229, 231-235, 243, 281, 286, 292, 296, 311
Pole-Carew, Gen. R 61, 62, 68, 95, 119, 134, 135, 138,
146, 158, 159, 182-184, 187, 189, 190
Poplar Grove 106, 109, 110, 113, 115
Poplar Grove (Modderrivierspoort), Battle of 115,
116
Porter, Col. TC 95, 101, 138, 142, 158
Potchefstroom 149, 157, 158, 161, 162, 173, 175, 178,
179, 183, 191-194, 206, 218, 224, 239, 269, 274,
275, 304, 321
Potgieter, Comdt. FJ 218, 283, 301, 319, 321
Potgieter, Field-cornet 325, 326
Pretoria 42, 50, 65, 69, 73, 74, 83, 86, 89-91, 93, 97, 109,
112, 113, 122, 123, 138-141, 143, 147, 150, 151,
153-156, 158, 159, 161-163, 167-170, 172-182, 186,
187, 189-191, 193, 196, 201, 202, 208, 216, 219,
222, 225, 227, 231, 232, 240, 243, 244, 254, 260,
262, 264, 270, 275, 296, 304, 307, 311, 312, 316,
321, 323, 326, 328-330, 332
Pretorius, MW 15, 215, 239
Pretorius, Maj. LJ 202
Pretyman, Gen. GT 118, 187
Prinsloo, Chief Comdt. M 38, 42, 79, 83, 91, 92, 170,
172-176
Prinsloo, Comdt. H 86, 123, 198, 223
Prinsloo, Gen. JJP 38, 57-60, 64
Prinsloo, Gen. M 207, 218, 280, 288
Prisoner of war camps 306
Pulteney, Col. 219, 266, 286, 296
Pypers, Comdt. SW 271, 272, 297

Q,R

Quaggafontein, Action at 266
Raglan, Lord 223
Ramsbottom, Dr AEW 62, 209
Rawlinson, Col. Sir HS 256, 261, 270, 273, 282, 314,
317-319, 322
Reitz 173, 174, 176, 177, 196, 236, 240, 242, 251, 252,
276, 277, 280, 287, 298, 303
Reitz, D 324
Reitz, FW 14, 16, 32, 34, 50, 115, 133, 147, 167, 192,
208, 230, 238, 245, 270, 278, 318, 327, 332
Reitzburg 173, 174, 176, 177, 196, 256
Rensburg Siding 75, 76, 79, 83, 112
Renoster River 143-147, 156, 176, 196, 210, 312
Renosterkop, Battle of 200, 201
Renosterpoort 174, 177, 181
Rhenosterfontein, Action at 263
Rhodes, CJ 10, 11, 16, 21, 35, 84, 95, 98, 100, 167, 251,
239, 313
Ridley, Brig. CP 138, 158, 160, 173
Rietfontein, Battle of 45, 46
Rietfontein, ZAR 185, 186, 217, 235, 252, 298
Rimington, Col. MF 260, 264, 266, 270, 273, 278, 280,
281, 284, 285, 298, 303, 311, 323
Roberts, Col. HR 169
Roberts, Field-Marshal, Lord FS 65, 67, 72, 73, 75, 76,
82, 90-95, 97, 99-101, 104-106, 109, 111-113, 118,
119, 121, 123, 129, 130, 132, 134-136, 138, 141,
143-145, 152-157, 167, 169-171, 173, 175, 176, 178-
180, 182, 186, 187, 190, 191, 193, 195, 198, 199,
202, 204, 214, 217, 226, 240, 255, 269, 276, 287
Roberts, Flank march 95, 97, 99
Roberts, Marches North 138, 139, 141-143, 147, 148,
150-152, 154, 155
Roberts, Marches East 156, 158-161, 172-175, 180,
182, 183, 189
Roberts, Proclamations 101, 106, 118, 120, 121, 143,

146, 149, 152, 153, 155, 160-162, 168, 174, 180, 185, 186, 188
Robinson, Sir H 10, 11
Roodewal Siding 144, 150, 153, 189
Roodewal Siding, Battle of 156, 161
Roodewal ZAR, Battle of 319
Rosebery, Lord 10, 11, 284, 314
Ross, Comdt. A 285, 303
Roux, Gen. PH 161, 163, 170-172, 174, 175, 191
Rudolph, Comdt. JS 311
Rundle, Gen. Sir HML 84, 134-136, 138, 139, 147-150, 173, 174, 183, 190, 208, 236, 237, 241, 286, 287
Rustenburg 161, 162, 167, 168, 171-173, 177-180, 189, 1190, 202, 240, 262, 268, 269, 271, 307

S
Salisbury, Lord Cecil 34, 52, 56, 67, 91, 114, 117, 171, 193, 221, 238, 240, 278, 298, 314
Sand River 140-142, 161
Sannaspost, Battle of 122, 123
Scheeper's Nek, Battle of 146
Scheepers, Capt (Comdt.) GJ 124, 179, 194, 201-203, 207, 230, 232, 233, 252, 271, 272, 277, 282, 284, 286, 294
Schiel, Comdt. A 43-45
Schimmelhoek, Action at 273
Schoeman's Drift 177, 178, 196
Schoeman, Comdt. D 101, 104, 108
Schoeman, Gen. HJ 53, 55, 79, 80, 82, 141, 175, 187-189, 202
Scheiner, Olive 16, 271, 295
Schriener, WP 16, 17, 19-21, 38, 39, 55, 136, 157, 160, 161, 184, 219, 240
Scobell, Col. HJ 253, 254, 263, 271, 278
Scorched Earth Policy 161, 199, 278, 301
Second Republican Invasion 207
Second Republican Offensive 197
Seddon, Prime Minister 327, 329
Selborne, Lord (W Palmer) 14, 17, 19, 20
Serfontein Siding 163, 172, 189
Settle, Brig. HH 113, 130, 189, 193, 209, 282
Shekleton, Col. HP 227, 229
Shelton, Col. WAD 317, 321
Shepstone, AJ 325
Shepstone, Sir T 14, 325
Sikhobobo, Chief 312, 313, 323, 325, 326
Silkaatsnek 154, 167, 169, 170, 176, 207, 234
Slangfontein, Action at 266
Slegtkamp, Capt HF 181, 191, 223
Smartt, Dr 35, 115, 330
Smit, Comdt. 297, 298, 300
Smith-Dorrien, Gen. HL 95, 115, 138, 142, 172, 179, 197, 198, 201, 214, 220-223, 233, 234
Smuts, State Attorney (Gen.) JC 15-17, 23, 24, 26, 27, 74, 133, 148, 153-155, 167, 179, 180, 196, 202, 205, 219, 220, 224, 225, 227, 228, 230, 231, 234, 238, 240, 245, 253, 254, 292, 296, 301, 306, 317, 321, 322, 324, 326, 329
Smuts, Invades the Colony 254, 256-258, 260-266, 269-272, 275, 277, 279, 285
Smuts, Reorganises 287
Smuts, Negotiations 15, 17, 23, 24, 325, 328-331
Smuts, Gen. T 91, 92, 121, 122, 157, 159, 170, 172, 179, 193, 254, 255, 260, 261, 271
Snyman, Gen. JP 29, 50, 52, 55, 84, 106, 109, 125, 142, 143, 158
Solomon, R 219, 328
Spence, Col. 147, 152
Spens, Col. 260, 266, 287, 288, 321, 323
Spijtfontein, Meeting at 251, 280
Spioenkop, Battle of 84, 86, 87, 89, 120
Spragge, Col. BE 148-153
Sprigg, Sir G 21, 162, 236, 324
Springbok 316, 322
Springhaansnek 136, 137, 199, 207
Spruyt, Comdt. (Gen.) CJ 80, 221, 254
Spytfontein, Action at 280
Standerton 155, 163, 202, 240, 245, 263, 275, 276, 288, 321, 322
Steenekamp, Comdt. LP 48, 268
Stephenson, Brig. TE 95, 102-104, 138, 158, 189, 271, 302
Steyn, Pres. MT 15-21, 26, 27, 30, 31, 34, 38, 40, 42, 52-55, 62, 65, 83, 91, 110, 113, 114, 116-121, 132, 134, 146, 152, 153, 155, 161, 162, 168, 170, 174, 180-182, 184, 189-191, 193, 196-199, 207, 215,

218, 227, 230, 238, 240, 242, 243, 245, 246, 251, 252, 261, 269, 277, 280, 282, 283, 288, 293, 303, 308, 311-313, 317, 318
Steyn, Admonishes ZAR 238, 245
Steyn, Escapes 252
Steyn, Illness 311, 331
Steyn, Inspiring 45, 63, 64, 85, 110, 111, 129, 142, 149, 153
Steyn, Negotiations 318, 321, 322
Steyn, Peace efforts 15-20, 26, 27, 31, 34
Steyn, Proclamations 38, 40, 42, 53-55, 120, 160, 216, 259, 276
Stormberg, Battle of 66
Stowe, (US), Col. 176
Surprise Hill, Sortie against 67
Suzerainty 11, 15, 23-25
Symonds, Gen. Sir WP 28, 38, 42, 43, 45, 46

T
Tabaksberg 219
Tabanyama, Battle of 84, 85, 87
Tafelkop, Action at 283-285
Talana, Battle of 43
Te Water, Dr TNG 16, 20, 136, 138
Thaba Nchu 119, 120, 122, 123, 135, 136, 138, 140, 141, 207, 219, 244, 265, 297, 307
Theron, Comdt. Jan H 199, 218, 233, 276, 277, 306, 322
Theron, DJS (Capt. Danie) 15, 109, 110, 113, 119, 120, 122, 132, 142, 153, 167, 171, 172, 176, 178, 179, 181, 183, 184, 186, 189
Thorneycroft, Col. TMG 86, 87, 89, 104
Trichard, Col. SPE 38, 42-44, 48, 122, 157, 208, 255, 285, 303, 326
Trichard, Comdt. PF 168, 216, 223
Tucker, Gen. C 70, 95, 116, 122, 137, 138, 266
Tugela, Battles 101, 103, 104, 106-111
Tugela River 82-84, 86, 89-91, 93, 96, 104, 108
Turner, Maj. Scot 46, 60, 62
Tweebosch (De Klipdrift), Battle of 298, 309
Tygerkloof, Action at 284
Tygerpoort, Battle of 178

U
Uitlanders 10, 15-19, 24, 25, 27, 30, 31
'Uitschudden' 206
Uitspanningsfontein, Action at 298, 300
Ultimatum, British 16, 26-29
Ultimatum, Republican 29, 34, 35
Urmston, Col. 284
Utrecht 167, 202, 209, 312

V
Vaal River 119, 122, 139, 140, 147, 148, 174, 176-178, 182, 194, 196, 233, 235, 237, 255-257, 266, 278, 288, 307, 308, 314
Vaalkrantz, Battle of 91-95
Vallentin, Maj. JM 292
Van As, Field-cornet S 267, 330
Van der Merwe, Comdt. P 264, 301
Van der Merwe, Dr 331
Van Deventer, Comdt. (Gen.) J 240, 241, 253, 254, 256-258, 261, 270-272, 276, 280, 287, 300, 301, 306, 316, 317, 324
Van Heerden, Comdt. CP 311, 328
Van Reenen, Comdt. GHP 323, 240, 243, 297
Van Rensburg, HCJ 45, 49-51, 53, 240
Van Rensburg, NPJJ "Siener" 236, 261, 309, 312
Vanrhynsdorp 217, 218, 221, 258, 279
Van Staden, Comdt. MP 205
Vandeleur, Col. CFS 262
'Veldponde' 296
Ventersburg 142, 147, 163, 197, 198, 201, 218, 229, 231, 240, 253, 275, 288, 297, 307
Venterskroon 178
Vereeniging 191, 323-325
Vereeniging Confrence 327, 328, 330
Vereeniging, Treaty of 332
Vermaak, JJP 187
Vermaas, Comdt. HCW 217, 227, 228
Vet River 139, 140
Victoria Cross 40, 44, 47, 48, 67, 69, 72, 73, 75, 80, 81, 102, 103, 107-109, 112, 117, 124, 134-136, 149, 154, 155, 163, 169, 173, 176, 178, 181, 184, 185, 193, 194, 198, 200, 205, 214, 219, 222, 225, 228, 239, 244, 251, 265, 267, 269, 279, 284, 285, 301
Victoria, Queen 10, 11, 13, 17, 19, 20, 25, 35, 131, 136,

148, 163, 191, 204, 217, 218, 220, 223
Viljoen, (Comdt.) Gen. Ben 29, 54, 59, 83, 92, 94, 148, 151, 153, 160, 170, 171, 181, 184, 193, 194, 199-201, 209, 214, 217, 223, 233-238, 240, 245, 247, 256, 257, 273, 294-296, 306
Viljoen, Gen. PR 163, 209, 282, 283, 316
Vilonel, Comdt. SG 31, 107, 122, 123, 170, 175, 303, 323
Visser, Comdt. JH 53, 56, 64, 73, 75, 79
Vlakfontein, Battle of 240, 241
Volunteers, Foreign 29, 42-44, 49, 83, 97, 110, 112, 116, 120, 131, 137, 140, 147, 189, 194, 209, 233, 270
Von Dalwig, Capt. FA 182
Von Donop, Col. SB 224, 272, 273, 301-304, 319, 320
Von Rennenkampf, Dr J 305, 311
Vryheid, Attack on 204

W
Wagon Hill (Platrand) 52, 80-82
Warren, Gen. Sir C 53, 70, 74, 83-89, 94, 98, 104, 106, 135, 139, 146-148, 152, 155, 157, 163, 222, 301
Warwick, Dr. P 11
Waterval Meeting 245, 246
Waterval-Boven 163, 164
Wauchope, Gen. AG 53, 55, 65, 67
Wavell, Gen. AG 95, 99, 138
Weilbach, Comdt. JD 29, 116, 154
Wernher, J 9, 12
Wessels, CH 118, 132
Wessels, Chief Comdt. CJ 51, 52
Wessels, Comdt. L 296, 304
Wessels, Comdt. W 200, 285, 303
Wessels, Gen. JB 129, 218
White, Gen. Sir GS 26, 31, 32, 35, 38, 43, 46-48, 69, 74, 80, 81, 106, 112, 113
Wildfontein, Action at 231
Wilhelmina, Queen 25, 26, 184, 194, 222
Williams, Maj. FA 286
Willow Grange, Battle of 57, 59
Wilmansrust, Battle of 243, 244
Wilson, Capt. G 40
Wilson, Gen. 274, 303
Wilson, Lady S (Churchill) 40, 41, 64
Windvoël, (Groom) 241
Wolmarans, ADW 17, 110, 118, 132, 157
Wolmarans, Comdt. MJ 234, 293, 307, 309
Wolmaransstad 218, 223-225, 238, 301, 302, 304, 306, 308, 311
Wolseley, Lord G 19, 32
Woodgate, Gen. ERP 86, 120
Woolls-Sampson, Col. A 11, 30, 256, 281, 293, 316
Worcester Congress 204
Wyndham, Col. 253, 286, 301
Wynne's Hill, Battle of 106, 107, 109, 111
Wynne, Gen. AS 106, 141, 282

X,Y,Z
Ysterspruit, Battle of 304, 308, 309
Yule, Gen. JH 45, 46
ZAR government 12, 14, 17, 21, 23, 24, 27, 28, 30, 35, 84, 109, 180, 181, 184, 186, 189, 192, 193, 196, 197, 199, 202, 215, 233, 235-240, 242-247, 251-253, 257, 258, 261, 264, 266, 271-277, 279, 281, 284, 285, 293-296, 301-303, 307, 309, 311-313, 317, 331